TOTALLY 2002 !!

Your Guinness World Records™2002 unique I.D. number is:

91299804-8341-48CA

Log on at www.guinnessworldrecords.com to see if you're a winner!!

GUINNESS
WORLD RECORDS™
2002

British Library cataloging-in-Publication Data.
A catalog record for this book is available from the British Library
ISBN 1-892051-06-0

Managing Editor
Antonia Cunningham

Editors
Jackie Freshfield
Carla Masson
Virginia Robins
James Bradley

Design Concept
Lesley Horowitz and Dominic Sinesio at Office Group NYC

Design and Production
Karen Wilks
Juliet MacDonald

Research Director
Chris Sheedy

Picture Manager
Betty Halvagi

Researchers
Stuart Claxton
Jerramy Fine
David Hawksett
Della Howes
Hein le Roux
Stewart Newport
Louise Whetter

Picture Librarian
Roger Wemyss Brooks

Picture Assistant
James Thackwell

Production Director
Patricia Langton

Research Assistants
Keely Hopkins
Jo Violette

Production Co-ordinator
David D'Arcy

Proofreading
Sasha Heseltine
Susan Niner Janes

Website
Jennifer Banks
Samantha Harris
John Harry
Anthony Liu
Joe Lynham
Simon Rasalingham
Daniel Stott

Americaniser
Marion Dent

Index
Indexing Specialists

Fulfilment Co-ordinator
Claire Curtice

Colour Origination
Colour Systems, London, UK

Printing and Binding
Printer Industria Grafica, SA, Barcelona, Spain

Director of Television
Michael Feldman

Vice President Media
Ian Castello-Cortes

ABBREVIATIONS & MEASUREMENTS

GUINNESS WORLD RECORDS uses both metric and imperial measurements
(UK metric in brackets). The only exception to this rule is for some
scientific data, where metric measurements only are universally accepted,
and for some sports data.

All currency values are shown in dollars with the sterling equivalent in
brackets except where transactions took place in the United Kingdom, when
this is reversed. Where a specific date is given, the exchange rate is
calculated according to the currency values that were in operation at the
time. Where only a year date is given the exchange rate is calculated from
December of that year. The billion conversion is one thousand million.

'GDR' (the German Democratic Republic) refers to the East German
state which unified with West Germany in 1990. The abbreviation is
used for sports records broken before 1990.

The Union of Soviet Socialist Republics split into a number of parts in
1991, the largest of these being Russia. The Commonwealth of Independent
States replaced it and the abbreviation 'CIS' is used, mainly for sporting
records broken at the 1992 Olympic Games.

ACCREDITATION

Guinness World Records Ltd has a very thorough accreditation system for
records verification. However, while every effort is made to ensure
accuracy, Guinness World Records Ltd cannot be held responsible for any
errors contained in this work. Feedback from our readers on any point of
accuracy is always welcomed.

GENERAL WARNING
Attempting to break records or set new records can be dangerous.
Appropriate advice should be taken first and all record attempts are
undertaken entirely at the participant's risk. In no circumstances will
Guinness World Records Ltd have any liability for death or injury suffered in
any record attempts. Guinness World Records Ltd has complete discretion
over whether or not to include any particular records in the book.

GUINNESS WORLD RECORDS™ 2002

www.guinnessworldrecords.com

introduction

TOTALLY 2002!!

To celebrate the launch of this year's new edition you can win PRIZES on **Guinnessworldrecords.com**.

Just go to the website, type in the UNIQUE number that you will find on the inside front cover and see if you're a winner! Good Luck! You can find a full set of rules and regulations on page 288.

This has been an amazing year at Guinness World Records and we've added hundreds of amazing new records and record categories. Check out Colin Winkelmann's amazing power-assisted BMX ramp jump (page 225), Mikael Bigersson's concrete-crushing feats (page 245), NFL-star Corey Dillon's rushing record (page 202), and Madonna's largest-ever live audience (page 172)!

Clockwise from top:
Most Expensive Washroom
Most Rhinestones on a Body,
Tina-Marie Stoker
Lil Bow Wow, Youngest US
No.1 solo rapper

It's not just new records – 2002 has more interactive features than ever before. You will have seen your favorite records on Guinness World Records *Primetime*, now in its third great year on FOX. You can spot these in the book wherever you see the 📺USA symbol.

And for those of you really into the details around a particular record, use the great new short-codes to go straight online and discuss them with other fans!

We really enjoyed putting this year's edition together – we hope you'll really love it too!

Clockwise from top:
Most Contortionists in a Box
Youngest NBA Player, Kobe Bryant
Sword Swallower, Brad Byers
Farthest Distance Shot with a Bow and
Arrow using the Feet, Hang Thu Thi Ngyuen
Most Tattooed Man, Tom Leppard
Mark Thompson, Guinness World Records
Primetime Host, with Skateboard Plummet
record holder, Brian Patch
Larry and Danny Ramos Gomez from the
World's Hairiest Family
Most Jumps by a Dog, Olive Oyl
Man with the Longest
Fingernails, Shridar Chillal

GUINNESS WORLD RECORDS™

how to use this book

Guinness World Records 2002 is even more action-packed than ever, with lots of new ways to find out more about our amazing records. As well as all the great new records that you have come to expect, this year's book is crammed with extra information and opportunities to interact with other Guinness World Records enthusiasts on our hot new website. Log on and find out what everybody is saying! Follow our symbols to find out what's been shown on TV and where we have superfast record links on the web to fast-track to your favorite pages!

SUBJECT URL
The URL, shown here, is a subject URL. If you go to our website at **www.guinnessworldrecords.com** and type this address in, it will take you straight to the section of the site devoted to Unusual Skills.

---

www.guinnessworldrecords.com/unusualskills

unusual skills

MOST FOOT-JUGGLING FLIPS OF A TABLE 🖵 USA
Chester Cable (USA) flipped a table 3.03 m (9 ft 11.75 in) long, 88.9 cm (35 in) wide and 69.2 cm (27.25 in) high a total of 17 times, using his feet, on 16 Oct 1998.

MOST FOOT-JUGGLING FLIPS OF A PERSON 🖵 FR
On 26 Oct 2000 Ali Bandbaz (Iran) 'jugged' his brother Massoud through 12 consecutive 360° revolutions, using only his feet. Ali lay on his back with Massoud sitting on his feet, and the pair completed each revolution in the same position.

LARGEST BUBBLE-GUM BUBBLE BLOWN WITH NOSE 🖵 USA
Joyce Samuels (USA) blew a bubble-gum bubble with a diameter of 27.94 cm (11 in) on 10 Nov 2000.

LARGEST BALLOON INFLATED WITH A TANDEM NOSE BLOW 🖵 USA
On 10 Nov 2000 Ryan Barker (USA) inflated an 118.11-cm (46.5-in) balloon held in his wife Marilee's mouth by blowing through her nose.

CATAPULT EARS 🖵 USA
On 29 Oct 1999 Monte Pierce (USA, left) shot an American 10 cent coin a distance of 3.306 m (10 ft 10.5 in), using his ear as a catapult. This is the furthest a coin has been propelled by an ear lobe. Monte began pulling at his ears as a child to relieve earache, and now, aged 20, can pull them up over his eyes, pull them down to meet under his chin, or roll them up like earplugs. His left ear stretches to a length of 12-12.7 cm (4.75–5 in), and his right ear to a length of 11.4 cm (4.5 in). He has perfect hearing, and doctors assure him that he is not damaging his ears in any way by performing these feats.

www.guinnessworldrecords.com/catapultears
◄— ACCESS CODE: ‹54633›

LONGEST-DISTANCE MARSHMALLOW NOSE BLOW 🖵 USA
The greatest distance that a marshmallow has been shot from one person's nostril and caught in another person's mouth is 4.96 m (16 ft 3½ in). Americans Scott Jeckel (the launcher) and Ray Perisin (the catcher) set this record on 13 Aug 1999.

FASTEST PANCAKE MARATHON
On 24 Oct 1999 Mike Cuzzacrea (USA) ('The Pancake Man') ran the 42.1-km (26.2-mile) Casino Niagara International Marathon in Buffalo, New York, USA, in 3 hr 2 min 27 sec, while flipping a pancake continuously in a frying pan. He came 46th out of 1,319 finishers.

FASTEST SANDWICH MADE USING FEET 🖵 USA
On 10 Nov 2000 Rob Williams (USA) made a bologna, cheese and salad sandwich in 1 min 57 sec, using just his feet.

LOUDEST BURP 🖵 UK
On 5 April 2000 Paul Hunn (UK) registered a burp of 118.1 dB – similar to being in the front row at a rock concert, and only slightly quieter than the noise made by an aeroplane on a runway.

MOST STEPS CLIMBED ON A BICYCLE
Javier Zapata (Colombia) broke his own world record by hopping up 943 steps on a bicycle, without touching the ground, on 20 May 2000. The feat took him 43 min 26 sec.

FASTEST TIME TO MEMORIZE A PACK OF CARDS
Andi Bell (UK) memorized a pack of 52 shuffled cards and repeated out loud the order in which they appeared in 34.03 seconds on 28 Aug 1998.

LONGEST TIME TENNIS BALL KEPT IN AIR WITH FEET
On 11 Nov 1999 Jacek Guzowski (Poland) kept a tennis ball up in the air, using only his feet, for 5 hr 28 min 59 sec. A counter showed that he touched the ball 35,000 times – an average of approximately 107 times per minute, or 1.8 times per second.

LARGEST SCORPION HELD IN MOUTH 🖵 USA
Dean Sheldon (USA) was able to hold a 17.78-cm (7-in) scorpion in his mouth for 18 seconds on 21 Dec 2000.

MOST SCORPIONS IN MOUTH 🖵 USA
Dean Sheldon (USA) put a total of 20 scorpions in his mouth, holding them there for 21 seconds, on 21 Dec 2000.

INSECT MORSEL MUNCHIES
Retired rat-catcher and part-time entertainer Ken Edwards (UK, left) ate 36 medium-sized cockroaches, in one minute on 5 March 2001, setting the record for the most cockroaches ever eaten by a human. Eating cockroaches is "like having an anaesthetic at the back of the throat" he says, as they let off a scent to ward away predators. His other bizarre stage acts include stuffing 47 rats down a pair of tights he was wearing, and inviting people to throw darts at a cork placed in his navel.
On 20 Oct 1998 Dr Norman Gary (USA) held 109 honeybees in his closed mouth for 10 seconds – but didn't eat them. Gary is Emeritus Professor at the University of California, USA, where his specialist subject is the behaviour of bees.

www.guinnessworldrecords.com/cockroacheater
◄— ACCESS CODE: ‹54654›

66

‹54654›

SUPERFAST RECORD ACCESS CODES
With this superfast access code, you can go straight to this creepy cockroach record.

HOTTEST
METAL IN MOUTH [USA]
On 18 Dec 1998 Yim Byung Nam held a silver-dollar-sized piece of metal, heated to 487.8°C (910°F), in his mouth for 14 seconds. When Yim spat it out, it was hot enough to fry bacon.

LONGEST TIME IN A
BOX BY THREE CONTORTIONISTS [FR]
Bonnie Morgan, Daniel Smith and Leslie Tipton (all USA) fitted into a box measuring 66.04 x 68.58 x 55.88 cm (26 x 27 x 22 in) and stayed there for 2 min 40 sec on 31 Jan 2001.

LONGEST
BASKETBALL SHOT MADE WITH HEAD [USA]
On 10 Nov 2000 Eyal Horn (Israel) shot a basketball with his head while standing 7.62 m (25 ft) from the backboard. He also scored a record 15 consecutive lay-ups (shooting and catching the ball with the head).

MOST CHERRY STEMS
KNOTTED IN ONE HOUR
On 4 Sept 1997 Al Gliniecki (USA) knotted 911 cherry stems with his tongue in one hour – an average of 15 stems per minute.

MOST SKIPS ON A
UNICYCLE IN ONE MINUTE [DE]
On 31 Aug 2000 Peter Rosendahl (Sweden) who resides in Germany, set the record for the most revolutions of a jump rope made on a unicycle. He managed 169 revolutions in just one minute.

GREATEST DISTANCE
TO SPIT A CRICKET [USA]
Danny Capps (USA) spat a dead cricket a total distance of 9.17 m (30 ft 1.2 in) on 26 June 1998.

FASTEST HUMAN
BEER BOTTLE OPENER [USA]
Daniel Lambert (Sweden) used his teeth to open 50 conventional crown-cap bottles on 11 March 2001. He achieved this in only one minute.

FASTEST TYRE FLIPPER [SE]
On 31 Jan 2001 in Stockholm, Sweden, Jorma Paananen (Sweden) completed a 20-m (65-ft) course – 10 m (32 ft 6 in) there and back – of flipping a Michelin Radial Steel Cord X26.5R25 (XHA) tyre in a time of 1 min 6 sec. The tyre weighed 420 kg (925.9 lb).

www.guinnessworldrecords.com/archeryfeet

AMAZING
FEET OF ARCHERY [USA]
Hang Thu Thi Nguyen (Vietnam, left) set the record for the furthest distance shot with a bow and arrow using the feet. On 12 Aug 1999 she hit a target that was 5 m (16 ft 5 in) away. Thu Hang, whose father is a lighting technician at Ho Chi Minh City Circus, first became interested in circus skills as a child. She spends three hours a day practising her act. Although shy by nature, Thu Hang is very focused and confident on stage.

ACCESS CODE: <54641>

GUINNESS WORLD RECORDS

CHAPTER SYMBOLS
Every chapter has its own symbols to identify it. These pages come from the chapter on Human Achievement.

WHAT'S BEEN ON TV?
These symbols show which records have been performed and shown on TV and in which country they originated.

[] USA – USA, FOX

[] FR – France, TF1

[] DE – Germany, ARD

[] SE – Sweden, TV3

[] FIN – Finland, NELONEN

[] UK – UK, LWT

SAY WHAT YOU THINK!
Now you have the chance to say what you think about some of the records in the book. This symbol means that there is a bulletin board on our website for the featured record. Get in there, see what everybody is talking about, and have your say!

INVESTIGATE MORE!
Every featured record in the book can be reached on the web with no sweat, if you type in this fast-track access code. If there is a TV symbol, check out whether there is a video to go with it!

ICON MENU
If you forget what each icon means, just look along here to find out.

GUINNESS WORLD RECORDS

how to use the web

Get a piece of the action when you log on to **http://www.guinnessworldrecords.com**. Choose from hundreds of crazy videos to watch, play games, discuss our amazing records with your mates, and catch the latest world record news. Here's how ...

GWR NEWS
Click here for the latest Guinness World Records news, gossip, and info – valiant attempts, records in progress, celebrity record breakers, hilarious failures, and lots more. With daily updated record news, there's always something to come back for.

FIND YOUR CATEGORY!
This year's Guinness World Records website is more exciting than ever with lots of new and exciting ways of finding out more about all our amazing records. Search the category menu to find the subject area you're looking for ...

Click on different menus to find records featured in the Guinness World Records book.

What do YOU think of these records?

Have your say with the fully interactive 'The Big Question'.

GO STRAIGHT TO THE ACTION
Go straight to your favorite record for even more amazing pictures and information using the access codes in this book!

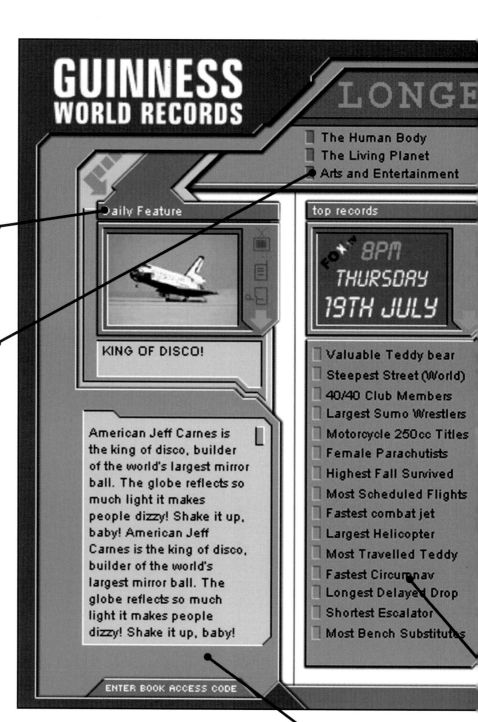

GUINNESS WORLD RECORDS

LONGE

- The Human Body
- The Living Planet
- Arts and Entertainment

Daily Feature

KING OF DISCO!

American Jeff Carnes is the king of disco, builder of the world's largest mirror ball. The globe reflects so much light it makes people dizzy! Shake it up, baby! American Jeff Carnes is the king of disco, builder of the world's largest mirror ball. The globe reflects so much light it makes people dizzy! Shake it up, baby!

ENTER BOOK ACCESS CODE

top records

FOX TV **8PM THURSDAY 19TH JULY**

- Valuable Teddy bear
- Steepest Street (World)
- 40/40 Club Members
- Largest Sumo Wrestlers
- Motorcycle 250cc Titles
- Female Parachutists
- Highest Fall Survived
- Most Scheduled Flights
- Fastest combat jet
- Largest Helicopter
- Most Travelled Teddy
- Fastest Circumnav
- Longest Delayed Drop
- Shortest Escalator
- Most Bench Substitutes

HOT BUTTONS
Amazed at what you've just seen? Hook up with some e-buddies and say what you think! Want to see more? Check out the video!

FANTASTIC SHORTCUTS
Use the access codes shown in *Guinness World Records 2002* to get straight to the action! Follow the directions on pages 6–7 and go directly to the record you want!

KEYWORD SEARCH
Use our keyword search to locate one of the thousands of Guinness World Records home pages.

INSTANT UPDATE
Hit the ticker tape when a world record flashes by and get the full details – instantly.

GREAT T-SHIRTS
Pick up some of the coolest, newest Guinness World Records T-shirts.

○○○○○ SEARCH ○○○○○

HOVERCRA

SHOP
GUINNESS
WORLD RECORDS

ame and Money   Human Achievements
World Matters   The Material World
Technology   Sports

favourite videos

top five videos

☐ Heaviest car balanced o
☐ Coin throwing - 24 hour
☐ Dog weaving
☐ Fastest pantomime hors
☐ First virtual newscaster

past favourites

☐ Fastest system frame scaff
☐ Most heads shaved in 4 ho
☐ Tallest paper cup
☐ Bow and arrow speed shoc
☐ Tallest tomato plant
☐ Heaviest train pulled
☐ Longest bicycle
☐ Largest accordion ensemt

interactive

top five game scores

nemo 22 55555
winboy 34
no doubt 56
poke y2 43
wormy 23

top 5 games

☐ nemo 22
☐ winboy
☐ no doubt
☐ poke-y2
☐ wormy

Contact Us

☐ Submit a Claim
☐ Enquires

PRIVACY   CREDITS   ABOUT US   CONTACT

The Video Vault

car balancing

the Video vault

HOME PICTURES ◄ ►

LAUNCH WINDOWS MEDIA PLAYER - 14.4KB - 56KB MODEMS
LAUNCH WINDOWS MEDIA PLAYER - ISDN, ADSL, CABLE, T1-T3 CONNECTIONS
LAUNCH REAL PLAYER - 14.4KB - 56KB MODEMS
LAUNCH REAL PLAYER - ISDN, ADSL, CABLE, T1-T3 CONNECTIONS

Windows Media Player

VIDEO VAULT
Choose from hundreds of great record film clips straight from the Guinness World Records video vault.

4

INTERACTIVE GAMES
Test your skill and see how you rank against all the other Guinness World Record challengers by playing our interactive games.

TOP RECORDS
Find the top records here, from the biggest, smallest, longest, highest, oldest, youngest, loudest, deepest, to the wettest, hottest, hairiest, fastest, slowest, coolest, smelliest, richest ...

WANT TO BREAK A RECORD?
Have you broken a Guinness World Record? Do you want to break a Guinness World Record? Send us your claim over the web for a fast response or contact us for information. You're only a click away, and you could be in next year's book ...

GUINNESS WORLD RECORDS™

contents

Josh Tenge – see page 225

Robonaut – see page 179

Alex Rodriguez – see page 201

Crash Bandicoot – see page 169

GUINNESS WORLD RECORDS

www.guinnessworldrecords.com/thehumanbody

the human body

extreme bodies

GREATEST HEIGHT DIFFERENCE BETWEEN A MARRIED COUPLE

When Fabien Pretou and Natalie Lucius (both France) walked down the aisle on April 14 1990, they became the married couple with the greatest difference in height. He is 6 ft 2 in (188.5 cm) tall, while she is only 3 ft 1 in (94 cm) – a difference of 3 ft 1.2 in (94.5 cm).

GREATEST WEIGHT DIFFERENCE BETWEEN A MARRIED COUPLE

Jon Brower Minnoch weighed 1,400 lb (635 kg) when he married his 110-lb (50-kg) wife, Jeannette, (both USA) in March 1978. At 1,289.7 lb (585 kg), this is the greatest recorded difference in weight for a married couple. Jon was also the heaviest person in medical history. He suffered from obesity as a child and by 1963, when he was 22 years old and 6 ft 1 in (1.85 m) tall, he weighed a huge 392 lb (178 kg). By Sept 1976 he weighed 974 lb (442 kg). He died in 1983, still weighing more than 798 lb (362 kg).

MOST WEIGHT GAINED BY A WOMAN

Doris James (USA) is alleged to have gained 324 lb (147 kg) in the 12 months before her death in Aug 1965. At this time she was age 38, weighed 675 lb (306 kg) and measured 5 ft 2 in (1.57 m) in height.

MOST WEIGHT GAINED BY A MAN

Arthur Knorr (USA), who was born in 1916 and died in 1960, gained a record 293 lb (133 kg) in the last six months of his life.

HEAVIEST WOMAN USA

Rosalie Bradford (USA) is claimed to have registered a peak weight of 1,199 lb (544 kg) in Jan 1987, age 43. After following a controlled diet, she weighed 282 lb (128 kg) in Feb 1994.

LIGHTEST PERSON

Lucia Xarate (1863–89, Mexico), an emaciated ateleiotic dwarf of 26.8 in (67 cm) who weighed 2.8 lb (1.1 kg) at birth, weighed only 4.7 lb (2.13 kg) at the age of 17. She had fattened up to 13 lb (5.9 kg) by her 20th birthday. The lightest recorded adults of normal height are those suffering from Simmond's Disease (*hypophyseal cachexia*). Losses of up to 65% of the original body weight have been recorded in females, with a 'low'

WASTING THOSE INCHES

Cathie Jung (USA, left) has a 15-in (38.1-cm) waist – the smallest waist on a living person. She is 5 ft 8 in (1.73 m) tall. Cathie and husband Bob worked together to develop her tiny waist as part of their enthusiasm for Victorian dress. At 38, the mother of three started wearing a 6-in (15-cm) wide training belt to reduce her waist gradually. She does not eat a special diet or exercise to maintain her waist.

The smallest waist ever of a person of normal height was 13 in (33 cm). Ethel Granger (UK) reduced to this measurement from a natural 22 in (56 cm) from 1929 to 1939, by wearing specially constructed corsets.

A measurement of 13 in (33 cm) was also claimed for French actress Mademoiselle Polaire (real name Emile Marie Bouchand) who died in 1939.

<54595> www.guinnessworldrecords.com/tinywaist ← ACCESS CODE

of 44 lb (20 kg) in the case of Emma Shaller (USA) who stood 5 ft 2 in (1.57 m). Edward C. Hagner, alias Eddie Masher (USA), is alleged to have weighed only 48 lb (22 kg) at a height of 5 ft 7 in (1.7 m). He was also known as the 'Skeleton Dude.'

HEAVIEST TWINS AT BIRTH

The world's heaviest twins were born to J.P. Haskin (USA) on Feb 20 1924. They had a combined weight of 27 lb 12 oz (12.6 kg).

CROWD PULLERS

The world's most elastic man is double-jointed Pierre Beauchemin (Canada, left), who earned the nickname 'Mr. Gumby' for his amazing ability to turn his arms and legs around in extremely contorted positions. Doctors believed that Pierre would be crippled by the time he was 30, but at 34 he continues to entertain people.

Gary Turner (UK) has skin that stretches further than that of any other known human being. His favorite trick is to stretch his neck skin over his mouth to create a human turtleneck, although this does not beat his stomach trick – on Oct 29 1999 he stretched the skin of his stomach 6.25 in (15.8 cm). Gary, who was born in 1964, has been entertaining people with this ability since school days.

<53928> www.guinnessworldrecords.com/elasticman ← ACCESS CODE

HEAVIEST TWINS

Billy Leon and Benny Loyd McCrary, alias McGuire (both USA), were normal in size until the age of six. In Nov 1978, just before their 32nd birthday, Billy and Benny weighed 743 lb (337 kg) and 723 lb (328 kg) respectively, and both had waists measuring 84 in (2.13 m). They became professional tag wrestling performers. When weighed before competitions, they clocked weights of up to 769 lb (349 kg).

LIGHTEST TWINS

Two sets of twins have been born with a combined weight of 30.33 oz (860 g). Roshan Maralyn (17.28 oz or 490 g) and Melanie Louise (13.05 oz or 370 g), were born to Katrina Gray (Australia) at the Royal Women's Hospital, Brisbane, Qld., Australia, on Nov 19 1993. Wendy Morrison (Canada) gave birth to Anne (14.81 oz or 420 g) and John (15.52 oz or 440 g) at Ottawa General Hospital, Ontario, Canada, on Jan 14 1994.

SHORTEST LIVING TWINS USA

The shortest living twins are John and Greg Rice (USA), born on Dec 3 1951. They are identical twins and both measure 2 ft 10 in (86.3 cm).

SHORTEST TWINS EVER

The shortest twins on record were Matyus and Béla Matina (Hungary, later USA; 1903–c.1935), who were both 2 ft 6 in (76 cm) tall.

SHORTEST LIVING MAN

Younis Edwan (Jordan) is believed to be 2 ft 1.5 in (65 cm) tall. He was born c.1971, and is the sixth sibling in a family of seven sisters and brothers.

SHORTEST MAN EVER

The shortest mature man for whose height there is independent evidence was Gul Mohammed (India). When examined at Ram Manohar Hospital, New Delhi, in 1990, he was found to be just 1 ft 10.5 in (57 cm) tall.

14

www.guinnessworldrecords.com/longlegs

A LONG STRETCH

At the age of 17, Sam Stacey (UK, right) has the world's longest verified legs. They measured 49.75 in (126.36 cm) in Jan 2001. Sam has always been taller than average and at the age of 17, she is 6 ft 4 in (2.08 m) – about the same height as her father. At a height of 5 ft 10 in (1.77 m), Sam's mother actually looks short. Her younger brother and sister are both of average height. Although Sam has occasionally considered a career in modeling, she is studying to become a nurse.

ACCESS CODE ‹56075› ←

He died at the age of 39 in 1997, after a long struggle with asthma and bronchitis.

SHORTEST LIVING WOMAN

Madge Bester (South Africa) is just 2 ft 1.5 in (65 cm) tall. Sadly, she suffers from *osteogenesis imperfecta* (characterized by brittle bones and deformities of the skeleton) and is confined to a wheelchair.

SHORTEST WOMAN EVER

The shortest-ever female was Pauline Musters (1876–1895), who measured 1 ft (30 cm) at the time of her birth in Ossendrecht, Netherlands, and 1 ft 9.6 in (55 cm) at the age of nine. A postmortem carried out after her death, from pneumonia and meningitis, at the age of 19 in New York City, showed her to be 2 ft (61 cm) tall, although there was evidence of elongation of the body after death.

TALLEST LIVING MAN 📺 UK

The tallest living man is Radhouane Charbib (Tunisia), who measures 7 ft 8.9 in (2.35 m). He is one of 11 brothers and sisters, who all measure a normal 5 ft 6 in (1.7 m).

TALLEST MAN EVER

The tallest man in medical history was Robert Wadlow (USA). When measured in June 1940, shortly before his death, he was 8 ft 11.1 in (2.72 m) tall. His greatest recorded weight was 491 lb (222.71 kg)

on his 21st birthday. He weighed 438 lb (199 kg) at the time of his death. His shoe size was 37AA (18.5 in or 47 cm long) and his hands measured 12.75 in (32.4 cm) from the wrist to the tip of the middle finger. His arm span was 9 ft 5.75 in (2.88 m) and his peak daily food consumption was 8,000 calories. At the age of nine, he was able to carry his father, Harold F. Wadlow, who stood 5 ft 11 in (1.8 m) and weighed 170 lb (77 kg), up the stairs of the family home.

TALLEST LIVING WOMAN 📺 USA

Sandy Allen (USA) is 7 ft 7.25 in (2.31 m) tall, making her the tallest living woman. A 6-lb-8-oz (2.95-kg) baby, her abnormal growth began soon after birth. She stood 6 ft 3 in (1.90 m) by the age of 10 and was 7 ft 1 in (2.16 m) by 16.

TALLEST WOMAN EVER

The tallest woman for whose height there is reliable evidence was Zeng Jinlian (China). She was 8 ft 1.75 in (2.48 m) tall when she died on Feb 13 1982, age 17.

LARGEST WAIST 📺 USA

The largest waist was that of Walter Hudson (USA), which measured 9 ft 11 in (3.02 m) at his peak weight of 1,201 lb (545 kg).

body parts

LARGEST BELLY CIRCUMFERENCE

Gut barger contestant David White (UK), also known as 'Mad Maurice Vanderkirkoff,' had a belly circumference of 54.2 in (137.7 cm) when measured on March 12 2001.

FEWEST TOES

The two-toed syndrome exhibited by some members of the Wadomo tribe of the Zambezi Valley, Zimbabwe, and the Kalanga tribe of the eastern Kalahari Desert, Botswana, is hereditary, via a single mutated gene.

MOST FINGERS AND TOES

An inquest held on a baby boy on Sept 16 1921 in London, UK, reported that he had 14 fingers and 15 toes. This condition, known as polydactylism, can be caused by any one of over 30 rare congenital medical syndromes (syndromes that are present at birth). The condition is relatively common, with as many as two in 1,000 births affected. These extra digits are most commonly fleshy bumps without any bones, but can be complete fingers or toes.

LIVING PERSON WITH MOST FINGERS

Godfrey Hill (UK) has 10 fingers and two thumbs. Born in 1928, when 12 pennies made a shilling, his extra fingers were an advantage at school where he topped the class at adding. His condition has won him attention around the world, especially in Tunisia, where he was mistaken for a descendant of Allah.

MOST DEVELOPED THIRD FOOT

José López (originally Mexico, now USA) has a third foot, consisting of an ankle and four toes, growing out from the ankle of his left leg.

HEAVIEST BRAIN

The heaviest brain ever recorded weighed 5 lb 1.1 oz (2.3 kg). It belonged to a 30-year-old male, and was reported by Dr. T. Mandybur of the Department of Pathology and Laboratory Medicine at the University of Cincinnati, Ohio, in Dec 1992. An average-size brain for an adult would weigh 2.8 to 3 lb (1.3 to 1.4 kg).

LONGEST NOSE

There are historical accounts that Thomas Wedders, who lived in the UK during the 1770s and was a member of a traveling freak circus, had a nose measuring 7.5 in (19 cm) long.

LIGHTEST BRAIN

The world's lightest normal (nonatrophied) brain weighed just 1 lb 8 oz (680 g). It belonged to Daniel Lyon (Ireland), who died in New York, in 1907, age 46. He was just over 5 ft (1.5 m) tall and weighed 145 lb (66 kg).

MOST VALUABLE TOOTH

In 1816 a tooth belonging to scientist Sir Isaac Newton (UK, 1642–1727) was sold in London for £730 ($3,633). This is approximately £25,000 ($35,700) in today's terms. It was purchased by an aristocrat who had it set in a ring.

HORRENDIX APPENDIX

The appendix (above) removed from the abdomen of Mr. Mahendra (India) on Aug 11 2000 measured a record 6.8 in (17.5 cm) in length. An average appendix measures just 3–4 in (8–10 cm long). The operation was performed by Dr. Teekappa at Vishwamanava Hospital, Birur, India.

On Oct 25 1998 surgeon Kadri Al-Ban (Yemen) removed the biggest bladder stone ever recorded from one of his patients in an operation at the Al-Kadri Clinic, Ibb, Yemen. Mohammed Ali A. Al-Muleiki (Yemen) had a vesical (bladder) stone that weighed a record-setting 9.15 oz (260 g), with a diameter of about 2.75 in (7 cm).

‹53572› www.guinnessworldrecords.com/appendix
← ACCESS CODE

GET IT OFF YOUR CHEST

Robert Earl Hughes (USA, left) had a chest measurement of 10 ft 4 in (3.15 m). His parents believed that a bout of whooping cough at the age of three months caused an endocrine imbalance that accounted for his incredible weight gain. At the age of six, he weighed 203 lb (92 kg). By 10 he weighed 378 lb (171 kg) and at age 25 he reached 896 lb (406 kg). In Feb 1958, just before his death, Robert weighed 1,067 lb (484 kg). His waist was 10 ft 2 in (3.1 m), and each upper arm was 3 ft 4 in (1.02 m) in circumference.

The largest muscular chest measurement is that of Isaac Nesser (USA) at 6 ft 2 in (1.88 m).

‹48481› www.guinnessworldrecords.com/bigchest
← ACCESS CODE

LONGEST MUSTACHE

The mustache of Kalyan Ramji Sain (India) spanned 133.4 in (3.39 m). In July 1993 the right side measured 67.7 in (1.72 m) and the left measured 65.7 in (1.67 m). The mustache had been growing since 1976.

LONGEST HAIR

 USA

The world's longest documented hair belongs to Ho Sateow, a tribal medicine man from Chiang Mai, Thailand. On Nov 21 1997 his hair was unraveled and it was officially measured at 16 ft 11 in (5.15 m) long. He had not had a haircut in over 70 years. He fell sick after cutting his hair when he was age 18 and vowed never to cut it again. The hair is washed annually with detergent and worn wound up in a fashionable beehive.

LONGEST-BEARDED MAN

The beard of Hans Langseth (Norway) measured 17 ft 6 in (5.33 m) at the time of his burial at Kensett, Iowa, in 1927. He started growing his beard at the age of 30 and it took 51 years to grow to this length. It grew at an average rate of 0.007 in (2 mm) per week, and was presented to the Smithsonian Institution, Washington D.C., in 1967.

LONGEST-BEARDED WOMAN
The beard of the 'Bearded Lady,' Janice Deveree (USA), was measured at 14 in (36 cm) long in 1884.

LONGEST-BEARDED LIVING WOMAN
📺 USA

Vivian Wheeler (USA) grew a full beard in 1990. The longest strand from the follicle to the tip of hair was measured at 11 in (27.9 cm) in 2000. Wheeler, who has married four times, was shaving her face at age seven.

LONGEST MALE FINGERNAILS
📺 USA

The world's longest fingernails are those of Shridhar Chillal (India), who last cut his fingernails in 1952. On July 8 1998 the nails on his left hand had a total length of 20 ft 2.25 in (6.15 m).

LONGEST FEMALE FINGERNAILS
📺 USA

The woman with the world's longest fingernails is Lee Redmond (USA). Her nails measure a total length of 21 ft 9 in (6.63 m). Lee has been growing her nails for 19 years. The longest nail is on her left thumb and measures 27 in (68.58 cm).

LARGEST GALL BLADDER
On March 15 1989 at the National Naval Medical Center in Bethesda, Maryland, Prof. Bimal C. Ghosh removed a gall bladder weighing a record-breaking 23 lb (10.4 kg) from a

69-year-old woman. This is more than three times the weight of an average newborn baby. The patient made a full recovery after the operation.

www.guinnessworldrecords.com/bigfeet

BIGFOOT
📺 USA

The biggest feet of a living person (excluding cases of the disease elephantiasis) are those of Matthew McGrory (USA, right) who wears US size 28.5 (UK size 28) shoes. Unsurprisingly, he has to have all his shoes custom-made to fit. Both his big toes measure 5 in (12.7 cm) in length, and his little toes are 1.5 in (3.81 cm) long.

LARGEST BICEP
The right bicep of Denis Sester (USA) measures 30 in (77.8 cm) when cold. He built up his amazing muscles by performing arm curls with a 150-lb (68-kg) bucket of sand. As a youngster he wrestled hogs weighing 400 lb (180 kg) on his parent's farm to get fit.

GUINNESS WORLD RECORDS™

age and youth

OLDEST LIVING WOMAN

Maude Farris-Luse (neé Davis) born on Jan 21 1887 in Morley, Michigan, USA, is the world's oldest living woman whose date of birth can be fully authenticated.

OLDEST PERSON EVER

The greatest fully authenticated age to which any human has ever lived is 122 years 164 days by Jeanne Louise Calment (France). She was born on Feb 21 1875 and died on Aug 4 1997.

THREE OF A KIND

Marjory Skeaping (née Scott), Sheila Botterill (neé Scott), and David Scott (UK, above) have been verified as the oldest triplets living in the world. They were born in Edinburgh, UK, on May 19 1920. Interestingly their uncle, aunt, and their mother's first cousin also celebrate their birthdays on May 19.

The longest-lived triplets ever recorded were Faith, Hope, and Charity Cardwell (USA) who were born on May 18 1899. Faith died first, on Oct 2 1994, aged 95 years 137 days.

The oldest quadruplets were the Ottmans (Germany). Adolf, Anne-Marie, Emma, and Elisabeth were born on May 5 1912. All four quads lived to the age of 79.

In Nov 2000 there were 992 sets of quadruplets worldwide. Identical quads are quite rare – only about 20 sets worldwide.

www.guinnessworldrecords.com/
oldtriplets

ACCESS CODE
‹54715› ←

Centenarians surviving beyond their 113th year are extremely rare. It is thought that only one 115-year life can be expected in 2.1 billion lives.

OLDEST MOTHER

Rosanna Dalla Corte (Italy), born in 1931, gave birth to a baby boy on July 18 1994 when she was 63. The baby was conceived through artificial insemination of donor eggs.

On Nov 7 1996, 63-year-old Arceli Keh (USA) gave birth to daughter Cynthia having undergone IVF treatment.

OLDEST MOTHER TO HAVE QUADRUPLETS

The oldest mother to have quadruplets is Merryl Thelma Fudel (Australia) who gave birth to three girls and one boy on April 18 1998, at the age of 55 years 286 days, at Sharp Memorial Hospital, San Diego, California. One baby died at birth due to respiratory failure.

OLDEST MALE TWINS

The oldest twins ever documented are Eli Shadrack and John Meshak Phipps (USA), born on Feb 14 1803 in Affington, Virginia. Eli died on Feb 23 1911 at the age of 108 years; his brother John died on Dec 10 1916 at the age of 113. The chance of identical twins both reaching and surpassing the age of 100 is about one in 700 million.

OLDEST LIVING MALE CONJOINED TWINS

Born in 1952, Ronnie and Donnie Galyon (both USA) are the oldest living conjoined male twins. For 36 years they traveled in side shows, carnivals, and circuses. In 1991 they retired and now live in Ohio.

OLDEST LIVING FEMALE CONJOINED TWINS

Masha and Dasha Krivoshlyapova (USSR), born on Jan 3 1950, are a rare form of conjoined twins – *dicephales tetrabrachius dipus* (two heads, four arms, and two legs). Now 51 years old, they reside in a Moscow old people's home.

IN SEVENTH HEAVEN

The most surviving children from a single birth is seven. The septuplets (above) were born eight weeks premature on Jan 14 1998 to 40-year-old Hasna Mohammed Humair (Saudi Arabia). There were four boys and three girls, the smallest of which weighed just under 2 lb (907 g).

Bobbie McCaughey (USA) also had septuplets on Nov 19 1997. Named Kenneth, Nathaniel, Brandon, Joel, Kelsey, Natalie, and Alexis, they weighed between 2 lb 5 oz and 3 lb 4 oz (1,048 g and 1,474.3 g) and were delivered at 31 weeks by cesarean in the space of 16 minutes.

‹48315› www.guinnessworldrecords.com/septuplets
         ← ACCESS CODE

OLDEST MALE CONJOINED TWINS EVER

Giacomo and Giovanni Battista Tocci (Italy) were born on Oct 4 1877 and lived to be 63 years old. They were separate above the waist, but shared an abdomen, pelvis, and two legs.

MOST LIVING ASCENDANTS

At her birth on May 16 1982, Megan Sue Austin (USA), all her parents, grandparents, and great-grandparents, plus five great-great-grandparents, were alive, making 19 direct ascendants.

GREATEST NUMBER OF DESCENDANTS

At the time of his death on Oct 15 1992, age 96, Samuel S. Mast (USA), had 824 living descendants. The roll call consisted of 11 children, 97 grandchildren, 634 great-grandchildren, and 82 great-great-grandchildren.

In polygamous countries, the number of a person's descendants can become incalculable. The last Sharifian emperor of Morocco, Moulay Ismail, who died in 1727, was reputed to have fathered a total of 525 sons and 342 daughters by 1703 and had his 700th son in 1721.

MOST COINCIDENT BIRTHDAYS IN A FAMILY

Ralph Betram Williams (USA) was born on July 4 1982. His father, grandfather, and, in 1876, his great-grandfather, were also born on July 4.

Veera Tuulia Tuijantyär Kivistö (Finland), who was born in 1997, shares her birthday of March 21 with her mother (1967), her grandfather (1940), and great-grandfather (1903).

MOST COINCIDENT BIRTHDAYS OF SIBLINGS

Catherine (1952), Carol (1953), Charles (1956), Claudia (1961), and Cecilia (1966) were born to Carolyn and Ralph Cummins (both USA) – all of them on Feb 20. The random odds against five single siblings sharing a birthdate are one in 17,797,577,730.

Heidi (1960), Olav (1964), and Leif-Martin (1968) Henriksen (Norway), all celebrate their birthdays on leap year day (Feb 29).

AGE BEFORE BEAUTY

At 112, Antonio Todde (right), born on Jan 22 1889 in Tiana, Sardinia, Italy, is the oldest living man in the world. He says his longevity is due to a lifetime of hard work and a daily glass of locally produced red wine. Sardinia's exceptionally high concentration of centenarians is attributed mainly to genes. Both Antonio's parents lived well into their nineties, and his four children are all in their eighties.

MOST SOUTHERLY BIRTH

Emilio Marcos Palma (Argentina) was born on Jan 7 1978 at the Sargento Cabral Base, Antarctica. To date, he is the only infant known to have been born on the icy southern continent.

LONGEST INTERVALS BETWEEN BIRTHS

The longest interval between the birth of two children to the same mother, but in separate pregnancies, is 41 years. Elizabeth Ann Buttle (UK) had a daughter, Belinda, in 1956 and a son, Joseph David, on Nov 20 1997, at the age of 60.

Jackie Iverson (Canada) gave birth normally to a boy, Christopher, on Nov 21 1993, a girl Alexandra, on Nov 29 1993, and was delivered (by cesarean) of another boy and girl, Matthew and Sarah, on Nov 30 1993. This period of nine days is the longest interval between the births of quadruplets.

MOST PREMATURE BABIES

On May 20 1987 James Elgin Gill was born to Brenda and James Gill (both Canada). 128 days premature, he weighed only 1 lb 6 oz (624 g).

Born on April 8 1996 in Riverside, Ohio, Devin and Dorraine Johnson (both USA) are the most premature twins. They were 119 days premature.

The most premature triplets are Guy, Kathryn and Marcus Humphrey (UK), born on Feb 28 1992 in Manchester, UK, 108 days early.

The greatest age to which any man has ever lived is 120 years 237 days. Shigechiyo Izumi, of Isen on Tokunoshima, an island 820 miles (1,320 km) south-west of Japan, was born on June 29 1865 and died on Feb 21 1986. He worked until he was 105. He drank *sho-chu* (distilled from barley) and took up smoking at the age of 70. He attributed his long life to 'God, Buddha, and the Sun.'

Kathryn Tepper (Australia) delivered a set of quadruplets on Feb 20 1997, a record 105 days early. They were Ben Stewart (1 lb 10.3 oz or 790 g), Hannah Elise (1 lb 6.9 oz or 680 g), Ryan Colin (1 lb 10 oz or 780 g), and Lisa Nicole (1 lb 8.5 oz or 735 g).

MOST PROLIFIC MOTHER

The wife of Feodor Vassilyev from Shuya, Russia, gave birth to 69 children in 27 confinements. A total of 16 pairs of twins, seven sets of triplets, and four sets of quadruplets were born between 1725 and 1765. Only two of the children failed to survive infancy.

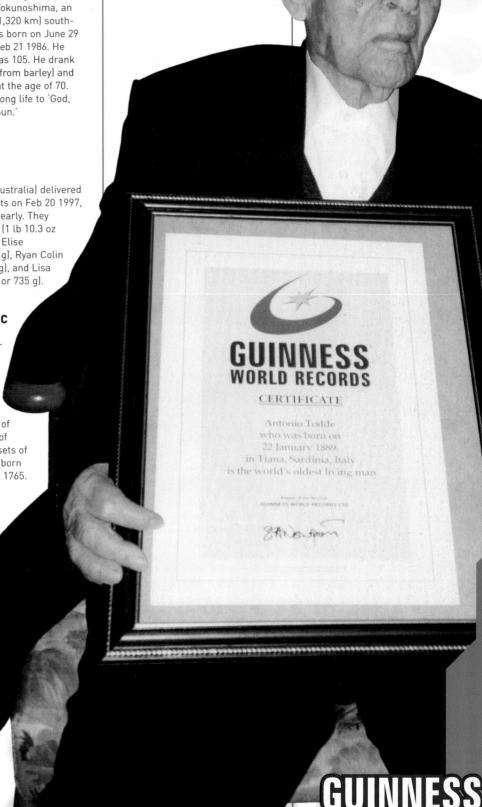

GUINNESS WORLD RECORDS CERTIFICATE

Antonio Todde who was born on 22 January 1889, in Tiana, Sardinia, Italy is the world's oldest living man

Keeper of the Records GUINNESS WORLD RECORDS LTD

GUINNESS WORLD RECORDS

body beautiful

COUNTRY WITH MOST PLASTIC SURGEONS

The USA has the world's most plastic surgeons, with approximately 5,965, followed by Brazil and then Japan, according to the International Confederation for Plastic, Reconstructive and Aesthetic Surgery. This figure is equal to almost half of the world's plastic surgeons. New York City has the highest concentration, but San Francisco is the city with the most plastic surgeons per capita.

MOST PLASTIC SURGERY

Cindy Jackson (USA) has spent $99,600 (£69,104) on 28 cosmetic operations over 15 years. Born in Ohio in 1955, Jackson has had three full face-lifts, two nose operations, knee, waist, abdomen, and jawline surgery, thigh liposuction, breast reduction and augmentation, and semipermanent makeup.

MOST EXPENSIVE SKIN BEAUTY TREATMENT

The 'Botaenica Dual-Mud Kit' made by a New York City luxury store is the most expensive skin beauty treatment in the world. It sold out after just four days at a price of $845 (£534) per unit. Each of the Dual-Mud systems was obtained from different geological compositions – the first from the Dead Sea and the second from the emanation of an Arctic Ocean floor volcanic vent, a very rare mud found only at this depth.

BODY TALK 📺 USA

Fashion designer Tina-Marie Stoker (USA) adorned the body of a model (left) with a record-breaking 29,540 rhinestones in Munich, Germany, on Jan 20 2000.

Adornment of a different kind makes Luis Antonio Agüero (Cuba), a record-holder as the world's most pierced man. He sports 230 piercings on his head and body. His face alone carries over 175 rings. Agüero uses a sterilized needle to do all his own piercing, and the 230 piercings have taken him 10 years.

The world's fastest henna artist is Ash Kumar (UK). On April 1 2001 he completed 96 traditional henna armband tattoos in one hour, at Cannon High School, Middlesex, UK.

‹54611› www.guinnessworldrecords.com/rhinestonebody
← ACCESS CODE

LARGEST LIP JEWELRY

The Ethiopian Mursi tribe is renowned for their practice of inserting large, circular clay plates behind the lower lips of their women as a sign of true beauty. At puberty, the lip is stretched with a clay plate, and the size is increased periodically. A girl's goal is to wear a plate at least the size of a teacup saucer (6 in or 15 cm in diameter), before she is married.

LONGEST NECK

The maximum known extension of a human neck is 15.75 in (40 cm). This was created by the successive fitting of copper coils, as practiced by the women of the Padaung or Kareni tribe of Myanmar (Burma) as a sign of beauty. Only initial discomfort is reported after the coils are fitted, yet the distance from earlobe to clavicle lengthens to more than double the average. The women's necks eventually become so long and weak that they cannot support their heads without the coils.

MOST WOMEN WITH BOUND FEET

In China, 38% of women aged 80 or older have bound feet. The practice of footbinding began in the Sung dynasty (960–976 AD) as a symbol of beauty. Chinese women's feet were bound tightly with strips of cloth to stop them from growing, so that their feet would resemble three-inch golden lotus flowers. By the time a girl turned three, all but the first of her toes were broken, and because of the cloth strips, her feet would grow no larger than 3.9 in (10 cm).

MOST VALUABLE PAIR OF 'FALSIES'

A pair of flesh-colored foam and cotton bra cups once belonging to film star Marilyn Monroe (USA), sold at auction for $5,000 (£3,450) in Bedford, New Hampshire, on April 15 2000. The 'falsies,' with nipple-shaped tips, were given to the Westwood Village Mortuary, Los Angeles, by Monroe's housekeeper, but were not used when preparing Marilyn's body for burial. They were rescued from the mortuary's bin by Allan Abbott, who kept them for 37 years, finally selling them for $2,100 (£1,500) in 1999.

MOST EXPENSIVE PERFUME

The world's most expensive perfume, launched in June 2000, is *Parfum VI*, designed by British perfumer Arthur Burnham. The 4-in (10.2-cm) bottle, made with platinum, 24-carat gold, rubies, and diamonds, costs $71,380 (£47,500) and was inspired by the Phantom VI Rolls-Royce. Only 173 bottles were made, and Michael Jackson and Mike Tyson were among the first to place orders.

LARGEST GLOBAL BEAUTY PAGEANT

As of Feb 2001, there were 89 entrants from 89 countries competing for the title of Miss World. India and Sweden have the most Miss World titles, with five each in the pageant's history.

BEAUTY PAGEANT WITH THE OLDEST CONTESTANTS

The 'Ms. Senior America' pageant is only open to women age 60 years or older. It was founded in 1971 to draw attention to the positive aspects of aging in response to the then bleak media image of America's elderly.

HEAVIEST MS. OLYMPIA CONTESTANT

Nicole Bass (USA) weighed 204 lb (92.5 kg) when she participated in the 1997 Ms. Olympia contest. As

BODY OF EVIDENCE

Although she no longer appears regularly on the catwalk, Elle MacPherson ('The Body'), is said to be the world's richest supermodel, worth a massive $38.12 million (£23 million). Her business interests include her own line of lingerie, 'Elle MacPherson Intimates.' Elle has also appeared in several films including *Sirens* (Australia/UK, 1994), *Jane Eyre* (USA, 1996), and *Batman & Robin* (USA, 1997). Most recently, she appeared in the US TV sitcom, *Friends*.

The largest international model agency is Elite Model Management. It is currently based in 22 countries around the world, with 11 offices in Europe and five in the USA. The company also has offices in Brazil, Hong Kong, and China.

‹52258› www.guinnessworldrecords.com/ellethebody
← ACCESS CODE

well as the heaviest, she is also the tallest-ever contestant, at 6 ft 2 in (1.87 m). Nicole was the overall winner of the 1997 NPC National Bodybuilding Championships before she went into Pro Wrestling. She is now working at independent shows worldwide. She has a 50-in (127-cm) chest, 30-in (76-cm) waist, 18-in (45.7-cm) arms, 28-in (71-cm) thighs, and 18-in (45.7-cm) calves.

MOST TATTOOED MAN 📺 USA

Tom Leppard (UK) has approximately 99.9% of his body covered in tattoos. Tom's all-body tattoo portrays a leopard-skin design – dark feline spots, with a leopardlike yellow tattooed on the skin in between. Tom now lives as a hermit on the Isle of Skye, UK, and estimates he has spent over £5,000 (about $7,000) on his amazing bodywork.

MOST TATTOOED WOMAN

The world's most tatooed woman is strip artiste Krystyne Kolorful (Canada). Tattoos cover 95% of her body and took 10 years to complete.

TALLEST HAIRDO

Ladies' hairdos literally reached their 'high point' in the mid-1770s when the French Queen Marie Antoinette's hair stood an amazing 36 in (91.44 cm) tall on her head. Ribbons, feathers, and other decorations made it even taller. These elaborate hairdos were expected to last a month – with unsavory results, since the hair had to be mingled with lard and whiting to keep it in place.

MOST HAIR 'UPDOS' STYLED IN ONE MINUTE 📺 DE

With only one minute on the clock, hairdresser Timo Zimmermann (Germany) twisted the hair of 22 women into a chignon-style 'updo,' using a chopstick-type implement, in Munich, Germany, on Dec 2 1998.

LARGEST FITNESS CHAIN

The world's largest fitness franchise is Curves International Inc., with over 1,700 locations throughout the USA. Curves opens a new location approximately every 12 hours and was founded in 1992. *Entrepreneur Magazine* ranked Curves the No.1 Top New Franchise and No.14 Fastest Growing Franchise in Jan 1999 and Jan 2000 respectively.

www.guinnessworldrecords.com/hairyboys

CROWNING GLORY 📺 USA

Victor 'Larry' and Gabriel 'Danny' Ramos Gomez (below) are 98% covered by a thick coat of fur, caused by a condition called hypertrichosis. The boys are very positive about their condition and have become stars in the Mexican National Circus, thanks to its owner Mundo Carpa. As Danny says,"We have learned that people who are different can still have dignity." Many others in their family – the De Jesus clan – also have hypertrichosis, earning them the title of 'the world's hairiest family.'

ACCESS CODE

‹53833› ←

GUINNESS WORLD RECORDS™

disease

RAREST DISEASE

The world's rarest disease is smallpox. In May 1978 the WHO (World Health Organization) registered zero cases in the previous six months worldwide. The last case of smallpox, in Aug 1978, resulted in death when a medical photographer at Birmingham University, West Midlands, UK, was infected by a sample kept for research purposes. There have been no cases since.

LEADING CAUSE OF DEATH

In industrialized countries, diseases of the heart and blood vessels (cardiovascular disease) currently account for over 50% of deaths. The most common of these are heart attacks and strokes, commonly due to atheroma (degeneration of the arterial walls) obstructing the flow of blood. Of the 53.9 million deaths in 1998, 16.71 million, or 31%, were caused by cardiovascular diseases.

MOST COMMON CAUSE OF SUDDEN DEATH

Coronary heart disease is the most common cause of sudden death. Smoking, high blood pressure, and high levels of cholesterol in food put an individual at high risk.

‹52507› www.guinnessworldrecords.com/badcigs
← ACCESS CODE

GOVERNMENT HEALTH WARNING

The world's most urgent health problems are tobacco-related. The WHO estimates that by 2020, tobacco-related illnesses including heart disease, cancer, lung disease (left), and respiratory disorders will be the world's leading killers, responsible for more deaths than AIDS, tuberculosis, road accidents, and suicide put together – around seven million people per year. Populations in developing countries face the greatest risk as 85% of all smokers will come from the poorer countries. Health-care costs associated with these illnesses result in a global net loss of $200 billion (£140 billion) per year.

WORST FLESH-EATING DISEASE

📺 USA

Dubbed the 'flesh-eating bug' by the media in May 1994, the rare and deadly necrotizing fasciitis (NF), has been around since World War I. The cunning *Streptococcus A* bacteria first attacks a layer of tissue below the skin, leaving gangrene in its wake, for which there is only one cure – surgical removal of the infected area. The mortality rate for patients contracting NF is 15%. But if NF combines with streptococcal toxic shock syndrome – severe pain and fever – the death rate soars to 70%.

MOST DISEASE OUTBREAKS

According to the 1999 WHO Report on Infectious Diseases, as of April 15 1999, the year 1998–1999 saw 45 reported outbreaks of cholera. The second was the potentially fatal meningococcal disease – infection of the spinal cord – with 29 reported outbreaks.

DEADLIEST AVIAN FLU OUTBREAK IN HUMANS

Avian flu, a strain of influenza previously only known to affect birds, was found to have infected 16 people in Hong Kong, China, in 1997. Four people died from the virus. This is the first virus to have been passed directly from birds to humans.

MOST VIRULENT DISEASE

Dengue, a viral disease carried by mosquitoes, and its more serious variant, dengue hemorrhagic fever (DHF), are probably the most widespread reemerging diseases. In 1998 there were 1.2 million cases of dengue and DHF reported. Over 15,000 of these cases led to deaths.

MOST COMMON NONCONTAGIOUS DISEASE

Periodontal diseases like gingivitis (inflammation of the gums) are the world's most prevalent non-contagious disease. Few people used to escape the effects of tooth decay but the 1981 level of 93% among UK schoolchildren had fallen to 55% by 1992. Sources state that up to one-third of American adults suffer from it.

LONGEST SNEEZING FIT

Donna Griffiths (UK) started sneezing on Jan 13 1981 at the age of 12, and sneezed an estimated million times in the next 365 days. She achieved her first sneeze-free day on Sept 16 1983 – the 978th day.

MOST NOTORIOUS CARRIER

The most publicized of all typhoid carriers is Mary Mallon (real name Maria Anna Caduff), known as 'Typhoid Mary,' who was born in Switzerland in 1855 and emigrated to the USA in 1868. In her job as a cook, she was the source of 53 typhoid outbreaks, including the

MAD, BAD, AND DANGEROUS TO HAVE

The most recently discovered infectious human disease is a new type of Creutzfeldt-Jakob disease (CJD, left), which leads to dementia. It is probably caused by a prion (a tiny piece of protein) transmitted from cattle suffering from the disease bovine spongiform encephalitis (BSE).

In 1999 the WHO recognized the southeast Asian Nipah virus as the newest virus. A Hendra-like paramyxovirus, it is clinically similar to Japanese encephalitis (JE), although probably not transmitted by mosquitoes but through direct contact with the tissue fluids of infected animals. This disease is associated with pig farming and has caused illness and death in both humans and pigs in Malaysia. The first human case of Nipah virus occurred in Sept 1998.

1903 epidemic of 1,400 cases in Ithaca, New York, and three deaths. She was placed under permanent detention at Riverside Hospital on North Brother's Island, East River, New York, from 1915 until her death from broncho-pneumonia on Nov 11 1938.

HIGHEST MORTALITY

The three diseases that are generally considered to be universally fatal are AIDS, rabies encephalitis, and plague. Acquired Immune Deficiency Syndrome (AIDS) is a fatal transmittable breakdown of the immune system, caused by the human immunodeficiency virus (HIV). HIV attacks and destroys the immune system, leaving the infected individual vulnerable to infections that will cause death. AIDS is the last stage of HIV infection, during which time these diseases have taken hold.

Rabies, a viral infection of the central nervous system, is commonly caused by being bitten by a rabid animal. The majority of rabies cases occur in wild animals like raccoons, bats, and foxes. Early symptoms in humans include fever, headache, and sickness, followed progressively by hallucinations, insomnia, anxiety, hypersalivation, and hydrophobia (fear of water). Death can occur within days of the start of symptoms, but with immediate treatment, chances of survival are high.

In the world's worst pandemic, the Black Death, an estimated third of the world's population died. From 1347 to 1351, this pneumonic form of plague (bacterial infection) spread through Asia, North Africa, and Europe, crossed the English Channel into England and Scotland, then went on into Norway, Sweden, Denmark, Iceland, and Greenland. It killed everyone who caught it – some 75 million people worldwide.

EARLIEST AIDS CASE

In Jan 1998 Dr. Tuofo Zhu (USA), from the Aaron Diamond AIDS Research Institute in New York, found the oldest known specimen of HIV in a blood sample taken in 1959 in Leopoldville, Zaïre (now Democratic Republic of Congo). This pinpoints the beginning of the AIDS (Acquired Immune Deficiency Syndrome)

epidemic to a decade earlier than first thought. Comparison of the specimen's genetic material to current strains suggest that HIV first crossed from monkeys to humans around that time. The HIV virus mutates very rapidly and charting its evolutionary changes will help to predict how much the virus will change in the future.

SMALLEST PARASITE

The smallest parasitic animals are various unicellular, protozoan parasites, some of which are only a few micrometers long. The smallest of these is *Pneumocystis carinii*, which is only about 0.02 in (0.5–1 mm) long. It inhabits the lungs and causes pneumonia in humans.

LONGEST-LIVING PARASITE

A life span of 27 years has been reliably recorded for the medicinal leech (*Hirudo medicinalis*). The length of a leech's body ranges from miniscule to about 8 in (20 cm), and longer when the animal stretches. The medicinal use of leeches dates back to antiquity and reached its peak in the first half of the 19th century. Hirudin, an extract from leeches, is used as a blood anticoagulant. The leech's saliva contains substances that anesthetize the wound and prevent the blood from clotting.

www.guinnessworldrecords.com/leprosy

ACCESS CODE

‹48530› ←

UNDER YOUR SKIN

Although plague and cholera are mentioned in the Old Testament of the Bible, leprosy (below) is thought to be the world's oldest disease. Cases of leprosy were described in ancient Egypt as early as 1350 BC. The disease is described by the World Health Organization (WHO) as 'a chronic infectious disease caused by the bacterium *Mycobacterium leprae*.' It mainly affects the skin, the peripheral nerves, mucosa of the upper respiratory tract, and the eyes, and it causes body mutilation.

Tuberculosis schistosomiasi, an infectious disease of the lungs, has also been seen in Egyptian mummies from the 20th dynasty (1250 to 1000 BC). Sophisticated techniques such as DNA extraction are now used to uncover the secrets of ancient illness. The first successful diagnosis was made from a Byzantine skeleton found in Turkey, which shows tuberculosis damage.

GUINNESS WORLD RECORDS™

medical marvels 1

MOST ARTIFICIAL JOINTS
Diagnosed with arthritis at the age of 13, Anne Davison (UK) had 12 major joints (both shoulders, elbows, wrists, hips, knees, and ankles) and three knuckles replaced by the age of 47. Her right knee was the first joint to be replaced, when she was 27 years old.

LONGEST TIME SURVIVED WITHOUT A PULSE
The longest time a human has survived without a pulse is three days. Julie Mills (UK) was at the point of death on Aug 14 1998 due to severe heart failure, when cardiac surgeons at the John Radcliffe Hospital, Oxford, Oxon., UK, used a special blood pump to support her for one week, during which time her heart fully recovered and the pump was removed. This was the first time a patient survived the procedure.

LARGEST PREGNANCY
In 1971 Dr. Gennaro Montanino (Italy) announced that he had removed 15 fetuses from the uterus of a 35-year-old woman who was four months pregnant. A fertility drug was responsible for this unique incidence of quindecaplets.

BABY IT'S YOU
Louise Brown (UK, left) was the world's earliest test-tube baby. Weighing 5 lb 12 oz (2.6 kg), she was delivered by cesarean section on July 25 1978 in Oldham General Hospital, Lancashire, UK. Louise's mother had been told for years that she could not have her own child. The miracle birth was thanks to the work of UK gynecologist Patrick Steptoe and two Cambridge doctors, Robert Edwards and Barry Bavister. The trio pioneered a new technique by which an egg could be taken from a woman's ovary and fertilized in a test tube before being returned to the womb to develop normally.

<53414> www.guinnessworldrecords.com/louisebrown ← ACCESS CODE

YOUNGEST PERSON TO RECEIVE A PACEMAKER
Stephanie Gardiner (UK) was just four hours old when she was implanted with a tiny pacemaker, which was the size of a stamp, on March 11 1995.

MOST PACEMAKERS IMPLANTED IN ONE PERSON
Mark D. Smith Jr. (USA) has used a record-breaking 18 pacemakers in his lifetime. His first pacemaker was implanted in Sept 1964, when he was just two years old and, because of complications over the years, he has had a grand total of five temporary and 13 permanent pacemakers implanted and replaced.

Pacemakers were invented in 1930, with the first implant performed on Oct 8 1958, only five years prior to Smith's first implant.

LONGEST WORKING PACEMAKER
The longest working pacemaker is a lithium-battery-powered Biotec 777 which was implanted in János Szilágyi (Hungary) on Jan 18 1979 and was last confirmed on April 7 2000 to be operating as normal.

LEAST BLOOD TRANSFUSED DURING A TRANSPLANT OPERATION
In June 1996 a transplant team led by surgeon Stephen Pollard (UK) at St. James University Hospital, Leeds, West Yorks., UK, performed a liver transplant on 47-year-old housewife Linda Pearson (UK) without a drop of blood being transfused. This operation usually requires up to 4.8–7.2 pints (2.3–3.4 liters) of blood, but as a Jehovah's Witness, Pearson could not receive any blood that was not her own.

RECIPIENT OF MOST BLOOD
A 50-year-old hemophiliac, Warren Jyrich (USA), was given a record 2,400 units of blood, equivalent to 285.3 gal (1,080 liters), when he underwent open-heart surgery at the Michael Reese Hospital, Chicago, Illinois, in Dec 1970. An average human body contains around 10.5 pints (5 liters) of blood.

OLDEST PATIENT TO UNDERGO AN OPERATION
The oldest age at which anyone has undergone an operation is 111 years 105 days. James Brett (USA) had a successful hip operation on Nov 7 1960, but died a year later of old age.

LARGEST GALLSTONE
The largest gallstone ever to be reported in medical literature weighed 13 lb 14 oz (6.29 kg) and

ARMS TRADE
At only four weeks old, Chong Lih Ying (Malaysia, left) was the youngest person to have a full limb transplanted when surgeon Dr. V. Pathmanathan (Malaysia) and his team of 55 transplanted her twin sister's left arm to her body in May 2000, during a 15-hour operation. Her twin sister, who was born with a severe brain abnormality, had no hope of survival before the operation. Chong was born with a deformed left arm and no hand. She was the first person in the world to undergo a transplant for a whole limb and was expected to create another medical first after not having to receive any carcinogenic drugs to prevent rejection of the limb. This was anticipated because Chong's identical twin had the same blood group and cell makeup as she did, making the operation a complete success.

 USA

www.guinnessworldrecords.com/handtransplant

HANDYMAN

The most amputations on the same arm have been endured by Clint Hallam (New Zealand, right), who has had his right hand amputated a total of three times. He first lost his hand in 1984 after an accident with a circular saw. Surgeons managed to reattach the severed limb but an infection developed and it was removed again in 1988. In Sept 1998 doctors performed a pioneering hand transplant on Hallam at a hospital in Lyons, France. However, he later requested that it be amputated once more as he was in continual pain. An operation to meet his demand successfully took place at a London hospital on Feb 2 2001.

ACCESS CODE

‹56505› ←

was removed from an 80-year-old woman at Charing Cross Hospital, London, UK, on Dec 29 1952.

LARGEST BRAIN TUMOR

A tumor weighing a record-breaking 1 lb 5 oz (570 g) was successfully removed from the brain of four-year-old Kaushal Choudhary (India) at Curewell Hospital, Indore, India, on May 25 2000. The child was admitted to hospital on May 24 2000 and was allowed to leave on May 30 2000.

LARGEST TUMOR REMOVED INTACT USA

The largest tumor ever removed intact was a multicystic mass from an ovary weighing 303 lb (137.6 kg). The giant growth had a diameter of 3 ft 3 in (1 m) and was removed in Oct 1991 from the abdomen of a 34-year-old woman. The operation was performed by Professor Katherine O'Hanlan of Stanford University Medical Center, California, and took over six hours.

MOST BENEFICIAL PARASITE TO HUMANS USA

The medical leech *Hirudo medicinalis*, traditionally used by doctors for bloodletting, has made a comeback. In 1991 a team of Canadian surgeons led by Dr. Dean Vistnes took advantage of the anticoagulants in leech saliva to drain away blood and prevent it from clotting during an operation to reattach a patient's scalp. The leeches used had been specially cultured in sterile conditions.

GUINNESS WORLD RECORDS

medical maruels 2

YOUNGEST DOUBLE HEART-VALVE TRANSPLANT

The youngest-ever double heart-valve transplant patient is Cameron Miles (UK), who was born with one heart valve missing and another not functioning. He was just three weeks old when he received a donor replacement on Dec 14 1998 and another on Dec 23 1998, at Leeds Gen. Infirmary, Leeds, West Yorks., UK.

YOUNGEST LIVER TRANSPLANT PATIENT

Five-day-old Baebhen Schuttke (Ireland) was given a new liver in an operation lasting seven hours at King's College Hospital, London, UK, after she collapsed with liver failure 24 hours after she was born.

YOUNGEST MULTIORGAN TRANSPLANT PATIENT

Sarah Marshall (Canada) was only six months old when she was given a liver, a bowel, a stomach, and a pancreas at London's Children's Hospital, Western Ontario, Canada, on Aug 7 1997. She had been born with an enlarged bladder, a small colon, and an abnormal bowel.

MOST HEART STOPPAGES IN AN OPERATION

Rudolph A. Cizmar (USA) died twice on the operating table on Sept 16 1999 at Baptist Memorial Hospital in Mississippi. He had to be given

electric shocks to restore a heart rhythm twice by doctors, once at 3:20 p.m. for 25 minutes, and again at 5:20 p.m. He made a full recovery.

LONGEST HEART STOPPAGE

The longest recorded heart stoppage is 3 hr 40 min in the case of Jean Jawbone (Canada), who at the age of 20 was revived by a team of 26, using peritoneal dialysis, on Jan 8 1977 at the Health Sciences Center, Winnipeg, Manitoba, Canada.

LONGEST SURVIVING KIDNEY TRANSPLANT PATIENT

The longest surviving kidney transplant patient is Johanna Rempel (Canada), who was given a kidney from her identical twin sister on Dec 28 1960 when she was 12 years old in an operation at the Peter Bent Brigham Hospital, Boston, Massachusetts. Both Johanna and her sister have continued to enjoy excellent health and both have had healthy children.

LONGEST SURVIVOR OF A PORCINE HEART-VALVE REPLACEMENT

An unnamed American lived a record 22 years, 8 months, and 22 days after a porcine (pig) aortic valve replaced a defective heart valve. He died on Dec 28 1998.

Harry Driver (UK) received a porcine aortic valve replacement on April 12 1978. It was still functioning on May 12 2000, a total of 22 years and one month later.

CHANGE OF HEART

On Nov 8 1996, one-hour-old Cheyenne Pyle (USA, left) became the youngest-ever recipient of a donor heart. The six-hour operation at Jackson Children's Hospital, Miami, Florida, involved draining her blood and cooling her body to 62.6°F (17°C), the temperature at which organs cease to function. Surgeons had an hour to complete the operation to prevent damage to her other organs.

Sophie Parker (UK) is the youngest recipient of two donor hearts. In 1992, age two, she underwent an operation at Harefield Hospital, London, UK, to give her a donor heart to complement her weak natural heart. In March 1998 her natural heart no longer functioned properly, so she had a second donor heart transplant to aid her donor heart.

<48446> www.guinnessworldrecords.com/youngestheartop
← ACCESS CODE

MOST ANEURYSMS SURVIVED

An aneurysm is a ballooning-out of the wall of an artery, vein, or the heart, due to weakening of the wall by disease, injury, or an abnormality present at birth, and is often caused or aggravated by high blood pressure. Sheryl Evette Kessee (USA) has survived surgery for a record-breaking three aneurysms – two of which burst in the front of her head and a third that was removed intact from behind her right ear.

MOST EXTENSIVE SKULL RECONSTRUCTION 📺 USA

Ahad Israfil (USA) holds the record for having the world's most extensive cranial reconstruction, after he was nearly killed by a close-range .357 Magnum revolver wound to the head when his employer mistook him for an intruder and shot him. A local surgeon, Dr. James Apesos, literally rebuilt Ahad's skull using a silicon mold and, after nearly a dozen separate operations, the reconstruction was complete.

MOST EXTENSIVE FACIAL PROSTHESIS 📺 USA

Leonard McQueeny (Australia) lost his nose and upper palate to a cancerous tumor and had them replaced with snap-on prosthetics made from silicon rubber and surgical-grade titanium.

SMALLEST SUBMARINE FOR MEDICAL USE

In 1999 German company microTEC produced a microsubmarine just 0.157 in (4 mm) in length with a diameter of 0.025 in (0.65 mm). Made with computer-guided lasers, it will be used to travel to sites of blockage or damage in blood vessels and repair them from within the body.

GREATEST NUMBER OF SEX-CHANGE OPERATIONS PERFORMED 📺 USA

Surgeon Stanley Biber (USA) has performed sex-change operations for 30 years in Trinidad, Colorado. He has conducted 3,000 male to female operations and over 250 female to

FAKING IT

The longest surviving recipient of an artificial heart (left) was William Schroeder (USA), who lived for 620 days from Nov 25 1984 until Aug 7 1986.

Made of plastic, aluminum, and polyester, the earliest artificial hearts date back to the 1950s. The best-known is the *Jarvik-7*, named after its designer, Robert K. Jarvik, an American physician. Designed to function like the natural heart, the *Jarvik-7* has two pumps (like the ventricles), each with a disk-shaped mechanism that pushes the blood from the inlet valve to the outlet valve.

The longest surviving recipient of a real heart was Dirk van Zyl (South Africa) who lived for 23 years 57 days after a heart transplant at the Groote Schuur Hospital, Cape Town, South Africa, on May 10 1971.

<48472> www.guinnessworldrecords.com/heart
← ACCESS CODE

www.guinnessworldrecords.com/descendant

BACK TO MY ROOTS

Adrian Targett (UK), the living link to the oldest-known family tree in the world, can trace his family back further than any other person. He has been shown to be a direct descendant, on his mother's side, of 'Cheddar Man,' a 9,000-year-old skeleton found in a cave in Cheddar Gorge, Somerset, UK. Scientists took a DNA sample from a molar from Cheddar Man and found a near perfect match in Adrian Targett, who lives less than half a mile away.

ACCESS CODE

‹48343› ←

male operations. The three-hour operation costs approximately $30,000 (£18,750).

LARGEST OBJECT REMOVED FROM HUMAN SKULL 📺 USA

The largest object removed from a human skull is a 8-in (20.32-cm) survival knife with a serrated blade, which was plunged into the head of 41-year-old Michael Hill (USA) on April 25 1998. Surgeons had to remove parts of Hill's skull to take the knife from his head successfully.

OLDEST SURGICAL PROCEDURE 📺 USA

Trepanation – the process of removing bone from the cranial vault – is the oldest surgical procedure practiced by mankind. The oldest evidence of trepanation was found at a 7,000-year-old burial site at Ensisheim, France, and belonged to a 50-year-old man.

MOST SUCCESSFUL ARTIFICIAL EYE

On Jan 17 2000 it was announced that Jeremiah Teehan (USA), who lost his sight 36 years ago due to a blow to his head, can now see again thanks to an artificial eye developed by William Dobelle, an American eye specialist who worked to create this device for approximately 30 years. The device consists of a miniature camera and ultrasonic rangefinder that feeds signals via two computers into electrodes planted in Teehan's brain.

GUINNESS WORLD RECORDS

against all odds

MOST LIGHTNING STRIKES SURVIVED

In the USA, the average number of deaths from lightning is just over 100 a year. Ex-park ranger Roy C. Sullivan (USA) was struck by lightning a record seven times. Sullivan's attraction for lightning began in 1942 (lost big toenail), followed by 1969 (lost eyebrows), July 1970 (left shoulder seared), April 16 1972 (hair set on fire), Aug 7 1973 (new hair refired and legs seared), June 5 1976 (ankle injured), and June 25 1977 (chest and stomach burns). Sadly, despite his many escapes, he died in 1983.

LONGEST SURVIVING HEADLESS CHICKEN

On Sept 10 1945 a Wyandotte chicken called Mike had its head chopped off but went on to survive for 18 months. Mike's owner, Lloyd Olsen (USA) fed and watered the headless chicken directly into his gullet using an eyedropper. Mike eventually choked to death in an Arizona motel. He now has a website dedicated to him: www.miketheheadlesschicken.org

GREATEST RESCUE WITHOUT LOSS OF LIFE

The greatest rescue without any loss of life was from the American vessel *Susan B. Anthony*, which was carrying 2,689 people, all of whom survived when it was sunk off the coast of Normandy, France, on June 7 1944.

<52780>

www.guinnessworldrecords.com/titanicbaby
← ACCESS CODE

THIRTEEN – LUCKY FOR SOME

Millvina Dean (UK, left) was just nine weeks old when she traveled third class on the cruiseliner *Titanic* with her parents and 18-month-old brother, Bertram. Millvina, along with her mother and brother, all managed to get into a lifeboat (No. 13) and survived when the 'unsinkable' ship sank after hitting an iceberg in the infamous 1912 tragedy. Her father, Bert, was not so fortunate and was among the 1,517 passengers who perished. Of the 706 passengers who traveled in third class, down in the bowels of the ship, only 178 survived – 75 of the 462 men, 76 of the 165 women, and 27 of the 79 children. In total there were 109 children on board the ship, 57 of whom were saved.

LONGEST SURVIVAL ALONE ON A RAFT

The longest recorded survival alone on a raft is 133 days by Second Steward Poon Lim (Hong Kong) of the UK Merchant Navy, whose ship, the *SS Ben Lomond*, was torpedoed in the Atlantic Ocean 565 miles (910 km) west of St. Paul's Rocks on Nov 23 1942. He was picked up by a Brazilian fishing boat off Salinópolis, Brazil, on April 5 1943, and was able to walk ashore.

LONGEST TIME ADRIFT AT SEA IN A FISHING BOAT

Fishermen Tabwai Mikaie and Arenta Tebeitabu, from the island of Nikunau in the Republic of Kiribati, survived for 177 days adrift at sea in their 13-ft (4-m) fishing boat. They were caught in a cyclone after setting out on a trip on Nov 17 1991 and were found washed ashore in Western Samoa, 111 miles (180 km) away, on May 11 1992. A third man on the boat died a few days before reaching Western Samoa.

LONGEST UNDERWATER SUBMERGENCE SURVIVAL

In 1986, two-year-old Michelle Funk (USA) made a full recovery after spending 66 minutes underwater, having fallen into a swollen creek.

DEEPEST UNDERWATER ESCAPE WITHOUT EQUIPMENT

The greatest depth from which an escape without any equipment has been made is 225 ft (68.6 m), by Richard A. Slater (USA) from the rammed submersible *Nekton Beta* off Catalina Island, California, on Sept 28 1970.

DEEPEST UNDERWATER RESCUE

The deepest-ever underwater rescue was that of Roger R. Chapman and Roger Mallinson (both UK) from the minisub *Pisces III*, in which they were trapped for 76 hours when it sank to 1,575 ft (480 m), 150 miles (240 km) southeast of Cork, Ireland, on Aug 29 1973. It was hauled to the surface on Sept 1 by the cable ship *John Cabot* after work by *Pisces V*, *Pisces II*, and the remote-control recovery vessel *CURV* (Controlled Underwater Recovery Vehicle).

FURTHEST VERTICAL SKI FALL

 USA

In April 1997, while competing in the 1997 World Extreme Skiing Championships in Valdez, Alaska, 25-year-old Bridget Mead (New Zealand) fell a vertical distance of nearly 1,312.4 ft (400 m), suffering bruises and severe concussion but no broken bones. At that time, Mead was the highest-ranked female extreme skier. Her doctors credit her survival to her excellent physical condition and to the fact that she was wearing a helmet.

LONGEST ELEVATOR FALL SURVIVED

On Jan 25 2000, US office workers Shameka Peterson and Joe Mascora dropped 40 floors – 400 ft (121 m) – in an elevator in four seconds down the Empire State Building, New York City, when their elevator cable failed. Stopping just four floors from the ground, both suffered only minor bruising.

HIGHEST G FORCE ENDURED VOLUNTARILY

The highest G value voluntarily endured is 82.6 G for 0.04 seconds by Eli L. Beeding Jr. (USA) on a water-braked rocket sled at Holloman Air Force Base, New Mexico, on May 16 1958. He was hospitalized for three days.

INVASION OF THE BODY SNATCHERS

A team of 21 firemen and one woman from the Malaysian Fire and Rescue service carried out the highest high-rise external snatch and rescue operation on April 17 1998. The rescue was from a gondola elevator that had stopped 1,241 ft (378.25 m) from the ground, on the 88th (top) floor of the Petronas Towers (left), Kuala Lumpur, Malaysia – the world's tallest office building. Due to strong winds and the building design, the 'victims' had to be carried down from the top to the ground in five stages – from the 88th to the 82nd floor, from the 82nd to the 73rd, from the 73rd to the 60th, from the 60th to the 6th, and from 6th to the ground. The entire operation, an exercise to test the competency and ability of the fire crew, took only 20 minutes.

<53086>

www.guinnessworldrecords.com/snatchrescue
← ACCESS CODE

HIGHEST G FORCE ENDURED INVOLUNTARILY

Racing driver David Purley (UK) survived a deceleration from 108 mph (173 km/h) to zero over 26 in (66 cm) in a crash at Silverstone Race Track, Northants., UK, on July 13 1977. He endured a G force of 179.8 G and suffered 29 fractures, three dislocations, and six heart stoppages. He recovered and continued racing.

LONGEST SURVIVAL WITHOUT FOOD AND WATER

The longest recorded case of survival without food and water is 18 days by 18-year-old Andreas Mihavecz (Austria). He was put into a holding cell in a local government building in Höchst, Austria, on April 1 1979 but was totally forgotten by the police. On April 18 1979 he was discovered close to death. Mihavecz had been a passenger in a crashed car.

LONGEST POSTEARTHQUAKE SURVIVAL BY A CAT

In Dec 1999, 80 days after an earthquake struck Taiwan on Sept 21 1999, killing an estimated 2,400 people, a cat was discovered alive after being trapped in the rubble of a collapsed building in Taichung, Taiwan. The cat, dehydrated and barely breathing, was treated immediately in a veterinary hospital and eventually made a full recovery.

LONGEST SURVIVAL WITH HEART OUTSIDE BODY

Christopher Wall (USA), born on Aug 19 1975, is the longest known survivor of the condition known as *ectopia cordis*, where the heart lies outside the body. The mortality rate is high, with most patients not living beyond 48 hours. The condition occurs in between 5.5 and 7.9 per one million live births according to the American Heart Association. Wall now works for a Philadelphia construction company.

LOWEST BODY TEMPERATURE

The lowest authenticated body temperature is 57.5°F (14.2°C) for two-year-old Karlee Kosolofski, (Canada) on Feb 23 1994. She had accidentally been locked outside her home for six hours in a temperature of -8°F (-22°C). Despite severe frostbite, which meant the amputation of her left leg above the knee, she has made a full recovery.

LOWEST PARACHUTE ESCAPE

RAF officer Terence Spencer (UK) achieved the lowest-ever aircraft escape when he was blown out of his aircraft at a height of 30–40 ft (9–12 m) over Wismar Bay, Germany, on April 19 1945. He managed to swim ashore but his plane crashed on land.

www.guinnessworldrecords.com/frostbite

WEATHER-ING THE STORM

On May 10 1996 Dr. Seaborn 'Beck' Weathers (USA, right) miraculously survived being left for dead on Mt. Everest when he was caught in a blizzard with winds up to 90-mph (145-km/h). The snowstorm claimed the lives of eight other climbers – the most deaths on Mt. Everest in a single day. Weathers lay exposed on the South Col for 16 hours, but revived and staggered to safety. He lost his right hand, some of his left hand, and his nose due to the frostbite caused by the bitter -40°F (-40°C) temperatures.

GUINNESS WORLD RECORDS

BULLETIN BOARD   GUINNESS WORLD RECORDS TV

www.guinnessworldrecords.com/fameandmoney

fame and money

movie stars

HIGHEST ANNUAL EARNINGS BY A FILM ACTRESS

According to the 2001 *Forbes* Celebrity 100 list, Julia Roberts (USA) earned more in 2000 than any other actress – an estimated $18.9 million (£13.3 million).

Julia Roberts is also responsible for the highest box-office earnings generated by any actress. Since 1987 her 24 films have earned a total box-office gross of $1,532.6 million (£1,054 million). Eight of her films have taken over $100 million (£71.4 million); the highest earner, *Pretty Woman* (USA, 1990), made $463.4 million (£331 million).

MOST BEST ACTOR OSCAR NOMINATIONS FOR THE SAME FILM

At the 1935 Academy Awards, three out of the four Best Actor nominees were from the same film. Clark Gable, Charles Laughton, and Franchot Tone (all USA) were all nominated for *Mutiny On The Bounty* (USA, 1935). However, it was fourth nominee Victor McLaglen (UK), who won the award for his role in *The Informer* (USA, 1935).

ACTOR WITH THE MOST OSCAR NOMINATIONS

Jack Nicholson (USA) has notched up a record 11 Oscar nominations since his 1958 film debut. Four were for Best Supporting Actor, with the remaining seven for Best Actor.

AND THE OSCAR GOES (AGAIN) TO...

Katharine Hepburn (USA, left) has been nominated for and won more Oscars than any other actor. She won the Best Actress Oscar for her roles in *Morning Glory* (USA, 1933), *Guess Who's Coming to Dinner* (USA, 1967), *The Lion in Winter* (USA, 1968), and *On Golden Pond* (USA, 1981). She has been nominated for an Oscar a record 12 times.

‹50660› www.guinnessworldrecords.com/oscarwinner
← ACCESS CODE

MOST BEST ACTOR OSCARS WON

Seven American actors have twice won the Best Actor Oscar at the Academy Awards. They are Spencer Tracy for *Captains Courageous* (USA, 1937) and *Boys Town* (USA, 1938); Fredric March for *Dr. Jekyll and Mr. Hyde* (USA, 1932) and *The Best Years of Our Lives* (USA, 1946); Gary Cooper for *Sergeant York* (USA,1941) and *High Noon* (USA, 1952); Marlon Brando for *On the Waterfront* (USA, 1954) and *The Godfather* (USA, 1972); Jack Nicholson for *One Flew Over the Cuckoo's Nest* (USA, 1975) and *As Good As It Gets* (USA, 1997); Dustin Hoffman for *Kramer vs. Kramer* (USA, 1979) and *Rain Man* (USA, 1988); and Tom Hanks for *Philadelphia* (USA, 1993) and *Forrest Gump* (USA, 1994).

MOST OSCAR NOMINATIONS WITHOUT WINNING

Actors Richard Burton and Peter O'Toole (both UK) have both been nominated seven times for the Best Actor award, but neither have won.

YOUNGEST OSCAR WINNER

The youngest Oscar winner is Tatum O'Neal (USA), who was age 10 years 148 days when she received the Best Supporting Actress award for *Paper Moon* (USA, 1973) on April 2 1974.

YOUNGEST WINNER OF A BEST ACTRESS OSCAR

Marlee Matlin (USA) was 21 years 219 days old when she accepted the Best Actress award on March 31 1987, for her role as a deaf-mute in *Children of a Lesser God* (USA, 1986).

YOUNGEST WINNER OF A BEST ACTOR OSCAR

Richard Dreyfuss (USA) won the Best Actor award on April 13 1978 for his performance in *The Goodbye Girl* (USA, 1977), age 29 years 166 days.

OLDEST WINNER OF A BEST ACTOR OSCAR

Henry Fonda (USA) won a Best Actor Oscar on March 29 1982 for his performance in *On Golden Pond* (USA, 1981), age 75 years 318 days.

OLDEST WINNER OF A BEST ACTRESS OSCAR

British-born actress Jessica Tandy won a Best Actress award for *Driving Miss Daisy* (USA, 1989) on March 29 1990, at the age of 80 years 295 days.

YOUNGEST RECIPIENT OF AN OSCAR

Shirley Temple (USA) won a special Juvenile award from the Academy on Feb 27 1935, age six years 310 days, the same year she became the youngest person to reach No.1 at the box office. She became the youngest, self-made dollar millionairess in 1938.

OLDEST WINNER OF AN HONORARY OSCAR

Comic genius Groucho Marx (USA) was 83 years 182 days old when he received an Honorary Award on April 2 1974. The wisecracking actor, famed for his greasepaint mustache, died on Aug 19 1977.

OLDEST ACTOR WITH AN OSCAR NOMINATION

American actor Richard Farnsworth, (1920–2000), was 79 years 270 days old when he was nominated for a Best Actor Oscar for his role in *The Straight Story* (USA, 1999) in Feb 2000.

OLDEST ACTRESS WITH AN OSCAR NOMINATION

British-born American actress Eva LeGallienne was 82 years 80 days old when she was nominated as Best Supporting Actress for her role in *Resurrection* (USA, 1980).

ONLY ACTORS TO WIN A BEST DIRECTOR OSCAR

In 1996 Mel Gibson (Australia) became the fifth actor to receive a Best Director Oscar, which he won for his film *Braveheart* (USA, 1995). He shares the record with Kevin Costner (USA) for *Dances with Wolves* (USA, 1990); Clint Eastwood (USA) for *Unforgiven* (USA, 1992); Woody Allen (USA) for *Hannah and her Sisters* (USA, 1986); and Robert Redford (USA) for *Ordinary People* (USA, 1980).

GET SHORTY!

The shortest adult actor in a supporting role is Verne Troyer (USA, left), known for his role as 'Mini-Me' in *Austin Powers: The Spy Who Shagged Me* (USA, 1999), who is 2 ft 8 in (81 cm) tall. His other films include *Men In Black* (USA, 1997) and *Fear and Loathing in Las Vegas* (USA, 1998).

The shortest adult actor in a lead role is 2-ft 9-in (83-cm) tall Philippino paratrooper and martial-arts expert Weng Wang, who stars in spoof Bond films *For Your Height Only* (Phil, 1979) and *Agent 00* (Phil, 1981).

The shortest actor with a star on the Hollywood Walk of Fame was Billy Barty (USA) who died in 2000. The 3-ft 9-in (113-cm) veteran of 130 films founded The Little People of America Inc., an organization that provides support and information for people of short stature.

‹54327› www.guinnessworldrecords.com/getshorty
← ACCESS CODE

MAY THE FORD BE WITH YOU

Actor Harrison Ford (USA, above) has been in a record 11 movies with international box-office takings of over $100 million (£71.4 million). His top five films are *Star Wars* (USA, 1977), $798 million (£570 million); *Return of the Jedi* (USA, 1983), $572.9 million (£409.2 million); *The Empire Strikes Back* (USA, 1980), $529.3 million (£378 million); *Indiana Jones and the Last Crusade* (USA, 1989), $494.8 million (£353.4 million); and *Raiders of the Lost Ark* (USA, 1981), $383.9 million (£274.2 million).

www.guinnessworldrecords.com/harrisonford

ACCESS CODE
‹54197› ←

FILM STAR WITH THE MOST FANMAIL

Silent movie star Charlie Chaplin (UK) received a record 73,000 fan letters in the first three days of his return home to London in 1921.

TALLEST ACTOR

Richard Kiel (USA), best known for his role as Jaws, the assassin with steel teeth, in the Bond films *The Spy Who Loved Me* (UK, 1977) and *Moonraker* (UK, 1979) stands 7 ft 2 in (2.18 m) tall.

TALLEST ACTOR IN A LEADING ROLE

Christopher Lee (UK), the tallest film actor in a leading role, is an awesome presence on set at 6 ft 5 in (1.94 m). He has been towering over movie lineups since his film debut in 1948. His first lead role was as Dracula in the 1958 film of the same name.

TALLEST ACTRESS IN A LEADING ROLE

Brigitte Nielsen (Denmark), Margaux Hemingway, Sigourney Weaver, and Geena Davis (all USA) are neck-and-neck for the tallest actress record, all at 6 ft (1.82 m) tall.

SHORTEST LIVING ADULT ACTRESS IN A LEADING ROLE

Linda Hunt (USA), who debuted in *Popeye* (USA, 1980), stands 4 ft 9 in (1.43 m) tall. She won an Academy Award in 1984 for her role as Billy Kwan, a male Eurasian cameraman in *The Year of Living Dangerously* (Australia, 1982), becoming the only actress to win an Oscar for playing someone of the opposite sex.

SHORTEST-EVER ADULT ACTRESS IN A LEADING ROLE

ET star Tamara de Treaux (USA), who died in 1990, was only 2 ft 7 in (77 cm) tall. She shot to fame after playing the role of ET in Steven Spielberg's *ET, The Extra-Terrestrial* (USA, 1982).

www.guinnessworldrecords.com/brucewillis

BUY HARD

Bruce Willis (USA, right) has the highest annual earnings for a film actor, earning an estimated $70 million (£46.89 million) in 2000 according to the 2001 *Forbes* Celebrity 100 list.

The highest fee earned by an actor in one film went to Jack Nicholson (USA), who was paid up to $60 million (£40 million) for playing the Joker in the hit film *Batman* (USA, 1989). His record paycheck was a percentage of the film's worldwide box-office takings of $413.2 million (£252 million).

Harrison Ford (USA) holds the record for the highest worldwide box-office earnings generated by an actor. He has acted in 25 films, generating total box-office earnings of $3,285 million (£2,315 million). Of these 25 movies, classic space epic *Star Wars* (USA, 1977), starring Ford as Captain Han Solo, has made the most money so far, taking a staggering $798 million (£570 million) worldwide.

ACCESS CODE
‹52230› ←

GUINNESS WORLD RECORDS™

tu stars

HIGHEST-EVER ANNUAL EARNINGS FOR A TV ACTOR
Jerry Seinfeld (USA) earned a record-breaking $267 million (£159.5 million) for appearing in the hit comedy *Seinfeld* in 1998.

HIGHEST-PAID TV COMEDY ACTOR PER EPISODE
Kelsey Grammer (USA), who plays psychoanalyst Frasier Crane in the TV comedy series *Frasier,* will be

paid a record-breaking $1.6 million (£1.1 million) per episode for the 2002 and 2003 series.

HIGHEST-PAID TV DRAMA ACTOR PER EPISODE
In Aug 1998 Anthony Edwards (USA), who plays Dr. Mark Greene in the American hospital drama *ER*, saw his salary rocket from $125,000 (£77,160) an episode to a record-breaking $400,000 (£246,913) per episode in a four-year deal totaling $35 million (£21,604,938).

HIGHEST ANNUAL EARNINGS FOR A TV TALK-SHOW HOST
Oprah Winfrey (USA) earned a record $150 million (£100,489,047) in 2000 according to the 2001 *Forbes* Celebrity 100 list. The series *Oprah* has over 22 million viewers and is seen in 113 countries. It has won a grand total of 34 Emmy Awards.

HIGHEST ANNUAL EARNINGS FOR A TV NEWS BROADCASTER
Barbara Walters (USA) reputedly earns over $13 million (£7.84 million) a year as news correspondent and coanchor for ABC's news magazine, *20/20*, *The Barbara Walters Specials*, and *The View*. Walters was the first woman to anchor the network nightly news and she has interviewed every US president since Richard Nixon. She made journalistic history by arranging the first joint interview of President Anwar Sadat of Egypt and Prime Minister Menachem Begin of Israel in Nov 1977.

HIGHEST ANNUAL EARNINGS FOR A MAGICIAN
David Copperfield (USA) had the highest annual earnings of any magician in 2000 with $60 million (£42.8 million). The host of TV shows for both ABC and CBS, his illusions have included making the Statue of Liberty vanish and walking through the Great Wall of China.

RICHEST TV QUIZ MASTER
Talk-show host Regis Philbin (USA), who is the quiz master for the US version of *Who Wants to be a Millionaire?*, earned a record $35 million (£25 million) in 2000.

LONGEST TIME PLAYING THE SAME TV ROLE
William Roache (UK) has played the character Ken Barlow without a break since the first episode of the British soap *Coronation Street* was broadcast on Dec 9 1960.

MOST APPEARANCES BY A TV EXTRA
Vic Gallucci (UK) did his first walk-on part in *The Bill* (UK) in 1989 and has since made over 819 appearances on the show as Detective Constable Tom Baker – the most appearances ever by a TV extra. With no lines to speak, he still arrives at work early to learn his 'lurking' moves, which involve shuffling papers and wandering around the set's coffee machine. Also known as 'Trev' which stands for Totally Reliable Extra Veteran, Vic can be seen in the background shots of almost every episode.

LONGEST CAREER AS A TV CHEF
Julia Child (USA) first appeared on US TV in 1963 in a series called *The French Chef*. Pioneering the art of French cuisine on television, the series was followed by numerous others, including *Master Chef*, *Baking at Julia's*, and most recently 22 episodes of *Julia and Jacques Cooking at Home* (1999) in which she teamed up with French chef Jacques Pepin.

LONGEST-SERVING ACTOR IN AN AUSTRALIAN SOAP
Three actors have appeared in the *Home and Away* TV series since it first aired in Australia on Jan 15 1988 – Norman Coburn who plays Donald Fisher, Ray Meagher who plays Alf Stewart, and Kate Ritchie who plays Sally Fletcher.

LONGEST PERFORMANCE CONTRACT IN RADIO AND TV
American entertainer Bob Hope (USA) completed the 60th year of his NBC contract on Nov 23 1996, making this the longest performance contract ever. As well as performing on radio, TV, and film, he has also entertained the US troops overseas in every war from World War II to the Gulf War.

MOST CELEBRITIES FEATURED IN A CARTOON TV SERIES
Since first appearing in 1987 as a series of 30-second spots produced by Matt Groening (USA) for the Fox network's *The Tracey Ullman Show*, *The Simpsons* has featured 240 celebrities including Dolly Parton, Buzz Aldrin, and Jerry Springer (all USA), and Stephen Hawking (UK).

LONGEST CAREER AS A CARTOON VOICEOVER ARTIST
Jack Mercer (USA) first provided the voice for the movie series *Popeye* in the film *Let You and Him Fight* in 1934. He continued to play the role for the next 45 years and 294 productions including the TV cartoons.

FIRST PERSON TO APPEAR ON A BRITISH TV AD
On Sept 22 1955, the opening night of UK Independent Television, Meg Smith (UK) beat 80 other actresses to

EXCELLENT SPELLING
Aaron Spelling (USA, above) has produced over 3,842 hours of television airtime since 1956, making him the most prolific TV producer of drama. This includes 3,578 hours of TV episodes and 264 hours of TV movies. His shows have included *Mod Squad*, the original 1970s *Charlie's Angels*, *Love Boat*, *Dynasty*, *Fantasy Island*, *Beverly Hills 90210*, *Melrose Place*, *Charmed*, and *All Souls*. It would take over four months to watch all his TV shows if you watched them back-to-back for 24 hours a day.

Spelling has also erected the largest Hollywood home, dubbed 'The Manor' by his family. The building occupies an area of 56,550 ft² (5,253 m²) and has 123 rooms. The house is currently valued at $37 million (£26.4 million) and includes a gymnasium, bowling alley, swimming pool, and skating rink. The previous house on the site, owned by Bing Crosby, was demolished to make way for Spelling's new house.

‹51566›
www.guinnessworldrecords.com/aaronspelling
← ACCESS CODE

MONKEY BUSINESS

The PG Tips advertising campaign, starring chimpanzees (above), began in 1956 and ran until 1994, making the chimps the most enduring commercial stars. They were first voiced by *Pink Panther* star Peter Sellers (UK) and have since starred in more than 100 commercials. The chimps put their individual fees of over £1,000 ($1,397) per commercial into a retirement fund set up by the company.

www.guinnessworldrecords.com/pgtips

ACCESS CODE

‹47906› ←

become Britain's first 'plug' girl – wielding a toothbrush in the 60-second ad for Gibbs SR toothpaste.

MOST STARS FROM DIFFERENT MUSIC STYLES ON ONE VIDEO

A charity recording of 'Perfect Day' by Lou Reed (USA), which was commissioned to show the diversity of music played on BBC television and radio, features a record-breaking 27 artists from 18 different musical genres. These include jazz (Courtney Pine), reggae (Burning Spear), country (Emmy Lou Harris), blues (Dr. John), pop (Boyzone), rap (Fun Lovin' Criminals), and classical music (Lesley Garrett). Lou Reed himself appears on the video.

MOST CONSECUTIVE BAFTA AWARDS

Robbie Coltrane (UK) has won a record three consecutive BAFTA (British Academy of Film and Television Arts) awards as 'Best Television Actor,' for his role as psychiatrist Gerry 'Fitz' Fitzgerald in Granada Television's series *Cracker*, from 1994 to 1996.

MOST TIMES MC AT THE ACADEMY AWARDS

American entertainer Bob Hope (USA) has served as Master of Ceremonies on Oscar night, alone and with others, a record-breaking 16 times and has taken part in 27 Academy Awards presentations. Hope himself received five Oscars during his acting career.

MOST DURABLE TV PRESENTER

Patrick Moore (UK) has presented the monthly *Sky at Night* without a break or a miss since April 24 1957. By May 2001 a total of 570 shows had been broadcast. Moore has received the OBE for services to astronomy, and in 1988 he received the CBE. His guests have included first man on the Moon, Neil Armstrong (USA), and rock star Brian May (UK).

www.guinnessworldrecords.com/jenniferaniston

GIRL POWER

The highest annual earnings from female TV acting roles are paid to Jennifer Aniston (right), Lisa Kudrow and Courteney Cox Arquette (all USA), who have played the leads in NBC's *Friends* since 1994. They all earned a record-breaking $15.3 million (£10.9 million) in 2000, according to the 2001 *Forbes* Celebrity 100 list. They and their male co-stars negotiated a salary of $750,000 (£525,714) per episode in 2000 for the seventh season.

ACCESS CODE

‹52644› ←

GUINNESS WORLD RECORDS

pop stars

LONGEST MUSIC VIDEO

Ghosts, Michael Jackson's (USA) 1996 part-feature film, part-music video, is 35 minutes long and was based on an original concept by cult horror writer Stephen King (USA).

MOST GRAMMY AWARDS WON IN A YEAR BY AN INDIVIDUAL

Michael Jackson took home a record eight Grammy Awards in 1984, including Best New Rhythm and

*NSYNC ARE ONE IN A MILLION

*NSYNC's (USA) 'No Strings Attached' 2000 US tour broke the record for the most tickets sold in a day when a record one million, valued at $40 million (£25,078,370), were sold on March 25 2000. The band sold out 51 of their 52 tour dates on the first day of sales.

The most successful tour of all time is The Rolling Stones' (UK) 1989 'Steel Wheels' tour of North America, which earned an estimated $310 million (£185 million) and was attended by 3.2 million people in 30 cities.

The largest paying audience ever attracted by a solo performer was an estimated 180,000–184,000, in the Maracanã Stadium, Rio de Janeiro, Brazil, to hear a gig by ex-Beatle Sir Paul McCartney (UK) on April 21 1990.

www.guinnessworldrecords.com/nsync

ACCESS CODE
‹56312› ←

Blues Song for hit single 'Billie Jean,' as well as several awards for writing, producing, and performing the legendary *Thriller* album.

FASTEST-SELLING ALBUM

The Beatles' (UK) album, *1*, sold a record 13.5 million copies around the world in its first month. Released on Nov 13 2000, it shifted 3.6 million copies on its first day alone. Although all the tracks on the disc were more than 30 years old, it was the biggest-selling album of 2000 in the UK and was No.1 in 35 countries.

FASTEST LIVE RECORDING TO RETAIL

A limited edition of Midge Ure's (UK) 'Dear God' single, including two live B-side tracks 'All Fall Down' and 'Strange Brew,' was delivered to retail just 81 hr 15 min after the songs were recorded at The Venue in Edinburgh, UK, on Nov 21 1988.

FASTEST RAPPER USA

Rebel XD, otherwise known as Seandale Price (USA), is the world's fastest rap artist. On June 24 1998 he rapped 683 syllables in 54.501 seconds, which works out at just over 12.5 syllables per second, beating his own previous record of 674 syllables in 54.9 seconds, or 12.2 syllables per second set in 1992.

GREATEST AGE RANGE IN A BAND

The 1997 Afro-Cuban All Stars album *A todo Cuba le Gusta* featured band members spanning four generations, ranging in age from 15 to 81. The oldest was flute player, Robert Egues, while the youngest was Julián Oviedo Sánchez (both Cuba), playing the timbales.

LARGEST SCREEN AT A ROCK CONCERT

The set for U2's (Ireland) 1997 'PopMart' tour featured the world's largest LED (light-emitting diode) screen. Measuring a gigantic 54 ft 8 in x 170 ft (16.7 x 51.8 m), the screen showed animation and pop-art masterpieces. Although U2 were originally identified with guitar-based

BACKSTREET BOYS MOVE INTO THE FAST LANE

The biggest-selling boy-band album of all time is the Backstreet Boys' (USA) *Millennium*, released in 1999, which had sales of 13 million by March 2001. The record entered the US Billboard Top 200 Album Chart at No.1 in June 1999. It sold 1,134,000 copies in its first week, shattering Garth Brooks's one-week sales world record. The Backstreet Boys earned an estimated $60 million (£43,148,714) in 1999, according to *Forbes* Celebrity 100 list (2000). The Backstreet Boys have emerged as the most successful boy-band of their generation, and their 1999 tour of the US drew 1.4 million fans.

‹56422› www.guinnessworldrecords.com/backstreetboys
← ACCESS CODE

anthems, the 1990s saw them experimenting with samplers, dance rhythms, and visual effects.

MOST SUCCESSFUL MALE COUNTRY SINGER

Garth Brooks (USA) is the most successful country artist of all time, with album sales of over 100 million since 1989. He is also the biggest-ever certified solo album artist in the USA.

Garth Brooks also holds the record for the highest-grossing country music tour with his three-year long 'Sevens' tour. Starting in March 1997, it grossed a record $105 million (£65.625 million). He played 350 shows in 100 cities, pulling crowds of around 55,000 fans at each concert.

MOST BRIT AWARDS WON BY AN INDIVIDUAL

Robbie Williams (UK) has won more BRIT (British Record Industry Trust) awards than any other artist or act. He has won 12 awards in total, both as a solo singer and as part of Take That. Recent awards include Best British Single and Best British Video (both for 'Rock DJ'), and British Male Solo Artist at the BRITS on Feb 26 2001.

OLDEST EUROVISION SONG CONTEST WINNER

The Olsen Brothers (Jorgan and Niels), representing Denmark, won the Eurovision Song Contest at ages 49 and 45 respectively. 'Fly On The Wings Of Love' won with 195 points in Stockholm, Sweden, on May 13 2000.

LONGEST-RUNNING GROUP WITH SAME LINEUP

The Beverley Sisters (UK) made their professional debut on Nov 13 1944, with Glenn Miller (USA) and the American Band of the AEF for the BBC's AEFP Broadcast in London. They are still regularly singing live after 57 years with the same lineup of Joy, Teddie, and Babs.

MOST MUSIC VIDEOS FOR ONE SONG

There are five different videos for the 1998 song 'Timber' by UK dance act Coldcut – the original mix, the EBN remix, the LPC remix, the Clifford Gilberto remix, and the Gnomadic remix. They offered the 'Timber' track to videomakers to encourage them to remix videos in the same way that dance music DJs and producers remix records.

MY BANK ACCOUNT IS THRILLING ME ...

The fastest–selling album by a female artist is Britney Spears' (USA) album, *Oops!...I Did it Again*, which sold a record 1.3 million copies in its first week of release in the US in June 2000. A further 612,500 copies were snapped up the following week. Britney Spears (right) earned $38.5 million (£25,457,225) in 2000, according to the *Forbes* Celebrity 100 list released on March 2 2001.

The record for the highest–ever annual earnings by a female artist is held by Celine Dion, who made more money in one year than any other woman in pop. According to the *Forbes* 1999 Celebrity 100 list, the French Canadian songstress, who sings in both English and French, earned an estimated sum of $56 million (£33.5 million) in 1998.

MOST SUCCESSFUL FEMALE SOLO SINGER

The most successful female solo artist is Madonna (USA), who has sold around 120 million albums and 40 million singles. Her total sales are more than any other female music star. Madonna has had 34 American Top-10 singles and 12 Top-10 albums. In the UK she's had 48 Top-10 singles and 14 Top-10 albums.

OLDEST RAPPERS

Japanese twin sisters Kin Narita and Gin Kanie were born on Aug 1 1892. For their 100th birthday in 1992, they recorded a 'granny-rap' record that entered the Japanese pop chart. Although Gin died of a heart attack in Jan 2000, they are still household names in Japan and, in the past, appeared regularly on TV and commercials.

HIGHEST ANNUAL EARNINGS BY A BOY-BAND

*NSYNC were the highest earning boy-band in 2000, with an estimated income of $42 million (£28,136,933), according to *Forbes* Celebrity 100 list.

HIGHEST ANNUAL EARNINGS BY A RAPPER

Dr. Dre (USA) has made more money than any other rapper in one year. According to the 2001 *Forbes* Celebrity 100 list, Dre earned $31.5 million (£21,102,700) in 2000.

BIGGEST-SELLING FEMALE LATIN ARTIST

Cuban-born singer Gloria Estefan is the most successful female Latin artist in the world, with total global sales estimated at more than 35 million. In the USA she has amassed eight gold albums, four of which – *Primitive Love, Let It Loose, Cuts Both Ways*, and *Greatest Hits* – have passed the three million sales mark.

BIGGEST-SELLING MALE LATIN ARTIST

Spanish vocalist Julio Iglesias is the world's most successful Latin music artist, with global album sales of more than 200 million. *Julio*, released in 1983, was the first foreign-language album to sell more than two million copies in the USA, and the only foreign-language record to go double platinum there.

HIGHEST-EVER ANNUAL POP EARNINGS

In 1989 Michael Jackson made the highest-ever earnings for a pop star in one year. He topped the *Forbes* list with an income of $125 million (£76,298,602).

HIGHEST-EVER ANNUAL EARNINGS BY A GIRL-BAND

The Spice Girls (UK) ranked 20th on *Forbes* list of 1998's 40 richest entertainers, with a group income of $49 million (£29.6 million).

HIGHEST ANNUAL EARNINGS BY A BAND

The Beatles, despite breaking up in 1970, were the highest-earning band in 2000, making $150 million (£100.49 million) according to the 2001 *Forbes* Celebrity 100 list.

RICHEST BAND

The Rolling Stones (all UK) are the richest band with a combined wealth of £400 million ($647 million). In 2000 lead singer Mick Jagger had an estimated fortune of £150 million ($243 million), followed by guitarist Keith Richards with £130 million ($210 million), drummer Charlie Watts with £65 million ($105 million) and guitarist Ronnie Wood with £55 million ($89 million).

GUINNESS WORLD RECORDS™

super rich

RICHEST BACHELOR

Larry J. Ellison (USA) is estimated to be worth $47 billion (£33 billion). He has been CEO of Oracle Corporation since he founded the company in 1977.

RICHEST PERSON

Bill Gates (USA), founder and chairman of Microsoft Corporation, is currently the richest person in the world. *Forbes* magazine estimated his wealth at $60 billion (£38 billion) in May 2000. Gates began computer programming when he was just 13. In 1986, at the age of 31, Gates became the youngest-ever dollar billionaire. For a few weeks in early 2000, Larry Ellison and Gates competed for the title of the world's richest person, but Gates soon reclaimed the title.

YOUNGEST SELF-MADE MILLIONAIRE

The youngest male ever to earn a million dollars was the child film actor Jackie Coogan (USA). Between 1923 and 1924 he earned $22,000 (£15,400) per week (in today's terms: $222,081 or £155,560) and retained about 60% of his films' profits. At 13 he was a millionaire. Unfortunately, his showbiz parents squandered his money and under California law at

GETTING THE WANG OF THINGS

Charles B. Wang (USA, left), founder and chief executive officer of Computer Associates International, earned $650,048,000 (£418,734,741) in the financial year 1999/2000 – a figure that includes his salary, bonus and stock gains. This is currently the highest annual earnings by a CEO. His total earnings over the five-year period 1996–2000 were $713,452,000 (£459,577,045). *Fortune* magazine has named Computer Associates as one of America's most admired companies and one of the best companies to work for in America. The company is a business-to-business technology and software solutions provider.

‹52160›
← ACCESS CODE
www.guinnessworldrecords.com/wang

the time, he had no rights to the money he made as a child. Jackie filed suit for around $4 million (£2.8 million) and, in 1939, was awarded just $126,000 (£88,278). The ensuing legal case (1938) led ultimately to the Child Actor's Bill, also known as the Coogan Act, to protect the earnings of child actors.

LARGEST ANNUAL INCOME

George Soros (USA), president and chairman of Soros Fund Management LLC, a private investment management firm, earned $1.5 billion (£1 billion) in 1995 alone. Most of his earnings came from profitable investments in offshore funds such as Quantum, Quantum Emerging Growth, Quota, and Quasar International.

RICHEST WORKING WOMAN

Abigail Johnson (USA), a senior vice president of FMR Corp. (Fidelity Investments), has a net worth of $7 billion (£4.4 billion), and is No.18 on the 2000 *Forbes* 400 US Rich list.

RICHEST WOMAN

Liliane Bettencourt (France), the heiress to the L'Oréal cosmetics fortune, has an estimated worth of $15.2 billion (£10.1 billion).

RICHEST INVESTOR

Warren Edward Buffett (USA), chairman of Berkshire Hathaway, is the world's richest investor, estimated to be worth $28 billion (£18.8 billion). He started playing the stock market at age 11. At 25, Buffett started his own investment company, the Buffett Partnership. In 1965 it

bought its first company, Berkshire Hathaway. Since then, the company's stock has increased by more than a stunning 300,000%.

RICHEST DESIGNER

Ralph Lauren (USA) has a personal fortune estimated at $1.7 billion (£1.03 billion) – the highest of any designer. The Ralph Lauren empire is currently valued at around $3 billion (£1.8 billion). Lauren was born Ralph Lifshitz in New York City, in 1939.

HIGHEST-EVER ANNUAL EARNINGS BY A SUPERMODEL

According to the 1999 *Forbes* Celebrity 100 list, Claudia Schiffer (Germany) earned a record $10.5 million (£6.3 million) in 1998.

HIGHEST ANNUAL EARNINGS BY A FILM PRODUCER

Hollywood producer and director George Lucas (USA) topped the 2001 *Forbes* Celebrity 100 list, having earned a record-breaking $250 million (£175 million) in 2000

THE WRITE PAY

According to the March 2001 *Forbes* Celebrity 100 list, Stephen King (USA, left) enjoyed estimated earnings of over $44 million (£29 million) in 2000 – the highest current annual earnings by an author. King wrote his first short story at the age of seven. Since then, his horror/sci-fi books have been translated into 33 languages and published in over 35 different countries. Over 300 million copies of his novels are in circulation.

In 1999 J.K. Rowling (UK) earned £24 million ($40 million) – the highest annual earnings by a children's author according to the 2000 *Forbes* Celebrity 100 list. In July 2000 *Harry Potter and the Goblet of Fire* saw a first printing of 5.3 million copies with advance orders of over 1.8 million, which has made Rowling one of Britain's richest women.

after the video release of *Star Wars: Episode 1 – The Phantom Menace* (USA, 1999).

RICHEST LUXURY GOODS MAKER

Bernard Arnault (France), who heads the luxury goods empire LVMH (Louis Vuitton Moët Hennessy), is worth an estimated $12.6 billion (£8.4 billion). LVMH owns high-profile luxury brands such as Christian Dior, Kenzo, Louis Vuitton, Guerlain, and Givenchy perfumes, as well as top drink brands, such as Dom Perignon and Hennessy.

RICHEST JEANS TYCOON

In 1999 Robert D. Haas (USA), the great-great-grandnephew of the founder of jeans manufacturer Levi Strauss Co., had amassed a fortune of $8.2 billion (£5 billion). As a result, he ranked 358 on the 1999 *Forbes* 400 list.

RICHEST ROYALS

King Fahd Bin Abdulaziz Alsaud (Saudi Arabia) is the richest monarch in the world, with an estimated personal wealth of $30 billion (£21 billion) in April 2001. The Saudi dynasty is also the richest royal family.

The richest European royal house is the Dutch House of Orange, which has an estimated wealth of $3.69 billion (£2.6 billion). Queen Béatrix of the Netherlands has an estimated net worth of $3.42 billion (£2.43 billion), making her the wealthiest queen in the world.

WEALTHIEST DOG

The largest legacy to a dog is $15 million (£10.5 million), bequeathed by Ella Wendel (USA) to her poodle, Toby, in 1931. This is equivalent to $169 million (£118 million) in today's terms.

www.guinnessworldrecords.com/masterp

PRODUCING THE GOODS

Master P. (USA, right), chief executive officer of No Limit Records and the world's richest music producer, is estimated to have a net worth of $56.5 million (£34.1 million). Born Percy Miller, Master P. opened his first record store in Richmond, California. He then founded his own record label, and his first release on No Limit Records, 'The Ghetto's Tryin' To Kill Me,' sold 100,000 copies. Although he no longer works as a solo artist, Master P. still works with the groups TRU and Da 504 Boyz. He has recently set up associated brands such as No Limit Films, No Limit Sports, No Limit Real Estate, and No Limit Clothing. The rapper also owns a chain of fast-food restaurants and gas stations in Louisiana.

ACCESS CODE

‹52302› ←

GUINNESS WORLD RECORDS

big money

RICHEST HINDU TEMPLE
The Tirupati Temple in Andhra Pradesh, India, has an astonishing annual income of $57.02 million (£35.2 million). The money comes mainly from collection boxes, but the most interesting source of income is human hair. Thousands of pilgrims donate their hair as a form of sacrifice and this is auctioned annually to wigmakers and chemical and fertilizer factories.

LARGEST FAMILY FORTUNE
The Oeri, Hoffman, and Sacher families of Switzerland, who jointly own Roche pharmaceuticals, have an estimated combined net worth of $11.5 billion (£8 billion).

MOST SPORTS TAX-EXILES LIVING IN ONE PLACE
Monaco has a record number of racing driver residents, including Ralf Schumacher (Germany), Pedro Diniz (Brazil), Johnny Herbert (UK), Mika Hakkinen (Sweden), David Coulthard (UK), Jacques Villeneuve (France), Alexander Wurz (Austria), Giancarlo Fisichella (Italy), and Rubens Barrichello (Brazil). A number of tennis players on the international circuit also live in the principality.

LARGEST DOWRY
In 1929 Bolivian tin millionaire Don Simon Iturbi Patío gave his daughter Elena Patío a dowry of $22.48 million

A GOOD TURN
On Sept 18 1997 Ted Turner (USA, left), the founder of CNN and vice president of Time Warner, announced that he was giving the United Nations (UN) $1 billion (£580 million) of his own money – the biggest-ever private cash donation to the UN. The money will be used to finance programs on behalf of refugees, children, the environment, and clearing landmines.

‹47802›
← ACCESS CODE
www.guinnessworldrecords.com/tedturner

(£8 million) – equal in 2000 to $400 million (£280 million). However, this did not make a major dent in his fortune of $606 million (£125 million) – the equivalent of $7,000 million (£5,000 million) in 2000.

LARGEST CASH PRIZE WON ON RADIO
Clare Barwick (UK) won £1,000,000 ($1,600,000) – the largest cash prize ever on radio – on Chris Evans's Virgin Radio show on Dec 17 1999. Clare correctly answered the question, "Which one of these two writers was really a woman – George Eliot or T.S. Eliot?" It was George, whose real name was Mary Ann Evans.

LARGEST DONATION TO A SINGLE UNIVERSITY
In Jan 2001 a record $250 million (£176 million) was given to the University of Colorado, Denver, by the chairman and cofounder of software manufacturer BEA Systems, Bill Coleman (USA).

LARGEST DONATION TO EDUCATION
In Dec 1993 philanthropist Walter H. Annenberg (USA) made the biggest donation to education in history. The publisher and diplomat split a record $365 million (£256 million) between three US universities and a US secondary school.

WEALTHIEST UNIVERSITY
In 2000 the endowment for Harvard University (USA) was $19 billion (£13 billion) – bigger than the annual operating budget of 142 of the world's countries, including Cuba, Jordan, and Lithuania. Graduates include seven US presidents. Fourteen Nobel Prize winners are Harvard faculty members.

BIGGEST NONPROFIT RACING CLUB
In 1998 the Hong Kong Jockey Club gave over $131.9 million (£93 million) to social and educational community projects, making it the biggest nonprofit racing club ever.

DEAD RICH
In the year 2000, 23 years after he died of a heart attack, the estate of Elvis Presley (USA, left) earned $35 million (£25 million), making him the richest dead celebrity. Elvis has sold more than one billion albums, generating large royalty checks for his family. He left daughter Lisa-Marie his Graceland mansion in Memphis, Tennessee, which earns $15 million (£10.5 million) annually in admission fees, while $5 million (£3.5 million) was earned by selling Presley-related articles such as T-shirts and toys. Elvis also earns through tourism with places like Heartbreak Hotel and Presley's restaurant in Memphis, as well as profits from posthumous appearances in advertisements for Lipton Iced Tea, Energizer batteries, and Apple Computer.

‹56563›
← ACCESS CODE
www.guinnessworldrecords.com/elvis

MOST EXPENSIVE CREDIT CARD
The American Express Centurion credit card, also known as the 'Black Card,' has an annual fee of $1,000 (£700) and is only open to those with a minimum salary of $215,000 (£150,000). The card has no spending limits and is offered by invitation only to selected individuals.

COMPANY WITH THE MOST MILLIONAIRES
In 2001 there were 10 millionaires in the investment bank Goldman Sachs, New York City. They have a combined wealth of $2,200 million (£1,551 million).

LARGEST SINGLE CASH BEQUEST
On Dec 12 1955 the Ford Foundation (USA) donated the world's biggest cash bequest of $500 million (then £178 million), to 4,157 educational and other institutions. This is the equivalent today of $4.2 billion (£2.4 billion).

LARGEST PAPER MONEY
The biggest paper money ever made was the one-guan note, which was issued between 1368 and 1399 in the Chinese Ming Dynasty. The note measured 9 x 13 in (23 x 33 cm) – bigger than a sheet of letter paper.

LARGEST RETURN OF CASH
In May 1994 Howard Jenkins (USA) discovered that an accidental transfer had credited his bank account with an extra $88 million (£62 million). The 31-year-old employee of a roofing company withdrew $4 million (£2.8 million) for a spending spree, but his conscience got the better of him and he returned the millions in full.

LARGEST ROBBERY BY A MUGGER
A mugger made off with treasury bills and certificates of deposit worth $435 million (£292 million) after attacking a broker's messenger in London on May 2 1990. But news of the theft spread to every major bank in the country, and none of them would accept the bills.

WINNER TAKES ALL

In Feb 1996 the New York State Supreme Court ruled that the actress Joan Collins (UK, above) could keep the $1.2 million (£845,000) advance for her unpublished novel *A Ruling Passion*. The publisher Random House (USA) had found her first draft unsatisfactory and sued her unsuccessfully for the return of the money – making this the world's biggest unreturned advance ever.

Joan Collins made more than 50 films before starring as the sultry Alexis in the hit 1980s television series *Dynasty*.

www.guinnessworldrecords.com/joancollins

ACCESS CODE

‹48299› ←

MOST MONEY RAISED BY AN INDIVIDUAL IN A MARATHON

Retired advertising executive John Spurling (UK) raised a record-breaking $1.87 million (£1.13 million) for charity by running the London Marathon on April 18 1999. With no previous experience, Spurling finished the race, raised the figure, and divided the money between two charities – the Animal Health Trust and the Lord's Taverners, a group of ex-international cricketers and celebrities who take part in cricket matches to raise money for charity.

www.guinnessworldrecords.com/billgates

BILLION-DOLLAR BILL

Bill Gates (USA, right), founder of computer giant Microsoft, and his wife Melinda donated $6 billion (£4.2 billion) to their charity, the Bill and Melinda Gates Foundation, in Aug 1999 – the largest-ever single private donation in history. The Foundation donates funds to global health-care programs, education, libraries, and community causes in the Pacific Northwest where Gates grew up.

In May 1999 the couple donated a record $25 million (£15.8 million) to AIDS and HIV research.

ACCESS CODE

‹55249› ←

MOST MONEY RAISED IN A SINGLE TELETHON

Between Sept 5 and 6 1999, the Jerry Lewis MDA (Muscular Dystrophy Association) telethon raised a record $53,116,417 (then £33,119,102) in pledges and contributions. About 64 million Americans in 26 million homes watched the program, which has become a Labor Day tradition. In 1998 the program became the first worldwide telethon, and the same year saw the launch of an Internet simulcast of the national broadcast, at www.mdausa.org.

GREATEST RANSOM

The greatest ransom ever, was a glittering hall full of gold and silver, paid in return for Atahualpa, the last emperor of the Incas, to the Spanish conquistador Francisco Pizarro. Paid from 1532 to 1533 at Cajamarca, Peru, the ransom would now be equivalent to $1.5 billion (£1 billion).

LARGEST FINE

A record fine was imposed on the US securities house Drexel Burnham Lambert in Dec 1988 for insider trading. The $650 million (£335 million) figure represented $300 million (£164 million) in direct fines, with the rest put into an account to satisfy claims of parties defrauded by Drexel's actions.

GUINNESS
WORLD RECORDS™

influential people

OLDEST LIVING ROYAL

Her Majesty Queen Elizabeth, The Queen Mother (UK), is the world's oldest living royal. She married Prince Albert (King George VI) on April 26 1923, and on his coronation, became the first British-born Queen Consort since Tudor times, as well as the Last Empress of India. She celebrated her 100th birthday on Aug 4 2000 and still enjoys a very full life. Since 1923, she has given only one interview.

YOUNGEST CURRENT QUEEN

The youngest current queen is HM Queen Rania Al-Abdullah of Jordan (b. Aug 31 1970). She is married to the head of state, King Abdullah Bin Al-Hussein.

LONGEST REIGN

Minhti, King of Arakan, which is now part of Myanmar (Burma), is reputed to have reigned for 95 years between 1279 and 1374. However the longest well-documented reign of a monarch is that of Phiops II, an Egyptian Sixth-Dynasty pharaoh. His reign began in c. 2281 BC, when he was six years old, and lasted about 94 years.

LARGEST PRESIDENTIAL ENTOURAGE

When former US President Bill Clinton visited China in June 1998, he was accompanied by an enormous entourage of 1,200 people. The crowd consisted of 200 secret-service agents, 150 military personnel, 30 senior delegates, 375 reporters, four White House TV crews, 150 support staff, and 70 senior aides or advisors.

MOST APPEARANCES ON THE COVER OF *TIME* MAGAZINE

Richard Nixon (37th President of the US) was featured on the cover of *Time* magazine a record 55 times.

LARGEST GATHERING OF WORLD LEADERS

The United Nations' Millennium Summit, held in New York City, from Sept 6 to 8 2000, was the largest-ever gathering of world leaders. It brought together 144 kings, presidents, prime ministers, and heads of state. There were over 1,300 official cars at the event, thousands of secret-service agents, and over 2,500 journalists. On the agenda was the crisis in the Middle East, education, technology, and multilateralism – the bringing together of different groups.

MOST ACCESSIBLE PRIME MINISTER

Danish premier Poul Nyrup Rasmussen, whose home telephone number is available to the public, is known to answer telephone queries from Danish citizens personally.

PRINCE CHARMING

His Royal Highness Prince William of Wales (above), grandson of HM Queen Elizabeth II of the United Kingdom, has more fan clubs devoted to him than any other royal in the world. As of April 2001, there were at least 72 clubs dedicated to admiring Britain's future monarch. All fan clubs are 'unofficial,' as they are not supervised by Buckingham Palace.

Prince William Arthur Philip Louis Windsor was born on June 21 1982, the elder son of the late Diana, Princess of Wales, and HRH The Prince of Wales. He has a younger brother, Harry (b. Sept 15 1984).

<56550>

www.guinnessworldrecords.com/william ← ACCESS CODE

LONGEST-SERVING FEMALE PRIME MINISTER

Sirimavo Bandaranaike was Prime Minister of Sri Lanka for a total of 17 years 208 days – from July 21 1960 to March 25 1965; from May 29 1970 to July 22 1977; and then again from Nov 12 1994 to Aug 10 2000.

YOUNGEST PRIME MINISTER

Swiss-born Dr. Mario Frick (b. May 8 1965), became Prime Minister of Liechtenstein at the age of 28 on Dec 15 1993.

MOST DESCENDANTS TO BECOME PRIME MINISTER

Jawaharlal Nehru became India's Prime Minister when the country attained independence in Aug 1947. He remained in power until his death in 1964. His daughter Indira Gandhi served as Prime Minister from 1966 to 1977, and again from 1980 to 1984, when she was assassinated by her bodyguards. Her eldest son, Rajiv Gandhi, became Prime Minister on his mother's death, and won the 1984 elections by a landslide victory. He served until 1989 but was also assassinated while campaigning for the premiership in 1991.

LARGEST HUMAN RIGHTS ORGANIZATION

Amnesty International has more than 1,200,000 members in over 100 countries, offices in more than 50 countries, and more than 4,200 local groups on every continent. The organization was founded in 1961 by Peter Benenson, a British lawyer, and originally began as a newspaper appeal called 'The Forgotten Prisoners.' As a result, over 1,000 letters flooded in supporting the idea of an international organization to protect human rights. In 1977 Amnesty International was awarded the Nobel Prize for Peace.

POWER TO THE PEOPLE

On Aug 28 1963 civil-rights leader Martin Luther King Jr. (USA, left) led more than 250,000 demonstrators in a march down the Mall in Washington D.C. The march was held to promote equal civil rights for all Americans, irrespective of race or color, and was the largest racial-equality rally ever held. From the steps of the Lincoln Memorial, King delivered his legendary "I have a dream" speech to the crowd.

Born in Atlanta, Georgia, on Jan 15 1929, Martin Luther King Jr. was a Baptist minister, a civil-rights activist, and winner of the Nobel Peace prize in 1964, at the time the youngest man ever to do so. He was assassinated on April 4 1968 in Memphis, Tennessee.

<54489>

www.guinnessworldrecords.com/martinlutherking ← ACCESS CODE

LARGEST CONSERVATION ORGANIZATION

With more than five million supporters and a global network of 27 national organizations and 21 program offices, the World Wide Fund For Nature (WWF) is the world's largest conservation organization. WWF and its members are committed to preventing the degradation of the natural world and to helping people live in greater harmony with nature. Since 1985 the WWF has invested over $1.165 billion (£729 million) in 11,000 projects in 130 countries.

LARGEST FEDERATION OF ENVIRONMENTAL GROUPS

Friends of the Earth International unites one million activists throughout the world, with member organizations in 68 countries and 13 affiliate groups – making it the world's largest federation of environmental groups. The federation aims to preserve the earth's ecological, cultural, and ethnic diversity by promoting environmentally sustainable development on local, regional, national, and global levels.

MOST PULITZER PRIZES

The Associated Press has received a record 45 Pulitzer Prizes. These have been awarded annually since 1917, after an endowment by newspaper publisher Joseph Pulitzer (USA) to recognize achievements in American journalism, letters, drama, and music.

MOST TEMPLES CONSECRATED BY ONE PERSON

His Holiness Pramukh Swami Maharaj (India), the spiritual master of the Swaminarayan Hindu Mission, consecrated (blessed) a record 386 temples in 11 countries between April 17 1971 and May 14 2001.

MOST INTERNATIONAL VISITS BY A POPE

The Pope is head of the Roman Catholic church. The visit by Pope John Paul II (Poland) to Kiev, Ukraine on June 25 2001 was his 126th trip abroad since he became Pope on Oct 16 1978, age 58. He was the first nonItalian chosen as Pope in 456 years and the youngest in the 20th century.

LONGEST-LIVED POPE

Of the Popes whose ages can be reliably confirmed, Leo XIII (Gioacchino Pecci, Italy) lived the longest. Born on March 2 1810, he was elected Pope on Feb 20 1878 at the age of 67. He died on July 20 1903 at the age of 93 years 140 days.

www.guinnessworldrecords.com/georgewbush

W MONEY

George W. Bush (inaugurated as the 43rd US president on Jan 20 2001, right), has assembled the wealthiest cabinet in American history by appointing more multimillionaires to the top rank of his government than any of his predecessors. Of the 16 full cabinet members at the heart of the Bush administration, 13 are millionaires, seven of whom own assets worth more than $10 million (£7 million). His cabinet has acquired the nickname 'tycoon's club.' Defense Secretary Donald Rumsfeld and Treasury Secretary Paul O'Neill each have declared assets of at least $61 million (£42.9 million), while Secretary of State Colin Powell has at least $18.5 million (£13 million).

ACCESS CODE

‹56549› ←

GUINNESS WORLD RECORDS™

big business

LARGEST SAVINGS BANK

The world's largest commercial and savings bank is Mizuho Holdings Inc. (Japan). According to recently released figures, the bank generated revenues of $76,851 million (£48,154 million) and profits of $1,843 million (£1,154 million) for 2000. Mizuho Holdings Inc. was created by the consolidation of the Dai-Ichi Kangyo Bank, Fuji Bank Ltd., and the Industrial Bank of Japan. It is the first bank to hold over a trillion dollars in assets.

HIGHEST TECHNOLOGY COMPANY VALUATION

On April 11 2000 Cisco Systems Inc. of San Jose, California, had a confirmed market capitalization of $503.4 billion (£317.7 billion). This places Cisco ahead of software giant Microsoft Corporation, whose share price suffered at the time, as a result of US judge Thomas Penfield Jackson's ruling against them over an anti-trust issue on 3 April 2000. This ruling was overturned in June 2001.

LARGEST CORPORATION

In 2000 General Motors of Detroit, Michigan, generated revenues of $184,632 million (£123,306 million) In the same year the company profits were $4,452 million (£2,982 million). General Motors is the world's largest automotive corporation and vehicle manufacturer.

SUPER MARKET!

Wal-Mart Stores Inc. (USA) had revenues of $191,329 million (£130,838 million) for the fiscal year ending Jan 31 2001, the largest revenues for a retail firm. The company had profits of $6,295 million (£4,304 million) for the fiscal year ending Jan 31 2001. As of March 31 2000, Wal-Mart had 4,003 retail locations in 10 countries, employing 1,140,000 people. Sam Walton opened the first Wal-Mart store in 1962 in Bentonville, Arkansas. A small-town storekeeper who had operated variety stores in Arkansas and Missouri, Walton dreamed up Wal-Mart as a discount store with a wide array of merchandise and friendly service. His son, S. Robson Walton (left), is now company chairman.

<49579> ← ACCESS CODE www.guinnessworldrecords.com/walmart

LARGEST CHECK

The largest amount paid with a single check is £2,474,655,000 ($3,971,821,324). The record-breaking check was issued on March 30 1995 as payment by Glaxo plc to Wellcome Trust Nominees Limited regarding the Trust's share in Wellcome plc. The Lloyds Bank Registrar's computer was unable to generate a check this big, so it was completed by an employee. The Lloyds typist was so overawed by the huge responsibility that she needed three attempts to write it correctly.

LAW FIRM WITH MOST LAWYERS

Clifford Chance LLP – created in Jan 2000 after the merger of Clifford Chance, Rogers Wells LLP, and Pünder, Volhard, Weber, and Axster, employs 7,400 staff, 3,580 of whom are fee-earning legal advisors and 652 are partners. The firm has 29 offices around the world and in 1999 had revenues of $1 billion (£625 million).

BIGGEST DAILY SALE OF A SINGLE STOCK

On Feb 11 2000 over 2.1 billion Vodafone shares were traded – the biggest-ever sale of a single stock.

LONGEST TRADING SUSPENSION

In 1914 the New York Stock Exchange ceased trading for four months and two weeks from July 31. The shutdown was due to the outbreak of World War I in Europe.

LARGEST AIRLINE CORPORATION

AMR Corporation, based in Fort Worth, Texas, is the world's largest airline corporation, with a workforce of 116,054, revenues of $19.7 billion (£13.1 billion), and profits of $813 million (£544 million) in 2000. The company has a fleet of nearly 700 jetliners, and its airlines serve around 170 destinations in the Americas, Europe, and the Pacific Rim.

LARGEST AEROSPACE COMPANY

The world's largest aerospace company is Boeing of Seattle, Washington. In 2000 the company generated revenues of $51.3 billion (£34.4 billion) with profits of $2.1 billion (£1.4 billion).

LARGEST BEVERAGE COMPANY

PepsiCo Inc., based in Purchase, New York, had revenues of $20,438 million (£13,692 million) in 2000 and profits of $2,183 million (£1,462 million). Beverage brands owned by PepsiCo include Pepsi, Mountain Dew, and Tropicana.

LARGEST CHEWING GUM COMPANY

The largest chewing gum company is the Wm. Wrigley Jr. Company based in Chicago, Illinois. In 2000 it had revenues of $2,145 million (£1,436 million) and profits of $328 million (£219 million). In total, the company accounts for around 50% of all US chewing gum sales.

LARGEST FAST-FOOD CHAIN

The McDonald's Corporation (USA) is the world's largest global food-service retailer. Revenues in 2000 were $14.2 billion (£9.5 billion), with profits totaling $1.9 billion (£1.2 billion), and the worldwide workforce was 364,000. McDonald's operates more than 28,000 restaurants (12,800 in the USA) in 120 countries worldwide. NonUS restaurants make up more than 60% of the company's sales and about

BABES IN TOYLAND

The world's largest toy manufacturer is Mattel Inc. of El Segundo, California. In 2000 the company, which employs 30,000 people, had revenues of $4,669 million (£3,127 million) and profits of a massive $430 million (£288 million). The company's best-known products include Barbie and Ken dolls (left), which are also now available in interactive games and software, Fisher-Price toys, and Matchbox cars. It has also licensed Disney and *Sesame Street* items.

The world's largest toy-retail chain is Toys 'R' Us Inc. of Paramus, New Jersey. The first Toys 'R' Us 'toy supermarket' opened in 1957, and the company now has 1,548 stores in 25 countries worldwide. It had revenues of $11,862 million (£8,111million) at the end of Jan 2001.

<57553> ← ACCESS CODE www.guinnessworldrecords.com/toptoys

50% of its profits. Brothers Dick and Mac McDonald pioneered the fast-food industry concept and later sold their business to their national franchise agent, Ray A. Kroc, who created the McDonald's Corporation.

LARGEST BRA MANUFACTURER

In 2000, US clothing and food conglomerate Sara Lee controlled 33% of the US bra market. The company enjoyed total sales of $17,511 million (£11,533 million) and profits of $1,222 million (£804 million) in 2000. Sara Lee owns the Wonderbra and Playtex brands, and its May 2000 takeover of UK firm Courtauld added the Berlei and Gossard brands to its portfolio.

LARGEST PR COMPANY

The largest public relations company in the world is US-based Burson-Marsteller, which enjoyed total revenues of more than $275 million (£171 million) in 1999. The company's most high-profile clients include Union Carbide, BP Chemicals, and the Exxon Corporation.

LARGEST ADVERTISING BILLBOARD

In Dec 2000 an advertising billboard measuring 77.7 ft (23.7 m) high and 433 ft (132 m) long, with a surface area of 33,661.58 ft² (3,128.4 m²), was erected on the side of Fort

Dunlop – the former Dunlop head-office building near Birmingham, West Midlands, UK. The construction cost was paid for by the Ford Motor Company Ltd. (USA) and Ford's six-month billboard campaign, installed by Mega Profile Ltd. (UK), cost $920,000 (£650,000).

LARGEST TELECOMMUNICATIONS COMPANY

The largest telecommunications company in the world is Nippon Telegraph and Telephone Corporation (NTT), based in Tokyo, Japan. In 2000 it had revenues of $97,956 million (£69,163 million) and profits of $2,821 million (£1,991 million).

www.guinnessworldrecords.com/bigmerge

TIME TO GET ONLINE

The world's largest merger was between America Online (AOL), the largest-ever internet company, and media corporation Time Warner. The $350-billion (£245-billion) deal was announced on Jan 10 2000 by AOL CEO Steve Case (right, on left of photo) and Gerald Levin, CEO of Time Warner (on right of photo). This merger created the world's largest media company, with a major portfolio of brands including AOL, Time, CNN, Warner Bros, Netscape, and Warner Music Group.

ACCESS CODE

‹53969› ←

GUINNESS WORLD RECORDS

buying and selling 1

MOST VALUABLE SOCCER MEDAL

The most that has ever been paid for a soccer medal is £124,750 ($177,280) for England goalkeeper Gordon Banks's 1966 World Cup winners medal, sold at Christie's, London, UK, on March 23 2001.

MOST EXPENSIVE GOLF CLUB

A 200-year-old Scottish putter sold for a record £106,000 ($150,000) at Christie's in Glasgow, Scotland, UK, on July 7 1998. It was bought by Titus Kendall (UK), a London antiques dealer, on behalf of Jaime Ortíz Patiño, a Bolivian millionaire, to display at the Valderrama Golf Club, which he owns in southern Spain.

MOST VALUABLE GOLF BALL

On July 1 1995 Jaime Ortíz Patiño paid a record £19,995 ($31,855) in Edinburgh, Scotland, UK, for a Victorian feathery ball. Golf was first played with leather balls stuffed with feathers and sticks tipped with horn.

MOST EXPENSIVE JIGSAW PUZZLE

The most expensive jigsaw puzzles in the world are the custom-made Stave Puzzles' Dollhouse Village puzzles, which cost a record $14,500 (£8,800) each in June 1999. The 2,640-piece jigsaws are handcut, one piece at a time, out of mahogany-backed plywood, by Steve Richardson (USA).

<43360> www.guinnessworldrecords.com/phantom
← ACCESS CODE

PHANTOM OF THE CAMERA

The prototype Phantom Camera Unit (left), designed by British inventor and MP Noel Pemberton Billing in 1946, was sold for £146,750 ($216,826) at auction by Christie's, London, UK, on Jan 16 2001 – making this the most valuable handheld self-contained camera in the world. The unit was designed for processing photographs on the move, and includes developing tanks, paper storage, and batteries. The camera also doubles up as an enlarger or projector.

The Phantom never went into production as the project stopped with Billing's death in 1948. The high price paid for the camera was due to the fact that the unit is unique. It was bought by a private photographic museum.

MOST VALUABLE ANTIQUE TOY

A toy hose sold for $182,545 (£128,333) at Christie's, New York City, on Dec 14 1991. The work is a handpainted tinplate replica of the 'Charles' hose reel, a piece of fire-fighting equipment. It measures 15 x 23 in (38.1 x 58.4 cm), and was made in the 1870s by George Brown & Co., Connecticut.

MOST VALUABLE DECK OF PLAYING CARDS

The highest price paid for one deck of playing cards is £99,000 ($143,352), by the Metropolitan Museum of Art, New York City, at Sotheby's, London, UK, on Dec 6 1983. The cards, dating from 1470, are the oldest complete handpainted set.

MOST VALUABLE ROBOT

A rare Masudaya Machine Man robot from the late 1950s was sold at Christie's, London, UK, in July 1999, for the record amount of £29,900

($47,203). The Machine Man is one of a set of early Japanese robots called 'The Gang Of Five.' These toys, which are about 15 in (38 cm) high, each have a lithographed tin body with graphics that resembled machine parts.

MOST VALUABLE TOY SOLDIER

A uniformed scale figure of Hitler's deputy, Rudolf Hess (Germany), was sold for £3,375 ($5,906) – the highest price ever paid for one toy soldier. The figure was among several sold by the Danish auction house Boyes in London, UK, on April 23 1991.

MOST VALUABLE PIANO

The greatest sum ever paid for a piano was £1.45 million ($2.1 million) by singer George Michael (UK) for a Steinway Model Z upright belonging to John Lennon (UK). The piano featured on Lennon's video 'Imagine' and was sold at an auction at the Hard Rock Café, London, UK, on Oct 17 2000.

MOST VALUABLE SINGLE MUSIC MANUSCRIPT .

A record £1.4 million ($2.3 million) was paid for a manuscript of German composer Robert Schumann's Second Symphony to a private collector at Sotheby's, London, on 1 Dec 1994.

MOST VALUABLE CARTOON POSTER

A film poster for Walt Disney's film Alice's Day at Sea, depicting Alice astride a fish above the waves, was sold at Christie's, London, UK, in April 1994 for a record £23,100 ($34,072). The film was the start of the series of 'Alice Comedies' – 56 silent cartoons created between 1924 and 1927.

MOST VALUABLE BLACK-AND-WHITE ANIMATION CELL

In 1989 a black-and-white acetate drawing from Walt Disney's Orphan's Benefit (USA, 1934), depicting Donald Duck being punched by an orphan, raised £171,250 ($327,858) at Christie's, London, UK.

MOST VALUABLE FILM COSTUME

A blue-and-white gingham dress worn by Judy Garland (USA) as Dorothy in the 1939 MGM film The Wizard of Oz was sold at Christie's, London, UK, on Dec 9 1999 for £199,500 ($324,188). The gingham pinafore bears a cotton wardrobe label inscribed in black ink 'Judy Garland 4228.' A New York real-estate agent bought the garment for 10 times more than the expected price.

SULTAN OF SPIN

The most expensive commercially produced yo-yos are the Cold Fusion yo-yo range (left), which cost between $150 and $250 (£90 and £150). The manufacturers, Playmaxx Inc., also produce a 24-carat gold-plated special-edition yo-yo, called the Gold Fusion, which sells for between $200 and $300 (£120 and £180). In 1998 Playmaxx Inc. generated approximately $96 million (£57.9 million) from yo-yo retail sales and earned the 'Craze of the Year' award from the British Toy Association.

Yo-yos date back as far as 400–500 BC in Greece, and early examples can be seen at the Metropolitan Museum of Art, New York City. According to the Playmaxx website, the French Emperor Napoleon Bonaparte was known to carry and use a yo-yo.

<52213> www.guinnessworldrecords.com/yoyo
← ACCESS CODE

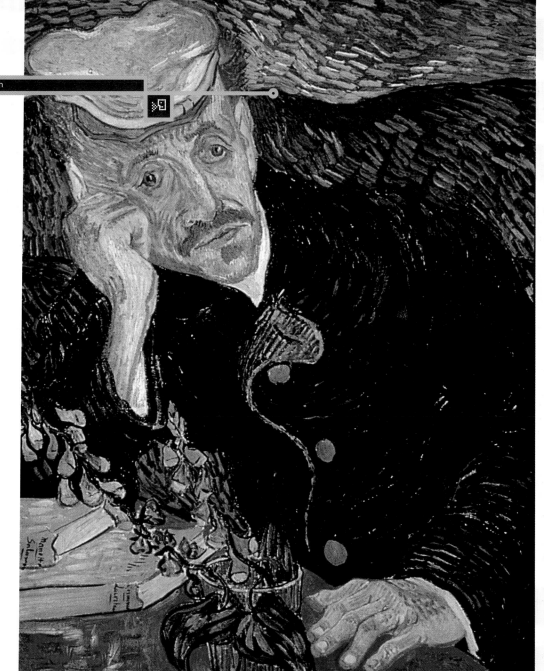

www.guinnessworldrecords.com/vangogh

PICTURE THIS

Portrait of Dr. Gachet (right), by Dutch artist Vincent van Gogh (1853–90), is the world's most valuable painting. It sold, in just three minutes, for a record sum of $82.5 million (£49.1 million) at Christie's, New York City, on May 15 1990. The artist completed this work just weeks before his suicide. The sitter, Dr. Paul-Ferdinand Gachet (France), was a friend and physician to van Gogh. Shortly before his death van Gogh had a burst of creativity, producing more than one painting a day, including several versions of Dr. Gachet.

ACCESS CODE

‹43323› ←

MOST VALUABLE FILM SHOES

The ruby slippers worn by Judy Garland (USA) in *The Wizard of Oz* (USA, 1939), sold at Christie's, New York City, on May 24 2000, for $666,000 (£450,920). The shoes were made of red silk overlaid with handsequinned georgette.

MOST VALUABLE JAMES BOND MEMORABILIA

The 1965 Aston Martin DB5, driven by Pierce Brosnan (UK) in *Goldeneye* (USA, 1995) sold for £157,750 ($228,264), at Christie's, London, UK, on Feb 14 2001. The car was bought by Max Reid (UK) as a Valentine's Day present for his wife.

LARGEST SALE OF CELEBRITY CARS

On June 5 2001 Sir Elton John (UK) auctioned 20 of his cars at Christie's, London, UK, raising £1,951,725 ($2,741,198). The top price paid was for a 1993 Jaguar XJ220 which sold for £234,750 ($329,706).

MOST EXPENSIVE SWISS ARMY KNIFE

An 18-carat gold Swiss army knife produced by Swiss jeweler Luzius Elmer has a retail price of $4,299 (£3,026). The Victorinox® Original Swiss Army™ pocketknife range, usually retails between $14 and $70 (£10 and £50).

MOST VALUABLE GUN

An 1873 .45-caliber Colt single-action army revolver, Serial No.1, was sold at Christie's, New York City, for a record-breaking $242,000 (£170,000) on May 14 1987. This is equivalent to $370,000 (£285,000) in the year 2000.

MOST VALUABLE PHONECARD

In Jan 1992 the first phonecard ever issued in Japan, and therefore a rare collectors' item, was bought for a record $52,430 (£28,000).

MOST EXPENSIVE SINGLE PURCHASE OF WHISKY

On Nov 16 2000 Norman Shelley (UK), paid £231,417 ($341,154) for 76 bottles of The Macallan malt whisky. The oldest whisky of the collection dated from 1856. The Macallan single-malt whisky has been made in Scotland since 1824.

MOST EXPENSIVE COW

The highest price paid for a live cow is $1,300,000 (£914,000) for a Friesian at auction in East Montpelier, Vermont, in 1985.

MOST EXPENSIVE POST-IT® NOTE

To celebrate the 20th anniversary of the Post-It® note, artists created mini-masterpieces on notes that were then auctioned online for charity. R.B. Kitaj's (USA) pastel-and-charcoal work sold for a record $925 (£640).

GUINNESS WORLD RECORDS™

buying and selling 2

MOST EXPENSIVE MEAL PER HEAD

In Sept 1997 three diners at Le Gavroche, London, UK, spent $20,945.92 (£13,091.20) on one meal. Only $345.92 (£216.20) went on food – cigars and spirits accounted for $1,352 (£845) and the remaining $19,248 (£12,030) was spent on six bottles of wine. The most expensive bottle, a 1985 La Romanée-Conti costing $7,920 (£4,950), was not to their liking so the generous group gave it to the restaurant staff. The diners began with a bottle of 1949 Krug champagne at $896 (£560) and followed it with clarets and burgundies – a 1985 DRC Montrachet at $2,240 (£1,400), a 1954 Château Haut Brion at $3,360 (£2,100), a 1967 Château d'Yquem at $1,712 (£1,070), and a 1961 Château Latour at $3,120 (£1,950).

MOST EXPENSIVE GLASS OF WINE

The most paid for a glass of wine is FF8600 ($1,382.80 or £982) for the first glass of 1993 Beaujolais Nouveau. The wine was released in Beaune, in the wine region of Burgundy, France. It was bought by Robert Denby in an auction at Pickwick's, a British pub in Beaune, on Nov 18 1993.

STAMP OF APPROVAL

The most valuable single stamp in the world is the Swedish 'Treskilling Yellow', a 3-skilling stamp (left). On Nov 8 1996 it was sold for a record Sw. Fr. 2,870,000 ($2,240,000 or £1,400,000) by David Feldman auctioneers, Geneva, Switzerland. The stamp, which should be green, was printed yellow and is the only one in existence, which makes it highly valuable to collectors. It was discovered by a schoolboy in 1885 among his grandfather's letters, and was first sold for just seven Swedish crowns – equivalent today to $1 or 70p. When sold in 1996, it became the world's most expensive item by weight.

<43309>
www.guinnessworldrecords.com/stamp
← ACCESS CODE

MOST EXPENSIVE WINE

The most expensive commercially available wine is the Château d'Yquem Sauternes (1787), priced between $56,000 (£39,363) and $64,000 (£44,985), depending on the retailer. Château d'Yquem Sauternes is a golden-colored dessert wine from France's Bordeaux region.

MOST EXPENSIVE FUNGUS

White truffle (*Tuber magnum pico*) is the world's most expensive edible fungus, fetching up to $1,500 (£1,047) per lb. They can only be found in the Italian regions of Piedmont, Emilia-Romagna, Tuscany, and Marches. Because they grow about a foot underground, they can only be located with the help of trained dogs.

MOST EXPENSIVE HAMBURGER

The 2001 Big Mac economic index, which compares the price of the classic McDonald's hamburger across the world, reveals that the Swiss pay the most for their burgers at $3.65 (£2.59). The price is over a dollar more than the $2.54 (£1.80) paid for a Big Mac in American McDonalds' restaurants.

MOST EXPENSIVE CAR REGISTRATION

License plate No.9 was sold at a Hong Kong government auction for $13 million (£9 million) on March 19 1994 to Albert Yeung Sau-shing. In Cantonese the pronunciation of the word 'nine' is identical to the word 'dog.' This license plate was considered lucky because 1994 was the Chinese Year of the Dog.

MOST EXPENSIVE PRIVATE JET

At $31 million ($45 million), the Gulfstream V-SP is the most expensive private jet ever made. It has a range of 6,750 nautical miles at long-range cruise speeds. The jet is powered by two Rolls-Royce BR-710 engines.

MOST EXPENSIVE MINI

The Mini Limo, an exclusive one-off commissioned by Rover Group and built by John Cooper Garages, cost £50,000 ($80,000) when it was delivered in Sept 1997. The two-door Mini boasts an £8,000 ($12,836) Alpine minidisc sound system and seats costing £6,000 ($9,627). The car also features a custom-built dashboard and interior, leather-bound Wilton carpets, lambswool rugs, self-closing and locking systems, and air-conditioning.

MOST EXPENSIVE COURSE

The Ivor Spencer International Finishing School for Young Ladies and Gentlemen, London, UK, began

DRESS TO IMPRESS

A flesh-colored beaded gown (left) worn by Marilyn Monroe when she sang 'Happy Birthday' to President Kennedy on May 19 1962, is the world's most valuable dress. It was sold on Oct 27 1999 for $1,267,000 (£885,904) at Christie's, New York City, New York, to dealers Robert Schagrin and Peter Siegel. It originally cost $12,000 (£4,200).

A diamond-encrusted bikini, valued at $194,458.97 (£123,409.90) was unveiled on March 22 2000 at Windsor Fashion Week by Prestons of Windsor, Berkshire, UK. In 1983 Sidney Smilove created the world's most expensive swimsuit – made from black nylon and lycra, with 19 diamonds (ranging from 0.5 to 0.003 carat) and 91 cultured pearls riveted in 14-carat gold settings. The swimsuit went on sale for $12,000 (£8,000).

<43411>
www.guinnessworldrecords.com/marilyn
← ACCESS CODE

a one-month 'finishing' course costing £77,500 ($111,092) in 1998. Students stay at one of London's finest hotels, travel on Concorde, and go to the ballet and opera. They also take lessons in etiquette, wine appreciation, and cooking.

MOST EXPENSIVE PEN

The world's most expensive pen is 'La Modernista Diamonds' made by Caran d'Ache, Geneva, Switzerland. The pricey pen was on sale in Harrods, London, UK, for £169,000 ($265,000) from Sept to Dec 1999. The rhodium-coated solid-silver pen has an 18-carat gold nib and is pavé-set with 5,072 diamonds totaling 20 carats. At the top of the cap 96 half-cut rubies are arranged to form the Caran d'Ache company monogram.

MOST EXPENSIVE HOUSE SALE

Eric Hotung's house at 6-10 Black's Link, Hong Kong, sold for HK$778.88 million ($101,909,312 or £62,767,500) on May 12 1997 to an anonymous buyer. Eric Hotung is an influential Hong Kong businessman, political adviser, and philanthropist.

MOST EXPENSIVE HOUSE PER UNIT AREA

Two Hong Kong properties, known as Genesis and Sky High, were bought by Wong Kwan for $2,826.54 per ft^2 (£18,793 per m^2) in Nov 1997.

MOST EXPENSIVE WEDDING CEREMONY

The wedding of Mohammed, son of Sheik Rashid Bin Saeed Al Maktoum, to Princess Salama, in Dubai in May 1981, lasted seven days and cost an estimated $44.5 million (£22 million). It was held in a custom-built stadium for 20,000 people. This amount is equivalent to $71 million (£50 million) in the year 2000.

MOST EXPENSIVE WATCH

The Supercomplication, a Patek Phillipe watch that belonged to banker Henry Graves Jr., became the most expensive timepiece ever sold when it fetched $11,002,500 (£6,820,450) on Dec 2 1999 at a Sotheby's auction, New York City, New York.

www.guinnessworldrecords.com/goldtoilet

ACCESS CODE

‹56573› ←

AWASH WITH MONEY

The world's most expensive washroom (right) was built by jeweler Lam Sai-wing for $3.5 million (£2.4 million) in his Hong Kong shop. It is made entirely out of gold and precious jewels. The toilet bowls, sinks, toilet brushes, toilet-paper holders, mirror frames, wall-mounted chandeliers, wall tiles and doors are all made out of solid 24-carat gold. In order to use the toilet, customers must spend at least $200 (£140) in Lam's shop.

GUINNESS WORLD RECORDS™

fashion

LARGEST FASHION SHOW AUDIENCE

More than two million people watched the Victoria's Secret Fashion Show, held at Cannes, France, in May 2000, by booting up and logging on to www.victoriassecret.com. Featuring models Tyra Banks (USA), Karen Mulder (Netherlands), and Stephanie Seymour (USA), it was hosted by Elizabeth Taylor (USA) and Elton John (UK) and raised over £1.25 million ($2 million) for AIDS research.

LONGEST CATWALK

A group of 111 fashion models walked the length of a 0.69-mile (1.111-km) catwalk, built in the Seacon Square shopping center car park, Bangkok, Thailand, between May 27 and 30 1998. The 5-ft 9-in-high (1.8-m) catwalk was built in 16 days by 150 workmen, and was sponsored by Anglo-Dutch conglomerate Unilever. When seen from the air, it spelled out the word 'Lux,' a Unilever soap brand.

MODEL FEATURED ON THE MOST MAGAZINE COVERS

Claudia Schiffer (Germany) was discovered in 1987 in a German disco at the age of 17 and has modeled ever since. She has graced the covers of more than 500 magazines, including Elle, Harper's Bazaar, Vogue, and Cosmopolitan. Claudia has also featured on the cover of Time Magazine and was the first model ever to feature on the cover of Rolling Stone magazine's 10 Most Beautiful Women edition.

MOST EXPENSIVE BRA

The Red Hot Fantasy bra burns a scorching $15-million (£10.57-million) hole in your purse. Created by Victoria's Secret, this explosive little number is alight with over 1,300 precious stones, including 300 carats of blazing Thai rubies set among diamonds. It is home-delivered by security guards in an armored truck.

HIGHEST HEELED SHOES COMMERCIALLY AVAILABLE

The highest heels commercially available boast a staggering combination of 11-in (27.9-cm) platforms and 16-in (40.6-cm) heels. Available in red or black leather and aptly named 'Vertigo,' the shoes sell for a steep $1,092 (£725). UK firm LadyBWear who make the shoes, warn that they cannot be held responsible for any injuries clients may sustain while wearing them.

MOST VALUABLE PAIR OF JEANS

In March 1997 Levi Strauss and Co. paid $25,000 (£15,616) to buy a pair of their own Levi® 501® jeans from New York vintage clothing store What Comes Around Goes Around. The jeans were found in a defunct Colorado coal mine and are believed to have been made between 1890 and 1901.

FILLING THE GAP

Don and Doris Fisher (both USA) founded Gap Inc. (left) in 1969, after Don had tried to exchange a pair of jeans and found a lack of organized clothes stores selling a sufficient range of jeans. By 2000, Gap had net sales of over $13.67 billion (£9.64 billion), and in May 2001 had 3,676 stores across the USA, Canada, UK, France, Germany, and Japan, making it the world's largest fashion-retail chain. It is currently rated No.174 in the Fortune 500 list, with a profile that has risen in recent years thanks to innovative advertising featuring songs from West Side Story and by Madonna (USA).

‹52438›   www.guinnessworldrecords.com/gap   ← ACCESS CODE

LARGEST SKATEWEAR COMPANY

Vans opened for business in 1966 in California, and by the late 1970s, Vans shoes were the top footwear of choice for the Californian skater community. Today they distribute their skatewear through over 126 company-owned retail stores in the USA and in over 80 countries worldwide.

LONGEST PEARL NECKLACE

A necklace measuring 354 ft (108 m) long, weighing 19 lb 2 oz (8.7 kg), and comprising 14,400 pearls, was assembled in the Japanese town of Ago-cho Yume-kaido with the help of tourists during the town's 1995 Campaign Project.

YOUNGEST HAUTE COUTURE DESIGNER

Yves Saint Laurent (France) began his design career at the age of 17. He first worked as assistant to fashion icon Christian Dior (France), but was named head of the House of Dior when Christian died four years later.

FINANCIAL BRIEFS

When it comes to cool contemporary threads, the brand-conscious bottoms of the world choose Calvin Klein, making it the world's best-selling designer underwear. In 1998 the company sold 30 million pairs of briefs and panties, worth $425 million (£256 million). The brand has been boosted with the help of a select list of celebrities from the worlds of fashion and music, such as Kate Moss (UK), Christy Turlington (USA), Macy Gray (USA), Moby (USA), and Marky Mark (USA) all lending their street-cred to the label. Calvin Klein (USA, left) founded the company in 1968. Although it makes its ready-made women's clothing its flagship, most of its income is actually generated from licensing the name to manufacturers of jeans, underwear, and fragrances.

‹52645›   www.guinnessworldrecords.com/calvinklein   ← ACCESS CODE www.guinnessworldrecords.com/ralphlauren

ACCESS CODE

POLO SPORT

The biggest-selling designer clothing brand in the world is US-based Ralph Lauren (as modeled by Gisele, Brazil, right), with annual global wholesales of $4.5 billion (£3.2 billion) in 2000. Boasting labels such as Polo Ralph Lauren, Polo Sport, and the Ralph Lauren Collection, the company has nearly 240 Polo shops and outlet stores worldwide, and also sells its designs through roughly 1,600 department stores and speciality shops.

‹52317› ←

Charles Frederick Worth (UK), who died in 1895, is the creator of the oldest designer label. He was the first designer to sign his work with a label and to show garments on live models. Worth moved from the UK to Paris, France, in 1845, where his talent for design was soon discovered by the ladies of the court of Napoleon III. His business continues today through the perfumes of the House of Worth, such as *Worth Pour Homme* and *Je Reviens*.

In 1962 he opened his own couture fashion house and in the 1970s expanded into ready-to-wear lines, household linens, and fragrances.

LONGEST WEDDING DRESS TRAIN

The world's longest wedding dress train measured 670 ft (204.1 m). Made by Hege Solli (Norway) for the marriage of Hege Lorence to Rolf Rotset (both Norway) on June 1 1996, the train needed 186 bridesmaids and page boys to carry it.

MOST EXPENSIVE TIARA

The world's most expensive tiara, designed by Gianni Versace (Italy) in 1996, is worth $5 million (£3.2 million), and features 100-carat diamonds set in yellow gold.

LARGEST G-STRING

Unveiled at the Body Shop's UK headquarters on March 15 2001, the world's largest G-string, a giant red and white cotton thong, was part of Comic Relief's 'Pants to Poverty' fund-raising campaign. It measured 30 x 15 ft (9.2 x 4.6 m).

LARGEST T-SHIRT

The UK's Spring Centre Trust Fund commissioned clothing firm Patz to make a giant white T-shirt measuring 95 ft 2 in (29 m) long and 78 ft 6 in (23.9 m) wide. Big enough to fill a cricket pitch, it was created to raise money for charities that support disabled children.

GUINNESS WORLD RECORDS™

www.guinnessworldrecords.com/humanachievements

human
achievements

early starters

YOUNGEST CONSULTANT

In April 2000 supermarket chain Tesco announced that it had hired seven-year-old Laurie Sleator (UK) to advise senior executives on the Pokémon craze. Laurie receives Pokémon products in return for his services.

YOUNGEST PHYSICIAN

Balamurali Ambati (USA) became the world's youngest doctor on May 19 1995, when he graduated from the Mount Sinai School of Medicine in New York City, USA, age 17. He also coauthored a book on AIDS with his older brother when he was 11.

YOUNGEST AUTHOR

Dorothy Straight (USA) was four years old when she wrote *How the World Began* in 1962. It was published in Aug 1964 by Pantheon Books.

YOUNGEST SINGER TO HAVE A NO.1 HIT

French singer Jordy (Lemoine) was just four-and-a-half years old when his single 'Dur Dur d'Etre Bébé' ('It's Hard To Be A Baby') reached No.1 in the French charts in Sept 1993. The song later entered the US Billboard chart.

YOUNGEST MUSICIAN TO PERFORM AT WOODSTOCK

On July 23 1999 11-year-old Ilan Rubin (USA) became the youngest musician to perform in the 30-year history of Woodstock, kicking off the festival's three-day run in Rome, New York. Ilan is a drummer in the ska-punk band F.o.N. (Freak of Nature), partly founded by his older brother, which he joined age nine.

YOUNGEST ROCK JOURNALIST

US director/writer/producer Cameron Crowe, who was born in 1957, began a career in journalism at the age of 15, writing for such publications as *Penthouse*, *Playboy*, and the *Los Angeles Times*. At 16, he joined the staff of *Rolling Stone* magazine, where he worked as a contributing editor and later as an associate editor, profiling influential musicians such as Bob Dylan, David Bowie, and Eric Clapton.

YOUNGEST PERSON TO HAVE A PLATINUM ALBUM

The youngest person to record a platinum album is Billy Gilman (USA), who was 12 years 3 months old when his debut album, *One Voice*, achieved sales of one million in the USA in Aug 2000. He is also the youngest artist to have topped the country sales chart, setting this record two months earlier with the album's title song.

YOUNGEST NBA PLAYER

Jermaine O'Neal (USA), the youngest ever NBA player, was 18 years 53 days old when he made his professional basketball debut for the Portland Trail Blazers on Dec 5 1996.

YOUNGEST WORLD SERIES BASEBALL PLAYER

The youngest World Series baseball player was Fred Lindstrom (USA), who was 18 years 339 days old when he played for the New York Giants (NL) on Oct 24 1924.

YOUNGEST SOLO CIRCUMNAVIGATOR

David Griffiths Dicks (Australia) was 18 years 41 days old when he returned to Fremantle, WA, Australia, on Nov 16 1996 after 264 days 16 hr and 49 min at sea.

YOUNGEST PERSON TO CLIMB MT. EVEREST

Shambu Tamang (Nepal) is the youngest person ever to ascend Mt. Everest. He reached the summit of the 29,035-ft-high (8,850-m) mountain at the age of 17 years 6 months and 15 days, on May 5 1973.

YOUNGEST RELAY TEAM TO SWIM THE CHANNEL

The youngest six-member relay team to cross the English Channel is the Thane District AAA team from Mumbai (Bombay), India, who swam from Shakespeare Beach, Dover, Kent, UK, to Cap Gris-Nez, France, in 11 hr 23 min on Aug 12 1996. The team members were Kaveri Thakur (13), Rahul Modi (13), Daniel Reuben (13), Gunjan Parulkar (14), Rashmi Sansare (14), and Siddesh Parab (14).

YOUNGEST PERSON TO HIKE THE APPALACHIAN TRAIL

Michael Cogswell (USA) was just six years old when he hiked the length of the Appalachian Trail with his mother and stepfather in 1980. It took the family eight-and-a-half months to finish the hike. The Appalachian Trail is the world's longest designated footpath, stretching from Katahdin, Maine, to Springer Mountain, Georgia – a distance of approximately 2,160 miles (3,476 km).

YOUNGEST SCHOOL GROUP TO VISIT THE NORTH POLE

On April 1 1998 eight pupils from Robertsbridge Community College, E Sussex, UK, flew to the magnetic North Pole in Nunavut Territory, Canada, accompanied by two teachers. The students, who were between 13 and 15, were required to complete research projects while on the expedition.

YOUNGEST PERSON TO VISIT BOTH POLES

Robert Schumann (UK) traveled to the North Pole on April 6 1992, age 10, and to the South Pole on Dec 29 1993, age 11. He arrived and left the North Pole by air, but reached the South Pole by mountain bike, having flown to within a short distance of his destination. He was accompanied by his father on both trips.

FANTASTIC GYMNASTICS

The youngest female world gymnastics champion is Aurelia Dobre (Romania, above), who won the women's overall world title age 14 years 352 days in Rotterdam, Netherlands, on Oct 23 1987. The overall competition involves gymnasts performing in four separate disciplines – beam, vault, floor, and uneven bars – with each discipline being marked individually. Inspired by the Romanian champion gymnast Nadia Comaneci, Dobre took up gymnastics at the age of six, making her debut in junior competitions in 1983. Her first World Championship in 1987 was also her most successful competition. She won three gold medals (the team event, the all-around competition, and the individual beam competition) and one bronze medal. She competed in the 1988 Olympic Games, winning silver in the team event, and repeated this achievement the following year in the World Championships. Dobre retired in 1990, at the age of 17, and now works as a choreographer and dance coach.

<45033>
www.guinnessworldrecords.com/gymchamp
← ACCESS CODE

LINED UP FOR VICTORY

Siobhan Dunn (UK, above) became the world's youngest line-dance champion when she won the Junior World Line Dance Championship in Nashville, Tennessee, at the boot-scootin' age of 6 years 6 months 11 days, in Jan 1998.

Two years later, the world's longest line dance involved 6,275 people (six rows of dancers, each 1 mile [1.6 km] long) in Tamworth, NSW, Australia on Jan 29 2000, dancing for a total of 6 min 28 sec.

www.guinnessworldrecords.com/linedancechamp

ACCESS CODE

‹53295› ←

YOUNGEST CHEF

Justin Miller (USA) is the world's youngest chef. He became nationally famous for his cooking prowess at the age of five, and published his own cookbook, *Cooking with Justin: Recipes for Kids (And Parents)*, at the of age seven. Justin is currently finishing his second cookbook, *Break an Egg*, and advises the Marriot Hotel chain on its children's menus.

www.guinnessworldrecords.com/bowwow

SNOOP PUPPY PUP

Born March 9 1987, Lil Bow Wow (USA, right) has been rapping since he was five. His single 'Bounce With Me' was the No.1 Rap single for eight weeks according to the Recording Industry Association of America, making him the youngest No.1 solo rapper on the US charts. His single 'Bow Wow (That's My Name)' was at No.55 on the Billboard Hot 100 singles chart. He was dubbed Lil Bow Wow by multimillion-selling rap superstar Snoop Doggy Dogg.

ACCESS CODE

‹56520› ←

YOUNGEST CONCRETE BLOCK BREAKER 📺 USA

David Chu Tan (Germany), trained by his father – a martial arts master – was 11 years old when he managed to break 24 concrete blocks with his head in 30 seconds, while doing a forward flip – one for every two blocks. He set this record on Dec 20 2000. David's father had been training David since he was a small child.

YOUNGEST GRADUATE

In June 1994 Michael Kearney (USA) became the world's youngest graduate when he obtained a BA in anthropology from the University of South Alabama, age 10 years, 4 months.

GUINNESS WORLD RECORDS

golden oldies

OLDEST ACTRESS

French actress Jeanne Louise Calment (1875–1997) played herself in the film *Vincent And Me* (1990) at the amazing age of 114. The movie is about a young girl who travels through time to 19th-century France to meet the famous painter Vincent van Gogh. Calment was one of the last living people to have known van Gogh in real life – she met him in 1888. When she died, age 122, she was the oldest person who had concrete proof of her date of birth.

OLDEST TV PERFORMER

Myrtle Wood (b.1900, Australia), still appears regularly on Australian television as a model on *Sale Of The Century*. She is best known for the character she played for 17 years – Granny Davis – the housewife who introduced sliced bread to Australian households in 1963.

OLDEST PROFESSIONAL PIANIST

Romanian concert pianist Cella Delavrancea (1887–1991) gave her last public recital at the age of 103 in 1990, receiving six encores.

OLDEST AUTHORS

Sisters and coauthors A. Elizabeth and Sarah Louise Delany published *The Delany Sisters' Book Of Everyday Wisdom* in Oct 1994, when Sarah Louise was a spectacular 105 years old and A. Elizabeth was 103. After A. Elizabeth died in 1995, Sarah wrote the sequel called *On My Own At 107*, which was published in 1997 by Kodansha America.

OLDEST ADOPTEE

Born in 1940, Paula Louise Daly Winter Dolan (USA) became the oldest person in the world to be adopted on Nov 5 1998, at the age of 58 years 5 months and 17 days. Her adopters were her aunt and uncle, John and Elizabeth Winter. Dolan had been disowned by her birth parents nearly 40 years earlier after she married a man of whom they did not approve.

OLDEST PILOT

Cole Kugel (b.1902, USA) is the oldest qualified pilot in the world at 99 years old. He was born one year before the legendary Wright Brothers took to the skies, and has been flying for the last 71 years. Cole is a member of the International Flying Farmers – where he is also the oldest member.

FAST AND FURIOUS

Jerry De Roye [UK, left], who was born Gerald Jones in 1927, is the world's oldest wall-of-death rider. He rides a 1927 V-Twin Indian Type 101 Scout motorbike, regularly giving 'trick 'n' stunt' performances. Prince Constantin von Lichtenstein is another death-defying pensioner. On Feb 15 2000, at the age of 88 years 54 days, he became the oldest person to have successfully ridden the Cresta Run. This 0.75-mile (1.2-km) ice run, in St. Moritz, Switzerland, is one of winter sport's legendary challenges. Riders lie headfirst on small toboggans to navigate a track that drops about 515 ft (157 m), with a gradient varying from 1:2.8 to 1:8.7. As racers reach speeds of up to 90 mph (145 km/h), great skill is required to negotiate the terrifying corners.

<48665> www.guinnessworldrecords.com/walloffdeath ← ACCESS CODE

OLDEST WINDSURFER

Charles Ruijter (b.1915) took up windsurfing at the age of 63 in 1978, and is still windsurfing around the lakes of his native Eindhoven, Netherlands. An experienced sailor and rower, great-grandfather Charles is entirely self-taught.

OLDEST COMPETITIVE WALKER

Philip Rabinowitz (b.1904) of Hout Bay, Cape Town, South Africa, is the world's oldest active competitive walker. He regularly competes in races over 12.5 miles (20 km).

OLDEST FEMALE IN-LINE SKATER

The oldest professional female in-line skater is Donna Vano (b.1953, USA). Donna has been competing since 1991, and also takes part in skateboarding and snowboarding competitions. Aggressive in-line skaters use a U-shaped ramp, from which they perform flips and other maneuvers.

SPRY AND NOT RETIRING

James Janssen (left, b.1921, USA) is the world's oldest lifeguard. A retired Catholic priest, he not only guards the pool at the Davenport Outing Club, Iowa, but also teaches swimming and water aerobics.

While Janssen has opted for a change of career in his retirement, other people have simply refused to retire at all. Dr. Ishwar C. Dalal (b.1900, India) is the world's oldest practicing physician, and has been a doctor since 1935. Leamon Ward (b.1910, USA) has been cutting hair professionally since July 1927, and is still working four-and-a-half days per week at his one-chair barber's shop in Keystone Heights, Florida, while Dr. Valanjattil Kuruvilla Mani (b.1910, India) has been practicing dentistry since 1935 and continues to do so.

<54621> www.guinnessworldrecords.com/lifeguard ← ACCESS CODE

OLDEST MOTORCYCLIST

On May 2 2000 Len Vale Onslow rode his motorcycle from his home in Birmingham, UK, a distance of 121 miles (194.9 km), to the gates of Buckingham Palace, London, UK, in order to receive a congratulatory telegram from the Queen – something that is given to every British person who reaches their 100th birthday. Len, who owns a motorbike store, has been riding motorcycles since he was seven years old.

OLDEST CIRCUMNAVIGATOR

In 1994, at the age of 82, Fred Lasby (USA) completed a solo around-the-world flight in his single-engined Piper Comanche. Leaving Fort Myers, Florida, on June 30, he flew 23,219 miles (37,366 km) westward, making 21 stops and arriving back at Fort Myers on Aug 20.

OLDEST PERSON TO COMPLETE A MARATHON ON EACH CONTINENT

American Bill Galbrecht (b.1928) has run a total of 56 marathons, including at least two on each of the seven continents. Most recently, he ran marathons on each of the continents between 1997, when he was 69, and 1999, when he was 71.

OLDEST SOLO TRANSATLANTIC SAILOR

Michael Richey (UK) was 80 years 25 days old when he arrived in Plymouth, Devon, UK, on July 31 1997, having sailed single-handedly from Newport, Rhode Island, USA. An expert navigator for the British

Navy during World War II, he has made a number of solo voyages in his boat *Jester* since 1966.

OLDEST PERSON TO CLIMB MT. KILIMANJARO

On Feb 11 1999, age 71 years 126 days, Dow Prouty (USA) became the oldest person to climb Mt. Kilimanjaro, Tanzania, Africa's highest mountain at 19,340 ft (5,895 m). Mr. Prouty was accompanied by his son and daughter and took six days to climb to the snowy summit.

OLDEST PERSON TO RAPPEL DOWN A BUILDING

On Nov 25 2000 great-grandmother Dorothy 'Dos' Williams (b.1916, UK), successfully rappelled down a 100-ft-high (30.5-m) building in Flintshire, Clwyd, UK. Sponsored by the North East Wales Search and Rescue Team, Mrs. Williams raised nearly £2,000 ($3,000) for cancer research.

OLDEST PERSON TO MAKE A SOLO SKYDIVE

Retired pilot Herb Tanner (USA) jumped unassisted from a single-engine plane in Cleveland, Ohio, on June 19 1998, age 92. He made the 3,500-ft (1,067-m) jump for the first time ever after receiving basic instruction and performing 10 practice jumps on a virtual reality simulator, with no worries about his artificial knees or hearing aid.

OLDEST TANDEM HANG GLIDER

The oldest person to hang glide with a tandem partner is Veronica Adams (b.1904, Australia), who was 94 years 92 days old when she made her flight over Helensburgh, NSW, Australia, on Nov 3 1998.

OLDEST MALE PARACHUTIST

Norwegian Bjarne Mæland (b.1899) made his first tandem parachute jump at the age of 100 years 21 days. He jumped from a height of 10,499 ft (3,200 m).

www.guinnessworldrecords.com/cher

CHER MAGIC

The oldest female singer to top the US chart is Cher (USA, right), who was 52 years old when her single 'Believe' reached No.1 in March 1999, staying in this position for four weeks. The song came from the album *Believe*, which was released in 1998 and was the biggest-selling of Cher's long career. Cher also holds the record for having the longest gap between No.1 hits on this chart, with her previous No.1, 'Dark Lady', topping the chart in 1974.

GUINNESS WORLD RECORDS

epic land journeys

GREATEST DISTANCE DRIVEN IN ONE YEAR

Two Opel Rekord cars, manufactured by the Delta Motor Corporation of Port Elizabeth, South Africa, covered a record distance of 356,063 miles (573,029 km) between May 18 1988 and May 18 1989. This is the equivalent of driving around the equator over 14 times. The cars did a daily average of 975 miles (1,570 km).

FASTEST AROUND-THE-WORLD CAR JOURNEY

Jeremy Levine, James Burke, and Mark Aylett (all UK) took 19 days 10 hr 10 min (not including the time spent aboard ships) to drive a taxi around the world. Starting at Buckingham Palace, London, UK, on June 16 2000 and arriving back on Oct 11 2000, they covered 18,119 miles (29,159 km). They journeyed through France, Italy, Greece, Bulgaria, Turkey, Syria, Jordan, Saudi Arabia, Australia, New Zealand, USA, and Spain; crossing the English Channel, Adriatic Sea, Red Sea, Indian Ocean, Tasman Sea, Pacific and Atlantic Oceans.

The first and fastest circumnavigation by car, made under the 1989 and 1991 rules and embracing more than an equator's length of driving, is held by Neena and Mohammed Salahuddin Choudhury (both India). Their 24,901-mile journey (40,075 road kms) took 69 days 19 hr 5 min from Sept 9 to Nov 17 1989.

FASTEST AROUND-THE-WORLD CYCLE TOUR

Tal Burt (Israel) cycled 13,253 miles (21,329 km) around the world solo in 77 days 14 hr, between June 1 and Aug 17 1992, starting and finishing in Paris, France. His average daily mileage was 172 miles (277 km).

<56015>

www.guinnessworldrecords.com/solarcar

← ACCESS CODE

SUN-DAY DRIVER

The longest solar-powered journey was made by the Radiance solar car (left), which traveled 4,376.62 miles (7,043.5 km) across Canada from Halifax to Vancouver in 29 days from July 1 to 29 2000. Built by the Queen's University Solar Vehicle Team of Ontario, Canada to an aerodynamic design, it runs on about as much energy as an average toaster, is less than 3.2 ft (1 m) high and is so flat that the driver literally has to lie down in it. The Radiance's journey cost less than CAN$5 (US$3.40), as opposed to the estimated CAN$3,000 (US$2,030) fuel costs for the truck that followed as a support vehicle.

Jay Aldous and Matt DeWaal (USA) cycled 14,290 miles (22,997 km) around the world from Salt Lake City, Utah, in 106 days, from April 2 to July 16 1984.

HIGHEST-ALTITUDE CYCLE RIDE

Siegfried Verheijke, Luc Belet (both Belgium), and Martin Adserballe (Denmark) rode their mountain bikes at an altitude of 22,992 ft (7,008 m) on the snowy slopes of the Muztagata peak in the Xinjiang province of China, on Aug 11 2000. It took them 14 days to reach the required altitude, carrying their disassembled mountain bikes, which weighed between 22 and 26 lb (10 to 12 kg), on the outside of their backpacks.

LONGEST UNICYCLE JOURNEY

Hanspeter Beck (Australia) unicycled 3,876.1 miles (6,237.96 km) from Port Hedland, Western Australia, to Melbourne, Vic, Australia, in 51 days 23 hr 25 min, from June 30 to Aug 20 1985.

LONGEST JOURNEY BY AUTORICKSHAW

Between Dec 17 1999 and June 23 2000, Ken Twyford and Gerald Smewing (both UK) traveled from Hyderabad, India, to Lancashire, UK, using a 145cc autorickshaw. These are lightweight, doorless vehicles with an average speed of 30 mph (50 km/h) widely used on the Indian subcontinent as taxis. This was a journey of 11,908 miles (19,165 km). Their route took them through India, Pakistan, Iran, Turkey, Greece, Italy, France, and England.

LONGEST BICYCLE WHEELIE JOURNEY

Between April 13 and June 25 1999, Kurt Osburn (USA) traveled 2,839.6 miles (4,569 km) from Hollywood, California, to Orlando, Florida. He used a standard 20-in (51-cm) BMX-style bicycle with a padded seat and 'fixed' wheel where the pedals pump backward and forward, like a unicycle. Osburn made the journey in 50-mile (80-km) stages at around 10 mph (16 km/h).

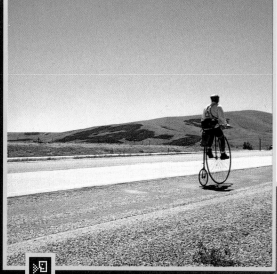

HIGH-WHEELER

The record for the fastest transAmerican journey on a penny-farthing bicycle is held by Steve Stevens (left, USA), who cycled from San Francisco, California, to Boston, Massachusetts, from May 26 2000 to June 23 2000 on an 1887 Rudge penny-farthing bicycle. It took him 29 days 9 hr and 3 min and he covered a total of 3,255 miles (5,238 k). Steve, 55, averaged an astonishing 112 miles (180 km) per day on a bike with solid rubber wheels and no suspension. With its 54-in-tall (1.37-m) front wheel, Steve's 1887 Rudge Light Roadster was considerably taller than his first bicycle, which he received age six. Steve restored his penny-farthing himself and says the transcontinental crossing had been his goal since taking up high-wheel cycling in the early 1990s.

<55918>

www.guinnessworldrecords.com/pennyfarthing

← ACCESS CODE

LONGEST RUN

Gary Parsons (Australia) ran 11,824.8 miles (19,030.3 km) in 274 days 8 min, beginning and ending in Brisbane, Qld, Australia, from April 25 1999 to Jan 25 2000. He ran around Australia in 197 days 23 hr 49 min on Nov 8 1999, having covered 8,947.3 miles (14,399.3 km). He then ran around Tasmania before returning to mainland Australia to complete the run. During his run he also set records for the fastest times to complete 10,000 km (6,213 miles): 135 days 9 hr 50 min; 15,000 km (9,320 miles): 205 days 23 hr 18 min; 10,000 miles (16,093 km): 221 days 1 hr 7 min.

SHORTEST TIME TO SKI DOWN MT. EVEREST

Ski instructor Davo Karnicar (Slovenia) skied from the summit of Mt. Everest to Base Camp in five hours on Oct 7 2000. He did not remove his skis during the descent from 29,028 ft (8,848 m) to 17,550 ft (5,350 m). It had taken him a month to reach the summit, stopping to acclimate to the extreme altitude.

LONGEST UNAIDED CROSSING OF ANTARCTICA

Alain Hubert and Dixie Dansercoer (both Belgium) are the first and only men to have crossed Antarctica

unaided. The 2,423-mile (3,900-km) journey took 99 days between Nov 4 1997 and Feb 9 1998 in temperatures consistently below 14ºF (-10ºC). With only skis and a parafoil, they averaged speeds of 28 mph (45 km/h) covering 1,180 miles (1,900 km) over the most favorable 20 days.

FASTEST ANTARCTIC CROSSING

Ranulph Fiennes, Oliver Shepard, and Charles Burton (all UK) completed the TransAntarctic leg of the 1980–82 TransGlobe Expedition in 55 days between Oct 28 1980 and Jan 11 1981. They used snowmobiles

to make the 2,600-mile (4,185-km) journey from Sanae to Scott Base, and reached the South Pole on Dec 15 1980. Their trip included a break of 17 days while they obtained permission to visit the Pole, and a four-day rest once they arrived there.

LONGEST DISTANCE SOLO CROSSING OF THE ANTARCTIC

Mitsuro Ohba (Japan) walked, skied, and parasailed a total of 2,376 miles (3,824 km) across Antarctica in 99 days, starting Nov 9 1998. Ohba began on Princess Astrid Coast on the South African side of Antarctica, and was aiming to reach Walgreen Coast on the Chilean side. He was picked up by a plane when bad weather forced him to abandon his attempt 124 miles (200 km) short of his target.

www.guinnessworldrecords.com/messner

ICE 'N' EASY DOES IT

Although there is no easy route up Mt. Everest, the south face is acknowledged to be less challenging than the north, with the final ascent passing over the South Col – the major pass between the Everest and Lhotse peaks. However, on this route climbers have to pass through the Khumbu Icefall (right), where unstable, house-sized ice blocks often crash down as a result of the Khumbu glacier moving beneath them.

In May 1978 Reinhold Messner (Italy), one of history's greatest mountaineers, and Peter Habeler (Austria), reached the summit of Mt. Everest without supplemental oxygen – via the deadly Khumbu Icefall.

Messner was the first person to climb the world's three highest mountains: Everest, K2, and Kanchenjunga. He has also climbed all 14 of the world's 26,250-ft (8,000-m) peaks.

ACCESS CODE

‹44794› ←

GUINNESS WORLD RECORDS

air and sea heroes

FASTEST AIR SPEED

The highest aircraft speed was recorded by Captain Eldon W. Joersz and Major George T. Morgan Jr (both USA) in a Lockheed SR-71A 'Blackbird' on July 28 1976. The flight took place over a 155-mile (250-km) course near Beale Air Force Base, California, and had an average speed of 2,193 mph (3,529.56 km/h) – about the same speed as a rifle bullet. In comparison, Concorde cruises at a mere 1,320 mph (2,124 km/h). A 'Blackbird' has flown from New York to London in 1 hr 55 min, compared with Concorde's average time of around 3 hr 50 min.

HIGHEST HORIZONTAL FLIGHT ALTITUDE

On July 28 1976, USAF Captain Robert C. Helt and USAF Major Larry A. Elliot (both USA) reached an altitude of 85,073.15 ft (25,929.031 m) in horizontal flight in a Lockheed SR-71A 'Blackbird' at Beale Air Force Base, California. This is approximately three times higher than the average Boeing 747 cruising at an altitude of 35,000 ft (10,660 m).

LONGEST BANZAI SKYDIVE

On Sept 2 2000 Yasuhiro Kubo (Japan) jumped from a plane at an altitude of 9,842.5 ft (3,000 m) without a parachute and was in freefall for 50 seconds before hooking on to a parachute that had been thrown out of the plane prior to his jump.

IN AT THE DEEP END

On May 13 2000 Audrey Mestre Ferrera (France, left) set the women's record for diving without breathing apparatus by descending to a depth of 410 ft (125 m) at Las Palmas, Canary Islands, Spain. She was underwater for a total of 2 min 30 sec. The record depth for a man is 498.7 ft (152 m), which was achieved by Loic Leferme (France) on June 22 2000 in Nice, France.

<55885>   www.guinnessworldrecords.com/onebreathdive
← ACCESS CODE

DEEPEST UNDERGROUND BALLOON FLIGHT

On May 6 2000 Krzysztof Rekas (Poland) used an AX-6 hot-air balloon to ascend the Staszica Chamber of Wieliczka salt mine near Krakow, Poland. Starting from an underground depth of 410.1 ft (125 m), it flew for four minutes, rising to a height of 6.98 ft (2.13 m) above the floor level of the chamber.

The altitude record for a hot-air balloon is 64,997 ft (19,811 m), set by Per Lindstrand (UK) in a Colt 600 hot-air balloon over Laredo, Texas, on June 6 1988.

LONGEST HUMAN-POWERED FLIGHT

Kanellos Kanellopoulos (Greece) kept his Daedalus 88 aircraft aloft for 3 hr 54 min 59 sec on April 23 1988 while pedaling the 71.53 miles (115.11 km) from Heraklion to Santorini, Greece. His flight ended when a gust of wind damaged the plane's tail and caused it to crash into the sea.

FASTEST AIRCRAFT CIRCUMNAVIGATION

The fastest circumnavigational flight under the FAI (Fédération Aéronautique Internationale) rules, was 31 hr 27 min 49 sec flown by an Air France Concorde between Aug 15 and 16 1995. Flight AF1995 flew east via Toulouse, Dubai, Bangkok, Guam, Honolulu, and Acapulco from JFK airport, New York.

HIGHEST PARAGLIDER

On Jan 6 1993 Robbie Whittal (UK) paraglided using bottled oxygen and achieved an amazing height gain of 14,849 ft (4,526 m) at Brandvlei, South Africa. At this record-breaking height, ice would have started to form on his clothing and glider.

LONGEST PARAGLIDING FLIGHT

Godfrey Wennes (Australia) paraglided 208.16 miles (335 km) from Mt. Borah to Enarra Station, Australia on Nov 16 1998.

UP, UP, AND AWAY

The first balloon to circumnavigate the globe nonstop was *Breitling Orbiter 3* (left), flown by Bertrand Piccard (Switzerland) and Brian Jones (UK). Taking off from Château d'Oex, Switzerland, on March 1 1999, it set the circumnavigation record in 15 days 10 hr 24 min. The flight continued until March 21, traveling a total of 25,361 miles (40,814 km) – 459 miles (739 km) longer than the equator. The entire flight took 19 days 21 hr 47 min and also set the gas and hot-air balloon distance and air duration records (under FAI rules).

The greatest distance for a solo balloon flight is 14,235 miles (22,909 km), set by Steve Fosset (USA). He took off from Mendoza, Argentina, on Aug 7 1998 but crashed into the Pacific on Aug 16 1998.

<44059>   www.guinnessworldrecords.com/circumballoon
← ACCESS CODE

FASTEST ATLANTIC CROSSING

The fastest Atlantic crossing was 2 days 10 hr 34 min 47 sec between Aug 6 and 9 1992 by the 223-ft (68-m) luxury yacht *Destriero* (*Warrior*). The gas turbine-propelled vessel maintained an average speed of 45.7 knots (52.6 mph or 84.6 km/h) despite weighing nearly 881,848 lb (400 tonnes). In comparison, the crossing of the *Mayflower* in 1620 took 66 days, and at the time of the *Titanic* (1912) the fastest crossing was still at least 4.5 days.

FASTEST CROSS-CHANNEL SWIM

Chad Hundeby (USA) swam across the English Channel from Shakespeare Beach, Dover to Cap Gris-Nez, France, on Sept 27 1994 setting a world record of 7 hr 17 min. The fastest France-England time is 8 hr 5 min set by Richard Davey (UK) in 1988.

HIGHEST SPEED ON WATER

On Oct 8 1978 Ken Warby (Australia) set the official record for the greatest speed on water with a top speed of 275.8 knots (317.55 mph or 511.11 km/h) in his unlimited hydroplane *Spirit of Australia* on Blowering Dam Lake, NSW, Australia. However, unofficially, he had also achieved the faster estimated speed of 300 knots (344.82 mph or 555 km/h) on Nov 20 1977.

FASTEST TRANSATLANTIC CROSSING BY ROWBOAT

Between Oct and Nov 1997 Phil Stubbs and Rob Hamill (both New Zealand) crossed the Atlantic from Tenerife to Barbados in just 41 days in their 21-ft (6.4-m) rowing boat. Despite having to anchor for two days to ride out a 60-mph (96-km/h) storm, they beat the previous record set in 1971 by Don and Geoff Allum (UK) by 32 days.

GREATEST DISTANCE BY PEDAL BOAT

Kenichi Horie (Japan) set a pedal-boating distance record of 4,460 miles (7,500 km), between Oct 30 1992 and Feb 17 1993, when he crossed the Pacific Ocean from Honolulu, Hawaii, to Naha, Okinawa, Japan.

WALKING ON WATER

In 1988 Remy Bricka (France, above) 'walked' across the Atlantic Ocean on skis 13 ft 9 in (4.2 m) long. Leaving Tenerife, Canary Islands, Spain, on April 2 1988, he covered 3,502 miles (5,636 km), arriving in Trinidad on May 31 1988. Remy made his two-month journey on polyester floats, with no fresh water or food supplies, eating plankton on the way. He was suffering from delirium when he arrived. In April 2000 he tried to 'walk' across the Pacific Ocean, from the USA to Australia. However, he encountered problems and had to abandon his plans.

www.guinnessworldrecords.com/oceanwalk

ACCESS CODE

<48769> ←

FASTEST SOLO SAILING CIRCUMNAVIGATION

Michel Desjoyeaux (France) circumnavigated the globe in 93 days 3 hr 57 min 32 sec during the 2000 Vendée Globe single-handed yacht race, starting and finishing at Les Sables d'Olonne, France. He covered a distance of 24,000 miles (38,600 km) from Nov 5 2000 to Feb 10 2001 in his yacht *PRB*. The Vendée Globe race follows the shortest and most treacherous route around the world – navigating south and around Antarctica before heading back north.

www.guinnessworldrecords.com/ellen

FANTASTIC VOYAGE

Ellen MacArthur (UK, right), age 24, broke the record for the fastest circumnavigation of the globe by a woman when she set a time of 94 days 4 hr 25 min 40 sec and finished second in the 2000 Vendée Globe single-handed yacht race, starting and finishing at Les Sables d'Olonne, France. She covered a distance of 24,000 miles (38,600 km) in her yacht *Kingfisher* between Nov 5 2000 and Feb 11 2001. She is also the youngest person to have completed one of the world's toughest sailing challenges.

ACCESS CODE

<56222> ←

FASTEST SOLO (UNAIDED) ROW ACROSS PACIFIC

Jim Shekhdar (UK) rowed across the Pacific Ocean in 273 days 13 hr and 12 min, starting from Ilo in Peru on June 29 2000, and ending near Brisbane, Australia, on March 30 2001. He made the estimated 9,100-mile (14,650-km) journey without outside support in his 33-ft (10-m) custom-built boat *Le Shark*.

DEEPEST MANNED OCEAN DESCENT

On Jan 23 1960 Dr. Jacques Piccard (Switzerland) and Lt. Donald Walsh, (USA) piloted the Swiss-built US Navy bathyscaphe *Trieste* to a depth of 35,799 ft (10,911 m) in the Challenger Deep section of the Mariana Trench. Challenger Deep, situated in the Pacific Ocean, is thought to be the deepest point on Earth.

DEEPEST CAVE SCUBA DIVE

On Aug 23 1996 Nuno Gomes (South Africa) scuba dived to a depth of 927.21 ft (282.6 m) at the Boesmansgat Cave, South Africa. His seven 23-gallon (88-liter) cylinders weighed 298 lb (135 kg) and used 14,458 gallons (54,730 liters) of mixtures of air, oxygen, nitrox, and trimix.

KING FISHER

GUINNESS
WORLD RECORDS

courage and endurance

HEAVIEST BED OF NAILS

On June 24 2000 Lee Graber (USA) was sandwiched between two beds of nails with a weight of 1,659 lb (752.5 kg) placed on top of the upper bed. He lay between the two beds for a total of 10 seconds.

MOST LAYERED BED OF NAILS

Lee, Todd, and Doreen Graber and Chris Smith (all USA) formed a layered four-person bed of nails at Tallmadge, Ohio, on Oct 8 2000. Lee Graber lay on a bed of nails on the ground, with Todd lying on top of a bed of nails on top of Lee, followed by Chris on a bed of nails on top of Todd, and finally Doreen on a bed of nails on top of Chris. The formation was held for 10 seconds after it had been created, with Lee supporting an estimated weight of 750 lb (340 kg).

LONGEST ONE-BREATH SWIM UNDER ICE

Wim Hof (Netherlands) swam 188.6 ft (57.5 m) under ice in a lake in Finland on March 16 2000. Although the water temperature was 21.2°F (-6°C), he did not use any special equipment, and wore only swimming trunks and goggles. The record attempt took 1 min 1 sec to complete.

LONGEST DISTANCE CYCLED UNDERWATER

Vittorio Innocente (Italy) cycled 3,937 ft (1,200 m) underwater up and down an Olympic-sized swimming pool in 23 min 54 sec in Chiavera, Italy, on April 12 2000. Vittorio's mountain bike was weighed down with 77.16 lb (35 kg) of lead, and the tires were filled with water. The bike was also equipped with four spoilers and two vertical plates to provide stability.

LONGEST UNDERWATER EXERCISE BIKE RIDE

Without the use of any breathing equipment, Benjamin Franz (Germany) was able to clock up a distance of 1,830 ft 7 in (558 m) in 1 min 33.5 sec on a submerged Kettler 'Racer' exercise bike in a single breath on Nov 6 2000.

LONGEST SUBMERGENCE

Michael Stevens (UK) remained underwater with no rest breaks for 212 hr 30 min from Feb 14 to 23 1986 using scuba gear and without surface air hoses.

<48740> www.guinnessworldrecords.com/longcrawl
← ACCESS CODE

FRONT CRAWL

The longest continuous voluntary crawl (with one or other knee in unbroken contact with the ground) is 31.44 miles (50.6 km), which was achieved by Peter McKinlay and John Murrie (both UK, left). They crawled around 115 laps of a running track, from March 28 to 29 1992. They broke the previous record by 3 miles (1.86 km) rather than the few yards they had planned because they crawled around the outside, rather than the inside, of the track. They raised over £2,500 ($4,400) for charity. They soaked their knees in running alcohol and trained for their record attempt for months in advance. Heavy-duty freezer gloves and miners' pads were worn to protect hands and knees, but they were still covered in bruises and blisters by the end.

LONGEST WATERSKIING SESSION

Ralph Hildebrand and Dave Phillips (Canada) waterskied for 56 hr 35 min 3 sec around Indian Arm, Canada, from June 10 to 12 1994. They waterskied a total of 1,337.4 miles (2,152.3 km) at an average speed of 30 mph (48 km/h). While waterskiing at night, infrared binoculars and spotlights were used.

GREATEST DISTANCE RUN CARRYING A BRICK

Arulanantham Suresh Joachim (Sri Lanka) holds the record for the longest recorded distance run while carrying a 10-lb (4.5-kg) brick continuously in the same ungloved hand in an uncradled downward position. The brick was carried nonstop with no breaks for 78.71 miles (126.67 km) around a circuit of 147 ft 6 in (45 m) at the Florence St. Mall Water Fountain, Hornsby, NSW, Australia, on Dec 11 to 12 1999.

MOST COBRAS KISSED CONSECUTIVELY

Gordon Cates (USA) kissed 11 of the world's most venomous snakes consecutively on Sept 25 1999. He kissed 10 monacle cobras and one 15-ft (4.57-m) King Cobra.

LARGEST NUMBER OF COCKROACHES IN A COFFIN

On Aug 12 1999 'Jungle' John Lamedica (USA) was placed in a Plexiglas™ coffin wearing only a pair of shorts and had 20,050 Giant Madagascan hissing cockroaches poured over him. He remained in the coffin for a minimum of 10 seconds.

BATHTUB-SITTING WITH MOST SNAKES

Jackie Bibby and Rosie Reynolds-McCasland (both USA) jointly hold the record for sitting in a bathtub with the most live rattlesnakes. On Sept 24 1999 these two experienced snake handlers sat in two separate bathtubs, each with 75 Western Diamondback rattlesnakes, for a minimum of 10 seconds.

LONGEST TATTOO SESSION

Matt O'Toole (USA) holds the record for enduring the longest tattooing session of 26 hr 49 min. Matt's tattooing began at 10 a.m. on July 31 and ended at 12:49 p.m. on Aug 1 2000. The tattoos, applied by tattoo artist Scott Lunn, cover Matt's back, thighs, chest, calves, right ankle, and right bicep, and include the Chinese symbols for 'pain' and 'suffering.'

FAITH, HOPE, AND CHARITY

Terry Fox (Canada, left), who had an artificial leg, ran from St. John's, Newfoundland to Thunder Bay, Ontario, Canada, in 143 days from April 12 to Sept 2 1980, covering 3,339 miles (5,373 km). He raised CAN$24.7 million (US$21.2 million) – the greatest amount ever raised by a charity walk or run. At 18, his right leg was amputated just above the knee due to bone cancer. Nonetheless, he decided to run across Canada to raise funds for cancer research. Unfortunately, Terry's cancer reappeared and he had to stop the run. He died on June 28 1981, age 22. His legacy, the annual Terry Fox Run, is the largest one-day cancer research fundraising event. Each year more than 1.2 million people participate. It has raised CAN$270 million (US$231.8 million) to date.

<47821> www.guinnessworldrecords.com/terryfox
← ACCESS CODE

LONGEST TIME SPENT BALANCING ON ONE FOOT

Arulanantham Suresh Joachim (Sri Lanka) balanced on one foot for a record 76 hr 40 min from May 22 to 25 1997. Under the rules, the disengaged foot may not be rested on the standing foot nor may any object be used for support or balance.

LONGEST TIME SPENT MOTIONLESS

Om Prakash Singh (India) stood without moving, except for involuntary blinking, for a continuous 20 hr 10 min 6 sec from Aug 13 to 14 1997. Singh, recovering from chicken pox, started his attempt on the eve of the golden jubilee of India's Independence, as an homage to unknown martyrs.

LONGEST STAY ON MT. EVEREST'S SUMMIT

In May 1999 Babu Chhiri Sherpa (Nepal) remained at the summit of Mt. Everest (29,028 ft or 8,848 m) for 21 hours without the use of bottled oxygen. Most climbers stay for under an hour. Chhiri, who made 10 successful ascents, climbed Everest just weeks later to become the first person to climb the mountain twice in the same season.

Babu Chhiri Sherpa also holds the record for the fastest ascent of Mt. Everest. He climbed from base camp to the summit via the south face in 16 hr 56 min on May 21 2000. Sadly, he died on Everest on April 29 2001.

LONGEST LIFEBOAT JOURNEY

In 1916, after his ship, *Endurance*, became trapped by the ice off the shores of Antarctica, Sir Ernest Shackleton (UK) abandoned ship with his 28-strong crew and, using three lifeboats, set course to Elephant Island, 100 miles (161 km) north. Once they were there, he selected five of his best men to direct the largest lifeboat, the 22.5-ft (6.85-m-long) *James Caird*, toward a whaling station in South Georgia, 800 miles (1,287 km) away. In a journey that is still regarded as the greatest in history, Shackleton and his men reached the island after 17 days, on May 19 1916, from where they sent a rescue ship for their stranded shipmates.

LONGEST CAR PUSH

Daniele Sangion and Giorgio Valente (both Italy) pushed a car 32.6 miles (52.47 km) in 24 hours on a 0.98-mile-long (1,590-m) track in Caorle, near Venice, Italy, on Oct 17 to 18 1998. The car pushed was a Fiat Uno 60 (1.1 liter) weighing 1,851.88 lb (840 kg).

LONGEST LADDER CLIMB

Ten firemen from the Bradford Shipley Fire Station, W Yorks, UK, collectively climbed a vertical height of 65.24 miles (105 km) up a standard fire-service ladder in 24 hours from Oct 6 to 7 2000. The ladder was 32.8 ft (10 m) high, so to set the record the team scaled it 10,500 times.

HIGHEST SLACKLINE WALK USA

Darrin Carter (USA) walked 100 ft (30.4 m) on a 1-in-wide (2.54-cm) line, 2,900 ft (883.9 m) above the ground at Yosemite National Park, California, on Aug 19 1999. Slack-lining is different from a tightrope walk in that under body weight the line sags significantly, whereas a tightrope has little or no sag.

LONGEST DISTANCE WALKING ON HANDS

In 1900 Johann Hurlinger (Austria) walked on his hands for 870 miles (1,400 km). In 55 daily 10-hour stints he walked from Vienna to Paris, averaging 1.58 mph (2.54 km/h).

www.guinnessworldrecords.com/iceman

ACCESS CODE

‹56038› ←

THE ICEMAN COMETH 📺 USA

Wim Hof (Netherlands, right) endured standing in a tube filled with ice-cubes for a record 60 min 24 sec on Dec 20 2000. Wearing only swimming trunks, he stood on a box so that his feet did not end up in a pool of water. Hof uses meditation, yoga, and breathing techniques to regulate his body temperature and keep it at a normal 98.6°F (37°C), even in extreme cold. Hof has been involved in various extreme outdoor activities for over 20 years, including rock climbing, canyoning, waterfall climbing, and ice diving.

GUINNESS WORLD RECORDS™

marathon efforts

LONGEST RADIO DJ MARATHON

DJ Greig Daines broadcast on Hospital Radio Chelmsford, which is based at St. John's Hospital, Chelmsford, Essex, UK, for 73 hr 33 min from Sept 6 to 9 2000. He played a total of 1,086 tracks, the first of which was Boo Radley's 'Wake Up Boo', and the last of which was 'Gold' by Spandau Ballet.

LONGEST RADIO QUIZ

Wilson Casey, a DJ at the radio station WKDY-A.M. in Spartanburg, South Carolina, spent 30 hours asking 3,303 trivia questions on air from Jan 9 to 10 1999. He used three phone lines for the event and estimated that 6,500 phone calls were fielded.

LONGEST CLAPPING SESSION

The record for continuous clapping (sustaining an average of 160 claps per minute, audible from 360 ft 11 in [110 m] away) is 58 hr 9 min, by V. Jeyaraman (India) from Feb 12 to 15 1988. The record was set to raise money for the Rotary Club of Madras North's polio immunization program, and for the Hindu Mission Hospital, Tambaram, India.

LONGEST KISS

On April 5 1999 Karmit Tzubera and Dror Orpaz (Israel) kissed for a record 30 hr 45 min to win a kissing contest held in Rabin Square, Tel Aviv, Israel.

DRUM UNTIL YOU DROP!

The world's longest drumming marathon lasted for 36 hours, and was undertaken by Steven Darvill (Canada, left) from Dec 31 2000 to Jan 2 2001 at Angel Auto Glass, North Vancouver, British Columbia, Canada. He played 490 songs. The team record is 24 hr 15 min, by eight drummers from Cambridge High School, Ohio, from Dec 29 to 30 2000.

‹54674› www.guinnessworldrecords.com/drummarathon
← ACCESS CODE

LONGEST LESSON

A Hungarian language and literature lesson taught at Leöwey Klára Grammar School, Pécs, Hungary, by Szabolcs Zalay, lasted for a record-breaking 24 hours from June 18 to 19 1999. It was attended by 34 students.

LONGEST MOVIE-WATCHING MARATHON

From Feb 18 to 20 2000, 14 people managed to watch films for 50 hr 55 min at the Grand Entertainment Global Village cinema in Bangkok, Thailand. The marathon began with an audience of 369 and 74 of them were able to stay awake long enough to break the previous record of 37 hr 25 min.

LONGEST TAI CHI MARATHON

On May 15 to 16 1999 Robin Nears, Keith Graham, and Jo Powell completed a tai chi marathon lasting 24 hours at St. James Square, Newport, Isle of Wight, UK.

LONGEST STREET THEATER MARATHON

From July 9 to 11 1999, 15 members of the Thisaigal Cultural Troupe (India) performed 12 plays on a stage outside Karuna Hospital, Madurai, India, for 57 hr 30 min.

LONGEST STATIC CYCLING MARATHON

Lisa Burke (South Africa) rode an exercise bike for a record-breaking 42 hr 15 min at the Bedfordview Health and Racquet Club, Bedfordview, South Africa, from Nov 11 to 13 2000.

GREATEST DISTANCE ON A STATIC CYCLE IN 24 HOURS

Between June 19 and 20 1999 Steven Renata (Australia) achieved a distance of 325 miles (523 km) on an exercise bike. The record was set during the International Fitness and Healthy Lifestyle Expo at the Sydney Expo Centre, Sydney, NSW, Australia.

GREATEST DISTANCE RIDDEN ON ESCALATORS

Arulanantham Suresh Joachim, who was born in Sri Lanka and now lives in Australia, traveled a total distance of 140 miles (225.4 km) up and down escalators at the Westfield Shopping Centre, Burwood, NSW, Australia, from May 25 to 31 1998. His ride lasted for 145 hr 57 min. Joachim is currently hoping to set up a charity to help children in need around the world.

GREATEST DISTANCE TRAVELED ON A POGO STICK

Ashrita Furman (USA) jumped a distance of 23.10 miles (37.18 km) on a pogo stick in 12 hr 27 min on June 22 1997. The record was set on the running track at Queensborough Community College, New York.

GREATEST DISTANCES TAP-DANCED

David Meenan (USA) tap-danced a record distance of 28.24 miles (45.44 km) in Red Bank, New Jersey, on Aug 31 1997. He traveled along a 0.5-mile (0.8-km) loop for seven hours, crossing railroad tracks and even having a guard stop a train for him.

MOST SKIPS IN 24 HOURS BY ONE PERSON

Ashrita Furman (USA) achieved 130,000 skips of a rope in a 24-hour period from Jan 23 to 24 1999. The attempt began at the Sheraton Hotel in Badung, Indonesia, and moved to the nearby Hotel Chedi after six hours. Ashrita took five-minute rest breaks per hour on a cumulative basis to preserve his strength.

DON'T CRY OVER SPILT MILK!

On April 22 to 23 1998 Ashrita Furman (USA, left) walked a distance of 80.96 miles (130.3 km) around Victory Field track, Forest Park, New York City, with a milk bottle balanced on his head. He continued for 23 hr 35 min, until he broke into a run and the milk bottle fell off. Ashrita Furman has set approximately 60 Guinness World Records – more than any other individual – and currently holds 12, as the others have been broken. A devout follower of spiritual leader Sri Chinmoy, he changed his name from Keith to Ashrita (Sanskrit for 'protected by God') in 1974. Ashrita currently manages a health food shop in Queens, New York City, and also works as the travel coordinator for Sri Chinmoy's international peace conferences.

GREATEST DISTANCE BY WHEELCHAIR IN 24 HOURS

Nik Nikzaban, who was born in Iran and now lives in Canada, wheeled himself a distance of 77.58 miles (124.86 km) in 24 hours between April 6 and 7 2000. The record was set on the running track at Handsworth Secondary School, North Vancouver, British Columbia, Canada. Nik spent six hours a day on his fitness regimen in preparation which included weight training, swimming and wheeling.

‹48721› www.guinnessworldrecords.com/bottlewalk

← ACCESS CODE

FEEL THE BURN!

The greatest distance run on a treadmill by a woman in 24 hours is 93.5 miles (150.5 km), by Patti Wixom (USA, above) at Gold's Gym, Amarillo, Texas, on March 28 1998. The idea for the record attempt came from the director of Gold's Gym, who noticed Patti's long training sessions on the treadmill and asked if she would like to try a 24-hour marathon.

The men's record is held by Rory Coleman (UK), who ran 100.78 miles (162.19 km) on a treadmill between Oct 17 and 18 1998. By his own admission, he is a former 'couch potato'.

www.guinnessworldrecords.com/treadmillrun

ACCESS CODE

‹51891› ←

GREATEST DISTANCE ON A SNOWMOBILE IN 24 HOURS

Randy Gravatt and Joe Williams (both USA) covered a distance of 1,189.7 miles (2,075.5 km) in 24 hours on trails around Island Park, Idaho, from Jan 27 to 28 1998.

MOST VERTICAL FEET SKIED IN 24 HOURS

Neal Weisenberg (Canada) skied 153,944 ft (46,920 m) from Feb 27 to 28 1999, at Kimberley Alpine Resort, British Columbia, Canada. He used a T-bar lift and made 102 runs from top to bottom – equal in distance to five times the height of Everest.

LONGEST BASKETBALL GAME

The longest game of basketball lasting a record-breaking 24 hours was played by the Suncoast Clippers at Maroochydore Eagles Basketball Stadium, Qld, Australia, from Nov 21 to 22 1998.

LONGEST CPR MARATHON

The world's longest cardiopulmonary resuscitation marathon took place between Sept 20 and 26 1998 at Merry Hill Shopping Centre, W. Midlands, UK. Two teams of two – Ben Albutt and Phil Watson, and Robert Cole and Darren Fradgley – performed CPR (15 compressions alternating with two breaths) on a dummy for 144 hours. The men were all members of the West Midlands Ambulance Service.

LONGEST ARCADE MACHINE DANCE MARATHON

Mark E.T. (Extra Tricks; UK) danced on Konami's Dancing Stage arcade machine for a record eight hours without stopping at the Trocadero, London, UK, on March 10 1999.

www.guinnessworldrecords.com/londonmarathon

RUN, BABY, RUN

The London Marathon, which has been run through the streets of London, UK, since 1981, raises more money for charity than any other single sporting event in the world. A record-breaking £24 million ($35.8 million) was raised on April 16 2000, the last Marathon for which figures are available, and over £100 million ($149 million) has been raised altogether. Pictured right is Jerry Hoare (UK), one of 31,542 runners to complete the 2000 Marathon, and one of 445,000 who have completed it since 1981.

ACCESS CODE

‹52445› ←

GUINNESS WORLD RECORDS

unusual skills

MOST FOOT-JUGGLING 📺 USA
FLIPS OF A TABLE
Chester Cable (USA) flipped a table that was 9 ft 11.75 in (3.03 m) long, 35 in (88.9 cm) wide, and 27.25 in (69.21 cm) high a total of 17 times in succession, using his feet, on Oct 16 1998.

MOST FOOT-JUGGLING 📺 FR
FLIPS OF A PERSON
On Oct 26 2000 Ali Bandbaz (Iran) 'juggled' his brother Massoud through 12 consecutive 360° revolutions, using only his feet. Ali lay on his back with Massoud sitting on his feet, and the pair completed each revolution in the same position.

LARGEST 📺 USA
BUBBLEGUM BUBBLE
BLOWN WITH NOSE
Joyce Samuels (USA) blew a bubble-gum bubble with a diameter of 11 in (27.94 cm) on Nov 10 2000.

LARGEST BALLOON 📺 USA
INFLATED WITH A
TANDEM NOSEBLOW
On Nov 10 2000 Ryan Barker (USA) inflated a 46.5-in (118.11-cm) balloon held in his wife Marilee's mouth by blowing through her nose.

SLINGSHOT EARS 📺 USA
On Oct 29 1999 Monte Pierce (USA, left) shot an American 10 cent coin a distance of 10 ft 10.5 in (3.306 m), using his ear as a slingshot. This is the furthest a coin has been propelled by an earlobe. Monte began pulling at his ears as a child to relieve earache, and now, age 20, can pull them up over his eyes, pull them down to meet under his chin, or roll them up like earplugs. His left ear stretches to a length of 4.75–5 in (12–12.7 cm), and his right ear to a length of 4.5 in (11.4 cm). He has perfect hearing, and doctors assure him that he is not damaging his ears in any way by performing these feats.

‹54633›
← ACCESS CODE   www.guinnessworldrecords.com/slingshotears

LONGEST-DISTANCE 📺 USA
MARSHMALLOW NOSEBLOW
The greatest distance that a marshmallow has been shot from one person's nostril and caught in another person's mouth is 16 ft 3.5 in (4.96 m). Americans Scott Jeckel (the launcher) and Ray Perisin (the catcher) set this record on Aug 13 1999.

FASTEST
PANCAKE MARATHON
On Oct 24 1999 Mike Cuzzacrea (USA), 'The Pancake Man' ran the 26.2-mile (42.1-km) Casino Niagara International Marathon in Buffalo, New York, in 3 hr 2 min 27 sec, while flipping a pancake continuously in a frying pan. He came 46th out of 1,319 finishers.

FASTEST SANDWICH 📺 USA
MADE USING FEET
On Nov 10 2000 Rob Williams (USA) made a bologna, cheese, and salad sandwich in 1 min 57 sec, using just his feet.

LOUDEST BURP 📺 UK
On April 5 2000 Paul Hunn (UK) registered a burp of 118.1 dB – similar to being in the front row at a rock concert, and only slightly quieter than the noise made by an airplane on a runway.

MOST STEPS
CLIMBED ON A BICYCLE
Javier Zapata (Colombia) broke his own world record by hopping up 943 steps on a bicycle, without touching the ground, on May 20 2000. The feat took him 43 min 26 sec.

FASTEST TIME TO MEMORIZE
A PACK OF CARDS
Andi Bell (UK) memorized a pack of 52 shuffled cards and repeated out loud the order in which they appeared in 34.03 seconds on Aug 28 1998.

LONGEST TIME TENNIS BALL
KEPT IN AIR WITH FEET
On Nov 11 1999 Jacek Guzowski (Poland) kept a tennis ball up in the air, using only his feet, for 5 hr 28 min 59 sec. A counter showed that he touched the ball 35,000 times – an average of approximately 107 times per minute, or 1.8 times per second.

LARGEST SCORPION 📺 USA
HELD IN MOUTH
Dean Sheldon (USA) was able to hold a 7-in (17.78-cm) scorpion in his mouth for 18 seconds on Dec 21 2000.

MOST 📺 USA
SCORPIONS IN MOUTH
Dean Sheldon (USA) put a total of 20 scorpions in his mouth, holding them there for 21 seconds, on Dec 21 2000.

INSECT MORSEL MUNCHIES
Retired ratcatcher and part-time entertainer Ken Edwards (UK, left) ate 36 medium-sized cockroaches, in one minute on March 5 2001, setting the record for the most cockroaches ever eaten by a human. Eating cockroaches is "like having an anesthetic at the back of the throat" he says, as they let off a scent to ward away predators. His other bizarre stage acts include stuffing 47 rats down a pair of pantyhose he was wearing, and inviting people to throw darts at a cork placed in his navel.

On Oct 20 1998 Dr. Norman Gary (USA) held 109 honeybees in his closed mouth for 10 seconds – but didn't eat them. Gary is Emeritus Professor at the University of California, where his subject of specialization is the behavior of bees.

‹54654›
← ACCESS CODE   www.guinnessworldrecords.com/cockroacheater

HOTTEST
METAL IN MOUTH
USA

On Dec 18 1998 Yim Byung Nam held a silver-dollar-sized piece of metal, heated to 910°F (487.8°C), in his mouth for 14 seconds. When Yim spat it out, it was hot enough to fry bacon.

LONGEST TIME
IN A BOX BY THREE
CONTORTIONISTS
FR

Bonnie Morgan, Daniel Smith, and Leslie Tipton (all USA) fitted into a box measuring 26 x 27 x 22 in (66.04 x 68.58 x 55.88 cm) and stayed there for 2 min 40 sec on Jan 31 2001.

LONGEST
BASKETBALL SHOT
MADE WITH HEAD
USA

On Nov 10 2000 Eyal Horn (Israel) shot a basketball with his head while standing 25 ft (7.62 m) from the backboard. He also scored a record 15 consecutive lay-ups (shooting and catching the ball with the head).

MOST CHERRY STEMS
KNOTTED IN ONE HOUR

On Sept 4 1997 Al Gliniecki (USA) knotted 911 cherry stems with his tongue in one hour – an average of 15 stems per minute.

MOST SKIPS ON A
UNICYCLE IN ONE MINUTE
DE

On Aug 31 2000 Peter Rosendahl (Sweden), who resides in Germany, set the record for the most revolutions of a jump rope made on a unicycle. He managed 169 revolutions in just one minute.

GREATEST DISTANCE
TO SPIT A CRICKET
USA

Danny Capps (USA) spat a dead cricket a total distance of 30 ft 1.2 in (9.17 m) on June 26 1998.

FASTEST HUMAN
BEER BOTTLE OPENER
USA

Daniel Lambert (Sweden) used his teeth to open 50 conventional crown-cap bottles on March 11 2001. He achieved this in only one minute.

FASTEST TIRE FLIPPER
SE

On Jan 31 2001 in Stockholm, Sweden, Jorma Paananen (Sweden) completed a 65-ft (20-m) course – 32 ft 6 in (10 m) there and back – of flipping a Michelin Radial Steel Cord X26.5R25 (XHA) tire in a time of 1 min 6 sec. The tire weighed 925.9 lb (420 kg).

www.guinnessworldrecords.com/archeryfeet

AMAZING
FEET OF ARCHERY
USA

Hang Thu Thi Ngyuen (Vietnam, left) set the record for the furthest distance shot with a bow and arrow using the feet. On Aug 12 1999 she hit a target that was 16 ft 5 in (5 m) away. Thu Hang, whose father is a lighting technician at Ho Chi Minh City Circus, first became interested in circus skills as a child. She spends three hours a day practising her act. Although shy by nature, Thu Hang is very focused and confident on stage.

ACCESS CODE

‹54641› ←

GUINNESS WORLD RECORDS

speed stunts

FASTEST BACKWARD WALK UP MT. KILIMANJARO

The fastest time for a solo backward walk up Mt. Kilimanjaro, Tanzania, was 72 hr by Jurgen Gessau (South Africa), from Marangu Gate to Ulhuru Peak, between July 20 and 23 1997.

FASTEST BACKWARD MILE

Donald Davis (USA) ran 1 mile (1.6 km) backward in 6 min 7.1 sec on Feb 21 1983.

FASTEST TRANS-USA BACKWARD RUN

Arvind Pandya (India) ran backward from Los Angeles, California, east across the USA to New York City, in 107 days, between Aug 18 and Dec 3 1984.

FASTEST 5-MILE MARCH WITH A BACKPACK

The fastest time in which anyone has run 5 miles (8 km) while carrying a 56-lb (25.4-kg) backpack is 36 min 49 sec, by Paddy Doyle (UK) at the Royal British Legion Runathon, Coventry, Warwickshire, UK, on May 9 1999.

FASTEST POGO STICK UP THE CN TOWER

Ashrita Furman (USA) pogo-sticked up the 1,899 steps of the CN Tower, Toronto, Canada, in 57 min 51 sec on July 23 1999 – approximately one step every two seconds.

MOST STEP-UPS IN ONE HOUR

The most step-ups completed in one hour is 4,135, by Manjit Singh (UK, 'the Ironman of Leicester') on a 15-in (38.1-cm) bench on April 4 1999.

MOST TRAMPOLINE DUNK SHOTS IN 30 SECONDS 📺 USA

Mark Odgers, Seth Botone, Shane Geraghty, Joseph Gibby, and Ben Ramsey (all USA) known as 'the Extreme Team' managed 15 somersaults from a trampoline, with a dunk shot into a basketball net in 30 seconds on Jan 21 2001.

FASTEST MIXED TEAM GARBAGE CAN RACERS

On Feb 21 1999 Aaron Viney and Olivia Jones (Australia) completed a 361-ft (110-m) wheeled-garbage can race in 48.53 seconds at Westfield Devils Junior Soccer Club, Launceston, Tas, Australia. The competitors had to sprint 33 ft (10 m) to their stationary bins before taking it in turns to be pulled over 164-ft (50-m) stretches of the course.

FASTEST TIME TO REFUEL

The record time for refueling an airplane with 102.7 gal (388.8 liters) of 100-octane avgas is 3 min 42 sec, which was achieved by the Sky Harbor Air Service line crew for a 1975 Cessna 310 (N92HH) on July 5 1992. The plane had landed at Cheyenne Airport, Wyoming, during an around-the-world race. It would normally take 10 to 15 minutes to refuel an aircraft of this type.

FASTEST BRIDGE BUILDERS

On Nov 12 1998 a team of British soldiers from 35 Engineer Regiment, based at Hameln, Germany, constructed a bridge across a 26-ft 3-in (8-m) gap using a five-bay single-story MGB (medium girder bridge) in 8 min 19 sec.

FASTEST LUMBERJACK TRIATHLON

The fastest time to complete the three disciplines of single buck, underhand chop, and tree fall, is 1 min 57 sec, by Werner Brohammer (Germany) on Aug 31 2000.

FASTEST TIME TO LAY A MILE OF COINS

On May 23 1998 at Ashbourne, Derbyshire, UK, eight members of the Ashbourne and District Lions Club laid out 79,200 pennies, weighing 550 lb (0.25 tonnes) in 4 hr 2 min.

FASTEST BEER-BOTTLE OPENERS 📺 DE

On April 2 1999 a team of three people, led by Alois Unertl of the Unertl Brewery, Mühldorf, Germany, opened 300 bottles of beer in 1 min 47 sec. Each person opened 100 bottles before passing the special opener to the next team member.

FASTEST PUMPKIN CARVER

On Oct 16 1999 Jerry Ayers (USA) carved 2,015 lb (914 kg), of pumpkins in 7 hr 11 min. The officials weighed all pumpkins with the minimum weight being 18 lb (8.1 kg).

Stephen Clarke (USA), carved a face into a 27.5-lb (12.47-kg) pumpkin in 1 min 14.8 sec on Dec 14 2000.

MOST BALLOON SCULPTURES IN ONE HOUR

John Cassidy (USA), made 367 different balloon sculptures in one hour, using 371 balloons. The record was set at Gator's Restaurant, Valley Forge, Philadelphia, on May 10 1999.

FASTEST HAIRCUT

On Nov 26 1999 Trevor Mitchell (UK), cut a full head of hair in 1 min 13 sec during the BBC TV South 'Children in Need' event.

FASTEST TYPIST ON A PC

Gregory Arakelian (USA), set a PC typing speed record of 158 wpm in the Key Tronic World Invitational Type-Off, which attracted about 10,000 entrants worldwide. He recorded this speed during the three-minute semi-final on Sept 24 1991, making only two errors.

FASTEST TIME TO MAKE A TV COMMERCIAL

A television commercial lasting 35 seconds advertising for the nonprofit foundation Creative for Children, made by Thomsen AG of

TREE-MENDOUS TREE CLIMBERS

The fastest time in which anyone has climbed a 29-ft 6-in (9-m) coconut tree barefoot is 4.88 seconds, by Fuatai Solo (Fiji, left) at the annual Coconut Tree Climbing Competition in Sukuna Park, Fiji, on Aug 22 1980. Climbing at this speed, Solo would be able to scale the Empire State Building, New York City, in just over four minutes. He was so pleased with his win – the third in succession – that he climbed the tree again, clutching the prize money of $100 (£43) in his mouth.

The record time for fir-tree climbing is held by Guy German (USA), who climbed up a 100-ft (30.5-m) fir spar pole, and down again, in 24.82 seconds during the 1988 World Championship Timber Carnival at Albany, Oregon. German also holds the record for treetopping, climbing up a spar pole of the same height and sawing off the top, which he achieved in an amazing 53.35 seconds in July 1989.

<48689>
www.guinnessworldrecords.com/treeclimb
← ACCESS CODE

KEN HE DO IT?
YES, HE CAN!

Ken Moss (UK, above), who lost his sight in 1992, set the blind land speed record of 131 mph (210.82 km/h) in a single-seater prototype MG EXF car on Oct 16 1999, at Boscombe Down, Wilts, UK. Sensors on the car gave guidance information to headphones in Ken's helmet, with bleeps in each ear telling him which way to steer.

www.guinnessworldrecords.com/
blinddriver

ACCESS CODE

‹55410› ←

Kiel, Germany, was created, filmed, and aired in a record-breaking 1 hr 19 min on Nov 4 1999.

FASTEST WINDOW WIPER

Terry Burrow (UK) cleaned three standard 45 x 45-in (1,143 x 1,143-mm) office windows set in a frame with a 11.81-in (300-mm) long squeegee and 2.3 gal (9 liters) of water in 9.91 sec on March 7 2001. The time taken to complete the windows was 8.91 sec, but two faults, each with a 0.5-second penalty, increased the overall time.

FASTEST RECITAL OF HAMLET'S SOLILOQUY

Sean Shannon (Canada) recited Hamlet's soliloquy 'To be or not to be' (260 words) in 23.8 sec (655 words per minute) on Aug 30 1995.

FASTEST 6.2-MILE (10-KM) BABY CARRIAGE PUSHING

The fastest time to finish the 6.2-mile (10-km) race to push a baby carriage is 34 min 26 sec by Mal Grimmett pushing his daughter Natalie, at the 1999 Olympic Dream fun run, Melbourne, Australia, on Nov 21 1999.

www.guinnessworldrecords.com/rocketluge

ROCKET MAN 📺 USA

Billy Copeland (USA, below), reached a record speed of 70 mph (112.65 km/h) on his rocket-powered street luge at Bakersfield, California, on May 15 1998.

A street luge is essentially a skateboard designed to be ridden lying down. Longer and wider than conventional boards, with bigger wheels, street luges are ridden feet first by riders who wear leather motorcycle clothing and crash helmets to protect themselves from harm if they tumble off at speed. The straighter the road, the faster the luge can go. For his record attempt, Copeland used eight rockets, but he has since tested 24 rockets attached to a set of triangular wings at the back of his luge. His ambition is to become the first street-luge rider ever to reach 100 mph (160 km/h). The rockets that he uses are similar to those used by hobbyists to launch rockets over 1 mile (1.6 km) into the air.

ACCESS CODE

‹53940› ←

GUINNESS WORLD RECORDS™

tests of strength

HEAVIEST HEAD BALANCE
The heaviest combined weight ever balanced on a person's head in one hour is 11,422 lb (5,180.09 kg). This record was achieved by John Evans (UK) on July 23 2000 when, in the course of an hour, he balanced 92 people in succession on his head for at least 10 seconds each.

HEAVIEST WEIGHT LIFTED WITH A HUMAN BEARD
Using only his beard, Antanas Kontrimas (Lithuania) lifted a total weight of 130.2 lb (59 kg) – the combined weight of a girl and the harness she was in – off the ground for 10.93 seconds on March 11 2001.

HEAVIEST VEHICLE HAIR PULL
On May 1 1999 at Bruntingthorpe Proving Ground, Leicestershire, UK, Letchemanah Ramasamy (Malaysia) pulled a Long Version Routemaster double-decker bus weighing 17,362 lb (7,874 kg) over a distance of 107 ft 9.5 in (32.85 m) using just his hair.

GREATEST WEIGHT BALANCED ON TEETH
Frank Simon (USA) balanced a 135-lb (61.23-kg) motorcycle, including a helmet, on his teeth for 14 seconds on April 27 1999, with only a tooth guard as protection.

MOST CONCRETE BLOCKS BROKEN WHILE LYING ON A BED OF NAILS
On April 27 2000 Paul Evans (UK) piled 26 concrete blocks weighing 286 lb (129.72 kg) on to his chest while lying on a bed of nails measuring 20 x 22 in (50.8 x 55.8 cm). The blocks were then smashed with a 6.35-kg (14-lb) sledgehammer. A karate teacher, Paul began training in martial arts as a Royal Marine in 1967 and first started performing on a bed of nails in 1979.

HEAVIEST TRAIN PULLED
On June 1 1999 strongman Juraj 'Duri' Barbaric (Slovakia) single-handedly pulled a 20-freight-car train full of scrap metal weighing 2 million lb (1,000 tonnes) a distance of 14 ft 9 in (4.5 m) along a railroad track at Kosice, Slovakia. On the day, he warmed up by pulling 590,520 lb (300 tonnes) for 10 ft (3 m), then 1,771,580 lb (900 tonnes) for 9.6 ft (2.95 m).

MOST CARS LIFTED
On Oct 3 1998 Mark Anglesea (UK) lifted the rear end of a Rover Mini Metro clear off the ground 580 times in one hour – an average of almost 10 lifts a minute – in Yorkshire, UK.

HEAVIEST ONE-ARM TRUCK-PULL
On March 29 2000 William Deandreis (France) pulled a 6,896-lb (3,128-kg) truck 5 ft (1.5 m), using only a single downward arm-wrestling move.

HEAVE HO!
The record for the most tug-of-war pulls in one hour by three teams was broken by 30 members of the Holland Tug-of-War Club (UK, left) on June 6 2000. The three teams of 10 – symbolizing the Staffordshire club's first 30 years – lifted a 937-lb (425-kg) weight (using a training rig) a total of 80 times in one hour. Each pull was over a distance of 22 ft 6 in (6.86 m). The teams took turns at the rope, and between them lifted the equivalent of a total of 74,957 lb (34 tonnes). Gantries or rigs are widely used by tug-of-war clubs for training and are trestlelike structures under which a weight is suspended by pulleys. A popular rural pastime in many parts of the world, tug-of-war was an Olympic event between 1900 and 1920.

‹55911› www.guinnessworldrecords.com/tugofwar
ACCESS CODE

MOST BOAT LIFTS
Sami Heinonen and Juha Räsänen (both Finland) continuously lifted a boat and 10 cheerleaders with a combined weight of 1,440 lb (653.2 kg) a total of 24 times on Oct 9 2000 (in Helsinki, Finland). The boat, a Buster XS, weighing 332 lb (151 kg), was lifted in an up-and-down motion to touch a bar 4 in (10 cm) high, ensuring the same distance was lifted every time.

HEAVIEST BOAT PULL
On Nov 19 1998 David Huxley (Australia), pulled the 20,012-lb (1,006-tonne) boat *Delphin*, with 175 cars and passengers, over 82 ft (25 m) in Rostock, Germany.

TIGHTEST FRYING PAN ROLL
Craig Pumphrey (USA) rolled a 12-in (30-cm) aluminum pan with his bare hands to a circle of 9.25 in (23.5 cm) in 30 seconds on Oct 16 1999.

LONGEST FIRE WALK
Gary Shawkey (USA) took 31 seconds to walk 165 ft (50.29 m) over burning embers of cedarwood with an average temperature of 982.22ºC (1,800ºF) at the Central Florida Fair in Orlando, Florida, on March 4 2000.

MOST TELEPHONE BOOKS TORN
Amanda Brutus (UK) tore nine *Yellow Pages* telephone books from top to bottom in three minutes at the Alliance & Leicester Group Property Services and Giro Services in Bootle, Liverpool, UK, on Nov 17 2000 in aid of the BBC TV *Children in Need* charity appeal. The exact time in which she set this record was 2 min 52.46 sec. Each book contained 1,007 pages.

MOST TIRES SUPPORTED
Gary Windebank (UK), supported 96 Michelin automobile tires in a free-standing 'lift' in Feb 1984. The total weight was 1,440 lb (653 kg). The tires used were Michelin XZX 155 x13.

KEEP ON TRUCKING
The one-hour team truck-pulling record was broken by 20 Atlas Gym Power Team strongmen (left) who pulled a 31,932-lb (15.966-tonne) dump truck a distance of 3.3 miles (5.31 km) in one hour on Oct 29 2000 in Kenosha, Wisconsin, USA. Gym owner Rhett Bobzien had the inspiration for this record while watching a strongman competition on TV. He went back to his gym and recruited 20 bodybuilders, all weighing over 198.5 lb (90 kg), and for weeks before the event Kenosha residents were treated to the sight of teachers, businessmen, factory workers, and law enforcement officers pulling their cars and pickup trucks around town. On the big day 10 men would pull while 10 would rest, but importantly, the pull didn't stop for the changeover.

‹56088› www.guinnessworldrecords.com/truckpull
ACCESS CODE

MOST ONE-ARM PUSH-UPS IN ONE MINUTE 📺 FR
Yvan de Weber (Switzerland) achieved 93 push-ups on one arm in one minute on Oct 26 2000.

MOST ONE-ARM PUSH-UPS IN FIVE HOURS
Paddy Doyle (UK) performed 8,794 one-arm push-ups in five hours on Feb 12 1996 in Birmingham, UK.

MOST PUSH-UPS IN ONE HOUR
An amazing 3,416 push-ups were performed in one hour by Canadian Roy Berger on Aug 30 1998 in Ottawa, Ontario, Canada.

MOST MILITARY BENCH PRESS LIFTS 📺 FI
On Oct 8 2000 Jani Riekkinen (Finland) lifted 149 lb (67.5 kg) 40 times, with his legs crossed and raised above the ground. Riekkinen weighed in at 147 lb (66.7 kg) according to the rules, two hours before the record attempt.

GREATEST DISPLAY OF LUNG POWER
Manjit Singh (UK) inflated a standard metereological balloon to a diameter of 8 ft (2.44 m), using only lung power, in 42 minutes on Sept 16 1998.

MOST BOARDS BROKEN
Sang-yun Lee (USA) broke 1,501 wooden boards by hand in one hour on Dec 12 1998 – equal to 2.4 boards per second. The boards measured 11 x 9 x 1 in (27.9 x 22.1 x 2.54 cm). The existing record had been 1,200 boards in seven hours.

MOST DECKS OF CARDS TORN
Scott Fraze (USA) ripped 13 decks of cards (52 cards plus two jokers per deck) in 30 seconds on Dec 21 2000.

GREATEST WEIGHT LIFTED WITH BOTH EARS
Dimitry Kinkladze (Georgia) lifted weights totaling 105 lb (48 kg) with his ears for 10 minutes on Nov 2 1997. A 70.56-lb (32-kg) weight hung from his left ear and a 35.28-lb (16-kg) weight hung from his right ear.

www.guinnessworldrecords.com/bottleblowup

CHAMPION WINDBAG 📺 FR
George Christen (Luxembourg, below) holds the record for the fastest time to blow up a standard hot water bottle until it bursts. He took 52.68 seconds to accomplish this on Dec 6 2000. To avoid air being forced back into the lungs, it is essential to breathe in through the nose and out into the bottle in a rhythmic way. Protective eye goggles must also be worn.

ACCESS CODE ‹52102› ←

GUINNESS WORLD RECORDS™

mass participation

MOST CHILDREN ON SPACE HOPPERS

On Oct 23 2000, to mark the launch of the *Guinness World Records* website, 520 children bounced simultaneously down Wembley Way, London, UK, on 520 rubber space-hopper toys.

LOUDEST CROWD ROAR AT AN OUTDOOR SPORTS STADIUM

On Oct 1 2000, during an NFL game between the Denver Broncos and the New England Patriots at the 76,123-seat Mile High Stadium in Denver, Colorado, a crowd roar was measured at 128.7 dB. In comparison, a car horn measures 110 dB and a rock concert generates 120 dB.

LARGEST 'YMCA' DANCE

On Nov 1 1997, 6,907 students from Southwest Missouri State University, Springfield, Missouri, danced to the song *YMCA* for five minutes while it was performed live by the famous group Village People. The record was set in the university's Plaster Stadium.

LARGEST HUG

The record for the world's largest hug was set by 899 bankers from Goldman Sachs at their IBD Global Conference

‹50475›

www.guinnessworldrecords.com/chickendance
← ACCESS CODE

CHICKEN!

An estimated 72,000 people took part in the world's largest Chicken Dance (left), which was staged during the Canfield Fair, Canfield, Ohio, on Sept 1 1996. The record was set as part of the Fair's 150th anniversary celebrations, and was chosen because the Fair's mascot is a rooster. For 10 minutes, all rides were paused and all vendors stopped working to dance to music blaring from sound systems. The crowd was led by the rooster mascot, members of the Fair's board, and a group of cheerleaders – many people even carried chickens as they danced.

in the huge ballroom of the Hilton International, New York City, New York on Dec 1 2000. The slogan for the event was 'One Team, One Hug.'

LARGEST TEA PARTY

On Oct 28 2000, 465 people gathered aboard the cruiser *The Spirit of Boston* on the Charles River, Boston, Massachusetts, to break the record for the world's largest tea party. A total of 85.4 gallons (323.4 liters) of tea were consumed – or approximately 1,138 cups.

MOST PEOPLE CRAMMED ON A BUS

On Oct 23 2000 a record-breaking 110 people crammed themselves onto a single-decker bus outside Cynthia's Bar and Restaurant, London, UK. The record was set as part of the launch of the *Guinness World Records* website.

LARGEST EASTER EGG HUNT

The world's largest-ever Easter egg hunt took place on March 20 1999, during the Vision Australia Foundation's annual Easter Fair at Kooyong, Vic, Australia. A total of 150,000 solid chocolate eggs were found by the 3,000 volunteers – this is an average of 50 eggs each. The hunt was so large that army troops had to be brought in to hide the eggs within the giant field of hay.

MOST PEOPLE WALKING ON STILTS

During the Zancothon '99 parade in Santiago de Cali, Colombia, on July 25 1999, 152 people age six to 37 walked on stilts for 1.86 miles (3 km).

LARGEST ACCORDION ENSEMBLE

The world's largest accordion ensemble consisted of 566 musicians playing the accordion for 22 minutes. The record was set during the International Folklore Festival in Diepenheim, Netherlands, on June 1 2000, and was organized by the Stedeker Dansers (Netherlands).

LARGEST JAPANESE DRUM ENSEMBLE

On Aug 9 1998 a record total of 1,850 musicians gathered to play *Yamabiko* on 1,845 Japanese drums at Irie Stadium, Muroran City, Japan. The 25-minute concert was held outside as the noise of the drums would have broken the windows of an indoor venue.

LARGEST ORCHESTRA

On May 15 2000 the world's largest orchestra, consisting of 6,452 student and professional musicians, all assembled at BC Place Stadium, Vancouver, British Columbia, Canada, to play 'Ten Minutes Of Nine,' an

SEEING DOUBLE?

On Nov 12 1999 – a national holiday marking the birth of Sun Yatsen, the first president of the Republic of China – a total of 3,961 pairs of twins gathered on the square of Taipei City Hall, Taiwan, to break the record for the largest gathering of twins (left). The event was organized by the Mayor of Taipei, Ma Ying-Jeou, and was meant to lift people's spirits following a large earthquake two months earlier. The twins came from as far away as the UK, Germany, India, and the USA, and ranged in age from one month to 88 years. National celebrities were also present, along with 37 sets of triplets and four sets of quadruplets. The participants lined up in a tree formation to symbolize the regrowth of areas damaged by the earthquake.

arrangement from Beethoven's Ninth Symphony. The orchestra was conducted by Bramwell Tovey, the music director of the Vancouver Symphony Orchestra.

LARGEST BARBECUE

On Oct 10 1993 a record 44,158 people attended a barbecue at Warwick Farm Racecourse, Sydney, NSW, Australia. More than 300,000 sausages, 100,000 steaks, and 50,000 chicken burgers were consumed, and over 481,000 cans of beer drunk. This is equivalent to 6.7 sausages, 2.25 steaks, 1.13 chicken burgers, and a whopping 10.89 cans of beer per person.

MOST PEOPLE SCUBA DIVING

On April 17 1999, at Saipan, Northern Mariana Islands (in the western Pacific Ocean), 215 people set a record for scuba diving at the same time and at the same location.

LARGEST GAY FESTIVALS

The Lesbian Gay Bisexual Transgender Pride Parade in San Francisco, California, and the Sydney Gay and Lesbian Mardi Gras in Sydney, NSW, Australia, each attract a minimum of 600,000 people annually.

MOST PARTICIPANTS IN A ONE-HOUR SWIMATHON

A record 2,533 people participated in BT Swimathon 2000, which took place at over 500 swimming pools across the UK between 6 and 7 pm on March 18 2000.

MOST PEOPLE BUNGEE JUMPING IN 24 HOURS

On Oct 26 2000, 505 people bungee jumped at the A.J. Hackett Bungy site at Cairns, Qld, Australia to raise money for charity. That is one bungee jump every 2.85 minutes.

---

www.guinnessworldrecords.com/tomatina

KILLER TOMATO ATTACK! USA

On the last Wednesday of every August, the town of Buñol, near Valencia, Spain, holds the world's largest food fight – its annual tomato festival, known as the *Tomatina* (below). At the 1999 event, 25,000 people spent one hour hurling approximately 264,554 lb (120 tonnes) of tomatoes at each other. The festival begins when the crowd cuts down a Serrano ham tied to the top of a greasy pole. Attendants then dump tomatoes on to the streets from the backs of trucks for participants to scoop up and throw at one another. By the time the food fight is finished, the town is saturated with sticky tomato paste, with rivers of tomato juice running down the streets. Finally, fire trucks hose down roads and buildings, while people head for makeshift public showers by the river. The *Tomatina* began by chance in 1944, when a truck dumped its load of tomatoes by accident.

ACCESS CODE ‹49067› ←

GUINNESS WORLD RECORDS

teamwork

CHECKMATE

On Oct 22 2000, 10,004 people set the record for the most people playing chess simultaneously as part of the Second Mexico City Chess Festival (above), a government initiative to bring cultural events out on to the streets for the people of the city. A team of 450 Mexican chess masters each played 20 to 25 members of the public, with 81% of the games won by the Masters, 13% won by the public, and 6% drawn. The festival opened at 10 a.m. and the last game finished at 5 p.m.

A national Mexican record was also established for the largest human logo representing an enormous chessboard. The previous record (made the previous year at the same event) was for 5,046 players.

The record for the most consecutive chess games played by one person is held by Willem van Roosmalen (Netherlands), who played 719 games from Nov 6 to 7 1998. He won 650, drew 37, and suffered only 32 defeats.

www.guinnessworldrecords.com/masschess

‹55923› ← **ACCESS CODE**

LARGEST 'STADIUM' WAVE

The largest 'stadium' wave was performed on June 24 2000 by 3,276 people. Organized by the West Sussex County Council Youth Service and the West Sussex Council for Voluntary Youth Services (both UK), the wave took seven minutes to complete and stretched for almost 3 miles (5 km).

MOST BAKED BEANS EATEN IN TWO MINUTES

On Nov 17 2000 a team of four people living in television's *Big Brother* house in Vilvoorde, Belgium, ate a total of 335 baked beans in two minutes – an average rate of nearly 42 baked beans (spiked and eaten one at a time) – every minute.

MOST VETS INVOLVED IN AN OPERATION

In Aug 1999 over 30 vets operated on Motola, a 38-year-old cow elephant who lost her left foot after stepping on a land mine on the Thai-Burma (Myanmar) border. It took Motola three days to cover the 60 miles (95.56 km) to reach the Hang Chat Elephant Hospital in Lampang, Thailand. Enough anesthetic to knock out 70 humans was used to put her to sleep. Vets at the Lampang Hospital said they were the worst wounds that they had ever seen at the medical center. Motola's operation cost $105,000 (£64,571.70), and was paid for by public donation. Animal experts hoped that once Motola had recovered from her surgery they would be able to fit a prosthetic device to enable her to walk again. Elephants are cultural icons in Thai culture.

MOST RECONSTRUCTIVE SURGERY UNDERTAKEN BY A MEDICAL TEAM

Between Feb 5 and April 14 1999, a team of volunteer doctors treated 5,139 patients in 18 countries as part of Operation Smile's 'World Journey of Hope.' The doctors repaired cleft lips and cleft palates as well as operating on facial burns, tumors, and injuries. Operation Smile was founded in 1982 by Bill Magee, a plastic surgeon, and his wife Kathy, a nurse, in Norfolk, Virginia.

LARGEST CIVILIAN AID CONVOY

Between Dec 1 and 4 1992, a convoy of 105 privately owned vehicles traveled from Dover, UK, to Zagreb, Croatia, carrying donated food and other aid to refugees of the Bosnian war. The round trip was nearly 2,000 miles (3,200 km) long and was accompanied by a 2-mile (3.2-km) police escort through Slovenia.

LONGEST STRETCHER-BEARING DISTANCE

Between May 27 and 30 1996, two teams of four men from 1 Field Ambulance, Canadian Forces Base, Calgary, Canada, carried a stretcher bearing a 140-lb (63.5-kg) 'body' a distance of 186.66 miles (300.4 km). They began in Edmonton, Alberta, and finished in Calgary, Alberta, 59 hr 19 min later.

LONGEST COAL-CARRYING DISTANCE

A team of eight men carried a 100-weight bag of coal (112 lb or 50.8 kg) over a distance of 80 miles (128.7 km) in 11 hr 28 min 33 sec on May 20 2000. The team did 387 laps of a 1,092.52-ft (333-m) circuit of the Dewsbury Hospital car park, W. Yorks, UK – just over 48 laps each.

FURTHEST 24-HOUR BABY CARRIAGE PUSH

Between Nov 22 and 23 1990, a 10-man team from the Royal Marines School of Music, Deal, Kent, UK, pushed a baby carriage containing an adult 'baby' for 24 hours over a distance of 271.7 miles (437.3 km).

FURTHEST 24-HOUR WHEELCHAIR PUSH

Between Sept 13 and 14 1999, 88 volunteers pushed wheelchair-bound Ian Kershaw and Keith Matthews (both UK) around the track of the Copeland Athletic Stadium, Cumbria, UK, covering a distance of 216.4 miles (348.2 km).

FURTHEST 24-HOUR LAWN-MOWER PUSH

Between Sept 13 and 14 1997, a team of four members of the Stowmarket and District Round Table, Suffolk, UK, pushed a standard lawn mower a distance of 101.24 miles (162.93 km) in 24 hours.

LARGEST GAME OF LEAPFROG

On Oct 8 2000 a total of 222 people took part in a single game of leapfrog, which was organized by Discovery Creek Children's Museum at Glen Echo Park, Maryland.

FASTEST YOUTH WOOLSACK-RACING TEAM

A youth team from Sir William Romney School (UK) completed the World Woolsack Championship race in a time of 3 min 20.01 sec in 1997 – faster than the men's team record of 3 min 27.34 sec set in 1991. The event, held annually at Tetbury, Glos, UK, involves teams of four relaying up and down a steep hill, carrying a 60-lb (27.21-kg) bag of wool on their shoulders.

MOST FOUR-WAY SKYDIVING FORMATIONS IN 35 SECONDS

On Sept 23 1999 Daniel Brodsky-Chenfeld, Jack H. Jeffries, Mark Kirkby, and Kirk Verners (all USA), all members of the Airspeed Arizona team, performed a record 39 skydiving formations in 35 seconds – less than one second for each formation – while falling at speeds approaching 150 mph (240 km/h) from a height of 10,000 ft (3,050 m). According to FAI (Fédération Aéronautique Internationale) rules, formations may be random but the sky divers must lose complete physical contact with each other between each formation.

FLIPPER CHARTS

The largest underwater press conference was held on June 20 1997 when a group of 12 journalists representing Spanish newspapers and TV dived to a depth of 52 ft 5 in (16 m), off El Hierro, Canary Islands, Spain, to be present at a 20-minute book launch of *Champion's Secrets* – an underwater photo manual, written by Carlos Virgili Ribé (left). The author spoke to the journalists using an underwater walkie-talkie. Some of the journalists were certified divers, but the rest had to take lessons in using scuba (self-contained underwater breathing apparatus) gear the day before the conference.

‹52178›
← ACCESS CODE
www.guinnessworldrecords.com/underwaterpress

FASTEST HOUSE DEMOLITION BY A TEAM

On Aug 18 1979, 13 members of the East Anglia Martial Arts Club (UK) demolished a seven-roomed brick house in just 61 minutes, using nothing but their hands and feet. Destruction took approximately 8.7 minutes per room.

MOST TRAMPOLINE SOMERSAULTS

On July 24 1999 a team of 20 people from Kirklees Rebound Trampoline Club at Huddersfield Sports Centre, W. Yorks, UK, completed 29,503 somersaults in five hours using two competition-standard trampolines. This is an average of just over 1,475 somersaults per person – almost five somersaults each per minute.

www.guinnessworldrecords.com/747pull

PULLING POWER

On Sept 27 2000, 60 British police officers pulled a Boeing 747-400 (right) over a record 328 ft (100 m) in 53.33 seconds at Heathrow Airport, UK. The 747 weighed 451,947 lb (205 tonnes), with each officer pulling 7,500 lb (3.4 tonnes). RUC, London Metropolitan, and City of London officers had trained by pulling horse-boxes and other vehicles in London's Hyde Park.

ACCESS CODE
‹48715› ←

GUINNESS WORLD RECORDS

www.guinnessworldrecords.com/thelivingplanet

the living planet

the uniuerse

<56351>
← ACCESS CODE
www.guinnessworldrecords.com/blackhole

MOST LUMINOUS STAR

Although it cannot be seen from Earth with the naked eye, the Pistol star (identified by the Hubble Space Telescope) is 10 million times more powerful than the Sun and, according to calculations, emits as much energy in six seconds as the Sun does in a year. Astronomers estimate it is 25,000 light years away from Earth and more than 325 times as big as the Sun, which has a diameter of 864,910 miles (1,391,940 km). Pistol is thought to be only 1–3 million years old, whereas the Sun is five billion years old.

SPACE ODDITY

Normal black holes weigh several times the mass of the Sun, but supermassive black holes (left) reside in the hearts of galaxies and can be as massive as several hundred million times that of the Sun. Astronomers believe that such a terrifying force exists at the center of the Milky Way, 30,000 light years away.

The closest black hole candidate, as announced on Jan 14 2000, is V4641 Sgr, which is only 1,600 light years from Earth. Its recent discovery was due to the dramatic changes in the intensity of X-ray radiation from V4641 Sgr as it sucks gas away from its companion star.

BRIGHTEST STAR SEEN FROM EARTH

Sirius A (Alpha Canis Majoris), or the Dog Star, is 8.64 light years away from Earth and is the brightest star visible in the night sky. A 'light year' is the distance that light travels in a year – roughly 6 trillion miles (9.5 trillion km). The distance between the Earth and Sirius is approximately 50 trillion miles (80 trillion km). Sirius has a mass 2.14 times that of the Sun, and is visually 24 times more luminous. It is also almost twice as hot, with a surface temperature of about 17,500°F (10,000°C).

NEAREST STAR

Excluding the Sun, the nearest star is the faint Proxima Centauri (Alpha Centauri C), a red dwarf, discovered in 1915, which is 4.23 light years or 2.49 x 10^{13} miles (4 x10^{13} km) away.

NEAREST STAR CLUSTER

The Hyades cluster in the constellation of Taurus (the Bull) is the nearest star cluster to our Solar System. It contains around 300 stars, which are roughly 150 light years away and have been estimated to be 625 million years old.

BRIGHTEST SUPERNOVA OF MODERN TIMES

In 1987 a giant star in the Large Magellanic Cloud (a satellite galaxy of our own Milky Way) exploded in the brightest supernova of modern times. It was easily visible to the naked eye despite its distance from the Earth – 168,000 light years away. Supernovae occur at the end of the life of a giant star. As the star runs out of hydrogen fuel, it begins to use heavier elements as its nuclear fuel. Eventually, iron forms in the core, preventing further fusion reactions. As the star shuts down, it collapses in on itself and immediately blows itself apart as a supernova.

FASTEST PULSAR SPIN RATE

Pulsars are the rapidly spinning collapsed cores of massive stars that have blown themselves apart in a supernova. Spherical in shape and the size of a small city, a pulsar is so dense that a teaspoonful would weigh a billion tonnes. For pulsars whose spin rates have been accurately measured, the fastest-spinning is PSR B1937+214, which

was discovered by a group led by Donald C. Backer (USA) in Nov 1982. It is in the minor constellation Vulpecula (Little Fox) 11,700 light years distant and has a pulse period of 1.5578064949 milliseconds, which is equivalent to a spin rate of 641.9282518 revolutions per second.

YOUNGEST PULSAR

A team of astronomers at Columbia University, led by Dr. Eric Gotthelf (USA), discovered the youngest pulsar in 1995. The superdense stellar corpse, called PSR J1846-0258, is located on the other side of our Milky Way galaxy, about 60,000 light years away, and is only 700 years old.

CLOSEST GALAXY TO THE MILKY WAY

The closest object to Earth that is not in our galaxy is the Sagittarius Dwarf Elliptical Galaxy – a huge collection of stars and clouds made of dust and gas, which is about 82,000 light years away. The discovery by R.A. Ibata, G. Gilmore and M.J. Irwin (all UK) was announced in April 1994.

THE COLDEST PLACE IN THE UNIVERSE

The Orion Nebula (left) – a vast diffuse cloud of gas and dust – is the brightest nebula in the night sky. Located in the 'sword' of the constellation of Orion, the nebula is the nearest star-formation region to the Earth and is visible to the naked eye as a fuzzy patch of light. It is around 1,500 light years away.

The Boomerang Nebula, a cloud of dust and gases 5,000 light years from Earth, is where the coldest place in the universe can be found. This 'cold spot,' at the outermost part of the huge wind created by the suction of an imploding star, has a temperature of -457.6°F (-272°C). Here the gases are believed to be expanding and cooling at 370,000 mph (595,457 km/h). Colder temperatures have been achieved in laboratories on Earth.

<55562>
← ACCESS CODE
www.guinnessworldrecords.com/orionnebula

LARGEST GALAXY

The central galaxy of the Abell 2029 galaxy cluster, 1,070 million light years distant in the constellation of Virgo, has a major diameter of 5,600,000 light years – 80 times the diameter of our own Milky Way galaxy – and a light output equivalent to two trillion (2×10^{12}) Suns.

FARTHEST OBJECT VISIBLE TO THE NAKED EYE

The most remote heavenly body visible with the naked eye is the Andromeda Galaxy in the constellation of Andromeda, which was first noted from Germany by Simon Marius in 1611. It is a spiral galaxy similar to our Milky Way, at a distance from Earth of about 2.2 million light years, and can be seen by the naked eye as a gray smudge. Seen through binoculars or a telescope, the bright gray smudge is the combined light from more than 200,000,000,000 stars, some of which are just like our Sun.

SMALLEST CONSTELLATION

The smallest constellation is Crux Australis (Southern Cross), which takes up an area covering just 0.16% of the sky. Until it was recognized as a constellation in 1679, it was officially part of the constellation of Centaurus. Crux Australis, which can only be seen from the southern hemisphere, is well known for the obvious difference in the color of its stars. Three of the brightest stars are all very hot blue stars, while the other is a red giant. This striking difference can easily be seen with the naked eye.

LARGEST CONSTELLATION

Of the 88 constellations, Hydra (Sea Serpent), is the largest, covering 3.16% of the sky. It contains at least 68 stars visible to the naked eye.

MOST MASSIVE EXTRASOLAR PLANET

The discovery of the massive planet HD168443 orbiting a star 123 light years away was announced in Jan 2001. Jupiter, the largest planet in our Solar System, weighs more than all of the other planets and moons combined. HD168443 is 17 times more massive even than Jupiter.

NEAREST EXTRASOLAR PLANET

On Aug 7 2000 a team of astronomers led by Dr. William Cochran of the University of Texas McDonald Observatory (USA), announced the discovery of the nearest planet outside the Solar System. The planet – probably slightly larger than Jupiter – orbits the star Epsilon Eridani. This star, at only 10.5 light years distant, is one of the closest stars to the Sun. It is a main sequence star, which means that it is in the main phase of its life span.

www.guinnessworldrecords.com/helixnebula

ACCESS CODE

‹56518› ←

GAS-TRONOMIC!

The Helix Nebula (NGC 7293, below) is the nearest planetary nebula to Earth, lying about 450 light years away in the constellation of Aquarius. It formed when a dying star cast off its outer layers as 'shells' of gas. These shells emit light as the gas is ionized by radiation from the star. They are called planetary nebulae because astronomers originally believed they were new planets, due to their often spherical shapes. The Helix Nebula covers an area around half the size of the full Moon but is not visible to the naked eye. Planetary nebulae are generally short-lived, lasting around 50,000 years before their expanding gases become too diffuse to be visible. This image was produced by the CFH12k CCD camera on the Canada-France-Hawaii telescope at Mauna Kea, Hawaii, which is specially designed to image large areas of sky at a time.

GUINNESS WORLD RECORDS

the solar system

FASTEST PLANET
Mercury is the speediest planet in the Solar System, orbiting the Sun at an average of 107,030 mph (172,248 km/h), which is almost twice as fast as the Earth. The speed, coupled with the fact that Mercury is much closer to the Sun than the Earth is, means that a year on Mercury (the time it takes for Mercury to circle the Sun) lasts just 87.99 days, or roughly three months.

HOTTEST PLANET
The planet Venus has the hottest surface of any planet in the Solar System, with an average temperature of around 896°F (480°C), which makes exploration by probes on the surface rather difficult. If you were to step on to the surface of Venus you would be simultaneously crushed by the pressure, incinerated by the heat, corroded by the sulfuric acid, and suffocated by the carbon dioxide.

LEAST DENSE PLANET
Saturn has no solid surface, making it the lightest planet in the Solar System. The planet is composed mostly of hydrogen and helium, the two lightest elements in the universe. It has an average density only 0.71

<55663>

www.guinnessworldrecords.com/greatredspot
← ACCESS CODE

ALL IN A SPIN
The Great Red Spot (left) on the planet Jupiter is the largest cyclone in the Solar System. It varies in size but can be up to 24,800 miles (40,000 km) long and 8,700 miles (14,000 km) wide. Three planets the size of Earth would fit along its length. This vast maelstrom has been raging for at least 300 years, ever since telescopes became powerful enough to see it from Earth, and it has probably lasted much longer. It rotates counterclockwise at a speed of around 270 mph (435 km/h). The striking orange color of the storm may be due to the presence of sulfur and phosphorus in the atmosphere.

times that of water. This means that if there was an ocean that was large enough, Saturn would float in it.

BRIGHTEST ASTEROID
The brightest asteroid is Vesta, which was discovered on March 29 1807. Vesta is the only asteroid that is visible to the naked eye from the Earth on a clear night. This is due to the brightness of its surface, its size, – which measures 358 miles (576 km) across – and the fact that it can come as close to Earth as 105 million miles (177 million km).

LARGEST SATELLITE
The largest satellite in the Solar System is Ganymede, one of four large moons that circle the planet Jupiter. It is 2.017 times as heavy as the Earth's Moon and has a diameter of 3,273 miles (5,267 km).

SATELLITE WITH THE THICKEST ATMOSPHERE
Saturn's biggest moon Titan has the thickest atmosphere of any moon in the Solar System, exerting a surface pressure of 1.44 bar, nearly 1.5 times that of the atmospheric pressure at the Earth's surface. It consists mainly of nitrogen gas and is the most similar atmosphere to our own. Titan is the only moon in the Solar System to have a thick atmosphere – an orange smog layer obscures our view of its surface.

LARGEST CANYON IN THE SOLAR SYSTEM
The Valles Marineris on Mars is the largest canyon in the Solar System. It has an overall length of around 2,800 miles (4,500 km). At its widest,

it is 370 miles (600 km) across and is also up to 4.3 miles (7 km) deep. The immense canyon system, first discovered by NASA's *Mariner 9* spacecraft in 1971, would span the USA from coast to coast.

LARGEST SUNSPOT GROUP
On April 8 1947 the largest sunspot group ever was found in the Sun's southern hemisphere. At its greatest length, it measured 187,000 miles (300,000 km) with a maximum width of 90,000 miles (145,000 km). It was roughly 36 times greater than the surface area of the Earth and visible to the naked eye, close to sunset.

LONGEST MEASURED COMET TAIL
The longest comet tail ever measured was 350 million miles (570 million km) long and belonged to the comet Hyakutake. This is more than three times the distance from the Earth to the Sun. The tail was discovered by Geraint Jones of Imperial College, London, UK, on Sept 13 1999, using data gathered by

RING BOUND
The giant planet Saturn has the most massive ring system (left) of all the planets in our Solar System. The intricate system of rings around the giant has a combined mass of around 9×10^{19} lb (4×10^{19} kg) – equivalent to 30 million Mt. Everests. All the other gas giants – Jupiter, Uranus, and Neptune – have rings as well, but none are as extensive nor as impressive as those of Saturn. The planet's rings consist of millions of tiny, independently orbiting particles of ice and dust. It is likely that they were formed several tens of millions of years ago, when a comet smashed into a small moon shattering it into countless pieces of debris, which became the rings. Although the rings span 270,000 km (167,770 miles) in diameter, they are only a few hundred meters thick.

www.guinnessworldrecords.com/saturnrings
<56287> ← ACCESS CODE

the ESA/NASA spacecraft *Ulysses* on a chance encounter with the comet on May 1 1996.

HIGHEST CLIFFS IN THE SOLAR SYSTEM

Verona Rupes, a cliff on Miranda, a small moon that circles the planet Uranus, is roughly 12 miles (20 km) high. This is approximately 10 times higher than the walls of the Grand Canyon on Earth. This height is particularly extraordinary given the smallness of Miranda, which has a diameter of only 265 miles (472 km). The cliff and other strange geological features on the surface may have been caused by Miranda being smashed to pieces by a comet and then reformed from the fragments.

FASTEST WINDS IN THE SOLAR SYSTEM

The planet Neptune has the fastest winds anywhere in the Solar System. Measured by NASA's *Voyager 2* probe in 1989, they gust at about 1,500 mph (2,400 km/h). This is about five times faster than the highest wind speed recorded for a tornado on Earth.

LARGEST RECORDED IMPACT IN THE SOLAR SYSTEM

Between July 16 and 22 1994 more than 20 fragments of comet Shoemaker-Levy 9 collided with the giant planet Jupiter. The greatest impact was made by the largest fragment, which measured around 2 miles (3-4 km) across. It exploded with the energy of roughly 600 times all the bombs in the world going off simultaneously – equivalent to 6 million megatons of TNT. The 20 fragments plowed into Jupiter's atmosphere at around 40 miles (60 km) per second, leaving enormous scars in Jupiter's turbulent, deep atmosphere.

COLDEST KNOWN GEOLOGICAL ACTIVITY

Active geysers on Triton, the planet Neptune's largest moon, blast freezing cold nitrogen gas several miles high into the atmosphere. Triton has a surface temperature of −391°F (−235°C) and is one of the coldest places in our Solar System with lakes of water that are frozen hard as steel.

LONGEST TOTAL SOLAR ECLIPSE

The longest total solar eclipse of recent date was on June 20 1955 (7 min 8 sec), visible west of the Philippines, although it was clouded out along most of its track. The maximum possible duration of an eclipse of the Sun is 7 min 31 sec. An eclipse of 7 min 29 sec should occur in the mid-Atlantic Ocean on July 16 2186.

LARGEST RECORDED SOLAR FLARE

On April 2 2001 at 9:51 p.m. GMT, the largest solar flare ever recorded erupted from the surface of the Sun. It originated from one of the largest groups of sunspots ever recorded. The flare sent out billions of tons of electrified gas and radiation into the Solar System. Some of this matter collided with the Earth's upper atmosphere, causing beautiful displays of the aurora, especially in the northern hemisphere.

www.guinnessworldrecords.com/io

GREAT BALLS OF FIRE

Io, one of the four biggest moons of Jupiter, is the most volcanic body in the Solar System. In 1979, NASA's *Voyager 1* probe took the first images of volcanic eruption plumes, some reaching hundreds of miles into space (right, taken by NASA's *Galileo* spacecraft on June 28 1997). Io is so active that it has 'turned inside out' at least once, with the outer layers being buried under newly erupted lava until they are so deep that they melt and reerupt on to the surface as new lava.

ACCESS CODE

‹54814› ←

planet earth

LARGEST GEODE
The largest geode (a mineral-lined cave) is near Almería, Spain. It is 26 ft (7.92 m) long, 6 ft (1.83 m) wide, 6 ft (1.83 m) high, and is about six million years old. Most geodes are small enough to fit in the palm of a human hand.

OLDEST EARTH FRAGMENT
A tiny crystal of zircon is the oldest fragment of Earth discovered so far. Between 4.3 and 4.4 billion years old, this tiny sample is 100 million years older than any previous discovery.

LONGEST RIVER
The Nile and the Amazon are the two longest rivers in the world. Which is longer is debatable. The Nile's official length is 4,160 miles (6,695 km), but it lost a few miles after the formation of Lake Nasser behind the Aswan Dam. The Amazon has several mouths, so its end point is uncertain. If the Para estuary – its most distant mouth – is included, the river's length is approximately 4,195 miles (6,750 km).

HIGHEST ACTIVE VOLCANO
The Ojos del Salado on the border between Chile and Argentina is the world's highest active volcano at 22,595 ft (6,887 m) high.

LARGEST VOLCANO CRATER
The world's largest volcano crater is Toba in Sumatra, Indonesia, covering 685 miles^2 (1,775 km^2). It is inactive and last erupted around 75,000 years ago.

LARGEST ACTIVE VOLCANO
Mauna Loa, Hawaii, USA, is 75 miles (120 km) long and 31 miles (50 km) wide, with lava flows that occupy more than 1,980 miles^2 (5,125 km^2) of the island. It has a total volume of 16,400 miles^3 (42,500 km^3), of which 84.2% is below sea level. It has averaged one eruption every 3.6 years since 1843, although none since 1984.

LARGEST OCEAN
Covering more than one-third of the Earth's surface at 64,186,000 miles^2 (166,241,700 km^2), the Pacific is the largest ocean in the world, with an average depth of 12,925 ft (3,940 m).

DEEPEST VALLEY
Asia's Yarlung Zangbo river valley stretching from Tibet to Bangladesh has an average depth of 16,405 ft (5,000 m) with its deepest point at 17,658 ft (5,382 m) – more than three times as deep as the Grand Canyon.

SMALLEST CONTINENT
Of all the continents (Europe, Africa, Asia, North America, South America, Australasia, Antarctica), the Australian mainland, with an area of 2,939,960 miles^2 (7,614,500 km^2), is the smallest.

MAKING WAVES
The Amazon river in South America (above) has the greatest flow of any river, discharging an amazing average of 7,100,000 ft^3/sec (200,000 m^3/sec) into the Atlantic Ocean, which increases to more than 12,000,000 ft^3/sec (340,000 m^3/sec) in full flood. The lower 900 miles (1,450 km) average 55 ft (17 m) in depth, but the river has a maximum depth of 407 ft (124 m). The Amazon is fed by over 1,000 tributaries and its flow is 60 times greater than that of the Nile. The Amazon accounts for about 20% of all the fresh water that drains into the world's oceans.

‹47578› www.guinnessworldrecords.com/riverflow ← ACCESS CODE

LARGEST CONTINENT
Asia is the largest continent in the world, covering an area of 17,388,686 miles^2 (45,036,492 km^2). Africa ranks second with a land area of 11,715,721 miles^2 (30,343,578 km^2).

TALLEST MOUNTAIN
Mauna Kea ('White Mountain') on the island of Hawaii is the world's tallest mountain. Its base begins on the floor of the Pacific Ocean and rises to a peak of 33,480 ft (10,205 m). Up to 19,685 ft (6,000 m) of the mountain is

under water and 13,795 ft (4,205 m) is above sea level. In total, from base to peak, it is 4,452 ft (1,357 m) taller than Mt. Everest.

HIGHEST MOUNTAIN PEAK
Mt. Everest's eastern Himalayan peak has a height of 29,030.8 ft (8,848 m) and is the highest point in the world. Mt. Everest was named after Colonel Sir George Everest (1790-1866), formerly Surveyor-General of India (1830-43).

LARGEST RIVER TO DRY UP
In 1997 and 1998, the Yellow River (Huang He), China's second-longest river, ran completely dry along its lower section for over 140 days in each year, leaving farmland parched and threatening the fall harvest. This problem was the result of below-average rainfall, increased irrigation, and the industrial demands of a growing population.

LARGEST STEAM RINGS
Sicily's active volcano Mt. Etna is the highest and most active volcano in Europe. A complex physical process causes it to emit huge steam rings (similar to smoke rings) measuring about 656 ft (200 m) across, that can

SOMEWHERE UNDER THE RAINBOW
The red sandstone Rainbow Bridge, in Lake Powell National Monument, Utah, (left) is the highest natural arch in the world. It is only 270 ft (82.3 m) long, but is a massive feature rising to a height of 290 ft (88.4 m) – nearly twice the height of the Statue of Liberty. Rainbow Bridge is composed of Navajo sandstone and was formed by an ancient stream on its way to the Colorado River, which eroded away some of the weaker sedimentary rock in the area, leaving the natural bridge behind. It is considered sacred by the local Native Americans and is visted by around 300,000 people a year.

‹47585› www.guinnessworldrecords.com/rainbowbridge ← ACCESS CODE last up to 10 minutes or so as they drift up to a height of about 3,300 ft (1,000 m) above the volcanic vent.

FASTEST MOVING GLACIER
Measuring 34 miles (54 km) long, 3 miles (4.8 km) wide, and up to 3,000 ft (910 m) high at some points, the Columbia Glacier between Anchorage and Valdez in Alaska, was calculated to be flowing at an average rate of 115 ft (35 m) per day in 1999. It has almost doubled its speed over the last 20 years,

possibly because of global warming, which causes the ice to loosen and move faster.

LARGEST SUBGLACIAL LAKE
Lake Vostok in Antarctica was discovered in 1994 by analyzing radar imagery of the icy continent. Buried under 2.5 miles (4 km) of the East Antarctic Ice Sheet, it is the oldest and most pristine lake on Earth, completely isolated from the rest of the world for at least 500,000 years. Covering an area of about 5,400 miles^2 (14,000 km^2), it has a depth of at least 330 ft (100 m).

www.guinnessworldrecords.com/lambertglacier

ICE COOL
Covering 11.4 % of the planet, glaciers are mainly found in Antartica and Greenland with about 5.2 million miles^2 (13.5 million km^2) of Antarctica made of snow and ice. Glaciers are large, moving masses of ice formed where the rate of snowfall is greater than the rate of snow melting. As snow piles up, it is compressed into ice by the weight of

ACCESS CODE

‹47591› ←

more snow falling on top of it, and begins to slowly flow downhill under the force of its own weight.

Covering up to 386,102 miles^2 (1 million km^2), the world's largest glacier is the Lambert Glacier (below) in the Australian Antarctic Territory. Lambert is up to 40 miles (64 km) wide and measures at least 440 miles (700 km) in length – longer than the state of Florida.

weather extremes

WARMEST YEAR
The warmest year since records began in 1880 was 1998, with global temperatures 3.3°F (0.57°C) higher than the averages recorded between 1961 and 1990. The 1990s as a whole was also the warmest decade on record, and contained the six warmest years ever. The second warmest year was 1997.

MOST FREAKISH TEMPERATURE RISE
On Jan 22 1943 the temperature at Spearfish, South Dakota, rose from –4°F (–20°C) at 7:30 a.m. to 45°F (7°C) at 7:32 a.m. – a record-breaking 49°F (27°C) in two minutes.

GREATEST TEMPERATURE RANGES
The world's greatest temperature ranges are found around the 'cold pole' in Siberia, Russia. Temperatures in Verkhoyansk have ranged 188°F (105°C), from –90°F (–68°C) to 98°F (37°C). The town is in the Republic of Sakha – an area of 1.19 million miles² (3.1 million km²) – and has a population of just one million, mainly because of its extreme climate.

COLDEST PLACES
The lowest outdoor temperature ever recorded is –128.6°F (–89.2°C), registered at the Vostok Scientific

SNOW JOKE
During a snowstorm at Fort Keogh, Montana, on Jan 28 1887, Matt Coleman discovered a snowflake that was 15 in (38 cm) wide and 8 in (20 cm) thick, which he later described as being 'larger than milk pans' in the magazine *Monthly Weather Review*. A mail courier caught in the same snowstorm witnessed the fall of these giant flakes over several miles.

‹53605›
www.guinnessworldrecords.com/snowflake
← ACCESS CODE

Station in Antarctica on July 21 1983. The coldest permanently inhabited place in the world is Oymyakon, a village in Yakutia, eastern Siberia, Russia, where temperatures can drop to as low as –94°F (–70°C). The average temperature in January, the coldest month, is –58°F (–50°C).

LONGEST ICE AGE
Geological evidence suggests that the Earth endured several ice ages early in its history. The longest and most severe of these occurred between 2.3 and 2.4 billion years ago and lasted around 70 million years. During this period, the entire Earth was probably covered in ice.

HIGHEST BAROMETRIC PRESSURE
Barometric pressure – the physical pressure exerted by the air on people – is measured in millibars. Pressure decreases as a person's altitude increases, since there is less of the Earth's atmosphere to weigh them

down. The highest-ever barometric pressure was 32 in of mercury (1,083.8 mb), recorded at Agata, Siberia, Russia, on Dec 31 1968. This reading, which would normally be expected at 1,968 ft (600 m) below sea level, is even more impressive by the fact that Agata is actually located 859 ft (262 m) above sea level.

GREATEST SNOWFALLS
Snow with a depth of 37 ft 7 in (11.5 m) was recorded at Tamarac, California, USA, in March 1911.

The most snow produced in a single snowstorm is 15.75 ft (4.8 m), which fell at Mt. Shasta Ski Bowl, California, between Feb 13 and 19 1959.

HEAVIEST HAILSTONES
The heaviest hailstones on record weighed up to 2.2 lb (1 kg) each. They are reported to have killed 92 people when they struck the Gopalganj district of Bangladesh on April 14 1986.

HIGHEST WATERSPOUT
The highest waterspout – a tornado that travels over water – was observed on May 16 1898 off Eden, NSW, Australia. A theodolite reading taken from the shore registered its height as 5,013 ft (1,528 m), and it was about 10 ft (3 m) in diameter. Waterspouts have been known to suck up fish from the sea and drop them back down on nearby towns.

MOST RAINY DAYS
Mt. Wai-`ale-`ale in Kauai, Hawaii, which is 5,148 ft (1,569 m) high, has up to 350 rainy days per year – giving an average rainfall of over 32.8 ft (10 m).

MOST THUNDERY DAYS
In the 10 years between 1967 and 1976, an average of 251 days of thunder per year was recorded in Tororo, Uganda.

MOST INTENSE RAINFALL
On Nov 26 1970, 1.5 in (38.1 mm) of rain fell on the Caribbean island of Guadeloupe in just one minute – the most rain ever recorded over that period of time.

The record for rainfall over a 24-hour period is 6 ft 1 in (1.85 m), at Cilaos on the Indian Ocean island of Réunion, between March 15 and 16 1952.

FASTEST WIND SPEEDS
The US National Severe Storms Laboratory recorded a 318-mph (512-km/h) wind speed associated with a tornado near Bridge Creek, Oklahoma, on May 3 1999. The measurement was taken 100–200 ft (30–60 m) above the ground.

The fastest surface (ground-level) wind recorded at a high altitude is 231 mph (371 km/h), which was registered at a height of 6,288-ft (1,916 m) at the summit of Mt. Washington, New Hampshire, on April 12 1934.

The low-altitude wind-speed record is 207 mph (333 km/h), recorded on March 8 1972 at the US Air Force base at Thule, Greenland (altitude 145 ft or 44 m).

BLOWN AWAY
Tornadoes form where there is lots of warm, humid air and winds that change direction. These conditions are quite common in central USA, where there is plenty of moist air coming from the Gulf of Mexico. Between April 3 and 4 1974, this area, which extends from central Texas (left) to Iowa and Nebraska, and is often called 'Tornado Alley,' experienced a record-breaking 148 tornadoes in 24 hours.
Surprisingly, the record frequency of tornadoes by area is in the UK where, in an average year, one tornado is reported for every 2,856 miles² (7,397 km²). The figure for the USA is one tornado for every 3,345 miles² (8,663 km²). The longest distance traveled by a tornado is 293 miles (471.5 km) across Illinois and Indiana on May 26 1917.

‹47480›
www.guinnessworldrecords.com/tornadoes
← ACCESS CODE

TAN-FASTIC!

Children in Arizona try to beat the heat by cooling off in a livestock water trough outside their home (above). Yuma, Arizona, is one of the two sunniest places in the world, experiencing an average of 4,055 hours of sunshine (out of a possible 4,456 hours) per year. Located at an altitude of 138 ft (42 m) above sea level, the town has a population of around 71,000, and is one of Arizona's fastest-growing cities.

From Feb 1967 to March 1969 St. Petersburg, Florida, recorded a record-breaking 768 consecutive sunny days.

www.guinnessworldrecords.com/ yuma

ACCESS CODE

‹47494› ←

www.guinnessworldrecords.com/wettest

RAINDROPS KEEP FALLING ON MY HEAD

The world's wettest place in terms of average annual rainfall is Mawsynram in Meghalaya State, India (right). It experiences 38.94 ft (11.87 m) of rain per year. Most of the rain occurs during the monsoon season, from June to September.

The second rainiest place is Cherrapunji, also in Meghalaya, which has an average annual rainfall of 37.5 ft (11.43 m) per year. Amazingly, outside the monsoon season it can also suffer from serious drought.

ACCESS CODE

‹47532› ←

CLOUD FORM WITH GREATEST VERTICAL RANGE

The cloud form *cumulonimbus* has been seen to reach a height of nearly 65,620 ft (20,000 m) in the tropics – nearly three times higher than Mt. Everest.

LONGEST-LASTING SEA-LEVEL FOGS

Sea-level fogs, which are defined as fogs that have a visibility of less than 3,000 ft (900 m), persist for more than 120 days per year on the Grand Banks, Newfoundland, Canada.

LONGEST-LASTING RAINBOW

On March 14 1994 a rainbow was visible over Wetherby, W Yorks, UK, for six hours between 9 a.m. and 3 p.m. Most rainbows usually last for only a matter of minutes.

amazing science

OLDEST EXTRACTED HUMAN DNA

In Jan 2000 scientists extracted DNA from the bone of a 60,000-year-old ancestor of modern humans. The skeleton, nicknamed 'Mungo Man,' was unearthed at Lake Mungo, Australia, in 1974. This controversially challenges the theory that we are all descended from a common African ancestor.

OLDEST LIVING BACTERIA

Uncontaminated bacteria trapped in suspended animation inside salt crystals for 250 million years (older than the dinosaurs) have been revived and cultured by US scientists. Designated 'Bacillus 2-9-3,' this species is 10 times older than the previous oldest revived bacteria.

HARDEST ELEMENT

Carbon (C) has many different allotropes (different configurations of atoms), but the diamond allotrope, which has an extremely strong lattice structure, has a value of 10 on Moh's relative scale of hardness (the highest value). Diamonds are formed at least 93 miles (150 km) beneath the Earth's surface, where the pressures and temperatures are great enough to force the carbon atoms to adopt this structure.

RAREST ELEMENT ON EARTH

Discovered in 1931, astatine, a member of the halogen group of elements, is the rarest element in the Earth's crust, with only around 0.9 oz (25 g) occurring naturally – roughly the weight of a hen's egg.

MOST DENSE MATTER

Scientists at the Brookhaven National Laboratory, USA, have created matter 20 times more dense than the nucleus of an atom. By smashing the nucleii of gold atoms together at almost the speed of light, they created subatomic particles that lasted for fractions of a second. Matter this dense may not have existed in the universe since its creation in the 'Big Bang,' which occurred 12–15 billion years ago.

FINEST BALANCE

The Sartorius Microbalance Model 4108, made in Germany, can weigh objects of up to 0.018 oz (0.5 g) to an accuracy of 0.01 micrograms, or 3.5×10^{-10} oz (1×10^{-8} g) – equivalent to around one-sixtieth the weight of the ink on one of the periods on this page.

SHORTEST FLASH OF LIGHT

In 1998 at the University of Groningen, Netherlands, Douwe Wiersma, Andrius Baltuska, and Maxim Pshenchnikov measured the shortest flash of light ever produced – it lasted for 4.5 femtoseconds (0.0000000000000045 seconds).

MOST POWERFUL X-RAY GENERATOR

The Z Machine at the Sandia National Laboratories, New Mexico, can, for a few trillionths of a second, reach the temperature of the Sun's surface and give a power output (in X rays) equal to approximately 80 times that of all the world's electrical generators combined.

LARGEST SCIENTIFIC INSTRUMENT

The Large Electron Positron (LEP) Storage Ring Collider at CERN, Geneva, Switzerland, which was created to examine the smallest particles of matter, is the world's largest scientific instrument (and arguably the largest machine.) Made up of a circular tube 12 ft 6 in (3.8 m) wide and 17 miles (27 km) long, the Collider is inside a giant donut-shaped tunnel 328 ft (100 m) in depth. Inside, electrons and positrons are accelerated around the 'donut' before colliding with each other to produce tiny subatomic particles that enable physicists to study the nature of the universe. The LEP began operating in 1989 and was officially closed down at 8 a.m. on Nov 2 2000.

MOST POWERFUL ELECTRIC CURRENT

In April 1996 scientists at Oak Ridge National Laboratory, Tennessee, sent a current of 13 million amps per in^2 (2 million amperes per cm^2) down a superconducting wire. Standard household wires carry a current of less than 6,450 amps per in^2 (1,000 amps per cm^2.)

FASTEST CENTRIFUGE

Ultracentrifuges are used to separate mixtures of organic substances. The highest man-made rotary speed was achieved at Birmingham University (UK) in 1975, which registered a speed of 4,500 mph (7,250 km/h). This maximum speed is more than three times faster than Concorde flying at typical cruising speed.

MOST ACCURATE VALUE OF PI

Pi (n), one of the most important numbers in mathematics, is always equal to half the circumference of a circle, divided by its radius. Pi is also an irrational number – ie it has infinite numbers after its decimal point, which follow no repeating pattern. This lack of a pattern has inspired mathematicians to calculate pi to more and more accurate values. The most decimal places to which pi has been calculated is 206,158,430,000 by Professor Yasumasa Kanada and Dr. Daisuke Takahashi (both Japan), who made the calculation by running two different computer programs in 1999.

HOTTEST FLAME

The hottest flame is produced by carbon subnitride (C_4N_2) which, at one atmosphere pressure, can generate a flame calculated to reach 9,010°F (4,988°C). The highest man-made temperature is 100,000 times hotter than this.

HIGHEST MAN-MADE TEMPERATURE

The highest man-made temperature is 950 million° F (510 million° C) – almost 30 times the temperature at the center of the Sun – attained on May 27 1994 at the Tokamak Fusion Test Reactor at Princeton, New Jersey. The high temperatures were produced using a deuterium-tritium plasma mix.

LOWEST MAN-MADE TEMPERATURE

In 1995 Eric Cornell and Carl Wieman (both USA) cooled atoms of rubidium to a record low temperature of less than 170 billionths of a degree above absolute zero – the coldest temperature possible.

LIGHT FANTASTIC

The solid substance with the lowest density is aerogel, a silicon-based solid that is 99% air and 1,000 times less dense than glass. Aerogel (left) resembles solid smoke in appearance and weighs only three times as much as air itself, yet a piece only 1 in (2.5mm) thick will protect a human hand from the heat of a blowtorch. The lightest of these aerogels, with a density of only 5 oz/ft^3 (0.005 g/cm^3), was produced at the Lawrence Livermore Laboratory, California. Aerogel is currently being flown on the Stardust planetary mission. Its unusual properties will allow tiny particles ejected from the tail of comet Wild 2 to be captured. The particles will strike the aerogel collectors at high velocities, will be slowed down by the frothy aerogel structure, and trapped intact inside the substance.

<47186>
www.guinnessworldrecords.com/aerogel
← ACCESS CODE

SMELLIEST SUBSTANCE

With a smell reminiscent of rotting cabbage, garlic, burnt toast, and sewer gas, the world's smelliest substances are the gases ethyl mercaptan (C_2H_5SH) and butyl seleno-mercaptan (C_4H_9SeH). They are toxic and in large doses will cause headaches, nausea, lack of coordination, and liver and kidney damage. Ethyl mercaptan is often added to odorless natural gas so that a gas leak can be detected.

MOST BITTER SUBSTANCE

Denatonium benzoate is the world's most bitter-tasting substance. It can be detected in dilution levels as low as one part in 500 million – a

PIGGY BANK

The greatest number of cloned piglets born in one litter is five. Millie, Christa, Alexis, Carrel, and Dotcom (above) were born on March 5 2000 in Blacksburg, Virginia. PPL Therapeutics Plc – the company that created Dolly the sheep, the first clone of an adult animal – produced the piglets as a result of nuclear transfer. This process involves transferring the nucleus of a body cell into an egg from which the nucleus and DNA have been removed. As pigs are physiologically one of the closest animals to humans, this is a potentially unlimited new source for human transplants.

www.guinnessworldrecords.com/pigclones

ACCESS CODE

‹54194› ←

www.guinnessworldrecords.com/genome

IT'S ALL IN THE GENES

The Human Genome Project is the largest-ever biology research collaboration. It completed the final sequence of the three billion 'letters' in the genetic code for a human being in Feb 2001. Humans share 99.99% of the code; 0.01% is the tiny percentage of genes which vary among humans – accounting for all the differences between people.

ACCESS CODE

‹56349› ←

dilution of one part in 100 million will leave a lingering taste. Higher levels are too bitter to be tolerated. It is used in products such as antifreeze to deter people from swallowing them.

SWEETEST SUBSTANCE

Thaumatin (or 'Talin'), obtained from arils (appendages found on seeds) of the *katemfe* plant (*Thaumatococcus daniellii*) from Africa is 615,000 times sweeter than sugar. It leaves a licoricelike aftertaste.

GUINNESS WORLD RECORDS™

natural disasters

MOST NATURAL DISASTERS IN ONE YEAR

Although not the most costly in terms of insurance and economic losses, the year 2000 holds the record for the most natural disasters as recorded by the world insurance industry. Extreme weather accounted for the bulk of the 850 reported catastrophes, with windstorms responsible for 73% of claims and floods for another 23%. The average number of annual natural disasters throughout the 1990s was 650.

GREATEST RECORDED IMPACT ON EARTH

A huge explosion that shook the Siberian region of Tunguska on June 30 1908 was so powerful that it was equivalent to 10–15 megatons of high explosive, and resulted in the devastation of a 1,500-mile^2 (3,900-km^2) area. The shock wave was felt up to 620 miles (1,000 km) away. The explosion was caused when an asteroid with a diameter of 98 ft (30 m), traveling faster than the speed of sound, disintegrated at an altitude of 6.2 miles (10 km). Although no one was killed, since the area was so sparsely populated, the same explosion over a major city would have resulted in millions of deaths.

<52457>
www.guinnessworldrecords.com/earthquake
← ACCESS CODE

COSTING THE EARTH

The earthquake that struck Kobe, Japan (left), in Jan 1995 resulted in record losses of 9,860 billion yen ($100 billion; £63 billion). Measuring 7.2 on the Richter scale, the quake killed more than 6,400 people and injured around 27,000. Over 106,000 buildings were damaged and hundreds of houses, particularly older wooden ones, collapsed. Japan's geographic location on the Pacific 'Rim of Fire' means that tremors are inevitable. Fortunately, Japan is relatively well prepared for this, and can draw on her large fiscal resources and modern construction techniques.

Despite these devastating statistics, asteroid collisions are – in theory – the most preventable of natural disasters, since it may now be possible to deflect their course.

MOST POWERFUL EARTHQUAKE

An earthquake that struck Chile on May 22 1960 had a magnitude of 8.3 on the Richter scale, making it the most powerful earthquake ever recorded. In Chile, it killed more than 2,000 people, injured 3,000, and left an estimated 2 million homeless. The resultant *tsunami* (giant wave) also caused massive damage, and was responsible for around 200 deaths thousands of miles away on the US west coast, in Hawaii, and Japan.

MOST PEOPLE KILLED BY AN EARTHQUAKE

It is thought that around 830,000 people died when an earthquake struck the Shanxi and Henan provinces of China on Feb 2 1556.

MOST PEOPLE KILLED BY LANDSLIDES

On Dec 16 1920 a series of landslides triggered by a single earthquake that hit Gansu Province, China, killed around 180,000 people.

DEADLIEST LAKE

In recent decades, toxic gases emanating from Lake Nyos in Cameroon, west Africa, have claimed an estimated 2,000 lives. On one night in Aug 1986 alone, between 1,600 and 1,800 people and countless animals were killed when a large quantity of carbon dioxide gas was naturally released from the lake. The exact source of these deadly gases is unknown, but they are thought to be either volcanic in origin or caused by the decomposition of organic material on the lakebed.

MOST PEOPLE KILLED BY A LIGHTNING STRIKE

On Dec 8 1963 a Boeing 707 jet airliner was struck by lightning near Elkton, Maryland, causing it to crash. A total of 81 passengers were killed.

MOST DESTRUCTIVE GEOMAGNETIC STORM

The most destructive geomagnetic storm on record is the 'Great Geomagnetic Storm' of March 13 1989, which was classified G5 (the most severe rating) on the space weather scale. The result of an abnormally strong solar wind, it caused large-scale disruption to the power grid in Canada and the USA, and even changed the orbit of a satellite.

GEYSER ATTACK

Formed in 1886 when the nearby volcano Tarawera erupted, the volcanic Waimangu Valley, New Zealand, contains the world's largest hot spring (left). In Aug 1903 one of the geysers in this area erupted, killing four people – the greatest number of fatalities in a geyser-related accident. The power of the eruption was such that the victims, who were standing 88.6 ft (27 m) away, were blown distances of up to 2,625 ft (800 m).
There are about 700 active geysers in the world. They occur in active volcanic regions, where groundwater can circulate deep underground, and becomes superheated by molten magma. Cracks and fissures in the overlying rock allow the hot water to erupt out of the ground as a geyser when the pressure builds up.

<47755>
www.guinnessworldrecords.com/geysererupt
← ACCESS CODE

HIGHEST TSUNAMI WASH

The highest *tsunami* (giant wave) ever reported was 1,719 ft (524 m) high and occurred along the fjord-like Lituya Bay, Alaska, on July 9 1958. Caused by a giant landslip, it moved at 100 mph (160 km/h). This wave was so high it would easily have swamped the Petronas Towers in Kuala Lumpur, Malaysia, which, at 1,483 ft (452 m), are the world's tallest office buildings.

LARGEST TIDAL BORE 🖵 USA

A tidal bore – caused when the Sun, Moon, and Earth align to form dramatic tidal conditions – is a solitary wave that travels with great speed up a narrow river, forcing the flow upstream. The world's largest tidal bore occurred in Hangzhou Bay, China, on Aug 18 1993. The bore was 30 ft (9.14 m) high and 200 miles (321.8 km) long, and pushed approximately 2 million gallons (9 million liters) of water per second toward the shore. It has been estimated that 100 people died as a result of the disaster.

MOST PEOPLE MADE HOMELESS BY FLOODS

During Sept 1978 monsoon rains in the Indian state of Bengal caused such extensive river flooding that, as a result, around 15 million people, out of a total population of 44 million, were made homeless. A total of 1,300 people and 26,687 cattle drowned, and 1.3 million homes were destroyed.

www.guinnessworldrecords.com/mitch

HURRICANE MITCH

Hurricane Mitch left more people homeless than any other cyclone when it struck Central America between Oct 26 and Nov 4 1998 (below). It caused 9,745 deaths and destroyed 93,690 dwellings, leaving approximately 2.5 million people dependent on international aid efforts. It began as a tropical depression on Oct 22 1998, and within four days had become a monster Category-Five storm on the Saffir–Simpson Hurricane scale.

The most powerful storm in the Caribbean Sea since Hurricane Gilbert in 1988, Mitch reached a maximum speed of 180 mph (290 km/h), gathering strength over the Caribbean Sea before hitting the coast of Honduras and moving slowly inland. The storm retained its Category-Five rating for 33 hours, the longest since Hurricane David sustained its fury for 36 hours in 1979.

ACCESS CODE

‹49208› ←

GUINNESS WORLD RECORDS

plant world

MOST DANGEROUS STINGERS

New Zealand's tree nettle (*Urtica ferox*) has killed dogs, horses, and at least one human. The tree nettle can grow to 9.84 ft (3 m) in height and has fine white stinging hairs on its green leaves. These inject potent toxins into the skin, the main ones being histamine, 5-hydroxytryptamine, acetylcholine, formic acid, and tryffidin. Australia's stinging trees (genus *Dendrocnide*), armed with large, hollow hairs on their leaves and twigs, are as feared as New Zealand's tree nettle. The worst, the gympie bush (*Dendrocnide moroides*), causes intense stabbing pains that can recur months later.

HIGHEST CHLOROPHYLL CONTENT

Chlorophyll is the green matter in plants that traps the energy from sunlight in order to process carbon dioxide. The chlorophyll content of the algae Kirin Chlorella M-207A7 (*Chlorella vulgaris*), measured on a dry-weight basis, is 6.7% and was discovered by Dr. Kouichi Nakanishi (Japan) in Jan 2000. For most plants, the chlorophyll content is between 0.6% and 1.2% on a dry-weight basis. Spinach, one of the darkest green vegetables, is still only 0.9%.

TALLEST DAFFODIL

A daffodil grown in 1979 by M. Lowe of Chessell, Isle of Wight, UK, reached an amazing height of 5 ft 1 in (1.55 m).

LARGEST CORK TREE

The largest cork tree is the 'Whistler Tree' in the Alentejo region of Portugal, which averages over 2,244 lb (1.02 tonnes) of raw cork per harvest – enough cork for 100,000 wine bottles. In comparison, an average cork tree produces enough cork each harvest for 4,000 wine bottles. Over 212 years old, the Whistler Tree has been producing cork every nine years since 1820, and it is anticipated that it will produce over one million corks in its lifetime.

SMALLEST FRUIT

The floating duckweed (genus *Wolffia*) – the world's smallest flowering plant – produces the world's smallest fruit. As the entire plant body is less than 0.04 in (1 mm) long, the mature fruit takes up a large proportion of its parent plant. The fruit of the *Wolffia augusta* is only 0.0098 in (0.25 mm) long and weighs about 0.00015 oz (70 micrograms), making it smaller than the individual cells of many plants and animals, and smaller than an average grain of table salt.

<55976>
www.guinnessworldrecords.com/seaweed
← ACCESS CODE

MEDITERRANEAN MENACE

Caulerpa taxifolia (left) is the world's fastest-growing seaweed, growing at a staggering rate of 3 in (8 cm) per day. *Caulerpa taxifolia* was released from the Oceanographic Institute of Monaco into the Côte d'Azur about 16 years ago and it now covers 15,000 acres (6,000 ha) of seabed off the French coast. It has also spread as far as California. In France, the worst hit country, experts have tried using aluminum and plastic sheeting to prevent sunlight from reaching it and thereby slowing its growth rate.

The longest species of seaweed is the Pacific giant kelp (*Macrocystis pyrifera*), which grows to around 197 ft (60 m) in length. Kelp is required for a healthy marine ecosystem.

GREATEST GIRTH OF A LIVING TREE

'El Arbol del Tule' in Oaxaca state, Mexico, is a 135-ft-tall (41-m) Montezuma cypress (*Taxodium mucronatum*) with a girth of 117 ft 6 in (35.8 m), measured 5 ft (1.52 m) above the ground. If 10 medium-sized cars were placed end-to-end in a circle, this would be about the same size as the girth of this tree. The largest girths are generally attributed to African baobab trees (*Adansonia digitata*).

LONGEST DISTANCE TRAVELED BY A DRIFT SEED

The longest documented drift range for any seed or tropical fruit is for a single Mary's bean (*Merremia discoidesperma*) that traveled over 15,000 miles (24,140 km) from the Marshall Islands in the Pacific Ocean to Norway. This distance could be traced as the seed is native to only a few Pacific locations and has been researched by the world's drift-seed authority, Dr. Charles R. Gunn (USA).

LARGEST FLOWER

The orange-brown and white parasite *Rafflesia arnoldi* has the largest of all blooms. These attach themselves to the cissus vines of the jungle in southeast Asia. Resembling a huge poppy, they measure up to 3 ft (91 cm) across, weigh up to 24.25 lb (11 kg) with petals 0.75 in (1.9 cm) thick. There are 16 known species of *Rafflesia* (named after Sir Stamford Raffles and Dr. Joseph Arnold) – the latest discovery is as recent as 1988.

LARGEST LEAF

The largest leaves of any plant are those belonging to the raffia palm (*Raffia farinifera* or *R. ruffia*) of the Mascarene Islands in the Indian Ocean, and the Amazonian bamboo palm (*R. taedigera*) of South America and Africa, whose leaf blades may be up to 65 ft 6 in (20 m) long, with petioles (the stalk that attaches a leaf to a plant) measuring 13 ft (4 m).

TALLEST CACTUS

The tallest cactus is the cardon (*Pachycereus pringlei*) found in the Sonoran Desert, Mexico, in April 1995. Still growing, it currently measures 63 ft (19.2 m) in height – almost the same as the length of a volleyball court.

SMELLIEST FLOWER

Also known as the 'corpse flower', the Sumatran *Amorphophallus titanum* releases an extremely foul odor, comparable to that of rotten flesh, which can be smelled from ⅔ mile (1 km) away.

TOP TOPIARY

Moirangthem Okendra Kumbi (India) has been shaping the shoots of a Sky Flower bush (*Duranta repens variegata*) in his 'Hedge to Heaven' garden since 1983. It has now grown to a height of 61 ft (18.59 m, left). Overall, with the help of a specially constructed ladder, he has cut 41 structural shapes, repeating a design of a rounded umbrella followed by two disks. Told that the Duranta plant would not grow past 20 ft (6 m), Moirangthem encouraged growth by pruning, redirecting new sprouts, and fertilizing the soil. At first, the plant was displayed at local exhibitions, but when it became too large to move, it was planted in its permanent, current location. Moirangthem still climbs the tall iron railings that hold the plant up, twice a day in order to look after it.

<53209>
www.guinnessworldrecords.com/topiary
← ACCESS CODE

MOST MASSIVE TREES

The all-time most massive tree was 'Lindsey Creek' tree, a coast redwood (*Sequoia sempervirens*) in California, which had a minimum trunk volume of 90,000 ft³ (2,549 m³) and a minimal total mass of 8 million lb (3,630 tonnes) – including its foliage, branches, and roots – roughly equal to the weight of 800 elephants. The tree blew over in a storm in 1905.

The world's most massive living tree is 'General Sherman,' the giant sequoia (*Sequoiadendron giganteum*) in the Sequoia National Park, California, which stands 275 ft (83.82 m) tall, has a diameter of 36 ft 5 in (11.1 m), and a girth of 31.3 m (102 ft 8 in). The trunk has a volume of 52,508 ft³ (1,487 m³). It is estimated to contain the equivalent of 606,100 ft (184,739 m) of timber, enough to make 5 billion matches, and is thought to weigh an estimated 4.4 million lb (2,000 tonnes).

LARGEST FUNGI

A fungus growing in the Malheur National Forest in the Blue Mountains, Oregon, covers 2,200 acres (890 ha) – an area equivalent to 1,220 soccer fields. The species *Armillaria ostoyae*, also known as honey mushroom, is calculated to be at least 2,400 years old.

The largest edible fungi, a giant puffball (*Calvatia gigantea*) measuring 8 ft 8 in (2.64 m) in circumference and weighing 48 lb 8 oz (22 kg), was found by Jean-Guy Richard (Canada) in 1987. A single basketball-sized puffball could produce enough spores in only a couple of generations to result in a puffball seven times the size of the Earth.

LARGEST SEED

The world's largest seed is the giant fan palm *Lodoicea maldivica*, commonly known as the double coconut or *coco de mer*, which is found wild only in the Seychelles. The single-seeded fruit can

www.guinnessworldrecords.com/talltree

ACCESS CODE

‹47342›

BRANCHING OUT

The tallest living tree is 'Mendocino Tree,' a coast redwood (*Sequoia sempervirens*, right). It is still growing at Montgomery State Reserve, California. In Sept 1998 it was 368 ft (112.01 m) tall, with a diameter of 10.3 ft (3.14 m). This height is the same as the length of the average soccer field. The tree is about 1,000 years old.

The oldest living tree is the 4,767-year-old bristlecone pine 'Methuselah' *Pinus longaeva* in the White Mountains, California.

take 10 years to develop and weigh up to 44 lb (20 kg) – equivalent to the weight of approximately six newborn babies. They grow on the palm until they become so heavy that eventually they fall to the ground.

SMALLEST SEED

The smallest seeds are those of epiphytic (nonparasitic) orchids, at 28,129.81 million seeds per oz (992.25 million per gram). As a comparison, grass pollens have up to 6 billion grains per oz (170.1 billion grains per gram).

GUINNESS WORLD RECORDS

animal extremes

LARGEST MAMMAL

The world's largest mammal is the blue whale (*Balaenoptera musculus*). They have an average length of 115 ft (35 m) and can weigh up to 287,000 lb (130 tonnes). A huge specimen caught in the Southern Ocean, Antarctica, on March 20 1947 weighed a massive 420,000 lb (190 tonnes) and measured 90 ft 6 in (27.6 m). A blue whale also has the largest offspring; the newborn calf is 20–26 ft (6–8 m) long and weighs 4,400–6,600 lb (2–3 tonnes).

LARGEST LAND MAMMAL

The largest land mammal is the male African bush elephant (*Loxodonta africana*). These huge beasts have an average shoulder-height of 9 ft 10 in–12 ft 2 in (3–3.7 m) and an average weight of 8,800–15,400 lb (4–7 tonnes). The heaviest recorded specimen was a bull shot in Mucusso, Angola, on Nov 7 1974, that had a projected standing height of 13 ft (3.96 m) and weighed a staggering 26,900 lb (12.24 tonnes). The tallest male African bush elephants are found in Namibia; the tallest recorded example was shot near Sesfontein, Namibia, on April 4 1978, after allegedly killing 11 people.

‹51472› www.guinnessworldrecords.com/condor
← ACCESS CODE

WATCH THE BIRDIE

The heaviest bird of prey is the Andean condor (*Vultur gryphus*, left), males of which average 20–27 lb (9–12 kg), with a wingspan of 10 ft (3 m). A weight of 31 lb (14.1 kg) was claimed for a California condor (*Gymnogyps californianus*) now preserved in the California Academy of Sciences, Los Angeles, but this species is generally smaller and rarely exceeds 23 lb (10.4 kg).

The longest feathers grown by any bird were recorded in 1972 on a Phoenix fowl or Yokohama chicken (*Gallus gallus*), whose tail covert measured 34 ft 9.5 in (10.6 m) – as long as a bus.

It measured 14 ft 6 in (4.42 m), had a projected height of about 13 ft 10 in (4.21 m), and weighed an estimated 17,600 lb (8 tonnes).

TALLEST MAMMAL

The tallest mammal is the giraffe (*Giraffa camelopardalis*), which is only found in Africa. On average, mature giraffe males grow to a height of around 18 ft (5.5 m). George, a Kenyan Masai bull (*Giraffa camelopardalis tippelskirchi*), who arrived at Chester Zoo, Cheshire, UK, on Jan 8 1959, was the tallest giraffe ever recorded. Standing 19 ft (5.8 m) tall, his horns almost grazed the roof of the 20-ft (6-m) high giraffe house when he was nine years old.

SMALLEST MAMMAL

The very tiny Kitti's hog-nosed bat (*Craseonycteris thonglongyai*) has a body no bigger than a large bumble-bee. It has a head-body length of only 1.14–1.30 in (2.9–3.3 cm), an average wingspan of 5.1–5.7 in (13–14.5 cm), and weighs just 0.06–0.07 oz (1.7–2.0 g). This tiny bat can be found in a few limestone caves on the Kwae Noi River, Thailand.

LARGEST CAMELIDAE

The dromedary or one-humped camel (*Camelus dromedarius*) is the largest even-toed hoofed mammal. Native to the Middle East, it survives as a wild animal in Australia and as a domestic animal elsewhere. It has an average head and body length of 7.5–11.5 ft (2.3–3.5 m), a shoulder height of 6–7 ft (1.8–2.1 m) (maximum 7 ft 11 in or 2.4 m) and weighs 992–1,521 lb (450–690 kg). Incredibly, the world's tallest man (Robert Wadlow) was taller, measuring 8 ft (2.72 m).

SMALLEST HIPPOPOTAMUS

The pygmy hippopotamus (*Choeropsis liberiensis*) is the smallest species of hippo, found mainly in Liberia, west Africa. Standing at human knee-height, pygmy hippos have an average head-body length of 4 ft 11 in–8ft 1 in (1.5–1.85 m), a shoulder height of 2 ft 3.5 in–3 ft 3.25 in (70–100 cm), and a weight of 353–606 lb (160–275 kg). In comparison, the average-sized hippopotamus is about 10 times bigger and weighs a heavy-duty 5,733 lb (2,600 kg).

LARGEST DEER

The world's largest deer is the Alaskan moose (*Alces alces gigas*). The largest specimen, a bull that stood 7 ft 8 in (2.34 m) and weighed an estimated 1,800 lb (816 kg), was shot in Canada in Sept 1897.

GONE TO POT!

The American or North Atlantic lobster (*Homarus americanus*, left) is the heaviest marine crustacean. On Feb 11 1977 a specimen weighing a staggering 44 lb 6 oz (20.14 kg) and measuring 3 ft 6 in (1.06 m) from the end of the tail fan to the tip of the largest claw, was caught off Nova Scotia, Canada, and later sold to a New York restaurant owner. The average weight of a lobster is usually 3 lb (1.4 kg).

The largest of all marine crustaceans (although not the heaviest) is the *taka-ashi-gani* or giant spider crab (*Macrocheira kaempferi*), found in the Pacific regions. A specimen with a claw-span of 12 ft 1 in (3.7 m) weighed 41 lb (18.6 kg). These spider crabs are part of a large group of slow-moving crabs that lie in wait to attack their prey.

‹51451› www.guinnessworldrecords.com/giantlobster
← ACCESS CODE

SMALLEST DEER

The smallest true deer (family *Cervidae*) is the tiny southern pudu (*Pudu puda*), which is 13–15 in (33–38 cm) tall at the shoulder and weighs 14–18 lb (6.3–8.2 kg). An endangered species, it is found on the slopes of the Andes mountains in Chile and Argentina.

LARGEST MAMMAL EYES

The Pygmy tarsier (*Tarsius pumilus*) from Southeast Asia has a head-body length of 3.3–6.3 in (8.5–16 cm) and huge forward-pointing eyes with a diameter of 0.6 in (1.6 cm). This eye-size is equivalent to eyes the size of a grapefruit in a human being. Tarsiers are also the only primates that can move their heads through 180 degrees to the left and to the right.

LARGEST WILD PIG

The largest wild pig is the extremely fierce giant forest hog (*Hylochoerus meinertzhageni*), which lives in central Africa. It has a head-body length of 4 ft 5 in–7 ft (1.3–2.1 m), a tail length of 12–17.75 in (30–45 cm), a shoulder height of 2 ft 9.5 in–3 ft 8.33 in (85–105 cm) and a weight of 287–606 lb (130–275 kg). They have sharp tusks and are highly dangerous when angry.

LARGEST OWL

The world's largest owl is the European eagle owl (*Bubo bubo*), which has an average length of 26–28 in (66–71 cm), a weight of 3.5–8.82 lb (1.6–4 kg), and a wingspan of more than 5 ft (1.5 m).

SMALLEST OWL

The world's smallest owl is the elf owl (*Micrathene whitney*) from southwestern USA and Mexico, averaging 4.72–5.5 in (12–14 cm) in length and weighing less than 1.76 oz (50 g).

HEAVIEST SCORPION

The black west African species *Pandinus imperator* can weigh up to 2 oz (60 g) and is between 5–7 in (13–18 cm) in length. This is the average length of an adult human hand.

www.guinnessworldrecords.com/greatwhite

FISHY TALES

The largest predatory fish is the rare great white shark (*Carcharodon carcharias*, below). Adult specimens average 14–15 ft (4.3–4.6 m) in length, and generally weigh 1,146–1,697 lb (520–770 kg). The world's biggest fish is the rare plankton-feeding whale shark (*Rhincodon typus*), which is found in the Atlantic, Pacific, and Indian Oceans. They can grow to a massive 59 ft (18 m). The whale shark also produces the largest fish egg.

ACCESS CODE

‹51342›

GUINNESS WORLD RECORDS™

dangerous beasts

MOST SUCCESSFUL PREDATOR

African hunting dogs, also called cape hunting dogs or dog hyenas (*Lycaon pictus*), hunt in packs and are successful in 50–70% of their hunts. This is consistently the highest figure in the mammalian world.

LARGEST LAND CARNIVORE

Adult male polar bears (*Ursus maritimus*) typically weigh 880–1320 lb (400–600 kg) and,

nose-to-tail, are 7 ft 11 in–8 ft 6 in (2.4–2.6 m) in length. Excellent swimmers, they have been known to swim 60 miles (about 100 km) to hunt seals. The polar bear has a stomach capacity of about 150 lb (68 kg) and is known to kill animals as large as walruses (1,100 lb or 500 kg) and beluga whales (1,320 lb or 600 kg) – the world's largest prey. Their digestive system is also more adapted for processing meat than plant material, making them the most carnivorous of all bear species.

Male Kodiak bears (*Ursus arctos middendorffi*), a subspecies of brown bear found on islands in the Gulf of Alaska, are more robustly built than the polar bear, but are usually shorter in length.

MOST FATALITIES FROM ANIMAL ATTACKS

On Feb 19 1945, 980 Japanese soldiers out of a group of 1,000 were killed by estuarine or saltwater crocodiles (*Crocodylus porosus*) after being forced to cross a 10-mile (16-km) mangrove swamp in order to join their infantry division. This is a survival rate of only 0.2 % – the worst-ever crocodile attack. The estuarine crocodile, found in Asia and the Pacific, is the world's largest reptile; adult males average 14–16 ft (4.2–4.8 m) long and weigh about 900–1,150 lb (408–520 kg). The largest authenticated specimens measured over 23 ft (7 m). Unauthenticated reports claim specimens up to 33 ft (10 m) in length.

Between 1764 and 1766, a wild wolf called the 'Beast of Gevauden' attacked dozens of people in the mountainous region of Lozère, France. More than 100 wolves were killed before the killer wolf was shot on Jan 19 1766. When it was cut open, the shoulder of a young child killed the previous day was found inside its stomach.

The Champawat Tigress – said to be responsible for 436 deaths in the Champawat district, India, between 1902 and 1907 – was one of the most notorious man-eating animals in India. She was eventually shot by Colonel Jim Corbett in 1907.

ARMED AND DANGEROUS

The longest horns of any living animal belong to the wild water buffalo (*Bubalus arnee*, above) of India, Nepal, Bhutan, and Thailand. The average spread is about 3 ft 3 in (1 m), but one bull shot in 1955 had horns measuring 13 ft 11 in (4.24 m) from tip to tip along the outside curve across the forehead.

The longest nonprehistoric tusks were obtained from an African elephant (*Loxodonta africana*) in Zaïre (now Democratic Republic of Congo) and are kept in the New York Zoological Society, New York City. The right tusk measures 11 ft 5 in (3.49 m) along the outside curve, and the left 11 ft (3.35 m). Together, they weigh 293 lb (133 kg).

The Gila Lizard (*Heloderma suspectum*) is the world's most dangerous lizard, with sharp teeth and enough venom to kill two adults.

www.guinnessworldrecords.com/buffalo

ACCESS CODE

‹51205› ←

RED FOR DANGER

The tiny, brightly colored poison dart frogs of South and Central America (*Phyllobates terribilis*, above) are the most poisonous frog species. They secrete some of the most deadly biological toxins known, including batrachotoxin, which affects the nervous system. A single drop in contact with the human body can block transmission of nerve impulses and may even stop the heart. This poison is used by native South and Central American tribes to coat arrowheads, hence the name. The 1.6–2-in-long (4–5-cm) frog produces enough toxin to kill 10 adult humans.

‹51322› www.guinnessworldrecords.com/poisonfrog ← ACCESS CODE

MOST FEROCIOUS FRESHWATER FISH

The piranha, especially of the genera *Serrasalmus* and *Pygocentrus*, is found in the rivers of South America. It has razor-sharp teeth and is the world's most ferocious freshwater fish. Attracted to blood and frantic splashing, piranhas can completely strip an animal as large as a horse of its flesh within minutes, leaving only the skeleton. Attacks are swift and comprehensive as they start eating their victim alive – piranhas will even often injure one another in the frenzy of an attack. On Sept 19 1981 more than 300 people were reportedly killed and eaten when an overloaded passenger-cargo boat capsized and sank as it was docking at the Brazilian port of Obidos.

MOST ELECTRIC FISH

The electric eel (*Electrophorus electricus*), a relative of the piranha, is the world's most electric fish. Measuring up to 6 ft (1.8 m) in length, it lives in rivers in Brazil and the Guianas, and can stun its prey with an electric shock of up to 650 volts – enough to light an electric bulb or to stun a human adult.

MOST VENOMOUS FISH

The stonefish (family Synanceidae), which lives on the bottom of the Indo-Pacific Ocean, is the world's most venomous fish. *Synanceia horrida* has the largest venom glands of any known fish. Any direct contact with its spiny fins, which contain a strong, toxic poison, can prove fatal.

MOST VENOMOUS EDIBLE FISH

The puffer fish (*Tetraodon*), of the Red Sea and Indo-Pacific region, is the most poisonous edible fish, secreting a venom that is 1,250 times deadlier than cyanide. However, when cooked properly, it is a Japanese delicacy called *fugu*. The Japanese consume 22 million lb (10,000 tonnes) of *fugu* a year, resulting in an average fatality rate of 70–100 people per year.

MOST POISONOUS BIRD

The hooded pitohui (*Pitohui dichrous*) from Papua New Guinea is the only known poisonous bird in the world. Discovered in 1990, scientists do not know why its feathers and skin contain the poison homobatrachotoxin (the same one secreted by the dart frogs of South America). Like many other poisonous animals, this bird emits a foul smell and is brightly colored.

MOST DANGEROUS BIRD

The most dangerous birds are the three species of cassowary (family Casuariidae) that live in New Guinea and northeastern Queensland, Australia. Standing up to 6 ft 7 in (2 m) tall, they have strong claws on the three forward-pointing toes of each foot. The inner toe has a 5-in-long (12-cm) spike for defensive purposes – it kicks out when cornered. They can leap into the air and kick, damaging vital organs or causing massive bleeding. Its kick is powerful enough to rip open a person's stomach or even kill.

MOST VENOMOUS MOLLUSC

The two closely related species of blue-ringed octopus, *Hapalochlaena maculosa* and *H. lunulata*, found on the coasts of Australia and southeast Asia, carry a neurotoxic venom so potent that their relatively painless bite can kill in a matter of minutes. With a radial spread of 4–8 in (100–200 mm), an individual carries enough venom to cause the paralysis (or even death) of 10 adult humans.

MOST VENOMOUS JELLYFISH

The transparent Australian sea wasp or box jellyfish (*Chironex fleckeri*) is the most venomous cnidarian and also one of the world's most venomous creatures, with enough poison to kill 60 people. Weighing an average of 13 lb (6 kg), and measuring 8–12 in (20–30 cm) across the bell, the jellyfish may have up to 60 tentacles, each one containing millions of poisonous nematocysts. At least 70 people have died from the venom in the last 100 years with death occuring in as little as four minutes.

www.guinnessworldrecords.com/venomviper

MIND YOUR STEP!

The Gaboon viper (*Bitis gabonica*, above) from tropical Africa, produces more venom than any other snake. A single adult male is thought to have enough venom to inject lethal doses into 30 people. As they also have the longest fangs of any snake, Gaboon vipers also inject the poison more deeply – one specimen measuring 6 ft (1.83 m) had fangs 2 in (50 mm) long.

The world's longest venomous snake, the king cobra (*Ophiophagus hannah*), from India and southeast Asia, is also highly dangerous and can deliver enough venom to kill an elephant or 20 people, through fangs almost 12 mm (0.5 in) long. Averaging 12–15 ft (3.65–4.5 m), the longest known specimen, captured in 1937, measured 18 ft 2 in (5.54 m) and later grew to 18 ft 9 in (5.71 m).

ACCESS CODE

‹51007›

GUINNESS WORLD RECORDS™

creepy crawlies

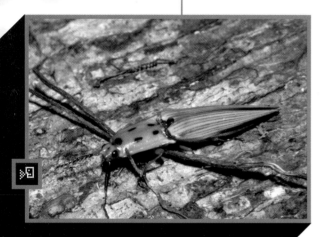

BEETLEMANIA!
The click beetle (*Athous haemorrhoidalis*, above) achieves the highest G-force of any insect without the use of its legs. The 'click' occurs when the beetle 'jackknifes' into the air to escape predators; it bends its head and prothorax backward and then straightens up suddenly with a snapping motion, shooting up to 6 in (15 cm) high and achieving a G-force of around 400 G. One beetle measuring 0.5 in (1.2 cm) in length and weighing 0.00014 oz (40 mg) jumped to a height of 12 in (30 cm) and was calculated to have endured a peak brain deceleration of 2,300 G by the end of the movement. G-force measures the change of speed over time, and gauges how fast a person, animal, or thing is accelerating from moment to moment. If sustained for longer than a few seconds, a G-force of between 4 and 6 G will cause a human being to black out. Astronauts on the space shuttle during liftoff experience a force of 3 G.

‹51294› www.guinnessworldrecords.com/clickbeetle
← ACCESS CODE

LARGEST MARINE SNAIL
The largest known marine gastropod is the trumpet or baler conch (*Syrinx aruanus*) of Australia. One specimen collected off Western Australia in 1979 had a shell 30.4 in (77.2 cm) long, with a maximum girth of 39.8 in (101 cm). It weighed nearly 40 lb (18 kg) when alive.

LONGEST EARTHWORM
The longest earthworm is the *Microchaetus rappi* of South Africa. In 1967 a giant specimen was found measuring 22 ft (6.7 m) in length (when naturally extended) and 0.8 in (2.03 cm) in diameter. The average length of this species is approximately 6 ft (1.8 m) when naturally extended.

LARGEST BUTTERFLY
The largest known butterfly is the poisonous Queen Alexandra's Birdwing (*Ornithoptera alexandrae*) of Papua New Guinea. Females may have a wingspan over 11 in (27.9 cm) and weigh more than 0.9 oz (25 g).

SMALLEST BUTTERFLY
The smallest butterfly is the South African dwarf blue (*Brephidium barberae*). It has a wingspan of 0.55 in (1.4 cm) and weighs less than 0.00035 oz (10 mg).

LARGEST COCKROACH
The largest cockroach is *Megaloblatta longipennis* of Colombia. A specimen belonging to Akira Yokokura (Japan) is 1.75 in (4.45 cm) wide and 3.8 in (9.7 cm) long. The average cockroach measures 0.24–3 in (0.6–7.6 cm) long.

LARGEST FLEA
There are around 1,830 species of flea, of which the largest known is *Hystrichopsylla schefferi*, first found in the state of Washington, in 1913. Females of this species grow to an average length of 0.3 in (0.76 cm). As a comparison, the common flea (*Pulex irritans*) has an average length of 0.04–1 in (0.1–2.54 mm).

The champion jumper among fleas is the cat flea (*Ctenocephalides felis*), which can reach a height of 13 in (34 cm) in a single jump – 130 times its height. This requires an acceleration of over 20 times that needed to launch a space rocket.

LARGEST WASP NEST
A wasp nest found by Yoichiro Kawamura (Japan) on May 18 1999 at Yonegaoka, Nahari Town, Japan, had a circumference of 8 ft (2.45 m) and weighed 17.6 lb (8 kg). The circumference was approximately three times the size of a basketball.

OLDEST FOSSIL ANTS
In 1998 a team of researchers from the American Museum of Natural History, New Jersey, announced the dating of the oldest fossil ants ever found. The extremely rare 92-million-year-old ants, discovered in 1967, are preserved in amber. They were found in a New Jersey location where some of the most important amber-encased fossils have been located.

OLDEST INSECT
The longest-lived insects are the splendor beetles (Buprestidae). On May 27 1983 a specimen of *Buprestis aurulenta* appeared from the staircase timber in the home of W. Euston of Prittlewell, UK, after at least 47 years as a larva.

LOUDEST INSECT
The African cicada (*Brevisana brevis*) produces a calling song with an average sound pressure level of 106.7 dB at a distance of 19.5 in (50 cm). As a comparison, the noise measured in the front row of a rock concert is 110 dB. Cicada songs play a vital role in communication.

LARGEST INDOOR SPIDER'S WEB
A spider's web 16 ft 6 in (5.08 m) long and 12 ft 4 in (3.80 m) wide, with an area of 208 ft² (19.35 m²), was discovered in the outbuilding of a 17th-century cottage in Newent, Glos, UK, in Jan 1999. The web, which hung suspended like a second ceiling 5.9 ft (1.8 m) off the floor, was probably built by a succession of eight-legged inhabitants.

STRANGEST INSECT DEFENCE SYSTEM
The bombardier beetle (genus *Brachinus*) stores two relatively benign chemicals in its body. When threatened, these chemicals mix with an enzyme, causing a violent chemical reaction and the release of considerable heat (up to 212°F or 100°C) from the anus. This spray of irritating gas can be turned on and off an amazing 500 times a second. This system is similar to the pulse jet engine that powered the World War II German V-1 flying bomb. However the V-1 could only pulse its jet 42 times per second.

MOST EXPENSIVE INSECT
A giant 7.9-cm (3.1-in) stag beetle (*Dorcus hopei*) is reported to have been sold for JPY 10,035,000 (£57,000; $90,000) at a Tokyo store on Aug 19 1999. A 36-year-old company president apparently bought it for his collection but refused to be identified for fear of being targeted by thieves.

FASTEST CATERPILLAR
The larvae of the mother-of-pearl moth (*Pleurotya ruralis*) can travel 15 in (38.1 cm) per second, as they curl into a ball and roll away when attacked. This is the caterpillar equivalent of 150 mph (241 km/h).

HIGHEST FLYING INSECT
The greatest height reported for migrating butterflies is 19,000 ft (5,791 m) for a flock of small tortoiseshells (*Aglais urticae*) seen over the Zemu Glacier in the eastern Himalayas. In comparison, the highest altitude recorded for a bird is 37,000 ft (11,300 m) for a Ruppell's vulture (*Gyps rueppellii*),

which collided with a commercial aircraft over the Ivory Coast, on Nov 29 1973.

MOST DESTRUCTIVE INSECT

The desert locust (*Schistocerca gregaria*) found in Africa, the Middle East, and western Asia measures only 1.7–2.4 in (4.5–6 cm) long, but it can eat its own weight in food every day. In a single day, a 'small' swarm of about 50 million locusts can eat enough food to sustain 500 people for an entire year.

RAREST INSECT

Scientists believe that there may only be 10 specimens of the flightless giant stick insect (*Phasmid drycelus australis*) in existence. They evolved before the dinosaurs and were presumed extinct for 80 years until rediscovery in Australia in Feb 2001.

www.guinnessworldrecords.com/goliathspider

WORLD WIDE WEB?

A male goliath bird-eating spider (*Theraphosa leblondi*) collected in Venezuela in April 1965 had a record legspan of 11 in (28 cm) – sufficient to cover a dinner plate. This species inhabits the rainforests of Surinam, Guyana, and French Guiana, but specimens have also been found in Venezuela and Brazil. They feed on rodents, killing their prey with their huge venom-producing fangs.

GUINNESS WORLD RECORDS

dinosaurs and mammoths

TALLEST DINOSAUR

The *Sauroposeidon* is thought to be the largest creature to have ever walked the Earth. Remains found in Oklahoma, in 1994, indicate that it stood 60 ft (18.28 m) tall, weighed 132,277 lb (60 tonnes), and had the longest neck of any known dinosaur, with vertebrae measuring up to 4 ft (1.2 m) long. *Sauroposeidon* was giraffelike in shape but was 30 times larger than the largest giraffe on record – as tall as a six-story building. It lived about 110 million years ago.

MAMMOTH TASK

The oldest intact mammoth is 'Jarkov' (above), estimated to be 23,000 years old, excavated by a group of French scientists in October 1999 in Siberia (Russia). It died at the age of 47 and would have stood 8.5 ft (2.6 m). Originally found by nine-year-old reindeer herder Guenadi Jarkov in 1997, the mammoth was subsequently named after his family. Much of the excavation work has been financed by the Discovery Channel. In 2000, the mammoth was airlifted to shelter in its 51,456-lb (23.34–tonne) frozen cube, with its two tusks sticking out of the ice – it is now in a cave being defrosted by scientists using hairdriers. Although only a small fraction of the block has melted, mammoth bones, hair, and other items have been found and sent around the world for analysis. Scientists plan to extract DNA to perform experiments.

www.guinnessworldrecords.com/mammoth

ACCESS CODE
‹53392 ←

LARGEST CARNIVOROUS DINOSAUR

A skeleton of the largest-ever predatory dinosaur was discovered in Neuquen, Argentina in 1995. *Giganotosaurus carolinii* (giant southern reptile) was 41 ft (12.5 m) long and weighed 17,637 lb (8 tonnes). The bones suggest that it was both taller and more heavily built than *Tyrannosaurus rex*. It walked the Earth around 110 million years ago – 30 million years before the *Tyrannosaurus rex*.

SMALLEST DINOSAUR

The chicken-sized *Compsognathus* (pretty jaw), of southern Germany and southeast France, measured 23 in (60 cm) from the snout to the tip of the tail and weighed about 6 lb 8 oz (3 kg). *Compsognathus* existed in the late Jurassic period, about 145 million years ago. It was a carnivore, eating small animals such as lizards and insects. Only two specimens have been found since 1859 – an adult in Germany and a juvenile in France.

HEAVIEST DINOSAUR

Argentinosaurus, a titanosaurid from Argentina, was probably the heaviest dinosaur. Estimates made in 1994, based on its massive vertebrae, suggest it may have weighed up to 220,462 lb (100 tonnes). The heaviest UK dinosaur was the diplodocid *Cetiosaurus oxoniensis*, which lived around 170 million years ago and weighed about 99,208 lb (45 tonnes), according to estimates based on part of a femur found in Bucks, UK.

LARGEST ARMORED DINOSAUR

Ankylosaurus, a herbivore protected with thick plates covering the skin, also had a double row of spikes running down from the back of its head to its club tail. Measuring 24.6–35.1 ft (7.5–10.7 m) long and 4 ft (1.2 m) tall, it even had plates to protect its eyes, with only its belly left unplated. With a width of up to 8 ft (2.5 m), it was also the widest known dinosaur. The last and largest of the ankylosaurids at 8,618.5 lb (4 tonnes), it lived in the late Cretaceous period, about 70–65 million years ago.

TAIL ENDING

The *Diplodocus* (double-beamed, above), a long-necked sauropod from the late Jurassic period 155–145 million years ago, had the longest tail of any dinosaur, with a length of up to 43 ft (13.1 m). The remains of a *Diplodocus carnegii* found in Wyoming, in 1899 would have measured 87.2 ft (26.6 m) long when alive, with much of that length made up by a long neck and an extremely long whiplike tail. It probably weighed 12,787–40,785 lb (5.8–18.5 tonnes), with an estimate of around 26,455 lb (12 tonnes) being the most likely.

‹56108›   www.guinnessworldrecords.com/longtaildino
← ACCESS CODE

THICKEST DINOSAUR SKULL

Pachycephalosaurus, a dome-headed herbivore that lived about 76–65 million years ago during the late Cretaceous period, had a skull measuring 2 ft (65 cm) long with a bone dome of 7.8 in (20 cm). In comparison, the thickest part of the human skull is 0.7 in (20 mm).

LONGEST PREHISTORIC SNAKE

The longest prehistoric snake was the pythonlike *Gigantophis garstini*, which inhabited what is now Egypt about 38 million years ago. Parts of a spinal column and a piece of jaw discovered at Fayum in the Western Desert indicate a length of about 36 ft (11 m). This is 3 ft 3 in (1 m) more than the current longest snake, the reticulated python (*Python reticulatus*).

LARGEST FOSSIL TRILOBITE

A fossil trilobite discovered in Canada measured over 27.5 in (70 cm) in length, more than 11.8 in (30 cm) longer than the previous largest trilobite. The discovery of this 445-million-year-old specimen was announced on Oct 9 2000.

LARGEST PREHISTORIC FLYING BIRD

In 1979 fossil remains of the giant *Argentavis magnificens*, which lived about 6–8 million years ago in what is now Argentina, were discovered 100 miles (160 km) west of Buenos Aires. The remains indicate a wing span of over 19 ft 8 in (6 m) – possibly up to 25 ft (7.6 m) – and a weight of about 176 lb (80 kg). In comparison, the albatross (*Diomedea exulans*), which has the largest wingspan of any living species of bird, measures 11 ft 11 in (3.63 m).

LARGEST PREHISTORIC INSECT

The largest prehistoric insect was the dragonfly *Meganeura monyi*, which lived about 280 million years ago. Fossil remains discovered at Commentry, France, indicate a wing expanse of up to 27.5 in (70 cm).

EARLIEST MAMMAL

In 1991 a partial skull of a mammal named *Adelobasileus cromptoni* (similar to a modern tree shrew) was found in 225-million-year-old rocks in New Mexico.

LONGEST PREHISTORIC TUSKS

The longest prehistoric tusks were those of the straight-tusked elephant *Hesperoloxodon antiques germanicus*, which lived in what is now northern Germany about two million years ago. The average tusk length in adult bulls was 16 ft 4.75 in (5 m).

HEAVIEST SINGLE FOSSIL TUSK

The heaviest recorded single fossil tusk weighed 330 lb (150 kg) with a maximum circumference of 35 in (89 cm), and belonged to an unknown species of mammoth. The specimen (in two pieces) is 11 ft 9 in (3.58 m) in length.

LARGEST PREHISTORIC ANTLERS

The prehistoric giant deer or Irish elk (*Megaloceros giganteus*), found in continental Europe as recently as 10,000 years ago, had the longest known antlers. One specimen, recovered from an Irish bog, had antlers measuring 14 ft (4.3 m) across, corresponding to a shoulder height of 6 ft (1.83 m) and a weight of 1,100 lb (500 kg). This compares to the largest recorded spread or 'rack' of antlers of any living species, which was 6 ft 6 in (1.99 m) from a moose (*Alces alces*) killed near the Stewart River, Yukon, Canada in Oct 1897.

DINOSAUR WITH THE MOST TEETH

The dinosaurs with the most teeth were the duck-billed *hadrosaurs* (bulky lizards). Despite being herbivores with toothless beaks, they had up to 960 self-sharpening cheek teeth in the side of their strong jaws for chewing tough plants. *Hadrosaurs* ranged in size from 10–40 ft (3–12 m) long.

www.guinnessworldrecords.com/trex

LARGE AND EXPENSIVE

One of the largest-ever carnivores, *Tyrannosaurus rex* (above) roamed the Earth during the last part of the Cretaceous Age, between 85 and 65 million years ago. The largest and most complete *T-rex* skeleton ever is 'Sue,' discovered in South Dakota, on Aug 12 1990 by fossil hunter Sue Hendrickson. The skeleton is 13 ft (4 m) tall and 41 ft (12.5 m) long and has a skull measuring 4.9 ft (1.5 m) long. She has 58 teeth in her powerful jaw, with each tooth measuring between 7.5 and 12 in (19 and 30 cm). Her estimated live weight is 14,110 lb (6.4 tonnes). The Field Museum, Chicago, purchased the skeleton at a public auction in 1997 for $8,362,500 (£5,174,014) – the world's highest price for a dinosaur skeleton – and have put her on permanent display.

ACCESS CODE

‹54658›

GUINNESS WORLD RECORDS

extraordinary animals

SLOWEST MAMMAL

The three-toed sloth of tropical South America (*Bradypus tridactylus*) has an average ground speed of 6–8 ft (1.8–2.4 m) per minute (0.07–0.1 mph; 0.1–0.16 km/h), but in the trees it can accelerate to 15 ft (4.6 m) per minute (0.17 mph, 0.27 km/h). Sloths seldom descend to the ground as they cannot walk and have to pull themselves along using their claws. Digestion for a sloth is also very slow, and it may take a month or more for food to pass from the stomach to the intestine.

LONGEST JOURNEY MADE BY A FISH

Two oyster toadfish (*Opsanus tau*), a species that inhabits the Northeast of the USA, traveled more than three million miles through space in the Discovery space shuttle mission STS-95. The fish were taken aboard to help scientists learn more about how bodies react to motion sickness.

BEST TREE-CLIMBING FISH

The climbing perch (*Anabas testudineus*), from South Asia, is remarkable for its walking and palm-tree climbing abilities. It will even walk to search for better habitat. The species has special gills that allow it to absorb atmospheric oxygen. Similarly mudskippers (of the Perciformes order like the perch) can live out of water for short periods and climb trees, holding on by their pectoral fins.

SPEEDY GONZALES

The ostrich (*Struthio camelus*, left), which is found on the plains of Africa, holds the record speed for a land bird of 45 mph (72 km/h) and has a stride that may exceed 23 ft (7.01 m). In comparison, over distances of up to 1,800 ft (550 m), the cheetah (*Acinonyx jubatus*) holds the overall animal speed record, maintaining a steady 60 mph (100 km/h) on level ground – almost the US highway speed limit. Cheetahs are found in Africa, Iran, Turkmenistan, and Afghanistan. The American antelope (*Antilocapra americana*) holds the long-distance speed record for an animal, with continuous speeds of 35 mph (56 km/h) for as far as 4 miles (6 km). It is found in the USA, Canada, and northern Mexico.

‹51481›
www.guinnessworldrecords.com/ostrich
← ACCESS CODE

LONGEST RODENT HIBERNATION

Arctic ground squirrels (*Spermophilus parryi*) hold the record for the longest hibernation by a rodent. They live in northern Canada and Alaska, and hibernate for nine months every year.

MOST COLD-RESISTANT ANIMAL

The Woodland frog, which lives north of the Arctic Circle, is the only animal that can survive being frozen. Glucose in the blood acts as an 'antifreeze,' which protects the frogs' vital organs, while the rest of the body freezes solid. Once the weather warms up, the frogs 'come back to life.'

MOST RADIATION-RESISTANT LIFEFORM

The bacterium *Deinococcus radiodurans* can repair damage to its chromosomal DNA and thus resist 1.5 million rads of gamma radiation, which is about 3,000 times the amount that would kill a human. If the bacteria

is cooled or frozen, it can take twice that amount. The bacterium survives and reproduces in environments lethal to any other organism and also resists high doses of ultraviolet radiation.

BEST ANIMAL REGENERATION

Sponges (Porifera) have the best powers of regeneration of any animal. If they lose a segment of their body, it will grow back and if a sponge is forced through a fine-meshed silk gauze, the separate fragments will reform into a full-size sponge.

SLOWEST GROWTH RATE

The slowest animal growth rate is that of the deep-sea clam (*Tindaria callistiformis*), which inhabits the North Atlantic ocean. It takes about 100 years to grow 0.3 in (8 mm) long.

MOST FEARLESS MAMMAL

The most fearless mammal is the ratel or honey badger (*Mellivora capensis*) found in the forest and brush country

of Africa, the Middle East, and India. It will defend itself against animals of any size, especially if they come too close to its breeding burrow. Its tough skin is impervious to the stings of bees, the quills of porcupines, and the bites of most snakes. The skin is also so loose that if a predator holds it by the scruff of the neck, the badger can turn inside its skin and bite its attacker until released.

STRONGEST ANIMAL

In proportion to their size, the strongest animals are the larger beetles of the family Scarabaeidae, which are found mainly in the tropics. In tests carried out on a rhinoceros beetle of the family Dynastinae, it was found to support 850 times its own weight on its back.

MOST DANGEROUS LOVE LIFE

The male brown antechinus (*Antechinus stuartii*), a marsupial mouse from eastern Australia, has a fatal sexual appetite. Each year the entire adult male population mates with as many females as possible. They rarely eat and spend their time fighting rival males. As a result, they all die within a matter of days, due to starvation, ulcers, or infection.

MOST AERIAL LAND BIRD

A common swift (*Apus apus*) completes a nonstop flight of 310,000 miles (500,000 km) between fledging and its first landing at a potential nesting site two years, and, in some cases, up to four years later. During this time it sleeps, drinks, eats, and even mates on the wing.

THE GOLDEN SHOT

The yellow-and-black banded archerfish (*Toxotes jaculator*, left) lurks near riverbanks in its native Thailand waiting for a suitable insect to alight on a water plant within its record 5-ft (1.5-m) water-spitting range. The fish shoots a pellet of water at the prey from its tubular-shaped mouth. If the fish misses, it is able to attempt again in quick fire. This semiautomatic hunting method is unique among animals and makes the archerfish the best aquatic marksman in the world.

The grotesque-looking Texas horned lizard, also known as the horned toad, or the horny toad, holds the record for the strangest defense mechanism among animals. When threatened, it can spray blood containing caustic irritants out of its eyes, warding off potential predators.

‹53943›
www.guinnessworldrecords.com/archerfish
← ACCESS CODE

www.guinnessworldrecords.com/koko

SAY 'CHEESE'!
In 1972, Koko – a gorilla born at San Francisco Zoo – was taught ASL (American Sign Language for the Deaf) by Dr. Francine Patterson. By 2000, Koko (right, in a photograph that she took of herself in a mirror) had a record working vocabulary of over 1,000 signs and understood roughly 2,000 words of English. She can refer to the past and future, argue, make jokes, and lie. Koko has told *Guinness World Records* that she is honored to hold the record for the gorilla most proficient in sign language and to be in this book.

ACCESS CODE

‹51137› ←

GUINNESS
WORLD RECORDS

fantastic pets

OLDEST CATS

Ma, a female tabby owned by Alice St. George Moore (UK) and Grandpa Rex Allen, a champion show cat owned by Jake Perry (USA) are the longest-living domestic cats ever recorded. Both felines were an amazing 34 years old when they died on Nov 5 1957 and April 1 1998 respectively. This is more than twice a cat's average life span.

HEAVIEST CATS USA

OT, short for 'Orange Thing,' owned by Tom Phillips (USA) is the world's heaviest living cat, weighing in at an amazing 40 lb 14 oz (18.55 kg) on Oct 30 1998, at the age of eight.

The heaviest domestic cat ever recorded was Himmy, a male tabby belonging to Thomas Vyse (Australia), who weighed 47 lb (21.3 kg) when he died in 1986 at the age of 10.

SMALLEST CAT

The smallest cat on record is a blue point Himalayan-Persian named Tinker Toy, who reached only 7.5 in (19 cm) when fully grown. He belongs to Katrina and Scott Forbes (USA).

HEAVIEST LIVING DOG

Kell, an English mastiff owned by Tom Scott (UK), is the heaviest living dog, weighing 286 lb (130 kg) on Aug 18 1999. She feeds on a boxer's diet, eating lots of protein, including chopped beef, eggs, and goats' milk.

HEAVIEST PIG

Big Bill, a Poland-China hog owned by W.J. Chappall (USA), weighed a record 2,552 lb (1,157.5 kg) before he died in 1933. He stood 5 ft (1.52 m) high at the shoulder, and was 9 ft (2.74 m) long.

OLDEST GOLDFISH

A goldfish named Tish, owned by Hilda and Gordon Hand (UK), lived for 43 years after Hilda's son Peter won him at a fairground in 1956. Tish was so old that his scales had turned from gold to silver by the time he died in 1999.

LARGEST PIGEON

A Canadian giant runt cock pigeon called Doc Yeck, owned by Leonard Yeck (Canada), weighed 4 lb (1.8 kg) on March 6 1999, with a chest width of 5 in (12.7 cm). Doc Yeck is twice the size and weight of an average pigeon of the same breed.

LARGEST HAMSTER LITTER

On Feb 28 1974 a hamster belonging to the Miller family (USA) gave birth to 26 baby hamsters. This is more than three times the average litter size, which is eight.

SHOW ME THE BUNNY!

Toby III (above), a black male English lop bred by Phil Wheeler (UK), holds the record for the longest rabbit ears – they are an astounding 29.7 in (75.6 cm) long and 7.18 in (18.24 cm) wide.

The largest rabbit ever recorded was in April 1980, when a five-month-old French lop doe weighing 26 lb 7 oz (12 kg) was exhibited at the Reus Fair in northeast Spain.

The smallest breeds – the Netherland and Polish Dwarf rabbits – are 10 times smaller than the lops, and weigh between 2 and 2.5 lb (0.9 kg–1.13 kg).

‹51129› www.guinnessworldrecords.com/rabbit
← ACCESS CODE

CAT WITH MOST TOES

Normal cats have five toes on each front paw and four toes on each hind paw, giving them a total of 18 toes. However, Twinkle Toes, a three-year-old owned by Gloria Boensch (USA), has a total of 25 toes – six on each of her hind paws, six on her left front paw, and seven on her right.

TURTLE WITH MOST HEADS

In 1999, Lin Chi-Fa, from southern Taiwan, discovered a three-headed turtle in his garden pond. Only two of its heads were fully developed. As the turtle is regarded as a sacred animal in Chinese folklore, Lin took it to a temple to be blessed, only to notice that it walked in a zig-zag fashion as its two fully developed heads could not agree on which direction to take.

MOST PROLIFIC CAT

A tabby cat named Dusty (USA), produced 420 kittens during her breeding life. This averages out at approximately 28 kittens a year over 15 years. She gave birth to her last litter (a single kitten) on June 12 1952.

HIGHEST FREESTYLE JUMP BY A DOG

On July 28 1999 during the Superdog Show at Klondike Days, Edmonton, Alberta, Canada, a Russian wolfhound named Wolf made a freestyle jump of 5 ft 3 in (160 cm). Wolf is owned and trained by Seanna O'Neill (Canada).

MOST ROMANTIC GUINEA PIG

Sooty, a three-year-old guinea pig (UK), became globally infamous when he escaped from his hutch and romanced 24 partners in a single evening. Following this impressive display of passion

LITTLE AND LARGE

The smallest living dog is a Yorkie named 'Big Boss' (left), owned by Dr. Chai Khanchanakom (Thailand). At one year old, he measured 4.7 in (11.94 cm) tall and 5.1 in (12.95 cm) long.

The smallest dog on record was a fist-sized dwarf Yorkshire terrier owned by Arthur Marples (UK), which stood just 2.5 in (6.3 cm) tall at the shoulder, and measured 3.75 in (9.5 cm). It died in 1945, just before its second birthday.

The tallest living dog, a Great Dane called Harvey, stands a massive 5 ft (1.54 m) at the shoulder. Owned by Charles Dodman (UK), Harvey eats a huge 7.9 lb (3.6 kg) of canned dog food a day. Great Danes usually average 2 ft 6 in (75 cm) at the shoulder.

‹51213› www.guinnessworldrecords.com/dogdwarf
← ACCESS CODE: ‹51213›

in Dec 2000, Sooty became the proud father of 43 baby guinea pigs. On Feb 14 2001 Sooty received a record 206 Valentine cards, some from as far away as New Zealand.

LONGEST DOG SWIM
On Sept 2 1995 two Labradors called Kai and Gypsy swam the 'Maui Channel Swim' from Lanai to Maui, Hawaii, with their owner, Steve Fisher (USA). They swam the 9.5-mile (15.2-km) course in 6 hr 3 min 42 sec.

DOG WITH THE LARGEST REPERTOIRE OF TRICKS
Chanda-Leah, a toy poodle owned and trained by Sharon Robinson (Canada), has a repertoire of 469 tricks, which includes playing the piano and fetching a tissue when someone sneezes.

FASTEST WEAVING DOG
A South African border collie named Jazz holds the speed record for weaving his way between 60 poles in an amazing 12.98 seconds. The record was set on Dec 4 1999.

FARTHEST JUMP BY A FROG
Santjie, a South African sharp-nosed frog (*Ptychadena oxyrhynchus*), jumped a total of 33.79 ft (10.3 m) in three jumps at a frog Derby held at Lurula Natal Spa, Paulpietersburg, KwaZulu-Natal, South Africa, on May 21 1977. This is about half the length of a basketball court.

BEST TALKING BIRD
A female African gray parrot (*Psittacus erythacus*) named Prudle won the 'Best talking parrot-like bird' title at the British National Cage and Aviary Bird Show for a record 12 consecutive years before retiring in 1976. Prudle came to the UK from Uganda in 1958 and boasted an amazing vocabulary of nearly 800 words.

MOST WELL-TRAVELED CAT
In Feb 1984 a cat called Hamlet escaped from his cage on a flight from Toronto and was caught behind some paneling. He stayed there

for seven weeks, traveling just under 600,000 miles (965,600 km), approximately the same distance as going around the world 24 times.

BRAVEST ANIMALS
A Saint Bernard dog named Barry saved the lives of more than 40 people during his 12-year career in the Swiss Alps. His rescues included that of a boy who lay half-frozen under an avalanche in which his mother had died. Barry spread himself across the boy's body to warm him and licked the child's face until he woke up, and then carried him to the nearest dwelling.

On May 19 1997 Murphy, an Australian Army donkey, was posthumously awarded the RSPCA Australia Purple Cross on behalf of all the donkeys that served in the 1915–16 Gallipoli campaign in World War I. Murphy carried thousands of wounded soldiers to the field hospitals.

In Dec 1999 Charlie, a three-year-old gray parrot, saved the lives of Patricia Tunnicliffe of Durham, UK, and her five children, after a fire started in their home caused by Christmas lights igniting curtains. Charlie's squawks and shouts woke Patricia, and she was then able to get her five children out of the house unharmed. Unfortunately, Charlie was not so lucky.

www.guinnessworldrecords.com/skydivedog

DOGGY DIVERS TAKE PLUNGE
Katie, a Jack Russell cross (UK, above), became the first record doggy diver when she dived with her owner from 12,000 ft (3,658 m) over southern England in Oct 1987. She still holds the UK title.

However, since then, a miniature dachshund, Brutus the Skydiving Dog, excelled with a jump from a plane at an altitude of 15,000 ft (4,572 m) above Lake Elsinore, California, on May 20 1997. Brutus currently boasts 71 skydives in his canine career.

ACCESS CODE
‹56167› ←

GUINNESS WORLD RECORDS

www.guinnessworldrecords.com/worldmatters

world
matters

the enuironment

MOST POLLUTED MAJOR CITY

Mexico City is the world's most polluted city, having serious problems with sulfur dioxide, suspended particulate matter, carbon monoxide, and ozone (in all of which the World Health Organization guidelines are exceeded), plus moderate to heavy lead and nitrogen dioxide pollution.

HIGHEST CARBON DIOXIDE EMISSIONS

The USA has the highest emissions of CO_2, one of the key gases responsible for the 'greenhouse effect.' In 1999 the USA emitted 11,000 billion lb (5,500 million tonnes) of CO_2.

LOWEST CARBON DIOXIDE EMISSIONS

Of the major industrialized nations in the western hemisphere, France has the lowest emissions of CO_2. In 1999 France emitted 800 billion lb (400 million tonnes) of CO_2. France's commitment to nuclear power helps cut fossil fuel-related CO_2 emissions.

LARGEST HOLE IN THE OZONE LAYER

In Sept 2000 a hole in the ozone layer was detected above Antarctica that

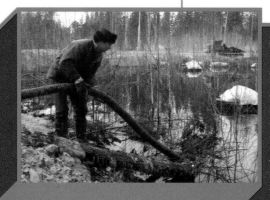

OIL DISASTER

Between Aug and Sept 1994 an area of the pristine Arctic tundra of the Komi Republic in Russia totaling 5,213 acres (2,110 ha) – the size of El Salvador – was contaminated with thousands of tons of oil flowing from damaged pipes transporting oil from an oil refining plant. Estimates of the amount of oil lost calculate that 31 million gal (117 million liters) were spilled. Known as the Usinsk accident (left), this is the worst case of land pollution that has ever occurred. The cost of the accident was estimated at more than 311 billion roubles ($10 billion).

‹49232›
www.guinnessworldrecords.com/oildisaster
← ACCESS CODE

measured about 11 million miles^2 (28.3 million km^2), which is roughly three times the size of the USA.

LOWEST OZONE LEVELS

Between Oct 9 and 14 1993 ozone levels reached a record low over the South Pole in Antarctica, when an average figure of 91 Dobson units (DU) was recorded. The Dobson unit measures the thickness of the ozone layer – 300 DU is considered to be adequate to shield the Earth from solar ultraviolet radiation and sustain biological systems as we know them.

Efforts are being made to reduce the global consumption of CFCs (chlorofluorocarbons) – the most prevalent ozone-depleting substance (ODS) – and it is hoped that by the year 2050 the ozone layer will have returned to safer, pre-1980 levels.

LARGEST WIND FARM

At Altamont Pass, California, the Pacific Gas and Electric Company has built a wind farm that covers 54 miles^2 (140 km^2) and has 7,300 wind turbines. Since 1981 the turbines have produced more than 6 billion kilowatt-hours of electricity – enough to give 800,000 homes power for one year.

LARGEST SOLAR ENERGY ROOF

The world's largest photovoltaic solar energy roof, which is 108,000 ft^2 (10,000 m^2), belongs to the Nordrhein-Westfalen Mont-Cenis Academy in Herne, Germany. The one megawatt roof has 3,185 solar cells, connected by 34 miles (55 km) of cabling, and yields over twice the annual power consumption of the building.

MOST ENERGY-EFFICIENT SUPERMARKET

J. Sainsbury PLC operates a 3,251-m^2 (35,000-ft^2) supermarket in Greenwich, London, UK, designed by architects Chetwood Associates. The supermarket's heating and electricity bill is 50% less than a normal supermarket of equivalent size. The store has a number of energy-saving features, including an on-site combined heat and power plant, wind turbines and photovoltaic cells.

LARGEST OFFSHORE OIL CONTAINMENT BOOM

An oil containment boom is a device used to contain oil spilled into the sea from pipelines, oil wells, tankers, and other vessels. Usually made of rubber, they inflate quickly to float on the surface of the water and prevent an oil slick from spreading. The biggest containment boom was developed by Ro-Clean Desmi in 2000 and is called the Ro-Boom 3500. It has an overall deflated width of 11 ft 5 in (3.5 m). In tests, it contained 95% of a 3,355-ft^3 (95-m^3) oil slick with a thickness of 5.5 in (14 cm). It can

SAY 'NO' TO OZONE

The SULEV-rated (Super Ultra-Low Emission Vehicle) Accord EX Sedan (left) which was developed by the Japanese company Honda, has the lowest emission levels of any gas-fueled car. Certified by the California Air Resources Board (CARB), a SULEV engine emits only 2.3 lb (1.04 kg) of ozone-forming hydrocarbons during 100,000 miles (161,000 km) of driving, which is about the same as spilling 32 fl oz (0.95 liters) of gas. This is an 86% reduction compared to a Low Emission Vehicle (LEV).

The rental company with the most low-emission cars is Kobe-Eco-Car (Japan), established on Jan 30 1999. It is dedicated to the rental of environmentally friendly vehicles and has a fleet of 53, made up of electric vehicles, compressed natural gas vehicles, and hybrid cars.

‹54216›
www.guinnessworldrecords.com/sulev
← ACCESS CODE

also contain oil traveling at speeds of up to 1.3 knots (1.5 mph or 2.4 km/h). The Ro-Boom can also contain and tow oil for long periods of time. It survived being towed for two weeks in the middle of winter and even contained oil in waves 23 ft (7 m) high.

LARGEST DEFORESTATION

Tropical forests are being cut down at a rate equivalent to 200 football fields every minute. The greatest rate of deforestation is in Jamaica where, in the 1980s and 1990s, 7% of its forests were cut down every year. In terms of size, Brazil has cleared the greatest amount of forest each year. In most years in the 1980s and 1990s, an area the size of Belgium (12,000 miles^2 or 30,500 km^2) was cleared and burned in the Amazon Basin of Brazil to create new pastures or farming land.

MOST CONTAMINATED LAKE

Lake Karachay in the Chelyabinsk province of Russia has accumulated 120 million curies of radioactivity and absorbed nearly 100 times more strontium 90 and caesium 137 than was released at Chernobyl in 1986. If a person stood on the shore of the lake he would receive a radiation exposure rate of 600 roentgens an hour. This is 2,000 times greater radiation than that emitted during a normal chest X ray and is strong enough to kill a person in an hour. The lake is near a Soviet nuclear facility called Mayak Chemical

Combine. The plant was shut down in 1990, but radiation emitted still either evaporates and is dispersed by the wind, or is absorbed by sand particles and sediment at the bottom of the lake.

MOST ACIDIC WATER

Normally pH values range from 0 to 14, with 7 (the pH factor of water) being neutral. The lower the number, the higher the acid level of the given substance. When sampled in 1990–91, water running through the Richmond Mine at Iron Mountain, California, had a pH value of -3.6. The source of the acid in the water was hot acid solutions dripping off colored stalactites in an abandoned copper and zinc mine.

www.guinnessworldrecords.com/tankerspill

KNOCKOUT BLOW TO COASTAL LIFE

On March 25 1989 the *Exxon Valdez* oil tanker collided with Bligh Reef in Prince William Sound, Alaska, spilling more than 11 million gal (41 million liters) of oil and causing the worst ever coastal damage in an environmental disaster. A total of 1,500 miles (2,400 km) of coast were polluted, and the diverse and populous marine ecosystem of the sound was devastated (below). Between 3,000 and 5,000 sea otters

ACCESS CODE

‹49233› ←

perished, and current otter populations continue to be contaminated by the toxic hydrocarbons from the oil pollution. Seabirds suffered losses of an estimated 1,000,000, and around 20 Orca whales were killed. The company was fined $5 billion (£3 billion), on top of a cleanup bill of $3 billion (£2 billion). The captain admitted that he drank three double vodkas before setting sail with the 900-ft (274.3-m) long ship.

GUINNESS WORLD RECORDS™

consumption and waste

HIGHEST GNI PER CAPITA

Of the 260 countries for which figures were available to the World Bank in 1999, Luxembourg was the country with the highest Gross National Income (the total dollar value of goods and services produced by a country in one year divided by its population) with a spending per person of 1,724,755 Luxembourg francs ($42,960/£26,577). Luxembourg is about the size of Greater London, UK, and has a population of only 429,080 (1999), 30% of which are foreign nationals. The GNI per capita for the UK is $23,590 (£14,593) and for the US is $31,910 (£19,740).

LOWEST GNI PER CAPITA

In 1999, Ethiopia had the lowest GNI per capita – 704,410 Ethiopian Birr ($100).

HIGHEST FOOD CONSUMPTION

Argentina consumes the most food per head, with each citizen consuming 183% of the 1996 FAO (United Nations Food and Agriculture Organization) recommended requirement. Portugal came second at 149%, followed by Ireland (142%), the USA, Hong Kong, Turkey, UAE, and Yugoslavia (all 140%).

LOWEST FOOD CONSUMPTION

According to the UN's food agency the country with the lowest food consumption is Tajikistan (formerly in the USSR). Each citizen consumes only 55% of the FAO recommended minimum daily requirement. Somalia comes second with 67%.

HIGHEST PER CAPITA COFFEE CONSUMPTION

The country that consumes the most coffee per capita is Finland, where 24.91 lb (11.3 kg) of coffee per person was consumed in 1998. The total amount of coffee consumed in Finland in 1998 was 127.8 million lb (58,000 tonnes). This is roughly equivalent to 1,737 cups of coffee per person per year, or five cups a day. The same year the USA consumed the greatest total amount of coffee in the world – an estimated 2.5 billion lb (1,148,000 tonnes), which is 9.26 lb (4.2 kg) or 646 cups annually per person.

HIGHEST TEA CONSUMPTION

Paraguay (population 5,359,000 in 1999) is the country that consumes the most tea per person – 25.79 lb (11.7 kg) of tea each in 1998, which is roughly 14.62 cups per person per day. The UK and Ireland came joint 7th. However, India consumes the most tea overall worldwide – drinking a massive 1.4 billion lb (640,000 tonnes) in 1998, compared with Paraguay's 1.3 billion lb (61,000 tonnes). China was second to India at 1.03 billion lb (466,000 tonnes); the UK consumed 321.8 million lb (146,000 tonnes).

A YEN FOR THE HIGH LIFE?

In 2000, for the ninth year, *The Economist* Intelligence Unit's biannual survey (to aid the calculation of salary packages for employees relocating overseas) revealed that Tokyo was the world's most expensive city. The survey is based on the varying costs of 90 shopping items in 126 cities. Taking New York as a median 100, Tokyo scored 164. Osaka, Japan, came second with 161, with Hong Kong third with 120. Oslo and Zurich came joint 5th as the most expensive European cities, followed by London in 7th place. New York was the most expensive US city, ranking 12th worldwide.

‹53711› www.guinnessworldrecords.com/highcosttokyo
← ACCESS CODE

HIGHEST CONFECTIONERY CONSUMPTION

According to a report by the candy manufacturers Cadbury and Trebor Bassett, the UK spent more than £5 billion ($8,252,500,300) on candy in 1997. The average UK resident ate 35 lb (16 kg) of candy that year, ahead of the USA's 22 lb (10 kg), France's 19 lb (9 kg), and Japan's 6.6 lb (3 kg). Londoners eat the least candy, spending £1.45 ($2.39) per person a week, while those living in the West Country and Wales spend the most with £2.09 ($3.44).

HIGHEST BOVINE MEAT CONSUMPTION

Argentina consumes the most bovine meat (beef and veal) per person. In 1998, each Argentinian ate 124.12 lb (56.3 kg) of bovine meat – a total of 4.5 billion lb (2,033,000 tonnes). Overall, however, in 1998 the USA consumed the most bovine meat – 26.5 billion lb (12,048,000 tonnes) – 97 lb (44 kg) per capita.

PARTY TIME

The Czech Republic is the world's leading beer consumer per capita, with each person drinking an average of 42.7 gal (160 liters) in 1998. The country as a whole consumed 436.68 million gal (1,653 million liters) during 1998. The USA consumed the greatest volume of beer in the world in the same year, drinking 6.439 million gal (24,376 million liters) – an average of 23.5 gal (89 liters) per person.

The record for the world's greatest per-capita wine consumption goes to Luxembourg with 16.7 gal (63.3 liters) per person. The smallest measurable wine consumer is Egypt, where the average yearly wine consumption is about 2 tablespoons.

‹46083› www.guinnessworldrecords.com/beerdrinkers
← ACCESS CODE

www.guinnessworldrecords.com/trash

TRASHED!

The USA produces most of the world's municipal waste, according to the Organization for Economic Cooperation and Development (1999), at an estimated figure of 1,587 lb (720 kg) per person. Fresh Kills landfill, on Staten Island, New York, (below), which covers 2,965 acres (1,200 ha) is the world's largest garbage dump, estimated to contain 220 million lb (100 million tonnes) of garbage. The site, just 15 miles (24 km) from the heart of Manhattan, is the size of 2,400 American football fields and is as high as a 17-story building. At its peak in the mid-1990s, 28.6 million lb (13,000 tonnes) of garbage was processed every day. Around 5.9 million lb (2,700 tonnes) of methane gas is released daily due to decomposition.

ACCESS CODE ‹49718›

HIGHEST HONEY CONSUMPTION

In 1998, in the Central African Republic, 6.61 lb (3 kg) of honey was consumed per person – a national total of 22 million lb (10,000 tonnes). However, the UK consumed the greatest amount of honey overall, getting through 50.7 million lb (23,000 tonnes), an average of 14.1 oz (400 g) per person.

HIGHEST CHEESE CONSUMPTION

The inhabitants of Greece ate an astonishing average of 60.63 lb (27.5 kg) of cheese per person in 1998. The country as a whole consumed 643.75 million lb (292,000 tonnes). Feta, Gaviera, Kasseri, and Myzithra are some of Greece's more popular cheeses. In the same year the USA consumed the most cheese in the world – a total of 8.5 billion lb (3,837,000 tonnes) – 30.86 lb (14 kg) per person.

HIGHEST ELECTRICITY CONSUMPTION

The USA used 3,235.9 billion kilowatts per hour in 1999. This is equal to almost a quarter of the total net electricity consumption of the entire world, which came to 12,832.7 billion kilowatts per hour.

LARGEST ENERGY CONSUMPTION

The USA is the world's largest consumer of both fossil fuels (coal, oil, and natural gas) and commercial energy (fossil fuels plus nuclear and hydro power). In 1998 it consumed a total of 1,937 Mtoe (million tonnes of oil equivalent) of fossil fuels and 2,147 Mtoe of commercial energy. In the same year, the total world energy consumption of fossil fuels was 7,624 Mtoe and the total world energy consumption of commercial fuel was 8,477 Mtoe.

HIGHEST SOLAR ENERGY USE

Switzerland has the highest per-capita solar usage in the world, with 1.82 watts per capita. In Germany 0.71 watts of solar power is used per capita, while Japan is in third place in terms of solar power usage with 0.65 watts per capita.

GUINNESS WORLD RECORDS

crime and punishment

BEST POLICE DOG

The world's top police dog is Trepp, a Golden Retriever, owned by Tom Kazo (USA). Trepp, short for Intrepid, has been credited with more than 100 arrests and the recovery of narcotics worth more than $63 million (£44 million). Within his first two months on the job, Trepp had sniffed 3,351 lb (1.52 tonnes) of unlawful substances. Trepp was once ordered to detect 10 hidden packets of drugs at a demonstration – and found 11.

OLDEST PRISONER

Bill Wallace is the oldest prisoner on record – he spent the last 63 years of his life in Aradale Psychiatric Hospital, Ararat, Vic, Australia. He shot and killed a man in Dec 1925 and, having been found unfit to plead, was transferred to the Mental Health Department in Feb 1926. He remained there until his death on July 17 1989, shortly before his 108th birthday.

LONGEST PRISON ESCAPE

The longest recorded escape by a recaptured prisoner was that of Leonard Fristoe, age 77, who escaped from the Nevada State Prison, Carson City, Nevada, on Dec 15 1923. Fristoe was turned in by his son on Nov 15 1969 at Compton, California. By then Fristoe had enjoyed nearly 46 years of freedom under the name of Claude R. Willis. His crime was killing two sheriff's deputies in 1920.

LONGEST STAY IN SOLITARY CONFINEMENT

Mordecai Vanunu (Israel) has spent nearly 12 years in a total isolation jail cell – the longest known term of solitary confinement in modern times. Born in 1955, Vanunu was convicted of treason for giving information about Israel's nuclear program to London's *Sunday Times* newspaper. He was held in isolation from 1986 until March 1998. Not long afterward, the prison gate was opened, and he finally walked away a free man.

‹54910›
www.guinnessworldrecords.com/prisonwedding
← ACCESS CODE

MOST COMMON METHOD OF EXECUTION

The most common method of execution is by firing squad, which is practiced in 73 countries. In 45 of these countries, this is the sole method of executing criminals. Hanging is the second most common method, and is practiced in 58 countries worldwide. Beheading is still practiced in three countries, while electrocution is practiced only in the USA.

NO GETTING AWAY WITH MURDER

The longest sentence imposed on a mass murderer was 21 consecutive life sentences and 12 death sentences. John Gacy (left) killed 33 boys and young men during a six-year killing spree from 1972 to 1978 in Illinois. He was sentenced by a Chicago jury on March 13 1980 and executed by lethal injection at Stateville Prison in Joilet, Illinois, on May 10 1994.

The most prolific female murderer in the western world was Elizabeth Bathori, who practiced vampirism on girls and young women. Throughout the 15th century, she is alleged to have killed more than 600 virgins in order to drink their blood and bathe in it – to preserve her youth. When her murderous career was discovered, she was walled up in her castle from 1610 until her death in 1614.

‹55421›
www.guinnessworldrecords.com/murdersentence
← ACCESS CODE

MOST SECURE PRISON

The United States Penitentiary, Administrative Maximum Facility 'Supermax' Prison, set in wasteland west of Pueblo, southern Colorado, is equipped with laser beams, 1,400 remote-controlled steel doors, motion detectors, pressure pads, and silent-attack dogs, and surrounded by razor wire and guard towers. With a 'level-6' security rating, inmates are often locked in their cells for 23 hours a day and for the remaining hour must wear leg-irons and handcuffs.

FOR BETTER OR FOR WORSE

One hundred and twenty inmates of Carandiru prison, São Paulo, Brazil, married their fiancées at the largest mass wedding ceremony in a prison on June 14 2000 (left). Officials and evangelical pastors made Carandiru's cell block 6 into a temporary church. The brides (who traditionally show up late for weddings) and the guests had to turn up two hours before the ceremony for a body search. The grooms wore jackets and ties. The only thing that gave them away as inmates were their beige trousers, which form part of the prison uniform. The Detention House, Carandiru's formal name, houses 7,400 inmates and is best known for a massacre by police in 1992 that left 111 inmates dead.

MOST PROLIFIC CANNIBAL

During the 19th century Ratu Udre Udre reportedly ate between 872 and 999 people. The Fijian chief had kept a stone to record each body eaten, and these are placed along his tomb in Rakiraki, northern Viti Levu, Fiji.

LARGEST ART ROBBERY

On April 14 1991, 20 paintings, worth around $500 million (£280 million), were stolen from the Van Gogh

Museum in Amsterdam, Netherlands. They were found in an abandoned car not far from the museum, just 35 minutes later.

LARGEST JEWEL HEIST

A three-man gang bearing machine-guns barged into the Carlton Hotel jewelry shop in Cannes, France, and stole gems with an estimated value of FF250 million ($45 million) on Aug 11 1994. This is the biggest recorded theft of jewels.

LONGEST-SERVING POLITICAL PRISONER

Kim Sung-myun served a lengthy 43 years and 10 months in prison in Seoul, South Korea, for supporting Communist North Korea. He was released at the age of 70 in Aug 1995, having never read a newspaper or watched television while in prison.

LARGEST CRIMINAL GANG

The Yamaguchi-gumi gang of the *yakuza* in Japan has 30,000 members. There are about 90,000 *yakuza* or gangsters altogether, in more than 3,000 groups. The *yakuza* carry on their business openly and even advertise for recruits.

LARGEST KIDNAP RANSOM

Two Hong Kong businessmen, Walter Kwok and Victor Li, paid gangster Cheung Tze-keung a record total of $206 million (£134 million) in return for their freedom after they were kidnapped separately in 1996 and 1997 respectively. Cheung was executed in China on Dec 5 1998.

www.guinnessworldrecords.com/oldsparky

ACCESS CODE

OLD SPARKY

'Old Sparky' (right), also known as the 'Texas Thunderbolt,' was the first chair used for electrocutions in Texas. It was built in 1923–24 by an inmate who was facing the death penalty, and used until 1964. Before 1923, hanging was the primary means of execution in Texas.

Between Jan 1974 and April 2001, Texas executed (now by lethal injection) a record 244 criminals – more than any other US state. Virginia follows with 82 executions and Florida is third with 51.

‹56558› ←

MOST PRISONERS

According to figures released by Amnesty International in Feb 2000 the prison population in the USA topped two million. This accounts for 25% of the world's prison population, yet the USA accounts for only 5% of the world's population. The USA's per capita prison population is 565 prisoners per 100,000 people.

LEAST PRISONERS

Slovenia is the country with the least prisoners. It has under 500 prisoners in a population of just under two million. Few offenders are jailed – instead community service, probation, and similar programs are employed. The Slovene prisoners represent a mere 25 out of every 100,000 of the population.

LARGEST PRISON SYSTEM

The US state of California has the biggest prison system in the industrialized world. The single state holds more inmates in its jails and prisons than do France, Great Britain, Germany, Japan, Singapore, and the Netherlands combined. More than 626 out of every 100,000 people in California are incarcerated.

MOST ARRESTS

By 1988, Tommy Johns of Brisbane, Qld, Australia, had been arrested a total of nearly 3,000 times for being drunk and disorderly in a public place. Ironically, he died in April 1988 at the age of 66, from a brain tumor rather than a alcohol-related illness.

LARGEST FRAUD

Porn webmaster Kenneth Taves (USA) is believed to have committed the largest fraud carried out by one person, with a total of $38 million (£23.3 million) in unauthorized credit card charges by 2001. Taves got hold of credit card numbers belonging to nearly four million consumers who had bought items from merchants with accounts at Charter Pacific. The 49-year-old resubmitted up to 800,000 of the credit card numbers to his merchant service with instructions to charge each account $19.95 (£12.25) per month. Taves pleaded guilty in federal court and faces a maximum penalty of 30 years in prison.

GUINNESS WORLD RECORDS

war and weapons

BLOODIEST SIEGE

The worst siege in history was when Leningrad, USSR (now St. Petersburg, Russia), was besieged by the German army for 880 days from Aug 30 1941 until Jan 27 1944. It was estimated that between 1.3 and 1.5 million defenders and citizens lost their lives. This number included 641,000 people who died of starvation in the city and 17,000 civilians who were killed by shelling. More than 150,000 shells and 100,000 bombs were dropped on the city.

I SPY

The smallest spy plane in existence is the palm-sized Black Widow (above), developed by AeroVironment of Monrovia, California, for possible reconnaissance use by ground combat troops. It has a wingspan of 6 in (15.24 cm), weighs just 2.8 oz (80 g), and carries a tiny color video camera weighing 0.07 oz (2 g). The Black Widow has a speed of 30 mph (50 km/h), a maximum range of 1.24 miles (2 km), and can stay airborne for 30 minutes. Although it has an autopilot, it will typically be controlled by a pilot navigating by live video relayed from its onboard camera. The entire ground control system and launcher fits into a briefcase-sized box. The solid wings are manufactured from lightweight expanded polystyrene foam and propulsion is provided by a battery-powered electric motor.

www.guinnessworldrecords.com/
spyplane

ACCESS CODE
‹56237› ←

HIGHEST BATTLEFIELD

Since 1984 the Indian and Pakistani armies have fought each other on the Siachen Glacier, in the disputed territory of Kashmir, at a height of up to 22,000 ft (6,700 m). At this altitude, they are higher than climbers standing on the summits of the tallest mountains in Africa, North America, Australasia, Europe, and Antarctica. Reports suggest that Pakistan spends as much as $588,000 (£354,000) a month and India about $1 million (£600,000) a month maintaining troops on the glacier.

SHORTEST WAR

The shortest war on record was between the UK and Zanzibar (now part of Tanzania) in 1896. On Aug 25 Sultan Hamid bin Thuwaini died. Two hours later, the self-appointed Sultan Seyyid Khalid bin Bargash broke into the palace and declared himself the new ruler. The Royal Navy, under the command of Rear Admiral Harry Rawson, delivered an ultimatum. At precisely 9 o'clock on Aug 27, three warships opened fire and in 45 minutes completely destroyed the palace and killed the usurper.

MOST HEAVILY ARMED TANK

The most heavily armed tanks in recent times are the Russian T-64, T-72, T-80, and T-90 tanks, which have a 4.92-in (12.5-cm) gun-missile launcher system.

LARGEST ARMY

The People's Liberation Army of China had 2.2 million service personnel as of May 2000.

LONGEST EMBASSY SIEGE

In Sept 1979 a crowd of about 500 people seized the US embassy in Tehran, Iran. Of the approximately 90 people inside the embassy, 52 remained in captivity until the end of the crisis 444 days later, making this the longest embassy siege ever. The American hostages were seized in response to the exiled Shah of Iran's admission to the USA for medical treatment. The hostage release coincided with President Reagan's inauguration day on Jan 20 1981.

ENEMY AT THE GATE

The greatest death toll in a battle has been estimated at 1,109,000 in the Battle of Stalingrad, USSR (now Volgograd, Russia, above), which started in the summer of 1942 and ended with the surrender of the German Sixth Army on 31 Jan 1943.

The 142-day battle of the Somme, France (1 July–19 Nov 1916) is in the same league. There are no exact figures, but the estimate for dead *and* wounded is calculated to have been at least 1,220,000 men, of which 398,671 were British (57,470 on the first day) and more than 800,000 were German and French.

www.guinnessworldrecords.com/battledeaths

‹46252› ← **ACCESS CODE**

BLOODIEST WAR

The most costly war in terms of human life was World War II (1939–45), in which the total number of fatalities, including battle deaths and civilians, is estimated to have been 56.4 million – roughly equivalent to the population of the UK.

HIGHEST DEATH TOLL FROM A NON NUCLEAR RAID

On March 10 1945 about 83,000 people were killed in an Allied bombing raid on Tokyo, Japan. Total Japanese fatalities in World War II were 600,000 killed by conventional weapons and 220,000 by the nuclear attacks on Hiroshima and Nagasaki.

GREATEST DEATH TOLL FROM A SINGLE CHEMICAL WARFARE ATTACK

The greatest number of people killed in a single chemical weapons attack is estimated at 4,000, when President Saddam Hussein of Iraq attacked members of his country's Kurdish minority at Halabja, Iraq, in March 1988. The attack was punishment for the support the Kurds had given to Iran in the Iran–Iraq war (1980–90).

LONGEST-RANGE AIR ATTACKS

Seven B-52G bombers, which took off from Barksdale Air Force Base, Louisiana, on Jan 16 1991, flew 14,000 miles (22,500 km) to deliver cruise missiles against targets in Iraq during the Gulf War. They refueled four times in flight, with the round-trip mission lasting 35 hours.

MOST SIBLINGS TO SERVE IN WORLD WAR II

Seven brothers from the Pritchard family (UK) served in the Armed Forces between 1939 and 1945. One, Ronald (Royal Navy), was killed in action in 1942. The six surviving sons were Idris (Royal Marines); Clifford (Parachute Regiment); Horace and David (Royal Artillery); James (Royal Army Service Corps); and Albert (Royal Pioneer Corps).

MOST EXPENSIVE PEACEKEEPING OPERATION

UNPROFOR (United Nations Protection Force) cost $4.6 billion (£2.97 billion) from Jan 12 1992 to March 31 1996, for peacekeeping duties in the former Yugoslavia.

www.guinnessworldrecords.com/vxgas

CHEMICAL ABUSE

VX gas is the most deadly chemical warfare agent – a mere 10 mg (a raindrop weighs around 80 mg) on the skin will kill most people. Some nations, such as Iraq, are thought to possess such weapons and if a threat is thought to exist, the military wears protective clothing. Pictured right is a US soldier wearing nuclear-biological-chemical warfare gear during an exercise in Egypt in 1989.

ACCESS CODE

‹47180› ←

GREATEST RANGE OF A GUN

The long-range gun that shelled Paris in World War I was the *Paris-Geschetz* 'Paris Gun,' with a caliber of 8.25 in (21 cm), a designed range of 79.5 miles (127.9 km), and an achieved range of 76 miles (122 km).

LARGEST AIR FORCE

The largest air force, in terms of aircraft, is that of the USA, which had 4,413 combat aircraft as of Sept 1999. This total includes 179 bombers, 1,666 fighter and attack aircraft, and 1,279 trainer aircraft.

MOST EXPENSIVE MILITARY AIRCRAFT

The US-made Boeing B-2 Spirit is priced at $1.3 billion (£780 million). A long-range multirole bomber, it is capable of delivering both conventional and nuclear munitions, and has a number of stealth characteristics that enable it to penetrate an enemy's defenses without being observed.

LARGEST DEFENSE CONTRACTOR

The world's largest producer of military and defense-related equipment is the Lockheed Martin Corporation (USA), which, in 1999, had global sales totaling $25.5 billion (£17.8 billion), with the US government its biggest customer.

HIGHEST RATE OF FIRE FROM A BALLISTIC WEAPON

The prototype 36-barrel gun built by Metal Storm of Brisbane, Australia, has a firing rate in excess of 1 million rounds per minute (16,666 bullets per second). Such high rates of fire are achievable because the rounds are fired electrically by computer, rather than by a 'hammer' detonator. In comparison, the fastest firing machine gun, the M134 minigun, fires at a rate of 6,000 rounds per minute.

MOST SOPHISTICATED HANDGUN

The O'Dwyer Variable Lethality Law Enforcement (VLE) prototype pistol, made by Metal Storm, has no moving parts, with projectiles fired electronically by a built-in computer processor. The gun can only be fired by someone wearing an authorized transponder ring, and is capable of firing up to three shots within 0.002 sec, equivalent to 60,000 rounds per minute. While it seems that only one shot has been fired, the results are far more deadly. In addition, the pistol provides audible and visual confirmation of its settings.

MOST DESTRUCTIVE NONLETHAL WEAPON

The BLU-114/B 'graphite bomb' deployed by NATO against Serbia in May 1999, disabled 70% of its power grid with minimal 'direct' casualties. A similar device was used during the Gulf War (1990–91) to knock out 85% of Iraq's electricity-generating capacity. These so-called 'soft bombs' work by exploding a cloud of hundreds of ultrafine carbon-fiber wires over electrical installations, causing the electrical systems to short-circuit and temporarily halt the supply.

HIGHEST DEFENSE SPEND

It is estimated that world spending on defense reached a peak of $1,000 billion (£681.523 billion) in 1986–87, about $200 (£136) per head of world population. Between 1993 and 1994 expenditure fell from $823 billion (£548 billion) to $795 billion (£529 billion) – a trend that has continued.

GUINNESS WORLD RECORDS

disasters

DANGER IN THE SKIES

The world's worst midair collision involving balloons occurred on Aug 13 1989, when two balloons (above) collided at a height of 2,000 ft (610 m), resulting in 13 fatalities. The two passenger balloons were launched a few minutes apart for a sightseeing flight over Alice Springs, Northern Territory, Australia. The basket of one of the balloons tore a hole in the fabric of the other, which then collapsed. The pilot and 12 passengers died.

The worst airship disaster involved the US Navy Airship Akron, which killed 73 people when it was ripped apart in a storm off the New Jersey coast on April 3 1933.

The worst midair collision involving an airplane happened when a Saudi Boeing 747 scheduled flight crashed with a Kazakh Ilushin 76 charter flight, killing 351 people. The crash occurred 50 miles (80 km) southwest of New Delhi, India, on Nov 12 1996.

<52449>
www.guinnessworldrecords.com/ballooncollision
← ACCESS CODE

WORST TUNNELING DISASTER

Between 1931 and 1935 at the Hawk's Nest hydroelectric tunnel, West Virginia, around 2,500 people were killed – the majority through exposure to rock dust that contained silica. Many of them contracted silicosis, a condition that decreases lung capacity and can lead to diseases like pneumonia and TB. This was the worst occupational-health disaster in American history.

WORST FAMINE DEATH TOLL

In the years between 1959 and 1961 approximately 40,000,000 people died from malnutrition in the Great Famine of China. In part, the famine was a direct result of unsuccessful new farming methods that were introduced by Chairman Mao after the formation of the People's Republic of China in 1949.

WORST ROAD ACCIDENT

On Nov 3 1982 a gas tanker exploded inside the Salang Tunnel, Afghanistan. Local estimates suggest that 176 people died (Western estimates quote over 1,100). Either way, it is the worst road accident ever. The Salang Pass, which is 67 miles (108 km) long, is one of the most expensive stretches of road in the world, having cost $42 million (£24 million) to build.

WORST NUCLEAR REACTOR DISASTER

At 1:23 a.m. local time on April 26 1986, a nuclear reactor disaster at Chernobyl's No. 4 reactor in the former USSR (now the Ukraine), resulted in an official Soviet death toll of 31 people. No systematic records were kept of subsequent deaths, but over 1.7 million people were exposed to varying amounts of radiation. A total of 135,000 people were evacuated, while another 850,000 people are still living in the contaminated regions. The contamination covers a total area of 10,900 miles^2 (28,200 km^2) in Russia and Belarus. An estimated 200,000 people were involved in the cleanup operation.

WORST YEAR FOR AIR CRASHES

In 1988 the average fatality rate for scheduled flights was 175 per million departures, making it the worst year for air crashes. The African continent had an average of 190 fatalities per million departures for scheduled flights; Latin America, including Mexico, had 70 to 80 fatalities per million departures; North America and Canada had 25 fatalities per million departures, followed by Europe, which had an average of six to seven fatalities per million departures. The risk of air fatalities has fallen by a third since then.

WORST SINGLE AIRCRAFT DISASTER

The crash of JAL's Boeing 747 flight 123, near Tokyo on Aug 12 1985, in which 520 passengers and crew perished, was the worst single-plane crash in aviation history.

WORST UNDERGROUND TRAIN DISASTER

On Oct 28 1995 about 300 people were killed (and at least 250 people injured), when their subway train caught fire in a tunnel at Baku, Azerbaijan. Official reports blamed the fire on an electrical malfunction. Some reports suggested a bomb. Many of the passengers were killed by carbon-monoxide poisoning, when toxic materials in the train carriages caught fire. Other victims were crushed in the ensuing panic.

WORST TRAIN DISASTER

On June 6 1981 more than 800 passengers died when seven cars of their passenger train plunged off a bridge into the Bagmati River at Samastipur, Bihar, India. Confusion exists over the exact cause – some reports claim that the train struck a buffalo, while others say that its brakes failed catastrophically. Some reports put the death toll at 900, although it could have been twice that number.

WORST PEACETIME SINGLE-SHIP DISASTER

The paddle steamer *Sultana* sank on the Mississippi River, Memphis, Tennessee, on April 21 1865, when her boilers exploded, with the loss of more than 1,650 lives. Poor recordkeeping at the time of boarding means that the actual number of passengers aboard the *Sultana* will always be unclear. Some historians believe that between 2,200 and 2,300 people were probably aboard. By law, she was allowed to carry only 376 people.

WORST SUBMARINE DISASTER

The French submarine *Surcouf* sank with 159 crewmen on board after it was rammed by US merchantman *Thompson Lykes* in the Caribbean on Feb 18 1942. At the time of her sinking, *Surcouf* was the world's largest submarine – 361 ft (110 m) long. Today's largest are the Russian Typhoon class nuclear submarines, which are 558 ft (170 m) in length.

WORST YEAR FOR FOREST FIRES

Deliberately lit forest fires made 1997 the worst year in recorded history for the destruction of the natural environment. The largest and most numerous forest fires were in Brazil, where they raged along a 1,000-mile (1,600-km) front near the Amazon rain forest. The Brazilian Government and the international community were put on the alert due to the severity of the situation.

The second most destructive forest fires in 1997 were in Indonesia, covering large areas of Southeast Asia with smog and resulting in over 40,000 people being hospitalized with breathing problems.

WORST DISASTER CAUSED BY MASS PANIC

Around 4,000 people were killed on June 6 1941 at an air-raid shelter in Chongqing, China. The crowd was leaving the shelter after an air raid when the warning siren sounded again. The 4,000 deaths were due to suffocation and trampling as the crowd tried to return to the shelter.

WORST MOUNTAINEERING DISASTER

On Peak Lenin (23,406 ft or 7,134 m) on the border between Tajikistan and Kyrgyzstan (then USSR), 43 people were killed in a massive ice and snow avalanche triggered by a small earthquake on July 13 1990. Only two of the expedition's climbers survived the mountaineering accident.

WORST DEATH TOLL FROM AN OFFSHORE OIL DISASTER

The largest offshore oil disaster occurred on July 6 1988 when a fire started on the Piper Alpha oil platform in the North Sea, killing 167 people.

WORST AVALANCHE DISASTERS

An estimated 40,000 to 80,000 men lost their lives during World War I in the Tyrolean Alps, after avalanches were triggered by gunfire. A total of 18,000 Austrian and Italian troops were lost in the Dolomite valleys of northern Italy on Dec 13 1916 after more than 100 avalanches ripped through the region.

WORST SPACE-RELATED DISASTER

In the greatest space-related disaster that took place on the ground, 91 people were killed when an R-16 rocket exploded during fueling at the Baikonur Space Center, Kazakhstan, on Oct 24 1960.

WORST MANNED SPACEFLIGHT DISASTERS

On Jan 28 1986 the worst manned spaceflight disaster occurred when *Challenger 51L* exploded 73 seconds after liftoff from the Kennedy Space Center, Florida, at a height of 46,000 ft (14,020 m). The crew of five men and two women died on board. NASA's other space shuttles were grounded for nearly three years while investigations took place to ensure that such a disaster never happened again.

Four people, all Soviet, have been killed during actual spaceflight – Vladimir Komarov of *Soyuz 1*, which crashed on landing on April 24 1967; and Georgi Dobrovolsky, Viktor Patsayev, and Vladislav Volkov died when their *Soyuz 11* spacecraft depressurized during reentry to the Earth's atmosphere on June 29 1971.

WORST INDUSTRIAL CHEMICAL DISASTER

Up to 4,000 people were killed and thousands more were left with permanent disabilities after a toxic cloud of methyl isocyanate (MIC) gas enveloped a settlement around the Union Carbide Corporation's pesticide plant in Bhopal, India, on Dec 3 1984. Reports claimed that the gas leak occurred after a disgruntled employee added water to a storage tank, causing heat and pressure to build up inside until the lethal gas escaped. After legal wranglings, the Indian Supreme Court made Union Carbide Corporation pay $470 million (£310 million) in compensation to the victims and their families.

www.guinnessworldrecords.com/concordecrash

CONCORDE TRAGEDY

On July 25 2000 an Air France Concorde (above) crashed, killing 113 people (all 100 passengers, nine crew members and four people on the ground). Concorde took off from Charles de Gaulle Airport, Paris, France, bound for New York City, USA. It was brought down soon after taking off by an explosion in one of its fuel tanks, which was pierced by rubber thrown up at high speed by a burst tire. The tire was punctured by a piece of metal on the runway. The aircraft nosedived and crashed into a three-story hotel near Gonesse. This is the third supersonic passenger jet accident and the one with the highest death toll.

ACCESS CODE

‹55378›

GUINNESS WORLD RECORDS™

explosions

MOST POWERFUL NUCLEAR EXPLOSION

The most powerful thermonuclear device so far tested is one dubbed 'Tsar Bomba' with a power equivalent to that of approximately 57 megatons of TNT, which was detonated by the former USSR above the remote Arctic island of Novaya Zemlya. The 56,000-lb (28-tonne) bomb was air-dropped at 8.33 a.m. GMT on Oct 30 1961. The shockwave circled the world three times, with the first circuit taking 36 hr 27 min. Some estimates put the power of this device at between 62 and 90 megatons.

GREATEST EXPLOSION EVER

Most astronomers now believe that the universe began about 12 billion years ago in a cataclysmic explosion that we now call 'Big Bang.' All the matter and energy in the universe had its origins in this event, along with time itself. One second after Big Bang, the temperature was around 10,000 million degrees – around 600 times hotter than the interior of the Sun.

LARGEST IMPACT ON EARTH

Most astronomers now believe that, 4.5 billion years ago, a planet the size of Mars collided with the young Earth. Some of the debris from this cataclysm went into orbit around the Earth and collected under its own gravity to form the Moon. The effect of this impact would have been devastating to the Earth. The entire crust of the planet would probably have been blasted off leaving Earth with a surface made solely of molten magma.

MOST POWERFUL SPACE-BASED NUCLEAR EXPLOSION

On July 9 1962 a 1.45-megaton nuclear explosion occurred in space 248 miles (399 km) above Johnston Island (Christmas Island) in the Pacific Ocean. The 16,655-lb (7,550-kg) warhead, codenamed 'starfish,' was launched by the US Air Force. The explosion was 100 times more powerful than the 1945 Hiroshima blast and formed its own artificial aurora as radioactive particles interacted with the Earth's magnetic field. The height of this detonation equals the orbital altitude of the Space Shuttle.

LARGEST NUCLEAR EXPLOSION CRATER

A 104-kiloton nuclear device was detonated at the Semipalatinsk Test Site, Kazakhstan, 583 ft (178 m) beneath the dry bed of the Chagan River on Jan 15 1965. It left a crater that was 1,338 ft (408 m) wide with a maximum depth of 328 ft (100 m). A major lake later formed behind the 65–114-ft (20–35-m) upraised lip of the crater, which was then cut through with earthmoving equipment to allow it to be used as a reservoir.

HEAVIEST NUCLEAR BOMB

The heaviest known nuclear bomb in operational service was the MK 17 carried by US B-36 bombers in the mid-1950s. It weighed 42,000 lb (19.05 tonnes) and was 24 ft 6 in (7.47 m) long. It had a maximum yield of 20 megatons, equivalent to a thousand Hiroshima bombs. The MK 17 design was tested in the 1954 Castle Romeo nuclear test at Bikini Atoll in the South Pacific, producing an 11-megaton blast.

DEEPEST UNDERGROUND NUCLEAR EXPLOSION

A 2.5-kiloton nuclear device was detonated at the bottom of a 9,350-ft-deep (2,850-m) shaft at a location 37 miles (60 km) south of Nefte-yugamsk, Siberia, Russia, on June 18 1985. This is roughly one-eighth the size of the Hiroshima atomic explosion (the Hiroshima bomb had a yield of 20 kilotons). The detonation was carried out in an attempt to stimulate oil and gas production in the area.

GONE BALLISTIC!

The most destructive ICBM (intercontinental ballistic missile) is the former USSR's SS-18 Model 5 (above), which is accurate to within 820 ft (250 m), and is armed with 10 MIRVs (multiple independently targetable reentry vehicles), each with a yield equivalent to 750 kilotons of TNT. During the Cold War the SS-18 was the most feared weapon in the Warsaw Pact armory. START 2 (Strategic Arms Reduction Talks) requires that all SS-18s, and other ICBMs with more than one warhead, are eliminated.

www.guinnessworldrecords.com/ballisticmissile
ACCESS CODE
<46277> ←

MOST NUCLEAR WEAPONS DETONATED SIMULTANEOUSLY

A minimum of eight nuclear weapons were detonated simultaneously in an underground tunnel at the Russian test site at Novaya Zemyla on Oct 24 1990. The simultaneous explosions were carried out for maximum power and to beat the deadline for the Soviet moratorium on nuclear testing

LARGEST SINGLE CONVENTIONAL EXPLOSION

The demolition of the German fortifications at Heligoland, a North Sea island, on April 18 1947 used a charge of 8,952,970 lb (4,061 tonnes). During both World Wars the island served as a major German naval base. The charge was detonated by a demolition team from HMS Lasso, which lay 9 miles (14.5 km) offshore.

HIROSHIMA HORROR

On Aug 6 1945, 155,200 people were killed when an atomic bomb was dropped on Hiroshima, Japan – the largest death toll from an atomic bomb. This figure includes radiation deaths within a year. This first atomic bomb – dropped on Japan by the USA with the intention to bring World War II to an end – had an explosive power equivalent to that of 27,560 lb (12.5 kilotons) of trinitrotoluene ($C_7H_5O_6N_3$), called TNT. Codenamed 'Little Boy' the bomb was 10 ft (3.04 m) long, weighed 9,000 lb (4,080 kg), and exploded 1,670 ft (509 m) above Hiroshima. The bomb completely devastated 4 miles² (10 km²) of the city as soon as it exploded. Over 65% of the city's structures were destroyed or damaged.

<49193>
www.guinnessworldrecords.com/atombomb
← ACCESS CODE

www.guinnessworldrecords.com/bigfirework

BIG BANGS

The world's largest firework was Universe I Part II (right), which exploded at the Lake Toyas Festival, Hokkaido, Japan on July 15 1988. The 1,543-lb (700-kg) shell burst to a diameter of 0.75 mile (1.2 km).

On Aug 15 1997 at the Battle of Flowers Moonlight parade, Jersey, Channel Islands, UK, a record 40,000 rockets were launched of which 39,210 simultaneously exploded.

‹48124› ←

LARGEST DEMOLITION

On May 26 1972, the 21-story Traymore Hotel, Atlantic City, New Jersey, was demolished by Controlled Demolition Incorporated, Maryland. This 600-room hotel had a cubic capacity of 6,403,926 ft³ (181,340 m³).

TALLEST STRUCTURE DEMOLISHED

The 1,202-ft 5 in (366.48-m) Omega Radio Tower, Trelew, Argentina, was demolished with explosives on June 23 1998 by Controlled Demolition Incorporated, Maryland. The tower was a steel-guyed transmitter that weighed 703,360 lb (314 tonnes). There were 34 separate explosive charges containing 21 lb (9.5 kg) of charge. In a carefully planned 11.5-second detonation sequence, the tower underwent an 'accordion collapse,' folding up and falling to the ground without damage to its base building.

TALLEST BUILDING DEMOLISHED

Controlled Demolition Incorporated, Maryland, used explosives to demolish the 25-story, 439-ft (150-m) tall Hudson Building in Detroit, Michigan, on Oct 24 1998. The building had a capacity of 2.2 million ft³ (62,297 m³). It took 2,278 lb (1,033 kg) of explosives detonating from the southwest corner to the northeast over a period of 9.5 seconds to reduce the venerable old department store to 660 million lb (270 million kg) of rubble. An estimated 50,000 people came to witness the destruction of this famous building.

GUINNESS WORLD RECORDS

www.guinnessworldrecords.com/thematerialworld

the material world

food and drink

LARGEST WINE TASTING
On Nov 22 1986 a record 4,000 wine tasters consumed 9,360 bottles of wine. The event was sponsored by local San Francisco television station KQED in California.

LARGEST MILKSHAKE
The Comfort Diners, Parmalat, USA, and the American Dairy Association made the world's largest milkshake of 6,000 gal (22,712 liters) in New York, on Aug 1 2000. This was the equivalent of 50,000 standard-sized milkshakes.

MOST VALUABLE FISH
The eggs of the Russian sturgeon (*Huso huso*) make it the most valuable fish in the world. A 2,706-lb (1,227-kg) female caught in the Tikhaya Sosna river in 1924 yielded 540 lb (245 kg) of best-quality caviar, worth $289,000 (£200,800) today.

MOST HOT DOGS EATEN IN 12 MINUTES
Kazutoyo 'The Rabbit' Arai of Saitama, Japan, ate 25 entire hot dogs and buns in 12 minutes to win the annual Nathan's Famous International Fourth of July Hot Dog Eating Contest on July 4 2000.

LARGEST BEER FESTIVAL
Munich's Oktoberfest 99, which took place from Sept 18 to Oct 5, was visited by seven million people, who consumed a record 1,532,197 gal (5.8 million liters) of beer in 11 beer tents, that stood on a site as large as 50 football fields.

LARGEST BURGER
Loran Green and Friends of Hi Line Promotions made a burger of pure Montana beef weighing 6,040 lb (2,740 kg) and measuring 24 ft (7.32 m) in diameter at the Sleeping Buffalo Resort, Saco, Montana, on Sept 5 1999. More than 3,500 people gathered to watch the burger cook for about two hours on a gigantic specially made grill.

LARGEST COOKIE
The largest cookie ever made was a chocolate chip cookie with a diameter of 81 ft 9 in (24.9 m) and a circumference of 256 ft (78.2 m), made by Cookie Time, Christchurch, New Zealand, on April 2 1996.

LARGEST BOWL OF SOUP
Wyler's, a division of Borden Foods Corporation (USA) prepared the world's largest bowl of beef and vegetable flavored soup with a volume of 661.99 gal (2,505.94 liters) on Oct 5 2000 to mark the company's 70th birthday.

MOST DIFFERENT DISHES ON DISPLAY
On Oct 27 2000 Bochasanwasi Akshar Purushottam Swaminarayan Sanstha (BAPS – a social spiritual organization) displayed 1,247

A SHIPLOAD OF CHOCOLATE
A chocolate model, in the shape of a traditional Spanish sailing ship (left), measuring 27 ft 10.5 in (8.5 m) tall, 42 ft 8 in (13 m) long, and 8 ft 2.5 in (2.5 m) wide, was made by Gremi Provincial de Patisseria, Confiteria i Bolleria School, Barcelona, Spain, in Feb 1991. It was the tallest chocolate model ever made and weighed 8,818 lb (4 tonnes). It was displayed at the Palacio de Alfonso XIII at the international fair *Tecnoalimentaria* in Feb 1991.

‹49162› www.guinnessworldrecords.com/chocship
← ACCESS CODE

GIMME S'MORE!
S'more – short for "Some more!" is a classic American campfire treat made of roasted marshmallows, Hershey bars, and Graham crackers. The largest s'more (above), weighing 789 lb (357 kg) was created at the Cape Hatteras KOA Kampground in Rodanthe, North Carolina, on June 19 1999. It contained 284 lb (128 kg) of Graham crackers, 374 lb (170 kg) of chocolate, and 131 lb (59 kg) of marshmallows (in all 10,000 marshmallows were roasted). It measured a lip-smacking 40 x 10 ft x 2 in (12 x 3 m x 5 cm).

‹53349› www.guinnessworldrecords.com/smore
← ACCESS CODE

different dishes of vegetarian food as an *Annakut* (offering) to mark the Hindu New Year. The record was set at the Shree Swaminarayan Mandir, Neasden, London, UK.

LARGEST HOT BREAKFAST
The Chinook Centre, Calgary, Alberta, Canada, organized a hot breakfast for 8,337 people in the Chinook Centre parking lot on July 8 2000 between 8:11 a.m. and 9:11 a.m. Food consumed consisted of 3,300 lb (1,500 kg) pancake mix; 1,980 lb (900 kg) ham; 107,586 fl oz (3,181.69 ml) orange juice; 105.6 gal (400 liters) maple syrup; 6,372 lb (3,171 kg) baked beans; and 45 lb (20.43 kg) ground coffee.

MOST OYSTERS EATEN IN THREE MINUTES
James Arney (UK) ate 64 oysters in three minutes at Bentley's Restaurant, London, UK, on Sept 1 2000. Arney ran out of oysters after 2.5 min so he could probably have eaten more, given the chance.

LARGEST PIZZA COMMERCIALLY AVAILABLE
Since June 1999, Original Brooks Pizza 2 for 1 Ltd, Alberta, Canada, has sold 200 pizzas measuring 3 x 4 ft (1 x 1.25 m) and weighing between 25 and 35 lb (11–16 kg). 'The Colossal' takes two people to make, 13 lb (5.89 kg) of bread dough for the crust and 8 lb (3.63 kg) of cheese for the topping.

LARGEST CURRY COOKED
Abdul Salam, owner and chef of the Eastern Eye restaurant, Lichfield, Staffs, UK, cooked a vegetable curry weighing 6,849.8 lb (3,106.5 kg) on July 17 2000. The curry fed about 7,500 people and the event raised £4,500 ($6,689) for charity.

FASTEST RICE EATER
Using chopsticks, Tae Wah Gooding (South Korea) ate 64 grains of rice, one by one, in three minutes. The

record was set at Peterborough Regional College, Cambs, UK, on Nov 7 2000 (National Curry Day).

LARGEST JAR OF JELLYBEANS

Goelitz Confectionery, makers of Jelly Belly jellybeans, made a jar containing 2,160,000 jellybeans at the Empress Casino, Hammond, Indiana, on Oct 15 1999. It weighed a massive 6,050 lb (2,744.23 kg) and measured a record-breaking 4 ft 6 in x 4 ft 6 in x 10 ft (1.37 x 1.37 x 3 m).

LARGEST TEQUILA SLAM

The world's largest tequila slam involving 154 people at Bar Madrid, London, UK, took place on Feb 10 2001 in order to raise money for the Alejandro Magno Boys' Home, Bolivia.

FASTEST SODA CRACKER EATER

Damian Howarth (UK) ate three soda crackers, in a record-

www.guinnessworldrecords.com/fastfood

ACCESS CODE

‹56570› ←

AMAZING GRAZING

In 2000 Americans spent a record $110 billion (£76 billion) on fast food, more than on higher education, personal computers, or new cars. On any one day approximately 25% of adults in the USA visit a fast-food outlet. The typical American eats about three burgers per week from one of the country's 300,000 fast-food outlets.

breaking time of 1 min 22.36 sec. He performed this feat on the set of Channel 4's *The Big Breakfast*, London, UK, on March 6 2001.

HIGHEST-ALTITUDE FORMAL MEAL

The highest altitude at which a formal meal has been eaten is 22,205 ft (6,768 m), a record set when nine members of the Ansett Social

Donald A Gorske (USA) ate his 17,500th McDonalds Big Mac on Feb 19 2001 – the most Big Macs ever consumed. On May 17 2001 he completed his 29th year of eating Big Macs on a daily basis, sometimes at a rate of nine a day. He and his wife celebrated their 25th wedding anniversary in 2000 after he proposed to her in 1975 at his favorite McDonalds.

Climbers from Sydney, NSW, Australia, scaled Mt. Huascarán, Peru, on June 28 1989. They took a three-course meal, wine, a Louis XIV dining table, chairs, and candelabra with them.

MOST CHILIES EATEN IN THREE MINUTES

Armando Martillana ate a record 550 chilies in three minutes at the annual Magayon Festival, Philippines, on May 28 2000. He won PHP50,000 ($1,042.75) in prize money. The chilies used for the competition were *capsicum frutescens* – one of the world's hottest chilies.

LONGEST CURRY DELIVERY

On Feb 23 2001 fast-food website, MadAboutCurry.co.uk arranged for a vegetable curry and a peshwari naan to be sent to Rachel Kerr (UK) from Newcastle-Upon-Tyne, Tyneside, UK, to Sydney, Australia, a distance of 10,811 miles (17,398 km) as the crow flies. It arrived three days later on Feb 26 2001.

GUINNESS WORLD RECORDS

big stuff 1

LARGEST GUACAMOLE DIP

The world's largest guacamole dip weighing 2,840 lb (1,288 kg) was created at The Town Theater, Michoacan, Mexico, on Nov 26 2000. The ingredients used were 2,205 lb (1,000 kg) avocado, 242.50 lb (110 kg) onions, 242.50 lb (110 kg) tomatoes, 33 lb (15 kg) chilies, 11 lb (5 kg) coriander, 26 lb (12 kg) salt, and 79.36 lb (36 kg) of limes.

LONGEST SUSHI

The world's longest *futomaki* (sushi roll) was created on Sept 23 2000 by 315 staff of the Toyota Motor Corporation, Japan, and 3,050 members of the local community at the Toyota Gijyutu Fureai Fesuta 2000 in Aichi, Japan. It measured 0.69 miles (1.11 km) long, weighed about 4,851 lb (2,200 kg), was 1.96 in (5 cm) in diameter, and took about an hour to make.

LARGEST DOG BISCUIT

The world's largest dog biscuit measured 7 ft 9.4 in (2.35 m) long, 1 ft 11.3 in (57 cm) wide, and 1 in (2.54 cm) thick. Produced by the People's Company Bakery in Minneapolis, Minnesota, on Aug 11 1999, the biscuit, weighing 8,849 lb (4,014 kg), was unveiled at the Phalen Pork Pavilion, St. Paul, Minnesota, for the annual Walk and Talk for Homeless Animals. It was broken up and eaten by about 100 dogs who had been in the walkathon.

LARGEST BOX OF CHOCOLATES

A calorie-laden 8,000 Disaronno Amaretto-filled chocolates, weighing 179 lb (81.2 kg) went into the world's largest box of chocolates, which was created in the shape of a heart and measured 15 x 15 x 2.5 ft (4.6 x 4.6 x 0.76 m) in New York City, on Feb 14 2000 to mark St. Valentine's Day. A total of 4,890 ft² (454.3 m²) of cardboard was used to make the box. When assembled, the full box of chocolates weighed 1,300 lb (590 kg).

LARGEST ALUMINUM CAN

On March 16 1999 the world's largest aluminum drinks can was first displayed in Sydney, Australia. Made by O'Brien Aluminium and launched on behalf of Guinness Australasia, the replica of a can of Draft Guinness had a capacity of 7,625 pints (3,608 liters), holding 8,200 times more beer than the 15.48-fl oz (440-ml) original. It was 14 ft 9 in (4.5 m) tall, 5 ft 10 in (1.8 m) wide, and weighed 661.39 lb (300 kg).

ENOR-MOUSE

In May 1998 students from Columbiana Career Center, Lisbon, Ohio, constructed a fully operational mousetrap measuring 9 ft 10 in (2.99 m) long and 4 ft 5 in (1.33 m) wide (left). The new record holder is over a third larger than the previous 6-ft 4-in (193-cm) record-breaking model built by physics lecturers Mel McDaniel and Joseph Melancon of the University of Texas. The Columbiana students built a full-scale replica of a Victor mousetrap, the world's most popular model. First patented a century ago, the steel-spring Victor, made in Litiz, Pennsylvania, has sold millions of units. A mouse in proportion to this massive mousetrap would be around 9.84 ft (3 m) long – the size of a small car.

<48095> ← ACCESS CODE www.guinnessworldrecords.com/mousetrap

LARGEST WOK

The world's largest wok, made by Tony Hancock (UK) measures 9 ft 7 in (2.93 m) in diameter and is 2 ft (0.60 m) deep. On March 16 2000 at Wing Yip Chinese restaurant and supermarket, Croydon, Surrey, UK, Tony Hancock demonstrated the use of the giant double-handed wok by stir-frying 882 lb (400 kg) of vegetables and noodles. The large wok rested on a 2-ft 2.4-in high (0.68-m) wok stand incorporating a propane burner carrier.

ARK DE TRIOMPHE!

Between Jan and Aug 1999 G.P. Reichelt (Germany), assisted by Ida Bagus Jiwartem (Bali), carved a 'Noah's Ark' measuring 4 ft 11 in (1.5 m) long, 2 ft 1 in (0.64 m) wide, and 7 in (0.18 m) high from a single piece of wood (left). Mr. Reichelt initially intended to carve an ark that would hold just 42 pairs of animals but then decided to aim to carve one that would house 100 pairs. The result of his efforts was an ark that holds a record-breaking 71 pairs of animals – all individually carved. Reichelt cut the original shapes of the animals and formed them roughly with a grinder, then he and Jiwartem did the finer carving, with Reichelt performing the final finishes.

<53394> ← ACCESS CODE www.guinnessworldrecords.com/ark

LARGEST BRUSSELS SPROUT

In Oct 1992 Dr. Bernard Lavery of Llanharry, South Wales, UK, grew a huge Brussels sprout that weighed an astounding 18 lb 3 oz (8.3 kg).

TALLEST CELERY PLANT

In 1998, Joan Priednieks of Bridgwater, Somerset, UK, grew a massive celery plant that measured 9 ft (2.74 m) tall. Normally these plants only grow to about 3 ft (91 cm).

LONGEST PENCIL

On Feb 15 1998 the Sri Chinmoy Marathon team (USA) made a pencil 20 ft 6 in (6.24 m) long and weighing 560 lb (254 kg). Six angled sections of pine were fitted together with a core of 3.25 in (8.25 cm) synthetic graphite running through it, forming a 13-in (33-cm) diameter. For the eraser, 35 lb (15.87 kg) of rubber was attached to one end with a sheet of aluminum. An electric plane sharpened the pencil so it could be used to write.

LONGEST CAN CHAIN

Bexley Make A Difference Day (MADD) group created the longest chain of aluminum cans using 12,756 cans at Queen Mary's Hospital, Sidcup, Kent, UK, on Oct 28 2000. The final length of the chain was 0.91 miles (1.47 km).

LONGEST GUM WRAPPER CHAIN

On March 11 1965 Gary Duschl of Ontario, Canada, began making a gum-wrapper chain. By March 31 2000 it measured 34,078 ft (10,387 m), was made up of 1,585,382 links from 792,691 wrappers, and weighed around 465 lb (211 kg).

LARGEST BAR OF CHOCOLATE

Between March 16 and 19 2000 at the Eurochocolate 2000 confectionery exhibition in Turin, Italy, Elah-Dufour United Food Companies Ltd made a scaled-up version of a chocolate bar, weighing an amazing 5,026 lb (2,280 kg). It measured 124 x 59 x 17.7 in (315 x 150 x 45 cm), equal to 22,800 4-oz (100-g) chocolate bars.

SNOW BUSINESS

Residents of Bethel, Maine, and surrounding towns, built an enormous snowman measuring 113 ft 7.5 in (34.63 m) high (right), over a period of 14 days, completing him on Feb 17 1999. The 10-story snowman named Angus (after Maine governor Angus King) was constructed using 197,762 ft³ (5,600 m³) of snow. He finally melted 15 weeks later on June 10 1999 – the date had been the subject of a sweepstake.

ACCESS CODE

‹48789› ←

LARGEST STICK OF CANDY

The Coronation Rock Company of Blackpool, Lancashire, UK, created the largest stick of candy weighing 936 lb (424.5 kg) and measuring 14 ft 9 in (4.49 m) long, with a circumference of 45 in (1.14 m) at their factory on Dec 6 2000. The candy was broken up and sold for charity.

JIGSAW PUZZLE WITH MOST PIECES

A puzzle consisting of 209,250 pieces, each measuring 0.59 x 0.59 in (1.5 x 1.5 cm), was completed at the Mulan Jigsaw Puzzle contest at the Grand Formosa Regent Hotel, Taipei, Taiwan. The overall measurement was 22 ft 1 in x 22 ft 10 in (6.75 m x 6.97 m).

GUINNESS WORLD RECORDS™

big stuff 2

BIGGEST NIGHTCLUB
The nightclub Privilege in Ibiza Spain, can hold 10,000 clubbers on its 69,965 ft² (6,500 m²) of dance space spread over three floors – altogether the size of a soccer field. Sheet glass at one end allows the morning sun to shine through. A swimming pool, fountains, gardens, trees, and plants add to the ambience in the club.

LARGEST PARAFOIL
The largest parafoil parachute ever flown has a span of 143 ft (43.6 m) giving it a surface area of 7,500 ft² (700 m²), nearly one-and-a-half times the size of the wings of a Boeing 747. Essentially a parachute that is 'inflated' by air pressure as it descends, the parafoil was developed by NASA to bring its X-38 spacecraft down to the surface after reentering the atmosphere. Most paragliders, which are also parafoils, have a surface area of 270–323 ft² (25–30 m²).

LARGEST CARDBOARD BOX
The world's largest corrugated cardboard box was constructed by Kappa Van Dam, a manufacturer of custom shipping cartons. It measured 22.9 ft (7 m) long, 8.5 ft (2.6 m) wide, and 7.87 ft (2.4 m) high, and was unveiled on Nov 20 1999 at Eindhoven market, Netherlands. The mammoth box was manufactured on mass-production equipment at the Kappa Van Dam production site, Helmond, Netherlands.

CALCULATED TO IMPRESS
The largest recognized abacus (left) measures 15.41 ft (4.7 m) long and 7.21 ft (2.2 m) high, contains 91 beads, and weighs 838 lb (380 kg). It was made by Spectrum for Math Year 2000 and unveiled at the Science Museum, London, UK, on Jan 23 2001. The abacus is regarded as a universal mathematical icon. The frame was built from aluminum, the poles from stainless steel, and the 91 shiny blue beads from plastic. According to Keith Greaves, head of the construction team, one problem was simply getting the huge abacus inside the Science Museum – it barely fit through the doors. The abacus originated between 600 and 500 BC in either Egypt or China. They were, in effect, the first-ever handheld calculators.

‹56104›
www.guinnessworldrecords.com/abacus
← ACCESS CODE

LARGEST FOUNTAIN
The world's largest fountain is the Suntec City Fountain of Wealth in Singapore. Its cast-bronze superstructure weighs 187,400 lb (85 tonnes) and stands 46 ft (14 m) high, while the base of the fountain has a total area of 18,116 ft² (1,683 m²). It cost around $6 million (£3.5 million) to build in 1997.

LARGEST FIREWORK WHEEL
The world's largest self-propelled vertical firework wheel measured 85 ft (25.95 m) in diameter, and was designed by the Newick Bonfire Society Ltd. It fired for 12 revolutions on Oct 30 1999 at Newick, E Sussex, UK.

BIGGEST BRAZIER
A brazier that was 26 ft (8 m) tall, 30 ft (9 m) wide, and weighed 55,115 lb (25 tonnes) was used to house the Millennium Beacon, lit on the River Thames, London, UK, on Dec 31 1999. The beacon (the biggest in a national

chain of about 2,000 beacons and bonfires) took 2,000 man-hours and eight weeks to construct. Although there is no official figure, reports state that the flame from this brazier, which was lit by Queen Elizabeth II, shot over 328 ft (100 m) into the air.

LARGEST PIGGY BANK
In Nov 1995 a giant pink piggy bank was constructed by the Canadian Imperial Bank of Commerce, Canada. Named Maximillion, it measured 15 ft 5 in (4.70 m) in length, 8 ft 8 in (2.64 m) in height, and 21 ft 4 in (6.52 m) in circumference.

LARGEST ACOUSTIC GUITAR
A fully functional acoustic guitar, measuring 28 ft 5 in (8.66 m) long and 3 ft 2 in (97.2 cm) deep, is exhibited at the Stradivarium exhibition in The Exploratory, Bristol, UK. The dimensions were enlarged from the proportions of a 18th-century classical guitar made by Antonio Stradivari (Italy).

ANGELIC PROPORTIONS
An angel (left) constructed from 2,946 glass bottles (still containing beer) and punctured metal sheets from which bottle caps had been made, was designed and built by artist Sergio Rodriguez Villarreal (Mexico). It measured 18 ft 3 in (5.57 m) high, 11 ft 9 in (3.6 m) wide, with a base diameter of 8 ft 2 in (2.5 m) and was displayed at Alfonso Reyes Avenue, Nuevo León, Mexico, in Jan 2000. This work of art holds the record for the largest Christmas angel sculpture. The artist was inspired by the creative spirit of Christmas to become a multiple Guinness record holder.
Villarreal also designed and built the largest-ever Christmas bauble, which measured 9 ft (2.75 m) tall and 7 ft 2 in (2.2 m) in diameter. It was displayed at Alfonso Reyes Avenue, Neuvo León, Mexico, in 2000.

‹48146›
www.guinnessworldrecords.com/angelsculpture
← ACCESS CODE

LARGEST CHANDELIER
The world's largest set of chandeliers was created by the Kookje Lighting Co Ltd of Seoul, South Korea. The set is 12 m (39 ft) high, weighs 10.67 tonnes (23,500 lb) and has 700 bulbs. Completed in Nov 1988, it occupies three floors of the Lotte Chamshil department store in Seoul.

LARGEST AXE
A steel axe measuring 60 ft (18.3 m) long, 23 ft (7 m) wide and weighing 15,400 lb (7 tonnes) was designed and built by BID Ltd of Woodstock, New Brunswick, Canada. It would take a 308,500-lb (140-tonne) lumberjack to swing the axe, and a crane was used to lift it into its concrete 'stump.'

LARGEST CLOCK
The world's largest clock is the astronomical clock in the Cathedral of St. Pierre, Beauvais, France, constructed between 1865 and 1868. It consists of 90,000 parts and is 40 ft (12.1 m) high, 20 ft (6.1 m) wide and 9 ft (2.7 m) deep.

LARGEST FOOTBALL
A football made from 560 ft² (52.03 m²) of PU leather and sewn by hand had a diameter of 11 ft 7 in (3.53 m) when measured on July 1 1999. Made by Tianjin Nanhua of Lisheng Sports Products Co, Beijing, China, the ball had 12,870 stitches, a circumference of 36 ft 4 in (11.075 m) and weighed 313 lb (142 kg). To be in proportion with this ball, a player would have to be around 28 m (92 ft) tall – as high as a six-story building.

LARGEST GREETING CARD

A giant freestanding Christmas card, as big as 4,500 regular-sized greeting cards put together, was made from one piece of card measuring a total of 2,700 ft^2 (251 m^2) or 98 ft 0.6 in x 27 ft 2 in (30 x 8.3 m) on Dec 3 1990 at University College, Dublin, Ireland. Once folded, the card front measured a record-breaking 49 ft 2 in x 27 ft 2 in (15 x 8.3 m).

LARGEST BEDFRAME

A total of 223 students, ages 14 to 18, lay side by side in three rows upon a mattress on a giant wooden bedframe measuring 26 ft 2 in x 32 ft 10 in (8 x 10 m). Starlight Ltd exhibited it at the Furniture World exhibition from Nov 14 to 18 2000 in Budapest, Hungary.

BIGGEST BRA

In Sept 1990 Triumph International Japan Ltd made a bra with an underbust measurement of 78 ft 8 in (24 m) and a bust measurement of 91 ft 10 in (28 m). It was made from 229 ft 7 in (70 m) of fabric, enough to make 1,000 regular-sized bras.

LONGEST SCARF

Karen Dengate (UK) began knitting a scarf on Oct 1 1997 and has spent three hours a day working on it since. When measured in March 2000 it was 571 ft 6 in (174.21 m) long and 7.5 in (19 cm) wide. She will carry on knitting.

TALLEST PAPER CUP

The tallest paper cup is 8 ft 3 in (2.53 m) high, and was created by Bunzl Disposables Europe with the help of Polarcup on Feb 1 2000 in Epsom, Surrey, UK. The cup was filled with 1,302.36 gal (4,930 liters) of water by the local fire department. To ensure that it was a scaled-up version of a normal paper cup, it was made with 13 layers of paper and had a watertight seam.

www.guinnessworldrecords.com/cowboyboots

IF THE BOOT FITS . . .

Texas, known for big ranches and big hats, is also home to the world's biggest pair of authentic cowboy boots. The boots (right) are 4 ft 6.75 in (1.38 m) tall and 3 ft 11 in (1.19 m) long. They were made by the co-owner of Rocketbuster Boots, El Paso, Texas, Marty Snortum. A team of 15, headed by designer Nevena Christi, used $5,000 (£3,463) of materials and took three months to make the brightly colored pair of boots, finishing them on Jan 13 1999. They weigh 100 lb (45 kg) and have soles stitched with nylon clothesline.

The world's largest shoe measures 10 ft 3 in (3.12 m) in length, 3 ft 5.5 in (1.05 m) in width, and 4 ft 0.8 in (1.23 m) in height. Zahit Okurlar (Turkey) used three-cows' worth of leather just for the sole. The right shoe was exhibited in Feb 2000 at the Konya International Shoe Fair.

Edmund Kryza (Poland) made a giant ladies' shoe 6 ft (1.84 m) long and 3 ft 8 in (1.12 m) high from 64 ft^2 (6 m^2) of artificial leather on May 8 1996.

ACCESS CODE

‹53153› ←

GUINNESS WORLD RECORDS

small stuff

SMALLEST NIGHTCLUB

The world's smallest nightclub is The Miniscule of Sound, London, UK, which is a box only 8 ft (2.4 m) long, 4 ft (1.2 m) wide, and 8 ft (2.4 m) high. Constructed in Aug 1998 from Dexion shelving and hardboard walls, and decorated with fake fur, strobe lighting, and a mirror ball, it contains a full DJ and sound system and a dance floor measuring only 21.5 ft^2 (2 m^2). The maximum capacity is 14 people including the DJ.

SMALLEST WINE GLASS

The smallest wine glass was unveiled on Dec 7 2000. Created by NEC (Japan), this tiny vessel measures just 2,750 nanometers across (one nanometer is one-billionth of a meter). This is approximately 20,000 times smaller than a conventional wine glass.

SMALLEST ABACUS

In Nov 1996 scientists at the IBM Research Division's Zurich laboratory (Switzerland) built an abacus with individual molecules as beads with a diameter of less than one nanometer (one-billionth of a meter). They formed rows of 10 molecules along steps one atom high, which acted as the rails for each molecule.

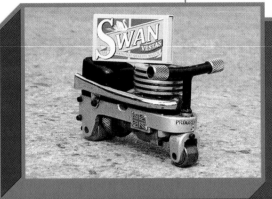

‹43595› ← ACCESS CODE

MICROMOTORCYCLE

Simon Timperley and Clive Williams of Progressive Engineering Ltd, Manchester, UK, designed and constructed the world's smallest motorcycle (left) with a wheelbase of 4.25 in (108 mm), a seat height of 3.74 in (95 mm), and with a wheel diameter of 0.74 in (19 mm) for the front and 0.94 in (24 mm) for the back. The bike was ridden a distance of 3.28 ft (1 m). All parts of the motorcycle were handmade, except for the engine, which had to be modified to fit on to the chassis. The 10 cc model aircraft engine buzzes at 13,000 rpm, pushing the cycle along at a sedate 2 mph (3.2 km/h).

www.guinnessworldrecords.com/micromotorcycle

SMALLEST PENKNIFE

The world's smallest fully-operational handmade penknife measures 0.3 in (8 mm) long and 0.1 in (3 mm) wide when closed. With the sharp blade snapped open, the knife extends to 0.5 in (14.5 mm) long and 0.09 in (2.5 mm) wide.

SMALLEST SCISSORS

In 1998 Ramesh Chand Dhiman (India) constructed, by hand, a pair of working scissors measuring just 0.12 in (3.12 mm) long and 0.08 in (2.17 mm) wide. Although they work, the scissors would be completely impractical for any kind of application. Ramesh Chand Dhiman also made the smallest razor blade in the world.

SMALLEST MICROPHONE

A silicon microphone only 40 microns (one micron is one-millionth of a meter) wide was produced by the Electrical Engineering and Physics departments of the University of Bilkent, Turkey. It is hoped it will be used in the medical technique of ultrasound scans.

SMALLEST PAPER MONEY

The smallest national note issued was the 10-bani note of the Ministry of Finance of Romania in 1917. Its printed area measured 1.08 x 1.49 in (27.5 x 38 mm). This is about one-tenth the size of a $1 bill.

SMALLEST RULER

A ruler used for measuring very small lengths in an electron microscope was developed in 1994 by John McCaffrey and Jean-Marc Baribeau of the Institute for Microstructural Sciences at the National Research Council, Canada. The smallest division on the ruler is 18 atoms wide and individual atoms are visible. It is so small that 10 of the rulers stacked end to end would equal the diameter of a human hair.

SMALLEST TEST TUBE

The world's smallest test tube – a nanotube – was made at the École Polytechnique Fédérale de Lausanne in Switzerland in 1996. Each tube is one micron long and has an internal diameter of less than 10 nanometers (10 billionths of a meter). End to end you could fit 15,000 of these nanotubes across your thumb.

SMALLEST HOLDING

Because of a legal technicality, the Electricity Trust of South Australia is the proprietor of a registered and separately delineated piece of land in Adelaide, South Australia, measuring just 1 in (25.4 mm) on all four sides, i.e. the same size as the average postage stamp.

THE BEE'S KNEES!

The Rutherford Appleton Laboratory, Oxfordshire, UK, created the world's smallest advertisement for Guinness World Records, measuring just 100 microns x 100 microns. It featured on a kneeband worn by a bee on Oct 25 2000 (left). Made from Kapton (a flexible and light plastic film), the letters, which were between 5 and 20 microns high read, 'Guinness World Records.com' and were made from deposited gold. As a comparison, a human hair on average measures between 40 and 100 microns in diameter. The whole process of making the advert took just half a day. The bee chosen had been selected from a colony of bees and was found dead at the bottom of the hive – so no harm was actually inflicted on a live bee.

‹55977› ← ACCESS CODE

www.guinnessworldrecords.com/microadvert

MINUTE SURVEILLANCE

The PC-53XP pinhole microvideo camera (below), manufactured by US-based video security firm Supercircuits, is the smallest color video camera commercially available in the world. It measures just 0.26 in³ (4.25 cm³) and provides full-color video pictures. Weighing just 0.25 oz (7 g), this camera outputs standard NTSC format images that are digitally controlled to give a high-quality picture despite being smaller than a sugar cube. The camera provides a horizontal resolution of 380 lines and consumes just 50 milliamps at 2 volts DC. When combined with the AVX-900T3 (also manufactured by Supercircuits), the result is the world's smallest wireless video camera. Ideal for covert operations and surveillance, the combined camera and transmitter (the AVX-900S5) can transmit color video over a distance of 750 ft (230 m).

SMALLEST BICYCLE

The world's smallest-wheeled rideable bicycle has a front wheel with a diameter of 0.43 in (11 mm) and a rear wheel of 0.51 in (13 mm). On Aug 11 1999 its constructor, Zbigniew Rózanek (Poland), rode it a distance of 16 ft (5 m).

SMALLEST CRYSTAL BOWL

A crystal bowl made by Jim Irish of Rathculliheen, Waterford, Ireland, measured 0.336 in (8.55 mm) wide, 0.18 in (4.6 mm) tall, 0.08 in (2.1 mm) thick, and was made with 208 cuts. It took eight hours to complete the bowl over a two-week period, working in 45 tiny segments. The bowl can fit six times on to one Irish penny.

SMALLEST GUITAR

The world's smallest guitar carved from a block of silicon and based on a Fender Stratocaster, measures just 10 micrometers long – ¹⁄₂₀ of the thickness of a human hair. Made in 1997 in just 20 minutes by scientists at Cornell University, New York, each of its six strings were 0.002 in (0.05 mm) thick and, when plucked, they vibrated at frequencies 1,000 times higher than the human ear can hear. The guitar is the same size as a human blood cell.

SMALLEST RETURNING BOOMERANG

A boomerang measuring 1.8 in (48 mm) long and 1.77 in (45 mm) wide, was successfully thrown by Sadir Kattan at the Australian National Boomerang Championships, Melbourne, Vic, on March 22 1997. The boomerang traveled past the qualifying 65.6 ft (20 m) and returned into the accuracy circles from where it had been thrown.

SMALLEST STEAM ENGINE

In 1993 a team of physicists at Sandia National Laboratories in Albuquerque, New Mexico, invented a microscopic steam engine that was 6 microns long and 2 microns wide. Despite the engine's tiny size, its makers say that it is powerful enough to work in all manner of microtools such as the tweezers and scalpels used in eye or brain surgery.

SMALLEST SHIP-IN-A-BOTTLE

Arthur V. Pedlar (UK) constructed the smallest ship-in-a-bottle in a medical phial 0.94 in (24 mm) long and 0.35 in (9 mm) wide, with a neck of 0.08 in (2 mm) in 1956. The galleon has three masts, five sails, and three flags and was inserted into the bottle in 28 pieces, each placed in position with a piece of fuse wire glued to a matchstick. The sea is sealing wax pulled into thin strands, the rigging is horsehair, and the hull of the galleon is made of cork. A lighthouse was also placed inside the bottle.

collections 1

LARGEST PRIVATE ROLLS-ROYCE FLEET

Sultan Hassanal Bolkiah of Brunei is believed to have the biggest private collection of Rolls-Royce cars, consisting of an estimated 150 vehicles. Together with his brother, Prince Jefri, the Sultan is reported to own a further 1,998 luxury cars.

LARGEST COLLECTION OF MODEL BUSES

Ben Bradshaw (UK) has collected a total of 153 individual model buses – both single and double-decker – since he was three years old. The manufacturers most represented are Mercedes Benz and Corgi, with 45 and 59 models respectively.

LARGEST COLLECTION OF MODEL RAILROAD VEHICLES

The largest collection of model railroad vehicles made by one person is the J.P. Richards Collection owned by the National Railway Museum in York, UK. There are 610 models in the collection, handmade to scale by James Peel Richards (UK).

LARGEST JET-FIGHTER COLLECTION

The world's biggest private jet-fighter collection numbers 110, and belongs to French winemaker Michel Pont. His hobby started in 1985, and includes Russian MiGs, British Jaguars, and French Mirages. He buys them from governments, although they are not allowed to be flown over French airspace.

LARGEST COLLECTION OF TELEVISIONS AND RADIOS

By Sept 22 1998 Göran Ågårdh (Sweden) had collected a record total of 10,060 televisions and radios.

LARGEST COLLECTION OF PENCILS

Emilio Arenas (Uruguay) has a collection of 5,500 different pencils, each printed with a distinct design, logo, or brand. Emilio also owns impressive collections of key rings, ashtrays, soft drink and beer cans, perfume bottles, pencil sharpeners, pins, matchboxes, and phone cards, all of which are on public display in four huge rooms in Emilio's house.

LARGEST BALLPOINT PEN COLLECTION

Angelika Unverhau (Germany) has a collection of ballpoint pens that in Oct 2000 numbered 205,050 units (excluding duplicates) and represents 146 countries. She has been collecting unusual pens since childhood, but decided to take her

SUPERMODELS

The record for the largest collection of model cars is held by Suhail Mohd. Al Zarooni of Dubai (UAE, above) who owns more than 1,500 miniature model cars. This huge collection – his passion since 1990 – is worth nearly $3 million (£2,100,000). Many of his models are rare cars such as Queen Elizabeth II's Rolls-Royces and some are painted in 24-carat gold. A large number of the cars are models from the 1960s – classic cars, police cars, and limousines – most of which he purchased in the UK and Europe. He often buys a real car to match a favorite model.

‹55947›
www.guinnessworldrecords.com/modelcars
← ACCESS CODE

hobby more seriously in 1990. She founded a club with 90 members from all over Germany who meet twice a year to trade pens and share pen-related experiences.

MOST BANK BILLS FROM DIFFERENT COUNTRIES

Shail Kumar and Larry and Dallys Arias Beebe (USA) share the record for the largest collection of bank bills – both with collections representing a grand total of 217 different countries.

LARGEST WINE AND CHAMPAGNE LABEL COLLECTION

Since 1984, Sophia Vaharis-Tsouvelekakis (Greece) has collected 15,403 labels from champagne and wine bottles, representing 50 different countries. She catalogs the labels using a special computer program that will not accept duplicate entries. She also has a unique, thermostat-controlled wine cellar where she stores thousands of bottles of wine and champagne.

LARGEST BOTTLE OPENER COLLECTION

Dale Deckert (USA) started his collection of 20,884 individual bottle openers representing 136 countries, after being discharged from the US Army in 1945. Including duplicates, the entire collection numbers 28,146.

LARGEST BAR TOWEL COLLECTION

Alan Alcott (UK) has collected 504 individual bar towels since 1977. When displayed end to end, these towels stretch 524 ft 2 in (159.77 m). Alan's longest bar towel is an Australian 'bar runner' from Castlemaine, which measures 9 ft 10 in (3 m) long.

PLANE CRAZY

The largest collection of handmade model airplanes is owned by Robert Humphrey of West Jordan, Utah (left). Robert's collection consists of 1,642 plastic airplane models all of which he has assembled himself. He has an emergency backup kit on hand for every single plane in case something should happen to it. Robert, born in 1952, built his first plane with his father's help in 1958. He subsequently received a model plane each year on his birthday. Robert now searches for rare models and his collection grows by about 100 airplanes every year. The plastic airplane models represent army forces, marine air forces, and air forces of 61 different nations.

‹55815›
www.guinnessworldrecords.com/modelplanes
← ACCESS CODE

LARGEST BEER BOTTLE COLLECTION

Ron Werner (USA) has collected 11,644 different beer bottles since 1982. Of these, 7,128 are unopened. He has sampled almost every one of his 1,704 brands of beer.

LARGEST GASOLINE-PUMP COLLECTION

The Fisogni Museum, Milan, Italy, currently houses 164 gasoline pumps. They range in age from a 1910 Tokheim self-measuring pump to a 1981 FIMAC Benaglia 'Lux 60 Puma' volumetric pump. There are 7,500 pieces of gasoline pumps, oil tanks, gadgets, and toys in the museum. Guido Fisogni has been building his collection for more than 30 years and is dedicated to documenting the history of technological improvements.

LARGEST STAR WARS MEMORABILIA COLLECTION

Jason Joiner (UK) started collecting *Star Wars* memorabilia as a 12-year-old, and has never stopped. A special effects expert who has worked on the *Star Wars* films made in the UK, he has a collection of over 20,000 *Star Wars* toys. In addition, Joiner has one of the original C3PO robots, an original R2D2, and an original Darth Vader costume. Only *Star Wars* creator George Lucas has a larger collection of props and costumes. Joiner hopes to open a museum to house some of his collection.

LARGEST SWATCH WATCH COLLECTION

Fiorenzo Barindelli (Italy) has a collection of 3,677 Swatch watches, which includes an example of every Swatch watch produced since 1983. His collection is on display at the World Museum 2000, Cesano, Italy.

www.guinnessworldrecords.com/gnomes

WHEREFORE ART THOU GNOMEO?

Since 1978, Ann Atkin (UK, above) has collected a record total of 2,010 gnomes and pixies, all of which live in a massive 4-acre (1.6-ha) Gnome Reserve in North Devon, UK. Some are fishing, others pushing wheelbarrows, some are musically inclined, mining, or gambling. Every year, for the last 18 years, over 25,000 visitors have donned hats to turn temporarily into gnomes to journey through the woodland. The largest gnome in the reserve is 45 in (115 cm) tall and the smallest is only 0.75 in (2 cm) tall. They are all brought out once a year for an annual bath and a new outfit.

GUINNESS WORLD RECORDS

collections 2

LARGEST LIBRARY
The United States Library of Congress (founded on April 24 1800) in Washington, DC, contains 125,198,175 items, including over 18 million books, 2.5 million recordings, 12 million photographs, 4.5 million maps, and 54 million manuscripts. The library occupies about 2.85 million ft² (265,000 m²) in the Capitol Hill buildings alone, with 532.2 miles (856.5 km) of shelving.

LARGEST FOUR-LEAF CLOVER COLLECTION
George J. Kaminski (USA) has single-handedly collected 72,928 four-leaf clovers since 1995. A total of 13,383 were collected from within the 5-acre (2-ha) prison yard, during his recreation time at the State Correctional Institution, Somerset, Pennsylvania, and a further 59,545 were collected from the prison yard at the State Prison in Houtzdale, Pennsylvania.

LARGEST COLLECTION OF BADGES
Daniel Hedges (UK) has collected 8,662 different badges. He began collecting when he was 14 years old. Danny's badges range from sassy

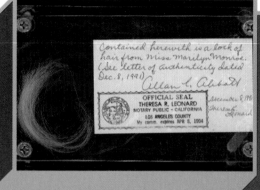

GENTLEMEN PREFER BLONDS
John Rezinkoff of Connecticut, has collected hair from 115 different historical celebrities. This collection of famous locks is insured for $1 million (£698,470) and includes tresses from the heads of Abraham Lincoln, John F. Kennedy, Marilyn Monroe (left), Albert Einstein, Napoleon, Elvis Presley, King Charles I, and Charles Dickens. He aspires to finding locks from Mark Twain and Shakespeare. Despite offers of up to $100,000 (£69,847) for individual items, the collection is not for sale. All hair specimens in Reznikoff's collection have documentation and/or DNA tests to back them up.

messages like 'no farting zone' to a much more elegant example from the Royal Enclosure at Ascot.

LARGEST AIRLINE SICKNESS BAG COLLECTION
Marketing and investment consultant Niek Vermeulen (Netherlands) has 2,112 airline sickness bags from 470 different airlines, topping a list of over 50 serious airline sickness bag collectors. He currently resides in Vietnam. His favorite is an airline sickness bag from a NASA space shuttle. Be it barf bag, vomit bag, motion sickness bag, hurl bag, spew bag, Sac Vomitoire, Sac pour mal de l'air, Bolsa de mareo, prullenzakje, Spucktüte, Spuckbeutel, Beg Mabuk Udara, Torba chorobowa, Etiquette bukuro, Oksennuspussi, Sacchetto Per Il Mal D'aria, Kräkpåse, Spypåse, Gero-Bukuro, Sanitarinis Maiselis ... whatever you call it, Vermeulen collects them all.

LARGEST FILM STILLS COLLECTION
The National Film Archive Stills Collection in London, UK, houses 6.5 million black-and-white stills and over 1 million color transparencies from over 80,000 films from all over the world.

LARGEST MOVIE CAMERA COLLECTION
The largest unique collection of movie cameras, with no duplicates, belongs to retired mailman Dimitrios Pistiola (Greece). He has accumulated 440 movie cameras dating from 1901 and has created a small museum for them.

MOST VALUABLE CAMERA COLLECTION
The record total for any camera auction is $424,090 (£296,043) for a collection of 'spy,' subminiature, and detective cameras sold at Christie's, London, UK, on Dec 9 1991.

LARGEST COLORED VINYL RECORD COLLECTION
Alessandro Benedetti (Italy) has collected 934 music records made of colored vinyl. His massive collection is made up of 647 LPs (601 colored, 46 with pictures) and 287 singles (255 colored, 13 with pictures, and 19 in unusual shapes).

LARGEST MENU COLLECTION
Daniel Barlow (USA) has been collecting restaurant menus for 52 years, and has accumulated 3,908 different menus. His favorites are a papyrus menu from Egypt, scroll-style menus from China, a menu from a floating restaurant in Hong Kong, and one from a Florida nudist resort. Daniel believes they depict change and progression in world cuisine.

HIT ME WITH YOUR RHYTHM STICK
The record for the largest autographed drumstick collection in the world is held by Peter Lavinger of New York, who has collected over 1,300 drumsticks since 1980 when he caught his first drumstick from the front row of a Good Rats concert. Although Peter is not a drummer himself, the origins of his drumsticks vary from rock to blues, country to folk, soul to ska, and reggae to jazz. He boasts drumsticks once used by Pink Floyd, The Beatles, R.E.M., Nirvana, The Doors, Fleetwood Mac, Pearl Jam, The Rolling Stones, and U2, plus hundreds more. In 1989, the collection was displayed in the New York Hard Rock Café and is currently on show at the Rock and Roll Hall of Fame and Museum in Cleveland, Ohio. His collection is worth over $1 million (£695,601).

www.guinnessworldrecords.com/navelfluff

NAVEL VICTORY

The largest collection of navel fluff belongs to plucky Australian Graham Barker, who has collected 0.54 oz (15.41 g) of his own navel fluff since 1984. "Some people gaze into their navel for inspiration: I look into mine and see navel fluff," says Graham Barker, who has collected the fluffy substance that forms in his bellybutton consistently for the last 16 years. When asked "why?" Graham simply replies, "why not?" Though he now owns two-and-a-half jars of this bizarre bodily by-product (one jar shown, right) Graham's ultimate goal is to collect enough fluff to stuff a pillow. He began his collection one day when he found himself cooped up in a youth hostel in Brisbane, Australia, extremely bored. Now Graham says collecting his navel fluff has become an ingrained, daily habit. He claims his navel fluff is in mint condition since he makes a point of immediately storing it in a jar to ensure that it remains uncontaminated.

LARGEST BANANA COLLECTION

Kevin Bannister's International Banana Club Museum in Altadena, California, houses 17,000 banana-related articles. The museum was opened in 1972 and has 9,000 members from 27 countries. The collection includes banana slippers, suits, games, pots, pipes, and puppets.

LARGEST BUNNY COLLECTION

Husband and wife Steve Lubanski and Candace Frazee (USA) have acquired 8,437 bunny-themed collectibles since they began collecting on Feb 14 1993.

LARGEST FROG COLLECTION

Wendy Scower (Canada) has accumulated a collection of 1,202 different frog items since she was 10 years old in 1967.

LARGEST PIG COLLECTION

Carl Kinney's collection of pig memorabilia contains 2,250 different items, including banks, books, toys, napkin rings, cookie jars, figurines, and comic books. Carl (USA) began collecting in 1978 to build upon his grandmother's collection, which was made up of 200 pig items.

LARGEST FRIDGE MAGNET COLLECTION

Louise J. Greenfarb (USA) has collected 29,000 refrigerator magnets. Her collection is displayed at the Guinness World Records Museum in Las Vegas, Nevada. Louise's magnets portray everything from food to US presidents, and such is her love of her collection that she even wants to be buried in her fridge.

LARGEST HANDCUFF COLLECTION

Locksmith Chris Gower (UK) has 530 pairs of antique and modern handcuffs that he has been collecting since 1968. They range from ancient slave shackles to the most up-to-date high-security cuffs. His favorite item in the collection is a famous pair of Plug Lock Figure '8' leg-irons from which Houdini, his big hero, failed to escape in 1903.

LARGEST VALID CREDIT CARD COLLECTION

Walter Cavanagh (USA) has collected 1,397 individual valid credit cards. The cost of acquisition to 'Mr. Plastic Fantastic' was nil, but the cards are worth more than $1.65 million (£1.15 million) in credit. Walter Cavanagh keeps them in the world's longest wallet – 250 ft (76.2 m) in length and weighing 38 lb 8 oz (17.49 kg). If laid end-to-end, Cavanagh's credit cards would reach to the top of a four-story building.

LARGEST COLLECTION OF PAPER AND PLASTIC BAGS

Heinz Schmidt-Bachem (Germany) has collected 150,000 plastic and paper bags since 1975. They range from simple plastic bags from a grocery store to bags from designer boutiques. His oldest bag dates from 1853 and is the first industrially manufactured paper bag ever made.

Navel Fluff 1994-97

GUINNESS WORLD RECORDS™

www.guinnessworldrecords.com/artsandentertainment

arts and entertainment

GUINNESS
WORLD RECORDS

movies 1

LONGEST FILM TAKE

The longest take in a movie makes up the whole of Kevin du Toit's noncommercial *BugNight* (USA, 1998). It consists of 84 minutes of a flashback at a diner where nine hostages are being held.

LONGEST TAKE IN A COMMERCIAL FILM

In *A Free Soul* (USA, 1931), there is a 14-minute uninterrupted monologue by Lionel Barrymore. Since a reel of camera film only lasts 10 minutes, it was achieved by using more than one camera.

LONGEST FILM EVER MADE

The longest film ever made was the 85-hour *The Cure for Insomnia* (USA, 1987), directed by John Henry Timmis IV. It premiered at The School of the Art Institute of Chicago, between Jan 31 and Feb 3 1987.

MOST COSTUME CHANGES FOR A FILM CHARACTER

Madonna changed costume 85 times in *Evita* (USA, 1996) and wore 39 hats, 45 pairs of shoes, 56 pairs of earrings, and 42 hair designs to transform her into Eva Perón, First Lady of Argentina. The costumes were designed by Penny Rose. After making thousands of samples, an army of costumemakers went to work, taking 14 weeks to stitch, sew, bead, and recreate Eva's wardrobe.

‹50750›
← ACCESS CODE
www.guinnessworldrecords.com/lostworld

JURASSIC ADVENTURES

Universal's *Jurassic Park: The Lost World* was given the widest release of any film in history when it opened on America's Memorial holiday weekend (May 23 1997) on more than 5,000 screens across the country, with some multiplexes showing the film simultaneously on six screens. This film was the sequel to *Jurassic Park* (USA, 1993), reuniting actors Jeff Goldblum and Richard Attenborough.

From May 26 1997 *Jurassic Park: The Lost World* (USA, 1997) took a four-day gross of $90.1 million (£54.9 million) from 3,281 screens. This is the all-time record for highest box-office gross on an opening weekend. (This figure excludes the preview night of $2.6 million (£1.5 million) from 1,755 theaters.)

LARGEST MAKEUP BUDGET

A total of $1 million (then £345,542) was budgeted for makeup in *Planet of the Apes* (USA, 1968). This would equal $4.95 million (£2.92 million) today. This amount represents nearly 17% of the film's total production cost of $5.8 million (£2,004,146). Today's equivalent value would be $28.71 million or £16.92 million.

MOST FILM EXTRAS

Over 300,000 extras appeared in the funeral scene of *Gandhi* (UK, 1982), the epic directed by Richard Attenborough. For this scene, 11 camera crews shot 20,000 ft (6,096 m) of film, more than the total footage of the final 188-minute released film. The edited funeral sequence ran for only 125 seconds of screen time.

MOST EXPENSIVE FILM MADE

Paramount's *Titanic* (USA, 1997) cost just over $200 million (£118,934,350) to make. The retelling of the UK's worst single ship disaster in peacetime became one of Hollywood's greatest triumphs. It was originally given a $125 million (£74,333,969) budget, and was due to have been released in July 1997, but postproduction problems set the date back to Dec 1997, which, in turn, added to the cost.

In terms of real costs (adjusted for inflation) the most expensive film ever made was *Cleopatra* (USA, 1963). Its $44 million (then £15,712,602) budget would be equivalent to $306,867,120 (£175,352,640) today.

ONLY FILM MADE WITHOUT A CAMERA

Artist Jose Antonio Sistiagas (Spain) is credited with the only full-length film made without a camera. He completed his 75-minute animated one-man production *Scope, Color, Muda* (Spain, 1970) in 17 months between 1968 and 1970. Sistiaga single-handedly painted directly on to the film stock, frame by frame.

MOST EDITED SCENE

Editor Lloyd Nosler (USA) compressed 200,000 ft (60,960 m) of film into a mere 750 ft (228.6 m) for the chariot race scene in *Ben Hur* (USA, 1925), starring Ramon Navarro – the most edited scene in cinema history with a ratio of 267:1 (film shot to film shown).

LARGEST PRODUCTION CREW FOR A FEATURE FILM

The largest number of craftsmen and technicians employed on a dramatic feature was 532 for the World War I flying story *Gunbus* (UK, 1986; USA title *Sky Bandits*). The crew built enormous sets for war scenes, constructed buildings that were to be exploded, and built airplanes similar to those used in 1917.

LONGEST PRECREDIT SEQUENCE

Before the opening title of Dennis Hopper's *The Last Movie* (USA, 1971), the precredits ran for 30 minutes.

LONGEST CREDIT SEQUENCE

The credits for Sergio Leone's *Once Upon a Time in the West* (Italy/USA, 1968) lasted for 12 minutes.

LONGEST FILM TITLE

The official title of Lina Wertmüller's film was *Un Fatto di sangue nel commune di Sculiana fra due uomini per causa di una vedova si sospetano moventi politici. Amore-Morte-Shimmy. Lugano belle. Tarantelle. Tarallucci é vino.* (Italy, 1979). It has 179 characters, including punctuation. The English title was *Revenge!*

AGAIN AND AGAIN AND AGAIN . . .

Director Stanley Kubrick demanded the record number of retakes for one scene in a film with dialog. The scene with Shelley Duvall in *The Shining* (USA, 1980), also starring Jack Nicholson (left), had an unbelievable 127 takes.

Marilyn Monroe did 59 takes of a scene in *Some Like it Hot* (USA, 1959) in which her only line of dialog was "Where's the Bourbon?"

The scene in Charlie Chaplin's *City Lights* (USA, 1931) in which a blind girl sells him a flower thinking that he is a wealthy tycoon, took 342 takes, and is the overall record for the film with the most retakes for one scene. This silent movie, generally considered to be Chaplin's best, was released three years after the start of the talkies.

‹54546›
← ACCESS CODE
www.guinnessworldrecords.com/retakes

HIGHEST BOX-OFFICE GROSS

Rising cinema ticket prices mean the all-time top-grossing movies are nearly all recent films. Although *Gone with the Wind* (USA, 1939) took just $393.4 million (then £88 million) at the international box office, in an inflation-adjusted list it comes top with a total gross of $3,785,107,801 (£2,365,692,376). In the USA alone, *Gone with the Wind* had 283,100,000 admissions compared to 130,900,000 for *Titanic* (USA, 1997).

LARGEST BOX-OFFICE LOSS

MGM's *Cutthroat Island* (USA, 1995), starring Geena Davis and directed by Renny Harlin, cost over $100 million (£63 million) to produce, promote, and distribute, and reportedly earned back just $11 million (£7 million).

LARGEST FILM BUDGET

The largest production budget given to a movie before filming started is $145 million (£93.428,437) for the war epic *Pearl Harbor*. Shooting began on April 3 2000 and the film, starring Ben Affleck, was released in May 2001.

HIGHEST-GROSSING SCIENCE-FICTION FILM

Star Wars (USA, 1977) originally took $513.7 million (£294.29 million) worldwide. In an inflation-adjusted list, the film comes second only after *Gone with the Wind* (USA, 1939), with an international gross of $1,561,189,344 (£975,743,340).

www.guinnessworldrecords.com/hannibal

ACCESS CODE

<56244> ←

MONEY SPINNERS

In its opening weekend (starting on Feb 9 2001) *Hannibal* (USA, 2001), directed by Ridley Scott and starring Anthony Hopkins and Julianne Moore (below), took $58 million (£40.1 million) from 3,230 screens. This is the highest box-office gross for a film with an over-18 rating on an opening weekend.

Opening in 2,970 cinemas, *Star Wars: Episode 1 – The Phantom Menace* (USA, 1999), reached the $100-million (£60.33-million) mark in a record five days from May 23 to 28 1999, breaking the previous record set by *Jurassic Park: The Lost World* for the fastest time to reach $100 million. When the preview was first released, cinemas reported that some people bought tickets, only to walk out once they had seen the *Star Wars: Episode I* preview.

HIGHEST-GROSSING AUSTRALIAN FILM

Crocodile Dundee (Australia, 1986), starring Paul Hogan and Linda Kozlowski, has grossed $328 million (£218 million) since its release.

HIGHEST-GROSSING UK FILM

The Full Monty (UK, 1997), released in Aug 1997, grossed a record total of $256.9 million (£160.5 million).

HIGHEST-GROSSING WESTERN

The Western *Dances with Wolves* (USA, 1990), directed by and starring Kevin Costner, has grossed $424.2 million (£297.6 million) at the international box office since being first released in the USA in Nov 1990.

HIGHEST-GROSSING HORROR FILM

The Exorcist (USA, 1973), which was directed by William Friedkin with a $12 million (then £4.89 million) budget, has taken a record $292.7 million (£205.3 million) at the international box office.

LARGEST ANNUAL FILM OUTPUT

India produces more feature-length films than any other country. In 1990 a record 948 films were produced and, in 1994, a total of 754 films were produced in a record 16 languages at the three major centers of production – Mumbai (Bombay), Calcutta, and Madras. Since the 1980s, traditional Hindi musical love stories have dominated the screen in India.

GUINNESS WORLD RECORDS

movies 2

LARGEST ASSEMBLAGE OF ANIMALS IN A FILM

Around the World in Eighty Days (USA, 1956) directed by Daniel Anderson and starring David Niven as Phileas Fogg, involved a total of 8,552 animals – 3,800 sheep, 2,448 buffalo, 950 donkeys, 800 horses, 512 monkeys, 17 bulls, 15 elephants, six skunks, and four ostriches.

MOST EXTENSIVE SCREEN TEST

To find the actress to play the role of Scarlett O'Hara in *Gone with the Wind* (USA, 1939), MGM shot 149,000 ft (45,415 m) of black-and-white test film and another 13,000 ft (3,962 m) of color with 60 actresses, none of whom got the part. After discarding 27 hours of test film, producer David O. Selznick narrowed the choice to four. Vivien Leigh eventually landed the part after shooting had already commenced. The total cost of the 162,000 ft (49,377 m) of tests was $105,000 (£23,452) – approximately the budget then of an average second feature film. Today this would be equivalent to $1.63 million (£1.16 million).

MOST FILM SEQUELS

The American film series 'Blondie', starring Penny Singleton in the title role of Blondie Bumstead, first hit the screen in 1939 with *Blondie Meets the Boss*, followed by 26 sequels, the last being *Beware of Blondie* (USA, 1950). Naturally a brunette, she bleached her hair especially for the role. She starred in an average two to three 'Blondie' films a year – the most made in a year was four in 1947.

SMALLEST FILM SET

The smallest film set was built for *Bill and Coo* (USA, 1947). It was filmed entirely in a model village mounted on a table measuring 30 ft x 15 ft (9.14 m x 4.57 m). The performers were love birds. The success of the film was rewarded with an Honorary Academy Award in 1948.

LARGEST INDOOR FILM SET

The UFO landing site built for Steven Spielberg's *Close Encounters of the Third Kind* (USA, 1977) was 90 ft (27 m) high, 450 ft (137 m) long, and 250 ft (76 m) wide. The structure included 4 miles (6.4 km) of scaffolding, 16,900 ft² (1,570 m²) of fiberglass, and 29,500 ft² (2,740 m²) of nylon canopy.

LONGEST FILM SERIES

The longest film series is the 103 features made in Hong Kong about the 19th-century martial arts hero Huang Fei-Hong, starting with *The True Story of Huang Fei-Hong* (HK, 1949). The latest production, after 46 years, was *Once Upon a Time in China 5* (HK, 1995).

LONGEST OSCAR SPEECH

The longest speech at the Oscars lasted 5 min 30 sec, and was made by Greer Garson at the 1942 Academy Awards on March 4 1943, after receiving Best Actress award for her title role in *Mrs. Miniver* (USA, 1942). Speeches have been restricted to 45 seconds since the 1990 Awards.

MOST PEOPLE THANKED BY AN OSCAR WINNER

When Olivia de Havilland won Best Actress for Josephine Norris in *To Each His Own* (USA, 1946) at the 1946 Academy Awards on March 13 1947, she thanked a record 27 people.

HORROR UPON HORROR

The character most often portrayed in horror films is Count Dracula, created by Irish writer Bram Stoker. One such portrayal of Dracula (left) is *Bram Stoker's Dracula* (USA, 1992). Representations of the Count or his immediate descendants outnumber those of his closest rival, Frankenstein, by 162 to 117.

The year 1972 was the most prolific year for horror films – it saw a record total of 189 horror films released. Of these, 83 came from the USA. The boom rapidly abated within three years, when only 58 screamers were produced in 1975. This was, however, the year that horror pictures took the largest share of film rentals, largely due to the overwhelming success of *Jaws* (USA, 1975).

<50723> www.guinnessworldrecords.com/dracula
← ACCESS CODE

LONG TIME NO SEE

Walt Disney Production's sequel *Return To Oz* (USA, 1985) was made 46 years after the original, *The Wizard of Oz* (USA, 1939), which starred Judy Garland and Jack Haley (left). This is the longest interval between an original and its sequel. The sequel was based on the second and third of Frank Baum's 14 Oz books, *The Land of Oz* and *Ozma of Oz*.

The record for the longest interval between an original film and a remake stands at 74 years 267 days in the case of *Seven Chances* (USA, 1925) directed by and starring Buster Keaton and *The Bachelor* (USA, 1999) directed by Gary Sinyor. Both films tell the story of Jimmie Shannon who has 24 hours in which to find a woman to marry in order to claim his recently deceased grandfather's fortune.

<50608> www.guinnessworldrecords.com/wizardofoz
← ACCESS CODE

MOST OSCAR NOMINATIONS FOR FOREIGN LANGUAGE FILM

The martial arts film *Wo hu zang long* or *Crouching Tiger, Hidden Dragon* (Taiwan, 2000), directed by Ang Lee and starring Yun-Fat Chow and Michelle Yeoh, was nominated for a record 10 Oscars on Feb 23 2001. Also nominated for Best Picture, Best Director, Music (Song), Writing (Adapted Screenplay), Film Editing, and Costume Design, it won Oscars for Best Foreign Language Film, Art Direction, Music (Score), and Cinematography.

MOST OSCAR NOMINATIONS FOR FOREIGN FILMS

France holds the record for having a film nominated in the Foreign Language Film category 31 times between 1956 and 2001. France has won the category on nine occasions, in 1958, 1959, 1962, 1966, 1972, 1973, 1977, 1978, and 1992.

MOST OSCAR NOMINATIONS WITHOUT WINNING

Art director Roland Anderson received 15 Oscar nominations for Art Direction but never won. Composer Alex North also had 15 nominations without winning, but was awarded an Honorary Oscar in 1986.

MOST OSCAR NOMINATIONS FOR A FILM

The most Oscar nominations a film has received is 14, given to *All About Eve* (USA, 1950) in 1951 and *Titanic* (USA, 1997) in 1998. *All About Eve* eventually won six Oscars, while *Titanic* came away with 11 – a record it shares with *Ben Hur* (USA, 1959).

PRETTY WOMAN

Julia Roberts (right) commanded a fee of $20,000,000 (£12,500,000) for her lead role in *Erin Brokovich* (USA, 2000). This makes her the highest-paid actress for a single film. Her previous highest fee was $17,000,000 (£10,625,000) for *Runaway Bride* (USA, 1999). On March 25 2001 she received an Oscar for Best Actress for portraying Erin Brokovich. Other big film hits include *Notting Hill* (UK, 1999), as well as *Pretty Woman* (USA, 1990).

ACCESS CODE

‹54705› ←

WESTERN HERO MOST OFTEN PORTRAYED ON SCREEN

William Frederick Cody, otherwise known as 'Buffalo Bill,' has been portrayed in a total of 48 films, first appearing in *Buffalo Bill* (Australia, 1909) and most recently portrayed by Keith Carradine in *Wild Bill* (USA, 1995).

MOST COSTUMES USED IN A FILM

The largest number of costumes used for any one film was 32,000 for *Quo Vadis?* (USA, 1951), starring Robert Taylor and Deborah Kerr.

MOST OSCAR NOMINATIONS FOR A LIVING PERSON

The composer John Williams has had 38 Academy Award nominations, making him the most-nominated living person. His first nomination was for Best Music, Scoring of Music, Adaptation, or Treatment for *Valley of the Dolls* (USA, 1967). His 38th nomination for Best Original Score was for *The Patriot* (USA, 2000) in 2001.

MOST OSCAR-WINNING GENERATIONS

The only family with three generations of Oscar winners are the Hustons. Walter Huston (1884–1950) won Best Supporting Actor for *The Treasure of the Sierra Madre* (USA, 1948); his son John (1906–1987) won Best Director for the same film and John's daughter Angelica (b. 1951) won Best Supporting Actress for *Prizzi's Honor* (USA, 1985).

MOST OSCAR WINS FOR ACTING AND WRITING

Emma Thompson won Best Actress in 1993 for her role in *Howards End* (UK, 1991) and was awarded Best Screenplay Written Directly for the Screen for *Sense and Sensibility* (USA/UK, 1995) in 1996, making her the first person ever to win Oscars for both acting and writing.

MOST OSCARS WON FOR BEST FOREIGN LANGUAGE FILM

Italy has won 12 Oscars for Best Foreign Language Film, the most recent being *Life Is Beautiful* (1997) at the 71st Academy Awards in 1999. The Italian Academy-Award winners have been as follows: *Mediterraneo* (1991), *Cinema Paradiso* (1989), *Amarcord* (1974), *The Garden of the Finzi Continis* (1971), *Investigation of a Citizen Above Suspicion* (1970), *Yesterday, Today and Tomorrow* (1964), Federico Fellini's *8½* (1963), *The Nights of Cabiria* (1957), *La Strada* (1956), *The Walls of Malapaga* (1950), and *The Bicycle Thief* (1949).

GUINNESS WORLD RECORDS

tu ads and production

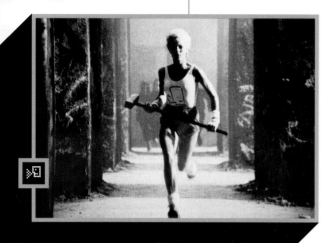

THE BIG APPLE

The most expensive TV ad ever made was a commercial for computer manufacturer Apple Macintosh (above), based on the novel *1984* by George Orwell. It cost $600,000 (£360,000) to produce and $1,000,000 (£600,000) to show during the NFL Super Bowl in Jan 1984. Its impact was so great and the recall so high that it is considered to be one of the most cost-effective commercials ever made. It was shown only twice – the other occasion was on a small station in the US in Dec 1983. It depicted an IBM world being overrun by a new machine – the Mac.

The highest rate for an ad broadcast during a TV series was a 30-second network spot during the commercial breaks for the last-ever episode of NBC's *Seinfeld*, starring Jerry Seinfeld. It cost $575,000 (£359,375) on May 14 1998. That is $15,000 (£9,225.09) more than the second-highest rate commanded by the medical drama *ER*.

<48001>
www.guinnessworldrecords.com/apple
← ACCESS CODE

LARGEST REVENUE BY A TV NETWORK ON A SINGLE DAY
Fox TV (USA) is reputed to have earned $150 million (£90.5 million) on Super Bowl Sunday (Jan 31 1999) – the most advertising revenue earned by a network in one day.

SHORTEST TV AD
A subliminal ad for Bon Marche's Frango sweets lasted four frames (there are 30 frames in a second) when it was aired on KING-TV's *Evening Magazine* (USA) on Nov 29 1993.

EARLIEST AD IN SPACE
On Aug 22 1997 an advertising campaign for Tnuva Milk showed cosmonaut Vasily Tsibliyev drinking milk aboard the Russian space station, Mir, making it the first ad to be filmed in space.

MOST TV ADS FOR ONE PRODUCT IN ONE NIGHT
On Oct 1 1996 Granada Sky Broadcasting (UK) aired all 17 versions of the Castlemaine XXXX ad.

LARGEST CAST OF BABIES FOR AN AD
A British television commercial made for the Vauxhall Astra car by Tony Kaye in 1996 featured 2,000 babies.

LARGEST SIMULTANEOUS TV AD PREMIER
The Ford Motor Company (USA) aired their two-minute *Global Anthem* advertisement on more than 140 pan-regional or local market networks in a record 190 countries on Nov 1 1999 at 9 p.m. local time.

BIGGEST TV AUDIENCE RATING SHARE
The final episode of *M*A*S*H*, *Goodbye, Farewell, and Amen*, was transmitted by CBS on Feb 28 1983 to 60.3% of all households in the USA. About 125 million people tuned in – 77% of the viewing public.

EARLIEST PROGRAM BUDGET
In 1936, Cecil Madden, program organizer and senior producer at Alexandra Palace, London, UK, was allotted a budget of £1,000 (then $4,971) for a week's entire television output for the BBC – equivalent today to £28,850 ($40,390). This, in part, accounted for the audience viewing pattern – one hour in the afternoons, one hour in the evenings, and no television on Sundays.

FASTEST VIDEO PRODUCTION
Live filming of the Royal Wedding of HRH Prince Andrew and Sarah Ferguson (UK) on July 23 1986 ended with the departure of the honeymoon couple from Chelsea Hospital by helicopter at 4:42 p.m. The first fully edited and packaged VHS tapes produced by Thames Video Collection were purchased from the Virgin Megastore in Oxford Street, London, UK, at 10:23 p.m. – 5 hr 41 min later.

HIGHEST EARNINGS FOR A TV PRODUCER
In 1999 David E. Kelley (USA), the creator of *Ally McBeal* and *The Practice*, became the world's highest-earning TV producer according to the 2000 *Forbes* Celebrity 100 list, after his earnings topped $118 million (£73.1 million).

HIGHEST EARNINGS FOR A TV WRITER
Larry David, cowriter and cocreator of the hit US comedy *Seinfeld*, earned an estimated $242 million (£146 million) in 1998. David left the show in 1996, returning to pen the final episode in 1998.

SHORTEST-LIVED TV MONOPOLY
The shortest-lived monopoly in the history of broadcasting was the BBC's *Breakfast Time*, launched on Jan 17 1983 on BBC1. It operated for 15 days before ITV introduced TV-AM on Feb 1 1983 as a rival.

LONGEST-SERVING CUSTOM-BUILT TRANSMITTING TOWER
A steel TV transmitting mast was erected in 1935 on top of the south-east tower of Alexandra Palace, London, UK, to the specifications of John Logie Baird, the BBC, and EMI-Marconi. It transmitted the world's first high-definition TV service from Nov 1936, and is still being used for BBC and ITV television and digital radio signals.

LONGEST TIME SPENT SUBTITLING A LIVE SHOW
The BBC's subtitling team employed eight stenographers, working shifts throughout the night, to bring verbatim subtitles of the BBC's *1997 Election Special* program to a deaf and hard-of-hearing audience. They worked for 17 hr 55 min from 9:55 p.m. on May 1 until 4 p.m. on May 2. The only break in the coverage was between 1:30 p.m. and 2 p.m., when local news programs were broadcast.

LARGEST TV AUDIENCE FOR A SPACE EVENT
The most televised event in space was the first moonwalk by the Apollo 11 astronauts in July 1969. It was watched on TV by an estimated 600 million people – a fifth of the world's population at the time.

LARGEST MUSIC TV NETWORK
MTV is beamed into 281.7 million households in 79 countries around the globe, which means it can be seen by one in four of the world's total TV audience.

LARGEST TV NETWORK
CNN International can be seen in 212 countries and territories through a network of 23 satellites. About

www.guinnessworldrecords.com/er

A COSTLY OPERATION

The most expensive TV program currently made is *ER*, America's No.1 prime-time show. It had a weekly audience of 33 million when, in Jan 1998, Warner Bros agreed to a three-year deal with NBC of a record $857.6 million (£536 million) for 22 episodes at $13.1 million (£8.2 million) per one-hour episode. Before the deal, NBC paid $1.6 million (£1 million) per episode, earning $16 million (£10 million) in advertising revenue. In April 2000, NBC paid a record $640 million (£400 million) for three more series until 2004, which works out at $9.6 million (£6 million) an episode. Pictured below are Goran Visnjic (left), as Dr. Luka Kovac, James Cromwell (center), as Bishop Stewart, and Erik Palladino (right), as Dr. Dave Malucci.

149 million households across the planet can tune in, making it the world's largest TV network.

MOST WATCHED TV NETWORK

The state-owned station China Central Television (CCTV) is transmitted to 84% of all Chinese viewers in China. It is estimated that over 900 million people in the country have access to television, making CCTV the world's most watched network. Its nine channels broadcast in Mandarin, Cantonese, English, and French.

MOST EXPENSIVE TV DOCUMENTARY SERIES PER MINUTE

It cost over £37,654 ($61,112) per minute to produce the BBC's documentary series *Walking with Dinosaurs* (Oct 1999), which depicts how dinosaurs lived, reproduced, and became extinct. The six-part series took more than two years to produce and cost £6.1 million ($9.9 million). It features computer graphics and animatronics with background footage filmed in locations around the world.

MOST EXPENSIVE TV RIGHTS

In June 1997, the Fox network paid a record $81 million (£50 million) for the TV rights to Steven Spielberg's film *Jurassic Park: The Lost World* (USA,1997) before it was even released on the international market. *Jurassic Park: The Lost World* was the sequel to *Jurassic Park* (1993).

GUINNESS WORLD RECORDS™

tv shows

MOST MONEY DONATED TO A TELETHON

On March 16 2001, UK supermarket chain Sainsbury's presented Comic Relief with a check for £4.5 million ($6.4 million) during *The Night of Comic Relief* on BBC1. Money was raised through the sales of Comic Relief products and staff fundraising.

MOST TV EPISODES SOLD

On May 31 1971 Granada Television sold 1,144 episodes of *Coronation Street* (UK) to CBKST Saskatoon,

MONEY MONEY MONEY

The largest cash prize ever won on television is £1 million, and has been given on three occasions. On Dec 24 1999, Ian Woodley (UK) won his million (then equivalent to $1,618,000) on Channel 4's *TFI Friday* quiz thanks to knowing that in the film *American Pie*, the pie was made from apples.

On Nov 19 2000 Judith Keppel (UK, above) won £1 million (then worth $1,423,000) on ITV's *Who Wants To Be A Millionaire?* She answered 15 questions correctly, the last being, "Which King was married to Eleanor of Aquitaine?" Her correct answer was "Henry II."

The show gave away another £1 million (then $1,439,500) on April 9 2001 to science teacher David Edwards (UK). He won the grand total on the question, "If you planted the seeds of *Quercus Robur*, what would you grow?" He answered correctly – "trees."

www.guinnessworldrecords.com/millionaire

ACCESS CODE

‹47849›

Saskatchewan, Canada. This number of episodes equaled 20 days 15 hr 44 min continuous viewing.

LONGEST FILM SHOWN ON TV

The longest film shown on television in a single day was the 8-hr-27-min epic *War and Peace* (USSR, 1967). It was transmitted by Mexico's Channel II on Feb 28 1981.

LONGEST-RUNNING CHILDREN'S MAGAZINE PROGRAM

The BBC's *Blue Peter* was transmitted for the first time from London's Lime Grove Studios on Oct 16 1958. There have been 29 presenters and 3,456 shows broadcast up to April 18 2001.

LONGEST-RUNNING CHILDREN'S PROGRAM

Since 1949, over 150,000 individual episodes of the TV show *Bozo the Clown* (USA) by Larry Harmon Pictures have been aired daily on 150 stations in the USA.

LONGEST-RUNNING POP SHOW

The first edition of the UK's *Top of the Pops* was presented by Jimmy Savile on Jan 1 1964 on BBC1 and is still running. Dusty Springfield, the Rolling Stones, the Dave Clark Five, the Swinging Blue Jeans, and the Hollies all appeared in the first program. The Beatles and Cliff Richard and the Shadows were shown on film. The program had reached its 1,939th edition on May 18 2001 and celebrated its 2000th edition in summer 2001.

LONGEST-RUNNING PRIME-TIME ANIMATED SERIES

The Simpsons (USA), created by Matt Groening, is the longest-running prime-time animated television show. Up to March 4 2001, 263 episodes had been shown on the Fox network in the USA.

LONGEST-RUNNING TV DRAMA

Granada's *Coronation Street* (UK) is the longest-running domestic drama

---

DON'T TRY THIS AT HOME!

USA

The world's most extreme game show is Japan's *Za Gaman* (above), or in English, *Endurance*. Contestants have to endure different types of mental and physical torture, such as standing on their heads with hot coals on their feet, or hanging between swinging cacti above a tank of snakes – the winners endure the challenge for the longest. *Za Gaman* is a prime-time series on the Fuji Network and is the No.1 show. In the test of endurance shown here, which took place on Jan 15 1998, the contestants braved the cold and doused themselves in freezing water during a heavy snowfall.

‹53821›

www.guinnessworldrecords.com/endurance

← ACCESS CODE

---

serial with the first episode shown on Dec 9 1960. The program is shown four times a week and up to April 16 2001 there had been a total of 5,021 episodes broadcast.

LONGEST-RUNNING TV SHOW

NBC's *Meet the Press*, which first transmitted in the USA on Nov 6 1947 and was subsequently shown weekly from Sept 12 1948, has had 2,649 shows aired up to Feb 4 2001.

LONGEST TV DOCUMENTARY ON A SINGLE SUBJECT

Every seven years since 1963, the '7 Up' documentary film series, shown on the UK's ITV, has followed the lives of the same 14 children selected from different social groups in the UK at the age of seven. The first in the series, *7 Up*, was followed by *7 times 7* (1970), which filmed the children at age 14. A further four installments have been added.

LONGEST TV TALK SHOW MARATHON

The record for the longest continuous talk show hosted by an individual is 24 hours. It is held by

---

Peter Imhof, who started at 1:30 p.m. on June 23 2000 and chatted to more than 450 people in front of a studio audience in Potsdam-Babelsberg on Germany's station SAT.1.

LONGEST UNINTERRUPTED LIVE TV BROADCAST

The Swiss television station Suisse 4 broadcast the 1996 Olympic Games held in Atlanta, Georgia, around the clock for 16 days 22 hr 45 min.

MOST DAYTIME SERIES EMMY NOMINATIONS IN A SEASON

A grand total of 21 nominations for Daytime Emmy Awards were given to the US soap opera *The Young and the Restless* (ABC) on March 11 1999. It won three awards at the ceremony on May 21 1999 for Supporting Actress in a Drama Series (Sharon Case); Younger Actress in a Drama Series (Heather Tom); and Drama Series Writing Team.

SHORTEST TV PROGRAM

Election Thoughts, a series of 15 programs just 30 seconds long, complete with titles, program content, credits, and original music score, were broadcast by Channel 4 during the three weeks leading up to the UK General Election of 1997.

LARGEST TV AUDIENCE FOR A WEDDING
On July 29 1981 the marriage of HRH Prince Charles to Lady Diana Spencer was seen by an estimated 750 million people in 74 countries. At the time the largest remote broadcast in British history, it had an audience in Britain of 39 million.

LARGEST TV AUDIENCE FOR A COMEDY
The final episode of the US television comedy *Seinfeld*, starring Jerry Seinfeld, was screened on May 14 1998, attracting 108 million viewers.

MOST POPULAR CHILDREN'S EDUCATIONAL PROGRAM
Sesame Street (USA) produced since Nov 10 1969 by the Children's Television Workshop, New York, is sold to 180 countries. This figure includes coproductions (such as *Open Sesame*) and dubbed versions.

CONTESTANT WITH MOST TV QUIZ APPEARANCES
Since March 1986, Marc Vanacker (Belgium) has appeared on 29 TV quiz shows that have been broadcast in Belgium, Germany, the Netherlands, and the UK. The shows include *Going for Gold* (Grundy Television) and *Einstein* (NCRV), and he has won a total of BFr 1,520,326, ($34,577), trips to the USA, Paris, and Vienna, and a car.

MOST SUCCESSFUL TV SOAP
The American TV series, *Dallas*, began quietly in 1978 with just five episodes. By 1980, it was watched by an estimated 83 million people in the US, giving it a then record 76% share of the television audience. It has been seen in more than 90 countries, often in dubbed versions. A sister series, *Knots Landing*, was made, but it did not achieve the same level of success.

MOST POPULAR TV GAME
The game show *Wheel of Fortune* is currently seen in 204 US markets, as well as in 54 overseas markets, with an estimated 100 million viewers a week. Since its 1983 syndication launch, the US show has awarded over $112 million (£70 million) in cash and prizes, averaging in excess of $7 million (£4.3 million) per year.

www.guinnessworldrecords.com/westwing

LANDSLIDE VICTORY
NBC's drama series *The West Wing* (below), which is set behind-the-scenes at the White House, won a record nine awards for a single season at the 52nd Annual Prime-Time Emmy Awards held from Sept 9 to 10 2000.

The series shared the record for the most nominated show with HBO's *The Sopranos* with 18. *The Sopranos* went home in 2000 with one win. Premiered on US television on Sept 22 1999, *The West Wing* was created by Aaron Sorkin, and stars Rob Lowe as the White House deputy communications director and speechwriter, as well as Moira Kelly, Bradley Whitford, John Spencer, Richard Schiff, Allison Janney, and Martin Sheen, who plays President Josiah Bartlet, a New Hampshire Democrat.

ACCESS CODE

‹51843› ←

GUINNESS WORLD RECORDS

stunts and special FX

BALLOONATIC! 📺 USA

On May 20 1998 Mike Howard (UK, above), walked, with no parachute, between two hot air balloons at the frightening height of 18,800 ft (5,486.4 m) – the highest altitude at which anyone has completed a balloon skywalk. The two balloons flew over Marshall, Michigan, with Howard balancing on a tiny beam 19 ft (5.79 m) long and only 3 in (7.62 cm) wide. By the time Howard finished his return journey across the beam, the hot air balloons had risen to 19,000 ft (5,791.2 m) and traveled over 65 miles (104 km) at a speed of more than 46.2 mph (74.4 km/h). The balloons were connected by two safety ropes and were piloted by Mike's wife Renée and his fellow balloonists Scott Lorenz, Steve Davis, and Doug Davis, who also filmed Mike's breathtaking steps through the sky, as did additional film crews in a helicopter above the action, and below on the ground.

<48863>
← ACCESS CODE   www.guinnessworldrecords.com/balloonwalk

MOST CLAY PIGEONS SHOT UPSIDE DOWN 📺 USA

Kimberly Rhode (USA) managed to shoot 21 out of 24 clay pigeons while she was hanging upside down in a 40-ft (12.19-m) clear tunnel on Dec 20 2000.

LARGEST TIGHTROPE PYRAMID

On June 27 and 30 1998 the children's high-wire act of the Peru Amateur Circus, Peru, Indiana, achieved an eight-person pyramid on a high wire 20 ft (6.09 m) above the floor of the circus arena.

MOST INVERTED FLAT SPINS 📺 USA

The most inverted flat spins made in one attempt is 78 at 14,764 ft (4,500 m) by Wayne Handley (USA). The record was set in a superlight stunt plane G202, on April 2 1999.

LONGEST HUMAN SUCTION SUSPENSION 📺 USA

By pressing a rice bowl on his abdomen, Cuong Chu-Tan of Saale, Germany, was able to create enough suction to suspend himself from a helicopter on a 16-ft 5-in (5-m) rope for 3 min 37 sec. He traveled for 0.5 miles (0.8 km) at a height of 200 ft (60.96 m) on Feb 27 2001.

LONGEST STRETCHED BUNGEE-JUMP CORD

Gregory Riffi made a bungee jump from a helicopter above the Loire Valley, France, in Feb 1992. His 820-ft (249.9-m) cord stretched to 2,001 ft (610 m) during the jump. This record refers to the length of the elastisized bungee cord at maximum elongation, so after freefall the cord stretched a further 1,181 ft (360.1 m) – greater than any cord used before.

LONGEST UNSTRETCHED BUNGEE-JUMP CORD

On Sept 19 1997 Jochen Schweizer (Germany) used a cord, that when unstretched, measured 931 ft 9 in (284 m). When he jumped from an SA 365 Dauphine helicopter at a height of 8,202 ft (2,500 m) over Reichelsheim, Germany, the cord stretched to 1,246 ft 8 in (380 m). Since this is the longest bungee cord ever used, the freefall distance and duration were longer than on any other bungee jump.

MOST SWORDS SWALLOWED

Martin Henshaw (USA) swallowed 14 swords simultaneously on April 6 2000 at Fremantle, Perth, Western Australia. The swords were 1.57 in (4 cm) wide, 23.19 in (58.9 cm) long, and weighed a total of 9.92 lb (4.5 kg). Another of Martin's acts includes cooking a sausage between his pectoral muscles by passing 240 volts of electricity through his body jewelry.

MOST CHAINSAWS JUGGLED 📺 SE

Karoly Donnert (Hungary) juggled three chainsaws, managing 12 rotations (36 throws) on Jan 30 2001.

HIGHEST JUMP WITHOUT A PARACHUTE BY A STUNTMAN

A.J. Bakunas (USA) jumped from 232 ft (70.7 m) on to an air mattress while doubling for Burt Reynolds in *Hooper* (USA, 1978). On Sept 9 1980, during the filming of *Steel* (USA, 1980), Bakunas was fatally injured when he fell from the top of a construction site in Lexington, VA.

HIGHEST FREEFALL BY A STUNTMAN

For the film *Highpoint* (Canada, 1979), stuntman Dar Robinson freefell from the record height of 1,100 ft (335 m), from a ledge at the summit of the CN Tower, Toronto, Canada. The freefall lasted six seconds before his parachute opened 300 ft (91.4 m) from the ground.

MOST EXPENSIVE AERIAL STUNT

Simon Crane (UK) performed one of the most dangerous aerial stunts ever when he moved between two

DOUBLE JEOPARDY

Vic Armstrong (UK) is the world's most prolific movie stuntman. He has been the stunt double for many top actors including Sean Connery, Donald Sutherland, Timothy Dalton, Roger Moore, Pierce Brosnan, and Harrison Ford (left). In a career spanning 30 years, he has performed stunts in over 200 films, including *Raiders Of The Lost Ark* (USA, 1981) and the Indiana Jones series. He has also coordinated stunts for movies such as *Tomorrow Never Dies* (UK/USA, 1997) and is married to stuntwoman Wendy Leech, whom he met when they doubled for the stars of *Superman* (USA, 1978).

<53683>
www.guinnessworldrecords.com/stuntman
← ACCESS CODE

jets at an altitude of 2.95 miles (4.75 km) for the movie *Cliffhanger* (USA, 1993). The stunt, performed only once because it was so risky, cost a record $1 million (£568,000). Sylvester Stallone, the film's star, is said to have offered to reduce his fee by the same amount to ensure that the stunt was made.

LARGEST COORDINATOR OF FILM AERIAL STUNTS

Flying Pictures (UK) has planned and coordinated air stunts for more than 200 feature films, including *Cliffhanger* (USA, 1993), *GoldenEye* (UK/USA, 1995), and *Mission Impossible* (USA, 1996).

LARGEST SPECIAL-EFFECTS BUDGET

The special-effects budget for Stanley Kubrick's movie *2001: A Space Odyssey* (USA, 1968) came to $6.5 million (£2,246,023), the equivalent of around $27 million (£19 million) today. This represents over 60% of the total $10.5 million (£3,628,191) production cost. Compared to *Star Wars – The*

Phantom Menace (USA, 1999), this would be the equivalent of spending $69 million (£48 million) of its $115 million (£81 million) budget on special effects.

LARGEST FILM STUNT BUDGET

More than $3 million (£1.87 million) of the $200-million (£125-million) budget for *Titanic* (USA, 1997) went toward film stunts. In the most complex scene, 100 stuntpeople leapt, fell, and slid 751 ft (229 m) as the ship broke in half and rose out of the water to a 90° angle. The exterior set was a 775-ft (236.22-m) long copy of *Titanic* – only 10% smaller than the actual ship.

MOST STILL CAMERAS USED IN A FILM SEQUENCE

When shooting the 'bullet-time' sequence during the filming of *The Matrix* (USA, 1999), 120 specially modified film cameras were used by directors Larry and Andy Wachowski to achieve a panning shot of Neo (Keanu Reeves) as he dodged bullets from a pursuer.

Slow-motion filming that used 12,000 frames a second was added to the still shots and normal filming, which were all computer-manipulated later.

MOST COMPUTER-GENERATED FILM EFFECTS

Pleasantville (USA, 1998) had 1,700 separate digital visual effect shots, compared to the average Hollywood

www.guinnessworldrecords.com/firewall

GREAT WALLS OF FIRE

On Oct 14 2000 the Marine Corps Air Station (MCAS) Miramar Explosive Ordnance Disposal Team created a wall of fire measuring a record 2,500 ft (762 m) in San Diego, California, during the MCAS Miramar Twilight Air Show. The fire wall (below) consisted of 334 5-gal (23-liter) bags of unleaded fuel connected by a detonation cord. Once this

ACCESS CODE

<56058> ←

film which has 50. The movie, about two 1990s' teenagers (always shown in color) who are transported into the black-and-white world of a 1950s' television show, was shot on color film. All color then had to be painstakingly removed from each frame where the characters and backgrounds were monochrome. The 82-minute film spent over a year in postproduction since every shot in the movie had to be adjusted.

MOST EXPENSIVE SPECIAL EFFECTS IN A MUSIC VIDEO

The video for 'What's It Gonna Be?' (1999) by Busta Rhymes and Janet Jackson, directed by Hype Williams, cost $2.4 million (£1.44 million) to produce. Inspired by the *Terminator* movies, computer-morphing effects, such as liquid being molded into different objects – including Busta – accounted for much of the expenditure. The track was taken from Rhymes' millennium-themed album *E.L.E. – The Final World Front*.

cord was lit the fire wall lasted for a few seconds as the fuel consumed itself almost immediately. The flames rose 200-300 ft (60-90 m) into the air and the heat of the blast could be felt from 1,250 ft (380 m) away. The length of the fire wall was equivalent to approximately 50 Greyhound buses placed end-to-end in a straight line.

music best sellers

GREATEST ADVANCE SALES FOR A SINGLE
'Can't Buy Me Love' by The Beatles (UK) sold 2.7 million copies before its release on March 21 1964.

BEST-SELLING CANTONESE POP FEMALE
Faye Wong (Hong Kong) had sold an estimated 9.7 million copies of her 20 albums by March 2000. Her most recent album, *Lovers & Strangers*, was released in Sept 1999 and has so far sold over 800,000 copies, reaching No.1 in Hong Kong, China, Taiwan, Singapore, and Malaysia.

BEST-SELLING GROUP EVER
The Beatles have amassed the greatest sales of any group, with all-time sales estimated by EMI at over one billion disks and tapes to date.

BEST-SELLING DRUM 'N' BASS ALBUM
New Forms by British act Reprazent has sold a total of 763,910 copies worldwide since its release in 1997. The Mercury Music Prize-winning debut album achieved sales of 250,000 in the UK alone.

BEST-SELLING COUNTRY SINGLE
'How Do I Live' by LeAnn Rimes (USA) is the best-selling single by a country artist in the USA, with sales of over 3 million. The single spent a record 33 weeks in the Top 10 and was still on the Country Sales chart in June 2001, a massive 208 weeks after it was released.

BEST-SELLING ALBUM BY A BRITISH GROUP
The best-selling album in the world by a British group is *The Wall* by the highly influential Pink Floyd, with global sales estimated at the 23 million mark. Released in 1979, the LP spent 15 weeks at the top of the US charts and was made into a movie starring Bob Geldof (Ireland) in 1982.

BEST-SELLING FILM SOUNDTRACK ALBUM
The best-selling movie soundtrack is *Saturday Night Fever* (USA, 1977), with sales of over 30 million. Taken from the film starring John Travolta (USA), this disco classic included an incredible six No.1 US hit singles.

BEST-SELLING SINGLE BY A GROUP
The best-selling single by a group is 'Rock Around the Clock' by Bill Haley and his Comets (USA), which sold an estimated 25 million copies. This track was recorded in 1954 and used as the title track to the hit movie *The Blackboard Jungle* (USA, 1955).

BEST-SELLING ALBUM EVER
The best-selling album of all time is the Quincey Jones-produced *Thriller* by Michael Jackson (USA), with global sales of over 47 million copies since its release in 1982.

BEST-SELLING CLASSICAL ALBUM
The world's best-selling classical album is *In Concert*, with global sales of 10.5 million copies to date. It was recorded by José Carreras, Placido Domingo, and Luciano Pavarotti in Rome on July 7 1990 during the 1990 World Cup Finals held in Italy.

BEST-SELLING REGGAE ALBUM
Legend by Bob Marley is the best-selling reggae album ever. The album topped the UK chart, selling 1.8 million copies, and sold more than 10 million in the USA despite never reaching the US Top 40. Marley was awarded the Jamaican Order of Merit after he died in 1981 and is officially known as The Honorable Bob Marley.

BEST-SELLING ALBUM IN AUSTRALIA
Best of ABBA, a compilation of hits by the Swedish pop group ABBA, has sold over 1.2 million copies in Australia since 1976.

BEST-SELLING ALBUM IN THE USA
The best-selling album in the USA by a group is *Their Greatest Hits 1971-75* by the Eagles, with total sales of over 27 million copies, beating the previous holder *Thriller*.

BEST-SELLING ALBUM ON UK CHART
The UK's best-selling album of all time is *Sgt. Pepper's Lonely Hearts Club Band* by The Beatles, with a reported 4.5 million sales since its release in June 1967.

BEST-SELLING AUSTRALIAN ALBUM
The best-selling album by an Australian act is AC/DC's *Back in Black* with estimated global sales of 19 million copies since 1980. Formed in 1973, in Sydney, NSW, Australia, this heavy metal act reportedly found their name after a band member's sister read the label on a vacuum cleaner.

BEST-SELLING COUNTRY ALBUM BY A GROUP
The best-selling album by a country group is *Wide Open Spaces* (1998) by the Dixie Chicks (USA), which has sold 10 million copies. Within 12 months of release, the album was certified as quadruple platinum.

BEST-SELLING LIVE ALBUM
Double Live by country star Garth Brooks (USA) is the best-selling live album in the USA with certified sales of 14 million (seven million double LPs) since being released on Nov 17 1998. Brooks won Entertainer Of The Year at the 1997 Country Music Awards.

COUNTRY COMES ON OVER
The best-selling album in the USA by a female solo artist is Shania Twain's record-breaking album *Come On Over* (1997), which has sold a total of 18 million copies in the USA and 30 million worldwide. The album was produced and cowritten by Twain's husband Robert 'Mutt' Lange and also holds the record for the best-selling country album in the USA by a solo artist. Born Eileen Regina Edwards in Canada in 1965, Shania (above left) is one of the few country artists who have made the successful crossover into pop. Her husband also produced *The Woman In Me* (1995), which was an enormous success, selling over 10 million copies by 1998 and including four Top 10 US country chart hits. She released *Come on Over* and won most of the country music awards, including the Entertainer Of The Year trophy, in 1997 – a phenomenal year for her. *Come on Over* remained in the Top 40 of the Billboard 200 chart 127 weeks after its release.

<56273>
www.guinnessworldrecords.com/shania
← ACCESS CODE

A P-LATIN-UM ARTIST

The best-selling album by a Latin artist is Carlos Santana's (above) *Supernatural* album, which has sold 14 million copies in the USA since its release in June 1999. Hailing from Mexico, Santana's musical career has now spanned five decades. His influential group, also known as Santana, has experimented with diverse cultural elements and sounds including blues, acid rock, Latin, African, and pop.

www.guinnessworldrecords.com/santana

ACCESS CODE
‹54238› ←

MOST PLATINUM CERTIFICATES

Elvis Presley holds the record for the most platinum certificates, with 54 since the Recording Industry Association of America (RIAA) introduced its sales-based awards on March 14 1958. The Beatles hold the group record for the most platinum certificates (awarded for sales of one million units) with 33.

BEST-SELLING SINGLE SINCE THE CHARTS BEGAN

The best-selling single since the UK chart records began (Nov 14 1952) is Elton John's (UK) 'Candle In The Wind 1997/Something About The Way You Look Tonight,' with worldwide sales of 33 million. As of Oct 20 1997 it had reached the top of the charts in 22 countries. 'Candle In The Wind 1997' was recorded as a tribute to Diana, Princess of Wales, and all Elton John's artist and PolyGram profits were donated to the Diana, Princess of Wales Memorial Fund.

BEST-SELLING SINGLE OF ALL TIME

'White Christmas,' written by Irving Berlin (USA) and recorded by Bing Crosby (USA) on May 29 1942, is the best-selling single of all time. It is estimated to have sold in excess of 50 million copies, although there are no exact figures available. If all formats such as 78s and albums are included, this figure rises to more than 100 million.

BEST-SELLING MUSIC VIDEO

The Making of Michael Jackson's Thriller, released in Dec 1983, is the world's best-selling music home video, with more than 900,000 units sold. The extravagant 14-minute-long *Thriller* was directed by John Landis (USA), and famously mocked the style of big-budget horror movies.

www.guinnessworldrecords.com/tlc

ALL SOULED OUT

The best-selling rap/hip hop album in the USA is *CrazySexyCool* (1994) by TLC, which achieved worldwide sales of 11 million copies, surpassing M.C. Hammer's *Please Hammer Don't Hurt 'Em* (1990), which sold 10 million copies. TLC is made up of Rozonda 'Chilli' Thomas, Tionne 'T-Boz' Watkins, and Lisa 'Left Eye' Lopes (right), all from Atlanta, Georgia. *CrazySexyCool*, which featured guest performances by Busta Rhymes (USA) and Phife of A Tribe Called Quest (USA), won two Grammy Awards for Best R&B Performance by a Duo/Group for 'Creep' and Best R&B Album. Other awards included two Billboard Music Awards, three Soul Train Music Awards, and a Blockbuster Entertainment Award. Chilli is quoted as saying that she wishes "to be the biggest female group of all time, to sell so many albums that it will be a few years before any other group can catch up"

ACCESS CODE

‹54252› ←

GUINNESS WORLD RECORDS

chart toppers

YOUNGEST NO.1 SOLO ARTIST ON US ALBUM CHART
Stevie Wonder (USA) was 13 years 3 months old when his album *Little Stevie Wonder – The Twelve Year Old Genius* (1963) topped the US charts.

YOUNGEST SINGER IN UK ALBUM CHART TOP 10
Lena Zavaroni (UK) was just 10 years 146 days old when she hit the album charts in March 1974 with *Ma,* which reached No.8.

ALL YOU NEED IS POP
The record for the most consecutive No.1 hits in the UK is held by The Beatles (above), who had 11 in a row between 1963 and 1966 (from 'From Me to You' through to 'Yellow Submarine'). They also share the record for most consecutive UK Christmas No.1 singles with the Spice Girls, both of whom have had three festive chart-toppers in a row. Formed in the late 1950s as The Quarry Men, The Beatles went through various lineups and name changes, with John Lennon, Paul McCartney, and George Harrison at the core before adding Ringo Starr on drums in 1962. Guided by manager Brian Epstein (UK) and the production skills of George Martin (UK) they became a worldwide sensation, causing hysteria among their fans and amassed the greatest record sales for any group with over one billion units sold.

www.guinnessworldrecords.com/beatles

ACCESS CODE
<50847> ←

FASTEST-SELLING DEBUT SINGLE ON UK CHART
Released on March 12 2001, 'Pure And Simple' by Hear'Say, the group consisting of the five winners of the UK's ITV *Popstars* series, became the best-selling debut single on the UK chart, with 549,823 sales in the first week, taking them straight to No.1. The group, consisting of Noel, Danny, Suzanne, Kym, and Myleene, are also the first-ever act to top the UK single and album charts simultaneously with their debut releases.

LONGEST SPAN OF UK NO.1 SINGLES
Cliff Richard (UK) has had a span of 40 years between his first and most recent No.1 singles on the UK chart – 'Living Doll' in 1959 and 'The Millennium Prayer' in 1999.

LONGEST WAIT FOR A US NO.1 SINGLE
Santana (Mexico) hold the record for the longest gap between their first chart entry – 'Jingle' in Oct 1969 – and their first No.1 – 'Smooth', which became the US No.1 in Oct 1999.

MOST UK CHRISTMAS NO.1 SINGLES
The Beatles have had four singles in the coveted Christmas top spot – 'I Wanna Hold Your Hand' (Dec 12 1963), 'I Feel Fine' (Dec 10 1964), 'Day Tripper/We Can Work it Out' (Dec 16 1965), and, last but not least, 'Hello Goodbye' (Dec 6 1967).

MOST CONSECUTIVE WEEKS AT NO.1 ON US SINGLES CHART
The record that has spent most consecutive weeks at No.1 on the US singles charts is 'One Sweet Day', a collaboration between Mariah Carey and Boyz II Men, (both USA), which topped the chart for 16 weeks in 1995.

MOST CONSECUTIVE SINGLES TO ENTER THE UK CHART AT NO.1 SINCE DEBUT
In 1999/2000, Irish boy-band Westlife became the only group to have their first seven singles enter the UK

HOUSTON, WE HAVE A RECORD BREAKER!
The record for the most consecutive No.1 singles on the US charts is seven, a total achieved by R&B vocalist/actress Whitney Houston (USA, above) between 1985 and 1988. The songs were 'Saving All My Love For You' (1985), 'How Will I Know' (1985), 'Greatest Love Of All' (1986), 'I Want To Dance With Somebody (Who Loves Me)' (1987), 'Didn't We Almost Have It All?' (1987), 'So Emotional' (1987), and 'Where Do Broken Hearts Go?' (1988). Born on March 27 1970, in Long Island, New York, Whitney's record sales total over 100 million copies worldwide to date.

www.guinnessworldrecords.com/whitney
<54592> ← ACCESS CODE

charts at No.1 when their single 'My Love' entered at the top spot on Nov 11 2000.

MOST UK NO.1 SINGLES BY A FEMALE GROUP
The most No.1 singles on the UK charts by a female group is nine by the Spice Girls, and was achieved on Nov 4 2000 when their double-A side single 'Holler/Let Love Lead The Way' reached the top spot.

MOST US NO.1 ALBUMS
The record for the most US No.1 albums is 19, by The Beatles – more than doubling the number of those held by closest rivals Elvis Presley (USA) and The Rolling Stones (UK) with nine each. 'The Fab Four' have now reached the top of the US album chart in five different decades.

MOST NO.1 SINGLES BY A SOLO ARTIST
Elvis Presley holds the record for the most No.1 hit singles by a solo artist. Since the beginning of the rock era in 1955, 'the King' has scored 17 UK No.1 hit singles and

18 in the USA, which stayed at No.1 for a grand total of 80 weeks – more than any other artist in the USA.

MOST UK NO.1 SINGLES
The Beatles and Elvis Presley both share the record for the most No.1 hit singles on the UK charts, with 17 chart toppers each.

MOST US NO.1 SINGLES
The Beatles have the most No.1 hits on the US singles chart with 20, the first of which was 'I Want To Hold Your Hand' on Feb 1 1964.

MOST WEEKS AT NO.1 ON AUSTRALIAN SINGLES CHART
The Beatles' 'Hey Jude' (1968) and ABBA's 'Fernando' (Sweden,1976) both spent 15 weeks at No.1 in Australia.

MOST WEEKS AT NO.1 ON UK ALBUM CHART
The soundtrack to *South Pacific* (USA, 1958) was the first No.1 album. It stayed at the top for 70 consecutive weeks from Nov 8 1958, eventually spending a record 115 weeks at No.1.

www.guinnessworldrecords.com/destinyschild

DESTINATION NO.1

The most weeks spent at No.1 on the US singles chart by a girl band is 'Independent Woman' by Grammy Award-winning R&B trio Destiny's Child (USA, right). It was released on Nov 20 2000, and spent a record 11 weeks at the top of the US chart. The song was the title track from the hit movie *Charlie's Angels*, and the first single by a US female trio to top the UK chart for over 26 years.

YOUNGEST MALE SOLO ARTIST TO ENTER AT NO.1 ON UK SINGLES CHART

The youngest male solo artist to enter the UK singles chart at No.1 is R&B singer Craig David (UK), who was 18 years 339 days old when his single 'Fill Me In' reached the top of the charts on April 9 2000, selling over 165,000 copies.

YOUNGEST SINGER AT NO.1 ON UK ALBUM CHART

Neil Reid (UK) was 12 years 9 months old when his self-titled debut album topped the chart on Feb 19 1972.

MOST SUCCESSFUL POP FAMILY

The Jackson family have scored 26 US No.1 singles – 13 by Michael, nine by Janet, and four by the Jackson 5, who achieved the first Jackson No.1 with 'I Want You Back' on Dec 6 1969.

MOST INTERNATIONAL CHARTS TOPPED BY AN ALBUM

Since being released on Nov 13 2000, the album *1* by The Beatles – a compilation of all of their UK and US No.1 singles – has topped the charts in 35 countries from Australia to Venezuela. Furthermore, it was the biggest album of the year in Australia, Germany, Ireland, Italy, Portugal, and the UK.

MOST UK NO.1 SINGLES BY A TEENAGE FEMALE ARTIST

Two artists share this record with three UK No.1 hits. Britney Spears (USA) was 18 years 158 days old when 'Oops! I Did It Again' became her third single to reach No.1 on May 7 2000; and Billie Piper (UK) was 17 years 242 days old when 'Day & Night' became her third No.1 debuting at the top of the charts on May 21 2000.

GUINNESS WORLD RECORDS

chart hits

MOST NO.1 SINGLES PRODUCED BY AN ADVERTISING CAMPAIGN

Seven songs have reached the No.1 position in the UK pop charts after having appeared on Levi Strauss and Co. TV advertisements. The chart successes include 'Stand By Me' by Ben E. King (USA), 'The Joker' by The Steve Miller Band and 'Inside' by Stiltskin. The seventh No.1 hit to be associated with Levi's TV adverts, 'Flat Beat' by French artist Mr. Oizo, entered at No.1 in Britain on April 3 1999 after selling nearly 284,000 copies.

LONGEST STAY ON UK ALBUM CHART

The longest stay on the UK album chart is a record 477 weeks by Fleetwood Mac's *Rumours*, released on Feb 26 1977. The album hit No.1 and included four entries on the singles chart, though none hit the Top 20.

LONGEST TIME SPENT AT US RAP NO.1 SPOT

'Hot Boyz' by Missy 'Misdemeanor' Elliott (USA) featuring guest rappers Nas, Eve, and Q-Tip, spent a record 18 weeks at the top of the US rap singles chart in 1999/2000.

LONGEST TIME SPENT ON UK SINGLES CHART

'My Way' by Frank Sinatra (USA) has spent 124 weeks on the UK chart since its original release on April 2

SINGING LA VIDA LOCA

The fastest-selling album of all time in Spain was *El Alma Al Aire* (The Bared Soul) by Alejandro Sanz (left), released in Oct 2000. A record 500,000 advance orders were taken and over one million copies were sold in its first week of release (equivalent to 20 million in the USA). A total of 800,000 were shipped to North and South America.

'Macarena' by Spanish duo Los Del Rio (Spanish for 'People of the River') is the most successful Latin single of all time, selling over 10 million copies worldwide. It topped the US chart for 14 weeks in 1996 and spent 60 weeks in the Top 100. Despite its huge success, an internet poll recently voted it, 'Most irritating summer single of all time,' and some US schools banned it due to its suggestive lyrics.

<56330>
www.guinnessworldrecords.com/sanz
← ACCESS CODE

1969 when it reached its peak position of No.5. It has since reentered the chart no fewer than 10 times.

LONGEST US CHART SPAN

The jazz trumpeter Louis Armstrong (USA) first appeared on a chart in 1926 with 'Muskrat Ramble.' His most recent entry came in 1988, with 'What A Wonderful World' after it was included in the film soundtrack to *Good Morning Vietnam* (USA, 1987), thus taking his span of hits to more than 61 years. He also holds the record for the longest gap between US album chart entries. His album *Satch Plays Fats* entered on Oct 1 1955 and *Ken Burns Jazz – The Definitive Louis Armstrong* entered in Jan 2001, 45 years 3 months later.

MOST US HIT ALBUMS BY A FEMALE ARTIST

Barbra Streisand (USA) holds the female record for the most albums to enter the US chart with 48, since her first *The Barbra Streisand Album* hit

the charts on Feb 25 1962, reaching No.8. Her most recent, *Timeless – Live in Concert* was released on Sept 19 2000 and reached No.21.

MOST US HIT SINGLES BY A MALE ARTIST

Elvis Presley (USA) had a record 149 hit singles on the Billboard Hot 100 between 1956 and 1996. He took his first step towards a musical career at the age of 10, when he won $5 (then £1.24) in a local singing contest in Tupelo, Mississippi, performing the Red Foley ballad, 'Old Shep.'

MOST UK HIT ALBUMS BY A MALE ARTIST

The record for the most UK album chart entries is held by Elvis Presley with 100 by Feb 2001.

MOST CONSECUTIVE WEEKS ON UK SINGLES CHART

Elvis Presley stayed on the UK chart with 13 hit singles, from 'A Mess of

Blues' in 1960 to 'One More Broken Heart for Sale' in 1963 for an unbroken 144 weeks on the chart.

MOST NEW UK HIT SINGLES IN ONE YEAR

British group The Wedding Present and Elvis Presley share this record with 12 new hits in the UK singles chart in one year, Elvis in 1957 and The Wedding Present in 1992. In both cases all 12 hit the Top 30.

MOST UK HIT SINGLES BY A MALE ARTIST

Cliff Richard (UK) has had 123 UK hit singles up to March 2001. His first hit was 'Move It,' which reached No.2 on Sept 12 1958 and his latest was 1999's No.1 'The Millennium Prayer.'

THE BEATLES, THE MONKEES, AND THE BEST BAND IN THE WORLD

The Beatles (UK), The Monkees (USA), Pearl Jam (USA) and U2 (Ireland, left), hold the record, with seven albums each, for having the most albums on the US chart (Top 200) at the same time. The Beatles achieved this on Jan 31 1981 in the aftermath of John Lennon's death with *Beatles 1967-1970*, *Beatles 1962-1966*, *White Album*, *Sgt. Pepper's Lonely Hearts Club Band*, *Rubber Soul*, *Abbey Road*, and *Love Songs*. The Monkees, whose success was based largely on their TV show, achieved their record in 1987. U2, Bono's self-proclaimed 'Best Band in the World' joined the Beatles and the Monkees as record-holders in the same year. Pearl Jam were the last to hit the spot on March 17 2001.

<56340>
www.guinnessworldrecords.com/mostalbums
← ACCESS CODE

MOST SIMULTANEOUS US ALBUM CHART ENTRIES IN A WEEK

Rock group Pearl Jam (USA) had seven different albums enter the US Top 200 chart on March 17 2001. They were part of a series of 23 albums recorded live at different venues around the USA during the group's world tour, and broke their own record of five entries, held five months before, from a series of 25 simultaneously released live albums from concerts across the world.

MOST WEEKS ON US COUNTRY CHART BY A FEMALE ARTIST

Patsy Cline's *12 Greatest Hits* (USA) was still on the US country catalog album chart in Feb 2001, 722 weeks after it first entered. The album spent 251 weeks (almost five years) at No.1 and sold over seven million copies. Cline died alongside country stars Hawkshaw Hawkins and Cowboy Copas in a light aircraft crash in March 1963, and her funeral was attended by 25,000 grieving fans.

MOST WEEKS SPENT ON UK SINGLES CHART

Elvis Presley's 111 hits have spent a total of 1,168 weeks on the UK singles chart since 'Heartbreak Hotel' debuted on May 11 1956. In the weeks after his death on Aug 16 1977, his record sales predictably rocketed and 'Way Down' proved a fittingly final UK No.1.

MOST WEEKS SPENT ON US ADULT CONTEMPORARY ALBUM CHART

Australian duo Savage Garden's single 'Truly Madly Deeply' spent a record 123 weeks on the US adult contemporary chart before it dropped out of the chart in May 2000. Their debut album sold 11 million copies.

MOST US SOLO NO.1 ALBUMS

Elvis Presley has had a record nine No.1 albums – *Elvis Presley* (1956), *Elvis* (1956), *Loving You* (1957), *Elvis Christmas Album* (1957), *GI Blues* (1960), *Something For Everybody* (1961), *Blue Hawaii* (1961), *Roustabout* (1964), and *Elvis – Aloha From Hawaii* (1973).

www.guinnessworldrecords.com/puffdaddy

THE MACK DADDY

Sean 'Puffy' Combs, a.k.a. Puff Daddy (USA, left), is the world's most successful rap producer, having been responsible for four singles that consecutively headed the US rap chart for a record 36 weeks in 1997. Stars he has worked with include Lil' Kim, Mariah Carey, and Usher. He took part in the record-breaking run himself with a tribute record to his friend Christopher Wallace, a.k.a. rapper Notorious B.I.G. who recorded for Puffy's record label Bad Boy. When B.I.G. was tragically shot, Puffy recorded a tribute single with B.I.G.'s wife, Faith Evans. 'I'll Be Missing You' was a massive international chart success and all proceeds were donated to his children.

ACCESS CODE

‹55719› ←

GUINNESS WORLD RECORDS

music facts and feats

MOST GRAMMY AWARDS WON BY AN INDIVIDUAL

The Hungarian-born British conductor, Sir Georg Solti (1912–97) won an all-time record of 31 Grammy awards (including a special Trustees award presented in 1967) between 1958 and 1997.

BEST-SELLING JAZZ ARTIST

The best-selling jazz artist is Kenny G (USA), who has sold an estimated 55 million albums worldwide to date.

THE CAT IN THE HAT

The best-selling funk album of all time is *Travelling Without Moving* by Jamiroquai (UK), which has sold more than seven million albums globally since its release in 1996. Jamiroquai, led by vocalist Jay Kay (above), have sold 11 million albums and have become one of the most sought-after live jazz funk acts in the world. The album spawned hit after hit in the UK, including 'Cosmic Girl,' 'Alright,' and 'Virtual Insanity,' and it saw them break the American market, collecting four US MTV awards and a Grammy in 1997. In 1998 Jamiroquai wrote 'Deeper Underground' for the Hollywood movie *Godzilla* and most recently released the 1999 album *Synkronized*. Their career started way back in 1992 when they released 'When You Gonna Learn' on a small independent London label, Acid Jazz, before they signed with Sony.

www.guinnessworldrecords.com/bestfunk

ACCESS CODE
‹54242› ←

This includes 12 million copies of *Breathless*, the best-selling jazz album of all time, released in 1992. Born Kenneth Gorelick, Kenny has won many awards, including Grammy, American Music Awards, Soul Train Awards, and World Music Awards.

MOST VALUABLE JAZZ INSTRUMENT

The most valuable jazz instrument is a saxophone, once owned by Charlie 'Bird' Parker (USA), which sold for £93,500 ($144,500), at Christie's, South Kensington, London, UK, on Sept 7 1994.

MOST VALUABLE VIOLIN

A violin made by Guarneri del Gesu (Italy) in 1742, and owned by the late Yehudi Menuhin (UK), was sold to an anonymous collector in Zurich, Switzerland, on Oct 29 1999. Swiss dealer Musik Hug said it sold for "approximately $1.25 million (£781,250) above what had ever been paid for a violin" – which was $1,585,452 (£947,500) in 1998.

HIGHEST ALTITUDE CONCERT

A concert commemorating the 150th anniversary of the death of composer Gaetano Donizetti (Italy) took place at a record height of 16,568 ft (5,050 m) above sea level, on Oct 24 1998 at the Laboratory-Observatory, a three-story glass and aluminum pyramid, in Mt. Everest's Khumba Valley, Nepal. The concert was performed by flutist Ombretta Maffeis and pianist Gianni Bergamelli.

GREATEST VOCAL RANGE

Marta Maria Kupeczik (Hungary) has a vocal range extending from great B Flat to D4, or from the male bass to the highest coloratura – an incredible range of more than four octaves.

LARGEST CD MUSIC EDITION

Great Pianists of the 20th Century, compiled by Philips, is the largest single edition ever recorded. It consists of 200 CDs and was released over 12 months starting Sept 1998. The edition features 74 pianists, the youngest of whom is Evgeny Kissin

THERE WERE 470 GLASS BOTTLES, SITTING ON THE WALL, 470 GLASS BOTTLES ...

On Oct 12 2000 in Toledo, Ohio, local flutists Patricia Rentner and Roselyn Smith broke the record for the largest bottle orchestra by blowing into a line of 470 strategically arranged glass bottles (above). Patricia conducts Ottawa Hills Flute Choir, while Roselyn is a flutist with the 555th Air National Guard of Toledo, Ohio. Both strayed from their normal repertoires to play a nursery-rhyme medley on the bottles including 'This Old Man,' 'Hickory Dickory Dock,' and 'Mary had a Little Lamb.'

www.guinnessworldrecords.com/glassbottles

‹50521› ← ACCESS CODE

(b. Oct 10 1971, Russia), and the oldest, deceased musician Ignaz Paderewski (1860–1941, Poland).

LARGEST ELECTRONIC KEYBOARD ENSEMBLE

The largest electronic keyboard ensemble consisted of 100 students and teachers from the Music School, Gorsium, Hungary, performing on keyboards programmed to sound like traditional orchestral instruments. They played Strauss's *Blue Danube* and Monti's *Monti Czardas* during the first Roland Keyboard Festival on June 2 2000, in the Pesti Vigado Concert Hall, Budapest, Hungary.

MOST GUITAR PARTS PLAYED SIMULTANEOUSLY BY AN INDIVIDUAL

On Jan 12 2000 Jack 'Hoss' Linneman (USA) played the four guitar parts – two types of rhythm, melody, and fill notes – of the tune 'Greenback Dollar' simultaneously on the *Jimmy Smart Show*. He played on a standard six-string Epiphone guitar and maintained a speed of 240 beats per minute, which works out at 36 notes per second.

LONGEST APPLAUSE

Spanish tenor Placido Domingo was applauded for a grand total of 1 hr 20 min through 101 curtain calls after a performance of *Otello* by Verdi at the Vienna Staatsoper on July 30 1991.

LARGEST SIMULTANEOUS PERCUSSION PERFORMANCE

The largest simultaneous percussion performance was *Beat This!*, an event organized as part of the BBC Music Live festival on May 29 2000. Across the UK, from 12–12:30 p.m., 2,140 people played a common percussive rhythm especially devised for the event. Groups were linked by radio or television to the TV center, and a live broadcast was shown on TV.

YOUNGEST WINNER OF THE BIGGEST MUSIC PRIZE

British composer Thomas Adès won the Grawemeyer Award for Music Composition in 2000 at the age of 28, to become the youngest and only the third British winner of the award. It is the world's largest single music writing award worth $200,000 (£125,000).

A SAW POINT FOR EMINEM

The record for the fastest-selling rap artist of all time is held by Detroit rapper Eminem. *The Marshall Mathers LP* sold a record 1.76 million copies in its first week in the US in May 2000. Seen by some people as a brilliant lyricist reflecting social problems in American society, and by others as a bad influence on adolescents worldwide who are influenced by his aggressive lyrics,

Eminem's records court controversy – his ode to an obsessive fan, 'Stan' proved an international smash hit. He is so popular that a search on the internet will offer at least 215,000 links. Tongue-in-cheek references to members of his own family in his songs have led to multimillion dollar lawsuits, dwarfed only by the even larger profits from his album and video sales, which show no sign of slowing down.

‹56305› ←

HIGHEST-PAID PIANIST

Wladziu Valentino Liberace (USA, 1917–87) earned more than $2 million (£716,845) for each 26-week season at Madison Square Garden, New York City, with a peak of $138,000 (then £49,285) for a single night's performance in 1954, equal to $1,085,252 (£775,180) today.

LARGEST ONE-MAN BAND

Rory Blackwell (UK), aided by his double left-footed perpendicular percussion-pounder, plus his three-tier, right-footed horizontal, 22-pronged differential beater, as well as his 12-outlet, bellow-powered horn-blower, played 108 different instruments (19 melody and 89 percussion), simultaneously in Dawlish, Devon, UK, on May 29 1989. The entire collection of instruments measured 15 x 12 ft (4.57 x 3.65 m).

LARGEST PIANO REPERTOIRE

Richard Järnefelt of Helsinki, Finland, has a repertoire of 3,000 songs that he can play from memory. The list consists mainly of pop songs but also includes classical pieces.

OLDEST PLAYABLE INSTRUMENT

Archeologists uncovered a 9,000-year-old Chinese bone flute and managed to play a tune on it. The flute, which is 8.6 in (22 cm) long, has seven holes, and is made from the leg bone of a red crowned crane. It was found at Jiahu, the site of an ancient farming village on the Yellow River flood plain, China.

LONGEST SYMPHONY

The symphony *Victory at Sea*, written by Richard Rodgers (USA) for the film of the same name, and arranged by Robert Russell Bennett (USA) in 1952, lasted 13 hours.

GUINNESS WORLD RECORDS

theatrical performance

HIGHEST THEATER BOX-OFFICE GROSS

Since first opening at Her Majesty's Theatre, London, UK, on Oct 9 1986, Andrew Lloyd Webber's (UK) musical *The Phantom of the Opera* has played in 18 countries and has taken $3.2 billion (£2 billion) at the box office. The second-highest grossing theater show ever is *Cats*, another Lloyd Webber musical, with a box-office take of $2 billion (£1.25 billion).

HIGHEST INSURANCE FOR A SHOW

When the musical *Barnum* opened at the London Palladium on June 11 1981, it became the most highly insured show in theater history. Producers put the total cover at £5 million (then $9,87 million) – £3 million (then $5,9 million) of which was the cost of insuring Michael Crawford (UK), who walked the high-wire and slid down a rope to the stage from the topmost box during the show.

MOST EXPENSIVE STAGE PRODUCTION

The stage adaptation of Disney's 1994 film *The Lion King* is the most expensive theatrical production ever. The Broadway production, which opened in Nov 1997, cost an estimated $15 million (£9.3 million).

GREATEST THEATRICAL LOSS

The Royal Shakespeare Company's musical *Carrie,* based on the Stephen King novel, closed after five performances on Broadway, New York City, on May 17 1988 at the huge cost of $7 million (£3,75 million). *King*, the musical about Martin Luther King, lost $5,13 million (£3 million) in a six-week run ending on June 2 1990, equaling the record London losses of *Ziegfeld* in 1988.

LONGEST THEATRICAL RUN

The longest continuous run of any show is Agatha Christie's (UK) *The Mousetrap*, which opened on Nov 25 1952. It had its 20,126th performance on April 23 2001 at St. Martin's Theatre, London, UK, and has grossed more than £20 million ($33.3 million) from more than 10 million theatergoers in its 49 years.

LONGEST-RUNNING MUSICAL

The off-Broadway musical *The Fantasticks*, by Tom Jones and Harvey Schmidt (both USA), opened on May 3 1960. By 2000, it had been performed a record 16,562 times at the Sullivan Street Playhouse, Greenwich Village, New York City.

SHORTEST PLAY

Nobel prizewinner Samuel Beckett (Ireland), author of one of the most influential plays in postwar drama, *Waiting For Godot* (1953), also wrote the shortest play in world drama, the 30-second *Breath* (1969).

LONGEST PLAY

The longest recorded theatrical production was *The Warp* by Neil Oram (UK), a 10-part play cycle that was performed at the Institute of Contemporary Arts, London, UK, between Jan 18 and 20 1979. Actor Russell Denton was on stage for all but five minutes of the 18-hr 5-min production.

FASTEST THEATRICAL PRODUCTION

Velvet Jacket Ltd's production of the musical *Oklahoma!* performed by Act 24 at The Playhouse, Edinburgh, UK, was put on stage 23 hr 55 min after the cast and crew first received the script at 8 p.m. on May 6 2000.

MOST TONY AWARDS

Harold Prince (USA) has won a total of 20 Tony Awards in 40 years. The Tony Award, named in honor of stage actress Antoinette Perry (USA), is one of theater's most coveted accolades. Harold Prince's record is made up of eight Tonys each for directing and producing, two as producer of the year's Best Musical, and two special Tony Awards.

MOST TONY AWARDS FOR AN ACTRESS

With five Tony Awards to her credit – her first win was in 1952 – Julie Harris (USA) has won more than any other actress. Julie Harris also holds the record for the most Tony Award nominations, with 10 over a period of 45 years. She made her Broadway debut in 1945.

MOST TONY AWARDS FOR A PLAY

Five plays have each won five Tony Awards – *A Man for all Seasons* by Robert Bolt (1962); *Who's Afraid of Virginia Woolf?* by Edward Albee (1963); *Child's Play* by Robert Marasco (1971); *Amadeus* by Peter Shaffer (1981); and *The Real Thing* by Tom Stoppard (1984).

MOST FREQUENTLY ADAPTED PLAY

A Day Well Spent, a one-act farce written by John Oxenford (UK) in 1835, has been adapted five times as follows – *Einen Jux will er sich machen* (1842) by Johann Nestroy; *The Merchant of Yonkers* (1938) by Thornton Wilder; *The Matchmaker* (1954) by Thornton Wilder; *Hello Dolly* (1963) by Jerry Herman and Michael Stewart; and *On The Razzle* (1981) by Tom Stoppard.

LARGEST SIMULTANEOUS PERFORMANCE OF ONE SHOW

At 7 p.m. on Nov 20 1999 the children's musical *The Rainbow Juggler* was performed in 56 theaters across the UK, Ireland, Germany, USA, and Australia by 4,568 Stagecoach Theater Arts students. The shows were staged to mark the 10th anniversary of the Convention on the Rights of the Child, and raised $78,947 (£50,000) for the United Nations Children's Fund (UNICEF).

LARGEST TAP DANCE

The greatest-ever number of tap dancers in a single routine was 6,776 outside Macy's department store on Fifth Avenue, New York City, on Aug 17 1997. The event was staged on 34th Street, with a two-minute routine to the tune of Irving Berlin's 'Puttin' on the Ritz.' The dancers' ages ranged from one year old to an impressive 91 years old.

MOST ROLES IN A SINGLE PLAY

For the play *For Love or Money*, put on at the Grand Theatre, Lancaster, UK, in Sept 2000 by the Lancaster Red Rose Amateur Operatic and Dramatic Society, Phil Gibson (UK) was credited for six production roles – original idea; composer; librettist; orchestration; chorus master; and the lead role of 'Sam.'

FLY BY NIGHT ACTOR?

Performing a stunt known in Japanese as *chunori*, kabuki actor Ichikawa Ennosuke (Japan, left) has flown across the stage and audience for 5,000 performances since April 1968. His record-breaking 5,000th stage flight was achieved on April 19 2000 at 3:08 p.m. at the Shimbashi Ebujo Theater in Tokyo, performing in *Shin Sankokushi*. Ennosuke plays a hero, who dies and flies to heaven with his lover in his arms. *Chunori*, performed using pulleys and a safety belt, was developed in Edo (Tokyo) in the 17th century and remained a popular stage trick for nearly three centuries. Ennosuke revived the stunt at the National Theater in Tokyo for the play *Yoshitsune and the Thousand Cherry Trees* and continued the *chunori* in numerous guises and drama throughout the following 32 years.

‹54812› www.guinnessworldrecords.com/chunori
← ACCESS CODE

HIGH CHAIRS
 USA

On Oct 16 1999 the Peking Acrobats (China, right) created the tallest human chairstack, measuring 21 ft (6.4 m) high, with six people stacked on to seven chairs. Once in place, they held a handstand for five seconds. The Peking Acrobats have performed together since 1952, mastering disciplines dating back to the Ch'in Dynasty (225–207 BC).

ACCESS CODE

‹54638› ←

MOST THEATER PERFORMANCES IN THE SAME ROLE

From Nov 1966 to June 1983, Kanbi Fujiyama (Japan) played the lead role in 10,288 performances as part of the comedy company Sochiku Shikigek.

MOST ACTING ROLES

Jan Leighton (USA) holds the record for playing the greatest recorded number of theatrical, film, and TV parts with 3,395 different roles to his credit since 1951. He owns over 200 wigs and hats, over 70 pairs of glasses, five Santa suits, and 36 pipes.

MOST PLAYS RUNNING SIMULTANEOUSLY BY ONE WRITER

Somerset Maugham (UK) set the record in 1908 when he had four plays running simultaneously in the West End, London, UK – *Lady Frederick* at the Court, *Jack Straw* at the Vaudeville, *The Explorer* at the Lyric, and *Mrs. Dot* at the Comedy.

VIETNAMESE VICTORY

Miss Saigon, the musical written by Alain Boubil and Claude-Michel Schonberg (both France) and produced by Cameron Mackintosh (UK), opened on Broadway in April 1991, having set a record of $36 million (£20.5 million) as the highest advance sales for a musical. The show includes a life-size helicopter, a 1959 Cadillac, and a cast of 44. *Miss Saigon*'s world première took place in London's Theatre Royal (above) on Sept 20 1989. The show opened in Tokyo in May 1992 and broke all box-office records there to become the longest consecutive-running musical in Japan.

MOST ACTORS SUSPENDED IN THE AIR SIMULTANEOUSLY

Período Doma, a show by the Argentinian dance-theater group De La Guarda, featured 33 actors suspended together in the air simultaneously. Five performances of *Período Doma* were watched by an audience of 14,000 at the Velódromo, Buenos Aires, Argentina, in April 1998.

MOST MEMBERS OF A FAMILY TO PERFORM ON STAGE TOGETHER

On June 12 1906 at Ellen Terry's (UK) Jubilee Matinée at the Drury Lane Theatre, London, UK, 22 members of the Terry family appeared in the ball scene from *Much Ado About Nothing*.

THICKEST MAKEUP

Chutti, the makeup unique to the Indian Kathakali dance-theater tradition, is built up using rice paste and paper and can extend 6 in (15 cm) from the face.

ACCESS CODE

‹50458› ←

GUINNESS WORLD RECORDS

www.guinnessworldrecords.com/harrypotter

POTTY ABOUT POTTER!

The first three books in J.K. Rowling's (UK) Harry Potter (right) series hold the record for the highest one-year sales for a book series. In 1999 the series sold over 18.5 million copies in the USA and over 4.5 million in the UK and Commonwealth. Rowling is also the first novelist to have three titles in the top four slots of the *New York Times* best-seller list for 16 weeks. Book four, *Harry Potter and the Goblet of Fire*, received record advance orders of 5.3 million copies.

ACCESS CODE

‹53728› ←

Authors. She read from *Harry Potter and the Goblet of Fire*. Canadian author Kenneth Oppel read from his novel *Silverwing*, while his compatriot Tim Wynne-Jones read from *The Boy in the Burning House*.

LARGEST BOOK-SIGNING EVENT

On Dec 3 1999, 60 Citron Press authors signed their books for the public at an event held at the Business Design Centre, London, UK. A total of 1,200 books were signed in two hours.

MOST OVERDUE LIBRARY BOOK

A German biography of the Archbishop of Bremen, published in 1609, was borrowed from Sidney Sussex College, Cambridge, UK, by Colonel Robert Walpole in 1668. Prof. Sir John Plumb found the book 288 years later in the library of the then Marquess of Cholmondeley at Houghton Hall, Norfolk, UK. He returned it, but was not fined.

BIGGEST INITIAL PRINT RUN FOR A NOVEL

J.K. Rowling's (UK) *Harry Potter and the Goblet of Fire*, the fourth in the record-breaking series, had an initial print run of 4.8 million copies, of which 3.8 million were printed in the USA (40 times as many as an average best-seller) and one million in the UK.

LARGEST PUBLICATION

The *Yongle Dadian* is a thesaurus compiled under the instructions of the Ming emperor Yongle in the 15th century. The 11,095 volumes containing 22,937 manuscript chapters (of which 370 still survive), were written by 147 Chinese scholars and subsequently revised by another 3,000 scholars between 1403 and 1408.

LARGEST ENCYCLOPEDIA

The largest encyclopedia in use is the *Arabic Legislations Encyclopaedia*, written by Mohamed Abu Baker Ben Younis (Greece). Its 200 volumes have a total of 164,000 pages and weigh 925 lb (420 kg). It contains every piece of legislation from all the Arab countries. The general index is contained in a further six volumes and there are also additional annexes.

LARGEST ENGLISH DICTIONARY

The second edition of the *Oxford English Dictionary* (1989) contains 21,543 pages in 20 volumes, consisting of over 231,000 main entries. The longest entry is for the verb 'set,' with over 60,000 words of text. In 1993 an annual series of *Additions Volumes* began, in which approximately 4,000 new vocabulary entries are listed. The dictionary is now also available on CD-ROM.

LARGEST DICTIONARY

Deutsches Wörterbuch (or *German Dictionary*), started in 1854 by Jacob and Wilhelm Grimm, best known for their collection of fairy tales, was completed in 1971 and consists of 34,519 pages in 33 volumes. It is available as a special order over the internet for around $1,695 (£1,200).

OLDEST PERIODICAL MAGAZINE

The oldest continuing periodical in the world is the Royal Society's *Philosophical Transactions*, first published in London, UK, on March 6 1665. Isaac Newton's rise to scientific prominence owes much to *Transactions* – he had 17 papers published in it. It also published work by Charles Darwin.

HEAVIEST MAGAZINE

The Feb/March 1999 issue of *Brides* magazine (UK) weighed 4 lb 5 oz (1.952 kg). It had 1,242 pages, including 1,065 pages of advertisements. This monster edition kept its usual cover price.

MOST EXPENSIVE MAGAZINE

Visionaire magazine (USA), established by Stephan Gan, Cecilia Dean, and James Kalian, is sold at $100 (£70) per issue, but can fetch $5,000 (£3,450) on the black market. The magazine format and theme varies with each edition but it generally combines fashion, photography, and art, and has no advertisements. The magazine always has a striking cover or case design, which in the past, has featured fabric, Plexiglas™, and even a jewelry box.

GUINNESS WORLD RECORDS™

art and sculpture

MOST PROLIFIC PAINTER

Pablo Diego José Francisco de Paula Juan Nepomuceno de los Remedios Crispín Cipriano de la Santísima Trinidad Ruíz y Picasso (1881–1973, Spain) was the most prolific of all painters in a career that lasted 75 years. Picasso produced about 13,500 paintings or designs, 100,000 prints or engravings, 34,000 book illustrations, and 300 sculptures or ceramics. His *oeuvre* has been valued at $709,600,000 (£500 million).

MOST VALUABLE 20TH-CENTURY PAINTING

Picasso's (Spain) *Woman With Crossed Arms* (1901-02) sold for a record $55 million (£38.47 million) on 8 Nov 2000 at a Christie's auction in New York City, New York, USA.

By May 9 1997 works of art by Pablo Picasso had been sold at auctions no fewer than 3,579 times. This makes him the artist with the most auction sales. The total value of these sales is $954,710,889 (£668, 817,963).

MOST STOLEN PAINTING

Jacob III de Cheyn (1632) by the Dutch artist Rembrandt van Rijn (1609–69), has been stolen from museums no fewer than four times. It was once found on the back of a bicycle, and once underneath a graveyard bench. It has been returned anonymously each time and, as a result, no one has ever been charged with theft.

Rembrandt's portrait of a tranquil young man is so well known that thieves would find it nearly impossible to sell.

MOST VALUABLE SCULPTURE

The Three Graces (1814) by Antonio Canova (Italy, 1752–1822) was jointly purchased by the Victoria and Albert Museum, London, UK, and the National Gallery of Scotland, Edinburgh, UK, for a record £7.5 million ($11.5 million) in 1994.

LARGEST COW ART EXHIBITION

CowPARADE began in Zurich, Switzerland, in 1998, to promote retail and the arts downtown. This event had 812 artistically painted life-size fiberglass cows, with names such as PiCOWso and Lady Cowdiva, exhibited along streets, on buildings, in parks, airport terminals, railroad stations, etc. – bringing in more than 1.5 million additional visitors to the city to experience the exhibit.

LARGEST ABSTRACT DRAWING BY TIRE MARKS

At an event called Burnout 2001, the world's largest abstract tire drawing was produced in the Melbourne Docklands (Australia) by eight drivers who burned tire marks on to an area of concrete measuring 229.6 x 98.4 ft (70 x 30 m). Thousands of excited spectators (art lovers and car lovers alike) watched as the drivers spun their wheels, where and as they pleased, in order to leave indelible rubber traces on the cement surface.

KIDS' STUFF

More than 200 children from Gaithersburg, Maryland, created the biggest-ever finger painting on July 19 1999. They used just their bare hands and feet to make the painting entitled *Ten Fingers, Ten Toes* (left), which measured 28 x 35 ft (8.53 x 10.66 m) in celebration of Sigma-Tau Pharmaceutical's first decade of commercial operation.

The world's largest jellybean mosaic, made from 210,000 STARBURST® jellybeans, was created by 60 children from Public School 166, New York City. The 320-ft² (29.7-m²) mosaic was designed by Stephanie Logsdon and made at the Children's Museum of Manhattan on April 18 and 19 2000. It was displayed on April 22 2000 at the 'Easter Eggstravaganza' in Central Park.

<54735>
www.guinnessworldrecords.com/fingerpainting
← ACCESS CODE

LARGEST FLORAL SCULPTURE

A sculpture created to resemble an aspirin package measured 249 ft 4 in x 86 ft 10 in (76 x 26.48 m) and was prepared and constructed in a week by 1,914 people, using 75,000 white chrysanthemums, 1,200,000 edelweiss, and 71,500 polybags of *Pangus kuning* leaves. The event was organized by advertising agency Ammirati Puris Lintas for PT Bayer on Oct 17 1999 in Jakarta, Indonesia.

LARGEST STONE SCULPTURE

The mounted figures of American confederate giants Jefferson Davis, Robert Edward Lee and Thomas Jonathan (Stonewall) Jackson are 90 ft (27.4 m) high and cover 1.33 acres (0.5 ha) on the face of Stone Mountain, near Atlanta, Georgia. Sculptor Roy Faulkner (USA) worked on the mountain face for eight years and 174 days, between Sept 12 1963 and March 3 1972, with a thermojet torch, working with Walker Kirtland Hancock (USA) and other helpers.

LARGEST ABSORBENT-COTTON SCULPTURE

In April 1999, after 11 months' work, Anant Narayan Khairnar (India) completed a sculpture of Mahatma Gandhi that was 7.5 ft (2.28 m) tall and weighed 44 lb (20 kg). Although it looks like marble, it is made entirely from white absorbent cotton soaked in chemicals to make it harden.

LONGEST SAND SCULPTURE

The longest sand sculpture ever made was the GTE Directories Ultimate Sand Castle, at 86,535 ft (26,375.9 m) long, built by more than 10,000 volunteers at Myrtle Beach, South Carolina, on May 31 1991.

LARGEST HORNET NEST SCULPTURE

Yoshikuni Shiozawa (Japan) created a model of Mount Fuji by joining together 160 hornet nests, containing around 160,000 live yellow hornets. It was 12 ft 4 in (3.766 m) high and 15 ft 7.4 in (4.8 m) wide at the base.

THE SKY'S THE LIMIT

The Statue of Liberty (left), the world's heaviest statue, weighs 54.31 million lb (24,635 tonnes) – 61,729 lb (28 tonnes) of copper, 249,122 lb (113 tonnes) of steel, and 53.99 million lb (24,493 tonnes) of concrete foundation. She stands 305 ft 1 in (92.99 m) from the ground to the tip of her torch; 354 steps inside lead up to the crown; her nose is 4ft 9 in (1.48 m) long; and her index finger 8 ft (2.44 m). It was made by Frédéric-Auguste Bartholdi, Richard Morris Hunt, and Alexandre Gustave Eiffel, and France gave it to the USA in 1885 to commemorate liberty and friendship.

The world's tallest statue is a bronze Buddha that is 394 ft (120 m) high, 115 ft (35 m) wide, and weighs 2.2 million lb (1,000 tonnes). It took seven years to build and was completed in Jan 1993 in Tokyo, Japan.

<54191>
www.guinnessworldrecords.com/statueliberty
← ACCESS CODE

MOST PAINT IN A PAINTING

In June 1998 the US duo The Art Guys (Michael Galbreth and Jack Massing) were commissioned to design a billboard entitled *ABSOLUTly A Thousand Coats of Paint*, to advertise the *Absolut* brand of vodka. The billboard, in Houston, Texas, features a 14-ft (4.3-m) tall picture of an *Absolut* bottle and was covered with 1,000 coats, or 1,984 lb (900 kg) of paint, in various colors. Artist Bernard Brunon did the painting over a nine-month period.

LARGEST PAINTING

ID Cultur completed a huge painting of the sea, the size of four American football fields (92,419 ft² or 8,586 m²) at The Arena, Amsterdam, Netherlands, on Aug 14 1996.

LARGEST 3-D BALLOON SCULPTURE

A display of 52,000 balloons in the shape of a football was shown at the Northampton Balloon Festival, Northampton, UK, between Aug 14 and 16 1998.

MOST BEADS IN A WORK OF ART

📺 USA

Liza Lou (USA) used 40 million glass beads to create a life-size kitchen and garden, first displayed at the Kemper Museum of Contemporary Art in Kansas City. If strung out, the beads would stretch about 380 miles (703.7 km), or the distance between Los Angeles and San Francisco.

LARGEST ART GALLERY

A person has to walk 15 miles (24 km) to visit each of the 322 galleries in the Winter Palace at the State Hermitage Museum in St. Petersburg, Russia, to see the nearly three million works of art and objects of archeological interest.

MOST BATTERIES IN A WORK OF ART

Gilberto Macías Enríquez (Mexico) has made a European medieval castle using 11,380 button-shaped batteries. He has been collecting batteries since 1988 and by recycling them in this way, he aims to make people aware of the high toxicity of the nitric acid used in them. He has already collected over 33,000 batteries.

www.guinnessworldrecords.com/carsculpture

LONG-TERM PARKING

The art sculpture containing the most whole cars (right) is entitled *Long-term Parking* and was commissioned by the Cartier Foundation in Jouy-en-Josas, France. The towering structure contains 60 cars embedded in 3.53 million lb (1,600 tonnes) of concrete, rising over 65.6 ft (20 m) into the air. The automotive sculpture was created by artist Armand Fernandez, better known as Arman, who is celebrated for his 'accumulation' artwork.

GUINNESS WORLD RECORDS

cartoons and animation

MOST VALUABLE COLOR ANIMATION CELL

One of the 150,000 color animation cells from Walt Disney's *Snow White and the Seven Dwarfs* (USA), which premiered on Christmas Eve 1937, was sold in 1991 for the record price of $222,525 (£115,000).

LARGEST CARICATURE

Paul Slattery (UK) drew a caricature of soccer player Alan Shearer (UK) that measured 62 x 30 ft 4 in (18.89 x 9.24 m) on a giant canvas. The drawing began with the subject's eye and was completed in three days. The caricature was hung off the Tyne Bridge, Newcastle, UK, and then auctioned to raise funds for the NSPCC (National Society for the Prevention of Cruelty to Children).

MOST EXPENSIVE CARTOON

DreamWorks' *Prince of Egypt* (USA, 1998) cost $60 million (£37.5 million) to make. With 350 artists and animators working on the project, it took four years to create. With a running time of 90 minutes, the film has 1,192 special effects. The four-minute 'Red Sea' sequence alone took 350,000 man-hours to complete.

LONGEST-RUNNING CARTOON SERIES

Between 1933 and 1957, Max Fleisher's (USA) *Popeye the Sailor Man* had 233 one-reelers and a single two-reeler, *Popeye the Sailor Meets Sinbad the Sailor* (USA, 1936). A further 220 *Popeye* cartoons were produced for TV by King Features from 1960 to 1962, followed by 192 *All New Popeye* cartoons made for the CBS Network from 1978 to 1983. The series was first aired on TV in Sept 1956, making it the longest-running syndicated cartoon series.

HIGHEST-GROSSING ANIMATION

Walt Disney's *The Lion King* (USA, 1994) is the animation with the highest box-office gross, taking in $777.9 million (£486.1 million). The film featured the voices of celebrities Rowan Atkinson (UK), Jeremy Irons (UK), and Whoopi Goldberg (USA). Walt Disney's first full-length feature film, *Snow White and the Seven Dwarfs* (USA, 1937), which took four years to make, took $184.9 million (then £37.38 million) at the box office worldwide. If inflation is taken into account, this would be the equivalent of $1.63 billion (£1.02 billion) today.

<53243>
← ACCESS CODE

SIZE ISN'T EVERYTHING

The smallest comic of all time is *Agent 327* (left), drawn and written by Martin Lodewijk (Netherlands). It was published by Comicshop Sjors in June 1999, measuring just 2.58 x 3.7 cm (1 x 1.4 in). Printed in full color, 2,000 copies of the 16-page comic were produced, and it was sold with a free magnifying glass. The record holder edition of the comic was called *Minimum Bug*.

www.guinnessworldrecords.com/smallestcomic

MOST CARTOON SERIES EPISODES

Harry Bud Fisher's (USA) *Mutt and Jeff*, which began as a supplement to *Pathé's Weekly* with the issue of Feb 10 1913, continued as separate weekly reels from April 1 1916 to Dec 1 1926. Allowing for a gap between 1923 and 1924, for which no titles have been traced, there were at least 323 *Mutt and Jeff* episodes shown at the movies. Several have been colorized and synchronized for video release, making them also the oldest cartoons in distribution.

MOST FAN MAIL IN HOLLYWOOD

Mickey Mouse was reported to have received 800,000 fan letters in 1933 – an average of 66,000 a month.

MOST CONSECUTIVE OSCAR NOMINATIONS

Walt Disney received nine consecutive Oscar nominations in the category Best Short Subject,

Cartoons, from 1942 to 1950, beginning the run with *Truant Officer Donald* (USA, 1941) and ending with *Toy Tinkers* (1949). From 1933 to 1940, Walt Disney was nominated for eight years in a row, including two films in 1933 and 1934, and three in 1939. During this period, he won a record eight consecutive times.

MOST EDITIONS OF A COMIC

The Mexican comic *Pepín*, which printed its first edition on March 4 1936 as a weekly anthology of comics, eventually became a daily and ran until Oct 23 1956 with a total of 7,561 issues. At the height of its popularity, sales were estimated at 320,000 copies a day, a number that doubled on Sundays.

LONGEST-RUNNING COMIC STRIP STILL SYNDICATED

The Katzenjammer Kids, Hans and Fritz, created by Rudolph Dirks (USA), was first published in the *New York Journal* on Dec 12 1897 and was inspired by 'Max und Moritz,' an 1860s' German children's story. This comic strip is the oldest still in syndication and is now drawn by cartoonist Hy Eisman (USA) and syndicated in 50 newspapers.

MOST PROLIFIC CARTOONIST

Joe Martin (USA), creator of *Mr Boffo*, *Willy 'n' Ethel*, *Cats with Hands*, and *Porterfield*, produces a total of 25 cartoon series, including single-panel cartoons and cartoon strips, totaling 1,300 cartoons a year. He has published 20,865 cartoons since 1978. Among hundreds of others, Martin's cartoons appear in newspapers such as the *Chicago Tribune*, the *San Francisco Chronicle*, and the *Boston Globe*.

LARGEST CARTOON MUSEUM

The International Museum of Cartoon Art in Boca Raton, Florida, has a collection of over 160,000 original animated drawings from 50 countries. The collection includes 10,000 books on animation and 1,000 hours of cartoons, interviews, and documentaries on film and tape. The museum covers 2,322.5 m² (25,000 ft²) and there is also a 250-seat theater.

ZORRO MAKES HIS MARK

Zorro, the world's most filmed cartoon character, was originated by Johnston McCulley (USA), and has been portrayed in 69 films. Wise, brave, charming, and romantic, Zorro was the first comic strip character to be the subject of a major feature film, *The Mark of Zorro* (USA, 1920) starring Douglas Fairbanks (USA). It appeared a year after the comic strip was printed, making Zorro the comic-strip character to make it fastest from strip to screen. The most recent Zorro movie, *The Mask of Zorro* (USA, 1998) starring Antonio Banderas (Spain, left), Anthony Hopkins, and Catherine Zeta-Jones (both UK) opened in the US on July 19 1998. It made $22.54 million (£13.69 million) in sales from 2,515 screens in its opening weekend.

<50724>
← ACCESS CODE

www.guinnessworldrecords.com/zorro

LONGEST COMIC STRIP

The longest comic strip measured 175 ft 6 in x 4 ft 11 in (53.5 x 1.5 m) and was made up of 20 panels. Drawn by 26 cartoonists on Oct 17 1999 in homage to the 16th-century Spanish humorist Quevedo, the strip was drawn during the *VI Muestra Iberoamericana de Humor Gráfico*, a cartoon festival held by the University of Alcalá, Spain.

MOST SWEARING IN AN ANIMATED MOVIE

The record for the most swearing ever featured in an animated movie

MOST COMIC READERS

In Japan, 40% of all printed material sold belongs to *manga* (the Japanese word for comic) sales. Throughout the 1990s, yearly sales of *manga* reached an average of 600 billion yen ($5.5 billion; £3.83 billion). Initially the *manga* storylines were primarily written for children (one of the characters with worldwide success is *Pokémon*), but about 50% of the material is now aimed at adults. *Manga* culture is so entrenched in Japanese society that it pervades every aspect of their lifestyle, from entertainment to design and education.

www.guinnessworldrecords.com/chickenrun

CHICK FLICK

The most plasticine (modeling clay) ever used in a movie was squeezed and shaped during the filming of Aardman Animation's *Chicken Run* (UK, 2000) in which animators used 5,247 lb (2,380 kg) of plasticine. The 82-minute *Chicken Run* also holds the record for the longest stop-motion film, made up of 118,080 separate stop-motion special effects shots. In comparison, a live-action feature would use 500 to 1000 shots. Each plasticine character on the miniature film set had to be adjusted 24 times for every second of film.

Pictured right is DreamWorks Pictures cofounder Jeffrey Katzenberg (USA) with stars of the movie, Rocky (left) and Ginger (right).

ACCESS CODE

‹54005› ←

is held by *South Park: Bigger, Longer, and Uncut* (USA, 1999), which included 399 swear words during its running time. Despite its 'uncut' label, it ran between 75 and 82 minutes depending on which country it was released in. It also included 128 offensive gestures and 221 acts of violence.

LONGEST-RUNNING COMIC

The children's comic weekly *Comic Cuts*, published from May 17 1890 to Sept 12 1953 in London, UK, ran for 63 years 128 days – 3,006 editions in total.

GUINNESS WORLD RECORDS

toys

LARGEST WATER PISTOL

The Monster XL water pistol of the Supersoaker line measures a record-breaking 39 in (99 cm) in length and can hold 162 fl oz (4.6 liters) of water. A pump-action stock pressurizes the water, which is fired from two nozzles that shoot to a range of around 33 ft (10 m).

FASTEST TIME TO SOLVE A RUBIK CUBE

Minh Thai, a 16-year-old Vietnamese refugee, won the World Rubik Cube Championship in Budapest, Hungary, on June 5 1982. His winning time was 22.95 seconds. Before the timer started, each contestant was allowed to lift the cube and look at it for 15 seconds. The best time out of three attempts determined the winner.

FASTEST TIME TO SOLVE A RUBIK CUBE BLINDFOLDED

Ralf Laue (Germany), solved a Rubik Cube while blindfolded in a record time of 5 min 42 sec on March 11 2001 in Los Angeles, California.

LARGEST RUBBER-BAND BALL

EdVenture Children's Museum, Columbia, South Carolina, made the world's largest rubber-band ball, weighing 2,450 lb (1,111 kg), out of about 500,000 rubber bands. The ball is 4 ft 4 in (1.32 m) high, 4 ft 6 in (1.37 m) wide, with a circumference

<48833>
www.guinnessworldrecords.com/lego
← ACCESS CODE

TOY STORY

A LEGO® tower built in Tallinn, Estonia, between Aug 18 and 21 1998 (left), reached a height of 81 ft 12 in (24.91 m) and contained 391,478 plastic, eight-stud LEGO® bricks with no adhesive to help them stick together. More than 6,000 children participated in the event, organized by A.S. Rekato Ltd to beat the previous record, set in Moscow, Russia, in July 1998, by 9 in (25 cm).

The longest LEGO® structure is a millipede, measuring 2,003.93 ft (610.8 m) and consisting of a total of 1,679,100 bricks. It was assembled by thousands of children at LEGOland® California, between July 8 and 13 2000. It has a total of 474 links and 948 legs. It was built in connection with the first LEGO® Maniac Kidvention.

of 14 ft 3 in (4.34 m). The project went from Dec 1 2000 to Feb 3 2001 and began with a single rubber band.

MOST CONSECUTIVE SWITCHES WITH ASTROJAX®

Maximilian Leidolf (Germany) performed a record 3,208 consecutive midair end-ball switches with a set of AstroJax®, (three spherical balls on a rope with the central ball acting as a yo-yo) in 24 min 52 sec on Feb 12 2000.

FASTEST YO-YO

The fastest time to complete 100 m while throwing and catching a yo-yo is 13.9 seconds by Taro Yamashita (Japan) at the Yolympics, New Hampshire, on May 25 1996.

MOST YO-YO TRICKS

Eddie McDonald, alias 'Fast Eddie' (USA), managed to complete a record-breaking 35 yo-yo tricks in one minute on July 22 1999.

GREATEST DISTANCE TRAVELED BY A MODEL CAR

The greatest distance traveled by a 1:64-scale car is 213.07 miles (342.9 km) in 24 hours. This was set by Team USA at Derby HO Racing Club, UK, under BSCRA (British Slot Car Racing Association) rules between Nov 15 and 16 1997.

Between July 5 and 6 1986, the North London Society of Model Engineers team achieved a 24-hour distance record of 305.94 miles (492.36 km) for a 1:32-scale car, a Rondeau M482C Group C sports car.

FASTEST RADIO-CONTROLLED MODEL CAR

The highest speed achieved by a radio-controlled model car is 59.09 mph (95.1 km/h) by an Audi TT Coupe (scale 1:10) controlled by Petri Kivikoski, Leo Hongisto, and Petri Väätäinen of the Audi Sport Team in Finland, on June 7 2000. It was 7.87 in (20 cm) wide, 15.74 in (40 cm) long, and weighed 4.41 lb (2 kg).

HIGHEST ALTITUDE BY A SINGLE KITE

Henry H. Clayton and A.E. Sweetland (both USA) flew a single kite at a height of 12,471 ft (3,801 m) at the Blue Hill Weather Station, Milton, Massachusetts on Feb 28 1898.

HIGHEST ALTITUDE BY A TRAIN OF EIGHT KITES

A record-breaking height of 31,955 ft (9,740 m) was reached by a train of eight kites over Lindenberg, Germany, on Aug 1 1919.

FASTEST KITE

The fastest speed attained by a kite was 120 mph (193 km/h) flown by Pete DiGiacomo (USA) at Ocean City, Maryland, on Sept 22 1989. The kite was a modified Super 10 Flexifoil. Readings were taken by a local police officer with a radar gun.

MOST FIGURE EIGHTS WITH A KITE

On Sept 25 1988 Stu Cohen (USA) achieved a record number of 2,911 figure eights with a kite in one hour at Ocean City, Maryland.

FASTEST POGO-STICK JUMPING

Ashrita Furman (USA) traveled one mile (1.6 km) on a pogo stick in 17 min 45 sec on the frozen runway of the Marambio Argentinian Research Base in Antarctica on Jan 15 2000. He set this record in Antarctica since he wishes to have a record for setting a record on each of the seven continents.

A FLYING TEDDY

Tornado Ted (UK, left) a teddy-bear mascot for the Northdale Horticulture Centre charity appeal (UK), flew a total distance of 156,539 miles (251,925 km) between Jan 6 and Sept 7 1998, making him the world's most well-traveled teddy bear. Traveling with the RAF, the USAAF, the Red Arrows, the Slovak, Hungarian and Austrian Air Forces, British Airways, Cathay Pacific, and British Midland, he flew in over 15 different types of aircraft, including Concorde, Tornado F3s, and VC10s, to raise money and awareness of the charity.

Ted has now gained celebrity status, including being made an honorary member of the Dutch Air Force 9G Club after flying in an F16. His latest flight was in a Hawk jet.

<48817>
www.guinnessworldrecords.com/tornadoted
← ACCESS CODE

160

MOST JUMPS WITH A POGO STICK

Gary Stewart (USA) jumped a record 177,737 times on a pogo stick at Huntington Beach, California, between May 25 and 26 1990.

LARGEST JIGSAW PUZZLES

The largest jigsaw puzzle measured 51,484 ft² (4,783 m²) and consisted of 43,924 pieces. It was assembled on July 8 1992 in Marseille, France.

The largest commercially available jigsaw puzzle is manufactured by Educa Sallent (Spain). It measures 7 ft 10.4 in x 4 ft 5.5 in (2.4 x 1.36 m) and has 10,000 pieces.

SMALLEST JIGSAW PUZZLE

The smallest commercially available jigsaw puzzle with a minimum of 1,000 pieces is manufactured by Educa Sallent (Spain). It measures 18 x 11 in (46 x 30 cm) and has 1,000 pieces. These puzzles are all made from recycled materials, with designs ranging from European landmarks to Disney and *Sesame Street* characters.

TALLEST K'NEX TOWER

K'nex Manufacturing built a toy tower measuring 101.3 ft (30.87 m) tall between June 5 and 6 1999. It was built on a 21-ft 6-in² (2-m²) base and contained 50,342 pieces.

TALLEST BUILDING BLOCK STRUCTURE

A pyramid measuring 82 ft 2 in (25.05 m) high was built of building blocks by a team of 800 people to commemorate the Taiwanese President Lee Teng-hui's inauguration. It was completed at Taipei, Taiwan, on May 18 1996.

HIGHEST OLLIE IN SKATEBOARDING

Danny Wainwright (UK) popped the highest ollie (jump) ever at 3 ft 8.4 in (1.13 m) off flat ground on Feb 6 2000 to win the Reese Forbes Ollie Challenge at the ASR Show, Longbeach, California.

HIGHEST SKATEBOARDING JUMP

The record for the highest-ever skateboarding jump is 5 ft 5 in (1.67 m) by Trevor Baxter (UK), set at Grenoble, France, on Sept 14 1982.

www.guinnessworldrecords.com/pinocchio

HANG LOOSE

The world's biggest string puppet is a jointed moveable Pinocchio (right), measuring 31 ft 9 in (10 m) tall. He was constructed by the Forum Town Decoration for Audio Visual Enterprises and displayed in Athens, Greece, on April 23 2000. Taking 82 days to build, Pinocchio was made from 551 lb (250 kg) of polyester, 330 lb (150 kg) of fiber-glass, 763 ft² (71 m²) of foam rubber, and 190 ft (58 m) of cloth including ropes and pulleys. The unveiling of the puppet was broadcast live on the internet.

GUINNESS WORLD RECORDS™

games and gambling

MOST FOOTBAG KICKS

Footbag, also known as hacky-sack, involves keeping a beanbag in the air using only your foot. Andy Linder (USA) managed 1,019 kicks of a footbag in five minutes on June 7 1996.

The world record for keeping a footbag airborne is 63,326 consecutive kicks in 8 hr 50 min 42 sec by Ted Martin (USA) at Lions Park, Mount Prospect, Illinois, on June 14 1997.

The doubles record is 132,011 consecutive kicks by Gary Lautt and Tricia George (both USA), at Chico, California, on March 21 1998.

FASTEST TIDDLYWINKS MILE

The fastest time for a tiddlywink to be propelled over a measured mile (1.6 km) is 2 hr 25 min 24 sec by a relay team of 23 people from AGS Home Improvements Ltd of Newton Abbot, Devon, UK, on Nov 20 1999.

FASTEST TIDDLYWINKS POTTING

Allen Astles from the University of Wales (UK) potted 10,000 winks in 3 hr 51 min 46 sec at Aberystwyth, Ceredigion, Wales, in Feb 1966.

<43436> ← ACCESS CODE

PASS 'GO' AND COLLECT $2 MILLION!

USA

An exclusive $2-million (£1.15-million) *Monopoly* set (left) was created by the jeweler Sidney Mobell, San Francisco, in 1988 – the most expensive *Monopoly* game ever. The board is made from 23-carat gold. Rubies and sapphires top the chimneys of the solid-gold houses and hotels, and the dice has 42 full-cut diamonds for spots!

By 1999, *Monopoly* had been played by 500 million people worldwide. *Monopoly* is the most played and best-selling board game in the world, sold in 80 countries, and produced in 26 different languages.

www.guinnessworldrecords.com/monopoly

YOUNGEST CHESS GRAND MASTER

Etienne Bacrot (France), age 14 years 59 days, became the youngest person to qualify as an International Grand Master on March 22 1997.

MOST SIMULTANEOUS CHESS OPPONENTS

The most games played simultaneously is 310 by Ulf Andersson (Sweden) at Alvsjö, Sweden, between Jan 6 and 7 1996. Of the 310 games played Ulf Andersson was defeated in only two.

SLOWEST CHESS MOVE

Francisco Torres Trois took 2 hr 20 min to play his seventh move against Luis Santos at Vigo, Spain, in 1980 – the slowest move since time clocks were introduced in the 19th century.

LEAPFROG OVER THE MOST STANDING PEOPLE

Andy Wiltz (USA) leapfrogged over 10 standing people during a local variety show at Seaman High School, Topeka, Kansas. All 10 people were over age 16 and over 5 ft (1.53 m) tall. Without using a trampoline, Wiltz had a running start before he pushed off the shoulders of the first person in line and flew through the air over all 10 heads.

MOST EXPENSIVE BOARD GAME

The most expensive commercially available board game is the deluxe version of *Outrage!* (by Imperial Games of Southport, Merseyside, UK). The game, which is based on stealing the Crown Jewels from the Tower of London, retails at £3,995 ($6,290).

LARGEST BOARD GAME

The world's biggest commercially available board game is *Galaxion*, created by Cerebe Design Int (Hong Kong). The board measures 33 x 33 in (83.8 x 83.8 cm).

LARGEST PRIZE IN A POKER TOURNAMENT

John Duthie (UK) won £1 million ($1,423,000) in the Ladbroke's Casinos Poker Million tournament held at the Hilton Casino, Douglas, Isle of Man, on Nov 19 2000.

Chris 'Jesus' Ferguson (USA) won $1.5 million (£995,000) in the 31st World Series of Poker tournament, held at the Binion's Horseshoe Casino, Las Vegas, Nevada, on May 15 2000.

LARGEST POKER POT

The largest pot accrued in a poker tournament is $4.5 million (£3.1 million) for the final hand of the 31st World Series of Poker between T.J. Cloutier (Canada) and eventual winner Chris 'Jesus' Ferguson (USA).

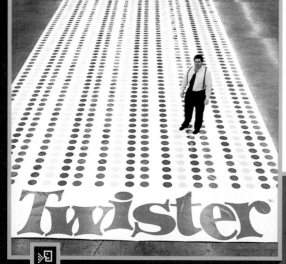

TWIST 'N' SHOUT!

The world's biggest *Twister* board (left), measuring 60 x 19 ft 8.5 in (18.28 x 6 m) was created by the digital printing company Vision International of Salt Lake City, Utah, in Feb 1998. The classic American party game was originally created by Milton Bradley in 1967, but on Feb 6 1998 it was simultaneously enjoyed by hundreds of Vision International employees. They intertwined their limbs with their coworkers' and twisted themselves into all sorts of contorted shapes before collapsing into heaps of laughter on the massive colored board.

The record number of participants in a game of *Twister* is 4,160 people at the University of Massachusetts, Amherst, on May 2 1987. The game was won by Allison Culler.

<49022> www.guinnessworldrecords.com/twistergame ← ACCESS CODE

LARGEST CASINO

Foxwoods Resort Casino in Ledyard, Connecticut, includes a total gaming area of 193,000 ft^2 (17,900 m^2). The casino features more than 5,800 slot machines, 17 different table games, and a 3,200-seat bingo hall.

BIGGEST SLOT-MACHINE WIN

On Jan 26 2000 cocktail waitress Cindy Jay scooped a record $34,959,458 (£21,258,282) on Megabucks for the world's largest slot-machine jackpot payout, at the Desert Inn Hotel's Casino, Las Vegas, Nevada.

LARGEST DENOMINATION PLAQUE

The largest denomination gaming plaque is valued at $10 million (£6.9 million) and is in use at The London Club at Aladdin, Las Vegas, Nevada.

BIGGEST LOTTERY WIN

The largest individual lottery win is a whopping $197 million (£122 million) by Maria Grasso (USA) for the Big Game lottery drawn on April 13 1999.

MOST MONEY WAGERED ON FLAT RACING

Of the $40 billion (£27.8 billion) wagered on horse racing worldwide, $17.2 billion (£11.9 billion) or 43% is placed in Japan. The biggest flat race in the Japanese racing calendar is the Arima Kinen race. It attracts wagers of around $636 million (£442 million).

LARGEST BRIDGE TOURNAMENT

More than 102,000 players played the same hands during the Epson World Bridge Championship at over 2000 centers worldwide on June 20–21 1992.

www.guinnessworldrecords.com/lasvegas

ACCESS CODE

‹56523› ←

LAS VEGAS OR BUST!

The city with the highest annual gross gaming revenue generated by casinos and entertainment complexes is Las Vegas, Nevada. In 2000, the revenue was an astounding $7,673,134,286 (£5,416,584,982).

Las Vegas is also home to the world's largest hotel. The MGM Grand Hotel/Casino has four 30-story towers with 5,005 rooms, and suites of up to 6,000 ft^2 (560m^2), on a site covering 112 acres (45.3 ha).

GUINNESS WORLD RECORDS

theme parks and rides

OLDEST AMUSEMENT PARK

Bakken, located in Klampenborg, Denmark, opened in 1583 and is currently the oldest operating amusement park in the world. In medieval Europe, most major cities featured what is the origin of the amusement park – a pleasure garden. These gardens were usually on the edges of the city, featuring live entertainment, fireworks, dancing, games, and some primitive amusement rides. Most closed down during the 1700s, and Bakken, located in woodland beside a lake, is the only one to survive.

MOST VISITED THEME PARK

Disneyland Tokyo is the most visited theme park in the world. An estimated 16.5 million people passed through its gates in 2000 (17.4 million in 1999). During the 1990s, the park had an estimated 179.11 million visitors, the most visited park of the decade. This is well above the total population of Japan (which is about 126 million).

LARGEST TEMPORARY AMUSEMENT PARK

The world's largest temporary amusement park springs up around the Oktoberfest Beer Festival in Munich, Germany, each year, and attracts up to 50 portable mechanical rides. The centerpieces of the amusement park are several world-class steel roller coasters, such as the five-inversion 'Olympia Looping Bahn.' This transportable roller coaster was designed by the world-famous Bavarian roller-coaster designer, Anton Schwarzkopf.

OLDEST ROLLER COASTERS

'Leap-The-Dips,' a traditional side-friction roller coaster at Lakemont Park, Altoona, Pennsylvania, was built by the Edward Joy Morris Company in 1902. It was closed to the public in 1985, seemingly at the end of its life, but was fully restored and reopened in 1999.

The oldest continually operating roller coaster is 'The Scenic Railway' at Luna Park, St. Kilda, Vic, Australia. It originally opened to the public on Dec 13 1912 and has remained in operation ever since. This traditional wooden roller-coaster was designed by La Marcus Adna Thompson (USA), who is regarded as the father of the modern roller coaster.

TALLEST ROLLER COASTER

'Superman The Escape' at Six Flags Magic Mountain, Valencia, California, a dual-track, vertical reverse-point, free-fall roller coaster, designed by Intamin AG of Switzerland, features 15-seater gondolas which, when launched along the track by means of a linear induction motor, reach a height of 415 ft (126.5 m) before falling vertically back along the same track at a speed of 100 mph (160 km/h).

TALLEST LOOPING ROLLER COASTER

'Viper' at the Six Flags Magic Mountain in Valencia, California, is 188 ft (57.30 m) high. It turns upside down seven times at a speed of 70 mph (112.65 km/h).

LONGEST WOODEN ROLLER COASTER

'The Beast,' built in 1979 at Paramount's Kings Island, near Cincinnati, Ohio, is the longest traditional wooden laminated-track roller coaster at 7,400 ft (2,286 m). A new roller coaster called 'Son of Beast' is being built and will hold the following records – tallest wooden roller coaster (218 ft or 66.5 m), tallest wooden roller coaster drop (214 ft or 65.2 m), fastest wooden roller coaster (78 mph or 125.5 km/h), most loops in a wooden roller coaster (although it will have only one). The loop is contained in a steel section incorporated into the laminated wooden tracks – standard wooden structures would not be able to withstand the forces of a loop.

COMING FULL CIRCLE

The 'British Airways London Eye' (above), designed by London architects David Marks and Julia Barfield, is the world's biggest observation wheel with a diameter and height of 443 ft (135 m). It had its first 'flight' on Feb 1 2000. The wheel turns continuously during normal operation. Each of the 32 fully enclosed high-tech capsules carries up to 25 passengers and completes a full 360° rotation every 30 minutes. At the highest point this giant wheel offers views across a 30-mile (48-km) radius of London, UK.

www.guinnessworldrecords.com/londoneye

ACCESS CODE
‹51872› ←

ROLLER COASTER WITH STEEPEST DROP

The steepest drop of any steel roller coaster in the world is at the 'Oblivion' in Alton Towers, UK, at 87.5°. The drop is 197 ft (60 m) long and the two-row cars reach a speed of up to 70 mph (113 km/h). Oblivion can take up to 1,900 riders per hour.

The record for the steepest drop in a wooden roller coaster is 58.5° and belongs to the 'Cyclone' in Astroland, New York City.

RIDING HIGH

Cedar Point Amusement Park, Sandusky, Ohio, (left, above), which dates back to 1870, has 68 rides – more than any other single amusement or theme park. This park also has the most roller coasters with 14 – two traditional wooden-track and 12 steel-track roller coasters featuring, among others, the 'Millennium Force,' which opened in 2000 and is taller than the Statue of Liberty.

A team of seven (left) holds the record for most roller coaster rides in 24 hours. Patricia Byron, Denise Lau Cortopassi, David Escalante, John Sutherland, David Curley, John Green, and Steven Wilson (all USA) rode on 40 different roller coasters at eight different parks from Oct 14 to 15 2000.

‹51868›   www.guinnessworldrecords.com/cedarpoint
← ACCESS CODE

EARLIEST FERRIS WHEEL

The original Ferris wheel, designed by engineer George Washington Gale Ferris Jr. (USA), was erected in 1893 in Chicago, Illinois. It had a maximum height of 264 ft (80 m) above the ground, with a diameter of 250 ft (76 m) and a circumference of 790 ft (240.8 m). Each of the 36 fully enclosed gondolas could carry up to 40 passengers in revolving chairs, and the wheel weighed 2.87 million lb (1,300 tonnes) unladen.

OBSERVATON WHEEL WITH BIGGEST CAPACITY

British naval officer Walter Bassett constructed his first and largest observation wheel for the Oriental Exhibition, Earl's Court, London, UK, in 1895. It had 10 first-class and 30 second-class cars, each carrying 30 people. It could carry up to a total of 1,200 passengers to a maximum height of 276 ft (84 m), but was scrapped in 1906.

FERRIS WHEEL WITH THE WIDEST DIAMETER

On March 18 1999 'The Cosmoclock 21' opened at Yokohama City, Japan. It is 328 ft (100 m) in diameter and 369 ft (112.5 m) high, equivalent to a 30-story building. It has 60 gondolas with eight seats in each. It is illuminated by laser beams and features acoustic effects by sound synthesizers. Fireworks are presented at 15-minute intervals to light up the wheel.

LONGEST MECHANICAL RODEO RIDE

Pauline Farrington (UK) was able to ride a mechanical bull set at level seven for a duration of 58.1 sec in Paris, France, on Sept 30 2000.

LONGEST VERTICAL DROP RIDE

At 'Drop Zone' at Kings Island theme park in Cincinnati, Ohio, the 40 riders are seated in a circle around a central pole. They fall for 262 ft 6 in (80 m) from a 300-ft (91.4-m) tower, reaching speeds of up to 65 mph (105 km/h). Only 141 ft (43 m) of the 262 ft (80 m) are free-falling. While braking, riders feel 4 G of force (four times the force of gravity), meaning that they effectively weigh four times their usual weight.

OLDEST CAROUSEL IN OPERATION

The world's oldest operating carousel is the Vermolen Boden-Karussel at Efteling Theme Park in Kaatsheuvel, Netherlands, and was built in 1865. It was originally powered by horses, but was later restored and is now electrically driven.

TALLEST SPEED WATER SLIDE

The tallest water slide in the world is 'Insane' at Beach Park, Fortaleza, Brazil, which is 135 ft (41 m) high. Riders reach speeds of up to 64.6 mph (104 km/h) in only 4 seconds – quite uncomfortable since the riders wear only their swimsuits. This slide is as tall as an 11-story building.

TALLEST ENCLOSED WATER FLUMES

The 'Turbo Twisters' at Myrtle Waves, Myrtle Beach, South Carolina, which opened in 1994, are 75 ft (22.8 m) high and 200 ft (61 m) long – the world's tallest tubular water flumes. Riders reach speeds of up to 34 mph (55 km/h) in complete darkness.

HIGHEST WAVE-POOL WAVE

The highest artificial waves are 9.18 ft (2.8 m) high, in the Valley of the Waves at Sun City, South Africa.

MOST WATERSLIDE FLUMES

The Splash Garden, Rokko Island, Kobe, Japan, has a record 50 waterslide flumes on a single tower.

LARGEST WAVE POOL

According to the World Waterpark Association, the largest wave pool, often called an artificial sea, covers 172,000 ft^2 or four acres (16,000 m^2) and can be found at Siam Park, Bangkok, Thailand.

www.guinnessworldrecords.com/steeldragon

BIG DIPPER 🖳 JP

The 'Steel Dragon' (left), which opened on Aug 1 2000 at Nagashima Spaland, Mie, Japan, is a noninversion steel-track gigacoaster, designed by Steve Okamoto. It is the fastest full-circuit roller coaster on earth and also holds the world records for the longest drop and the longest track. It lifts riders 311 ft 8 in (95 m) before dropping them 306 ft 9 in (93.5 m), while accelerating to 92.5 mph (149 km/h). Before completing the amazing 8,133 ft (2,479 m) of track, riders have additional 243-ft (74-m) and 210-ft (64-m) hills ahead of them. In total, riders are dropped 1,200 ft (365 m).

ACCESS CODE ‹55358› ←

GUINNESS WORLD RECORDS™

technology

GUINNESS
WORLD RECORDS™

computers 1

FASTEST-SELLING PC GAME

The role-playing PC game *Diablo II* by Blizzard Entertainment sold more than one million copies within the first two weeks of being released in June 2000. By Jan 2001 it had sold 2.75 million copies worldwide. The original *Diablo* role-playing computer game has sold more than 2.3 million copies since its release in 1997.

OLDEST GIGA PET

The world's oldest-known Giga Pet is Elvis, owned by Jessica Troiano (USA). According to its manufacturer, Tiger Electronics, Elvis' 'life' began on July 3 1997. It claimed the record on Jan 13 1998, at the age of 194 days, when its batteries ran out.

BEST-SELLING COMPUTER

About 30 million Commodore 64 computers were sold between the model's launch in 1982 and its commercial decline in 1993. The computer contained 64K RAM, 16K graphics, and 16K sound.

LENGTHIEST COMPUTATION FOR A YES/NO ANSWER

In 1986, the 20th Fermat number, $2^{220}+1$ (named after mathematician Pierre de Fermat 1601–65) was tested on a CRAY-2 supercomputer to see if it was a prime number. After 10 days, the answer 'no' came back, making this the longest ever computer computation to give a yes/no answer.

MINIMUM CREDIT

Just 60% the size of a credit card, the smallest computer keyboard with a full complement of alphanumeric, symbol, and command keys was patented on March 18 1997 by David Levy (USA). The keyboard (left) has 64 keys, which are big enough to be operated with a thumb, yet the whole device measures just 3 x 1.2 in (7.62 x 3 cm).

<47158>
← ACCESS CODE
www.guinnessworldrecords.com/tinykeyboard

BEST-SELLING SOCCER GAME

The FIFA series of games, developed by EA Sports (USA), have sold more than 16 million units. Launched in PC format on Nov 27 1998, the game features a full pop soundtrack, including recording artists such as Fatboy Slim (UK).

SHORTEST COMPUTER INSTRUCTION MANUAL

The Apple iMac personal computer comes with an instruction manual that consists of just six pictures and 36 words, allowing the computer to live up to the sales pitch that a user can just take it out of the box and plug it in.

LARGEST COMPUTERISED ROBOT DOG

The RS-01 RoboDog, manufactured by RoboScience (UK), measures 32 x 26 x 14 in (82 x 67 x 37 cm). RoboDog has an internal computer and connects remotely to the internet via a radio transmitter. It can monitor and read out emails sent to its owner, and responds to voice commands.

BEST-SELLING FLIGHT SIMULATOR

MS Flight Simulator was released by Microsoft in April 1992 and had sold a total of 21 million units by June 1999. *Flight Simulator 2000* allows players to 'fly' Concorde, the Boeing 737-400 and Boeing 777-300, the Learjet 45, the Bell 206B JetRanger helicopter, and the Sopwith Camel.

BEST-SELLING DRIVING SIMULATOR

Gran Turismo Real Driving Simulator, a Sony PlayStation game, had sold a record seven million units worldwide by Feb 2000. The game was developed by Polyphony Digital, a satellite company of Sony Computer Entertainment. A sequel, *Gran Turismo 2*, was launched in 1999, and *Gran Turismo 2000* is one of the headline titles showcasing the 'Emotion Engine' processor of the PlayStation2, which was released in Japan on March 4 2000.

LARGEST COMPUTATION

SETI@home, which was launched by the University of California at Berkeley, California, on May 17 1999, had made a total of 7.7×10^{20} (or 300 billion billion) computer calculations as of July 2000. SETI@home is a scientific experiment that harnesses the power of hundreds of thousands of internet-linked computers in the search for extraterrestrial intelligence. Participants download and run a free program that analyzes data from radio telescopes.

FASTEST COMPUTER

The fastest supercomputer is the RS/6000 *ASCI White*, which was completed by IBM in June 2000. The size of two basketball courts, this supercomputer is capable of 12 trillion calculations per second. It has more than six trillion bytes (terabytes) of memory along with 160 terabytes of storage memory – enough to hold six times the whole book collection of the US Library of Congress – the largest library in the world. In one second it could solve a problem that would take one person with a calculator 10 million years to complete. The purpose of *ASCI White* is to allow the testing of nuclear weapons using computer simulations instead of detonating actual bombs.

MOST 'HUMAN' COMPUTER PROGRAM

A computer running the program *Albert* was awarded the 1999 Loebner Prize for the 'most human' computer system after convincing 11% of judges that it was a real person. *Albert* won $2,000 (£1,250) for its author, Robby Garner (USA). *Albert* is a program that a user can communicate with using human speech and is capable of holding a quirky, spontaneous conversation full of sarcastic and witty one-liners.

BIGGEST SCANNER

The SLC972C color scanner, produced by Widecom Group Inc of Brampton, Ontario, Canada, has a 6-ft (1.82-m) scan width. Unveiled at

YU'RE IN THE MONEY

The most expensive computer game to be developed is the Dreamcast game *Shenmue*, which cost over $20 million (£12 million). The project (left) took seven years to complete and was the brainchild of Yu Suzuki (Japan), the head of Sega's game-development AM2 division. Suzuki built his reputation on arcade titles – credits include *Virtual Fighter* (1993), *Virtual Racing* (1992), and *Out Run* (1986).

Shenmue is about a Japanese high-school student who begins a quest to avenge the death of his father. The game is polished with ultrarealistic scenery, in-depth plot, and martial arts fighting. There are also over 200 characters to interact with, all of whom lead their own lives within the game.

<53483>
ACCESS CODE
www.guinnessworldrecords.com/dreamcast

PERSONAL BEST

The Compaq H3360 iPaq Pocket PC (above), a PDA (personal digital assistant) launched in 2001, it has a 206-MHz processor and a 240 x 320-pixel touch-sensitive color LCD screen, making it the most powerful PDA in the world. It has 64MB of RAM and 16MB of ROM, and weighs 6 oz (170 g), including its battery.

The Palm range of Personal Digital Assistants from 3Com are the best-selling PDAs, having sold over five million units since their launch in 1996. 3Com dominates the US market for PDAs, with a 73.6% market share as of Jan 2000.

www.guinnessworldrecords.com/pda

ACCESS CODE
‹53693› ←

a California trade show in May 1999, it is targeted at people who work in industries such as automotive and aircraft manufacturing and shipbuilding, who deal with huge drawings that require a scanning capacity of this size.

FASTEST-SELLING VIDEO GAME

The Nintendo Game Boy title *Pokémon Yellow* was released in the USA on Oct 18 1999 and had sold one million copies within

10 days. If you played each one of the 100 million Game Boys that exist in the world for just 60 seconds without stopping, it would take 190 years.

BEST-SELLING HANDHELD GAME SYSTEM

The world's most popular video game system is the Nintendo Game Boy, which sold more than 100 million units between 1989 and 2000 – an average of more than 1,000 units per hour. Nintendo currently occupies more than 99% of the US market through its *Game Boy*, *Game Boy Pocket*, and *Game Boy Color* units. More than 1,000 Game Boy titles are now available worldwide.

www.guinnessworldrecords.com/playstation

CRASH BANDICOOT WALLOP

The fastest-selling video game console is Sony's PlayStation2 (PS2) with a record 980,000 units of the game, which features the character Crash Bandicoot (right), being sold in the 48 hours following its release on March 4 2000. That is more than 10 times the sales scored by the original PlayStation console over the same period when it was launched in 1996. The console currently costs JPY39,800 ($369.62; £233.50). The character Crash Bandicoot was developed by Naughty Dog (USA), a company of 10 people.

ACCESS CODE
‹53538› ←

GUINNESS WORLD RECORDS™

computers 2

LARGEST NUMBER CRUNCHED

The largest number ever 'crunched' is $(10^{211}-1) / 9$, i.e. multiply 10 by itself 211 times, subtract 1 from the total, and then divide the result by 9. The number consists of 211 digits, all of which are ones. A group called 'The Cabal,' led by Herman teRiele, found two factors (whole numbers by which a larger number can be divided) to this massive figure. The factors themselves were 93 and 118-digits long. Number crunching, or 'factorization' as it is known, is very useful in writing complex codes and in coded military communications.

LARGEST PERSONAL COMPUTER MANUFACTURER

In 1998, US firm Compaq sold a total of 13,275,204 PCs – the equivalent of one every 2.38 seconds. Compaq provides the systems for 75% of the world's cashpoint transactions and 60% of all lotteries.

FIRST PROGRAMMABLE ELECTRONIC COMPUTER

The 1500-valve Colossus, formulated by Prof. Max Newman and built by T.H. Flowers, was run in Dec 1943 at Bletchley Park, Bucks, UK, to break codes created by the German-made Lorenz-Schlussel-zusatz 40 machine, or 'Tunny' as the British called it. Colossus was not declassified until Oct 25 1975.

MOST DAMAGING VIRUS

The CIH virus or 'Chernobyl' virus has affected one million PCs since it was first triggered on April 26 1998, the 12th anniversary of the nuclear reactor disaster in Chernobyl, USSR. According to the Taipei authorities, the virus was written by Chen Ing-hau, whose initials make up the name of the virus. CIH irreversibly alters a computer's BIOS chip, which is soldered on to the motherboard. The damage can make a computer totally useless.

<54029> ← ACCESS CODE
www.guinnessworldrecords.com/applemacchief

MOST CHARACTERS HANDLED BY SOFTWARE

Japan's Personal Media Corporation has developed a computer operating system called B-right/V2, which is capable of handling 128,175 different characters as part of its TRON code system. This includes most of the characters in all the world's alphabets, and special characters such as braille. The program was launched in 1999 and runs on all IBM PC-compatible computers.

BEST CHESS COMPUTER

IBM's Deep Blue was the first computer to beat a chess grandmaster when it defeated Gary Kasparov (Azerbaijan) in Feb 1996. The victory was part of a six-match series that Kasparov ultimately won 4–2. In 1997, a new and improved Deep Blue returned to beat Kasparov in a second series. The computer, which could consider a mind-boggling 200 million positions a second, won the series by 3.5 points to Kasparov's 2.5.

CORE VALUE

Steve Jobs (USA, left), the Chief Executive Officer and cofounder of Apple Computer Inc, is the world's worst-paid CEO, receiving a salary of just $1 (62 pence) a year. But the Apple chief gets a lot more than his annual core wage – in Jan 2000 Jobs received a Gulfstream luxury airliner and 10 million stock options for agreeing to stay with Apple as its permanent chief executive. From Jan 31 2000 he could exercise the options to buy and sell half of these 10 million shares. Jobs codesigned the Apple II computer, which ignited the personal computer revolution in the 1970s. He then led the development and marketing of the Macintosh computer in the 1980s, presiding over the growth of Apple into a $2-billion (£1.4-billion) company.

BEST-SELLING GAMES CONSOLE

The Sony PlayStation console had sold around 79.61 million units worldwide by Jan 2001, making it the world's best-selling games console. Sony Computer Entertainment Inc spent more than $300 million (£181 million) developing the console, which runs hit games such as *Tomb Raider* and *Final Fantasy VII*. Around 430 million PlayStation software units have been produced.

LOVESICK COMPUTERS

The virulent 'I Love You' computer virus (left) was the most widespread the world has ever known. It was first detected in Hong Kong on May 1 2000. Within four days it had mutated into three different generations. The Love Bug combined sophisticated programming with a cunning appeal to the human psyche. When users opened the 'I Love You' attachment, the virus was instantly forwarded to all the addresses in the victim's e-mail directory. Governments, multinational corporations, and small businesses were all affected. At its height, the virus forced the closure of the White House and US State Department e-mail networks. Figures published on May 8 2000 by Trend Micro Inc. showed that 'I Love You' had infected 3.1 million computers worldwide.

<52411> ← ACCESS CODE
www.guinnessworldrecords.com/lovebug

MOST ADVANCE ORDERS FOR A VIDEO GAME

More than 325,000 US consumers put down advance orders and deposits for the Nintendo 64 game, *The Legend of Zelda: Ocarina of Time*. The game hit the stores on Nov 23 1998.

BEST-SELLING GAME

The Nintendo game *Super Mario Brothers* has sold a total of 40.23 million copies worldwide since its launch in 1983.

LONGEST-RUNNING COMPUTER GAME CHARACTER

Nintendo's 'Mario' character, a plumber by trade, first appeared in the arcade version of *Donkey Kong* in 1981. Mario has since made an appearance in over 70 games, although he is a 'playable' character in only around 30 of these. In the original *Donkey Kong* game, Mario was a carpenter initially called 'Jumpman,' but he was renamed after the president of Nintendo noticed the character resembled his landlord, Mario. The character's look owes a lot to the limitations of early computer technology. On the low-resolution hardware of the early 1980s, it was easier to animate a moustache than a mouth, and a cap was easier to draw than hair.

MOST PARTICIPANTS IN A VIDEO-GAME TOURNAMENT

On March 24 1996 a record 9,066 people participated in Compile Corporation's second annual 'Puyo Puyo' tournament, held at Makuhari Messe, Hiroshima, Japan.

MOST ADVANCED GAMES CONSOLE

Microsoft's Xbox, which launched in the US in Fall 2001, is powered by a 733 MHz Intel chip, the fastest of any games console. The Xbox's graphics processor, which runs at 250 MHz, is also the field leader. The Xbox's rivals, the Sony PlayStation 2 and the Nintendo Gamecube, have clock speeds of 300 and 405 MHz respectively. The PlayStation 2 has a graphics chip that runs at 150 MHz. The Gamecube's graphics chip runs at 202.5 MHz. The PlayStation 2, however, also supports DVD and audio CD formats.

MOST TREES WITH MICROCHIPS

During 1999, 90,000 trees in Paris, France, were implanted with tiny 1.4 in (3-cm) glass and carbon-fiber electronic microchips. The chips were programmed with information about each individual tree's health. The microchip-tagging system allowed the city's tree surgeons to identify trees in need of treatment more precisely. About 1,200 trees die every year in Paris due to the effects of human and car pollution, winter salting, and dehydration.

FASTEST E-COMMERCE SET-UP

In 1999, Computer Experts of Brighton, UK, set up the website http://www. jcamping.instant-net.co.uk and received its first order in a record-breaking time of 20 min 6.83 sec.

OLDEST COMPUTER

The first fully automated, software-driven computer was designed and run by Tom Kilburn and Freddie Williams (both UK) on June 21 1948. They used a 17-instruction program on a machine called 'Baby,' which calculated the highest factor of 2^{18}. 'Baby' is 16 ft (4.87 m) long, 7 ft (2.13 m) high, and 2 ft (0.6 m) deep, and its wires and vacuum tubes occupied an entire room. The computer had 1,024 bytes of memory and could work out seven instruction types. 'Baby' could perform a maximum of 700 operations per second – modern machines can carry out tens of millions.

www.guinnessworldrecords.com/minimouse

ACCESS CODE: ‹56137› ←

MINI MOUSE

The smallest computer mouse is the Cat Eye FinRing (right). Made by Luckytech Technology (Taiwan), it is worn on the index finger like a ring. The wireless device is powered by two small batteries and it has three thumb-operated buttons. The user's finger movement is tracked by internal sensors, and information is transmitted to a receiver plugged into the computer's mouse port. Users can roam up to 26 ft 3 in (8 m) away from the receiver and still control the cursor accurately.

BIGGEST STORAGE CAPACITY

Ted Williams (UK) has invented a new type of double-sided solid-state memory that can hold as much as 1,742 gigabytes/in^2 (270 gigabytes/cm^2) of random access memory (RAM). This means that it could hold 10.8 terabytes on a chip the size of a credit card. Solid-state memory involves no moving parts.

THINNEST DIGITAL DISK

The *ThinDisc*, introduced on Dec 1 2000, is five times thinner than normal CDs or DVD disks. Designed to be played in virtually any CD or DVD drive, the *ThinDisc* is also very flexible and can be wrapped around a soda can without breaking.

EARLIEST COMPUTER GAME

Spacewar was the earliest computer game, first implemented between 1961 and 1962 at the Massachusetts Institute of Technology, on a PDP-1 computer. It was a space combat game in which two ships, revolving around a central star, had to shoot each other down. Written for fun by students at MIT, this game was an important precursor to all modern computer games. The PDP-1 computer first became available in 1960 and cost $120,000 (£56,900) – the equivalent today of $930,000 (£654,000). Fifty units were sold in total. The PDP-1 was the ancestor of the microcomputer and was designed for use in scientific institutions. It had a memory of 4K, and operators used a keyboard and paper tape to input data into it.

GUINNESS WORLD RECORDS™

LONGEST-RUNNING WEBCAM

Computer scientists at Cambridge University (UK) were so frustrated with trekking down the corridor to find that the coffee pot was empty, that they rigged up a camera and a computer so that they could see instantly if there was any coffee left. In Nov 1993 Daniel Gordon hooked the camera up to the World Wide Web, where live images of the now-famous coffee pot have been available ever since at web address: www.cl.cam.ac.uk/coffee/qsf/coffee.html. It will be turned off in late 2001.

HIGHEST ANNUAL ADVERTISING REVENUE

The year 2000 saw a rise in internet advertising revenues to a record $2.9 billion (£1.94 billion), a 52.6% increase on 1999 figures.

LARGEST INTERNET ADVERTISER

The largest internet advertiser in 2000 was General Motors, which spent $47.9 million (£32.09 million), a 96.5% increase on their advertising expenditure in 1999.

LARGEST BRAND ADVERTISER

The bookstore Barnes & Noble (USA) spent $15,903,892 (£10,654,446) on brand advertising in 2000, a 55.8% increase on their advertising expenditure in 1999.

WRIST BANDS

The smallest MP3 player and watch is the SV-SD75 by Panasonic (left), which measures 2 x 1.9 x 0.59 in (50.8 x 49.2 x 15.0 mm). It comes with 64MB memory on an SD memory card and is designed to be worn as a watch or around the neck. It connects to a home PC using a USB cable and, since it has no moving parts, it will never 'jump' or 'skip' while playing music.

<56559>

www.guinnessworldrecords.com/mp3player

← ACCESS CODE

INDUSTRY SECTOR WITH MOST INTERNET ADS

The industry sector that spent the most on internet advertising in the year 2000 with a combined expenditure of $542,155,702 (£363,204,731) was media and advertising. Retail came second, spending a grand total of $510,853,232 (£342,234,362).

WEBSITE WITH HIGHEST ADVERTISING REVENUE

Yahoo! Inc, based in Sunnydale, California, generated an advertising revenue of $442,336,726 (£296,333,306) from their website Yahoo.com in 2000, according to Competitive Media Reporting (CMR).

COSTLIEST E-MAIL

In 1997, a subsidiary of US-based petroleum company Chevron Corporation paid $2.2 million (£1.3 million) to settle a sexual-harassment lawsuit filed by four female employees. Evidence presented by the women's lawyers included e-mail records listing 25 reasons why beer is supposedly better than women. In settling, Chevron Corporation denied the women's allegations.

EARLIEST LIVE DEBUT PERFORMANCE OF A CLASSICAL WORK ONLINE

On Nov 19 1997 Sir Paul McCartney (UK) performed his new classical work, the 75-minute symphonic poem *Standing Stone*. It was broadcast live from Carnegie Hall, New York City, in a multifaceted presentation of radio, TV, interactive online interview, and internet audio and video broadcast across the World Wide Web.

BIGGEST FINE FOR AN INTERNET CRIME

US antiabortion activists who operated a site called The Nuremberg Files, containing 'Wanted' posters with the names and addresses of doctors who perform abortions, had to pay more than $107.7 million (£65 million) in damages on Feb 3 1999.

SMALLEST WEB SERVER

The web page of the Wearables Laboratory at Stanford University, California, is supported by Jumptec's DIMM-PC, a 'matchbox' server measuring a tiny 2.7 x 1.7 x 0.25 in (6.86 x 4.32 x 0.64 cm), making it only slightly higher and wider than a box of matches but just one-third of the thickness. The server weighs a mere 0.71 oz (20 g).

BIGGEST MULTILINGUAL WEB BROADCAST

In Dec 1997 the opening and closing ceremonies of the Third Conference of the Parties of the United Nations Framework Convention on Climate Change, which took place in Kyoto, Japan, were broadcast at the same time via the internet in seven languages — Arabic, Chinese, English, French, Japanese, Russian, and Spanish.

BIGGEST INTERNET GOLF TOURNAMENT

More than 11,000 players signed up for the 1999 Jack Nicklaus Online Golf Championship. The final round was held on Dec 10 1999. Chet Stone (USA) won the title and $5,000 (£3,492) after 36 holes of matchplay on a digitally rendered version of the golf course at the Pelican Hill Golf Club, California.

BIGGEST SCHOOL INTERNET PROJECT

The world's biggest school internet project is Tesco SchoolNet 2000 (UK), launched in Sept 1998. The aim of the project is to create an electronic 'Domesday Book' for the 21st century, made up of children's investigations into their local communities. By March 2001 up to 133,986 pupils and 17,312 schools had registered. The project was meant to finish at the end of 2000, but is so popular that it is continuing.

ACCESS ALL AREAS

A record 11 million people watched Madonna (left) perform a concert at the Brixton Academy, London, UK, on Nov 28 2000. It was broadcast live on the internet by Microsoft Network online. MSN e-mailed their 75 million Hotmail users to let them know of the event and also had homepage promotions in 17 different languages on more than 30 internet sites across the world.

The largest concert that took place exclusively via the internet was on Sept 24 1998. Roger Taylor and five band members performed a 45-minute gig at the Cyberbarn, Thursley, Surrey, UK. The audience consisted of a record 9,804 people who logged on via the internet – which was the only way to see the concert.

<54431>

www.guinnessworldrecords.com/madonna

← ACCESS CODE

LARGEST URL

The largest internet URL ever to be displayed is www.rawmart.com. A global commodities trading site, its

TRADING PLACES

If you can't find what you want in a shop, the Internet Mall (above) has a record 27,000 on-screen virtual shops and more than one million subscribers in the UK alone. It is available in more than 150 countries, with products ranging from popcorn to car insurance.

The most expensive internet domain name – business.com – was sold by entrepreneur Marc Ostrofsky (USA) on Dec 1 1999 for $7.5 million (£4.6 million). This tops the $3.3 million (£2,340,000) paid by Compaq for altavista.com and the $3 million (£2,130,000) paid for wine.com.

www.guinnessworldrecords.com/
internetmall

ACCESS CODE
<54144> ←

www.guinnessworldrecords.com/napster

NAPPY DAYS

Shawn Fanning (USA, right) was a 19-year-old computer science student at Northeastern University, Boston, Massachusetts, when he wrote the source code for the music file-sharing program Napster in mid-1999. Napster has since become the world's fastest-growing internet company, with more than 32 million users worldwide. The program got its name from Shawn's high-school nickname – the Napster – a reference to his perpetually 'nappy' (messy) hair.

ACCESS CODE
<90746> ←

name was painted on the side of the carrier ship *E-Trader* in letters 13.45 ft (4.1 m) high in July 2000. The full address was 389 ft (118.59 m) long.

LONGEST URL

The longest URL belongs to http://llanfairpwllgwyngyllgogerychw yrndrobwllllantysiliogogogoch.co.uk/, a site about an ancient rural village in North Wales, UK, called Llanfairpwllgwyngyllgogerychwyrn-drobwllllantysiliogogogoch. The name means 'Saint Mary's Church in the hollow of the white hazel, near a rapid whirlpool and the church of Saint Tysilio of the red cave.'

MOST ATTACKS IN A HACKING COMPETITION

A total of 5.23 million attacks were recorded during eWeek's 17-day-long Openhack III competition, in which

the latest security software, Pitbull, from Argus Systems Group Inc was probed for weaknesses by the hacking community. Despite the offered prize of $50,000 (£35,000), not one hacker was able to penetrate Pitbull. During Openhack I and II, the software that was being tested was successfully accessed.

MOST SEARCHED-FOR SPORTSWOMAN

The Russian tennis player Anna Kournikova is reported to be the most searched-for sportswoman on the internet.

MOST SEARCHED-FOR SPORTSMAN

The American golfer Tiger Woods is reported to be the most searched-for sportsman on the internet.

MOST REMOTE CONCIERGE

Anna Morris (USA) works 80 miles (130 km) from the hotel where she is employed as a concierge. Guests at the Westin Hotel, Santa Clara, California, speak to Anna via an interactive webcam and she can see guests via a camera in the hotel. So instead of driving through heavy traffic each day, she can work from home.

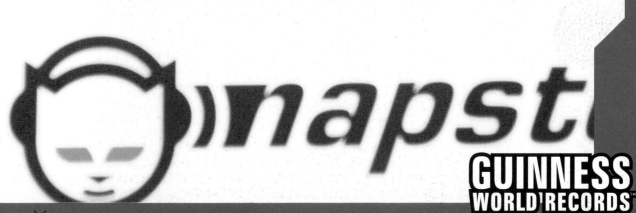

GUINNESS WORLD RECORDS

internet 2

MOST DOWNLOADED CYBERPET

More than 14 million people worldwide have downloaded *MOPy*, a lifelike pet fish screensaver, since it was first released in Oct 1997.

MOST CYBERSTAR VARIATIONS

There are an estimated 2,000 variations of *Dancing Baby*, a cyberstar originally created as an animated 3-D graphics model in Oct 1996 by Kinetix, a subsidiary of Autodesk Inc. (USA). *Dancing Baby* is the only character originated on the internet that has achieved a popular following prior to its appearance in mainstream media. The internet spurred the creation of new variations of *Dancing Baby* by amateur animation artists on hundreds of websites. The official *Dancing Baby* page has an average monthly view rate of 55,000.

HIGHEST CYBERSTAR MERCHANDISE SALES

During 1998 *Dancing Baby* T-shirt sales in the USA totaled more than $2.8 million (£1.7 million) wholesale. Music CD sales exceeded $425,000 (£256,000) wholesale, while international and US wholesale figures of the electronic *Dancing Baby* doll topped $550,000 (£331,845). Other merchandise across the USA, Australia, and Europe grossed over $900,000 (£543,019).

ONE FOR THE BOOKS

Amazon.com (left), founded in 1994 by Jeff Bezos (USA), opened its virtual doors in July 1995 and has now sold products to more than 13 million customers in over 160 countries, making it the largest online bookshop. It has a catalog of 4.7 million books, CDs, and videos, including titles currently out of print. Although there are over three million books actively in print, no one could build a bookstore large enough to hold them. The largest known conventional bookstores carry 170,000 titles. When Bezos started this business, he worked out of an office from his garage in Seattle, Washington – wrapping book orders himself and delivering them to the post office in the family car.

<53961>
www.guinnessworldrecords.com/amazondotcom
← ACCESS CODE

MOST QUESTIONS ASKED ONLINE

On May 17 1997 Sir Paul McCartney was asked over three million online questions in 30 minutes. Fans questioned him during a web event to promote his album *Flaming Pie*.

MOST STOCK TRADING ONLINE

During Jan 2000, 44.6% of all stock trading in South Korea was executed online, according to the Korea Securities Dealers Association. A record total of 51,000 billion won ($45.5 billion or £28.1 billion) worth of stocks listed on the Korea Stock Exchange and the Kosdaq were traded online.

LARGEST SINGLE E-COMMERCE TRANSACTION

Internet tycoon Mark Cuban (USA) bought a Gulfstream V business jet over the internet in Oct 1999. The jet changed hands for $40 million (£25 million).

LARGEST FREE E-MAIL PROVIDER

Hotmail is the world's largest free web-based e-mail service provider and had more than 70 million subscribers in April 2001. Every day Hotmail adds 100,000 new users. It is available in 230 countries and has 12 million unique logins per month.

EARLIEST REGISTERED DOMAIN NAME

Symbolics.com was the first domain name ever registered, according to NetNames Ltd. It was registered on March 15 1985.

MOST POPULAR TOP-LEVEL DOMAIN

'.com' is the most popular top-level domain. It is used by 22.3 million hosts, out of a possible 35.3 million in existence worldwide in April 2001. There are no general restrictions relating to who can register because '.com' is a top-level domain (TLD) and is considered to be global.

LARGEST CONCENTRATION OF DOMAIN NAMES

The greatest concentration of domain names is in the New York Metropolitan area. These domain names account for 4.8% of the world's total.

LARGEST HOLDER OF DOMAIN NAMES

US company Namezero holds a record 1,307,300 domain names – more than any other company in the world.

YOUNGEST INTERNET COUNTRY CODE

Palestine, still battling for international recognition as an independent state, acquired autonomy in cyberspace on March 22 2000. The Internet Corporation for Assigned Names and Numbers (ICANN), which regulates net addresses, granted the Palestinian National Authority its own two-letter suffix for online real estate. As with other so-called country codes, such as '.fr' for France and '.it' for Italy, the Palestinian group will be able to register addresses under its own domain, '.ps'.

MOST POPULAR COUNTRY-LEVEL DOMAIN

As of March 2001 the most popular country-level domain is '.uk' (United Kingdom) with over two million domain registrations, according to NetNames Ltd. The UK is closely followed by Germany ('.de'). Although America has the most internet sites, few of them use '.us' in their URL.

EASY DOES IT

easyEverything (left) in Times Square, New York City, is the world's biggest internet café. It opened on Nov 28 2000 and has 760 computer terminals. The 17,130-ft² (5,221-m²) cybercafé has two floors of PCs offering internet access to the web 24 hours a day, seven days a week. The New York café was the first easyEverything to open in the USA. Previously, branches had been confined to Europe. By April 2001 there were 21 easyEverything internet cafés around the world – five in London, two in Amsterdam, two in Barcelona, and one each in New York, Edinburgh, Glasgow, Manchester, Brussels, Antwerp, Rotterdam, Berlin, Munich, Rome, Paris, and Madrid. The creator of easyEverything is Greek-born, UK-based businessman, Stelios Haji-Ioannou.

<55978>
www.guinnessworldrecords.com/cybercafe
← ACCESS CODE

MOST VOTES RECEIVED BY A WEBPAGE

Between 2 p.m. on Oct 4 and midday on Nov 11 1999, the MTV Europe Music Awards website (www.mtv-vote.com), powered by Compaq, registered 1,643,863 votes. The site featured a built-in spam-trap to prevent hackers from setting up an automated voting system to register thousands of bogus votes.

MOST ELECTRONIC BIRTHDAY GREETINGS

To mark the birthday of 'Posh Spice' (Victoria Beckham), a website on www.dotmusic.com was reserved for birthday greetings from 2 p.m. on April 9 until 2 p.m. on April 10 2000. In 24 hours 2,600 messages were received from all over the globe.

MOST DAY-TO-DAY WEBSITE VISITS

The Microsoft Corporation website www.msn.com received 10.5 billion page views in March 2000, according to web statisticians, alexa.com. Of this total figure, 62% of page views came from Microsoft's free e-mail provider, www.hotmail.msn.com.

MOST VISITED ROYAL WEBSITE

The memorial page of the official website of the British monarchy was visited by 14 million people in Sept 1997, following the death of Diana, Princess of Wales. A record 580,000 messages of condolence were also left on the site.

MOST VISITED WEBSITE FOR AN EVENT

During the Fédération Internationale de Football Association (FIFA) World Cup held in France between June 10 and July 12 1998, the official website, www.france98.com, received a record total of 1,137,218,296 hits.

On June 29 1998 this website received a record 235,356 hits in one minute alone. On June 30 1998 this site received 10,290,429 hits in just 60 minutes. On the same date it also had a record 73,030,828 hits in 24 hours.

HIGHEST PERCENTAGE OF AIRLINE TICKETS SOLD OVER THE INTERNET

The airline company easyJet sells 86.6% of all of its tickets via its website www.easyjet.com (as of March 2001). The airline specializes in flights in Europe and keeps the prices of tickets to a minimum by selling directly to its customers, by using less congested airports, and by only using one type of aircraft, the Boeing 737-300.

www.guinnessworldrecords.com/battledotnet

BATTLE IT OUT

Battle.net, owned by Blizzard Entertainment, provides players of games such as *Diablo 2* (featuring characters such as The Sorceress, right) and *Starcraft*, with an internet arena where they can play multiplayer games on the web. Since its launch in 1997, its popularity has risen to over 8.2 million active accounts that log more than six million games daily. Peak concurrent usage tops more than 210,000 players per day. This is the largest free online game service.

ACCESS CODE

‹56574› ←

GUINNESS WORLD RECORDS™

gadgets

SMALLEST PERSONAL DIGITAL ASSISTANT

The REX PC Companion, built in 1998 by Franklin Electronic Publishers, Burlington, is the size and weight of a credit card – 3.4 x 2.1 x 0.25 in (8.6 x 5.3 x 0.63 cm) and 1.4 oz (39.7 g). You can slide it into any compatible laptop computer and then download. REX can also store up to 2,500 personal items, such as names, addresses, and appointments.

MOST VERSATILE PEN

The Space Pen range made by Fisher Space Pen Co. (USA) uses special nitrogen-pressurized cartidges to dispense viscoelastic ink. This allows these pens to work perfectly upside down, and under a wide range of environmental conditions including extreme heat and cold, underwater, and even the zero gravity of space. They were first used in space on the *Apollo 7* mission in 1968 and have become the standard pen for astronauts, including those currently working on the International Space Station. Before the Space Pen was invented, astronauts used pencils when they wanted to write anything in space. The ink is pressurized at nearly 50 psi and is fed to a tungsten carbide

WATCH OUT!

The smallest-ever GPS watch is the Casio PAT2GP-1V (left), measuring 2.3 x 2.0 x 0.8 in (58.5 x 51.5 x 21.0 mm). It receives data from the constellation of Global Positioning System (GPS) satellites in order to pinpoint the location of the wearer within an accuracy of 33 ft (10 m), anywhere on Earth. It can be connected to a home computer to plan map routes, which can be stored in the watch itself.

The Casio WQV1D-8CR is the most advanced digital watch camera and weighs only 1.12 oz (32 g). Its 1 MB of memory allows up to 100 pictures, 28,000 pixels each, to be taken and stored. Images can also be uploaded to a PC.

‹56399› www.guinnessworldrecords.com/gpswatch
← ACCESS CODE

ballpoint. Inside the cartridge, the ink has a consistency similar to that of thick rubber cement. The shearing action of the ballpoint rolling in its socket liquifies the ink, allowing it to flow out like any normal ballpoint pen.

MOST 'INTELLIGENT' PEN AND PAPER

The Swedish company Anoto has created a digital pen that allows the user to digitally store up to 50 fully written pages in its memory. This can be transferred directly to a

nearby computer or (via bluetooth technology) straight to any computer in the world over the internet. The pen writes on special digital paper that enables the pen to locate its exact position on the paper. The paper is divided into a grid system with squares of 0.08 x 0.08 in (2 x 2 mm). Inside each square is a pattern of dots that is different depending upon where one looks on the paper. The huge number of possible dot combinations means that, theoretically, a single sheet of paper larger than Asia and Europe combined could be created, and the pen would still know exactly where it was.

PUBLICATION WITH THE MOST USELESS INVENTIONS

Chindogu (Japanese for 'weird tool') is the art of inventions that appear to be useful but, on closer inspection, reveal their utter uselessness. Kenji Kawakami (Japan) has written *101 Unuseless Japanese Inventions*, containing *chindogu* inventions such as tiny dusters that slip on to a cat's paws, enabling it to clean dusty surfaces as it walks around.

MOST ENERGY-EFFICIENT SHOE

The Electric Shoe Company (founded by Trevor Baylis (UK) and Texon Int) aims to develop a shoe that generates electricity through the act of walking. In Aug 2000 prototypes were tested by Trevor Baylis and John Grantham (UK) during a 75-mile (120-km) trek into the Namibian desert. At the end of the walk, Baylis made a phone call to Richard Branson in the UK, using a mobile phone that had been charged by the shoes.

MOST SUCCESSFUL MECHANICAL RADIO

In 1993 inventor Trevor Baylis (UK) created a spring system that, when wound for several seconds gave several minutes airplay. Freeplay Energy refined his idea and have to date produced 2.5 million units of these self-sufficient windup radios.

LIGHTEST BINOCULARS

The Minolta UCIII binoculars weigh just 4.23 oz (120 g) and are available

WALKING AWAY WITH THE GLORY

The Walkman was developed by The Sony Corporation in 1979 and has proved to be the most successful portable music system ever. The first model on the market was the TPS-L2. Cassette Walkman sales to April 2001 total between 200 and 250 million units. Up to April 1999 the CD Discman had sold 54 million units and the MiniDisc Walkman 6.9 million units. As the Sony Walkman has evolved through the years, it has become more and more compact. The Sony NW-E3 (left) is the latest version and has no moving parts. This MP-3 player measures 3.18 x 1.26 x 0.57 in (8.1 x 3.2 x 1.46 cm) and weighs 1.16 oz (33 g). It has 64 MB of Flash memory embedded, can be connected to a PC via a USB connection, and can store up to two hours of music.

‹56519› www.guinnessworldrecords.com/walkman
← ACCESS CODE

with magnifications of six and eight. The 6 x 16 version can focus on objects just 3.3 ft (1 m) away.

MOST ADVANCED HOLOGRAPHIC UNDERWATER CAMERA

The HOLOMAR underwater holographic camera was developed by a team led by Aberdeen University, Scotland (UK). It can record 3-D images of objects as small as 100 microns across in up to 100 liters (26 gallons) of water.

LARGEST MOBILE-PHONE PENETRATION

Finland is the country with the greatest mobile-phone penetration. There are 651 cellular telephone subscribers for every 1,000 people.

www.guinnessworldrecords.com/thincamera

THROUGH THICK AND THIN

The Ultra-Pocket digital camera (below), designed and developed by SMaL Camera Technologies in Massachusetts, is only 0.2 in (6 mm) thick and weighs a mere 0.14 lb (63.3 g) – including the lithium-ion rechargeable battery. This, the thinnest camera ever, is the size of a credit card and can store approximately 40 color images on the included 8 MB MultiMediaCard.

This card can also be upgraded to a larger memory capacity. Images can be uploaded to a PC via a USB cable. The camera's full dimensions are 3.4 x 0.2 x 2.1 in (85.6 x 6 x 54 mm). The Ultra-Pocket was introduced at the International Consumer Electronics Show 2001 in Las Vegas, Nevada, on Jan 8 2001.

ACCESS CODE

‹56541› ←

PENKNIFE WITH MOST BLADES

The Year Knife was made in 1822 by Joseph Rodgers & Sons (UK). Initially, it had 1,822 blades – one for every year. The tradition of adding a new blade for every year was continued. Stanley Works (UK) Ltd. of Sheffield, South Yorks, UK, restored the knife in 1999 and added a final silver blade to mark the coming of the year 2000.

SMALLEST VIDEO TRANSMITTER

The AVX900T3 measures 0.36 x 0.75 x 0.20 in (0.9 x 1.9 x 0.5 cm) and is manufactured by Supercircuits of Texas. Designed to be used in covert operations and microrobotics, it can transmit video images over a distance of more than 750 ft (230 m), despite being smaller than the average thumb and weighing less than 0.35 oz (7.1 g).

S M a L
ULTRA-POCKET *DIGITAL*

Autobrite™ Exposure

SMaL Lens 6.3mm

GUINNESS WORLD RECORDS™

robots

MOST EXPENSIVE DOMESTIC ROBOT

The most expensive commercially available domestic robot is the TMSUK IV robot, developed by the Japanese Thames company. It was first exhibited in Tokyo, Japan, on Jan 23 2000. The 220-lb (99.8-kg) humanoid robot stands 4 ft (1.22 m) high and costs $43,037 (£30,000). It is totally obedient, can be controlled remotely by mobile phone, runs errands, and even gives massages.

FASTEST INDUSTRIAL ROBOT

The LR Mate 100I high-speed conveyance robot can carry objects for up to 1.86 miles (3 km), can move up and down 1 in (2.5 cm), and can move back and forth over 12 in (30 cm) in just 0.58 seconds. Its speed and movement capabilities enable fast and precise loading and unloading in factory and assembly situations. The robot was developed by Japanese company Fanuc in 1997 and is estimated to be 79% faster than previous models.

LARGEST ROBOTIC ARM IN SPACE

The Canadarm 2, built by the Canadian Space Agency measures 57.7 ft (17.5 m) in length and weighs 3,618 lb (1,641 kg). It was attached to the International Space Station on April 22 2001 during a spacewalk by US astronaut Scott Parazynski and Canadian astronaut Chris Hadfield.

HANDLE WITH CARE

The most advanced robotic hand available is the BH8-262 BarrettHand (left), launched by Barrett Technology Inc. (USA), in April 2001, which has three articulated fingers. Unlike more conventional robotic grippers, which work with a simple pincer movement, the BH8-262 can move its three fingers independently over their full range in either direction in less than one second. Weighing just 2.6 lb (1.18 kg), the hand can apply a force of up to 4.4 lb (2 kg) at each fingertip, allowing it to pick up and handle a variety of objects. The BarrettHand does not need to be physically customized for each specific job. Instead, all changes to its function can be accomplished using software.

‹56227› www.guinnessworldrecords.com/robothand
← ACCESS CODE

MOST HUMANOID ROBOT

The 5-ft 3-in (1.6-m) P3 robot was launched by the Japanese company Honda in 1997. P3 resembles a normal human, with arms and legs. It can walk sideways and backward, as well as walk up and down stairs and on sloped floors. The robot, with its 3-D sight, can also turn its head, step over obstacles, change direction, and correct its balance if pushed. It took 150 engineers, 11 years, and $80 million (£49 million) to produce and was designed to be used in nursing or in tasks too dangerous or strenuous for humans to do – such as bomb disposal.

MOST WIDELY USED INDUSTRIAL ROBOT

PUMA (Programmable Universal Machine for Assembly), designed by Vic Schienman (Switzerland) in the 1970s and manufactured by Swiss company Staubli Unimation, is the most commonly used robot in university laboratories and automated assembly lines.

MOST EMOTIONALLY RESPONSIVE ROBOT

Kismet, created by Cynthia Breazeal (USA) at the Massachusetts Institute of Technology, is a robotic head powered by 15 networked computers and 21 motors. It is designed to recognize different emotions while interacting with humans and to respond to them. Nine of the 15 computers are used to control Kismet's vision alone.

MOST SUCCESSFUL BIONIC EAR

In 1978, 48-year-old Rod Saunders (Australia) was the first person to be fitted with a bionic ear (or cochlear implant). Saunders had become profoundly deaf after a head injury. Designed by the Department of Otolaryngology at the University of Melbourne, Vic, Australia, the prototype became available commercially in 1982. By 2000 more than 20,000 people worldwide had bionic ears, including more than 10,000 children. The bionic ear, made by Australian firm Cochlear Limited, has been implanted in 10 times more patients than its nearest rival.

MOST ADVANCED ROBOTIC ARM

In 1997 the US company Barrett Technology Inc. developed a $250,000 (£153,000) robotic arm, complete with cables that act like human tendons, which can hold weights of up to 11 lb (5 kg) in any position. The arm has a total of seven gearless joints, driven by brushless motors. Potential uses include cleaning, assisting people in and out of the bath, opening doors, and preparing meals.

MOST ADVANCED CYBERNETIC LIMB IMPLANT

On Aug 24 1998 Kevin Warwick of the University of Reading, Berkshire, UK, had a cybernetic silicon chip implanted in his forearm. This enabled a computer to monitor him, using signals transmitted from the chip. Kevin was able to operate computers and other electronic items such as lights and heaters without actually touching them.

BEST-SELLING ROBOT LAWNMOWER

The RL500 Robomower, developed and manufactured in Israel by Friendly Robotics, has sold over 5,000 units worldwide. It retails for under $1,450 (£1,000). This battery-powered 'cutting-edge' gardener can cut an area equivalent to a tennis court on a single charge.

ROBOHOP!

Sandia National Laboratories, USA, have developed experimental 'hopper' robots (left) that use combustion-driven pistons to jump to heights of 29.5 ft (9 m). These small robots have potential applications in planetary exploration, where several hoppers could be released by a lander to survey the surrounding landscape. The idea for these robots came from Rush Robinett (USA) of Sandia's Intelligent Systems and Robotics Center while he was catching grasshoppers to use in trout fishing. The high-jumping hoppers could theoretically travel 100 hops on a single tank of fuel. On planetary bodies like the Moon and Mars, where the force of gravity is lower, these hoppers would be able to jump higher and travel further.

‹56526› www.guinnessworldrecords.com/jumpingrobot
← ACCESS CODE

MOST LIFELIKE ROBOT FISH

The world's most lifelike robot fish has been developed by Mitsubishi Heavy Industries in Japan in a four-year project. A whole series of robot fish have been constructed, and only the closest inspection can distinguish them from the real thing. Future applications include the development of superfast submarines and robot fish that could scour the oceans detecting sources of pollution. Mitsubishi is also developing robotic replicas of extinct fish for use in virtual aquariums.

FASTEST-SELLING ENTERTAINMENT ROBOT

When Sony Corporation's pet robot dog (AIBO Entertainment Robot ERS-110) made its debut on Sony's Japanese website on May 31 1999, 3,000 – retailing at $2,066 (£1,439) each – were sold within 20 minutes. AIBO ('partner' in Japanese) is 11 in (27.9 cm) tall and can recognize its surroundings with a built-in sensor. It can be programmed to perform tricks or 'play' on its own. On June 1 1999, 2,000 AIBOs became available over the internet in America, and the initial rush to buy the robot caused webservers to crash.

CHEAPEST ROBOT

The world's cheapest robot cost just $1.75 (£1.15) since it was made from the remains of a Sony Walkman at the Los Alamos National Laboratory, New Mexico, in 1996. Walkman was just 5 in (12.7 cm) tall and was highly unpredictable. In tests it was reported that the robot struggled to get free when its legs were held without being programmed to do so, and without making the same movement twice.

LARGEST ROBOT EXHIBITION

The International Robot Exhibition held every two years in Tokyo, Japan, demonstrates new and important feats of technology. The Oct 1999 event saw over 700 human exhibitors, both private and corporate, take part in displaying their latest robots.

LARGEST PERMANENT DISPLAY OF COLLECTIVE ROBOTS

A unique set of three small collective robots (i.e. are programmed to act as a team) are permanently housed in the Wellcome Wing of the Science Museum in London, UK. Visitors can control the movements of one of them using a joystick, and the other two can be instructed either to mimic, line up with, follow, or run away from the lead robot.

www.guinnessworldrecords.com/robonaut

MEET THE REAL C3PO

The most advanced robot astronaut is NASA's Robonaut (right). This prototype mechanical astronaut is designed to assist space travelers with vital and dangerous tasks, particularly during spacewalks. Anticipated to fly in space for the first time within the next few years, it has dexterous humanlike hands, stereo vision, and a single leg to allow it to move easily around the exterior of the International Space Station, where it will be deployed on a permanent basis. The design of Robonaut's crude nervous system – a web of sensors, software, and circuits – was borrowed from human anatomy. Since there is no 'brain' required in the small head, engineers concentrated most of the controls and command structures in a mechanical backbone. Cameras in Robonaut's head beam visual information to spectacles worn by a NASA technician, who can then direct the robot's arms and fingers by moving his own hands inside gloves wired with sensors linked directly to the robot. This gives the robot the full range of maneuvers.

ACCESS CODE

‹56386› ←

GUINNESS WORLD RECORDS

space exploration

MOST PEOPLE IN SPACE AT ONE TIME

On March 14 1995 a record 13 people were in space at the same time – seven Americans aboard the US *STS 67 Endeavour*; three CIS cosmonauts aboard the Russian *Mir* space station; and two CIS cosmonauts and a US astronaut aboard the CIS *Soyuz TM21*.

SMALLEST PLANETARY BODY EVER LANDED UPON

The *NEAR-Shoemaker* spacecraft landed on asteroid Eros on Feb 12 2001. The spacecraft transmitted 69 images of the surface of Eros during its descent, showing details of rocks that were just inches across.

LARGEST TELESCOPE

The twin Keck Telescopes, on the summit of Hawaii's Mauna Kea volcano, are the world's largest optical and infrared telescopes. Each one is eight stories high and weighs 661,000 lb (2,998 tonnes) Both have a mirror 32 ft (9.8 m) wide, made up of 36 hexagonal segments that together create a single reflective surface. With this telescope, you would be able to see a golf ball 93.2 miles (150 km) away.

‹46910›
← ACCESS CODE

www.guinnessworldrecords.com/spacewalk

SPACED OUT

The longest spacewalk was made by astronauts Jim Voss (left) and Susan Helms (both USA), who spent 8 hr 56 min outside in space on March 11 2001. Their job was to make room on the International Space Station for the Italian cargo module *Leonardo*, launched into space by the space shuttle *Discovery*. Around 11,000 lb (five tonnes) of equipment were included in *Leonardo*'s payload. When construction is completed, the station will measure 316 ft (96.3 m) from end to end. Sixteen nations are involved in the station's construction – one of the largest international nonmilitary collaborations in history.

LARGEST SOLAR PANEL ARRAY IN SPACE

On Dec 5 2000 astronauts on the space shuttle *Endeavour* deployed the first of four sets of solar panels to provide electrical power to the International Space Station. The remaining sets will be added over the next few years, making the station one of the brightest objects in the night sky – outshone only by the Moon, the brightest planets, and the star Sirius. Unfurled, the panels span 240 ft (73 m) and generate 64 kW of electricity between them (enough to power 30 households).

HEAVIEST ROCK RETURNED FROM SPACE

The only rock samples returned to Earth from space are Moon rocks brought back during the Apollo program. Of these, the largest was sample number 61016 nicknamed 'Big Muley,' returned by *Apollo 16*. It has a mass of 25.79 lb (11.7 kg).

LONGEST MANNED SPACEFLIGHT

The longest manned spaceflight was made by Valeriy Poliyakov (Russia), who was launched to the *Mir* space station aboard *Soyuz TM18* on Jan 8 1994 and landed in *Soyuz TM20* on March 22 1995, after a spaceflight lasting 437 days 17 hr 58 min 16 sec.

SHORTEST MANNED SPACEFLIGHT

Alan Bartlett Shepard (USA) boarded *Mercury-Redstone 3* on May 5 1961. His suborbital mission lasted only 15 min 28 sec because the *Redstone* booster rocket upon which his *Freedom 7* capsule was launched was not powerful enough to reach orbit. Instead, *Freedom 7* went up and down in an arc trajectory. Shepard reached an altitude of 116.5 miles (187.49 km) and during the flight he was subjected to acceleration forces 11 times stronger than the force of gravity.

MOST DISTANT IMAGE OF EARTH

On Feb 4 1990, after 12.5 years in space, NASA's *Voyager 1* spacecraft turned its camera back toward the Sun and the planets of the Solar System, to take photographs of our home planet from a distance of 4 billion miles (6.5 billion km). The photos were transmitted back to NASA and showed the Sun as a bright star and the Earth as a pale blue dot.

MOST POWERFUL GAMMA RAY TELESCOPE

Launched in 1991, the Compton Gamma Ray Observatory is the most powerful gamma ray telescope to date. It weighed 37,475 lb

MOON'S-TRUCK

The lunar speed record was set by the manned *Apollo 16* Rover, driven by John Young (USA, left), who achieved 11.2 mph (18 km/h) downhill. He also set the manned distance record with 21 miles (33.8 km). John Young is one of NASA's most experienced astronauts and has been called the 'Godfather of Space.'

The furthest distance traveled on another planet is 23 miles (37 km). The record was set on the surface of the Moon by the unmanned Soviet *Lunokhod 2* Rover between June 16 and 23 1973. *Lunokhod 2* moved during the lunar day, using its solar panels to charge its batteries, and hibernated during the long lunar night. Over four months, the Rover transmitted over 80,000 TV pictures and 86 panoramic images back to Earth.

‹46948› www.guinnessworldrecords.com/lunarspeed

www.guinnessworldrecords.com/mir

A MIR TRIFLE!

The heaviest man-made object to reenter the Earth's atmosphere is the Russian space station *Mir* (right). It was taken out of orbit during a successful controlled reentry of the Earth's atmosphere on March 23 2001. After an amazing 15 years in space, the 286,600-lb (130-tonne) outpost broke into thousands of incandescent pieces that splashed down in the Pacific Ocean, east of New Zealand.

‹56485› ←

(15.4 tonnes) and was placed in a low orbit around the Earth on April 5 1991 by the space shuttle *Atlantis*. After nine years of observation it was guided to a controlled reentry into the Earth's atmosphere and burned up on June 4 2000.

FURTHEST RESTING PLACE

On July 31 1999 the American *Lunar Prospector* spacecraft crashed on to the surface of the Moon, carrying a polycarbonate container holding 1 oz (28 g) of the remains of Dr. Eugene Shoemaker (USA). Brass foil inscribed with some of the images of Shoemaker's pioneering work in planetary science was wrapped around the container. This first lunar 'funeral' was a fitting tribute to the man who trained *Apollo* astronauts to become lunar field geologists.

LARGEST SPACE LABORATORY

The largest single research laboratory ever launched was the US *Skylab* in 1973, which was 82 ft (24.9 m) long and weighed 59,000 lb (26,762 kg). It was the largest man-made object to reenter the Earth's atmosphere until *Mir* reentered in 2001.

LONGEST SPACE FLIGHT BY A DOG

The two dogs Veterok (Little Wind) and Ugolek (Little Piece of Coal) spent 22 days orbiting the Earth during the Soviet *Kosmos 110* mission (launched Feb 22 1966). This record was not surpassed by humans until the *Skylab 4* mission in 1974.

GUINNESS WORLD RECORDS™

aircraft

LARGEST HELICOPTER EVER

The Russian Mil Mi-12 weighed 227,737 lb (103.3 tonnes) and was 121 ft 48 in (37 m) long. It was powered by four 6,500-hp (4,847-kW) turboshaft engines and had a rotor diameter of 219 ft 10 in (67 m). A prototype was demonstrated in 1971 but it never entered service.

LARGEST HELICOPTER IN PRODUCTION

The largest helicopter in service is the Russian Mil Mi-26, with a maximum takeoff weight of 123,458 lb (56 tonnes). Its overall length is 131 ft (40 m) and the eight-bladed rotor has a diameter of 105 ft (32 m). It can be converted into an assault-troop carrier or can carry up to 80 stretchers.

FASTEST HELICOPTER CIRCUMNAVIGATIONS

John Williams and Ron Bower (both USA) flew around the world in a Bell 430 helicopter in 17 days 6 hrs 14 min 25 sec at an average speed of 57.02 mph (91.76 km/h). They left Fair Oaks, London, UK, on Aug 17 1996 and flew westward, against prevailing winds, arriving back on Sept 3 1996.

Jennifer Murray (UK) circumnavigated the globe solo in a Robinson R44 helicopter in 99 days, from May 31 to Sept 6 2000, at an average speed of 10.55 mph (16.99 km/h). Her journey began and ended at Brooklands airfield, Weybridge, Surrey, UK, and covered 30 countries.

LONGEST HELICOPTER HOVER

Doug Daigle, Brian Watts, and Dave Meyer of Tridair Helicopters, and Rod Anderson of Helistream, Inc. (all USA), maintained a continuous hover in a 1947 Bell 47B model for 50 hr 50 sec between Dec 13 and 15 1989.

LARGEST OBJECT TRANSPORTED BY AIR

The largest single objects to be transported by air are the 122.17-ft (37.23-m) NASA space shuttles, which are 'piggybacked' on top of modified Boeing 747s from alternative landing strips back to Cape Canaveral. The shuttles – *Columbia*, *Discovery*, *Atlantis*, and *Endeavour* – weigh 220,500 lb (100 tonnes) each.

LARGEST CARGO AIRCRAFT

The aircraft with the largest cargo hold is the Airbus A300-600ST Super Transporter ('Beluga'). The cargo deck has a volume of 49,440 ft³ (1,400 m³), and is 123 ft 8 in (37.7 m) long, with a maximum height and width of 23 ft 3 in (7.1 m). Its maximum payload weight is 103,607 lb (47 tonnes). The main section of the cargo bay is two stories high, and longer than a basketball court.

HEAVIEST AIRCRAFT

The aircraft with the heaviest takeoff weight is the Antonov An-225 ('Mriya', meaning Dream) at 1.323 million lb (600 tonnes). The aircraft lifted a payload of 344,582 lb (156,300 kg) to an altitude of 40,715 ft (12,410 m) and covered a distance of 1,305 miles (2,100 km) on March 22 1989. In comparison, the maximum takeoff weight of a Boeing 747-400 ('Jumbo') is 874,990 lb (396.89 tonnes).

LARGEST WINGSPANS

The eight-engined 425,490-lb (193-tonne) Hughes H4 Hercules flying boat, more commonly known as the 'Spruce Goose,' had the largest wingspan of any aircraft ever constructed. Its wingspan was 319 ft 11 in (97.51 m) and its length 218 ft 8 in (66.65 m). It was raised 70 ft (21.3 m) into the air in a test run of 2,999 ft (914 m) by Howard Hughes, off Long Beach Harbor, California, on Nov 2 1947, but never flew again. At 240 ft 6 in (73.3 m), the Ukranian Anotov An-124 has the largest wingspan of any modern aircraft. In comparison, the Boeing 747-400 has a wingspan of 211 ft 5 in (64.4 m).

FASTEST COMBAT JET

The fastest combat jet is the Russian Mikoyan MiG-25 fighter (code name 'Foxbat'). The reconnaissance 'Foxbat-B' has been tracked by radar at Mach 3.2 (2,110 mph or 3,395 km/h). It has a wingspan of 45 ft 9 in (13.95 m), is 78 ft 2 in (23.82 m) long, and has an estimated maximum takeoff weight of 82,450 lb (37.4 tonnes).

LARGEST WATER BOMBER

The largest firefighting aircraft is the Russian-made Ilyushin 76TD air tanker, which can carry 11,000 gal (42,000 liters) of water or fire retardants. Owned by the Russian ministry for Civil Defense, Emergencies, and Elimination of Consequences of Natural Disasters (EMERCOM), five such aircraft are available at short notice for humanitarian missions and leasing to governments and organizations around the world. In one 8-10 second pass it is capable of soaking an area 0.75 miles (1,200 m) long and 295 ft (90 m) wide with water.

BOMBER WITH GREATEST WINGSPAN

The 10-engined Convair B-36J ('Peacemaker') had a wingspan of 230 ft (70.1 m), the longest ever for a bomber, and a maximum takeoff weight of 410,000 lb (185 tonnes). The B-36J has been out of service since the late 1950s, when it was replaced by the Boeing B-52.

HEAVIEST BOMBER

The former Soviet four-jet Tupolev Tu-160 ('Blackjack') bomber has a takeoff weight when fully loaded with bombs of 606,250 lb (275 tonnes). Its empty weight is 242,500 lb (110 tonnes). The 'Blackjack' has a maximum speed of Mach 2.05 (1,350 mph or 2,200 km/h) and is 177.5 ft (54.1 m) long, with a wingspan of 182.7 ft (55.7 m).

LARGEST PROPELLER

The largest airplane propeller ever to fly was the 22.6-ft (6.9-m) diameter Garuda propeller, attached to the Linke-Hofmann R II, which flew in 1919. It was driven by four 260-hp (195-kW) Mercedes engines and turned at only 545 rpm. Today's small aircraft propellers are roughly 6.56 ft (2 m) in diameter, and turn at approximately 2,500 rpm.

BLACKBIRD JOINS THE JETSET

The USAF Lockheed SR-71 ('Blackbird'), a reconnaissance aircraft (left), is the world's fastest airplane, with a top speed in excess of Mach 3 (1,979 mph or 3,185 km/h) although the exact figure is classified. The two-seater aircraft flew top-secret missions for nearly 25 years, making its first flight on Dec 22 1964. The fastest transatlantic flight record is 1 hr 54 mins 56.4 secs, by Major James V. Sullivan and Major Noel F. Widdifield (both USA), flying a 'Blackbird' eastward on Sept 1 1974. The average speed for the New York–London stage of 3,461.53 miles (5,570.8 km) was 1,806.96 mph (2,908.02 km/h).

The Lockheed SR-71 'Blackbird' was decommissioned by the USAF in 1990, but several reentered service for NASA in 1995 for research purposes.

<43994>
← ACCESS CODE

www.guinnessworldrecords.com/fastjet

www.guinnessworldrecords.com/pathfinder

HIGH FLYER

The highest-flying propeller-driven aircraft is the remotely controlled, solar-powered *Pathfinder* flying wing, which reached an altitude of over 80,000 ft (24,384 m) above the Hawaiian Islands on Aug 6 1998. At around 600 lb (270 kg) *Pathfinder* weighs less than a quarter of most cars, and it is small wonder that such craft are sometimes called 'lighter-than-air.' The *Helios* Prototype (below) is a similar, but larger, flying wing based on the *Pathfinder*, which its designers hope will ultimately reach an altitude in excess of 100,000 ft (30,480 m). The third aircraft in the family, *Helios*, is currently undergoing testing and is designed to stay aloft for months at a time, at heights of between 50,000 to 70,000 ft (15,000 to 21,000 m).

ACCESS CODE

‹56393› ←

SPACE TRAVEL

The largest passenger aircraft in development is the Airbus A380 (above), launched in Dec 2000 and expected to enter service by 2007. It has a wing-span of 261 ft 10 in (79.8 m) and is 239 ft 6 in (73 m) long. It will have a maximum takeoff weight of 1.23 million lb (560 tonnes) and will carry 555 passengers in considerable comfort, since its size allows for facilities such as casinos, bars, and gyms.

The Boeing 747-400 holds the record for the greatest capacity, holding a maximum of 566 people, but it is a smaller plane, with a wingspan of 212 ft 11 in (64.9 m), and a length of 231 ft 7 in (70.6 m).

www.guinnessworldrecords.com/
airbus

ACCESS CODE

‹56382› ←

FASTEST BOMBER

The US variable-geometry, or 'swing-wing' General Dynamics FB-111A has a maximum speed of Mach 2.5, which is two-and-a-half times the speed of sound (1,650 mph or 2,655 km/h).

The Russian swing-wing Tupolev Tu-22M, which is known to NATO as 'Backfire,' has an estimated speed of Mach 2, but may reach Mach 2.5.

LARGEST AIRSHIPS

The world's largest airships were the 471,568 lb (213.9-tonne) German *Hindenburg* (LZ 129) and *Graf Zeppelin II* (LZ 130), both of which were 803 ft 10 in (245 m) long with a hydrogen gas capacity of 7,062,100 ft³ (200,000 m³). The *Hindenburg* first flew in 1936, exploding and crashing on May 6 1937 at Lakehurst, New Jersey, and the *Graf Zeppelin II* first flew in 1938.

FASTEST FLYING BOAT

The Martin XP6M-1 *SeaMaster*, the US Navy four-jet-engined minelayer flown from 1955 to 1959, was the fastest flying boat ever built, with a top speed of 646 mph (1,040 km/h).

EARLIEST AIRPLANE HOP

On Oct 9 1890 the first hop by a manned airplane entirely under its own power was made when Clément Ader (France) flew in his *Éole* for about 164 ft (50 m) at Armainvilliers, France. It was powered by a lightweight steam engine of his own design, which developed about 20 hp (15 kW), but the flight was neither sustained nor controlled.

EARLIEST JET FLIGHT

The first flight by an airplane powered by a turbojet engine was made in the Heinkel He 178, piloted by Flugkapitän Erich Warsitz, at Marienehe, Germany, on Aug 27 1939. Despite its success, it was not until toward the end of World War II, in 1944, that the jet-propelled Messerschmidt Me 262 entered service as Germany's first active jet fighter.

LARGEST PAPER AIRCRAFT

The largest flying paper aircraft was constructed by a team of students from the Faculty of Aerospace Engineering at Delft University of Technology, Netherlands. It had a wingspan of 45 ft 10 in (13.97 m),

and was flown on May 16 1995. It was launched indoors and flew a distance of 114 ft 2 in (34.8 m). Founded in 1940, the 1,300-student Faculty, is equipped with a wind-tunnel test center and a supercomputer center and works with aerospace giants Airbus and Boeing.

MOST AIRCRAFT BUILT

The Cessna Aircraft Company of Wichita, Kansas, has been the world's most productive aerospace company, with total production of 182,804 aircraft by the end of 2000. Company founder Clyde Cessna built and flew his first airplane in 1911.

GUINNESS WORLD RECORDS™

ships and submarines

FASTEST SAILING VESSEL

On Oct 26 1993 the trifoiler *Yellow Pages Endeavour* reached a record speed of 46.52 knots (53.57 mph or 86.21 km/h) on a timed run of 1,640 ft (500 m) at Sandy Point near Melbourne, Vic, Australia.

FASTEST REGULAR ATLANTIC CROSSING

The fastest regular commercial Atlantic crossings were by the liner *United States*. On her maiden voyage between July 3 and 7 1952 from New York to Le Havre, France, and Southampton, UK, she averaged 35.39 knots (40 mph or 65.95 km/h) over 3 days 10 hr 40 min. The *United States* was decommissioned in 1969 and today is anchored in Philadelphia, Pennsylvania.

LARGEST BATTLESHIPS IN ACTIVE SERVICE

The largest battleships ever used in active service were the *USS Missouri* and *USS Wisconsin*. They were 887 ft (270 m) long and had a full-load displacement (the amount of water they displace when fully loaded) of 130 million lb (58,930 tonnes). Weapons included nine 16-in (40.6-cm) guns, which were used in

‹43704› ← ACCESS CODE

www.guinnessworldrecords.com/clipper

SAIL OF THE CENTURY

Taller above the waterline than a 15-story building, the *Royal Clipper* (left) is 439 ft (133.8 m) in length and has five masts and 42 sails, which use 56,000 ft² (5,202 m²) of canvas. This makes her the largest square rigger in service. Weighing 11 million lb (5,000 tonnes), she has a crew of 106 and can carry up to 228 passengers in luxury accommodations. Facilities include three swimming pools, a piano lounge, deluxe shops, a spa and gym, a large dining room, and a forward observation lounge for up to 90 people. The *Royal Clipper* cruises in the Caribbean and the western Mediterranean.

the Gulf War in 1991 and were capable of firing 2,700-lb (1,225-kg) projectiles a distance of 23 miles (39 km).

OLDEST COMMISSIONED WARSHIP IN USE

Ordered in 1758, the *HMS Victory* took six years to build and is the oldest serving warship still in commission, retaining her own captain, officers, and crew. Docked at the Portsmouth Historic Dockyard, Hampshire, UK, *HMS Victory* looks the same today as she did at the Battle of Trafalgar in 1805.

LARGEST CRUISE LINER 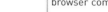 FI

The *Voyager of the Seas* is the world's largest cruise liner, measuring 1,020 ft (310 m) long and 157.5 ft (48 m) wide. She weighs 317.4 million lb (144,000 tonnes), has a crew of 1,181, and a total capacity of 3,114 passengers. The ship has its own five-story theater with 1,350 seats, plus a golf course, an ice skating rink, and a wedding chapel.

MOST MASTED SAILING SHIP

The only seven-masted sailing schooner ever built was the *Thomas W. Lawson,* measuring 375 ft (114.4 m) long. It was built at Quincy, Massachusetts, in 1902, and was wrecked off the Isles of Scilly, Cornwall, UK, in 1907.

TALLEST MAST

The 157-ft (47.9-m) sloop *Hyperion*, built by Wolter Huisman (Netherlands), has a mast 193 ft (59 m) high. *Hyperion* was commissioned in 1995 by Jim Clark (USA), the founder of internet browser company Netscape.

MOST POWERFUL ICEBREAKERS

The most powerful icebreakers are the *Rossiya*, *Sovetskiy Soyuz*, and *Oktyabryskaya Revolutsiya*. Built in Leningrad (USSR), now St. Petersburg, Russia, in 1985, the *Rossiya* weighs 51.7 million lb (23,460 tonnes) and has 75,000-hp (55.930-kW) nuclear engines.

LARGEST WING-IN-GROUND VEHICLE

Built by the Soviet Central Design Bureau of Hydrofoil Vehicles in the 1960s, the 1.9 million-lb (540-tonne) *Caspian Sea Monster* was the largest wing-in-ground (WIG) effect vehicle ever built. A cross between an aircraft and a hovercraft, it skimmed just above the waves at speeds of up to 311 mph (500 km/h). It was powered by 10 turbofan jet engines, but was destroyed in a crash in 1980.

LARGEST SHIPWRECK

The 708 million-lb (321,186-tonne) VLCC (very large crude carrier) *Energy Determination* blew up and

DHOW AMAZING!

Al Hashemi II, a wooden Arabic dhow (left) built and owned by Radisson SAS Hotels Resorts, Kuwait, is a record 263 ft 7 in (80.4 m) long and 61 ft 3 in (18.7 m) wide. This richly decorated traditional Arabic cargo ship is held together by approximately 78,737 lb (80 tonnes) of handmade nails and bolts, and is used as a conference and reception venue. It was completed in Jan 2000. Dhows are traditional wooden ships with distinctive triangular sails, common in the Persian Gulf and Indian Ocean ports. *Al Hashemi II* was the brainchild of Husain Marafie, one of the owners of the Radisson SAS hotel. It is modeled on a cargo-carrying dhow of the Baghlah type, built by his great-grandfather and named *Al Hashemi* in the late 19th century.

PLANE SAILING

ACCESS CODE

‹43675› ←

The warships with the largest full-load displacement are the Nimitz-class US Navy aircraft carriers *USS Nimitz, Dwight D. Eisenhower, Carl Vinson, Theodore Roosevelt, Abraham Lincoln, George Washington, John C. Stennis, Harry S. Truman,* and *Ronald Reagan* (below), the last five of which displace approximately 217.2 million lb (98,550 tonnes). They are 1,092 ft (332.9 m) long, have 4.49 acres (1.82 ha) of flight deck, can hit speeds over 30 knots (35 mph or 56 km/h), and are driven by four nuclear-powered 260,000-shp (194,000-kW) geared steam turbines.

Tasked with a multimission attack/antisubmarine warfare role, the *Nimitz* has four C-13 Mod 1 catapults, or 'cats,' that propel aircraft off the flight deck. These can accelerate even the heaviest carrier-based aircraft to speeds of 170 mph (273 km/h) from a standing take-off and launch one aircraft every 20 seconds.

broke in two in the Strait of Hormuz, Persian Gulf, on Dec 12 1979. The ship was not carrying cargo at the time, but the hull value alone was $58 million (£26 million).

EARLIEST SURVIVING VESSEL

The earliest surviving vessel is a pine logboat or dugout found in Pesse, Netherlands, which has been dated to around 6315 BC. It is now in the Provincial Museum, Assen, Netherlands. The second oldest surviving vessels are a fleet of 12 funeral riverboats discovered in 1991 at Abydos, Egypt, which have been tentatively dated to around 3000 BC.

FASTEST SUBMARINE

The Russian Alpha class nuclear-powered submarines had a top speed of over 40 knots (50 mph or 74 km/h), and were believed to be capable of diving to 2,500 ft (760 m). Only one now remains in service.

MOST SUBMARINES

The largest navy in the world in terms of submarines is the Russian navy, with 128 (92 nuclear) in 1997.

LARGEST SUBMERGED NUCLEAR CARGO

On Oct 6 1986 Russian nuclear submarine K-219 (Project 667-A Yankee Class) sank in the Atlantic Ocean 600 miles (965 km) north of Bermuda. The submarine carried two nuclear reactors and 16 nuclear missiles, making it the largest cargo of this type resting in the sea, at a depth of 19,000 ft (5,800 m).

GUINNESS WORLD RECORDS™

trucks, trains and buses

STAR TRACK:
TO BOLDLY GO WHERE NO STREETCAR HAS GONE BEFORE

The world's oldest streetcars in revenue service are cars 1 and 2 of the Manx Electric Railway (above), running regularly on the 17.7-mile (28.5-km) line between Douglas and Ramsey, Isle of Man, UK. They date back to the opening of the railroad in 1893. The MER is a popular tourist attraction on the island, as the journey provides views of the coastline.

The city of St. Petersburg, Russia, has the most extensive streetcar system, with 2,402 cars on 64 routes covering 429.1 miles (690.6 km) of track. St. Petersburg is Russia's second-largest city and former capital. It is also known as the 'Streetcar Capital of the World.' The first horse-drawn streetcar began moving freight in the outskirts of the city in 1854. The system grew in the 19th and 20th centuries, but in recent years sections of the track have been dug up to make way for roads.

‹43477› www.guinnessworldrecords.com/trams
← **ACCESS CODE**

FASTEST TRUCK WHEELIE FR
Patrick Bourny (France) drove his modified truck cab in a wheelie at a speed of 55.92 mph (90 km/h) at Lure, France, on Oct 21 2000.

FASTEST MONSTER TRUCK
The highest recorded speed ever reached by a monster truck is 69.3 mph (111.5 km/h), achieved by Dan Runte (USA) in his vehicle 'Bigfoot 14' on Sept 11 1999 at Symrna Airport, Nashville, Tennessee. The record was set in the run-up to the longest-ever monster truck ramp jump of 202 ft (61.6 m). The same truck and driver also hold the record for the highest monster truck jump, reaching 24 ft (7.3 m) on Dec 14 1999.

LARGEST DUMP TRUCK
The world's largest two-axle dump truck is the T-282, manufactured by the Liebherr Mining Equipment Co. (USA). It has a payload capacity of 720,910 lb (327 tonnes), or more than one-and-a-half times its own weight.

LONGEST ROAD TRAIN
The longest line of trailers pulled by a single truck stretched 2,003 ft 7 in (610.7 m). The 45 trailers were pulled by a Kenworth Tri-Drive Cab model K100G, driven by

Greg Marley (Australia) along the Great Eastern Highway at Merredin, Western Australia, on April 3 1999.

FASTEST LONDON UNDERGROUND CIRCUIT
The record time for doing a tour of all 272 stations on the London Underground is 19 hr 57 min 47 sec. Robert Robinson, Chris Loxton, Chris Stubley, Chris Whiteoak, Olly Rich, and Adam Waller Berks (all UK) made the journey on March 16 2000.

FASTEST TRAIN JOURNEY
The West Japan Railroad Company runs its 500-Series-Nozomi bullet trains (*Shinkansen*) at an average speed of 162.7 mph (261.8 km/h) on the line between Hiroshima and Kokura on the island of Honshu. The Nozomi, meaning 'dream,' entered service in 1997 and each train can carry up to 1,324 people.

FASTEST RAIL SYSTEM
The highest speed recorded on a national rail system is 320.2 mph (515.3 km/h), by the French SNCF high-speed train TGV *Atlantique*, traveling from Courtalain to Tours on May 18 1990.

FASTEST MAGLEV VEHICLE
The highest recorded speed of a Maglev (magnetically levitated) train is

343 mph (552 km/h), by the MLX01 on the Yamanashi Maglev Test Line between Otsuki and Tsuru, Japan, on April 14 1999. Operated by the Central Japan Railroad Company and Railroad Technical Research Institute, the record-breaking Maglev harnesses the power of magnetism to lift itself off the ground and move forward, with electromagnets made from superconductive metals.

LONGEST JOURNEY BY A RUNAWAY TRAIN
On March 26 1884 eight coal cars were set in motion by high winds in Akron, Colorado, and ran a distance of 100 miles (160 km) on the Chicago, Burlington & Quincy Railroad, east of Denver, Colorado. The cars are thought to have reached a maximum speed of 66 mph (106 km/h) on a downhill stretch. A freight engine gave chase and brought them under control.

FURTHEST DISTANCE TRAVELED BY TRAIN
Mona Tippins (USA) traveled a record 79,024 miles (128,492 km) by rail, without duplicating any part of her journey, between Oct 7 1994 and Feb 11 1997. She visited 33 countries in North America and Europe.

THE LONG AND WINDING UNDERGROUND RAILROAD

The most extensive underground rail system is the New York City subway (USA, left), covering a total track distance of 842 miles (1,355 km). This includes 186 miles (299 km) of track in yards, workshops, and storage, as well as 230 miles (370 km) of actual transportation routes. The network serves about 1.3 billion passengers per year and, with 468 stations, has more stations than any other system. Trains operate 24 hours a day, seven days a week, throughout the city, and on an average weekday cover around 1 million miles (1.6 million km).

www.guinnessworldrecords.com/newyorksubway

‹43824›   ← ACCESS CODE

FURTHEST DISTANCE TRAVELED BY TRAIN IN SEVEN DAYS

Andrew Kingsmell, Sean Andrews, and Graham Bardouleau (all UK) traveled 13,105 miles (21,090 km) on the French national railroad from Nov 28 to Dec 5 1992, with a total journey time of 6 days 22 hr 38 min.

LONGEST FREIGHT TRAIN

The world's longest freight train, measuring 4.8 miles (7.3 km) long and made up of 660 cars, a tank car, and a caboose made a run on the Sishen-Saldanha railroad in South Africa from Aug 26 to 27 1989. Moved by a total of nine 50-kV-electric and seven diesel-electric locomotives, it traveled 535 miles (861 km) in 22 hr 40 min. It took 4.3 miles (7 km) to come to a complete standstill after the brakes were first applied.

LARGEST LAND VEHICLE

The largest land vehicle is the 31.3 million-lb (14,196-tonne) RB293 bucket-wheel excavator, an earthmoving machine made by MAN TAKRAF of Germany. Used in a strip coal mine in the German state of North Rhine Westphalia, it is 722 ft (220 m) long, 310 ft (94.5 m) tall at its highest point, and can shift 8.475 million ft³ (240,000 m³) of earth a day. It has 18 buckets attached to a massive wheel. As the wheel revolves the buckets scoop up and dump soil.

LARGEST BUS FLEET

Andhra Pradesh State Road Transport Corporation (India) has the largest bus fleet in the world. As of Oct 31 1999, the company owned 18,397 buses.

www.guinnessworldrecords.com/fireengine

THE BACKDRAFT BUSTERS

📺 USA

The world's fastest fire engine is the rocket-powered Hawaiian Eagle (below), owned by Tom Seydel (USA). It reached a speed of 407 mph (655 km/h) in Brainerd, Florida, on July 11 1998. The vehicle is a 1941 truck, powered by two Rolls-Royce Bristol Viper engines, each boasting 6,000 hp (4,500 kW) and generating 12,000 lb (5,450 kg) of thrust.

ACCESS CODE

‹53934›   ←

The fire engine with the greatest pumping capacity is the 860-hp (640-kW), eight-wheel Oshkosh firetruck manufactured by Oshkosh Truck Corporation, Wisconsin. It can discharge a record 49,900 gal (189,000 liters) of foam through two turrets in just 150 seconds. This powerful pumping vehicle weighs 132,277 lb (60 tonnes) and is used for aircraft and runway fires.

KEEP BACK 300 FEET OR ELSE

GUINNESS WORLD RECORDS™

cars

BEST-SELLING SPORTS CAR

Mazda has manufactured a record 531,890 MX-5 Miata sports cars since production began in April 1989.

FASTEST PRODUCTION CAR

The highest speed achieved by a standard production car is 240.25 mph (386.7 km/h), by a McLaren F1, driven by Andy Wallace (UK) at the Volkswagen Proving Ground, Wolfsburg, Germany, on March 31 1998. Only 100 of these supercars have been manufactured.

The McLaren F1 is also the most powerful standard production car ever produced, accelerating to 60 mph (96 km/h) in 3.2 seconds.

FASTEST DIESEL-POWERED CAR

The Mercedes C111–III, powered by a five-cylinder three-liter diesel engine reached a top speed of 203.3 mph (327.3 km/h) in tests on the Nardo Circuit, Italy, from Oct 5 to 15 1978.

FASTEST STEAM CAR

On Aug 19 1985 Robert E. Barber (USA) broke the 79-year-old record for a steam car when *Steamin'*

FIRST-CLASS TRAVEL

The greatest confirmed price paid for a car is $15 million (£8.41 million) for the 1931 Bugatti Type 41 Royale Sports Coupé (left), sold by Nicholas Harley to the Meitec Corporation of Japan on April 12 1990.

A Bugatti also holds the record for the largest car ever produced – the Bugatti Royale Type 41, built by the Italian Ettore Bugatti. First made in 1927, it has an eight-cylinder engine with a capacity of 778 in³ and is over 22 ft (6.7 m) in length. Perhaps the only thing more remarkable than the massive bulk of this car is its rarity – only six were ever produced.

‹43465›   www.guinnessworldrecords.com/priceycar
← ACCESS CODE

Demon, built by Barber-Nichols Engineering Co., reached a speed of 145.58 mph (234.33 km/h) at Bonneville Salt Flats, Utah.

FASTEST SOLAR-POWERED CAR

The highest recorded speed for a solar/battery-powered vehicle is 83.88 mph (135 km/h) achieved by the Star Micronics solar car, *Solar Star*. The car was driven by Manfred Hermann (Australia) on Jan 5 1991 at Richmond RAAF Base, NSW, Australia.

FASTEST ROCKET-ENGINED CAR

The Blue Flame, a rocket-powered four-wheeled vehicle driven by Gary Gabelich (USA) reached a speed of 631.366 mph (1,016.086 km/h) on the Bonneville Salt Flats, Utah, on Oct 23 1970. The car was powered by a liquid-natural-gas/hydrogen-peroxide engine, which could develop thrust of up to 22,000 lb (9,979 kg).

FASTEST ELECTRIC CAR

On Oct 22 1999 *White Lightning Electric Streamliner*, an electric car driven by Patrick Rummerfield (USA), achieved a speed of 245.951 mph (395.821 km/h) at the Bonneville Salt Flats, Utah. With its slender, aerodynamic carbon-fiber body, the 25-ft (7.62-m) *White Lightning* looks more like a rocket than a car and can reach a speed of 100 mph (161 km/h) in eight seconds.

FASTEST LAND SPEED

The *Thrust SSC*, driven by Andy Green (UK), broke the sound barrier and achieved the one-mile (1.6-km)

land-speed record on Oct 15 1997. It reached a top speed of 763.03 mph (1,227.99 km/h) in the Black Rock Desert, Nevada.

HIGHEST REVERSE-DRIVING SPEED

Alistair Weaver (UK) reached a speed of 86 mph (138.4 km/h) in reverse, driving a Caterham Seven Blackbird at Bruntingthorpe Proving Ground, Leicestershire, UK, on March 7 2001. Weaver reached his record speed in 16.63 seconds, accelerating to 60 mph (96 km/h) in 9.32 seconds, a respectable rate even for cars traveling forward.

LONGEST CAR

The world's longest car is the 26-wheeled limo designed by Jay Ohrberg (USA). It is 100 ft (30.5 m) long and features include a king-sized water bed and a swimming pool with diving board. It is designed to be driven as a rigid vehicle but it can be changed to 'bend' in the middle. Its main purpose is for use in films and exhibits.

MINI DRIVER

The longest journey in a Mini was achieved by Duncan Mortimer (UK), who drove 22,655.4 miles (36,460.3 km) around the world in his bright yellow 1978 Mini Clubman 1275 GT (left) between May 25 1999 and Feb 13 2000. Starting in New York, and finishing back home in England, Duncan's journey took him through parts of the USA, Australia, India, Pakistan, Iran, Turkey, Greece, Italy, France, and England.

The greatest number of people to fit in a Mini was achieved on July 3 2000, when a total of 18 women crammed into a Mini Cooper outside the National Indoor Arena in Birmingham, West Midlands, UK, beating the previous record, set by the Reading Ladies' Rugby Club (UK), by one person.

LIGHTEST CAR

Louis Borsi (UK) has built and driven a 21-lb (9.5-kg) car with a 2.5-cc engine. It is capable of 15 mph (25 km/h).

OLDEST MANUFACTURED CAR

The Morgan 4/4 celebrated its 65th birthday in Dec 2000. Produced by the Morgan Motor Car Company of Malvern, Worcestershire, UK, (founded 1910), all Morgans are handbuilt and production time is an average of 23 days. The company's total production for all four of its models is around 540 per year. There is still a six-to-eight-year waiting list for delivery.

MOST EXPENSIVE PRODUCTION CAR

The world's most expensive car is the Mercedes Benz CLK/LM, which costs $1,547,620 (£957,093). It has a top speed of 200 mph (320 km/h) and can travel from 0 to 62 mph (100 km/h) in 3.8 seconds.

HEAVIEST CAR

The world's heaviest car is the Soviet-built (now Russian-built) Zil-41047 limousine with a 12.73-ft (3.88-m) wheelbase which weighs 7,353 lb (3,335 kg). A 'stretched' Zil was used by former USSR President Mikhail Gorbachev until Dec 1991. It weighed 13,227 lb (6 tonnes), including 3 in (75 mm) of armor-plating. The first

Zil was produced in 1936 for Soviet dictator Stalin. The side mirrors were removed since they were redundant – no one dared to pass him. Russian President Vladimir Putin imported two Zils to the UK for his visit in 2000.

HIGHEST CAR MILEAGE

The highest recorded mileage for a car is 1,882,559 miles (3,029,685 km) for a 1966 Volvo P-1800S owned by Irvin Gordon (USA) up to April 2001. He bought the car in 1966 and used to make a daily 124-mile (201-km) round trip to work. In 1998 he said that "it still handles like a new car."

AMPHIBIOUS CIRCUMNAVIGATION BY CAR

On May 8 1958 Ben Carlin (Australia) arrived in Montreal, Quebec, Canada, in his amphibious jeep *Half-Safe*, having completed a circumnavigation of 39,000 miles (62,765 km) over land and 9,600 miles (15,450 km) by sea or river – the only amphibious vehicle ever to achieve this.

LONGEST RAMP JUMP LANDING ON WATER

Philippe Leveque (Belgium) jumped a distance of 187 ft (57 m) in his car from a ramp into a river at Tournai, Belgium, on Oct 10 2000. When the car was fully submerged, Leveque got out of the vehicle unharmed.

LONGEST RAMP JUMP 📺 USA

The longest ramp jump in a car, with the car landing on its wheels and continuing to drive, is 237 ft (72.23 m), by Ray Baumann (Australia) in a VH Valiant at Ravenswood International Raceway, Perth, Western Australia, on Aug 23 1998.

Ray Baumann also achieved the furthest ramp jump ever with a standard trailer attached to the back of his car. For this record he launched from a ramp and landed on a collection of burned-out cars that acted as a cushion. The event took place at the Ravenswood International Raceway, Perth Ravenswood, Australia, on Oct 4 1999.

www.guinnessworldrecords.com/caracceleration

FAST AND FURIOUS

The fastest road-tested acceleration recorded is 0–60 mph (0–96 km/h) in 3.07 seconds by a Ford RS200 *Evolution* (below), driven by Graham Hathaway (UK) at the Millbrook Proving Ground, Bedfordshire, UK, on May 25 1994. They were developed in the 1980s to compete in the high-performance Group B Rally competition. Although most RS200s were equipped with turbocharged 109.8 in³ engines, the *Evolution* models had a 128.1 in³

powerplant, capable of an incredible 650 hp (485 kW).

The record for the highest speed achieved by a car, where the engine is connected to a transmission that drives the wheels, is 409.986 mph (659.808 km/h), the average over two runs, with a peak speed of 432.692 mph (696.331 km/h), achieved by Al Teague (USA) in *Spirit of '76* on Bonneville Salt Flats, Utah, on Aug 21 1991.

ACCESS CODE

‹43547› ←

bikes and motorbikes

THREEWHEELING

The world's largest tricycle (above) was designed and constructed by 16 students at Bay de Noc Community College, Michigan, in July 1998. The front wheel had a diameter of 15 ft 3 in (4.67 m), the back wheels measured 7 ft 3 in (2.23 m), and the trike had an overall height of 23 ft 4 in (7.13 m). It cost about $6,000 (£4,200) to build, with cash donated by local businesses and residents, and was ridden 250 ft (76 m) during testing. Chuck Gold, the Dean of Technology at the college, needed the help of a fire-truck ladder and crane to help him reach the trike's seat, which is 20 ft (6 m) off the ground. In reality, the seat is for show, with the two riders sitting nearer to the ground between the trike's back wheels.

The greatest number of penny-farthing bicycles freestanding in a line with the riders holding hands is 69 by members of the Velocipede Society at Evandale, Tasmania, Australia, on Feb 26 2000.

<43650> www.guinnessworldrecords.com/3wheelers
← ACCESS CODE

HIGHEST MOTORCYCLE JUMP

The highest motorcycle jump ever was achieved by Tommy Clowers (USA) on Jan 21 2001. Clowers achieved a height of 25 ft (7.62 m) from the top of a 10-ft (3.04-m) ramp after a run-up of 40 ft (12.19 m) at Van Nuys Airport, California.

LARGEST MOTORCYCLE WEDDING PROCESSION

Peter Schmidl and Anna Turcekova (Slovakia) had a wedding procession of a record-breaking 597 motorcycles when they got married in Bratislava, Slovakia, on May 6 2000.

LONGEST MOTORCYCLE RIDE BY A COUPLE

Jim Rogers and Tabitha Estabrook (both USA) drove 57,022 miles (91,766 km), covering six continents between March 1990 and Nov 1991.

LONGEST MOTORCYCLE RAMP JUMP

On July 9 2000 Jason Rennie (UK) jumped 253 ft (77.1 m) on a Yamaha YZ250 at Donington Park Grand Prix Circuit, Leicestershire, UK, beating the record by Doug Danger (USA) that had stood for nine years.

LONGEST REVERSE MOTORCYCLE JUMP

Roger 'Mr Backward' Riddell (USA) jumped seven cars – a record distance of 60 ft (18 m) – riding backward on a 650-cc Honda motorcycle in May 1987.

LONGEST RAMP-TO-TRUCK MOTORCYCLE JUMP

USA

The longest ramp-to-truck jump on a motorcycle is 135 ft (41.1 m) into a 7 x 20-ft (2.13 x 6.09-m) van traveling at 60 mph (96 km/h). The jump was made by Roger Wells (USA), on a Honda CR500 on Sept 17 1999.

LONGEST MOTORCYCLE JUMP WITH PASSENGER

On Nov 12 2000 Jason Rennie (UK) jumped his Yamaha YZ250 motorcycle a record distance of 96 ft (29.26 m), with his girlfriend Sian Phillips on the back at Rednall airfield, Shropshire, UK.

BIGGEST PARADE OF TRIUMPH MOTORCYCLES

The greatest number of Triumph motorcycles in a single parade is 313 for the Rally of the Tigers at Chislehurst, Kent, UK, on July 12 1998. The title refers to one of Triumph's famous models, the Tiger.

EARLIEST MOTORCYCLE

The earliest internal combustion-engined motorized bicycle was a wooden-framed machine built at Bad Cannstatt, Germany, between Oct and Nov 1885. It had a top speed of 12 mph (19 km/h). Known as the *Einspur*, it was lost in a fire in 1903.

GREATEST ENGINE EFFICIENCY

The best fuel-economic performance achieved with a road-legal vehicle is 1,015 mpg (0.28 liters per 100 km) by a motorized tricycle, invented and driven by James Ouchterlony (UK), in the Shell Mileage Marathon at Silverstone, Northants, UK, in 1998.

KING OF THE ROAD

Emilio Scotto (Argentina, left) completed the longest-ever journey on a motorcycle, covering over 457,000 miles (735,000 km) between Jan 17 1985 and April 2 1995. Riding a Honda Gold Wing motorcycle, he circumnavigated the planet both clockwise and counterclockwise, visiting 214 countries and traveling a distance equivalent to a round-trip to the moon.

The first woman to circumnavigate the world solo on a motorcycle was Monika Vega (Brazil) on a Honda 125-cc. She covered 51,885 miles (83,500 km) and visited 53 countries between March 7 1990 and May 24 1991.

‹43612› ← **ACCESS CODE** www.guinnessworldrecords.com/motorbikes

www.guinnessworldrecords.com/roadski

IRON IN THE SOLE ☐ UK

On April 18 1999 Gary Rothwell (UK, below) road-skied at a record speed of 156.3 mph (251.54 km/h). This daredevil stunt involved climbing from the seat to the rear of a speeding motorcycle and hanging off the back, using 0.07 in (2 mm) titanium-soled boots as 'skis,' In addition to 'skiing' behind the motorcycle with metal shoes, Gary's full repertoire consists of a series of courageous motorcycle tricks and stunts that often seem to defy the laws of physics. He can ride backward while lying down and steering only with his feet. He also does wheelies while sitting on the handlebars and multiperson wheelies with as many as 12 people on board.

ACCESS CODE ‹53432› ←

MOST EXPENSIVE MOTORCYCLE

The most expensive production motorcycle in the world is the Morbidelli 850 V8, retailing at 180,000,000 Italian Lira ($79,425 or £56,665) in 2000. The motorbike was styled by Pininfarina, a company best known for its work for Ferrari.

LONGEST STANDING BIKE JUMP ☐ FR

Marc Caisso (France) achieved a standing bike jump distance of 9.51 ft (2.9 m) on Oct 26 2000.

MOST BMX 360° FRONT-WHEEL SPINS IN A MINUTE ☐ SE

Using a standard freestyle BMX bike and balancing on just the front wheel, Andreas Lundqvist (Sweden) completed 34 continuous rotations in a minute on Feb 2 2001.

MOST EXPENSIVE SCOOTER

The world's most expensive production scooter is the Yamaha XP500 Tmax, currently available at an on-the-road price of $8,958 (£6,199). The scooter boasts the largest disk brakes and most powerful engine ever for a production scooter, with a top speed of 105 mph (168 km/h).

LONGEST PEDAL-POWERED VEHICLE

Roger Dumas (USA) built a 55-seater 'bicycle,' 140.67 ft (42.875 m) long, made of several bicycle frames welded together and supported by wheels at regular intervals along its length. It was pedaled a distance of 3,235 ft (986 m) by 52 members of Dumas' family in Augusta, Maine, on July 29 2000.

FASTEST BICYCLE

The highest speed ever achieved on a bicycle is 166.944 mph (268.831 km/h) by Fred Rompelberg (Netherlands) at Bonneville Salt Flats, Utah, on Oct 3 1995. He was towed until he reached 50 mph (80 km/h) and then continued under his own power, protected by the slipstreaming effect of the lead vehicle.

FASTEST 31 MILES CYCLING BACKWARD

On Aug 28 1999 Matthew Poynter (Canada) covered 31 miles (50 km) on a bicycle in 2 hr 52 min 11 sec, while facing backward. For the attempt, he sat on the handlebars and pedaled backward.

GUINNESS WORLD RECORDS

travel and transport

LONGEST ESCALATORS

The world's longest escalator system is Hong Kong's Central Hillside Escalator Link. The 2,624-ft-long (800-m) system of covered moving walkways carries commuters from the Mid-Levels district to the Central Market, which is near the waterfront on Hong Kong Island. After the morning rush, the escalator direction is reversed for the rest of the day.

SHORTEST ESCALATOR

The world's shortest escalator is the 32-in (83.4-cm) moving walkway at Okadaya More's Shopping Mall at Kawasaki-shi, Japan. It was installed by Hitachi Ltd and is 20 times smaller than the average escalator.

BUSIEST AIRPORT

The world's busiest airport for both international and domestic passengers is Hartsfield International Airport in Atlanta, Georgia. In 1999, 78,092,940 passengers passed through its doors. The highest-ranked nonUS airport was London Heathrow, with 62,263,365 annual passengers.

LONGEST AIR TICKET

The longest-ever single air ticket measured 39.37 ft (12 m) and was issued to Bruno Leunen (Belgium) in Dec 1984 for a 53,206-mile (85,623-km) round trip, using 80 airlines with a total of 109 stopovers.

<48606>
← ACCESS CODE

GO THE DISTANCE

The world's most traveled couple are Dr. Robert Becker and his wife Carmen (USA, left), both of whom have visited all of the sovereign countries and all but six of the nonsovereign or other territories, making a grand total of 234. The Emperor of Japan once gave Bob a shirt while on his travels, and the careful couple have only lost their luggage once, while in Korea.

Frederick W. Finn (UK) had flown more air miles than anyone else, with a record distance of 11,960,000 miles (19,247,750 km) by 2000. Finn commutes regularly from London to New Jersey, and also holds the record for the most flights as a supersonic passenger, having made 714 Atlantic crossings on Concorde.

www.guinnessworldrecords.com/traveltwo

FASTEST TRIP FROM LONDON TO NEW YORK

The speed record from central London, UK, to New York City, by helicopter and Concorde, is 3 hr 59 min 44 sec, set by David J. Springbett and David Boyce (both UK). The return journey took them 3 hr 40 min 40 sec. Both journeys were taken between Feb 8 and 9 1982.

FASTEST TRIP AROUND THE WORLD

Michael Bartlett and David J. Springbett (both UK) successfully circumnavigated the globe on scheduled flights in a record-breaking 62 hr 15 min between March 18 and 21 2000. In total they covered 25,484 miles (41,010 km) on their journey between London, Ti Tree Point, Auckland, Los Angeles, Chicago, Madrid, and London. The rules of this 'antipodal' record mean that the record holders have to pass through two points on the globe that are exactly opposite one another, and Springbett and Bartlett used Ti Tree Point (New Zealand) and Madrid (Spain) as their two antipodal points of reference.

HIGHEST AIRPORT

Situated in a mountainous region known as 'the roof of the world,' Bangda Airport in eastern Tibet lies at 15,548 ft (4,739 m) above sea level. Bangda also holds the record for the longest runway, at 18,045 ft (5,500 m).

LOWEST INTERNATIONAL AIRPORT

The lowest international airport is Schiphol, Amsterdam, Netherlands, at 15 ft (4.5 m) below sea level.

BUSIEST AIRLINE

The busiest scheduled domestic and international airline in the world is Delta Air Lines (USA). In 1999 Delta carried 105,534,000 passengers, the majority of whom (98,298,000) went to destinations within the USA. United Airlines and American Airlines were second and third, with 87,049,000 and 81,452,000 passengers respectively.

BUSIEST INTERNATIONAL AIRLINE

According to the International Air Transport Association (IATA), British Airways (UK) is the world's largest carrier of international passengers, with 36.609 million annual passengers. German airline Lufthansa is in second place, with 27.287 million passengers.

BUSIEST INTERCONTINENTAL AIR ROUTE

The world's busiest intercontinental route is London–New York, with over 3.82 million passengers flying the 3,442 miles (5,539 km) between these two cities annually.

BUSIEST INTERNATIONAL ROUTE

The world's busiest international scheduled air route runs between Hong Kong and Taipei, Taiwan, with 3.96 million passengers recorded in 1999 by the International Civil Aviation Organization. In 1997 the world's 25 top airports handled a total of 968 million passengers.

WIDEST ROAD

The world's widest road is the Monumental Axis, running for 1.8 miles (2.4 km) from the Municipal Plaza to the Plaza of the Three Powers in Brasilia, Brazil. The six-lane boulevard was opened in April 1960 and is 820.2 ft (250 m) wide.

TOWERING OVER THE COMPETITION

France (left) attracts more tourists than any other country. According to the World Tourism Organization, France received 73 million foreign tourists in 1999, representing 11.2% of the global market and easily outnumbering its own population of 59 million.

As a whole, Europe is the world's most popular destination for international tourists, with 379.8 million arrivals in 1999, accounting for 58.4% of the world total.

The USA spends more on foreign tourism than any other nation, with $54 billion (£32.56 billion) spent while traveling in 1999, down from $56.1 billion (£33.82 billion) in 1998. Germany and the UK hold second and third place in the spending stakes respectively.

<46014>
www.guinnessworldrecords.com/mosttourists
← ACCESS CODE

MOST LANES IN ONE ROAD

The San Francisco–Oakland Bay Bridge Toll Plaza has 23 lanes (17 westbound) serving the bridge in Oakland, California.

STEEPEST STREET

The world's steepest public road is Baldwin Street in Dunedin, New Zealand, which has a maximum gradient of 1:1.266 (38° or 42.2%). Baldwin Street is so steep that there are warning signs discouraging motorists from attempting to drive up it. In comparison, San Francisco's steepest streets, Filbert Street and 22nd Street, both have a maximum gradient of 1:1.853 (28.35° or 31%).

NARROWEST STREET

The world's narrowest street is in the village of Ripatransone in Italy. It is called Vicolo della Virilita (Virility Alley) and is 16.9 in (43 cm) wide.

GREATEST TRAFFIC DENSITY

International Road Federation statistics show that Monaco is the country with the highest number of vehicles in relation to its road network. In 1996, the most recent year for which statistics are available, there were 480 vehicles for each kilometer of road in the principality. If all the vehicles were parked behind one another on Monaco's streets, nearly half would have nowhere to park.

BIGGEST 'SPAGHETTI' JUNCTION

The most complex road interchange in the world is the 2/22/57 Interchange (known unofficially as the Orange Crush Interchange) in Orange County, California. It consists of 34 routes on just two levels and has an average daily traffic flow of 629,000 vehicles. The most complex interchange on the British road system is that at Gravelly Hill, north of Birmingham on the Midland Link Motorway section of the M6, opened on May 24 1972. Popularly known as 'Spaghetti Junction,' it includes 18 routes on six levels (together with a diverted canal and river).

GREATEST ROAD MILEAGE

According to the International Road Federation, the country with the greatest length of road is the United States (all 50 states), which had 3,944,788 miles (6,348,227 km) of graded roads in 1999. India had 2,062,839 miles (3,319,664 km) and Brazil 1,071,867 miles (1,724,924 km) of graded roads.

www.guinnessworldrecords.com/spacetourist

OUT OF THIS WORLD!

US businessman Dennis Tito (right, center) paid the Russians a reported $20 million (£14 million) to visit the International Space Station (ISS) as it orbited above the Earth. He took off on April 28 and returned on May 6 2001. Tito's 'vacation' can officially be called the most expensive tourist trip ever because he paid for it entirely out of his own pocket. Previous civilians who have made the trip into space have either been active crew members such as Helen Sharman (UK) and Salman al-Saud (Saudi Arabia), or have been paid for by an employer, as was the case with Japanese broadcaster Yoyohiro Akiyama.

The largest space-launch vehicle was the *Saturn V*, used to send astronauts to the Moon between 1968 and 1972. It was 363 ft (110.6 m) long.

The smallest satellite-launch vehicle was *Pegasus*, a three-stage booster, which was 50.85 ft (15.5 m) long. *Pegasus* has now been succeeded by an operational *Pegasus XL* version. The original *Pegasus*, first launched in 1990, was air-launched from an aircraft.

GUINNESS WORLD RECORDS

buildings and structures 1

LARGEST CINEMA

The largest cinema in the world is the Radio City Music Hall, New York City, which opened on Dec 27 1932 with 5,945 (now 5,910) seats. It was designated a New York City landmark in 1979 and a National Historic Landmark in 1987. More than 300 million people have passed through its art deco doors.

OLDEST ICE THEATER

The oldest custom-built ice theater is the Ice Drome at Blackpool Pleasure Beach, Lancashire, UK, which opened in Oct 1937. The theater has been in continuous use ever since.

LARGEST AMPHITHEATER

The Flavian amphitheater or Colosseum of Rome, Italy, completed in 80 AD, covers 5 acres (20,000 m²) and has a capacity of 87,000. It has a maximum length of 613 ft (187 m) and a maximum width of 574 ft (175 m). At the height of Rome's power, the Colosseum was the site of countless battles between gladiators, slaves, and wild beasts. The arena was even flooded to recreate naval battles.

SOUTHERNMOST LIGHTHOUSE

In 1884 the Argentine navy built a lighthouse on the Isla de los Estados, 100 nautical miles from Cape Horn

TEMPLE-TASTIC

The largest Buddhist temple in the world is Borobudur, central Java, Indonesia (left), built between 750 and 842 AD. The 14.83-acre (6-ha) stone structure is 113 ft (34.5 m) tall. The temple is built in three layers – a pyramidal base with five concentric square terraces, a cone with three circular platforms, and, at the top, a monumental bell-shaped stupa.

<49868>
www.guinnessworldrecords.com/borobudur
← ACCESS CODE

in Patagonia. The light guided ships and boats as they sailed through the Magellan Strait. Abandoned in 1902, the lighthouse has now been rebuilt and continues to operate.

SMALLEST CHURCH

The world's smallest church is Santa Isabel de Hungría, in Colomares, at Benalmádena, Málaga, Spain. Built out of polychromed stone, it was consecrated on April 7 1990 and has a total floor area of 21.1 ft² (1.96 m²). Mass is held on special occasions, and only one person can fit in to pray at a time.

FURTHEST BUILDING RELOCATION

The linked five-story Gem Theater and Century Club building in Detroit, Texas, was moved five blocks away – a distance of 1,850 ft (563 m) – on 72 dollies, each with eight rubber tires. It took 25 days to move the 6.061 million-lb (2,750-tonne) building, beginning on Oct 16 1997.

HEAVIEST BUILDING RELOCATED

On March 1 1998 the 8.157 million-lb (3,700-tonne) Empire Theater, New York City, was transported on rails 170 ft (51.81 m) west, as part of the 42nd Street Development Project. Moving at less than 1 ft (30 cm) a minute, it was transferred in less than five hours on to temporary foundations by hydraulic cylinders along eight rails.

TALLEST STRUCTURES

The tallest structure ever was the guyed Warszawa Radio mast at Konstantynow, Poland, which was 2,120 ft 8 in (646.38 m) tall before it collapsed during renovation work on Aug 10 1991. It was designed by Jan Polak (Poland) and weighed 1.102 million lb (550 tonnes).

The tallest structure that is still standing, is a stayed television transmitting tower, between Fargo and Blanchard, North Dakota, which is 2,063 ft (629 m) tall.

TALLEST BUILDING

The free-standing CN Tower in Toronto, Ontario, Canada, which rises to 1,815 ft 5 in (553.34 m), is the tallest building. At 1,150 ft (351 m) it has a revolving restaurant from which you can see 75 miles (120 km).

TALLEST OFFICE BUILDING

The Petronas Towers in Kuala Lumpur, Malaysia, became the world's tallest office building in March 1996, when stainless steel pinnacles measuring 241 ft (73.5 m) long were placed on top of the 88-story towers, bringing their height to 1,482 ft 8 in (451.9 m). Since these spires are nonfunctional, the Sears Tower, Chicago, Illinois, can still boast the highest occupied story.

TALLEST HOTEL

The Grand Hyatt Shanghai in Pudong, China, is the tallest hotel in the world. It occupies the top 35 floors of the 88-story Jin Mao Tower and contains the world's highest health club on the 57th floor.

HIGHEST-ALTITUDE HOTEL

The Hotel Everest View above Namche, Nepal – the town closest to Everest base camp – is located at a record height of 13,000 ft (3,962 m) above sea level. The hotel commands an excellent view of the Himalayas, including Mt. Everest, the world's highest mountain.

HIGHEST-ALTITUDE RESTAURANT

The highest restaurant in the world is on the mountain summit at the Chacaltaya ski resort, Bolivia, 17,520 ft (5,340 m) above sea level. Lake Titicaca, the world's highest navigable lake, can be glimpsed through the restaurant windows.

LARGEST ADMINISTRATIVE BUILDING

The Pentagon, in Arlington, Virginia, covers the largest ground area of any office building. Built to house the US Defense Department's offices, the exterior side of each wall is 921 ft (281 m) long, and the perimeter measures 4,610 ft (1,405 m) long. Its five stories enclose a total floor area

THE BIGLOO

The largest igloo ever built is the Ice Hotel in Jukkasjärvi, Sweden (left), 124 miles (200 km) north of the Arctic Circle. It has a total floor area of 43,055 ft² (4,000 m²), with the capacity to sleep up to 150 guests per night. It was first built in 1989 as the 'Art-ic' exhibition, with a 645 ft² (60 m²) gallery. It has been rebuilt every November since 1990, increasing in size each year. It opens in Dec and usually stays open until the end of April or the beginning of May, depending on the weather. The temperature inside the hotel hovers between 25° and 16°F (-4° and -9°C) depending on the weather outside. It currently features ice sculptures, a cinema, saunas, an ice chapel, and an ice bar. The guests even have to sleep on ice beds, but thankfully they are covered with thick reindeer pelts.

<52782>
www.guinnessworldrecords.com/igloo
← ACCESS CODE

SMALL IS BEAUTIFUL

The smallest house in the world is a 19th-century fisherman's cottage (above) at The Quay, Conwy, Wales, UK, which consists of two tiny rooms downstairs, a staircase, and a tiny bedroom – everything in fact but a bathroom. It has only 72 in (1.82 m) of frontage, is 122 in (3.09 m) high, and measures 100 in (2.54 m) deep. An average-height man could just manage to lie across its width. At the beginning of the century the owner, Robert Jones, traveled across Britain measuring all small houses to prove that his was really the smallest.

www.guinnessworldrecords.com/tinyhouse

ACCESS CODE
‹50055› ←

of 149.2 acres (604,000 m²), and the corridors total 17.5 miles (28 km) in length. A total of 23,000 military and civilian employees work in the building. It was completed on Jan 15 1943 and cost an estimated $83 million (£57.89) to build.

LARGEST INDUSTRIAL BUILDING

The largest multilevel industrial building that is a single structure, is the container freight station of Asia Terminals Ltd. at Hong Kong's Kwai Chung container port. The 15-level building has a total area of 9,320,868 ft² (865,937 m²).

LARGEST ANCIENT CASTLE

The largest ancient castle in the world is Prague Castle in the Czech Republic, which dates back to the 9th century. It is an irregular oblong polygon with an axis of 1,870 ft (570 m) and an average diameter of 420 ft (128 m), giving a surface area of 18 acres (72,800 m²).

SMALLEST DETACHED HOUSE

Thimble Hall, located in the Peak District village of Youlgreave, Derbyshire, UK, holds the record for the smallest detached house, externally measuring 11 ft 10 in (3.63 m) by 10 ft 3 in (3.14 m) and 12 ft 2 in (3.7 m) high. It was reputedly occupied by a family of eight in the 19th century.

LARGEST MOSQUE

The world's largest mosque is Shah Faisal Mosque, near Islamabad, Pakistan. The total area of the complex is 46.87 acres (189,700 m²), with the covered area of the prayer hall being 1.19 acres (4,800 m²). It can accommodate 100,000 worshipers in the prayer hall and courtyard and a further 200,000 people in the adjacent grounds.

www.guinnessworldrecords.com/largestwindows

EXTREME PANE

The largest windows in the world are those in the Palace of Industry and Technology at Rond-point de la Défense, Paris, France (below). The three matching windows, made up of a large number of panes of glass, have an extreme width of 715 ft (218 m) and a maximum height of 164 ft (50 m). The Palace of Industry and Technology was built by General de Gaulle's government in the late 1950s as a national exhibition center. It spearheaded

ACCESS CODE
‹49682› ←

LARGEST TRADITIONAL HINDU TEMPLE OUTSIDE INDIA

The largest traditionally built Hindu temple outside India is the Shree Swaminarayan Mandir, Neasden, London, UK, which covers an area of 65,344 ft² (6,071 m²) and is built with 26,300 pieces of stone. Opened on Aug 20 1995, it was carved by 1,526 craftsmen in India and then reassembled in London a year later.

the redevelopment of the La Défense area of the city, and was soon surrounded by offices, shops, and apartment buildings. Its three windows are 0.6 in (15 mm) thick, and were manufactured by the Chantereine-Thourotte factory outside Paris.

The largest sheets of glass ever manufactured were two identical panes 71 ft (21.64 m) long and 9 ft 6 in (2.9 m) wide, made by the Saint-Gobain Co. in France and installed in their Chantereine factory at Thourotte, France, in Aug 1996.

GUINNESS WORLD RECORDS™

buildings and structures 2

SMALLEST COMMERCIAL THEATER

The Theatre of Small Convenience, Malvern, Worcestershire, UK, a former Victorian gentleman's toilet, seats 12 people and covers an area of 109.1 ft² (10.14 m²). It opened on Nov 6 1999 and is used by amateur and professional performers.

LARGEST OPERA HOUSE

The Metropolitan Opera House at Lincoln Center, New York City, is the biggest opera house in the world, with a capacity of 4,065 people. The auditorium is 451 ft (137 m) deep, and the stage measures 230 ft (70 m) wide and 148 ft (45 m) deep.

LARGEST OBELISK

The obelisk of Pharaoh Tuthmosis III was brought from Aswan, Egypt, by Emperor Constantinus in 357 AD and repositioned in the Piazza San Giovanni in Laterano, Rome, Italy, on Aug 3 1588. The obelisk stands up to 107 ft 7 in (32.81 m) high and weighs 1,003,102 lb (455 tonnes).

DEEPEST UNDERWATER MAILBOX

The world's deepest underwater mailbox is located 32.8 ft (10 m) beneath the waters of Susami Bay, Japan. Sports divers can post special waterproof plastic postcards in the mail box, which is officially part of the Susami post office and opened daily.

‹49728› ← ACCESS CODE

www.guinnessworldrecords.com/djoser

ETERNAL TRIANGLE

The Djoser Step Pyramid (left) at Saqqâra, Egypt, is the world's oldest pyramid. It was constructed by Imhotep (Djoser's royal architect) during the Third Dynasty (around 2,630 BC) to a height of 204 ft (62 m) and is thought to be the first tomb in Egypt to have been built entirely out of stone.

The world's largest pyramid, and the largest monument ever constructed, is the Quetzalcóatl Pyramid at Cholula de Rivadavia, 63 miles (101 km) southeast of Mexico City, Mexico. It is 177 ft (54 m) tall, and its base covers an area of nearly 45 acres (18.2 ha). Its total volume has been estimated at 4.3 million yd³ (3.3 million m³), compared with the volume of 3.1 million yd³ (2.4 million m³) for the Pyramid of Khufu or Cheops, at Giza, Egypt.

More than 4,273 undersea letters were collected in the mailbox's first year of operation in 1999.

MOST ROOMS IN HOUSE

The house with the most rooms is Knole House, near Sevenoaks, Kent, UK, which is believed to have had 365 rooms, one for each day of the year. Built around seven courtyards, its total depth from front to back is about 400 ft (120 m). Building began in 1456 by Thomas Bourchier, Archbishop of Canterbury, and the house was extended by Thomas Sackville, first Earl of Dorset, around 1603. Knole is now administered by the National Trust.

LARGEST DOOR

The four doors in the Vehicle Assembly Building near Cape Canaveral, Florida, reach a record-breaking height of 460 ft (140 m). The building is used by NASA to assemble and prepare space vehicles.

LARGEST TENT

An enormous tent covering an area of 188,350 ft² (17,500 m²) was erected by the firm of Deuter from Augsburg, Germany, for the Welcome Expo in Brussels, Belgium, in 1958.

HIGHEST-ALTITUDE PRE-FABRICATED ROAD BRIDGE

The highest-altitude road bridge is a 18,380-ft (5,602-m-high) Bailey bridge invented by Sir Donald Bailey which was made up of pre-fabricated sections. Erected in Aug 1982 near Khardung-La, in Ladakh, India, it is 98 ft (30 m) across. Such bridges played a major role in the Allied invasion of Nazi-occupied Europe, enabling speedy river crossings even after the retreating Germans had dynamited established bridges.

LONGEST BRIDGE

At 23 miles (38.42 km), the longest bridge in the world is the Second Lake Pontchartrain Causeway, which joins Mandeville and Metairie,

Louisiana. Completed in 1969, the causeway is so long that it is possible to stand in the middle of it and be unable to see land in either direction.

LONGEST CABLE SUSPENSION BRIDGE

The Tsing Ma Bridge in Hong Kong, opened to the public in May 1997, has a span of 4,518 ft (1,377 m), making it the longest suspension-bridge span for combined road and railroad traffic.

TALLEST BRIDGE

The towers of the Akashi-Kaikyo Bridge, between Honshu and Awaji islands, Japan, rise to a height of 984 ft (299 m) and their foundations extend 230 ft (70 m) beneath the seabed. The suspension cables are 3 ft (1 m) thick. The bridge has been built to withstand winds of 50 mph (80 km/h), as well as earthquakes of 8.5 on the Richter scale.

LARGEST WALL OF BOOKS

On Nov 30 2000 a wall made of 649,000 books designed by Luz Darriba (Spain), was unveiled in Lugo, Spain. It has an area of 127,014 ft² (11,800 m²), took 6,000 people 100 days to build, and was built on a structure 19.7 ft (6 m) long.

LARGEST TEPEE

The world's largest tepee is 42 ft (12.8 m) high, 252 ft (76.8 m) in circumference, and has a diameter of 50 ft (15.2 m). It was built by Dr. Michael Doss (USA) of the Crow

UP THE GARDEN PATH

The largest beachfront garden in the world (left) stretches from Emissario Submarino, next to Urubuquecaba Island, to the entrance of the port channel between São Vicente and Santo Amaro Islands in Santos, Brazil. It covers an area of 2,355,143 ft² (218,800 m²) and has 719 flowerbeds, 1,746 trees, and the path running through it is 17,214 ft (5,247 m) long.

The world's largest garden is arguably the one created by André Le Nôtre at Versailles, France, in the late 17th century for Louis XIV. The magnificent formal gardens and parkland were created in what had been a muddy swamp. They cover over 15,000 acres (6,070 ha) of which the famous formal garden covers 247 acres (100 ha).

‹52135› ← ACCESS CODE

www.guinnessworldrecords.com/beachgarden

www.guinnessworldrecords.com/gettymuseum

‹50947› ←

STATE OF THE ART

The Getty Center in Los Angeles, California (below), is the world's most expensive museum, and is funded by a $4.3-billion (£2.4-billion) trust established after the death of oil tycoon J. Paul Getty in 1976. It cost an unprecedented $1 billion (£600 million) to build and took 13 years to construct on its 10-acre (4.04-ha) hilltop site, offering views to the city and the sea. It covers 1 million ft² (93,000 m²) and was designed by Richard Meier (USA).

Getty first opened a museum to the public in 1954 in the grounds of his Malibu home. The first art to be displayed consisted of antiquities and French decorative art and paintings. In 1974 he constructed a new villa for the display of his collections.

The new building, which opened in 1997, also holds the record for the largest museum acquisitions budget. It was first established with an initial budget of $700 million (£300 million) in Jan 1974. Today the museum has an annual budget of over $100 million (£70.4 million), which is used for acquisitions for its 38 galleries.

Indian Reservation, Montana, and is a Crow Nation tepee modeled directly on one owned by Chief Medicine Crow.

LARGEST SHOWER

The largest shower in the world was built at Jones Beach State Park, New York, on May 27 2000. It measures 80 ft 3.5 in (24.47 m) long, 8 ft (2.43 m) wide, and 3.65 m (12 ft) tall, big enough for up to 200 people to shower simultaneously.

LARGEST SHOPPING CENTER

West Edmonton Mall in Edmonton, Alberta, Canada, covers an area of 5.3 million ft² (492,387 m²). The mall contains over 800 stores and services, as well as 11 major department stores. Parking is provided in the world's largest

parking lot for over 20,000 vehicles. The mall also has the world's largest indoor amusement park, indoor water park, and man-made lake.

TALLEST CHIMNEY

The coal power-plant No. 2 stack at Ekibastuz, Kazakhstan, is 1,378 ft (420 m) tall. The diameter tapers from 144 ft (44 m) at the base to 46 ft 7 in (14.2 m) at the top.

LARGEST HANGING BASKET

Jos de Troyer (Belgium) created a hanging basket measuring 34.4 ft (10.5 m) in diameter and weighing 99,207 lb (45 tonnes) in Ghent, Belgium. It went on display on April 20 2000 and is hanging above the Emile Braunplein square in Ghent's historic center. A special flower beer was brewed to celebrate the occasion.

GUINNESS WORLD RECORDS™

www.guinnessworldrecords.com/sports

sports

baseball

HIGHEST OLYMPIC BATTING AVERAGE

Luigi Carrozza (Italy) hit .571 at the 1996 Olympic Games, Atlanta, Georgia, making this the highest batting average achieved by a player during an Olympic tournament.

MOST GAMES WON BY A PITCHER AT AN OLYMPICS

The greatest number of games won by a pitcher at an Olympic Games tournament is three by Chieh-Fu Kuo Lee (Chinese Taipei) in 1992, Seth Greisinger (USA), and Omar Luis (Cuba) in 1996, and Ryan Franklin (USA) in 2000. A pitcher is credited with winning the game when he pitches for the majority of the inning in which his team scores the winning run.

MOST STRIKEOUTS AT THE OLYMPICS

The most strikeouts thrown by a pitcher in an Olympic Games is 27 by Tomohito Ito (Japan) at Barcelona, Spain, in 1992.

MOST HITS BY A PLAYER IN OLYMPICS

The most hits at an Olympic Games tournament by a player is 20 by Omar Linares (Cuba) at Barcelona, Spain, in 1992, and again at Atlanta, Georgia, in 1996.

BORN TO RUN

The most home runs in a career was achieved by Henry Louis 'Hank' Aaron (USA, left) with 755 home runs; 733 for the Milwaukee Braves (1954–65) and Atlanta Braves (1966–74) in the National League, and 22 for the Milwaukee Brewers (AL) from 1975 to 1976. Born in 1943, Aaron grew up in a segregated neighborhood in Mobile, Indiana. From a young age he was determined to play professional baseball, and taught himself the game at the local playground. With no team at his high school, Aaron played in local amateur leagues until he was eventually recruited by the Milwaukee Braves. There he became one of the first black players to cross the color divide that was then in force.

‹45657› ← ACCESS CODE www.guinnessworldrecords.com/aaron

MOST HOME RUNS AT THE OLYMPICS

The record for the most home runs hit by an individual at an Olympic Games tournament is nine (in nine games) by Orestes Kindelan (Cuba) at Atlanta, Georgia, in 1996.

MOST MAJOR LEAGUE TEAM TITLES

There are two leagues in US baseball, the National League (NL) formed in 1876 and the American League (AL) formed in 1901. The champions of each league meet in the World Series, and the best players meet in an All Star Game: NL v. AL.

The greatest number of title wins of the American League is 37 by the New York Yankees between 1921 and 2000.

The record for the most National League titles is 18, held by the L.A. Dodgers (formerly the Brooklyn Robins and the Brooklyn Dodgers).

MOST WORLD SERIES WINS

The World Series was first staged unofficially in 1903, and officially since 1905. The most wins is 26 by the New York Yankees (AL) between 1923 and 2000 from a record-breaking 37 Series appearances.

MOST WORLD SERIES PLAYED

The most Series played is 14 by Lawrence Peter 'Yogi' Berra (USA) playing for the New York Yankees (AL) between 1947 and 1963.

MOST HOME RUNS IN A WORLD SERIES GAME

The most home runs in a World Series game is three by George Herman 'Babe' Ruth (USA) playing for the New York Yankees (AL) on Oct 6 1926 and again on Oct 9 1928, and by Reggie Jackson (USA) also playing for the New York Yankees (AL) on Oct 18 1977. Babe Ruth's impact on baseball remains unsurpassed, and he has been called 'the greatest player of all time.'

MOST HOME RUNS IN A SINGLE GAME

The most home runs hit in a major league game is four, first achieved by Robert Lincoln Lowe (USA) for Boston (NL) v. Cincinnati (NL) on May 30 1894. The feat has been achieved a further 11 times since then, most recently on Sept 7 1993 by Mark Whiten (USA), for St. Louis (NL) playing against Cincinnati (NL).

LONGEST HOME-RUN HIT

The longest measured home run hit for a major league game is 634 ft (193 m) by Mickey Mantle (USA) for the New York Yankees (AL), against the Detroit Tigers (AL) at Briggs Stadium, Detroit, Michigan, on Sept 10 1960.

MOST BASE HITS IN CAREER

Pete Rose (USA), nicknamed 'Charlie Hustle,' made the most base hits in a career, with 4,256 achieved for Cincinnati (NL), followed by Philadelphia (NL), Montreal (NL), and Cincinnati (NL) from 1963 to 1986.

MOST STOLEN BASES IN CAREER

'Man of Steal' Rickey Henley Henderson (USA) has stolen the greatest number of bases (when the batter gets to the next base without needing to hit the ball) in a baseball career. He notched up a record 1,376 stolen bases between 1979 and 2001 for, in sequence, Oakland (AL), New York (AL), Oakland (AL), Toronto (AL), Oakland (AL), San Diego (NL), Anaheim (AL), San Diego (NL), Oakland (AL), New York (NL), Seattle (AL), and San Diego (NL).

HIT AND RUN

The USA major league record for home runs in a season is 70 by Mark McGwire (USA, left) of the St. Louis Cardinals (NL) in 162 games in 1998. Born in Pomona, California, in 1963, Mark McGwire attended Damien High School where he played basketball and golf as well as baseball. He graduated in 1981 and went to the University of Southern California before turning professional. Initially he played pitcher but when his hitting power became apparent, he switched to third base. He was a member of the US Olympic team that won silver in 1984, when baseball was a demonstration sport, and he has reached the World Series three times with the Oakland Athletics (AL). McGwire is active in charity work, frequently appearing at charity golf tournaments.

‹45653› ← ACCESS CODE www.guinnessworldrecords.com/mcgwire

MOST STRIKEOUTS IN A CAREER

Nicknamed 'The Ryan Express,' Nolan Ryan (USA) playing for New York (NL), California (AL), Houston (NL), and Texas (AL), pitched a record 5,714 strikeouts during his career, from 1966 to 1993.

Nolan Ryan also achieved the most strikeouts in a season when he fanned 383 batters in one season in 1973, playing for California (AL).

MOST STRIKEOUTS IN ONE GAME

A record-breaking 20 strikeouts were pitched in one major league game of nine innings by Roger 'The Rocket' Clemens, playing for Boston (AL) v. Seattle (AL) on April 29 1986 and v. Detroit (AL) on Sept 18 1996; by Kerry Wood for Chicago (NL) v. Houston (NL) on May 6 1988; and most recently by Randy Johnson for Arizona (NL) against Cincinnati (NL) on May 8 2001.

MOST GAMES WON BY A PITCHER

The pitcher with the most games won in a career is baseball legend Denton True 'Cy' Young (USA), with 511 games won between 1890 and 1911 for Cleveland (NL), St. Louis (NL), Boston (AL), Cleveland (AL), and Boston (NL). He pitched a record total of 7,356 innings in the 749 games of his career.

MOST SHUTOUTS IN A PITCHER'S CAREER

The pitcher with the most shutouts (when the opposition fails to score a single run) in a career is Walter Perry Johnson (USA) playing for Washington (AL) with 110 shutouts achieved from 1907 to 1927. Nicknamed 'Big Train,' Johnson has been ranked as one of the fastest-ever pitchers.

MOST CONSECUTIVE GAMES

One of the most respected players in the game, Cal Ripken Jr. (USA) played 2,632 consecutive games for the Baltimore Orioles (AL) between May 30 1982 and Sept 19 1998.

MOST GAMES PLAYED

Pete Rose (USA) played in 3,562 games and was at-bat 14,053 times for the Cincinnati Reds (NL), the Philadelphia Phillies (NL), and the Montreal Expos (NL). After retiring from playing, Rose served as Reds' manager, steering the team to four consecutive second-place finishes.

MOST WORLD CUP TEAM WINS

Instituted in 1938, the World Cup has been won a record 21 times by Cuba in 1939–40, 1942–43, 1950, 1952–53, 1961, 1969–73, 1976, 1978, 1980, 1984, 1986, 1990, 1994, and 1998. Baseball was introduced into Cuba in 1866 and it continues to flourish there.

www.guinnessworldrecords.com/rodriguez

BALL PARK FIGURE

The richest baseball contract, based on the average annual salary for the duration of the contract, is the $25.2 million (£16.8 million) earned by Alex Rodriguez (USA, right) of the Texas Rangers (AL). This earned him $252 million (£168 million) over 10 years and was signed in Dec 2000. He made his major league debut in 1994, age 18, at shortstop for the Seattle Mariners (AL), one of the youngest-ever players to start a game in this position. He was also the youngest-ever shortstop for an All Star Game, playing in 1996, age 20.

ACCESS CODE

‹45664›

GUINNESS WORLD RECORDS

american football

HIGHEST NFL SCORE

The highest score ever in a regular season National Football League (NFL) game occurred when the Washington Redskins beat the New York Giants by 73 points to 41 in Washington, D.C., on Nov 27 1966. The aggregate score of 114 points is also a world record.

LONGEST FIELD GOAL

The longest field goal kicked in an NFL game is 63 yd by two players – Tom Dempsey for the New Orleans Saints on Nov 8 1970, and Jason Elam for the Denver Broncos on Oct 25 1998.

LONGEST PASS

A 99-yd-long pass has been achieved on eight occasions in NFL history and has always resulted in a touchdown. The most recent was a pass from Brett Favre to Robert Brooks, for the Green Bay Packers when they played the Chicago Bears on Sept 11 1995.

MOST TOUCHDOWNS IN AN NFL GAME

The most touchdowns scored in an NFL game is six by Ernie Nevers for the Chicago Cardinals against

‹47871›
← ACCESS CODE

www.guinnessworldrecords.com/superbowl

TV AUDIENCE BOWLED OVER

The biggest-ever TV audience for an American Football game was 138.5 million for the NBC transmission of Super Bowl XXX between the Dallas Cowboys and the Pittsburgh Steelers on Jan 28 1996 (left). It is estimated that 45% of all US homes tune in to the annual Super Bowl, and the game is estimated to reach about 100 million viewers. In 1998 a 30-sec advertising slot for Super Bowl XXXII between the Denver Broncos and the Green Bay Packers cost a record $1.3 million (£909,746) – four times the price of a normal advertising slot at a similar time.

the Chicago Bears on Nov 28 1929; by William Jones for the Cleveland Browns against the Chicago Bears on Nov 25 1951; and by Gale Sayers for the Chicago Bears against the San Francisco 49ers on Dec 12 1965.

MOST FIELD GOALS

The most field goals scored by an individual in an NFL game is seven, by Jim Bakken for the St. Louis Cardinals against the Pittsburgh Steelers on Sept 24 1967; and Rick Karlis for Minnesota Vikings against the L.A. Rams on Nov 5 1989.

MOST YARDS GAINED

Glyn Milburn gained a record 404 combined net yards for the Denver Broncos against the Seattle Seahawks on Dec 10 1996. Milburn received Pro Bowl honors in 1995 when he led the NFL with a 27-yd average on kickoff returns and has not missed one game, playing in 96 consecutive games.

MOST TOUCHDOWN PASSES

The most touchdown passes thrown in the same NFL game by the same player is seven; by Sid Luckman for the Chicago Bears on Nov 14 1943; Adrian Burk for the Philadelphia Eagles on Oct 17 1954; George Blanda for the Houston Oilers on Nov 19 1961; Y. A. Tittle for the New York Giants on Oct 28 1962; and Joe Kapp for the Minnesota Vikings on Sept 28 1969.

MOST YARDS GAINED RUSHING IN AN NFL GAME

Corey Dillon rushed for a record 278 yd for the Cincinnati Bengals against the Denver Broncos on Oct 22 2000.

MOST PASSES CAUGHT IN AN NFL GAME

Tom Fears of the L.A. Rams caught 18 passes in an NFL game against the Green Bay Packers on Dec 3 1950. Frears was inducted into the American Football Hall of Fame in 1970.

MOST YARDS PASSING IN AN NFL GAME

Norm Van Brocklin of the L.A. Rams passed for 554 yd against the New York Yanks on Sept 28 1951. Van Brocklin, a quarterback, was inducted into the American Football Hall of Fame in 1971.

MOST YARDS RECEIVING IN AN NFL GAME

Willie Lee Anderson of the Los Angeles Rams had a record 336 receiving yards in an NFL game against the New Orleans Saints on Nov 26 1989. He caught a total of 15 passes and helped the Los Angeles Rams to a 20–17 victory after 6 min 38 sec of overtime, when his 26-yd pass reception laid the ground for the game-winning field goal.

THE GOLDEN BOYS

Jerry Rice of the San Francisco 49ers (left) holds the record for the most touchdowns in a professional career, with 187 between 1985 and 2000. He also holds the Super Bowl career records for touchdowns (seven), yards gained receiving (512), and pass receptions (28). Born in Starkville, Mississippi, in 1962, Jerry Rice first came to prominence at Mississippi Valley State University, setting a college career record of 4,693 yards gained as receiver. He joined the San Francisco 49ers in 1985 forming one of the NFL's best passing partnerships with Joe Montana. Rice was voted Most Valuable Player (MVP) in the 1989 Super Bowl and has recently joined the Oakland Raiders. The 49ers also share the record for the highest attendance for a regular season game with a crowd of 102,368 when they played the L.A. Rams at the L.A. Coliseum, California, on Nov 10 1957.

www.guinnessworldrecords.com/dallascowboys

DALLAS DYNASTY

The greatest number of Super Bowl wins is five; by the Dallas Cowboys (1972, 1978, 1993, 1994, and 1996) and by the San Francisco 49ers (1982, 1985, 1989, 1990, and 1995). The Super Bowl was first held in 1967 between the winners of the NFL and the AFL. The Dallas Cowboys (right), nicknamed 'America's Team,' are the most successful team in the history of the NFL, and have appeared in eight Super Bowls in total.

MOST HOME GAMES OF DIFFERENT TEAMS SEEN BY AN INDIVIDUAL

Paul Sansone (USA) attended a home game for each of the 30 NFL teams in the 1998 season. Paul embarked on his tour of the teams in aid of the American Cancer Society.

HIGHEST ATTENDANCE

The greatest number of spectators at any game is 103,985, for Super Bowl XIV between the Pittsburgh Steelers and the L.A. Rams at the Rose Bowl, Pasadena, California, on Jan 20 1980.

MOST YARDS RUSHING IN A CFL CAREER

George Reed rushed for a Canadian Football League (CFL) career-record 16,116 yd for the Saskatchewan Roughriders, 1963–75.

MOST CFL TOUCHDOWNS

The most touchdowns scored in a career is 137, by George Reed for the Saskatchewan Roughriders between 1963 and 1975.

MOST CFL POINTS SCORED

Lui Passaglia scored 3,984 points for the BC Lions between 1976 and 2000. During this time Passaglia played in a record-breaking 408 games.

GUINNESS WORLD RECORDS

basketball

MOST POINTS IN AN NBA GAME

The most points ever scored by an individual in an NBA (National Basketball Association) game is 100. Wilt Chamberlain (USA) set the record while playing for the Philadelphia Warriors against the New York Knicks on March 2 1962. In NBA games, a successful shot is worth three points, except for shots taken within an area near to the basket. Throws from this area, which is marked with a semicircle drawn from the end of the court to a radius of 20.5 ft (6.25 m), are worth two points. Violations can be penalized with free throws, which are worth one point.

HIGHEST SCORE IN AN NBA MATCH

The highest points total in an NBA match is 370. This occurred when the Detroit Pistons (186) beat the Denver Nuggets (184) at Denver on Dec 13 1983. Overtime was played after regulation time ended in a 145-145 tie.

HIGHEST POINT AVERAGE IN AN NBA CAREER

The highest point-scoring average per game for players exceeding 10,000 points is 31.5 by Michael Jordan (USA). Jordan scored 29,277 points in 930 games for the Chicago Bulls between 1984 and 1998.

MOST GAMES PLAYED IN AN NBA CAREER

Between 1976 and 1997 Robert Parish (USA) played 1,611 regular-season games. He achieved this over 21 seasons and with four different teams – the Golden State Warriors (1976–80), Boston Celtics (1980–94), Charlotte Hornets (1994–96), and Chicago Bulls (1996–97).

MOST POINTS IN AN NBA CAREER

The most points scored in an NBA career is 38,387 (at an average of 24.6 points per game) by Kareem Abdul-Jabbar (USA) from 1969 to 1989. This includes 15,837 field goals scored in regular-season games, and 5,762 points scored in play-off games.

MOST POINTS IN AN NBA SEASON

The most points ever scored in an NBA season is 4,029 by Wilt Chamberlain (USA) for the Philadelphia Warriors in the 1961/62 season. (His career average was 30.1 points per game.)

MOST GAMES PLAYED IN AN NBA SEASON

The most complete games played in an NBA season is 79 by Wilt Chamberlain (USA) for the Philadelphia Warriors in the 1961/62 season. Chamberlain was on court for a record total time of 3,882 minutes.

MOST CONSECUTIVE NBA GAMES

From Nov 19 1986 to March 20 2001, A. C. Green (USA) played a total of 1,177 consecutive games. During this time Green played for four teams – the Los Angeles Lakers, Phoenix Suns, Dallas Mavericks, and Miami Heat.

MOST WINS IN AN NBA SEASON

The most wins in an NBA season is 72 by the Chicago Bulls in the 1995/96 season.

MOST CONSECUTIVE WINS

The record for the most consecutive NBA wins is held by the Los Angeles Lakers. The Lakers won a record-breaking total of 33 NBA games in succession from Nov 5 1971 to Jan 7 1972.

MOST NBA TITLES

The Boston Celtics have won more NBA Championship titles than any other team. They have taken the title a total of 16 times, winning in 1957, 1959–66, 1968/69, 1974, 1976, 1981, 1984, and 1986.

OLDEST NBA PLAYER

The oldest player to participate in an NBA game is Robert Parish (USA, b. Aug 30 1953). Parish played his last game with the Chicago Bulls age 43 years 231 days on April 19 1997.

TALLEST NBA PLAYER

The tallest player in NBA history is Gheorghe Muresan (Romania) of the Washington Bullets. Muresan measures up at 7 ft 7 in (2.31 m). He made his professional debut in 1994.

TALLEST BASKETBALL PLAYER

Suleiman 'Ali Nashnush was reputed to be 8 ft 0.25 in (2.45 m) tall when he played for the Libyan national team in 1962.

MOST PARALYMPIC WOMEN'S BASKETBALL GOLD MEDALS

The most Paralympic titles won is three, by Canada. The Canadians took the title in 1992, 1996, and 2000.

MOST MEN'S WHEELCHAIR BASKETBALL WORLD CHAMPIONSHIP TITLES

The most World Championship wins is five, by the USA, who won in 1979, 1983, 1986, 1994, and 1998. The first Championships were held in 1973, and the most recent were played in 2000. Twelve men's teams and eight women's teams competed at the 2000 Championships.

MOST WOMEN'S WHEELCHAIR BASKETBALL WORLD CHAMPIONSHIPS

Canada has won the women's wheelchair basketball title twice, in 1994 and 1998. The first Championships were held in 1990.

WOMEN ON TOP!

The US women's basketball team has won the Olympic gold medal a record-breaking four times. They took the title in 1984, 1988, 1996, and 2000. Teresa Edwards (USA, left) has been a member of every American Olympic gold medal winning team.

Women's basketball was introduced as an Olympic sport in 1976 at the Montreal Olympics. The USSR entered the inaugural competition with an unbeaten international winning streak stretching back to 1958. The Soviets extended this unbeaten run by taking gold in both the 1976 Games and at the 1980 Moscow Olympics. Their dominance of the competition was confirmed in 1980 by a record-breaking 66-point margin of victory over the Italian team, whom they beat 119–53. The American team, however, has won the women's basketball gold at every Olympics since 1980, excluding 1992, when the Commonwealth of Independent States (CIS) took the title.

<45627>
← ACCESS CODE
www.guinnessworldrecords.com/womensbasketball

CHECK THE
RARE CHAIR-FLAIR!

The US men's wheelchair basketball squad (above) have taken a record five Paralympic titles. They won in 1960, 1964, 1972, 1976, and 1988. Wheelchair basketball is largely identical to the standing game. The basket is set at the same height and the court is the same size. Wheelchair basketball demands high levels of skill and physical fitness.

www.guinnessworldrecords.com/
chairflair

ACCESS CODE
‹56470› ←

MOST WOMEN'S
BASKETBALL WORLD
CHAMPIONSHIPS

The USSR and the USA have both won the women's Basketball World Championships a record-breaking six times. The Soviet Union took the title in 1959, 1964, 1967, 1971, 1975, and 1983. The USA won in 1953, 1957, 1979, 1986, 1990, and 1998. The first women's World Championship was staged in 1953.

MOST MEN'S BASKETBALL
WORLD CHAMPIONSHIPS

Yugoslavia has won the most men's Basketball World Championships, taking the title a total of four times – in 1970, 1978, 1990, and 1998. The first men's Basketball World Championships were held in 1950.

MOST MEN'S BASKETBALL
OLYMPIC GOLD MEDALS

The USA has won a record-breaking 12 men's Olympic basketball titles. The sport was first played at the Games in 1936, and the US team won 63 consecutive matches after its introduction.

The USA's 36-year-long winning streak ended in Munich (West Germany) in 1972, when they lost 50–51 to the USSR in a hotly disputed final.

MOST CONSECUTIVE
FREE THROWS

On April 28 1996 Ted St. Martin (USA) scored a record-breaking 5,221 consecutive free throws. The record was set in Jacksonville, Florida.

LONGEST THROW

On April 8 1996 Iain McKinney (UK) scored with a record-breaking long-distance throw of 90 ft 6 in (27.6 m). The shot was thrown for the Sheffield Sharks during an exhibition game at Ponds Forge, Sheffield, UK.

FURTHEST BASKETBALL
DUNK SHOT FROM
A TRAMPOLINE

Joseph Gibby (USA) successfully dunked a basketball by leaping from a trampoline placed 19 ft (5.79 m) from the net's backboard. The dunk shot was sunk on Jan 21 2001 at Van Nuys Airport, California.

HIGHEST
DUNK SHOT

On April 1 2000 Michael 'Wild Thing' Wilson (USA) of the Harlem Globetrotters successfully dunked a

www.guinnessworldrecords.com/bryant

LAKERS RECRUIT
YOUNG HOOP-FUL

The youngest player ever to start an NBA game is Kobe Bryant (USA, above), the son of former NBA player Joe 'Jellybean' Bryant. The record-breaker started for the Los Angeles Lakers on Jan 28 1997, age just 18 years 158 days. His first match was against the Dallas Mavericks. Bryant is also the youngest player ever to have appeared in an NBA All Star game. He played in the 1998 match, age 19 years 169 days.

ACCESS CODE

‹56524› ←

regulation-sized basketball through a basket set at a height of 12 ft (3.65 m).

FURTHEST
DISTANCE DRIBBLED

Jamie Borges (USA) dribbled a regulation basketball for a distance of 96.89 miles (155.9 km) in 24 hours at Barrington High School, Rhode Island, between May 3 and 4 1998.

MOST
BASKETBALLS DRIBBLED

The most basketballs dribbled simultaneously is five, by Joseph Odhiambo (USA). He dribbled two on each hand and one between his feet.

LARGEST ATTENDANCE
FOR A BASKETBALL MATCH

A total of 80,000 people attended the European Cup Winners Cup final between AEK Athens and Slavia Prague on April 4 1968. AEK Athens beat Slavia Prague 89 to 82.

MOST FREE THROWS
SCORED IN 10 MINUTES

On Oct 12 1998 Jim Connolly (USA) scored 280 free throws from 326 attempts, in 10 minutes at St. Peter's School, Pacifica, California.

GUINNESS WORLD RECORDS

ice hockey

MOST INDIVIDUAL WINS IN CONSECUTIVE NHL GAMES
Gerry Cheevers (Canada) holds the record for the most consecutive individual NHL (National Hockey League) wins, with 32 for the Boston Bruins in the 1971/72 season.

MOST GOALS SCORED IN AN NHL SEASON
Wayne Gretzky (Canada) scored a record-breaking 92 goals for the Edmonton Oilers in the 1981/82 NHL season.

MOST GOALS SCORED BY AN INDIVIDUAL IN AN NHL GAME
The greatest number of goals scored by any individual in an NHL game is seven by Joe Malone (Canada) for the Quebec Bulldogs v. Toronto St. Patricks in Quebec City, Canada, on Jan 31 1920.

MOST POINTS SCORED IN AN NHL CAREER
The most points scored in an NHL career is 2,857 by Wayne Gretzky (Canada) for the Edmonton Oilers, Los Angeles Kings, St. Louis Blues, and New York Rangers between 1979 and 1999. This massive points total is from 894 goals and 1,963 assists, achieved in 1,487 games.

MOST POINTS SCORED IN A FULL NHL SEASON, INCLUDING PLAY-OFFS
The most points scored in a full NHL season, including the play-offs, is 255 points by Wayne Gretzky (Canada) for the Edmonton Oilers in the 1984/85 season. The points total consists of 90 goals and 165 assists.

MOST POINTS SCORED IN AN NHL SEASON
Ice hockey legend Wayne Gretzky (Canada) scored 215 points for the Edmonton Oilers in the 1985/86 season. The points total includes 163 assists.

HIGHEST PERCENTAGE OF WINS IN AN NHL SEASON
The highest percentage of wins to games in an NHL season was 87.5%, achieved by the Boston Bruins with 38 wins in 44 games in 1929/30.

MOST GOALTENDING SHUTOUTS IN AN NHL CAREER
The most goaltending shutouts in an NHL career were by Terry Sawchuk, while playing for Detroit, Boston, Toronto, Los Angeles, and the New York Rangers from 1949 to his death in 1970. He did not concede a single goal in 103 of his games.

WINGING IT
The most wins in an NHL season is 62 by the Detroit Red Wings (team member Sergei Fedorov above, left) in the 1995/96 season. Between 1935 and 1955, the team won seven Stanley Cups and boasted some of the all-time best players. Following the team's 1955 win, it hit a 42-year barren patch, the team's famed stability disappeared, and they changed coaches and players frequently. 1993 saw a new era of stability when coach Scotty Bowman joined and reversed the fortunes of a team that had become known as the 'Detroit Dead Things' because of their inability to win.

‹44947›
www.guinnessworldrecords.com/redwingwin
← ACCESS CODE

HIGHEST SCORE IN AN ICE-HOCKEY GAME
The highest score in a World Championship game was Australia's 58–0 win over New Zealand at Perth, WA, Australia, on March 15 1987.

FEWEST DEFEATS IN A SEASON
In the 1976/77 season, the Montreal Canadiens lost just eight games, the fewest in a season of 70 or more games, from 80 played (60 wins and 12 ties), earning a record 132 points.

BROTHERLY LOVE
The longest undefeated run for a team in an NHL season is 35 games – 25 wins and 10 ties – established by the Philadelphia Flyers (left) between Oct 14 1979 and Jan 6 1980. The Philadelphia Flyers came into existence on June 5 1967 as part of the NHL's expansion. Fittingly, the team that comes from the 'City of Brotherly Love' is known to treat its players as part of a 'family.' The team was an instant success, topping the division in their first season. In the 1970s they became known as the 'Broad Street Bullies' for their aggressive on-ice presence. The Flyers had consecutive Stanley Cup wins in 1974 and 1975 – their only successes in this particular competition.

‹44948›
www.guinnessworldrecords.com/phillyflyers
← ACCESS CODE

LONGEST GAME
The longest ice hockey game was 19 hr 8 min 44 sec, played by a team of 34 in the Labatt Blue NHL Pick-up Marathon at Red Deer, Alberta, Canada, beween 23 and 24 Feb 2001.

MOST STANLEY CUP WINS
The Montreal Canadiens have won the Stanley Cup a record 24 times. They won in 1916, 1924, 1930–31, 1944, 1946, 1953, 1956–60, 1965/66, 1968/69, 1971, 1973, 1976–79, 1986, 1993, from a record 32 finals.

MOST INDIVIDUAL STANLEY CUP WINS
Henri Richard (Canada) has a record 11 Stanley Cup wins to his credit between 1956 and 1973, playing for the Montreal Canadiens. He was on the winning side in 1956–60, 1965, 1966, 1968–69, 1971 and 1973.

MOST GOALS SCORED IN A STANLEY CUP GAME
Five players (all Canadian) share the record for the most goals scored in a Stanley Cup game. Five goals each were scored by Newsy Lalonde for Montreal v. Ottawa on March 1 1919; by Maurice Richard for Montreal v. Toronto on March 23 1944; by Darryl

Glen Sittler for Toronto *v.* Philadelphia on April 22 1976; by Reggie Leach for Philadelphia *v.* Boston on May 6 1976; and by Mario Lemieux for Pittsburgh *v.* Philadelphia on April 25 1989.

QUICKEST GOAL SCORED

The quickest goal scored in an NHL game occurred after five seconds. This record is shared by three players – Doug Smail (Canada) for the Winnipeg Jets *v.* St. Louis Blues at Winnipeg on Dec 20 1981; Bryan Trottier (Canada) for the New York Islanders *v.* Boston Bruins at Boston on March 22 1984; and Alexander Mogilny (USSR, now Russia) for the Buffalo Sabres *v.* Toronto Maple Leafs at Toronto on Dec 21 1991.

MOST OLYMPIC TEAM GOLD MEDALS

Ice hockey was first contested at the 1920 Olympics, and the USSR have a record eight wins: in 1956, 1964, 1968, 1972, 1976, 1984, 1988, and 1992 (as the CIS).

Women's ice hockey was first contested at the 1998 Winter Olympics. The USA defeated Canada to win gold.

MOST INDIVIDUAL OLYMPIC GOLDS

The most individual Olympic ice-hockey golds won is three, achieved by Soviet players Vitaliy Davydov, Anatoliy Firsov, Viktor Kuzkin, and Aleksandr Ragulin, who each won gold in 1964, 1968, and 1972; Vladislav Tretyak, who won gold in 1972, 1976, and 1984; and by Andrey Khomutov, who won gold in 1984, 1988, and 1992.

MOST WORLD CHAMPIONSHIP WINS

The Ice Hockey World Championships were first held for amateurs in 1920, in conjunction with the Olympic Games. Since 1976, the World Championships have been separate and open to professionals. The USSR won 22 world titles between 1954 and 1990 (and Russia won in 1993), including the Olympic titles of 1956, 1964, and 1968.

World Championships for women have been held since 1990, and have been won on each occasion by Canada, in 1990, 1992, 1994, 1997, 1999, 2000, and 2001. In winning the seven titles, the team has not lost a single game.

www.guinnessworldrecords.com/roygoaltend

PUCKER UP

The most NHL career wins by a goaltender is 481 by Patrick Roy (Canada, right) of the Colorado Avalanche, up to March 22 2001. This record was set on Oct 17 2000 in a game against the Washington Capitals, and Roy continues to play. The previous record holder was Terry Sawchuk. Throughout Roy's 16-year career he has only missed one season's play-offs, in 1994/95, and has been on the Stanley Cup winning side twice with the Canadiens in 1986 and 1993, and once with the Avalanche in 1996. A sporty child, he decided on becoming a goaltender at the age of eight after watching the sport on television and liking the look of the goaltender's uniform.

GUINNESS WORLD RECORDS

golf

BIGGEST PRIZE MONEY FOR A TOURNAMENT

The Players Championship, contested from March 23 to 27 2000 at Sawgrass, Florida, had a total prize pool of $6,113,400 (£3,835,250), with $1.08 million (£677,500) going to the winner, who was Hal Sutton (USA).

HIGHEST CAREER EARNINGS ON THE US LPGA TOUR

The record career earnings for a woman on the US Ladies Professional Golf Association (LPGA) tour belong to Annika Sorenstam (Sweden), with $6,957,044 (£4,874,371) earned between 1993 and April 2001.

MOST BRITISH OPEN TITLES

Harry Vardon (UK) won six British Open titles in 1896, 1898, 1899, 1903, 1911, and 1914. He started out as caddy, rose progressively to the top, and became one of golf's first international celebrities. Amazingly, he won two of the Opens after contracting tuberculosis.

MOST US OPEN TITLES

Willie Anderson, Bobby Jones Jr., Ben Hogan, and Jack Nicklaus have all won the US Open four times – Willie Anderson (USA) in 1901 and 1903–05; Bobby Jones (USA) in 1923, 1926, 1929, and 1930; Ben Hogan (USA) in 1948, 1950, 1951, and 1953; and Jack Nicklaus (USA) in 1962, 1967, 1972, and 1980.

HITTING THE JACKPOT

Jack Nicklaus (USA, left) won a total of six US Masters titles – more than any other golfer – in 1963, 1965, 1966, 1972, 1975, and 1986. He is considered by many to be the greatest golfer in the history of the sport. After turning professional in 1962, he dominated the golfing world during the 1960s and 1970s. Nicklaus became the first player to take his career earnings to the $2-million (then £816,000) mark in 1973, and in 1986 became the oldest player to win the Masters, at the age of 46.

Jack Nicklaus and Walter Hagan (USA) jointly hold the record for most US PGA titles won, with five titles each. Walter Hagan won in 1921 and 1924–27, and Jack Nicklaus in 1963, 1971, 1973, 1975, and 1980.

‹55734› www.guinnessworldrecords.com/jacknicklaus ← ACCESS CODE

MOST RYDER CUP WINS BY A TEAM

The biennial Ryder Cup professional match between the USA and Europe (British Isles or Great Britain prior to 1979) was instituted in 1927. The USA has won 24 to 7 (with two draws) up until 1999.

MOST RYDER CUP WINS BY AN INDIVIDUAL

Nick Faldo (UK) has won 23 out of 46 matches and also holds a record 25 points scored, having halved four other matches.

Arnold Palmer (USA) holds the US record for most matches won, with 22 out of 32 played. Billy Casper scored a US record 23.5 points from 37 matches.

MOST SOLHEIM CUP WINS

The female equivalent of the Ryder Cup is contested biennially between the top professional players of Europe and the USA, and was first held in

1990. The USA has won four times, in 1990, 1994, 1996, and 1998, with Europe winning in 1992 and 2000.

MOST SOLHEIM CUP WINS BY AN INDIVIDUAL

Dottie Pepper (USA) has won 13 out of 20 matches between 1990 and 2000. Laura Davies (UK) has won 13 out of 23 matches in the same period. The most points scored is 14, by both Davies and Pepper.

LOWEST SCORE OVER 18 HOLES BY A MAN

At least five players have played a long course (over 6,500 yd or 5,950 m) in a score of 58. Shigeki Maruyama (Japan) shot a round of 58 (29 + 29), which included 11 birdies and one eagle, in a qualifying event for the 2000 US Open, at Woodmont Country Club, Rockville, Maryland, (par 71, 6,539 yd or 5,979 m) on June 5 2000. (A birdie is one under par for the hole; an eagle is two under par; and an albatross three.)

The US Professional Golf Association (PGA) tournament record for 18 holes is 59. This is jointly held by Al Geiberger, Chip Beck, and David Duval (all USA). Al Geiberger scored 30 + 29 in the second round of the Danny Thomas Classic, on the 72-par (7,249-yd or 6,628-m) Colonial GC course, Memphis, Tennessee, on June 10 1977. Chip Beck played a score of 59 in the third round of the Las Vegas Invitational, on the 72-par (6,979-yd or 6,381-m) Sunrise GC course, Las Vegas, Nevada, on Oct 11 1991. David Duval scored 31 + 28 in the final round of the Bob Hope Chrysler Classic, La Quinta, California, on Jan 24 1999.

LOWEST SCORE OVER 18 HOLES BY A WOMAN

The lowest recorded score on an 18-hole course (over 5,600 yd or 5,120 m) for a woman is 59 by Annika Sorenstam (Sweden) in the 2001 Standard Register PING at Moon Valley Country Club, Phoenix, Arizona, on March 16 2001.

LOWEST TOTAL SCORE OVER 72 HOLES BY A WOMAN

The lowest four-round total in a US LPGA Championship event is 261. It is held by two people – Se Ri Pak (South Korea) with 71, 61, 63, 66 at the Jamie Farr Kroger Classic, Sylvania, Ohio, held from July 9 to 12 1998; and Annika Sorenstam (Sweden) with 65, 59, 65, 68 in the 2001 Standard Register PING at Moon Valley Country Club, Phoenix, Arizona, held from March 15 to 18 2001.

KARRIE'D AWAY

In 1999 Karrie Webb (Australia, left) had the highest season's earnings on the US LPGA tour. She won a record total of $1,591,959 (£1,115,387). Karrie began playing golf at the age of eight. By the time she had turned professional in 1994, she had already represented Australia six times in international competition. Webb qualified for the LPGA tour despite playing with a broken bone in her wrist. During her rookie season in 1996, she won four tournaments, making her the second most successful rookie ever. She was the first woman to reach the $1-million mark in a single season, winning this sum in only 10 months and 3 days.

‹53361› www.guinnessworldrecords.com/karriewebb ← ACCESS CODE

FASTEST ROUND OF GOLF BY AN INDIVIDUAL

The fastest round played when the golf ball comes to rest before each new stroke is 27 min 9 sec by James Carvill (UK) at Warrenpoint Golf Course, Co. Down, Ireland (18 holes; 6,154 yd or 5,628 m) on June 18 1987.

FASTEST ROUND OF GOLF BY A TEAM

The Fore Worcester's Children team of golfers completed 18 holes in 9 min 28 sec at the Tatnuck Country Club, Worcester, Massachusetts, on Sept 9 1996. They scored 70.

BEST GOLF-BALL CONTROL

Jonas Belander (Sweden) managed to keep a regulation golf ball aloft, alternating touches between two sandwedge golf clubs, for 13 min 47 sec on Feb 3 2001.

GREATEST DISTANCE BETWEEN TWO ROUNDS OF GOLF IN ONE DAY

Nobby Orens (USA) played at Stockley Park, Uxbridge, Greater London, UK, as well as Braemar Country Club, Tarzana, California – 5,954 miles (9,582 km) apart – on July 20 1999.

HIGHEST-ALTITUDE SHOT

Vladímir Mysík (Czech Republic) played a shot from the peak of Gasherbrum I, 26,470 ft (8,068 m), Karakoram Range, Kashmir (on the border of India and Pakistan), on July 9 1997.

LARGEST TRAP

The world's biggest trap (called a 'bunker' in the UK) is Hell's Half Acre on the 585-yd (535-m) seventh hole of the Pine Valley course, Clementon, New Jersey, built in 1912. It is generally regarded as the world's most difficult course.

LIGHTEST GOLF CLUB

The lightest full-size golf club is the driver JBeam Win.1, manufactured by Japan Golf Equipment Co. Ltd. of Tokyo, Japan, which weighs just 7.75 oz (220 g). The titanium head weighs 5.64 oz (160 g), the carbon-fiber shaft 1.23 oz (35 g), and grip 0.88 oz

(25 g). The Japanese golf market is the world's second largest golf market, with a size of $1,670 million (£1,016 million) at wholesale in 1998, as estimated by a private research institute. Golf is the largest segment of the overall Japanese sporting-goods market.

LONGEST GOLF HOLE

The longest hole in the world is the seventh hole (par 7) of the Satsuki GC, Sano, Japan, which measures 964 yd (881 m).

MOST GOLF BALLS HIT IN ONE HOUR

Sean Murphy (Canada) drove a record 2,146 balls over 91 m (100 yd) and into a target area at Swifts Practice Range, Carlisle, Cumbria, UK, on June 30 1995.

www.guinnessworldrecords.com/tigerwoods

WHAT A TIGER!

The all-time career earnings record on the US PGA circuit is held by Tiger Woods (USA, right) with $23,767,307 (£16,652,285), between Aug 1996 and March 2001. Eldrick 'Tiger' Woods was born on Dec 30 1975. His interest in golf started at an early age – at six months, he would imitate his father's swing as he hit balls into a net, and at the age of two he putted with Bob Hope on *The Mike Douglas Show*. Since turning professional in 1996, Woods has emerged as one of the most gifted players in the history of golf, becoming the only player to achieve a grand slam, as well as being the game's highest-ever earner.

The record for the highest season's earnings for the US PGA tour is also held by Tiger Woods. In 2000 he won a total of $9,188,321 (£6,437,698).

In June 2000 Tiger Woods won the US Open by 15 strokes. This is a record for a major tournament. He finished the tournament with a total of 272, an amazing 12 under par.

ACCESS CODE

‹53362› ←

GUINNESS
WORLD RECORDS™

soccer 1

LARGEST FOOTBALL TOURNAMENT

The second Bangkok League Seven-a-side Competition, which was held from Jan 9 to April 25 1999, was contested by a record 5,098 teams (35,686 players).

MOST SUCCESSIVE NATIONAL LEAGUE CHAMPIONSHIPS

The greatest number of successive National League Championships is 11 by Al-Ansar Sporting Club, Lebanon, from 1988 to 1999. For all 11 championships, the team was coached by Adnan Mekdashi and presided over by the same club president, Salim Diab.

MOST SOCCER MATCHES PLAYED

Peter Shilton (UK) made a record 1,390 senior appearances, including a record 1,005 league appearances – 286 for Leicester City (1966–74); 110 for Stoke City (1974–77); 202 for Nottingham Forest (1977–82); 188 for Southampton (1982–87); 175 for Derby County (1987–92); 34 for Plymouth Argyle (1992–94); one for Bolton Wanderers (1995); and nine for Leyton Orient (1996–97); one league play-off; 86 FA Cup; 102 League Cup; 125 internationals; 13 under-23; four Football League XI; and 53 various European and other club competitions.

MOST CAREER GOALS

The most goals ever scored in a career is a record 1,279 by Edson Arantes do Nascimento (Brazil), who is better known as Pelé. He set his record between Sept 7 1956 and Oct 1 1977 in 1,363 games. His best year was 1959 when he scored 126 goals, and the Milésimo (1,000th) came from a penalty for his club Santos at the Maracanã Stadium, Rio de Janeiro, Brazil, on Nov 19 1969 when playing his 909th first-class match.

<45617> ← ACCESS CODE

MOST GOALS BY A TEAM IN ONE GAME

The highest score recorded in a first-class match is 36. This occurred in a Scottish Cup tie between Arbroath v. Bon Accord on Sept 12 1885, when Arbroath won 36–0 at home.

HIGHEST SCORE IN A NATIONAL CUP FINAL

In 1935 Lausanne-Sports recorded the highest-ever score in a national cup final when they beat Nordstern Basel 10–0 in the Swiss Cup final, but later lost by the same scoreline at the hands of Grasshopper-Club (Zurich) in the 1937 Swiss Cup final.

FASTEST GOAL

Goals scored in three seconds or less after the kickoff have been claimed by a number of players. From video evidence, Ricardo Olivera (Uruguay) scored in 2.8 seconds for Río Negro against Soriano at the José Enrique Rodó stadium, Soriano, Uruguay, on Dec 26 1998. When the referee blew his whistle, Olivera blasted the ball toward goal when he saw the goalkeeper was off his line.

FASTEST TIME TO SCORE THREE GOALS (HAT TRICK)

The fastest time taken to score three goals is 2 min 13 sec by Jimmy O'Connor (Ireland) for Shelbourne against Bohemians at Dallymount Park, Dublin, Ireland, on Nov 19 1967.

THE REAL DEAL

The most European Champions Cup (instituted in 1957) wins is eight by Real Madrid (Spain, left), in 1955/56, 1956/57, 1957/58, 1958/59, 1959/60, 1965/66, 1997/98, and 1999/2000. Named by FIFA as Team of the Century in 1998, Real Madrid's remarkable success can be traced back to the arrival of its 10th president, Santiago Bernabéu, in 1943, and it was his dream of turning them into the best team in the world that led him to pursue the best players and coaches to share in his vision.

Real Madrid also own the world's most expensive player, winger Luis Figo (Portugal), who was transferred for a record 9.90 billion pesetas ($52,892,754 or £37 million) from Barcelona in July 2000.

www.guinnessworldrecords.com/realmadrid
← ACCESS CODE

MOST CONSECUTIVE HAT TRICKS

The most consecutive league games in which a player has scored hat tricks in a national top division side is four by Masashi Nakayama for Jubilo Iwata in the Japanese League – First Stage. He scored five goals against Cerezo Osaka at Nagai Stadium on April 15 1998, four goals against Sanfrecce Hiroshima at Jubilo Iwata Stadium on April 18 1998, four goals against Avispa Fukuoka at Kumamoto City Stadium on April 25 1998, and three goals against Consadole Sapporo at Jubilo Iwata Stadium on April 29 1998.

YOUNGEST PLAYER TO SCORE A HAT TRICK

The youngest scorer of a hat trick in UK football was Tommy Lawton, age 17 years 5 days, for Burnley v. Spurs at Turf Moor on Oct 10 1936. The youngest player to score a hat trick in the Premiership is Michael Owen, (UK), age 18 years 62 days, for Liverpool v. Sheffield Wednesday on Feb 14 1998.

MOST GOALS SCORED BY A GOALKEEPER IN ONE GAME

Paraguayan goalkeeper José Luis Chilavert scored a hat trick of penalties for Vélez Sarsfield in their 6–1 defeat of Ferro Carril Oeste in the Argentine professional league.

MOST GOALS SCORED FROM A CORNER

The most goals anyone has scored in a match direct from a corner is two by Luis 'Gita' Barroso (Portugal)

RIO GRANDE

Rio Ferdinand (UK, left) became the world's most expensive defender in Nov 2000 when he joined Leeds United from West Ham United in a deal worth £18 million ($25.6 million). Born on Nov 8 1978, in London, UK, Rio Ferdinand joined West Ham United as a schoolboy in 1994. He made his senior debut in 1996 and has since established himself as a regular in the senior England squad.

The most expensive goalkeeper of all time is Angelo Peruzzi (Italy), who was transferred from Juventus to Inter Milan (both Italian clubs) in June 1999 for a record fee of $17.4 million (£10.5 million), a full $4.3 million (£3 million) more than his nearest rival Fabien Barthez (France) who was bought by Manchester United (UK) from Monaco for £7.5 million ($11.66 million).

<54326> www.guinnessworldrecords.com/riogrande
← ACCESS CODE

for FC de Famalicão against SC Olhanese in a Portuguese Cup match, July 2 1946.

LONGEST TIME WITHOUT A GOALKEEPER CONCEDING A GOAL

Thomas McKenna (UK), of Folkestone Invicta Under-13s, played 1,417 minutes without conceding a goal, from Sept 24 1995 to May 5 1996.

LONGEST THROW-IN

The longest throw-in is 158 ft 0.4 in (48.17 m) achieved by Michael Lochner (USA) at Bexley High School, Ohio, on June 4 1998.

FASTEST INDOOR SOCCER BALL KICK

The fastest indoor soccer ball kick is 68 mph (109.43 km/h), by Moroccan international footballer Hassan Kachloul of Southampton FC, UK, on April 27 2000.

LONGEST PENALTY SHOOT-OUT

In the Freight Rover Trophy Southern Section quarterfinal between Aldershot Town and Fulham at Aldershot, Surrey, UK, on Feb 10 1987, a total of 28 penalty kicks were taken after the match had finished 1–1 after normal and overtime. Seven penalties were missed, with Aldershot winning 11–10.

LONGEST CONTROL OF A SOCCER BALL

Ricardinho Neves (Brazil) juggled a regulation soccer ball for 19 hr 5 min 31 sec nonstop with his feet, legs, and head and without the ball ever touching the ground at the Los Angeles Convention Center, California, on July 15 and 16 1994. The longest duration by a woman is 7 hr 5 min 25 sec by Cláudia Martini (Brazil) at Caxias do Sul, Brazil, on July 12 1996.

MOST SOCCER BALL TOUCHES IN 30 SECONDS

The greatest number of touches of a soccer ball in 30 seconds, while keeping the ball in the air, is 136 by Ferdie Adoboe (USA), at Fort Lowell Park, Tucson, Arizona, on

Jan 22 1999. On the same occasion, Adoboe completed 262 touches in just one minute.

MOST UNDISCIPLINED FOOTBALL MATCH

On Nov 3 1969, in the cup match between Tongham Youth Club, Surrey *v.* Hawley, Hants (both UK), the referee booked all 22 players, including one who went to hospital, and a linesman.

FURTHEST DISTANCE TRAVELED BY TEAMS

The furthest distance traveled between two clubs in the top division of a professional national league is 2,961 miles (4,766 km) between the home grounds of L.A. Galaxy, Los Angeles, California, and New England Revolution, Foxboro, Massachusetts, in the US Major League.

MOST VALUABLE FOOTBALL SHIRT

The red football shirt worn by striker Geoff Hurst (UK) during the 1966 World Cup final between England and Germany was sold for £91,750 ($134,393) at Christie's, London, UK, on Sept 28 2000.

www.guinnessworldrecords.com/manunited

UNITED THEY STAND

Manchester United Football Club (below), in the English Premier League, is the world's most valuable football club. They had a market capitalization of over £1 billion ($1.59 billion) on March 8 2000 – the first football club ever to reach that milestone. Their finest hour came in 1999 when their victory over Bayern Munich in the European Champion's League final completed the treble (they also won the FA Cup and the Premier League) – a unique achievement in English soccer.

ACCESS CODE

‹54710›

KEANE 16

GUINNESS WORLD RECORDS

soccer 2

MOST WORLD CUP WINS

FIFA (Fédération Internationale de Football Association), founded on May 21 1904, instituted the first World Cup on July 13 1930, in Montevideo, Uruguay. It is held quadrennially and Brazil has won a record-breaking four times, in 1958, 1962, 1970, and 1994.

MOST WOMEN'S WORLD CUP WINS

Initiated in 1991, the women's World Cup also takes place quadrennially. The USA won in 1991 and 1999. The winner in 1995 was Norway.

YOUNGEST PLAYER IN A WORLD CUP TOURNAMENT

The youngest person ever to play in a World Cup final match is Norman Whiteside (UK), who played for Northern Ireland v. Yugoslavia, age 17 years 41 days, on June 17 1982.

MOST WORLD CUP APPEARANCES

Antonio Carbajal (Mexico) appeared in a record five World Cup final tournaments, keeping goal for Mexico in 1950, 1954, 1958, 1962, and 1966, and playing 11 games in all.

<56488>
← ACCESS CODE
www.guinnessworldrecords.com/kristinelilly

WOMEN'S WORLD

The most international soccer appearances by a woman for a national side is officially 225 by No.13 player Kristine Lilly (USA, left) between 1987 and 2000.

In the women's international game, the highest score ever recorded is 21–0. This incredible score has occurred on four occasions – Japan v. Guam at Guangzhou, China, on Dec 5 1997; Canada v. Puerto Rico at Centennial Park, Toronto, Canada, on Aug 28 1998; and Australia v. American Samoa and New Zealand against Samoa, both at Mt. Smart Stadium, Auckland, New Zealand, on Oct 9 1998.

This record was equaled by Lothar Matthäus (Germany), who played in 1982, 1986, 1990, 1994, and 1998, playing a record 25 games in total.

FASTEST GOAL IN A WORLD CUP MATCH

The quickest goal in a World Cup final match was after 15 seconds by Vaclav Masek (Czechoslovakia) v. Mexico at Viña del Mar, Chile, on June 7 1962. In a preliminary match, Davide Gualtieri scored after seven seconds for San Marino v. England at Bologna, Italy, on Nov 17 1993.

YOUNGEST SCORER IN A WORLD CUP FINAL

The youngest scorer in a World Cup final match is Edson Arantes do Nascimento (Brazil), known as Pelé, who scored for Brazil against Wales, at Gothenburg, Sweden, on June 19 1958, age 17 years 239 days. A Brazilian hero, he is also known as Perola Negra (Black Pearl).

MOST FEDERATIONS IN FIFA WORLD CUP QUALIFIERS

A record 198 federations registered to play the FIFA qualifiers for the 2002 Soccer World Cup, to be played jointly in South Korea and Japan. The exceptions were the soccer federations of North Korea, Burundi, Niger, Afghanistan, and New Guinea. In terms of revenue and viewing figures, the World Cup is the world's largest single-sport competition.

MOST FUTSAL WORLD CUP TITLES

Since it was first held in 1989, Brazil holds the record for the most wins at the Futsal (indoor soccer) World Cup,

which is held every four years, with three in 1989, 1992, and 1996.

MOST EUROPEAN CHAMPIONSHIPS

Germany has won the European Championships a record three times, in 1972, 1980, and 1996 (the first two as West Germany).

A women's Championship was held for the first time in 1984. Germany holds the record for the most wins, winning four times in 1989, 1991, 1995, and 1997.

MOST EUROPEAN CUP-WINNERS CUPS

The European Cup-Winners Cup, contested until 1999 by the winners of European National Cups, has been won a record four times by Barcelona in 1979, 1982, 1989, and 1997. One of the top soccer clubs in the world, Barcelona has won every major European competition and is the only club in Europe to have taken part annually since 1955 when European competitions were first introduced.

KEEP THE BALL ROLLING

The oldest player to take part in a World Cup match was Albert Roger Milla (left, centre) for Cameroon v. Russia on June 28 1994, age 42 years 39 days. He also scored in the match, making him the oldest scorer in the finals. Africa's Soccer Player of the Year in 1976, Milla moved to France in 1977 and won the French Cup with Monaco in 1980 and with Bastia in 1981. He retired from international soccer having won 81 full caps, but was persuaded to rejoin the Cameroon squad for the 1994 tournament.

The oldest player to take part in an international game was William Henry 'Billy' Meredith (UK), who played outside right for Wales v. England at Highbury, London, UK, on March 15 1920, age 45 years 229 days. He played internationally for a record span of 26 years.

DOUBLE WHAMMY

Two records were broken at the same time when the highest score ever in an international match was achieved by Australia *v.* American Samoa during the Oceania Group One World Cup qualifying match at Coffs Harbour, NSW, Australia, on April 11 2001. Australia won 31–0 with Archie Thompson (Australia, right) scoring 13 goals in the match – the most goals ever scored by an individual in a World Cup match.

ACCESS CODE

‹56656›

MOST AFRICA CUP OF NATIONS WINS

The record for the most wins at the Africa Cup of Nations, which is held every two years, is four. It is held jointly by Ghana (1963, 1965, 1978, 1982) and Egypt (1957, 1959, 1986, 1998). The Africa Cup began in 1957 and had just three entrants. Now there are 49 participants.

MOST ASIAN CUP WINS

The most wins in the Asian Cup is three; by Iran in 1968, 1972, and 1976; and by Saudi Arabia in 1984, 1988, and 1996.

MOST CONCACAF CHAMPIONSHIPS

Costa Rica has won the CONCACAF Championships (Confederation of North, Central American, and Caribbean Association Football) 10 times between 1941 and 1989.

A women's version, held for the first time in 2000, was won by the USA.

MOST COPA AMERICA CHAMPIONSHIPS

Argentina has won the South American Championship (Copa America since 1975) a record 15 times between 1910 and 1993.

MOST GOALS IN A MATCH BY ONE PLAYER

On Dec 13 1942 Stephan Stanis (France), playing for Racing Club de Lens *v.* Aubry-Asturies, in Lens,

France, scored 16 goals – the most goals scored by one player in a match. The most goals scored by one player in a match at the Olympics is 10, a record shared by Sofus Nielsen playing for Denmark *v.* France (final score 17–1) in the 1908 London Olympic Games and Gottfried Fuchs of Germany, who beat Russia 16–0 in the 1912 Stockholm Olympic Games.

MOST INTERNATIONAL APPEARANCES

Hossam Hassan (Egypt) has made the most international appearances, representing his national team 156 times between 1985 and 2001.

FASTEST INTERNATIONAL THREE GOALS

Japanese international Masashi 'Gon' Nakayama scored three goals in 3 min 15 sec against Brunei during an Asian Cup qualifying match played on Feb 16 2000. Nakayama netted the ball after 1 min, 2 min, and 3 min 15 sec.

LARGEST MATCH ATTENDANCE

The greatest crowd attendance at a soccer match numbered 199,854 people at the Brazil *v.* Uruguay World Cup match in the Maracanã Municipal Stadium, Rio de Janeiro, Brazil, on July 16 1950.

LONGEST CLEAN SHEET IN SOCCER

The longest that any goalkeeper has succeeded in keeping goals out of his net in top-class competition is 1,275 minutes (just over 14 matches) by Abel Resino (Spain) of Atlético Madrid from Dec 10 1990 to April 1 1991.

The record in international matches is 1,142 minutes (nearly 13 matches) for Dino Zoff (Italy) from Sept 1972 to June 1974.

The British club match record is 1,196 minutes by Chris Woods (UK) for Glasgow Rangers from Nov 26 1986 to Jan 31 1987.

GUINNESS WORLD RECORDS

tennis

MOST GRAND SLAM SINGLES TITLES

Between 1960 and 1973 Margaret Court (*née* Smith, Australia) won 24 grand slam tournament singles tennis titles. She won 11 Australian Open titles, five US Open titles, five French Open titles, and three Wimbledon titles.

MOST GRAND SLAM MEN'S SINGLES TITLES

Pete Sampras (USA) won 13 grand slam tournament singles tennis titles between 1990 and 2000. These include seven Wimbledon titles, four US Open titles, and two Australian Open titles. When he won his first US Open in 1990, he became the youngest man to have done so, at 19.

BEST MALE GRAND SLAM PLAYERS

The only man to hold all four Championships (Wimbledon, US, Australian, and French Open Championships) simultaneously was Don Budge (USA) in 1938. He also won Wimbledon and the US Open in 1937, giving him six successive grand slam tournaments. The first man to

have won all four of the world's major Championship singles was Fred Perry (UK) when he won the French title in 1935. The only man to achieve the grand slam twice was Rod Laver (Australia) as an amateur in 1962 and again in 1969 when the titles were open to professionals.

BEST FEMALE GRAND SLAM PLAYERS

Four women have achieved the grand slam – Maureen Connolly (USA) in 1953; Margaret Court (Australia) in 1970; and Martina Navrátilová (USA) in 1983 and 1984. (These three also won six successive grand slam tournaments.) The fourth was Steffi Graf (Germany) in 1988, when she also won the women's singles Olympic gold medal. Pam Shriver (USA) won a record eight successive grand slam tournament women's doubles titles with Navrátilová, and 109 successive matches in all events from April 1983 to July 1985.

MOST WIMBLEDON WINS

Pete Sampras (USA) won seven Wimbledon men's singles tennis titles in 1993–95 and 1997–2000. This record was set after the Challenge Round was abolished in 1922. Before this, William Charles Renshaw (UK) won seven men's singles titles in 1881–86 and 1889.

Martina Navrátilová (USA) won a record nine Wimbledon women's singles tennis titles in 1978, 1979, 1982, 1983, 1984, 1985, 1986, 1987, and 1990.

The most Wimbledon doubles tennis titles is 19, held by Elizabeth Montague Ryan (USA) who won them between 1914 and 1934. The 19 titles consist of 12 women's doubles titles and seven mixed doubles titles. The seven mixed doubles titles is a record in itself.

Billie-Jean King (*née* Moffitt, USA) won a record 20 Wimbledon titles between 1961 and 1979, consisting of six singles, 10 women's doubles, and four mixed doubles titles. This is the most Wimbledon titles won

by a woman. King helped form the Women's Tennis Association (WTA) in 1974, becoming its first president.

The most Wimbledon tennis titles won by a man is 13 by Laurie Doherty (UK), consisting of five singles titles (1902–06) and eight men's doubles titles (1897–1906). For his men's doubles titles he was partnered by his brother Reginald Frank Doherty (UK).

MOST FRENCH OPEN WINS

Margaret Court (Australia) holds the women's record with 13 French Open titles between 1962 and 1973, consisting of five singles titles, four doubles titles, and four mixed doubles titles.

Henri Cochet (France) holds the men's record with nine titles at the French Open. He won four singles titles, three doubles titles, and two mixed doubles titles between 1926 and 1930.

Björn Borg (Sweden) won the French Open men's singles title a record six times, in 1974–75 and 1978–81.

Chris Evert (USA) won the French Open women's singles title seven times – in 1974, 1975, 1979, 1980, 1983, 1985, and 1986. She was voted the Women's Sports Foundation's greatest athlete of the past 25 years in 1985 and won the WTA Award in 1992.

MOST US OPEN WINS
The most US Open singles tennis titles won by a man is seven and is shared by Bill Tilden (USA) in 1920–25 and 1929; Richard Sears (USA) in 1881–87; and William Larned (USA) in 1901, 1902, and 1907–11.

The most US Open singles titles won by a woman is eight by Molla Mallory (née Bjurstedt, USA) in 1915–18, 1920–22, and 1926.

The most US Open titles won by a man is 16 by Bill Tilden (USA), including seven men's singles, 1920–25 and 1929.

The most US Open titles won by a woman is 25 by Margaret Du Pont (USA), who won 13 women's doubles, nine mixed doubles, and three singles titles from 1941 to 1960. The women's doubles titles were won with Louise Brough (USA) as her partner.

MOST AUSTRALIAN OPEN WINS
The most Australian Open singles tennis titles won by a man is six. This was won by Roy Emerson (Australia) in 1961 and 1963–67. In total he won 12 grand slam singles titles and 16 grand slam doubles titles.

The most Australian Open tennis titles won by a woman is 21 by Margaret Court (Australia) who won the women's singles 11 times (1960–66, 1969–71, and 1973), the women's doubles eight times (1961–63, 1965, 1969–71, and 1973), and the mixed doubles twice (1963 and 1964).

The most Australian Open women's doubles titles won is 16 by Thelma Long (née Coyne, Australia), who won 12 women's doubles and four mixed doubles titles.

MOST DAVIS CUP WINS
The most wins in the Davis Cup, the men's international team championship, is 31 by the USA between 1900 and 1995. The most appearances for Cup winners is eight by Roy Emerson (Australia), 1959–62, 1964–67. Bill Tilden (USA) played in a record 28 matches in the final, winning a record 21 (17 out of 22 singles and four out of six doubles). He was in seven winning teams in 1920–26 and then four losing teams in 1927–30.

LONGEST MATCH
The longest match in a grand slam tournament is 5 hr 31 min between Alex Corretja (Spain) and Hernán Gumy (Argentina), in the third round of the French Open on May 31 1998. Corretja eventually won 6–1, 5–7, 6–7, 7–5, 9–7.

MOST CONSECUTIVE SERVES
The most consecutive 'good' serves (without a double fault) is 8,017 by Rob Peterson (USA) at Port Aransas, Texas, on Dec 5 1998. The attempt lasted 10 hrs 7 min.

www.guinnessworldrecords.com/kournikova

GAME, SET, AND MATCH
The youngest-ever winner of a Federation Cup match is Anna Kournikova (Russia, right). On April 25 1996, when she was only 14 years old, she beat Anna-Karin Svensson (Sweden) 6-0, 6-3, helping Russia to defeat Sweden 3-0. Anna began playing tennis at the age of five and turned professional in 1995.

GUINNESS WORLD RECORDS™

athletics

MOST WORLD RECORDS IN ONE DAY

Jesse Owens (USA) set six world records in 45 minutes at Ann Arbor, Michigan, on May 25 1935 with a 9.4-sec 100-yd race at 3:15 p.m.; a 26-ft 8.25-in (8.13-m) long jump at 3:25 p.m.; a 20.3-sec 220-yd race at 3:45 p.m. (which included a separate record for the 200 m); and a 22.6-sec 220-yd low hurdle race at 4 p.m. (which also included a separate record for the 200-m hurdle).

LONGEST TRACK EVENT WINNING SEQUENCE

For over a decade Ed Moses (USA) dominated the men's 400-m hurdling event. His remarkable record of 122 consecutive wins began on Sept 2 1977 and ended when he was beaten by Danny Harris (USA) in Madrid, Spain, on June 4 1987. Moses' domination of the sport was such that at one time he held the 13 fastest times ever recorded.

LONGEST FIELD EVENTS WINNING SEQUENCE

Iolanda Balas (Romania) won a record 150 consecutive competitions at the high jump between 1956 and 1967 in National, European, World, and Olympic Championships.

MOST SUCCESSFUL IAAF GOLDEN LEAGUE INDIVIDUAL

The only athlete to have twice won a share of the jackpot in the IAAF (International Amateur Athletics Federation) Golden League is runner Hicham El Guerrouj (Morocco). For the jackpot, an athlete must win five of the seven IAAF Grand Prix meetings in a season and remain undefeated. Originally the jackpot was $1 million (£670,000) but it is currently 110 lb (50 kg) of gold.

OLDEST OLYMPIC ATHLETICS GOLD MEDALIST

The oldest athlete to win an Olympic title was Irish-born Patrick Joseph 'Babe' McDonald (USA) who was age 42 years 26 days when he won the 56-lb (25.4-kg) weight throw at Antwerp, Belgium, on Aug 21 1920.

The oldest female champion was Lia Manoliu (Romania) who was age 36 years 176 days when she won the discus event at the Mexico City Olympics on Oct 18 1968, with a throw of 191 ft 6 in (58.28 m).

YOUNGEST OLYMPIC ATHLETICS GOLD MEDALIST

The youngest Olympic athletics gold medalist was Barbara Pearl Jones (USA) who, at 15 years 123 days, was part of the 4 x 100-m relay team that won the gold at Helsinki, Finland, on July 27 1952.

The youngest male champion was Robert Bruce Mathias (USA) who

was age 17 years 263 days when he won the decathlon at the Olympic Games held in London between Aug 5 and 6 1948.

OLDEST SPORTING WORLD-RECORD BREAKER

The oldest person to set an official world record in sports was Gerhard Weidner (Germany), who set a 20-mile walk record of 2 hr 30 min 38.6 sec on May 25 1974, age 41 years 71 days.

YOUNGEST ATHLETICS WORLD-RECORD HOLDER

The youngest male to set an official world record is Thomas Ray (UK), who was 17 years 198 days when he set a pole-vault record of 11 ft 2.75 in (3.42 m) on Sept 19 1879.

The youngest female athletics record breaker is Wang Yan (China) who set a women's 5,000-m walk record of 21 min 33.8 sec when age 14 years 334 days on March 9 1986.

MOST INDOOR ATHLETICS WORLD CHAMPIONSHIP GOLD MEDALS

Iván Pedroso (Cuba) holds the record for the most individual titles with five, won in the long jump in 1993, 1995, 1997, 1999, and 2001.

The most individual golds by a woman is four by Stefka Kostadinova (Bulgaria) in the high jump in 1985, 1987, 1989, 1993; and Gabriela Szabo (Romania) for the 3,000 m in 1995, 1997, 1999 and the 1,500 m in 1999.

MOST ATHLETICS WORLD CHAMPIONSHIP GOLD MEDALS

The World Championships were inaugurated in 1983 in Helsinki, Finland. The most golds won to date is nine by Michael Johnson (USA), who won the 200 m in 1991 and 1995, the 400 m in 1993, 1995, 1997, and 1999, and the 4 x 400-m relay in 1993, 1995, and 1999.

The most World Championship gold medals won by a woman is five, by Gail Devers (USA). She won the 100 m in 1993, the 100-m hurdle in 1993, 1995, and 1999, and the 4 x 100-m relay in 1997.

MOST CROSS-COUNTRY RUNNING WORLD CHAMPIONSHIPS

The individual women's World Championship Cross-country race has been won five times by Grete Waitz (Norway), in 1978–81 and 1983.

The greatest number of men's individual victories is five by John Ngugi (Kenya) in 1986–89 and 1992; and Paul Tergat (Kenya) in 1995–99.

The greatest number of team victories in the World Cross-country Championships (first held in 1973) is 15 by Kenya, between 1986 and 2000.

The record for team victories in the World Cross-country Championships is held by the USSR, who won a record eight women's team victories in 1976–77, 1980–82, and 1988–90.

LONGEST-EVER RUNNING RACE

The longest race ever staged was the 1929 3,635-mile (5,850-km) transcontinental race from New York City to Los Angeles, California. Johnny Salo (Finland) won in 79 days, running from March 31 to June 17 1929. His time of 525 hr 57 min 20 sec (averaging 6.91 mph or 11.12 km/h) left him only 2 min 47 sec ahead of Pietro Gavuzzi (UK).

LONGEST ANNUAL RUNNING RACE

The longest race staged annually is the Sri Chinmoy 4,989-km (3,100-mile) race, held on a 400-m track in Jamaica, New York. The fastest time to complete the race is

IN THE LONG RUN

The fastest time for a men's half-marathon (13 miles 192.5 yd or 21.097 km) is 59 min 5 sec by Paul Tergat (Kenya, left). This record was set in Lisbon, Portugal, on March 26 2000.

The women's official half marathon record is 66 min 43 sec by Masako Chika (Japan) in Tokyo, Japan, set on April 19 1997.

Paul Tergat also holds the record for the most individual wins in the men's IAAF Half Marathon World Championships. He won in 1999 and 2000.

Tegla Loroupe (Kenya), holds the record for wins in the same event for women. She won in 1997, 1998, and 1999.

The most wins by a team at the same event is six by the Kenyan men's team in 1992–95, 1997, and 2000, and the Romanian women's team 1993–97 and 2000.

GREENE FLASH

Sprinter Maurice 'The Phenomenon' Greene (USA, right) always shaves his head before big races. He currently holds the world records for the indoor 50-m and 60-m sprints and the men's 100 m. He won the gold medal in the 4 x 100-m relay as part of the USA relay squad at the 2000 Sydney Olympics.

ACCESS CODE

<51642> ←

46 days 17 hr 2 min 6 sec by Istvan Sipos (Hungary) who ran from June 13 to July 28 1998, taking breaks at his own discretion.

OLDEST MARATHON

With a continuous 104-year history, the Boston Marathon is officially the oldest. The first Boston Marathon took place on April 19 1897, inspired by the Olympic Marathon the previous year.

GOING FOR GOLD

The most medals won in the biennial World Championships by a woman is 14 by Merlene Ottey (Jamaica, above) who won three gold (4 x 100-m 1991; 200 m 1993 and 1995); three silver (100 m 1993 and 1995, 4 x 100-m 1995), and eight bronze (100 m 1987–1991; 200 m 1987,1991, 1997; 4 x 100-m 1983, 1993).

The most World Championship medals won by a man is 10 by Carl Lewis (USA). He won eight gold (100 m, long jump, and 4 x 100-m 1983; 100 m, long jump, and 4 x 100-m 1987; 100 m and 4 x 100-m 1991); one silver (long jump in 1991); and one bronze (200 m in 1993).

ACCESS CODE

<45730> ←

MOST MARATHON FINISHERS

The record number of confirmed finishers in a marathon is 38,706 at the centennial Boston Marathon on April 15 1996.

FASTEST 100 X ONE-MILE RELAY RACE

The men's record for 100 miles by 100 runners is 7 hr 35 min 55.4 sec by the Canadian Milers Athletic Club at York University, Toronto, Ontario, Canada, on Dec 20 1998.

The women's record is 9 hr 38 min 39.14 sec by the Anderson College Athletics Club of San Francisco at Foothill College, Los Altos Hills, California, on June 15 1997.

MOST PARTICIPANTS IN A RELAY RACE

The most participants in a relay race is 7,175, (287 teams of 25), for the 175-km *Batavierenrace* run from Nijmegen to Enschede, Netherlands, which was run on April 24 1999. This annual race starts at midnight and takes about 18 hours to complete with each runner carrying a microchip to register each completed section.

FASTEST TRANSAMERICA RUN

The fastest time recorded for the transAmerica (San Francisco to New York) run is 46 days 8 hr 36 min by Frank Giannino Jr. (USA) who ran the 3,100 miles (4,989 km) from Sept 1 to Oct 17 1980.

The women's transAmerica record is 69 days 2 hr 40 min by Mavis Hutchinson (South Africa) who ran from March 12 to May 21 1978.

GUINNESS WORLD RECORDS™

olympics

LONGEST SPAN AS MALE OLYMPIC COMPETITOR

The longest span of an Olympic competitor is 40 years. Ivan Joseph Martin Osiier (Denmark) competed in fencing (1908–32 and 1948); Magnus Andreas Thulstrup Clasen Konow (Norway) in yachting (1908–20, 1928, and 1936–48); Paul Elvstrom (Denmark) in yachting (1948–60, 1968–72, and 1984–88); and Durward Randolph Knowles (UK 1948, then Bahamas) in yachting (1948–72 and 1988).

LONGEST SPAN AS FEMALE OLYMPIC COMPETITOR

The longest span as an Olympic competitor for women is 28 years and both record holders competed in dressage. Anne Jessica Ransehousen (née Newberry, USA) competed in 1960, 1964, and 1988 and Christilot Hanson-Boylen (Canada) in 1964–76, 1984, and 1992.

MOST CONSECUTIVE OLYMPIC TEAM GOLD MEDALS WON

The most successive gold medal wins in Olympic history is six by Aladár Gerevich (Hungary), who was a member of the winning saber team from 1932–60.

BIGGER AND BETTER DOWN UNDER

The very successful Summer Olympic Games held from Sept 15 to Oct 1 2000 in Sydney, NSW, Australia, had a record number of participants. The Games (opening ceremony, left) were attended by 11,084 athletes, of which 4,245 were women.

The 2000 Sydney Games also holds the record for the most countries participating in the Summer Olympics. A total of 199 countries took part. The Sydney Games also saw the most medal-winning countries at an Olympic Games, with 80 countries winning at least one medal.

<44741>
← ACCESS CODE www.guinnessworldrecords.com/sydney2000

MOST CONSECUTIVE OLYMPIC INDIVIDUAL GOLD MEDALS WON

The only Olympians to win four consecutive individual titles in the same event are Al Oerter (USA) for discus 1956–68, and Carl Lewis (USA) for long jump 1984–96. However, Raymond Clarence Ewry (USA) won both the standing long jump and the standing high jump at four games in succession in 1900, 1904, 1906, and 1908. (This is if the Intercalated Games of 1906, which were staged officially by the International Olympic Committee, are included).

Paul Elvstrom (Denmark) also won four successive gold medals at monotype yachting events between 1948 and 1960, although there was a class change (1948 Firefly class, 1952–60 Finn class).

MOST CONSECUTIVE GOLD MEDALS WON BY A WOMAN

The most consecutive Olympic gold medals won by a woman is four by Birgit Fischer (née Schmidt, Germany) for canoeing. She first competed at the Olympic Games held in South Korea in 1988, and also participated at the Sydney Olympics in 2000.

MOST MEDALS WON AT THE SUMMER GAMES

The USA has won more medals than any other country in the history of the Summer Olympic Games, 1896–2000. A total of 2,112 medals have been won during this time. Of these, a record 872 were gold.

The USA is the country that has won the most gold medals at a single Games. They won 83 gold

medals at the XXIIIrd Olympic Games held in Los Angeles, California, in 1984.

The USA also holds the record for the most medals won at a single Games. They were awarded 242 medals at the IIIrd Olympic Games, held at St. Louis, Missouri, in 1904.

MOST MEDALS WON AT THE WINTER GAMES

Norway has won a record total of 239 medals in the history of the Winter Olympic Games, 1924–98.

The most medals won by a country at a single Winter Olympic Games is 29 by the Soviet Union (USSR) at the XVth Winter Games at Calgary, Alberta, Canada, in 1988. This total was equaled by Germany at the XVIIIth Winter Games held at Nagano, Japan, in 1998.

The Soviet Union (USSR) has won the most gold medals at the Winter Olympic Games, with 87. They also won a record 13 gold medals at a

ERIC THE EEL

Eric Moussambani (Equatorial Guinea, left) clocked the slowest-ever recorded time in Olympic history for the 100-m freestyle, with a time of 1 min 52.72 sec at the Sydney Games on Sept 19 2000. Remarkably he won his heat, the two other participants in the heat having been disqualified for false starts. Eric, who acquired the nickname 'Eric the Eel' for his unique swimming style, had never seen an Olympic-size (50-m) pool before and had only learned to swim nine months previously. Training for the Games had been done in Equatorial Guinea's unique 20-m pool and in local rivers. Sadly his time was outside the qualifying time and he was eliminated from the competition. His time was over seven seconds slower than the gold-winning time for the men's 200-m freestyle.

single Winter Games, the XIIth Winter Olympiad held at Innsbruck, Austria, in 1976.

MOST MEDALS WON AT THE PARALYMPICS

Since the first Summer Paralympics, held in 1960 in Rome, Italy, the most medals won by a country is 1,938 by the USA. This includes a record 693 gold medals.

Since the first Winter Paralympics, held in 1976 at Örnsköldsvik, Sweden, Austria has won the most medals with a total of 250. The country that has won the most gold medals at the Winter Paralympic Games is Norway, with a total of 97.

MOST PARTICIPANTS AT A PARALYMPIC GAMES

The Paralympic Games held in 2000 in Sydney, NSW, Australia, saw more athletes than any other Paralympics, with a total of 3,824. The participants came from a record 125 countries.

www.guinnessworldrecords.com/redgrave

ACCESS CODE

‹55805› ←

ROW, ROW, ROW YOUR BOAT

The most consecutive Olympic gold medals ever won in an endurance event is five by Steve Redgrave (UK). Redgrave (below, center) won a gold medal in rowing at five consecutive Olympic Games, from 1984 to 2000. He has also won a record nine World Championships. These were for coxed pair in 1986, coxless pair in 1987, 1991, 1993–95, and coxless four in 1997–99.

Redgrave took up rowing at school in Marlow, Bucks, UK, after having proved himself talented at all other sports. He left school age 16 and devoted himself to training, but liked to unwind with a game of golf at his local club. In 1989 he took up bobsledding and was a member of the crew that won the British four-man Championship that year. Steve Redgrave was knighted for services to rowing on May 1 2001.

MOST OLYMPIC MEDALS WON BY A MAN

The most Olympic medals won by a man is 15 medals by the gymnast Nikolay Andrianov (USSR). In 1972–1980, between the ages of 19 and 27, he won seven gold, five silver, and three bronze medals.

MOST OLYMPIC MEDALS WON BY A WOMAN

The most Olympic medals won by a woman is 18 by gymnast Larisa Semyonovna Latynina (USSR). In 1956–64, between the ages of 21 and 29, she won nine gold, five silver, and four bronze medals.

GUINNESS WORLD RECORDS™

auto sports

MOST MAJOR NASCAR RACE WINS

Of the four major races in the NASCAR (National Association for Stock Car Auto Racing) series – the Daytona 500, Winston 500, Southern 500, and Coca Cola 600 – three US drivers share the record for winning three races in one season – Dave Pearson (1976), Bill Elliott (1985), and Jeff Gordon (1997). In 1969, Lee Roy Yarbrough (USA) won all three of the races contested that year – the Winston 500 was run for the first time in 1970.

FAST MOVER

Alain Prost (France, above) holds the record for the most Grand Prix points in a Formula 1 driving career, with 798.5 points from 199 races, between 1980 and 1993.

He also holds the record for the most Grand Prix victories by a driver. He won 51 out of a total of 199 races between 1980 and 1993. He has appeared a record number of times on the podium, stepping up 106 times to claim a first, second, or third place. Not surprisingly, as the world's greatest Formula 1 driver, his nickname is 'Professor of the Track.'

He retired from competitive racing in 1992 and since then has continued working in Formula 1, first as PR advisor for Renault and then as an advisor for McLaren. In 1997 he bought the Ligier team, renaming it Prost in 1998.

www.guinnessworldrecords.com/prost

ACCESS CODE
‹44854› ←

MOST NASCAR RACE VICTORIES

Richard Petty (USA) has achieved the most victories in a NASCAR career, winning 200 out of a possible 1,184 races, between 1958 and 1992.

MOST NASCAR TITLES

The most titles won in the annual NASCAR Championship is seven; by Richard Petty (USA), in 1964, 1967, 1971–72, 1974–75, and 1979 and Dale Earnhardt (USA), in 1980, 1986–87, 1990–91, and 1993–94.

MOST NASCAR POLE POSITIONS IN CAREER

The greatest number of pole positions (starting the race from the front after qualifying as the fastest driver) achieved in a NASCAR career is 126 by Richard Petty (USA), from 1958 to 1992.

MOST COCA COLA 600 RACE VICTORIES

Darrell Waltrip (USA) has achieved the greatest number of wins of the Coca Cola 600 – the longest race in the NASCAR series – winning five in 1979–80, 1985, and 1988–89.

MOST DAYTONA 500 RACE VICTORIES

The most wins of the Daytona 500 – the richest race in the NASCAR series with a prize of $10 million (£6.9 million) – is seven by Richard Petty (USA), in 1964, 1966, 1971, 1973–74, 1979, and 1981.

MOST SOUTHERN 500 RACE VICTORIES

The greatest number of wins of the Southern 500 – the oldest race in the NASCAR series, first run in 1950 – is five by Cale Yarborough (USA), in 1968, 1973–74, 1978, and 1982.

MOST WINSTON 500 RACE VICTORIES

Dale Earnhardt (USA) has achieved the greatest number of wins at the Winston 500 – the fastest race in the NASCAR series – with four victories, in 1990, 1994, 1999, and 2000.

GET RICH QUICK

The highest earnings in a NASCAR career is $41,445,551 (€29,011,885) by Dale Earnhardt (USA, above), between 1975 and 2001. Tragically, Dale was killed during the 2001 Daytona 500 race on Feb 18 2001. His son, Dale Jr., is following in his father's tire tracks, as Dale followed in his father Ralph's, so the Earnhardt name continues in NASCAR racing.

Al Unser Jr. (USA) holds the record for the highest earnings purely from winning races in the CART (Championship Auto Racing Teams) Championship. He had won $18,828,406 (£13,179,884) to the end of the 2000 season.

www.guinnessworldrecords.com/earnhardt
‹56448› ← **ACCESS CODE**

MOST CART CHAMPIONSHIP TITLES

The greatest number of wins in the CART (Championship Auto Racing Teams) National Championship is seven by A.J. Foyt (USA), in 1960–61, 1963–64, 1967, 1975, and 1979.

MOST POLE POSITIONS IN CART RACES

The greatest number of pole positions achieved in a CART racing career is 67 by Mario Andretti (USA) between 1965 and 1994.

MOST WORLD RALLY CHAMPIONSHIP RACE WINS IN A SEASON

The most World Rally Championship race wins in a season is six by Didier Auriol (France), in 1992. He took up rallying in 1979, following in the footsteps of his elder brother.

MOST WORLD RALLYING CHAMPIONSHIP TITLES

The most World rallying title wins is four, shared by Juha Kankkunen 1986–87, 1991, and 1993 and Tommi Makinen (both Finland) 1996–99.

YOUNGEST WORLD RALLY CHAMPION

The youngest World Rally champion is Colin McRae (UK), who was age 27 years 89 days when he won the title in 1995.

YOUNGEST FORMULA 1 GRAND PRIX WINNER

The youngest Formula 1 champion is Bruce McLaren (New Zealand), who won the US Grand Prix at Sebring, Florida, on Dec 12 1959, age just 22 years 104 days.

OLDEST FORMULA 1 WORLD CHAMPION

Juan Manuel Fangio (Argentina) won his last World Championship for the Mercedes-Benz team on Aug 4 1957, age 46 years 41 days, the oldest-ever Formula 1 champion.

YOUNGEST FORMULA 1 WORLD CHAMPION

The youngest-ever Formula 1 world champion was Emerson Fittipaldi (Brazil), who won his first World Championship on Sept 10 1972, age 25 years 273 days.

MOST GRAND PRIX FORMULA 1 WINS BY A MANUFACTURER

The greatest number of Grand Prix race wins by a manufacturer is 139 by Ferrari (Italy), out of a total number of 656 races. Ferrari won all seven races in 1952 and the first eight (of nine) in 1953 – an unbroken record for a manufacturer.

MOST WINS BY A MANUFACTURER IN A FORMULA 1 SEASON

In 1998 McLaren (UK) achieved the most wins by a manufacturer in a season, with 15 out of a possible 16 Grand Prix victories. Ayrton Senna (Brazil) took eight wins and Alain Prost (France) seven. The McLarens, powered by Honda engines, amassed over three times the points of their nearest rival, Ferrari.

FASTEST SPEED FOR A FUNNY CAR DRAG RACER

All drag races are run over 440 yd (402 m). John Force (USA) reached a top speed of 324 mph (521.50 km/h) from a 440-yd standing start in a '99 Ford Mustang at Gainesville, Florida, on March 21 1999.

FASTEST TIME FOR A FUNNY CAR DRAG RACER

The fastest time to cover 440 yd in a funny car is 4.788 sec by John Force (USA), driving a '99 Ford Mustang, at Houston, Texas, on April 11 1999.

FASTEST SPEED FOR A PRO STOCK MOTORBIKE

The top speed for a gasoline-driven piston-engined (Pro Stock) motorcycle is 191.45 mph (308.15 km/h) by Matt Hines (USA) on a '95 Suzuki GSX-R on 31 Oct 1999.

FASTEST TIME FOR PRO STOCK MOTORBIKE

On May 19 2000 Matt Hines (USA) covered 440 yd on a Pro Stock motorbike in a record time of 7.138 seconds on a '95 Suzuki GSX-R, at Englishtown, New Jersey.

TOP SPEED FOR A NHRA DRAG RACER

The highest speed reached by a NHRA (National Hot Rod Association) drag racer over 440 yd is an amazing 326.92 mph (526.11 km/h) by Tony Schumacher (USA) on Oct 22 1999.

FASTEST TIME FOR A TOP-FUEL DRAGSTER

The fastest time to cover 440 yd in a top-fuel dragster is 4.48 seconds by Gary Scelzi (USA), at Houston, Texas, on Oct 31 1999.

www.guinnessworldrecords.com/formula1

WINNING FORMULA

The most Grand Prix victories in a year is nine by Michael Schumacher (Germany, right) in 1995 and 2000 and Nigel Mansell (UK) in 1992.

Mansell quit Formula 1 to race Indy cars in 1993, becoming the first rookie to win the IndyCar title.

Schumacher's career began at the age of four when he discovered go-carting. He was runner-up in the Junior World Championships at the age of 16, and two years later he became European champion. After 15 years of go-cart racing, he switched to racing cars, and in 1990 became the Mercedes-Benz team driver in the Sports Car World Championship and the German Formula 3 champion. In 1991, at the Belgian Grand Prix, he made his debut as a driver for the Formula 1 Jordan team and his F1 career was born.

GUINNESS WORLD RECORDS™

bike sports

MOST TOUR OF ITALY WINS

The greatest number of *Giro d'Italia* (Tour of Italy) wins is five and is shared by Alfredo Binda (Italy) in 1925, 1927–29, and 1933; Fausto Coppi (Italy) in 1940, 1947, 1949, and 1952–53; and Eddy Merckx (Belgium) in 1968, 1970, and 1972–74.

MOST TOUR OF SPAIN WINS

The most wins in the *Vuelta a España* (Tour of Spain) cycling race is three, by Tony Rominger (Switzerland), from 1992 to 1994.

GREATEST DISTANCE CYCLED IN 24 HOURS

The 24-hr record behind pace is 1,216.8 miles (1,958.2 km) by Michael Secrest (USA) at Phoenix International Raceway, Arizona, on April 26 and 27 1990.

MOST WORLD CHAMPIONSHIP TITLES WON BY A WOMAN

Jeannie Longo (France) won 12 World Championship titles from her first in 1985 to her last in 1997. During this time, she won five road race titles, the only woman ever to do so, with four coming in consecutive years from 1985 to 1989. The remainder of her titles came in the time trial, points, and pursuit events.

LARGEST CYCLING EVENT

The most participants in a cycling event is 48,615 for Udine Pedala 2000, organized by Rolo Banca 1473 at Udine, near the Slovenian border, Italy, on June 11 2000. The cyclists completed a circuit measuring 18.2 miles (29.3 km) around Udine.

FASTEST TRANSAMERICA CROSSING BY A TWO-MAN CYCLE TEAM

The fastest transAmerica crossing by a two-man cycle team was 7 days, 9 hr, and 56 min by Ricardo S. Arap and Alexandre Ribeiro (both Brazil) from July 22 to 30 1998. They traveled 3,000 miles (4,828 km) at an average speed of 17.8 mph (28.6 km/h).

GREATEST DISTANCE CYCLED IN ONE HOUR

The official UCI (Union Cycliste Internationale) one-hour record from an unassisted standing start is 30.722 miles (49.441 km) held by Chris Boardman (UK), in Manchester, England, on Oct 27 2000.

The official UCI one-hour record by a woman from an unassisted standing start is 28.02 miles (45.094 km) by Jeanie Longo (France) in Mexico City, Mexico, on Dec 7 2000. She also won a 1996 Olympic road-race gold medal.

I LIKE TO RIDE MY SUPERBIKE

The record for the most World Superbike Championship titles won is four by Carl Fogarty (UK, above). Known as the Lion King, he made his racing debut in 1983, but did not record his first win until 1985, when he won the Manx 250GP. Racing for Ducati, he won his first World Superbike Championship in 1994, and repeated the feat the following year. He moved from Ducati to Honda in 1996 but only managed a fourth place in the Championship. Fogarty returned to Ducati in 1997, finishing runner-up in that season, before taking the title for two consecutive years again in 1998 and 1999.

<52800>
www.guinnessworldrecords.com/superbike
← ACCESS CODE

MOST PROFESSIONAL WORLD CHAMPIONSHIP TITLES

The most professional World Championship cycling titles won by a man is 10 by Koichi Nakano (Japan), in the professional sprint event between 1977 and 1986.

MOST WORLD CHAMPIONSHIP SPEEDWAY TITLES

Hans Hollen Nielsen (Denmark) has been the most successful rider in World Championship competitions, with eight Team (formerly Pairs), nine team, and four individual World titles, for a record 21 Championship titles in total.

MOST SPEEDWAY WINS

The most individual World Speedway Championship wins is six by Ivan Mauger (New Zealand), in 1968–70, 1972, 1977, and 1979.

MOST APPEARANCES IN SPEEDWAY FINALS

Barry Briggs (New Zealand) appeared a record 18 times in the World Speedway Championship finals between 1954 and 1972. Briggs won four times in 1957, 1958, 1964, and 1966.

MOST WORLD CHAMPIONSHIP POINTS

Barry Briggs (New Zealand) scored a record 201 points in 87 World Championship appearances between 1954 and 1972.

MOST WORLD TRIALS CHAMPIONSHIP TITLES

The record for the most World Trials Championships won is seven, held by Jordi Tarrés (Spain), in 1987, 1989–91, and 1993–95.

LANCE IN FRANCE

The fastest average speed in the Tour de France is 25.026 mph (40.276 km/h) by Lance Armstrong (USA, left) in 1999.

The greatest number of wins in the Tour de France is five, shared by Jacques Anquetil of France (1957 and 1961–64), Eddy Merckx of Belgium (1969–72 and 1974), Bernard Hinault of France (1978–79, 1981–82, and 1985), and Miguel Induráin of Spain (1991–95).

The closest Tour de France race ever was in 1989. After 2,030 miles (3,267 km) and 23 days (July 1–23) of racing, Greg LeMond (USA) completed the Tour in 87 hr 38 min 35 sec, beating Laurent Fignon (France) in Paris by only eight seconds.

<45315>
www.guinnessworldrecords.com/tourdefrance
← ACCESS CODE

MOST SUPERBIKE WINS BY A MANUFACTURER

The record for the most superbike races won by a manufacturer is 161 by Ducati, between 1989 and 1999. Ducati also holds the record for the most World Superbike Championship titles, with eight from 1991 to 1996 and 1998 to 2000.

MOST WORLD PAIRS CHAMPIONSHIP TITLES

The World Pairs Championships have been held unofficially since 1968, and officially since 1970. They were renamed the World Team

www.guinnessworldrecords.com/poleposition

ACCESS CODE

MAGNIFICENT MEN ON THEIR FLYING MACHINES

The world record for the most pole positions achieved in the World Superbike Championship is 25 by Troy Corser (Australia, right), between 1996 and March 2001. In 1996 he won the World Superbike Championship, age 24, the youngest-ever winner of the title. Corser has consistently taken third place ever since.

<52808> ←

Championships in 1994, and have been won a record nine times by Denmark: 1979, 1985–91, 1995.

MOST WORLD MOTORCYCLE CHAMPIONSHIP 125CC TITLES

The most World Motorcycle Championship 125cc titles won is seven by Angel Roldán Nieto (Spain), in 1971, 1972, 1979, and 1981–84.

MOST WORLD CHAMPIONSHIP SIDECAR TITLES

The most World Motorcycle Championship sidecar titles won is

seven by Rolf Biland (Switzerland), in 1978, 1979, 1981, 1983, and 1992–94. Biland was runner-up in the 1980 and 1982 Championships.

MOST MOTORCYCLE CAREER RACE WINS IN A SINGLE CLASS

The record for the most World Motorcycle Championship career wins in a single class is 79, set by Rolf Biland (Switzerland) in the sidecar class.

MOST WORLD MOTORCYCLE CHAMPIONSHIP TITLES

The record for the most World Motorcycle Championship titles is 15, held by Giacomo Agostini (Italy), with seven 350cc titles between 1968 and 1974, and eight 500cc titles from 1966 to 1972 and in 1975.

MOST NATIONAL SIDECAR TITLES

Milcho Georgiev Mladenov (Bulgaria) is the holder of a record-breaking 16 consecutive Bulgarian national titles in motorcycle sidecar class 500cc, between 1981 and 1999.

MOST MOTORCYCLE CAREER RACE WINS

The most World Motorcycle Championship career race wins is 122 (68 at 500cc class and 54 at 350cc class), held by Giacomo Agostini between April 24 1965 and Sept 25 1977.

MOST WORLD MOTORCYCLE CHAMPIONSHIP 250CC TITLES

The most World Motorcycle Championship 250cc titles won is four by Phil Read (UK), in 1964, 1965, 1968, and 1971.

GUINNESS WORLD RECORDS

extreme sports 1

LONGEST RAPPEL

On Nov 2 1993 a team of four Royal Marines (all UK) set a rappelling distance record by rappelling 3,627 ft (1,105.5 m) down the Boulby Potash Mine, Cleveland, UK. They started their descent 25 ft (7.6 m) below ground level, and rappelled deeper to finish at the bottom of the shaft.

GREATEST RAPPELLED DISTANCE DOWN A BUILDING

The record for rappelling down a building is 1,465 ft (446.5 m), by two teams of 12 representing the UK Royal Marines and the Canadian School of Rescue Training. All 24 rappelled to the ground from the Space Deck of the CN Tower, Toronto, Ontario, Canada, on July 1 1992.

LONGEST ROPE SLIDE

The greatest distance covered in a rope slide is 5,730 ft (1,746.5 m), by Lance-Corporal Peter Baldwin (UK) of the Royal Marines and Stu Leggett (Canada) of the Canadian School of Rescue Training. They slid from the summit of Mt. Gibraltar, Alberta, Canada, down to ground level on Aug 31 1994. For some of the descent, they both reached speeds in excess of 100 mph (160 km/h).

ON THE ROPES?

The world's longest Tyrolean traverse (a static rope running over an obstacle such as a canyon or a river) measured 3,128 ft 3 in (953.63 m) and spanned the Elbe River between Belveder and Dolni Zleb, Czech Republic. The traverse was erected by the Czech Speleological Emergency Service, and was crossed by Zdenek Kadlec (Czech Republic, left), who pulled himself along the rope upside down, while attached to a harness, in 59 min 6 sec on July 3 1998. This distance beat the previous record set the year before by their Slovak counterparts.

<44786>
www.guinnessworldrecords.com/tyrolrope
← ACCESS CODE

FASTEST FREE CLIMBER 📺 USA

Dan Osman (USA) climbed the 400-ft (120-m) 'Lover's Leap' rock face at Lake Tahoe, California, in 5 min 52 sec. He achieved this amazing feat without using ropes or harnesses on May 29 1997.

LONGEST ROPE JUMP 📺 USA

Dan Osman (USA) made a 1,000-ft (305-m) rope jump at the 'Leaning Tower' rock formation in Yosemite National Park, California, on Oct 12 1998. Dan's jump involved him free-falling for hundreds of feet until a rope tied to his full-body harness stopped his fall. Tragically, he died less than three weeks after setting this record, while attempting another jump at the same location.

LONGEST CLIMB BY A HUMAN FLY

The record for the longest climb by a 'human fly' was set on May 25 1981, when Daniel Goodwin (USA) climbed 1,454 ft (443.2 m) up the outside of the Sears Tower, Chicago, Illinois. For this death-defying feat, he used only a system of suction cups and metal clips for support.

FASTEST GRASS-SKIER

The grass-skiing speed record is 57.21 mph (92.07 km/h), by Klaus Spinka (Austria) at Waldsassen, Germany, on Sept 24 1989.

HIGHEST LAND YACHT SPEED

The highest land yacht speed recorded is 116.7 mph (187.8 km/h), by Bob Schumacher (USA) on *Iron Duck* at Ivanpah Dry Lake, Prim, Nevada, on March 20 1999. The yacht was designed and built by Bob Dill in Burlington, Vermont.

HIGHEST INDOOR HALF-PIPE JUMP ON IN-LINE SKATES 📺 FR

Taïg Khris (France) made an in-line skate jump of 10 ft 2 in (3.1 m) from a half-pipe on Dec 6 2000.

MOST IN-LINE SKATE BACK FLIPS 📺 USA

Jason Stinsmen (USA) achieved an in-line skate double-back flip using a ramp at Van Nuys Airport, California, on Jan 20 2001.

HIGHEST 'AIR' ON A SKATEBOARD

Danny Way (USA) pulled off a 16-ft 6-in-high (5-m) 'method air' jump from a half-pipe at Brown Field, San Diego, California, on Aug 3 1998. A method air is one of the most straightforward of the aerial tricks: the front hand grabs the heel edge,

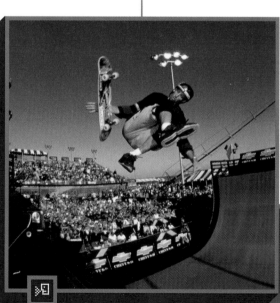

SPIN DOCTOR

Tony Hawk (USA, left) completed the world's first-ever 900-degree spin on a skateboard from a half-pipe during the 1999 X Games, held in San Francisco, California, on June 27 1999. The so-called '900' entails two-and-a-half airborne rotations, and Hawk remains the only person to have achieved it in competition. As a youth, he seemed an unlikely athlete, but his love of skateboarding inspired him to overcome his weak build and he had turned pro by the age of 14. Hawk is one of the few skateboarders to have achieved superstar status and has merchandise and computer games bearing his name. His autobiography, *Hawk: Occupation Skateboarder*, was published in Aug 2000.

ON A ROLL

Skateboarder Josh Tenge (USA, right), performed an amazing record-breaking back flip while on a sandboard on May 20 2000. The flip measured 44 ft 10 in (13.6 m). The record was set at the X-West Huck Fest, Sand Mountain, Nevada. Sandboarding is related to surfing and dates back as far as the 1940s. Sandboards run on laminated thermoplastics (Formica™) and, when waxed, can reach speeds in excess of 50 mph (80 km/h).

ACCESS CODE

‹54689› ←

both knees are bent, and the board is pulled up behind the rider. In the half-pipe, the rider's body can become parallel with the ground.

HIGHEST SKATEBOARD 📺 USA DROP ON TO A QUARTER PIPE

Jason Ellis (Australia) achieved the highest skateboard drop on to a quarter pipe from a height of 28 ft (8.53 m) at Van Nuys Airport, California, on Jan 21 2001.

LONGEST 📺 USA SKATEBOARD JUMP

Brian Patch (USA) jumped a record distance of 56 ft (17.06 m) on his skateboard at Van Nuys Airport, California, on Jan 21 2001.

FASTEST SKATEBOARDER

The highest speed ever recorded by a skateboarder is 78.37 mph (126.12 km/h) by Roger Hickey (USA) on a course near Los Angeles, California, on March 15 1990. He was riding in a prone position.

With an amazing speed of 62.55 mph (100.66 km/h), Gary Hardwick (USA) holds the record for the fastest speed reached in the standing position, which he achieved at Fountain Hills, Arizona, on Sept 26 1998.

FASTEST SANDBOARDERS

Erik Johnson (USA) achieved a record sandboarding speed of 51 mph (82 km/h) during the Sand Master Jam at Dumont Dunes, California, on April 12 1999.

The fastest female sandboarder is Nancy Sutton (USA), who achieved a speed of 44.7 mph (71.94 km/h) at Sand Mountain, Nevada, on Sept 19 1998.

MOST DOWNHILL MOUNTAIN BIKING WORLD CHAMPIONSHIPS

Nicolas Vouilloz (France) holds the record for the most Downhill World Championship wins with seven – three in the Junior Championships from 1992 to 1994 and four in the senior class from 1995 to 1998.

Anne-Caroline Chausson (France) holds the record in the women's event, also with five wins – two in the Junior Championships (1994 and 1995) and three in the senior class (from 1996 to 1998).

HIGHEST MOTOCROSS STEP-UP JUMP

On Aug 18 2000 Tommy Clowers (USA) achieved a record-breaking height of 35 ft (10.67 m) in the X Games Motocross Step-Up event. Essentially a 'high jump' on motorbikes, the sport involves riders trying to clear a bar placed at the top of a steep takeoff ramp. Clowers' feat is the equivalent of jumping on to the roof of a two-story building.

LONGEST POWER- 📺 USA ASSISTED BMX RAMP JUMP

Professional stunt rider Colin Winkelmann (USA) achieved a ramp jump of 116 ft 11 in (35.63 m) on his BMX bicycle at the Agoura Hills, California, on Dec 20 2000. His BMX was towed behind a motorcycle at a speed approaching 60 mph (100 km/h) – to give him the necessary velocity – before being released just before he hit the ramp.

MOST 📺 USA BACKFLIPS FROM A SINGLE SCOOTER JUMP

Jarret Reid (USA) managed a scooter back flip, landing with both feet on the scooter, when traveling from a ramp at a height of 18 ft (5.48 m). The record was achieved at Van Nuys Airport, California on Jan 21 2001.

GUINNESS WORLD RECORDS™

extreme sports 2

MOST HELICOPTER SKYSURFING SPINS ⊡UK

The most helicopter spins in the skysurfing position (spinning upside down with a board attached to the feet) is 64 in 20 seconds by Chris Gauge of St. Agnes, Cornwall, UK, in the skies above the Aerodrome Sierra Morena, Spain, on March 31 1999.

LONGEST DISTANCE BY KITE SURFER

Three surfers from kite manufacturer Flexifoil International crossed the English Channel using kite surfers – custom-made boards with 52.7-ft² (4.9-m²) two-blade traction kites. Chris Calthrop and Andy Preston (both UK) crossed the 23.2 nautical miles (42.9 km) from Hythe, Kent, UK, to Wissant, France, on Sept 17 1999, in 2 hr 30 min, while Jason Furness (UK) completed the record-breaking journey in three hours.

LONGEST PARACHUTE DROP

The longest-ever parachute drop is 40 min by Lt. Col. Wm. H. Rankin (USA), of the US Marine Corps, due to thermal updrafts, on July 26 1956.

FURTHEST FREEFALL DROP ⊡USA

The longest-ever freefall was by Capt. Joseph W. Kittinger, who dropped 84,715 ft (25,820 m) from a balloon at 102,800 ft (31,330 m), at Tularosa, New Mexico, on Aug 16 1960. The maximum speed reached in rarified air was 625 mph (1,006 km/h) at 90,000 ft (27,400 m), which is slightly faster than the speed of sound. He fell for 4 min 37 sec before his parachute was deployed automatically.

MOST PARACHUTE JUMPS IN 24 HOURS

The most descents made in 24 hours (in accordance with United States Parachute Association rules) is 476, by Jay Stokes (USA), at Yuma, Arizona, from Nov 12 to 13 1999. There were medics on hand who quizzed Jay to ensure that he was alert enough to keep jumping.

HIGHEST BASE JUMP

On Aug 26 1992 Nicholas Feteris and Glenn Singleman (both Australia) jumped from a ledge known as the 'Great Trango Tower,' Pakistan, which stands at 19,300 ft (5,880 m).

LONGEST BUNGEE JUMP

On Sept 19 1997 the renowned stuntman and bungee jumper Jochen Schweizer (Germany), jumped from an SA 365 Dauphine helicopter for a total distance of 3,320 ft (1,012 m) above Reichelsheim, Germany. Schweizer leapt from the helicopter

at 8,200 ft (2,500 m), then cut the rope, and went into a freefall, finally parachuting to safety near Frankfurt.

HIGHEST COMMERCIALLY OPERATED BUNGEE JUMP

The highest commercial bungee jump in the world is from the 708-ft-high (216-m) Bloukrans River Bridge, South Africa. Jumpers typically freefall for five seconds before the bungee cord begins to slow their fall. However, the jump usually lasts a further four

seconds, taking the total length jumped to between 525 and 590 ft (160 to 180 m).

LONGEST WATERFALL ⊡USA DESCENT IN A CANOE

The longest descent over a waterfall by canoe is 98.4 ft (30 m) by Tao Berman (USA) at the Upper Johnstone Canyon Falls in Banff National Park, Alberta, Canada, on Aug 23 1999.

LONGEST WATER-SKI JUMP

The International Water Ski Federation record for the longest ski jump is 232.6 ft (70.9 m) by Jimmy Siemers (USA) at the Tri-Lakes Late Bloomer event at Zachary, Louisiana, on Oct 22 2000.

The record for the longest jump by a woman is 172.9 ft (52.7 m) by Toni Neville (Australia) at the US Open event at Sacramento, California, on June 25 2000.

LONGEST BAREFOOT WATER-SKI JUMP

The world record for the longest barefoot water-ski jump is 84.6 ft (25.8 m) by Jon Kretchman (USA) in the USA in Aug 1998.

A MIGHTY FLIGHT IN A MICROLIGHT

Colin Bodill (UK, above) circumnavigated the globe in his Mainair Blade 912 Flexwing microlight aircraft in 99 days from May 31 to Sept 6 2000, starting and landing at Brooklands airfield, Weybridge, Surrey, UK. Colin covered approximately 21,750 miles (35,000 km), passing over 30 countries on his journey. In 1997 he won the gold medal in the microlight category at the first-ever World Air Games held in Turkey.

The highest altitude achieved in a microlight is 31,890 ft (9,720 m) by Serge Zin (France), at Saint Auban, France, on Sept 18 1994.

‹52011› www.guinnessworldrecords.com/microlight ← ACCESS CODE

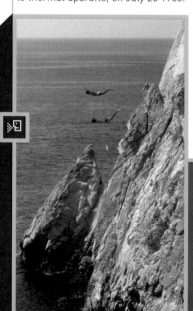

IN AT THE DEEP END

The highest regularly performed headfirst dives are those of professional divers, between 12 and 50 years old, from La Quebrada, Acapulco, Mexico. They have been diving headfirst from a record height of 115 ft (35 m) into a mere 12 ft (3.6 m) of crashing water since 1934. La Quebrada (left) is a rock formation with a large crevice between the two cliffs. It was formed when a cliff top was dynamited and split in two and its name means 'the break in the rocks.' This feat is equivalent to jumping off a 10-story building in a vertical freefall, although the divers must also clear the edge of the cliffs by 27 ft (8.2 m) to avoid jutting base rocks and wait for a wave to fill the channel to deepen the water.

‹48667› www.guinnessworldrecords.com/divers ← ACCESS CODE

www.guinnessworldrecords.com/surf

SURFER DUDES

The women's professional surfing title (instituted 1979) has been won a record four times by Frieda Zamba (USA) in 1984–86 and 1988; Wendy Botha (Australia, formerly South Africa) in 1987, 1989, and 1991–92; and Lisa Andersen (Australia, below) in 1994–97. Andersen pulled out of the 1998 season, citing chronic back troubles, but returned to the professional fray late in 1999, finishing fourth in the 2000 season. Combining prodigious talent with glamor, she is often credited with helping to popularize the sport among women.

The World Professional men's title has been won six times by Kelly Slater (USA), in 1992 and 1994–98, making him the man with the most World titles for surfing.

LONGEST DISTANCE SKI FLYING

The International Water Ski Federation record for ski flying (a more extreme form of water-ski jumping) is 298.9 ft (91.1 m), by Jaret Llewellyn (Canada) at the Big Air Challenge event at Orlando, Florida, on May 14 2000.

The record for ski flying by a woman is 218.5 ft (66.6 m), a distance achieved by both Toni Neville and Emma Sheer (both Australia) at the America's Cup event at West Palm Beach, Florida, in Sept 2000.

MOST WAKEBOARDING INVERTS IN ONE MINUTE

On Aug 30 1999 Julz Heany achieved 15 inverts (somersaults) in one minute on a wakeboard measuring 49 in (125 cm) long, and 15.5 in (39.8 cm) wide. Wakeboarding involves being pulled behind a speed boat, but with both feet attached to a small board, which gives great freedom for performing tricks.

FASTEST WATER-SKIERS

The fastest water-skiing speed recorded is 143.06 mph (230.26 km/h) by Christopher Massey (Australia) on the Hawkesbury River, Windsor, NSW, Australia, on March 6 1983.

Donna Patterson Brice set a women's record of 111.11 mph (178.8 km/h) at Long Beach, California, on Aug 21 1977.

MOST BODYBOARDING CHAMPIONSHIPS

Mike Stewart (USA) has won nine World Championships, eight National tour titles, and 21 Pipeline Bodyboarding Championships.

winter sports 1

FASTEST SNOWBOARD ON A BOBSLED RUN

Reto Lamm (Switzerland) surfed down a bobsled run on his snowboard at a record speed of 49.7 mph (80 km/h) in Nov 1998.

MOST SNOWBOARDING CHAMPIONSHIP TITLES

Karine Ruby (France) has won a record three Championship titles (including Olympic titles). She won the giant slalom in 1996, the Olympic title in 1998, and the snowboard cross (a race between four riders over a downhill course) in 1997.

LONGEST SNOWBOARDING VERTICAL DESCENT

On April 20 1998 Tammy McMinn (USA) snowboarded down a slope at Atlin, British Columbia, Canada, 101 times, making a total vertical descent of 305,539 ft (93,124 m).

MOST US OPEN SNOWBOARDING WINS

The greatest number of half-pipe victories at the US Open has been achieved by Terje Haakonsen (Norway) with three wins in 1992, 1993, and 1995.

FASTEST SNOWBOARDING SPEED

The fastest recorded speed reached by a snowboarder is 125.44 mph (201.907 km/h) by Darren Powell (Australia) at Les Arcs, France, on May 2 1999.

MOST OLYMPIC BIATHLON GOLDS

In the biathlon – shooting and Nordic (cross-country) skiing – the most Olympic individual titles won is two by Magnar Solberg (Norway) in 1968 and 1972; and Frank-Peter Rötsch

<44485>
← ACCESS CODE
www.guinnessworldrecords.com/goldberger

ONE JUMP AHEAD

The longest competitive ski jump by a man is 738 ft (225 m) by Andreas Goldberger (Austria, left) at Planica, Slovenia, on March 18 2000. The day before, his previous world record of a 731-ft (223-m) jump had been broken by 18-year-old Austrian Thomas Hoerl. Goldberger is reported as to have admitted that the wind played in his favor when he regained the title the next day. He has also won the World Cup three times in 1993, 1995, and 1996.

The women's record is 367 ft (112 m) by Eva Ganster (Austria) at Bischofshofen, Austria, on Jan 7 1994. She began skiing competitively when she was 10 years old.

(GDR) in 1988 at 10 km and 20 km. Aleksandr Tikhonov (USSR) won four relay golds at 7.5 km in the biathlon in 1968 and 1980, and a silver for the 20 km in 1968.

Anfissa Restzova (Russia) and Myriam Bédard (Canada) hold the most Olympic titles in the women's biathlon competition. Restzova won gold for the 7.5 km in 1992, and another in the 4 x 7.5 km in 1994; Bédard won gold in the 7.5 km and the 15 km in 1994.

MOST BIATHLON CHAMPIONSHIP TITLES

Frank Ullrich (GDR) has won a record six individual Biathlon World titles, with four victories at 10 km, from 1978 to 1981, including the 1980 Olympics, and two wins at 20 km, between 1982 and 1983.

GREATEST DISTANCE COVERED IN NORDIC SKIING IN 24 HOURS

A Nordic ski is only attached to the point of the toe of a boot, which resembles a running shoe. The furthest distance achieved by a Nordic skier in 24 hours is 258.2 miles (415.5 km), by Seppo-Juhani Savolainen (Finland) between April 8 and 9 1988 at Saariselkä, Finland.

The women's distance record for Nordic skiing in 24 hours is 206.92 miles (333 km), held by Kamila Horakova (Czech Republic) between April 12 and 13 2000 at the Canmore Nordic Centre, Alberta, Canada.

MOST NORDIC SKIING TITLES

Bjørn Dæhlie (Norway) has won the most Nordic skiing titles (including the Olympics) with a total of 17, consisting of 12 individual and five relay wins between 1991 and 1998. Dæhlie won a record 29 medals in total (gold, silver, and bronze) between 1991 and 1999.

The most Nordic skiing titles won by a woman is 17, achieved by Yelena Välbe (Russia). She won 10 individual and seven relay titles between 1989 and 1998. With an additional seven silver and bronze medals, her total of 24 is a record.

X-TREME MEASURES

The Winter X (extreme) Games were launched by ESPN in 1977 and feature ice climbing, snow mountain biking, free-skiing, skiboarding, snowboarding, and snowcross. Shaun Palmer (USA, left) has won a record three gold medals in the Boarder X (a race between four riders over a downhill course) discipline at the Winter ESPN X Games in 1997, 1998, and 1999. Shaun took up snowboarding, age 14, and turned professional three years later. The women's record for the most X Games snowboarding medals is six, by Barrett Christy (USA). Christy took the gold medal in the Big Air (jump tricks off a ramp) event and the silver medal in the Slopestyle (performing tricks on a slope that has rails and other props) discipline at the 1999 Winter X Games.

MOST WORLD CUP RACE WINS

The most World Cup wins for Alpine individual events is 86 (46 giant slalom and 40 slalom, from a total of 287 races) by Ingemar Stenmark (Sweden) between 1974 and 1989, including a men's record of 13 in one season between 1978 and 1979. Ten of these were part of a record 14 successive giant slalom wins from March 18 1978, his 22nd birthday, to Jan 21 1980.

Annemarie Moser (Austria) achieved a women's record for 62 individual event wins from 1970 to 1979. She had a record 11 consecutive downhill wins from Dec 1972 to Jan 1974.

MOST WORLD CUP DOWNHILL WINS

Franz Klammer (Austria) won a record-breaking 25 downhill races between 1974 and 1984.

MOST WORLD CUP FREESTYLE WINS

The most overall titles won by a woman in the World Cup is 10 by Connie Kissling (Switzerland) between 1983 and 1992.

The most men's overall titles in the World Cup is five by Eric Laboureix (France) between 1986 and 1988 and between 1990 and 1991.

MOST FREESTYLE SKIING TITLES

The first Freestyle World Championships were held at Tignes, France, in 1986, with titles being awarded in ballet, moguls, aerials, and combined (a combination of results from the other disciplines). Edgar Grospiron (France) has won a record three titles – moguls in 1989 and 1991, and aerials in 1995. He also won the Olympic freestyle title in 1992.

The most World titles for a woman is also three, achieved by Candice Gilg (France), who won the moguls in 1993, 1995, and 1997.

FASTEST OLYMPIC SKIING SPEED

The fastest average speed in the Olympic downhill race was 66.62 mph (107.24 km/h) by Jean-Luc Cretier (France) at Nagano, Japan, on Feb 13 1998.

FASTEST SKIING SPEED

The fastest speed for a skier is 154.147 mph (248.105 km/h) by Harry Egger (Austria) at Les Arcs, France, on May 2 1999.

The fastest speed by a female skier is 145.71 mph (234.528 km/h) by Karine Dubouchet (France) at Les Arcs, France, on May 2 1999.

MOST NATIONS CUPS WON

The Nations Cup, awarded for the best combined results of men and women taking part in the World Cup, has been won a record-breaking 22 times by Austria in 1969, from 1973 to 1980, in 1982, and from 1990 to 2001.

MOST SKI FLIPS (SOMERSAULTS) IN 10 MINUTES

Tommy Waltner (USA) completed 23 front inverted aerial jumps, within 10 minutes, on April 25 2000. The event took place on Aspen Mountain, Colorado, in order to raise money for Tommy's 'Loops for Lupus' (a disease of the immune system) campaign, which aims to heighten awareness of the condition. He achieved his record at the age of 50.

www.guinnessworldrecords.com/ruby

ACCESS CODE

‹55454› ←

JEWEL IN THE CROWN

Snowboarding became an Olympic sport in 1998 and is part of the Fédération Internationale du Ski. A World Cup series began in 1995, with World Championships inaugurated the following year. Karine Ruby (France, below) has won the greatest number of World Cup Snowboarding titles, with 14 victories consisting of the overall from 1996 to 1998 and 2001, the slalom between 1996 and 1998, the giant slalom from 1995 to 1998 and 2001, and snowboard cross between 1997 and 2001.

The most men's titles won in the World Cup is five by Mathieu Bozzetto (France), made up of the overall from 1999 to 2000 and the slalom/parallel slalom from 1999 to 2001.

winter sports 2

FASTEST LUGEING SPEED

The fastest-ever recorded, photo-timed lugeing speed is 85.36 mph (137.4 km/h) by Asle Strand (Norway) on May 1 1982 at Tandådalens Linbana, Sälen, Sweden.

MOST FOUR-MAN BOBSLED WINS

The World Four-man Bobsled title has been won a record-breaking 20 times by Switzerland, in 1924, 1936, 1939, 1947, 1954–57, 1971–73, 1975, 1982–83, 1986–90, and 1993. These include five Olympic victories, in 1924, 1936, 1956, 1972, and 1988.

MOST TWO-MAN BOBSLED WINS

Switzerland has won the two-man bobsled title a record 17 times – in 1935, 1947–50, 1953, 1955, 1977–80, 1982–83, 1987, 1990, 1992, and 1994. These include four Olympic wins in 1948, 1980, 1992, and 1994.

MOST MEDALS WON IN INDIVIDUAL BOBSLED EVENTS

The greatest number of individual World Bobsled titles won is 11, achieved by Eugenio Monti (Italy) between 1957 and 1968. He did this by winning eight two-man titles as well as three four-man titles, becoming the most successful bobsledder in the history of these two events.

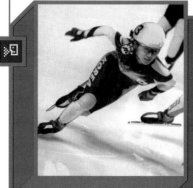

THE FAST LANE

The most victories in the women's Short-track Speed Skating Championships have been achieved by Sylvie Daigle (Canada), in 1983 and between 1988 and 1990; and Yang Yang (China, left), between 1998 and 2001.

In the men's Championships, the holder of the most titles is Marc Gagnon (Canada), from 1993 to 1994, 1996, and 1998.

<44915>
www.guinnessworldrecords.com/daigle
← ACCESS CODE

MOST INDIVIDUAL OLYMPIC BOBSLED MEDALS

Bogdan Musiol (GDR) has won the most individual bobsled medals, with seven accumulated between 1980 and 1992 – one gold, five silver, and one bronze. During his bobsled career, Musiol took part in four Olympic Games and never came home without a medal.

MOST BOBSLED OLYMPIC GOLD MEDALS

The most Olympic gold bobsled medals won by an individual is three and is shared by Meinhard Nehmer (GDR) and Bernhard Germeshausen (GDR) in the 1976 two-man, 1976 and 1980 four-man events. Following his retirement in 1991, Nehmer became the coach of the US bobsled team.

FASTEST CRESTA RUN FROM JUNCTION

The Cresta Run course, at St. Moritz, Switzerland, is a 3,977-ft- long (1,212-m) ice run with a drop of 514 ft

(157 m). It has two start points – at Junction (when the full length cannot be run due to snowfall) and at Top (the whole run). Johannes Badrutt (Switzerland) set a record from Junction (2,921 ft or 890 m) of 41.02 seconds on Jan 17 1999.

FASTEST CRESTA RUN COMPLETION TIME

The fastest-ever recorded time to complete the Cresta Run is 50.09 seconds at an average speed of 54.13 mph (87.11 km/h), achieved by James Sunley (UK) on Feb 13 1999.

Mrs. J.M. Baguley (UK) was the last woman to ride the Cresta in a race on Jan 13 1925. Women were banned from riding on Jan 6 1929 because it was considered too dangerous.

FASTEST 16-ENDER

Curling is played between two teams of four players each. The object is to push a 44-lb (20-kg) stone down a sheet of ice toward a ring of

concentric circles. A team scores a point for each stone that is closest to the center of the rings. A match consists of eight ends, with each player throwing two stones for a total of 16 – hence a 16-ender. Curling teams led by Hammy McMillan (UK) completed the fastest end in 6 min 49.90 sec at the 16-ender National Finals in Stirling, Scotland, UK, on Dec 22 1999.

MOST WORLD CURLING CHAMPIONSHIP TITLES

The most World Curling titles have been won by Canada with a record 26 titles – in 1959–64, 1966, 1968–72, 1980, 1982–83, 1985–87, 1989–90, 1993–96, 1998, and 2000.

Canada's women's team has won 12 titles – in 1980, 1984–87, 1989, 1993–94, 1996–97, and 2000–01.

MOST OLYMPIC GOLD SPEED-SKATING MEDALS

Lidiya Pavlovna Skoblikova (USSR) has won the greatest number of Olympic speed-skating gold medals with six victories – two in 1960 and four in 1964.

The greatest number of Olympic gold speed-skating medals won by a man is five. The record is shared between Clas Thunberg (Finland) who won his medals in the 1924 and 1928 Games; and Eric Arthur Heiden (USA), who won all his gold medals at Lake Placid, New York, in 1980.

MOST OLYMPIC SPEED-SKATING MEDALS

The most Olympic speed-skating medals won by a man is seven. This record is shared by Clas Thunberg (Finland) and Ivar Ballangrud (Norway). Thunberg, in addition to winning a record five golds, won one silver and one tied bronze between 1924 and 1928; and Ballangrud won four golds, two silvers, and a bronze medal between 1928 and 1936.

MOST WORLD CHAMPIONSHIPS SINGLE DISTANCE SPEED SKATING

Gunda Niemann-Stirnemann (Germany) has won the most women's titles at the World Single Distance Championships with

BACKSEAT DRIVER

The most World Championship Lugeing titles won (including the Olympics) is six by Georg Hackl (GDR/Germany, left), in a single-seater, in 1989, 1990, 1992, 1994, 1997, and 1998. Stefan Krausse and Jan Behrendt (both GDR/Germany) have won a record six two-seater titles, in 1989, 1991–93, 1995, and 1998.

The most Olympic gold luge medals won by a woman is two by Steffi Walter (GDR), with victories at the women's single-seater luge event in 1984 and 1988.

The most World Championships in lugeing won by a woman is four, by Margit Schumann (GDR), in 1973–1975 and in 1977. She also won the Olympic gold medal in 1976.

<45550>
www.guinnessworldrecords.com/hackl
← ACCESS CODE

SPEED DEMON

The most World Championship titles won in women's speed skating is eight by Gunda Niemann-Stirnemann (Germany, above), between 1991 and 1993 and from 1995 to 1999. Very popular in her homeland, she is nicknamed the 'Ice Queen' and has won several major sporting awards in Germany, including the German Athlete of the Year in 1995.

The greatest number of men's World Speed-skating titles is five, and is shared by Oscar Mathisen (Norway) from 1908 to 1909 and from 1912 to 1914; and by Clas Thunberg (Finland) in 1923, 1925, 1928–29, and 1931.

www.guinnessworldrecords.com/
niemann-stirnemann

ACCESS CODE

‹44913› ←

11 victories – the 1,500 m (1997), the 3,000 m (1996–1999, 2001), and the 5,000 m (1997–2001).

The most titles won by a man is seven, achieved by Gianni Romme (Netherlands) in the 5,000 m (1998–2000) and 10,000 m (1996–98 and 2000). He was helped to success by an innovative new skate design.

MOST OLYMPIC FIGURE-SKATING MEDALS

The greatest number of Olympic gold figure-skating medals won is three, a record that is shared by Gillis Grafstrom (Sweden) who won in 1920, 1924, and 1928; by Sonja Henie (Norway) – whom Grafstrom trained – at the Winter Olympics of 1928, 1932, and 1936; and by Irina Rodnina (USSR) – who won three pairs figure-skating gold medals with two different partners. In 1972 she won the gold medal skating with Alexei Ulanov

(USSR), and in 1976 and 1980 she won gold skating with Alexandr Zaitsev (USSR). Following retirement from the sport in 1980, Rodnina now coaches in California, and has trained the 1995 World Figure Skating champions.

GREATEST DISTANCE SKATED IN 24 HOURS

Martinus Kuiper (Netherlands) skated a record-breaking distance of 339.68 miles (546.65 km) in 24 hours at Alkmaar, Netherlands, between Dec 12 and 13 1988.

MOST CONTINUOUS SPINS ON ICE

The greatest number of continuous spins made on one foot on ice is 60 rotations achieved by Neil Wilson (UK) at the Spectrum Centre, Guildford, Surrey, UK, on July 1 1997.

MOST X GAMES ICE-CLIMBING MEDALS

Kim Csizmazia (USA) has won a record three X Games gold medals for ice climbing – the difficulty medal in 1998 and 1999, and the speed medal in 1998.

www.guinnessworldrecords.com/coomber

NO BONES ABOUT IT

Alex Coomber (UK, right) holds the most skeleton sled titles with two World Cups and one World Championship. The skeleton sled will be contested at the Winter Olympic Games, at Salt Lake City, Utah, in Feb 2002 after an absence of 54 years. For the first time there will be a women's competition with current women's World Cup champion Alex Coomber a favorite for success.

Coomber successfully defended her World Cup title during the 2000/01 season. She could not,

however, retain her World Championship title success of 2000, losing to Maya Pedersen (Switzerland) by just 7/100 seconds at the 2001 Championships.

The sport of skeleton sledding originated at the Swiss resort of St. Moritz in the 1800s and is noted for its headfirst style of riding. The sport got its name from the early metal toboggans that were used. People commented that they looked like skeletons.

ACCESS CODE

‹56666› ←

GUINNESS WORLD RECORDS

water sports

BOLD GOLD

Krisztina Egerszegi (Hungary, above) has won more Olympic gold medals for individual swimming than any other person. She won a record five gold medals, for 100-m backstroke (1992), 200-m backstroke (1988, 1992, and 1996), and 400-m medley (1992). In 1988, when she was only 14 years old, she won silver and gold medals at the Seoul Olympic Games.

The most individual Olympic gold medals awarded to a man for swimming are four. This record is jointly held by Charles Meldrum Daniels (USA) for 220-yd freestyle (1904), 440-yd freestyle (1904), 100-m freestyle (1906, 1908); Roland Matthes (GDR) for 100-m backstroke (1968, 1972) and 200-m backstroke (1968, 1972); Mark Spitz (USA) for 100-m and 200-m freestyle, and 100-m and 200-m butterfly (all 1972); Tamás Daryni (Hungary) for 200-m medley (1988, 1992) and 400-m medley (1988, 1992); and Aleksandr Popov (Russia) for 50-m freestyle (1992, 1996) and 100-m freestyle (1992, 1996).

<44333> www.guinnessworldrecords.com/egerszegi

← ACCESS CODE

MOST CONSECUTIVE OLYMPIC GOLD MEDALS FOR SWIMMING

Only two swimmers have won the same event on three occasions. Dawn Fraser (Australia) won the 100-m freestyle in 1956, 1960, and 1964, and Krisztina Egerszegi (Hungary) won the 200-m backstroke in 1988, 1992, and 1996.

MOST GOLD MEDALS FOR SWIMMING AT ONE OLYMPIC GAMES BY A WOMAN

Kristin Otto (GDR) won six golds for swimming. They were for the 50-m freestyle, the 100-m freestyle, the 100-m backstroke, the 100-m butterfly, the 4 x 100-m freestyle, and the 4 x 100-m medley in 1988.

MOST OLYMPIC GOLD MEDALS FOR SWIMMING BY A MAN

Mark Spitz (USA) won a total of nine Olympic gold medals. They were for 100-m and 200-m freestyle (1972), 100-m and 200-m butterfly (1972), 4 x 100-m freestyle (1968 and 1972), 4 x 200-m freestyle (1968 and 1972), and 4 x 100-m medley (1972). All but one of these performances (the 4 x 200-m freestyle of 1968) were new world records. He also won a silver (100-m butterfly) and a bronze (100-m freestyle) in 1968, for a record of 11 medals in total.

Spitz's record seven medals at one Games in 1972 was equaled by Matt Biondi (USA) who took five gold, one silver, and one bronze in 1988. Biondi has also won a record 11 medals in total, winning a gold in 1984 and two golds and a silver in 1992.

MOST OLYMPIC MEDALS FOR SWIMMING BY A WOMAN

The most medals won by a woman is eight. Dawn Fraser (Australia) won four golds and four silvers (1956–64); Kornelia Ender (GDR) won four golds and four silvers (1972–76); and Shirley Babashoff (USA) won two golds and six silvers (1972–76).

MOST OLYMPIC GOLD MEDALS FOR CANOEING BY A MAN

Gert Fredriksson (Sweden) won a record six Olympic gold medals from 1948 to 1960. He added a silver and a bronze for a record eight medals.

MOST OLYMPIC GOLD MEDALS FOR CANOEING BY A WOMAN

The most golds won by a woman is seven by Birgit Fischer (née Schmidt, GDR/Germany) between 1980 and 2000. She has also won three silvers for a record total of 10 medals.

MOST WORLD AND OLYMPIC TITLES FOR CANOEING BY A MAN

The record of 13 World and Olympic titles is jointly held by Gert Fredriksson (Sweden, 1948–60), Rüdiger Helm (GDR, 1976–83), and Ivan Patzaichin (Romania, 1968–84).

MOST WORLD AND OLYMPIC TITLES FOR CANOEING BY A WOMAN

In addition to her five Olympic titles, Birgit Fischer (née Schmidt) has won 29 World titles between 1979 and 1998, to make a record 34 titles overall.

LONGEST CANOE JOURNEY WITH PORTAGES

Verlen Kruger and Steven Landick (both USA) traveled a distance of 28,043 miles (45,129 km), starting from Red Rock, Montana, and finishing at Lansing, Michigan, from April 29 1980 to Dec 15 1983. They traveled via the Missouri, Great Lakes, Atlantic Coast, Gulf of Mexico, Mississippi, through Canada and Alaska, down the Pacific Coast to the Gulf of California, up the Colorado River, and back to Michigan. All portages (carrying the canoe) were human powered.

LONGEST CANOE JOURNEY WITHOUT PORTAGES

Without portages or aid of any kind, the longest canoe journey is 6,102 miles (9,820 km) by Richard H. Grant (USA) and Ernest Moose Lassy (USA). They circumnavigated the eastern USA via Chicago, New Orleans, Miami, New York, and the Great Lakes between Sept 22 1930 and Aug 15 1931.

HIGHEST CANOE SPEED OVER 200 M

At the 1998 World Championships held in Szeged, Hungary, the Hungarian four won the 200-m title in a time of 31.155 sec. This represents an average speed of 14.36 mph (23.11 km/h).

HIGHEST CANOE SPEED OVER 1,000 M

The German four-man kayak Olympic champions covered 1,000 m in 2:51.52 to win gold in Atlanta, Georgia, on Aug 3 1996. This represents an average speed of 13.04 mph (20.98 km/h).

MOST OLYMPIC GOLD MEDALS FOR YACHTING

The first sportsman ever to win individual gold medals for yachting in four successive Olympic Games was Paul B. Elvstrom (Denmark) in the firefly class in 1948 and the finn class in 1952, 1956, and 1960. He also won eight other World titles in a total of six classes.

LONGEST SOLO NONSTOP YACHTING RACE

The world's longest nonstop solo sailing race is the Vendée Globe Challenge, which starts and finishes at Les Sables d'Olonne, France. The first one took place on Nov 26 1989. The distance currently sailed without stopping is 22,500 nautical miles (25,881 miles or 41,652 km). The race is for single-handed yachts, between 50 and 60 ft long.

MAKING WAVES

The world record for the women's long-course 4 x 100-m freestyle relay is 3:36.61, by the US Olympic team, consisting of Amy van Dyken, Dara Torres, Courtney Shealy, and Jenny Thompson (left; from left to right). The time was set at the Olympic Games in Sydney, NSW, Australia, on Sept 16 2000. The US team broke the world record that had stood for six years. Jenny Thompson, who swam the fastest leg, has been a member of the winning relay team at the last three Olympic Games, equaling the record achievement of fellow American Matt Biondi.

‹52934› ← ACCESS CODE

www.guinnessworldrecords.com/usswimteam

www.guinnessworldrecords.com/ianthorpe

IAN THORPEDO

The fastest time set in the men's 400-m freestyle race is 3:40.59 by Ian Thorpe (Australia, below) at the Olympic Games in Sydney, NSW, Australia, on Sept 16 2000. Since March 2001 he also holds the world records for 200-m freestyle (1:44:69) and 800-m freestyle (7:41:59). He is regarded as one of the greatest swimmers the world has ever seen.

ACCESS CODE

‹52321› ←

BIGGEST RIVER-BORE RIDES

The longest recorded rides on a river bore have been set on the Severn bore, UK. The official British Surfing Association record for riding a surfboard is 5.7 miles (9.1 km) by David Lawson (UK), from Windmill Hill to Maisemore Weir, on Aug 29 1996.

MOST WORLD TITLES FOR WINDSURFING

World Championships were first held in 1973 and windsurfing (also known as sailboarding) was added to the Olympic Games in 1984. The winner was Stephan van den Berg (Netherlands), who also won five World titles between 1979 and 1983.

MOST SOUTHERLY ESKIMO ROLL

On Feb 3 1998 Christopher Patalano (UK) performed an eskimo roll (rotating through 360°) in icy waters at 77° 04.8'S. Sea temperatures in the area are normally little more than just above 32°F (0°C).

FURTHEST WHITEWATER SWIM

On June 5 1999 Thom Stanton (USA) swam up the James River in Virginia, from Mayo Island to Bosher's Dam, a distance of 7.5 miles (12.07 km). Armed only with flippers and web-fingered gloves, Stanton swam, dragged, and clawed his way up the Class II–IV+ rapids of the Falls of the James. Stanton took breaks totaling 29 min 24 sec. The event, without breaks, lasted 5 hr 50 min 30 sec.

BIGGEST SEA-WAVE RIDES

Four to six times each year rideable surfing waves break in Matanchen Bay near San Blas, Nayarit, Mexico, which makes surfing rides of around 5,700 ft (1,700 m) possible.

MOST CONTINUOUS ROTATIONS UNDER WATER

Virginie Dedieu (France), a bronze medalist in synchronized swimming at the Sydney Olympics, completed 22 rotations in one breath in Paris, France, on Oct 26 2000.

GUINNESS WORLD RECORDS

rugby

FASTEST INTERNATIONAL RUGBY LEAGUE TRY

The record for the fastest try in an international match is 15 seconds, by Bobby Fulton for Australia v. France at Odsal Stadium, Bradford, UK, on Nov 1 1970.

The fastest try in a rugby league match was by Lee Jackson (UK), who scored after nine seconds for Hull v. Sheffield Eagles in a Yorkshire Cup semifinal at Don Valley Stadium, Sheffield, UK, on Oct 6 1992.

HIGHEST RUGBY LEAGUE SCORE

The record for the highest score in a rugby league match is held by Ngati Pikiao of Rotorua. The team beat Tokoroa United 148–0 in a Bay of Plenty Rugby League under-17s league match at Pikiao, New Zealand, on July 10 1994.

MOST AMATEUR RUGBY LEAGUE TRIES SCORED IN A SEASON

Richard Lopag (UK) has scored the most tries in an amateur rugby league season, with 142 in the 1998/99 season for the Deighton Juniors under-9s side, West Yorkshire, UK. Richard started playing for the team at the age of five. His grandfather spotted the youngster's talent and, with the record books in mind, began compiling the statistics.

‹44564›
← ACCESS CODE
www.guinnessworldrecords.com/ausrugby

UP AND UNDER – DOWN UNDER

First held in 1954, the Rugby League World Cup has been won by Australia (left) a record eight times. They won the cup in 1957, 1968, 1970, 1977, 1988, 1992, 1995, and 2000, as well as a win in the International Championship of 1975.

Australia also holds the record for the most wins of the Webb Ellis Trophy (the Rugby Union World Cup). Instituted in 1987, Australia won the 1991 and 1999 contests and is the only team to have won it more than once. An early form of rugby is believed to have been played in Australia since the 1820s, although the first rugby club at Sydney University was not established until 1864. The Australian Rugby Union was formed in 1949.

MOST POINTS IN AN INTERNATIONAL RUGBY LEAGUE MATCH

The greatest number of points scored in a professional game is 48 (16 goals, 4 tries) by Hazen El Masri of Lebanon v. Morocco in a World Cup qualifying match at Avignon, France, on Nov 17 1999.

YOUNGEST INTERNATIONAL RUGBY LEAGUE PLAYER

The youngest international player in a rugby league match is Paul Newlove (UK), who played in the first Test for the UK against New Zealand on Oct 21 1989 at Old Trafford, Manchester, UK, age 18 years 72 days.

LONGEST RUGBY LEAGUE DROP GOAL

The longest drop goal in a rugby league match is 183 ft (56 m) by Joseph 'Joe' Lydon (UK) for Wigan, v. Warrington in a Challenge Cup semifinal at Maine Road, Manchester, UK, on March 25 1989.

HIGHEST RUGBY UNION POSTS

The world's highest rugby union goal posts measure 110 ft (33.54 m) and are at the Roan Antelope Rugby Union Club, Luanshya, Zambia. This is equivalent to 12 buses on top of one another.

HIGHEST ATTENDANCE AT A RUGBY UNION MATCH

The largest paying attendance for an international rugby match is 109,874 for New Zealand's 39–35 victory over Australia at Stadium Australia, Sydney, NSW, Australia, on July 15 2000.

MOST SUCCESSFUL RUGBY UNION TEAM

The Feilding Senior 4ths of New Zealand played 108 successive games without defeat from 1984 to 1989. At junior level, the Chiltern minirugby side played 213 games without defeat, from their formation as an under-8s side on Sept 29 1985 to April 8 1990.

FASTEST RUGBY UNION TRY

The fastest try was scored in just eight seconds by Andrew Brown (UK) for Widden Old Boys v. Old Ashtonians at Gloucester, UK, on Nov 22 1990.

INTERNATIONAL RUGBY UNION APPEARANCES

Frenchman Philippe Sella played in a record-breaking 111 internationals for France between 1982 and 1995. In the 13 years since his first appearance against Romania, Sella scored 30 tries and appeared in three World Cups, winning a runner-up medal in 1987.

MOST INTERNATIONAL RUGBY UNION PENALTIES

The greatest number of penalties successfully kicked in an international is nine by Keiji Hirose for Japan v. Tonga (44–17) in Tokyo, Japan, on May 9 1999; and by Andrew Mehrtens for New Zealand v. Australia (34–15) in Auckland, New Zealand, on July 24 1999.

I GET A KICK OUT OF VIEW

Neil Jenkins (UK, left) has scored the most rugby union international points in a career with a record 1,052 points in 86 matches for Wales (1,011 points in 83 matches) and British Lions (41 points in 3 matches), between 1991 and March 2001. Much of this tally comes from Jenkins's formidable kicking skills, to the extent that he has become the most prolific goal kicker in the history of international rugby.

The longest recorded successful drop goal in rugby union history is 269 ft (82 m) by Gerald 'Gerry' Hamilton Brand for South Africa v. England at Twickenham, London, UK, on Jan 2 1932. This was taken 19.69 ft (6 m) inside the England 'half,' 164 ft (50 m) from the posts, and it dropped over the dead ball line.

MOST INTERNATIONAL RUGBY UNION TRIES

The most tries in an international career is 64 by David Campese, in 101 internationals for Australia between 1982 and 1996. Campese is Australia's most capped player, (i.e. selected to play for the national team). In 1996 he was awarded a UNESCO (United Nations Educational, Scientific, and Cultural Organization) prize as one of the most outstanding sportsmen of the century.

‹52110›
← ACCESS CODE
www.guinnessworldrecords.com/kickrugby

MOST WINS IN THE HONG KONG SEVENS

The record for the greatest number of wins in the Hong Kong Rugby Union Sevens is held by Fiji, with nine wins in 1977–78, 1980, 1984, 1990–92, and 1998–99. In 1997 the contest was replaced by the World Cup Sevens and was also won by Fiji. The world's most prestigious international competition for seven-a-side teams, the first Hong Kong tournament was held in 1976.

MOST WOMEN'S HONG KONG SEVENS TITLES

The women's version of the world's most famous seven-a-side rugby competition was first held in 1997, and New Zealand has won the title a record four times, in 1997, 1999, 2000, and 2001.

MOST INDIVIDUAL POINTS SCORED IN A RUGBY UNION WORLD CUP MATCH

The most points scored in a match by an individual is 45 by Simon Culhane for New Zealand v. Japan (145–17) at Bloemfontein, South Africa, on June 4 1995. In the same match, Culhane scored a match-record 20 conversions. The final score earned New Zealand the record for most points scored by a team in a World Cup match. They also scored a record 21 tries during the match.

MOST INDIVIDUAL POINTS IN A RUGBY UNION INTERNATIONAL

On Oct 27 1994 Ashley Billington (Hong Kong) scored a record-breaking 50 points from 10 tries in the Rugby Union World Cup qualifying match between Hong Kong and Singapore at Kuala Lumpur, Malaysia, on Oct 27 1994.

MOST OUTRIGHT INTERNATIONAL CHAMPIONSHIP TITLES

England has won the Rugby International Championship more times than any other international side, with 23 outright wins between 1884 and 2000. This does not take into account any ties, because the title is then shared.

www.guinnessworldrecords.com/tryrugby

A GOOD TRY

Jonny Wilkinson (UK, above) holds the record for the most individual points scored in a Rugby Union International Championship match. His record-breaking 35 points in the England v. Italy (80–23) game at Twickenham, London, UK, on Feb 17 2001, consisted of four penalties (three points each), nine conversions (two points each), and a try (five points).

The 13 goals he kicked in this match are a record for an International Championship match. England's 80 points in this game was also the highest team score in a Rugby Union International Championship match.

The highest score for a Rugby League International is Australia's defeat of Russia (110–4) during the Rugby League World Cup at Hull, Yorkshire, UK, on Nov 4 2000.

ACCESS CODE

‹53873›

GUINNESS WORLD RECORDS

cricket

MOST WORLD CUP CATCHES
The most catches by a fielder is 14, by Steve Waugh (Australia) in 32 matches between 1987 and 1999.

The most catches in a tournament is eight by Anil Kumble (India) in 1996.

The most catches in a match is four by Chris Cairns (New Zealand) v. United Arab Emirates at Faisalabad, Pakistan, on Feb 27 1996.

MOST WORLD CUP RUNS
The most runs scored by an individual in World Cup matches is 1,083, by Javed Miandad (Pakistan) in 33 matches, from 1975 and 1996.

The greatest number of runs scored in a World Cup tournament is 523 by Sachin Tendulkar (India) in 1996.

The highest individual score in a World Cup match is 188 not out by Gary Kirsten (South Africa) v. the United Arab Emirates at Rawlpindi, India, on Feb 16 1996.

MOST WICKET-KEEPING DISMISSALS IN WORLD CUP
The most dismissals by a wicket-keeper in the World Cup is 29 by Moin Khan (Pakistan), in 20 matches between 1992 and 1999.

The most dismissals by a wicket-keeper in a tournament is 16 by Jeff Dujon (West Indies) in 1983.

The most dismissals in a match by a wicket-keeper is five by Syed Kirmani (India) v. Zimbabwe at Leicester, UK, on June 11 1983; Jimmy Adams (West Indies) v. Kenya at Pune, India, on Feb 29 1996; Rashid Latif (Pakistan) v. New Zealand, Lahore, Pakistan, on March 6 1996; Nayan Mongia (India) v. Zimbabwe at Leicester, UK, on May 19 1999; and Ridley Jacobs (West Indies) v. New Zealand at Southampton, UK, on May 24 1999.

MOST WINS IN WORLD CUP
The greatest number of wins is two by the West Indies, in 1975 and 1979; and Australia in 1987 and 1999.

MOST EXTRAS IN A ONE DAY INTERNATIONAL
The most extras conceded in a One Day International is 59 by the West Indies (eight byes, 10 leg byes, four no balls, and 37 wides) v. Pakistan at Brisbane, Australia, on Jan 7 1989; and Scotland (five byes, six leg byes, 15 no balls, and 33 wides) v. Pakistan at Chester-le-Street, Durham, UK, on May 20 1999.

HIGHEST INDIVIDUAL SCORE IN A ONE DAY INTERNATIONAL
The highest individual score is 194 by Saeed Anwar for Pakistan v. India, at Madras, India, on May 21 1997.

HIGHEST MARGIN OF VICTORY IN A ONE DAY INTERNATIONAL
The largest victory margin is 233 runs by Pakistan v. Bangladesh (320–3 to 87), at Dhaka, Bangladesh, on June 2 2000.

MOST ONE DAY INTERNATIONAL MATCHES PLAYED
The most matches played is 334 by Mohammad Azharuddin (India), between 1985 and 2000.

HIGHEST AND LOWEST SCORES IN ONE DAY MATCHES
The highest team score achieved in a World Cup match is 398–5 by Sri Lanka v. Kenya at Kandy, Sri Lanka, on March 6 1996.

The lowest team score is 45 by Canada v. England at Old Trafford from June 13 to 14 1979.

LOWEST TEAM SCORE IN A ONE DAY INTERNATIONAL
The lowest innings total is 43 by Pakistan v. the West Indies at Newlands, Cape Town, South Africa, on Feb 25 1993.

MOST ONE-DAY INTERNATIONAL CATCHES IN A CAREER
The greatest number of catches by a fielder is 156 in 334 matches by Mohammad Azharuddin (India), between 1985 and 2000.

MOST ONE DAY INTERNATIONAL WICKETS TAKEN IN A CAREER
The most wickets taken is 440 (av. 23.81), by Wasim Akram (Pakistan) in 316 matches from 1985 to Feb 2001.

HIGHEST BATTING AVERAGE IN FIRST-CLASS CRICKET
Don Bradman (Australia) holds the record for the highest batting average of 95.14, playing for New South Wales, South Australia, and Australia between 1927 and 1949 (28,067 runs in 338 innings, including 43 not outs).

MOST 150S SCORED AGAINST TEST-PLAYING NATIONS
On March 26 2000, during the third day of the second Test between New Zealand and Australia, Australian captain Steve Waugh became the first man to score 150 runs in an innings against each of the eight Test-playing nations. Waugh went on to lead Australia to victory by six wickets, thereby setting a new Australian record for consecutive Test-match victories (nine).

HIGHEST BATTING AVERAGE IN TEST CRICKET
Don Bradman (Australia) has the highest average of 99.94, playing for Australia in 52 Tests (6,996 runs in 80 innings) between 1928 and 1948.

MOST RUNS IN FIRST-CLASS CRICKET
Jack Hobbs (UK) scored a record 61,237 (av. 50.65) runs playing for Surrey and England between 1905 and 1934.

MOST RUNS IN TEST CRICKET
Allan Border (Australia) scored 11,174 runs in 156 Tests (av. 50.56) between 1978 and 1994.

MOST RUNS OFF AN OVER
The first batsman to score 36 runs off a six-ball over was Garfield Sobers (West Indies) off Malcolm Andrew Nash for Nottinghamshire v. Glamorgan at Swansea, UK, on Aug 31 1968. His feat was emulated by Ravishankar Jayadritha Shastri for

MAD ABOUT BATS
Sachin Tendulkar (India, left) has scored the most centuries in One Day Internationals during his career, with a record 28 centuries, having played 268 matches between 1989 and 2001.
He has also scored the most runs in One Day Internationals, amassing a grand total of 10,179 (av. 42.58) in 268 matches, from 1982 to 2001.
Sachin Ramesh Tendulkar, born on April 24 1973 in Mumbai (Bombay), India, is regarded by many to be the world's greatest batsman currently playing and has been compared to legendary Australian Don Bradman for his finesse and impeccable technique. Among his greatest assets, Tendulkar shows great timing and power, with the addition of a mental strength that has been tested in a number of international games.

<51995> www.guinnessworldrecords.com/bats ← ACCESS CODE

236

ACCESS CODE

‹45379› ←

BOWLED OVER!

The best bowling analysis in a One Day International is 7–30 by Muttiah Muralitharan (Sri Lanka, right) v. India at Sharjah, on Oct 27 2000.

Wasim Akram (Pakistan) has taken the most wickets in World Cup matches, with 43 in 32 matches from 1987 to 1999.

The most wickets in a single tournament is 20 by Geoff Allott (New Zealand) and Shane Warne (Australia), both in 1999.

The best bowling figures in a World Cup match is 7–51 by Winston Davis (West Indies) v. Australia at Headingley, W Yorks, UK, from June 11 to 12 1983.

Courtney Walsh (Jamaica) has taken the greatest number of Test-match wickets with 519 (av. 24.44 runs per wicket) in 132 matches between Nov 1984 and April 2001.

Mumbai (Bombay) v. Baroda at Mumbai (Bombay), India, on Jan 10 1985 off the bowling of Tilak Raj Sharma (India).

MOST CONSECUTIVE DUCKS

The greatest number of consecutive 'ducks' (when a batsman scores zero) in Test cricket is the five ducks achieved by Bob Holland (Australia), between Aug and Nov 1985 and Ajit Agarkar (India), between Dec 1999 and Jan 2000.

HIGHEST BATTING AVERAGE

The highest batting average in a league season is 330 by Colin Gill (UK) for Plymstock 2nd XI in 1998. Gill batted 10 times and was dismissed just once.

HIGHEST TEST SCORE

Sri Lanka scored a record 952 for six, v. India at Colombo, Sri Lanka between Aug 4 and 6 1997.

England scored a record 903 runs for seven wickets declared in 15 hr 17 min, v. Australia at The Oval, London, between Aug 20 and 23 1938.

LOWEST TEST INNINGS TOTAL

The lowest innings total in Test cricket is 26 by New Zealand v. England at Auckland on March 28 1955.

PUSHING OUT THE BOUNDARIES

Seven women's Cricket World Cups have been staged since 1973. The greatest number of World Cup titles is four won by Australia, in 1978, 1982, 1988, and 1997. England won in 1973 and 1993 and New Zealand was victorious in 2000. The picture above shows Karen Rolton (Australia) in action while scoring 154 not out during the Australia v. Sri Lanka match in the 2000 World Cup, which was played at Hagley Oval, Christchurch, New Zealand. Australia beat Sri Lanka by 200 runs but were in turn beaten by New Zealand.

www.guinnessworldrecords.com/
cricketwomen

ACCESS CODE

‹45357› ←

GUINNESS WORLD RECORDS™

ball sports 1

MOST MEN'S OLYMPIC HANDBALL TITLES

The USSR (the Unified Team from the republics of the former USSR) has won the men's Olympic handball title three times in 1976, 1988, and 1992.

MOST WOMEN'S OLYMPIC HANDBALL TITLES

The USSR and South Korea have both won the women's Olympic handball title twice. The USSR triumphed in 1976 and 1980, and South Korea won in 1988 and 1992.

HIGHEST MEN'S OLYMPIC HANDBALL SCORE

The highest handball team score in an Olympic match is 44, reached by Yugoslavia v. Kuwait at the 1980 Games in Moscow, USSR (now Russia). Sweden shares the record with a 44 score against Australia at the 2000 Olympics in Sydney, NSW, Australia.

HIGHEST WOMEN'S OLYMPIC HANDBALL SCORE

The record for the highest score by a female handball team at the Olympics is 45, by Austria v. Brazil at the 2000 Games in Sydney, NSW, Australia.

HIGHEST HANDBALL SCORE

The USSR reached the highest-ever score in an international handball match when they beat Afghanistan 86–2 in Hungary in Aug 1981.

THE KNOCK-IT-IN-THE-NET KNOCKOUTS

The Australian netball team (left) is one of the most successful teams in the history of Australian sport. The wonder women have won the World Championships a record eight times – in 1963, 1971, 1975, 1979, 1983, 1991, 1995, and 1999. As well as being world champions, they are also Open winners and were the first team to win the official Commonwealth Games gold medal in 1998. Every year, 20 athletes are picked for the Australian netball squad after the Qantas Netball Nationals have ended. They train throughout the year and a team of 12 is selected to represent Australia. The current team is captained by Kathryn Harby who plays all three defensive positions and was 1995's Netballer of the Year.

<44764>
www.guinnessworldrecords.com/netball
← ACCESS CODE

MOST WOMEN'S HANDBALL WORLD CHAMPIONSHIPS

Romania, Germany, and the USSR have all won three women's Handball World Championship titles. The Romanians were the outdoor victors in 1956 and 1960, and the indoor champs in 1962. Germany won indoors in 1971, 1975, and 1978. The USSR also tasted victory indoors in 1982, 1986, and 1990.

MOST WORLD CHAMPIONSHIP NETBALL GOALS SCORED

Irene van Dyk (South Africa) has scored the most goals at a Netball World Championship contest. Over the course of the 1995 tournament she put the ball in the net 543 times.

HIGHEST NETBALL WORLD CHAMPIONSHIP TEAM SCORE

The Cook Islands are the highest scoring Netball World Championship team. They beat Vanuatu 120–38 on July 9 1991 in Sydney, NSW, Australia.

MOST AFL TITLES

Australia has three major football leagues – the AFL (Australian Football League), the South Australian National Football League, and the Western Australian Football League. The AFL is the biggest and has been won by the Carlton Blues 16 times between 1906 and 1995. Port Adelaide has had 36 South Australian NFL wins from 1884 to 1991 and East Fremantle had 30 Western Australia FL wins between 1900 and 1998.

MOST AFL CAREER GOALS

The most goals scored in an AFL career is 1,357, by Tony Lockett between 1983 and 1999. He averaged five goals per match.

LARGEST AFL GRAND FINAL CROWD

The most people to attend an AFL Grand Final is 121,696. They watched Carlton beat Collingwood at the Melbourne Cricket Ground, Victoria, Australia, on Sept 26 1970.

HIGHEST TEAM SCORE IN AN AFL MATCH

The highest team score in the Australian Football League is 239 (37–17) reached by Geelong v. Brisbane on May 3 1992.

HIGHEST AGGREGATE SCORE IN AN AFL MATCH

The highest aggregate score (combined scores of both sides) in an Australian football match is 345 points, reached when St. Kilda beat Melbourne 204–141 on May 6 1978.

MOST MEN'S WORLD VOLLEYBALL CHAMPIONSHIP TITLES

The USSR has won six men's Volleyball World Championships. They were the victors in 1949, 1952, 1960, 1962, 1978, and 1982.

MOST WOMEN'S OLYMPIC VOLLEYBALL TITLES

The USSR has won four women's volleyball Olympic titles, in 1968, 1972, 1980, and 1988.

MOST MEN'S OLYMPIC VOLLEYBALL TITLES

The USSR has won a record three men's Olympic volleyball titles. The team won in 1964, 1968, and 1980. Introduced into the Olympics in 1964 for both men and women, volleyball has been dominated by the Russians. They have only come away from the Olympics without a medal twice – in 1992 in Barcelona and 1996 in Atlanta. In 1984 they boycotted the games.

YOU'VE REALLY GOT TO HAND IT TO THEM . . .

Sweden (left, playing Australia at the 2000 Sydney Olympics) has won the most men's indoor handball titles, with four wins in 1954, 1958, 1990, and 1999. Romania equals the record with victories in 1961, 1964, 1970, and 1974. Germany has won the outdoor title five times between 1938 and 1966. Handball originated in Germany in the 1920s and developed from the basics of soccer, with 11-a-side teams using their hands instead of their feet. It was originally an outdoor sport, played on a soccer-sized field. An indoor seven-a-side version developed and is the game solely played today. The original sport was only ever once contested at the Olympics, in 1936, with the indoor version introduced to the games in 1972.

<45019>
www.guinnessworldrecords.com/handball
← ACCESS CODE

BRILLIANT BRAZILIAN BEACH-BALL BABES!

Brazil is the holder of the most Beach Volleyball World Championship titles. The tournament was first staged for both men and women in 1997, and is held biennially. Brazil won both titles, for men and women (below), in 1997 and 1999.

Beach volleyball began in the 1920s. Its birthplace is generally recognized as Santa Monica, California. Courts were set up on the beach and standard six-a-side games were played. The sport soon became widespread in the USA, with interest spreading to Europe when American troops played on the beach during and after World War II. The format of the current game, two-a-side, was played during the 1930s, with the first official two-man competition at State Beach, California, in 1947. Long before hitting the beach, volleyball had been invented as 'Mintonette' in 1895 by a YMCA physical training instructor as a noncontact alternative to basketball, which had begun four years earlier.

MOST INTERNATIONAL WATER POLO GOALS

The most goals scored by an individual in an international water polo match is 13, achieved by Australia's Debbie Handley, when her team beat Canada 16–10 at the World Championship tournament in Guayaquil, Ecuador, in 1982.

MOST OLYMPIC WATER POLO TITLES

Hungary has won the most men's Olympic water polo titles, with six victories in 1932, 1936, 1952, 1956, 1964, and 1976. The sport is thought to have originated in Hungary, and the national team dominated international competitions from the early 1930s until the 1980s.

MOST WATER POLO WORLD CHAMPIONSHIPS

Three countries have won the Water Polo World Championship tournament twice – the USSR in 1975 and 1982; Yugoslavia in 1986 and 1991; and Italy in 1978 and 1994.

MOST GOALS SCORED IN A KORFBALL WORLD CHAMPIONSHIP

The most goals scored in a Korfball World Championship tournament is 191 by the Netherlands in 1999. Korfball was invented in 1901 by an Amsterdam schoolmaster, Nico Broekhuysen, and is similar to netball and basketball. The big difference is that it is designed to be played by mixed teams. Broekhuysen wanted it to be a game in which boys and girls in his school could compete at the same level. It is the world's only real mixed sport and was first demonstrated in 1902 in Holland.

MOST KORFBALL WORLD CHAMPIONSHIP TEAM WINS

The Netherlands have won the most Korfball World Championships since the tournament began in 1978. They have taken home the title a record five times in 1978, 1984, 1987, 1995, and 1999.

NARROWEST MARGIN OF VICTORY IN A KORFBALL WORLD CHAMPIONSHIP

The narrowest margin of victory in the final of the Korfball World Championships is one. There have been two such slim wins – in 1978 when the Netherlands defeated Belgium 14–13, and in 1991 when Belgium defeated the Netherlands 11–10.

HIGHEST KORFBALL SCORE IN A WORLD CHAMPIONSHIP FINAL

The highest team score in the final of the Korfball World Championships is 23 when the Netherlands beat Belgium 34–11 in 1999.

MOST KORFBALL WORLD GAMES TITLES

The Netherlands has won a record four Korfball World Games titles, with victories at every tournament held so far, in 1985, 1989, 1993, and 1997.

GUINNESS WORLD RECORDS

ball sports 2

MOST MEN'S TABLE TENNIS OLYMPIC GOLDS

Liu Guoliang (China) won a record two gold medals at the 1996 Atlanta Olympics, one in the singles, and one in the doubles with Kong Linghui.

MOST WOMEN'S TABLE TENNIS OLYMPIC GOLDS

Deng Yaping (China) has clinched a record four Olympic titles. She won gold in the women's singles in 1992

MOST TABLE TENNIS HITS IN ONE MINUTE

Between them, Jackie Bellinger and Lisa Lomas (both UK) broke the record for the most table tennis hits in one minute. They tapped the ball across the table to each other a total of 173 times at the Northgate Sports Center, Ipswich, Suffolk, UK, on Feb 7 1993.

and 1996, and two in the women's doubles, with Qiao Hang, in 1992 and 1996. She has won a total of 18 World titles during her 10-year career.

MOST MEN'S TEAM TABLE TENNIS WORLD CHAMPIONSHIP TITLES

The Chinese and Hungarian men's table tennis teams have won the most World Championship titles. They have taken home the coveted Swaythling Cup 12 times. China triumphed in 1961, 1963, 1965, 1971, 1975, 1977, 1981, 1983, 1985, 1987, 1995, and 1997. Hungary won in 1926, 1928–31, twice in 1933 (when two tournaments were held), and once in 1935, 1938, 1949, 1952, and 1979.

MOST WOMEN'S TEAM TABLE TENNIS WORLD CHAMPIONSHIP TITLES

China has won the most women's team Table Tennis World titles, with 13 Corbillon Cup victories. They first won in 1965, then followed with eight successive biennial wins from 1975 to 1989 and further victories in 1993, 1995, 1997, and 2000.

MOST MEN'S TEAM SQUASH WORLD CHAMPIONSHIPS

The Australian men's squash team has clinched the World Championship title a record six times. They won in 1967, 1969, 1971, 1973, 1989, and 1991. They share the record with Pakistan, who triumphed in 1977, 1981, 1983, 1985, and 1993.

MOST WOMEN'S TEAM SQUASH WORLD CHAMPIONSHIPS

The Australian women's team has won a record six World Championships, in 1981, 1983, 1992, 1994, 1996, and 1998.

MOST WOMEN'S SQUASH WORLD CHAMPIONSHIPS

Susan Devoy (New Zealand) has won the most women's Squash World Championship titles. She has been the World Open champion four times – in 1985, 1987, 1990, and 1992.

FASTEST SHUTTLECOCK SMASH

In tests at Warwickshire Racquets and Health Club, Coventry, UK, on Nov 5 1996, Simon Archer (UK) hit a shuttlecock at a record speed of 162 mph (260 km/h).

MOST BADMINTON SINGLES WORLD CHAMPIONSHIP TITLES

Four Chinese players have won a record two individual Badminton World titles. Yang Yang won the men's singles twice, in 1987 and 1989. The women's singles have

been won by Li Lingwei in 1983 and 1989; Han Aiping in 1985 and 1987; and Ye Zhaoying in 1995 and 1997.

MOST BADMINTON WORLD CHAMPIONSHIP TITLES

Park Joo-bong (South Korea) has won five World Championship Badminton titles. He triumphed in the men's doubles in 1985 and 1991, and in the mixed doubles in 1985, 1989, and 1991.

MOST WOMEN'S TEAM BADMINTON WORLD CHAMPIONSHIP TITLES

China has won the most women's team Badminton World Championships, taking home the Uber Cup seven times – in 1984, 1986, 1988, 1990, 1992, 1998, and 2000.

SHORTEST BADMINTON MATCH

Ra Kyung-min (South Korea) tasted badminton victory in the fastest time ever when she beat Julia Mann (UK) 11–2, 11–1, in six minutes, during the 1996 Uber Cup in Hong Kong, on May 19 1996.

HIGHEST SCORE IN MEN'S INTERNATIONAL FIELD HOCKEY

The Indian men's field hockey team beat the USA with the highest-ever score of 24–1, in California, at the 1932 Olympic Games. The unstoppable Indian team won an unbroken string of six Olympic gold medals between 1928 and 1956. At the 1936 Games in Berlin, Adolf Hitler was so impressed by the skill of Indian captain Dhyan Chand that he tried to buy his stick.

MOST MEN'S INTERNATIONAL FIELD HOCKEY APPEARANCES

From his debut in 1985 to Jan 2001, Jacques Brinkman (Netherlands) played field hockey for his country a record 337 times.

MOST WOMEN'S INTERNATIONAL FIELD HOCKEY APPEARANCES

Karen Brown (UK) played field hockey for England and Great Britain 355 times between 1984 and 1999.

KNOCK ME DOWN WITH A FEATHER!

Indonesia has won the most men's team Badminton World Championships. The team has taken home the Thomas Cup a record 12 times – in 1958, 1961, 1964, 1970, 1973, 1976, 1979, 1984, 1994, 1996, 1998, and 2000, with Hendrawan (above) a key player in clinching the last two trophies. The Thomas Cup is named after Sir George Thomas, a winner of 21 All-England titles, who donated the trophy in 1940. However, the competition did not actually begin until after World War II, in 1949. It was held every three years until 1982, when it became a biennial event. The competition is contested by teams of six, who play five singles and four doubles matches in each contest. Badminton gets its name from Badminton House in the UK, where it was played by the Duke of Beaufort's family in the 19th century. Its origins come directly from the children's game of battledore and shuttlecock, and a similar game played in China over 2,000 years ago.

<45671>

www.guinnessworldrecords.com/badminton

← ACCESS CODE

SQUASH THE OPPOSITION

Pakistan's Jahangir Khan (above) has won the most Squash World Open titles. He has triumphed a record six times between 1981 and 1985, and in 1988. He is considered the most successful player in the history of squash. The son of Roshan Khan, winner of the 1956 British Open, Jahangir started playing squash at the age of 10 and won his first World amateur title at 15.

www.guinnessworldrecords.com/squash

ACCESS CODE
‹44362› ←

MOST ALL-IRELAND HURLING FINAL WINS

The greatest number of All-Ireland Championships won by one team is 28 by Cork, from 1890 to 1999.

LARGEST CROWD AT A HURLING MATCH

A record crowd of 84,865 spectators turned out for the All-Ireland Hurling final between Cork and Wexford at Croke Park, Dublin, in 1954.

LONGEST HIT IN HURLING

The greatest distance for a hurling 'lift and stroke' hit is a record 387.16 ft (118 m), credited to Tom Murphy of Three Castles, Kilkenny, Ireland, during a 'long puck' contest in 1906.

MOST SHINTY TEAM WINS

Similar to the Irish sport of hurling, the mainly Scottish sport of shinty has its own champion of champions. The Newtonmore team from Highland, UK, has won the Camanachd Association Challenge Cup a record 28 times between 1907 and 1986.

HIGHEST MEN'S LACROSSE SCORE

The highest score in a Lacrosse World Cup match is Scotland's 34–3 win over Germany on July 25 1994 in Greater Manchester, UK. In the World Cup Premier division, the record score is the USA's 33–2 win over Japan at Greater Manchester on July 21 1994.

HIGHEST WOMEN'S LACROSSE SCORE

The highest score by an international female lacrosse team was notched up by Great Britain and Ireland when they beat Long Island 40–0 during their 1967 tour of the USA.

MOST WOMEN'S LACROSSE WORLD CHAMPIONSHIPS

The US women's team has won a record five Lacrosse World titles. They won the World Championships in 1974, and went on to win the World Cup (which replaced the World Championships) in 1982, 1989, 1993, and 1997.

MOST MEN'S LACROSSE WORLD CHAMPIONSHIPS

The USA has won seven of the eight Lacrosse World Championships in 1967, 1974, 1982, 1986, 1990, 1994, and 1998. Canada won the other, in 1978, beating the USA 17–16.

www.guinnessworldrecords.com/hockey

STICK AT IT

The most women's Field Hockey Champions' Trophies have been won by Australia (right). The team has triumphed a record five times – in 1991, 1993, 1995, 1997, and 1999. First held in 1987, the tournament takes place every two years, with the world's top six teams competing against one another to take home the coveted cup.

ACCESS CODE
‹45007› ←

GUINNESS WORLD RECORDS™

animal sports

MOST THREE-DAY BADMINTON WINS

The Badminton Three-Day Event has been won six times by Lucinda Jane Green (*née* Prior-Palmer, UK) on Be Fair (1973), Wide Awake (1976), George (1977), Killaire (1979), Regal Realm (1983), and Beagle Bay (1984).

BIGGEST CAREER WINNINGS BY A RACEHORSE TRAINER

Trainer Wayne Lukas (USA) began training horses full-time in 1967. He won $177 million (£118 million) in horse racing during his career. He was also awarded the Eclipse Award four times by the National Thoroughbred Racing Association for Trainer of the Year. His total winnings for 1988 was $17,842,358 (£11,947,234) – the biggest amount won in one year by a trainer.

HIGHEST-PRICED RACEHORSE

On July 23 1985 Robert Sangster (UK) and partners paid $13.1 million (£9 million) for yearling Seattle Dancer at Keeneland, Kentucky.

FASTEST RACEHORSE

The highest race speed recorded is 43.26 mph (69.62 km/h) or 20.8 sec for 804 m (0.5 miles), by Big Racket in Mexico City, on Feb 5 1945, and Onion Roll at Thistledown, Cleveland, Ohio, on

GOOD FORTUNE

From 1974 to April 2000 jockey Christopher McCarron (USA, left) won a total of $236 million (£148 million) – the greatest amount won in a horse-racing career. McCarron regards his Kentucky Derby win on Alysheba as a career highlight. He was also a regular rider of John Henry. In 1994 he posted his 6,000th win at Hollywood Park, California.

‹55548›
www.guinnessworldrecords.com/mccarron
← ACCESS CODE

Sept 27 1993. The record for 2,414 m (1.5 miles) is 37.82 mph (60.86 km/h) by 3-year-old Hawkster (carrying 121 lb or 54.9 kg) at Santa Anita Park, Arcadia, California, on Oct 14 1989 with a time of 2 min 22.8 sec.

HIGHEST HORSE JUMP

The official Fédération Equestre Internationale record for high jump is 8 ft 10 in (2.47 m) by Huaso, ridden by Alberto Larraguibel Morales (Chile) at Viña del Mar, Santiago, Chile, on Feb 5 1949.

HIGHEST INDOOR HORSE JUMP

On June 9 1991 Optibeurs Leonardo, ridden by Franke Sloothaak (Germany), at Chaudefontaine, Switzerland, jumped a record 7 ft 9 in (2.4 m).

BEST RODEO ATTENDANCE

The largest rodeo in the world is the National Finals Rodeo (USA), organized by the Professional Rodeo

Cowboys Association (PRCA) and the Women's Professional Rodeo Association (WPRA). The 1991 finals had a paid attendance of 171,414 for 10 performances – the highest ever.

MOST SUCCESSFUL RODEO BULL

The top-bucking bull, Red Rock, dislodged 312 riders between 1980 and 1988, and was finally ridden to the eight-second bell by world champion Bull Rider 1987, Lane Frost (USA), on May 20 1988. Red Rock, a red brindle Brahma-Hereford mix bull, had retired at the end of the 1987 season but still continued to make guest appearances.

BIGGEST FIRST PRIZE FOR A GREYHOUND RACE

The biggest first prize for a greyhound race is $125,000 (£87,000), won by Ben G. Speedboat in the Great Greyhound Race of Champions at Seabrook, New Hampshire, on Aug 23 1986.

FASTEST GREYHOUND

The fastest speed at which a greyhound has been timed is 41.83 mph (67.32 km/h) or 400 yd (366 m) in 19.57 seconds by Star Title on the straightaway track at Wyong, NSW, Australia, on March 5 1994.

HIGHEST JUMP BY A DOG

The canine high-jump record for a leap and scramble over a smooth wooden wall (without ribs or other aids) is 12 ft 2 in (3.72 m), achieved by an 18-month-old Lurcher dog named Stag, at the annual Cotswold Country Fair in Cirencester, Glos., UK, on Sept 27 1993. The dog is owned by Mr. and Mrs. P.R. Matthews (UK).

LONGEST SLED-DOG RACING TRAIL

The longest sled-dog race is the 1,243-mile (2,000-km) Berengia Trail from Esso to Markovo, Russia, which started as a 155-mile (250-km) route in April 1990. Now established as an annual event, the fastest time to complete the trail was achieved in 1991 by Pavel Lazarev (Russia) in 10 days 18 hr 17 min 56 sec. Lazarev's time is equivalent to an average rate of 5 mph (8 km/h).

OLDEST SLED-DOG RACING TRAIL

The oldest established sled-dog trail is the 1,049-mile (1,688-km) Iditarod Trail from Anchorage to Nome, Alaska, which has existed since 1910 and has been the route of an annual race since 1967. The fastest time, 9 days 58 min 6 sec, was set by Doug Swingley (USA) between March 6 and 14 2000. This is equivalent to an estimated average rate of 5 mph (8 km/h).

GREATEST DISTANCE FLOWN BY A PIGEON

The greatest distance flown in a competitive career is 25,508 miles (41,050 km) between 1990 and 1997 by Brazilian Beauty, a blue-check hen, owned by Robert Koch (South Africa).

HIGHEST-PRICED PIGEON

A four-year-old cock bird, winner of the 1992 Barcelona International race and

SPORT OF KINGS . . . . . . KINGS OF SPORT

Of the five Polo World Championships contested, three have been won by Argentina – the record for the most Polo World Championships won by one country. They won in 1987 in Argentina, in 1992 in Chile, and in 1998 in the USA. World Championships are held every three years under the auspices of the Federation of International Polo (FIP). Mariano Uranga (left) was one of the Argentinian team members who competed in the World Cup Polo held in Australia in March 2001.

The highest aggregate number of goals scored in an international match is 30, when Argentina beat the USA 21–9 at Meadowbrook, Long Island, New York, in Sept 1936.

‹54456›
www.guinnessworldrecords.com/polochamps
← ACCESS CODE

FABULOUS FERRET
On July 11 1999 at the North England Ferret Racing Championships held in Blythe, Northumberland, UK, an albino ferret named Warhol (above), owned by Jacqui Adams (UK), ran the 32-ft (10-m) tube race in a record 12.59 sec – beating 150 other ferret competitors. The fact that this was his very first race, makes this achievement even more remarkable. At the time of the race, Warhol weighed 6 lb (2.7 kg). Ferrets belong to the weasel family and have elongated bodies, short legs, and a long, bushy tail.

www.guinnessworldrecords.com/ferret

ACCESS CODE

‹53067› ←

subsequently named Invincible Spirit, was sold for £110,800 ($160,000) – the highest sum ever paid for a pigeon. Louella Pigeon World (UK) bought the bird from Martin Biemans (Netherlands) in July 1992.

FASTEST SNAIL RACE
The annual World Snail Racing Championships, held in July at Congham, Norfolk, UK, is conducted on a 13-in (33-cm) circular course outside St. Andrew's Church. The runners race from the center to the perimeter. Some race several times as they are divided into heats to cater for the 150 snail competitors who enter every year. The all-time record holder is Archie, trained by Carl Bramham, who sprinted to the winning post in 2 min 20 sec in 1995. Like all great racing champions, he was sent to stud in a cabbage patch.

www.guinnessworldrecords.com/camelfight

CAMEL COMBAT
At the 1994 Camel Wrestling Festival in Selçuk, Turkey, 20,000 people gathered to watch 120 dromedaries wrestle in a 2,000-year-old stadium in the city of Ephesus. This was the largest audience that has ever attended a camel-wrestling festival. Camel wrestling (below) is one of Turkey's oldest forms of entertainment. A male wrestling camel is brought before a female in the arena. As a courtship ritual the male immediately drops to the ground and writhes in front of the female.

ACCESS CODE

‹56083› ←

She is then taken away and replaced by a male, provoking a jealous battle for the female. As camels are expensive, muzzles are used so they do not seriously harm one another. Two breeds of camel are crossed to obtain the *tulu*, the camel used in wrestling.

The owner of a winning camel collects a cash prize of $60 (£40) as well as a carpet. There are approximately 1,200 wrestling camels in Turkey, and the sport extends over the Marmara, Aegean, and Mediterranean coasts of western Turkey.

GUINNESS WORLD RECORDS

combat and martial arts

HIGHEST ATTENDANCE AT A BOXING MATCH

The greatest paying attendance at any boxing match is 132,274 for four World title fights at the Aztec Stadium, Mexico City, on Feb 20 1993, headed by the successful WBC super lightweight defense of Julio César Chávez (Mexico) over Greg Haugen (USA).

The highest nonpaying attendance is 135,132 at the fight between Tony Zale and Billy Pryor (both USA) at Juneau Park, Milwaukee, Wisconsin, on Aug 16 1941.

LOWEST ATTENDANCE AT A BOXING MATCH

The smallest attendance at a World Heavyweight title fight was 2,434, at the Cassius Clay (Muhammad Ali) v. Sonny Liston (both USA) fight at Lewiston, Maine, on May 25 1965.

MOST JUDO WORLD TITLES WON BY A MAN

David Douillet (France) has won six World and Olympic titles – Over 95 kg (1993, 1995, and 1997), Open (1995), the Olympic Over 95 kg (1996), and Over 100 kg (2000). Yasuhiro Yamashita (Japan), who won nine

AND THE WREST IS HISTORY

A student of literature, opera, and ballet, Aleksandr Karelin (Russia, left) began wrestling at the age of 13. He quickly achieved success and was world junior champion in 1987. He has won 12 World titles in the Greco-Roman Under-130-kg class in 1988 to 1999 – more than any other wrestler. In addition to his World titles, Karelin has won Olympic gold medals at Seoul, Barcelona, and Atlanta as he continued to dominate world Greco-Roman wrestling. He developed a maneuver known as the 'reverse body lift,' with which he would slam his opponents to the mat. He is regarded as a national hero in Russia.

consecutive Japanese titles between 1977 and 1985, has won five World and Olympic titles – Over 95 kg (1979, 1981, and 1983), Open (1981) and the Olympic Open category (1984). He retired undefeated in 1985 after 203 successive wins.

MOST OLYMPIC GOLD MEDALS FOR JUDO

The only men to have won two Olympic gold medals are Wilhelm Ruska (Netherlands) for Over 93 kg and Open (1972), Peter Seisenbacher (Austria) for 86 kg (1984 and 1988),

Hitoshi Saito (Japan) for Over 95 kg (1984) and Open (1988), Waldemar Legien (Poland) for 78 kg (1988) and 86 kg (1992), David Douillet (France) for Over 95 kg (1996) and Over 100 kg (2000), and Tadahiro Nomura (Japan) for 60 kg (1996 and 2000).

MOST JUDO WORLD TITLES WON BY A WOMAN

Ingrid Berghmans (Belgium) has won a record six women's World titles for Open (1980, 1982, 1984, and 1986) and Under 72 kg (1984 and 1989).

MOST JUDO THROWS IN 10 HOURS

Patrick Hurley and Tony Cox (both UK) of the Leeds Central Aikido Club completed 46,261 judo and aikido throwing techniques in a 10-hour period at the Aireborough Leisure Centre, Leeds, UK, on May 30 1998.

RAREST SUMO LOSS

On May 13 2000, during the May tournament at the Kokugikan, Sumida-ku, Tokyo, Japan, *sandanme*

rikishi Asanokiri (Japan) lost a bout against opponent Chiyohakuho (Japan) because his loin cloth fell off – the first time in the 83 years since the introduction of the rule that a bout has been settled in this fashion. The fight was stopped after a ringside Sumo elder saw Asanokiri's genitals exposed when his *mawashi* (belt) fell off. *Mawashi* are about 26 ft (8 m) long and are wrapped tightly several times around the wrestlers' expansive bodies.

HEAVIEST LIVING ATHLETE

The heaviest living athlete in the world is Sumo wrestler Emmanuel 'Manny' Yarborough (USA). He stands 6 ft 8 in (2.03 m) tall and weighs a colossal 704 lb (319.3 kg).

HIGHEST MARTIAL ARTS KICK

The highest martial-arts kick measured is 9 ft 8 in (2.94 m) by Jessie Frankson (USA), who kicked a target with a pin attached, which in turn burst a balloon, on Dec 21 2000.

QUITE A HEAVYWEIGHT!

Up to May 2001, Ricardo López (Mexico, left) has remained unbeaten throughout his professional career, with 48 wins and one draw out of 49 fights over a total of 16 years and 8 months. No other boxer has been able to remain unbeaten for such a long period of time.

Joe Louis (USA) holds the record for the longest reign of a boxing world champion. His heavyweight duration record of 11 years 252 days undefeated stands for all divisions. When he died in 1981, he was considered one of the greatest fighters of all time.

Tony Canzoneri (USA) was world light-welterweight champion from May 21 to June 23 1933. This period of 33 days is the shortest for a boxer to have won and lost the world title in the ring.

CHAMP CHYNA

The highest earnings by a female wrestler in a year, as reported by the *Forbes* Celebrity 100 list, is $1 million (£700,000) by 'Chyna' (right) in 2000. Chyna's real name is Joanie Laurer (USA). She was born on Dec 27 1971 and started lifting weights when she was 15. In 1995 she went on to train with Walter 'Killer' Kowalski. She is a full-time professional wrestler, who has been a member of the World Wrestling Federation (WWF) since 1997. She was the first woman in the history of the sport to complete the Royal Rumble Match in 1999. In the same year she also became the first female intercontinental champion and was voted by her fans as WWF's Diva of the Year. Outside the ring she has appeared three times in NBC's *3rd Rock from the Sun* and in Sept 2000 released her video, *Chyna Fitness: More than Meets the Eye*. In 2001 she released her autobiography, *If Only They Knew*.

ACCESS CODE

‹56478› ←

MOST KICKBOXING WORLD TITLES

Don 'The Dragon' Wilson (USA) has won 11 World titles in three divisions (light-heavyweight, super light-heavyweight, and cruiserweight) and for six sanctioning organizations (WKA, STAR, KICK, ISKA, PKO, and IKF).

MOST CONCRETE BLOCKS SE BROKEN IN ONE MINUTE

Mikael Bigersson (Sweden) smashed 21 concrete blocks by hand in one minute on Feb 3 2001 in Stockholm, Sweden. The blocks, each measuring 23.62 x 7.87 x 2.7 in (60 x 20 x 7 cm), were stacked in piles of one, two, three, four, five, and finally six high.

MOST CONCRETE BLOCKS SMASHED IN A GROIN BREAK USA

On Aug 12 1998 a record two concrete blocks were placed over martial-arts expert Cliff Flenoy's (USA) groin and then smashed with a sledgehammer by another person, in Los Angeles, California.

LARGEST KARATE AUDIENCE

The Sabaki Challenge is the standard for bare-knuckle full-contact karate in the USA. This tournament has a live audience of 7,500 as well as millions of television viewers all over the world.

MOST SHEETS OF GLASS BROKEN IN KARATE USA

With a single karate chop, Maurice Elmalem (USA) broke 50 glass sheets, each measuring 3.875 in (9.84 cm) wide, 15 in (38.1 cm) long, and 0.16 in (0.4 cm) thick, in Los Angeles, on March 12 2001. The sheets were spaced using blocks measuring 3.5 in (8.9 cm) long, 0.5 in (1.27 cm) wide, and 0.125 in (0.32 cm) thick. To avoid being cut, Elmalem had to use twice the power he uses to break wood.

SLOWEST TAI-CHI WALK

The greatest time taken to travel 32 ft (10 m) using tai chi is 54 min 30 sec by Ken Poole (Canada) at the SlowDown ShowDown Race, Toronto, Canada, on Feb 6 1999.

FASTEST 100-MAN KUMITE KARATE

On March 22 1995 Francisco Alves Filho (Brazil) defeated 100 consecutive opponents in full-contact knockdown fighting in 3 hr 8 min. He won 26 fights by *Ippon* (full points), won 50 by decision, drew 24, and lost none. The One Hundred Man Kumite is the ultimate test in Kyokushin karate and is unique to this discipline. It involves fighting 100 opponents in full-contact knockdown fighting, with each bout lasting two minutes. If knocked down for more than five seconds, you would fail – even if it were your last fight.

GUINNESS WORLD RECORDS™

gymnastics and weights

MOST PUSH-UPS IN ONE MINUTE

Sgt. Paul Dean (UK) of the Royal Marines achieved a record 116 push-ups in one minute at the Marine Training Base, Lympstone, Devon, UK, on July 25 2000.

MOST PARALLEL BAR DIPS IN ONE HOUR

Simon Kent (UK) achieved 3,989 parallel bar dips at Farrahs Health Centre, Lincoln, UK, on Sept 5 1998.

FASTEST MILE DOING FORWARD ROLLS

Ashrita Furman performed one mile (1.6 km) of gymnastically correct forward rolls in 19 min 11 sec, around Victory Field Track in Forest Park, New York, on Nov 25 2000.

MOST CONSECUTIVE FORWARD ROLLS

Ashrita Furman performed 8,341 forward rolls in 10 hr 30 min over 12.22 miles (19.67 km) from Lexington to Charleston, Massachusetts, on April 30 1986.

MOST CARTWHEELS IN ONE MINUTE

The most complete cartwheels achieved in 60 sec is 48 by Brianna Schroeder (USA) at the GymCarolina Gymnastics Academy, Raleigh, North Carolina, on Nov 1 1997.

FASTEST 50-M REVERSE SOMERSAULTS

On Aug 31 1995 Vitaliy Scherbo (Belarus) somersaulted backward for a record 164 ft (50 m) in 10.22 sec at Makuhar Messe Event Hall, Chiba, Japan.

MOST ROTATIONS ON A POMMEL HORSE

Tyler Farstad (Canada) completed 97 consecutive double-leg circles on a pommel horse at Surrey Gymnastic Society, Surrey, British Columbia, Canada, on Nov 27 1993.

MOST SQUAT THRUSTS IN ONE HOUR

The most squat thrusts in one hour is 3,743 by Paddy Doyle (UK) at the Stamina Boxing Kickboxing Gym, Erdington, Birmingham, W. Midlands, UK, on May 4 1998.

MOST VAULTS IN ONE HOUR

A team of 10 gymnasts from the Blue Falcons Gymnastic Display Team of Chelmer Valley High School, Chelmsford, Essex, UK, completed a world-record 4,095 vaults in one hour (6.8 vaults each per minute) on Dec 2 1999.

YOU'RE BARRED!

The heaviest weight lifted in the women's 53-kg snatch weightlifting competition is a record-breaking 100 kg by Yang Xia (China, above) at the Olympic Games in Sydney, Australia, on Sept 18 2000. Yang also achieved an Olympic and world record-breaking 125 kg in the women's 53-kg clean and jerk weightlifting competition on the same day. These two weights are combined to calculate the total weight lifted. With a combined weight of 225 kg in the women's 53-kg category, Yang takes her record-breaking tally to three world records and three Olympic records.

‹51810› www.guinnessworldrecords.com/barred ← ACCESS CODE

YOUNGEST INTERNATIONAL GYMNAST

Pasakevi Voula Kouna (b. Dec 6 1971) was age 9 years 299 days at the start of the Balkan Games at Serres, Greece, on Oct 1 1981, when she represented Greece.

MOST OLYMPIC MEDALS WON BY A FEMALE GYMNAST

The most Olympic gymnastic medals won by a woman is 18 by Larisa Latynina (USSR) who won six individual gold medals, three team gold medals, five silver, and four bronze medals at three Olympic Games, between 1956 and 1964.

MOST OLYMPIC MEDALS WON BY A MALE GYMNAST

The most Olympic gymnastic medals won by a male is 15 by Nikolay Andrianov (USSR) between 1972 and 1980. Andrianov won seven gold, five silver, and three bronze medals.

MOST INDIVIDUAL OLYMPIC GOLD MEDALS WON

The most men's individual gold medals won is six. Boris Shakhlin (USSR) won one in 1956, four (two shared) in 1960, and one in 1964; and Nikolay Yefimovich Andrianov (USSR) won one in 1972, four in 1976, and one in 1980.

24-HOUR DEADLIFT

A deadlifting record of 6,917,886 lb (3,137,904 kg) was set by a team of 10 at the Pontefract Sports and Leisure Centre, W. Yorks, UK, between May 3 and 4 1997.

The individual 24-hour deadlift record is 1,004,595 lb (455,677.5 kg) by Steph Smit at Warren's Health Club, Pietermaritzburg, South Africa,

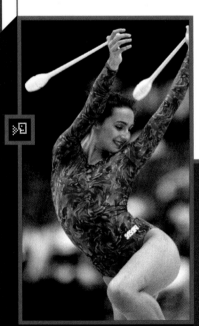

SHE'S GOT RHYTHM

The most individual World All-around Rhythmic Gymnastics titles is three, a record shared by María Petrova (Bulgaria, left), in 1993, 1994, and 1995 (shared), and Maria Gigova (Bulgaria) in 1969, 1971, and 1973 (shared). The all-around competition involves each competitor performing in four separate gymnastic disciplines chosen out of a possible five – rope, ball, ribbon, hoop, and clubs – with each discipline being marked individually.

The most individual Olympic gold gymnastics medals won by a woman is seven by Vera Cáslavská (Czechoslovakia). She won three gold medals in Tokyo, Japan, in 1964 and four (one shared) in Mexico City, in 1968.

‹45037› www.guinnessworldrecords.com/rhythmicgym ← ACCESS CODE between Sept 13 and 14 1997. In a deadlift, the lifter has to lift the bar from the floor, lock the knees, and stand erect with shoulders back. The bar is not lifted above the head or to the shoulders, and the arms are held straight down.

MOST TIMES OWN BODYWEIGHT LIFTED

Lamar Gant (USA) deadlifted a record-breaking five times his own bodyweight, lifting 660 lb (299.5 kg) while weighing 131 lb (59.5 kg) in 1985.

Cammie Lynn Lusko (USA) is the only woman to lift more than her bodyweight with one arm. She lifted 131 lb (59.5 kg) with a bodyweight of 128.5 lb (58.3 kg), at Milwaukee, Wisconsin, on May 21 1983.

HEAVIEST DEADLIFT WITH THE LITTLE FINGER

The heaviest deadlift with the little finger is 197.5 lb (89.6 kg) by Barry Anderson (UK) on Oct 14 2000 at the Bass Museum, Burton-upon-Trent, Staffordshire, UK. Competing in the Masters division for contestants between the ages of 65 and 69 in the 200.5-lb (100-kg) weight class, Barry lifted the weight with the little finger of his right hand.

www.guinnessworldrecords.com/weights

HEAVY METTLE

The most Olympic weightlifting gold medals won is three by Pyrros Dimas (Greece, right), and Turkey's Naim Suleymanoglü. Dimas won his gold medals in Barcelona, Spain, in the 82.5-kg weight class (1992); in Atlanta in the 83-kg weight class (1996); and in Sydney, Australia in the 85-kg weight class (2000).

MOST BODY RAISES IN ONE HOUR

The greatest number of body raises on a gymnastic bar (from hanging vertically to lying horizontally on the bar) in one hour is 493 by Tomasz Szanca (Poland) at Szczecin, Poland, on May 23 1999.

24-HOUR BENCH PRESS

A bench press record of 10,469,964 lb (4,748,283 kg) was set by a nine-man team at the Pontefract Sports and Leisure Centre, W. Yorks, UK, between April 11 and 12 1998.

MOST WORLD CHAMPIONSHIP POWERLIFTING TITLES

The winner of the most women's World Championship Powerlifting titles is Natalya Rumyantseva (Russia) with seven at 82.5 kg, from 1993 to 1999.

LONGEST STATIC WALL SIT

Rajkumar Chakraborty (India) stayed in an unsupported sitting position against a wall for 11 hr 5 min at Panposh Sports Hostel, Rourkela, India, on April 22 1994.

GUINNESS WORLD RECORDS

sports reference

BASEBALL

AL – American League
NL – National League

LONGEST BASEBALL THROW BY A WOMAN

296 ft (90.2 m), Mildred Ella Zaharias, (USA), July 25 1931

WORLD SERIES

MOST RUNS BATTED IN

6, Robert Richardson (New York AL), Oct 8 1960

MOST SERIES PLAYED BY A PITCHER

Game: 11, Whitey Ford (New York AL), 1950–64

MOST STRIKEOUTS

Game: 17, Robert Gibson (St. Louis NL), Oct 2 1968

PERFECT GAME (9 INNINGS)

Donald James Larsen (New York AL) v. Brooklyn, Oct 8 1956

MOST VALUABLE PLAYER AWARDS

2, Sandy Koufax (Los Angeles NL, 1963, 1965); Bob Gibson (St. Louis NL, 1964, 1967); and Reggie Jackson (Oakland AL, 1973, New York AL, 1977)

MAJOR LEAGUE PITCHING RECORDS

MOST NO-HIT GAMES

Career: 7, Nolan Ryan, 1973–91

MOST PITCHED SHUTOUT GAMES

110, Walter Johnson (Washington AL), 1907–27

MOST GAMES WON

Consecutive: 24, Carl Owen Hubbell (New York Giants NL), 1936–37
Season: 60, Hoss Radbourn (Providence NL), 1884
Career: 511, Cy Young (Cleveland NL, St. Louis NL, Boston AL, Cleveland AL, Boston NL), 1890–1911

TOTAL INNINGS

7,356, Cy Young (Cleveland NL, St. Louis NL, Boston AL, Cleveland AL, Boston NL), 1890–1911

MAJOR LEAGUE BATTING RECORDS

MOST RUNS BATTED IN

Inning: 7, Edward Cartwright (St. Louis AL), Sept 23 1890
Season: 191, Lewis Robert Hack Wilson (Chicago NL), 1930
Career: 2,297, Henry Hank Aaron, 1954–76

MOST RUNS

Season: 196, William Robert Hamilton (Philadelphia NL), 1894
Career: 2,245, Tyrus Raymond Ty Cobb, 1905–28

MOST TOTAL BASES

Game: 12, James Bottomley (St. Louis NL), Sept 16 1924; and Mark Whiten (St. Louis NL), Sept 7 1993
Career: 6,856, Henry Hank Aaron, 1954–76

AMERICAN FOOTBALL

SUPER BOWL RECORDS

MOST FIELD GOALS

Game: 4, Don Chandler (Green Bay Packers), 1968; and Ray Wersching (San Francisco 49ers), 1982
Career: 5, Ray Wersching (San Francisco 49ers), 1982–85

MOST PASSES COMPLETED

Game: 31, Jim Kelly (Buffalo Bills), 1994
Career: 83, Joe Montana (San Francisco 49ers), 1982, 1985, 1989–90

MOST PASSES CAUGHT

Game: 11, Dan Ross (Cincinnati Bengals), 1982; and Jerry Rice (San Francisco 49ers), 1989
Career: 28, Jerry Rice (San Francisco 49ers), 1989–90, 1995

MOST POINTS

Game: 18, Roger Craig (San Francisco 49ers), 1985; Jerry Rice (San Francisco 49ers), 1990, 1995; Ricky Watters (San Francisco 49ers), 1995; and Terrell Davis (Denver Broncos), 1998
Career: 42, Jerry Rice (San Francisco 49ers), 1989–90, 1995

MOST VALUABLE PLAYER AWARDS

3, Joe Montana, San Francisco 49ers, 1982, 1985, 1990

MOST TOUCHDOWN PASSES

Game: 6, Steve Young (San Francisco 49ers), 1995
Career: 11, Joe Montana (San Francisco 49ers), 1982, 1985, 1989–90

MOST TOUCHDOWNS

Game: 3, Roger Craig (San Francisco 49ers), 1985; Jerry Rice (San Francisco 49ers), 1990, 1995; Ricky Watters (San Francisco 49ers), 1995; and Terrell Davis (Denver Broncos), 1998

MOST PASSING YARDS

Game: 414, Kurt Warner (St. Louis Rams), Jan 30 2000
Career: 1,142, Joe Montana (San Francisco 49ers), 1982, 1985, 1989–90

MOST RECEIVING YARDS

Game: 215, Jerry Rice (San Francisco 49ers), 1989

MOST RUSHING YARDS

Game: 204, Timmy Smith (Washington Redskins), 1988
Career: 354, Franco Harris (Pittsburgh Steelers), 1975–76, 1979–80

NFL RECORDS

MOST COMBINED NET YARDS

Season: 2,535, Lionel James (San Diego Chargers), 1985
Career: 21,803, Walter Payton (Chicago Bears), 1975–87

MOST FIELD GOALS

Season: 39, Olindo Mare (Miami Dolphins), 1999
Career: 461, Gary Anderson, Pittsburgh Steelers (1982–94), Philadelphia Eagles (1995–96), San Francisco 49ers (1997), Minnesota Vikings (1999–2000)

MOST PASSES COMPLETED

Season: 404, Warren Moon (Houston Oilers), 1991
Career: 4,967, Dan Marino (Miami Dolphins), 1983–2000

MOST PASSES RECEIVED

Season: 123, Herman Moore (Detroit Lions), 1995
Career: 1,281, Jerry Rice (San Francisco 49ers), 1985–2000

MOST POINTS

Season: 176, Paul Hornung
(Green Bay Packers), 1960
Career: 2,059, Gary Anderson,
Pittsburgh Steelers (1982–94),
Philadelphia Eagles (1995–96),
San Francisco 49ers (1997),
Minnesota Vikings (1999–2000)

MOST TOUCHDOWN PASSES

Season: 48, Dan Marino
(Miami Dolphins), 1984
Career: 420, Dan Marino
(Miami Dolphins), 1983–99

MOST TOUCHDOWNS

Career: 180, Jerry Rice (San
Francisco 49ers), 1985–99

MOST YARDS
GAINED PASSING

Season: 5,084, Dan Marino
(Miami Dolphins), 1984
Career: 61,631, Dan Marino
(Miami Dolphins), 1983–99

MOST YARDS
GAINED RECEIVING

Season: 1,848, Jerry Rice
(San Francisco 49ers), 1995
Career: 19,247, Jerry Rice
(San Francisco 49ers), 1985–2000

MOST YARDS
GAINED RUSHING

Season: 2,105, Eric Dickerson
(Los Angeles Rams), 1984
Career: 16,726, Walter Payton
(Chicago Bears), 1975–87

BASKETBALL

NBA – National Basketball Association

HIGHEST
SCORING AVERAGE

NBA play-off career: 33.4
(5,987 points in 179 games),

Michael Jordan,
Chicago Bulls, 1984–98
NBA season: 50.4 points per
game, Wilt Chamberlain,
Philadelphia Warriors, 1961/62

MOST BASKETBALL
FIELD GOALS

NBA game: 36, Wilt Chamberlain,
Philadelphia Warriors,
March 2 1962
NBA season: 1,597, Wilt
Chamberlain, Philadelphia Warriors,
1961/62

MOST POINTS
SCORED BY A TEAM

NBA quarter: 58, Buffalo Braves,
Oct 20 1972
NBA half: 107, Phoenix Suns,
Nov 11 1990
NBA game: 186, Detroit Pistons,
Dec 13 1983

MOST FREE
THROWS SCORED

NBA game: 29, Wilt
Chamberlain, Philadelphia
Warriors, March 2 1962; and
Adrian Dantley, Utah Jazz,
Jan 5 1984

GREATEST WINNING MARGIN

NBA game: 68 points (148–80), Cleveland Cavaliers, Dec 17 1991

MOST NBA MINUTES PLAYED

Career: 57,446 min, Kareem Abdul-Jabbar, Milwaukee Bucks (1969–75) and Los Angeles Lakers (1975–89)

MOST NBA PLAY-OFF APPEARANCES

Career: 237, Kareem Abdul-Jabbar, Milwaukee Bucks (1969–75), and Los Angeles Lakers (1975–89)

GOLF

MOST MAJOR GOLF TITLES

British Amateur: 8, John Ball (UK), 1888, 1890, 1892, 1894, 1899, 1907, 1910, 1912

US Amateur: 5, Bobby Jones Jr. (USA), 1924, 1925, 1927, 1928, 1930

US Women's Amateur: 6, Glenna Vare (USA), 1922, 1925, 1928–30, 1935

US Women's Open: 4, Betsy Earle-Rawls (USA), 1951, 1953, 1957, 1960; and Mickey Wright (USA), 1958, 1959, 1961, 1964

BEST SCORES

US Open Score, 18: Any round 63, Johnny Miller (USA), June 17 1973; Jack Nicklaus (USA), June 12 1980; and Tom Weiskopf (USA), June 12 1980

US Open Score, 72: 272, Jack Nicklaus (USA), 63, 71, 70, 68, June 12–15 1980; Lee Janzen (USA), 67, 67, 69, 69, June 17–20 1993; and Tiger Woods (USA), 65, 69, 71, 67, June 13–16 2000

The Open Score, 18: Any round 63, Mark Hayes (USA), July 7 1977; Isao Aoki (Japan), July 19 1980; Greg Norman (Australia), July 18 1986; Paul Broadhurst (UK), July 21 1990; Jodie Mudd (USA), July 21 1991; Nick Faldo (UK), July 16 1993; and Payne Stewart (USA), July 18 1993

The Open Score, 72: 267 (66, 68, 69, 64), Greg Norman (Australia), July 15–18 1993

US Masters Score, 18: Any round 63, Nick Price (Zimbabwe), 1986; and Greg Norman (Australia), 1996

US Masters Score, 72: 270 (70, 66, 65, 69), Tiger Woods, 1997

US PGA Score, 18: 63, Bruce Crampton (Australia), 1975; Raymond Floyd (USA), 1982; Gary Player (South Africa), 1984; Vijay Singh (Fiji), 1993; Michael Bradley (USA), 1995; Brad Faxon (USA), 1995; and José Maria Olazábal (Spain), 2000

US PGA Score, 72: aggregate 267, Steve Elkington (Australia), 68, 67, 68, 64, 1995; and Colin Montgomerie (UK), 68, 67, 67, 65, 1995

TENNIS

AGE RECORDS

YOUNGEST CHAMPIONS

French Open, doubles pair: 15 yr 339 days, Andrea Jaeger, and 16 yr 296 days, Jimmy Arias (both USA), 1981

French Open, singles: 16 yr 169 days, Monica Seles (Yugoslavia, now USA), 1990

French Open, men's singles: 17 yr 109 days, Michael Chang (USA), 1989

Australian Open, singles: 16 yr 117 days, Martina Hingis (Switzerland), 1997
Australian Open, men's singles: 17, Rodney Heath (Australia), 1905
Wimbledon: 15 yr 282 days, Martina Hingis (Switzerland), in women's doubles with Helena Sukova (Czech Republic), 1996
Wimbledon, women's singles: 15 yr 285 days, Charlotte Dod (UK), 1887

Wimbledon, men: 17 yr 227 days, Boris Becker (West Germany), 1985
US Open: 15 yr 139 days, Vincent Richards, (USA), 1918 (men's doubles)
US Open, women's singles: 16 yr 271 days, Tracey Austin (USA), 1979
US Open, men's singles: 19 yr 28 days, Pete Sampras (USA), 1990

YOUNGEST WORLD TENNIS NUMBER ONE
Women: 16 yr 182 days, Martina Hingis (Switzerland), March 31 1997
Men: 20 yr 234 days, Marat Mikhailovich Safin (Russia), Sept 17 2000

YOUNGEST WIMBLEDON PLAYER
Match winner: 14 yr 89 days, Jennifer Capriati (USA), 1990
Seeded competitor: 14 yr 89 days, Jennifer Capriati (USA), 1990

OLDEST CHAMPIONS
French Open: 42 yr 88 days, Elizabeth Ryan (USA), 1934 (women's doubles)
French Open, singles: 34 yr 301 days, Andrés Gimeno (Spain), 1972
Australian Open: 46 yr 60 days, Norman Everard Brookes (Australia), 1924 (men's doubles)

Australian Open, singles: 37 yr 62 days, Kenneth Robert Rosewall (Australia), 1972

GRAND SLAM RECORDS

MOST DOUBLES PARTNERSHIP TITLES
Women: 20 (12 US, 5 Wimbledon, 3 French), Althea Louise Brough (USA) and Margaret Evelyn du Pont

(*née* Osborne, USA), 1942–57; and Martina Navratilova (USA) and Pam Shriver (USA), 7 Australian, 5 Wimbledon, 4 French, 4 USA, 1981–89

Men: 12 (5 Wimbledon, 4 Australian, 2 French, 1 US), John Newcombe (Australia) and Tony Roche (Australia), 1965, 1976

ATP TOUR RECORDS

MOST WINS
Doubles: 7, John McEnroe and Peter Fleming (both USA), 1978–84
Singles: 5, Ivan Lendl (Czech Republic), 1982, 1983, 1986, 1987

MOST QUALIFICATIONS
ATP tour: 16 (14 consecutive), Jimmy Connors (USA), 1972–85, 1987, 1988

ATHLETICS

WOMEN'S INDOOR RECORDS

50 M
5.96, Irina Privalova (Russia), Madrid, Spain, Feb 9 1995

50-M HURDLES
6.58, Cornelia Oschkenat (GDR), Berlin, Germany, Feb 20 1988

60 M
6.92, Irina Privalova (Russia), Madrid, Spain, Feb 11 1993 and Feb 9 1995

60-M HURDLES
7.69, Lyudmila Narozhilenko (Russia), Chelyabinsk, Russia, Feb 4 1993

200 M
21.87, Merlene Ottey (Jamaica), Liévin, France, Feb 13 1993

400 M
49.59, Jarmila Kratochvílovà (Czechoslovakia), Milan, Italy, March 7 1982

800 M
1:56.40, Christine Wachtel (GDR), Vienna, Austria, Feb 13 1988

1,000 M
2:30.94, Maria Mutola (Mozambique), Stockholm, Sweden, Feb 25 1999

1,500 M
4:00.27, Doina Melinte (Romania),
East Rutherford, NJ, USA, Feb 9 1990

1 MILE
4:17.14, Doina Melinte (Romania),
East Rutherford, NJ, USA, Feb 9 1990

3,000 M
8:32.88, Gabriela Szabo (Romania),
Birmingham, UK, Feb 18 2001

5,000 M
14:47.36, Gabriela Szabo (Romania),
Dortmund, Germany, Feb 13 1999

4 X 200 M RELAY
1:32.55, SC Eintracht Hamm, West
Germany (Helga Arendt, Silke-Beate
Knoll, Mechthild Kluth, Gisela Kinzel),
Dortmund, Germany, Feb 19 1988;
LG Olympia Dortmund, Germany
(Esther Moller, Gabi Rockmeier,
Birgit Rockmeier, Andrea Phillip),
Karlsruhe, Germany, Feb 21 1999

4 X 400 M RELAY
3:24.25, Russia (Tatyana Chebykina,
Svetlana Goncharenko, Olga
Kotlyarova, Natalya Nazarova),
Maebashi, Japan, March 7 1999

3,000-M WALK
11:40.33, Claudia Iovan (Romania),
Bucharest, Romania, Jan 30 1999

PENTATHLON
4,991 points, Irina Belova (Russia),
Berlin, Germany, Feb 14–15 1992,
60-m hurdles: 8.22; **High jump:**
6 ft 4 in (1.93 m); **Shot:** 43 ft 5.5 in
(13.25 m); **Long jump:** 21 ft 10.5 in
(6.67 m); **800 m:** 2:10.26

LONG JUMP
24 ft 2 in (7.37 m), Heike Drechsler
(GDR), Vienna, Austria, Feb 13 1988

TRIPLE JUMP
49 ft 8.75 in (15.16 m), Ashia Hansen
(UK), Valencia, Spain, Feb 28 1998

HIGH JUMP
6 ft 9.5 in (2.07 m), Heike Henkel
(Germany), Karlsruhe, Germany,
Feb 9 1992

POLE VAULT
15 ft 5 in (4.70 m), Stacy Dragila
(USA), Pocatello, Idaho, USA,
Feb 17 2001

SHOT PUT
73 ft 10 in (22.50 m), Helena
Fibingerová (Czechoslovakia),
Jablonec, Czechoslovakia,
Feb 19 1977

MEN'S INDOOR RECORDS

50 M
5.56, Donovan Bailey (Canada),
Reno, NV, USA, Feb 9 1996; and
Maurice Greene (USA), Los Angeles,
USA, Feb 13 1999

50-M HURDLES
6.25, Mark McCoy (Canada), Kobe,
Japan, March 5 1986

60 M
6.39, Maurice Greene (USA),
Madrid, Spain, Feb 3 1998 and
March 3 2001

60-M HURDLES
7.30, Colin Jackson (UK),
Sindelfingen, Germany, March 6 1994

200 M
19.92, Frank Fredericks (Namibia),
Liévin, France, Feb 18 1996

400 M
44.63, Michael Johnson (USA),
Atlanta, USA, March 4 1995

800 M
1:42.67, Wilson Kipketer
(Denmark), Paris, France,
March 9 1997

1,000 M
2:14.96, Wilson Kipketer (Denmark),
Birmingham, UK, Feb 20 2000

1,500 M
3:31.18, Hicham El Guerrouj
(Morocco), Stuttgart, Germany,
Feb 2 1997

1 MILE
3:48.46, Hicham El Guerrouj
(Morocco), Ghent, Belgium,
Feb 12 1997

3,000 M
7:24.90, Daniel Komen (Kenya),
Budapest, Hungary, Feb 6 1998

5,000 M
12:50.38, Haile Gebrselassie
(Ethiopia), Birmingham, UK,
Feb 14 1999

4 X 200 M RELAY
1:22.11, Great Britain (Linford
Christie, Darren Braithwaite,
Ade Mafe, John Regis), Glasgow,
Scotland, UK, March 3 1991

4 X 400 M RELAY
3:02.83, USA (Andre Morris,
Dameon Johnson, Deon Minor,
Milton Campbell), Maebashi,
Japan, March 7 1999

5,000-M WALK
18:07.08, Mikhail Shchennikov
(Russia), Moscow, Russia,
Feb 14 1995

HEPTATHLON
6,476 points, Dan Dion O'Brien (USA),
Toronto, Canada, March 13–14 1993
60 m: 6.67; **Long jump:** 25 ft 8.5 in
(7.84 m); **Shot:** 52 ft 6.5 in (16.02 m);
High jump: 6 ft 11.75 in (2.13 m);
60-m hurdles: 7.85; **Pole vault:**
17 ft 0.75 in (5.20 m); **1,000 m:** 2:57.96

LONG JUMP
28 ft 10 in (8.79 m), Carl Lewis (USA),
New York, USA, Jan 27 1984

TRIPLE JUMP
58 ft 6 in (17.83 m), Aliecer Urrutia
(Cuba), Sindelfingen, Germany,
March 1 1997

HIGH JUMP
7 ft 11.5 in (2.43 m), Javier
Sotomayor (Cuba), Budapest,
Hungary, March 4 1989

POLE VAULT
20 ft 2 in (6.15 m), Sergei Bubka
(Ukraine), Donetsk, Ukraine,
Feb 21 1993

SHOT PUT
74 ft 4 in (22.66 m) Randy Barnes
(USA), Los Angeles, USA,
Jan 20 1989

WOMEN'S OUTDOOR RECORDS

100 M
10.49, Florence Griffith-Joyner (USA),
Indianapolis, USA, July 16 1988

100-M HURDLES
12.21, Yordanka Donkova (Bulgaria),
Stara Zagora, Bulgaria, Aug 20 1988

200 M
21.34, Florence Griffith-Joyner (USA),
Seoul, South Korea, Sept 29 1988

1 HOUR
18,340 m, Tegla Loroupe (Kenya), Borgholzhausen, Germany, Aug 7 1998

20,000 M
1:05:26.6, Tegla Loroupe (Kenya), Borgholzhausen, Germany, Sept 3 2000

25,000 M
1:29:29.2, Karolina Szabó (Hungary), Budapest, Hungary, April 23 1988

30,000 M
1:47:05.6, Karolina Szabó (Hungary), Budapest, Hungary, April 23 1988

4 X 100 M RELAY
41.37, GDR (Silke Gladisch, Sabine Rieger, Ingrid Auerswald, Marlies Gohr), Canberra, Australia, Oct 6 1985

4 X 200 M RELAY
1:27.46, United States 'Blue' (LaTasha Jenkins, Chryste Gaines, Nanceen Perry, Torri Edwards), Philadelphia, USA, April 29 2000

4 X 400 M RELAY
3:15.17, USSR (Tatyana Ledovskaya, Olga Nazarova, Maria Pinigina, Olga Bryzgina), Seoul, South Korea, Oct 1 1988

4 X 800 M RELAY
7:50.17, USSR (Nadezhda Olizarenko, Lyubov Gurina, Lyudmila Borisova, Irina Podyalovskaya), Moscow, Russia, Aug 5 1984

HEPTATHLON
7,291 points, Jacqueline Joyner-Kersee (USA), Seoul, South Korea, Sept 23–24 1988
100-m hurdles: 12.69;
High jump: 6 ft 1.25 in (1.86 m);
Shot: 51 ft 10 in (15.80 m);
200 m: 22.56; **Long jump:** 23 ft 10.25 in (7.27 m); **Javelin:** 149 ft 10 in (45.66 m); **800 m:** 2:08.51

LONG JUMP
24 ft 8 in (7.52 m), Galina Chistyakova (USSR), Leningrad, USSR, June 11 1988

TRIPLE JUMP
50 ft 10.25 in (15.50 m), Inessa Kravets (Ukraine), Gothenburg, Sweden, Aug 10 1995

HIGH JUMP
2.09 m (6 ft 10.25 in), Stefka Kostadinova (Bulgaria), Rome, Italy, Aug 30 1987

POLE VAULT
15 ft 5 in (4.70 m), Stacy Dragila (USA), Pocatello, USA, April 27 2001

SHOT PUT
74 ft 3 in (22.63 m), Natalya Lisovskaya (USSR), Moscow, Russia, June 7 1987

DISCUS
252 ft (76.80 m), Gabriele Reinsch (GDR), Neubrandenburg, Germany, July 9 1988

HAMMER
249 ft 6 in (76.07 m), Mihaela Melinte (Romania), Rüdlingen, Germany, Aug 29 1999

400 M
47.60, Marita Koch (GDR), Canberra, Australia, Oct 6 1985

400-M HURDLES
52.61, Kim Batten (USA), Gothenburg, Sweden, Aug 11 1995

800 M
1:53.28, Jarmila Kratochvílova (Czechoslovakia), Munich, Germany, July 26 1983

1,000 M
2:28.98, Svetlana Masterkova (Russia), Brussels, Belgium, Aug 23 1996

1,500 M
3:50.46, Qu Yunxia (China), Beijing, China, Sept 11 1993

1 MILE
4:12.56, Svetlana Masterkova (Russia), Zurich, Switzerland, Aug 14 1996

2,000 M
5:25.36, Sonia O'Sullivan (Ireland), Edinburgh, Scotland, UK, July 8 1994

3,000 M
8:06.11, Wang Junxia (China), Beijing, China, Sept 13 1993

3,000-M STEEPLECHASE
9:40.20, Cristina Iloc-Casandra (Romania), Reims, France, Aug 30 2000

5,000 M
14:28.09, Jiang Bo (China), Beijing, China, Oct 23 1997

10,000 M
29:31.78, Wang Junxia (China), Beijing, China, Sept 8 1993

GUINNESS WORLD RECORDS

JAVELIN
227 ft 11 in (69.48 m), Trine Solberg-Hattestad (Norway), Oslo, Norway, July 28 2000

MEN'S OUTDOOR RECORDS

100 M
9.79, Maurice Greene (USA), Athens, Greece, June 16 1999

110-M HURDLES
12.91, Colin Jackson (UK), Stuttgart, Germany, Aug 20 1993

200 M
19.32, Michael Johnson (USA), Atlanta, Georgia, USA, Aug 1 1996

400 M
43.18, Michael Johnson (USA), Seville, Spain, Aug 26 1999

400-M HURDLES
46.78, Kevin Young (USA), Barcelona, Spain, Aug 6 1992

800 M
1:41.11, Wilson Kipketer (Denmark), Cologne, Germany, Aug 24 1997

1,000 M
2:11.96, Noah Ngeny (Kenya), Rieti, Italy, Sept 5 1999

1,500 M
3:26.00, Hicham El Guerrouj (Morocco), Rome, Italy, 14 July 1998

1 MILE
3:43.13, Hicham El Guerrouj (Morroco), Rome, Italy, July 7 1999

2,000 M
4:44.79, Hicham El Guerrouj (Morocco), Berlin, Germany, Sept 7 1999

3,000 M
7:20.67, Daniel Komen (Kenya), Rieti, Italy, Sept 1 1996

3,000-M STEEPLECHASE
7:55.72, Bernard Barmasai (Kenya), Cologne, Germany, Aug 24 1997

5,000 M
12:39.36, Haile Gebrselassie (Ethiopia), Helsinki, Finland, June 13 1998

10,000 M
26:22.75, Haile Gebrselassie (Ethiopia), Hengelo, Netherlands, June 1 1998

20,000 M
56:55.6, Arturo Barrios (Mexico, now USA), La Flèche, France, March 30 1991

1 HOUR
21,101 m, Arturo Barrios (Mexico, now USA), La Flèche, France, March 30 1991

25,000 M
1:13:55.8, Toshihiko Seko (Japan), Christchurch, New Zealand, March 22 1981

30,000 M
1:29:18.8, Toshihiko Seko (Japan), Christchurch, New Zealand, March 22 1981

4 X 100 M RELAY
37.40, USA (Michael Marsh, Leroy Burrell, Dennis A. Mitchell, Carl Lewis), Barcelona, Spain, Aug 8 1992; USA (John Drummond Jr., Andre Cason, Dennis Mitchell, Leroy Burrell), Stuttgart, Germany, Aug 21 1993

4 X 200 M RELAY
1:18.68, Santa Monica Track Club, USA (Michael Marsh, Leroy Burrell, Floyd Wayne Heard, Carl Lewis), Walnut, CA, USA, April 17 1994

4 X 400 M RELAY
2:54.20, USA (Jerome Young, Antonio Pettigrew, Tyree Washington, Michael Duane Johnson), New York, USA, July 23 1998

4 X 800 M RELAY

7:03.89, Great Britain (Peter Elliott, Garry Peter Cook, Stephen Cram, Sebastian Coe), London, UK, Aug 30 1982

4 X 1,500 M RELAY

14:38.8, West Germany (Thomas Wessinghage, Harald Hudak, Michael Lederer, Karl Fleschen), Cologne, Germany, Aug 17 1977

DECATHLON

9,026 points, Roman Sebrle (Czech Republic), Götzis, Austria, May 26–27 2001
Day 1
100 m: 10.64; **Long jump:** 26 ft 7.25 in (8.11 m); **Shot:** 50 ft 3.5 in (15.33 m); **High jump:** 6 ft 11.25 in (2.12 m); **400 m:** 47.79
Day 2
110-m hurdles: 13.92; **Discus:** 157 ft 2.5 in (47.92 m); **Pole vault:** 15 ft 9 in (4.80 m); **Javelin:** 230 ft 2 in (70.16 m); **1,500 m:** 4:21.98

LONG JUMP

29 ft 4.5 in (8.95 m), Mike Powell (USA), Tokyo, Japan, Aug 30 1991

TRIPLE JUMP

60 ft 0.25 in (18.29 m), Jonathan Edwards (UK), Gothenburg, Sweden, Aug 7 1995

HIGH JUMP

8 ft 0.5 in (2.45 m), Javier Sotomayor (Cuba), Salamanca, Spain, July 27 1993

POLE VAULT

20 ft 1.75 in (6.14 m), Sergei Bubka (Ukraine), Sestriere, Italy, July 31 1994

SHOT PUT

75 ft 10.25 in (23.12 m), Randy Barnes (USA), Los Angeles, USA, May 20 1990

DISCUS

243 ft (74.08 m), Jürgen Schult (GDR), Neubrandenburg, Germany, June 6 1986

HAMMER

284 ft 7 in (86.74 m), Yuriy Sedykh (USSR, now Russia), Stuttgart, Germany, Aug 30 1986

JAVELIN

323 ft 1 in (98.48 m), Jan Zelezný (Czech Republic), Jena, Germany, May 25 1996

CYCLING

WOMEN'S WORLD RECORDS

UNPACED STANDING START

500 m: 34.017, Felicia Ballanger (France), Bogotá, Colombia, Sept 29 1995
3 km: 3:30.816, Leontien Zijlaard-van Moorsel (Netherlands), Sydney, Australia, Sept 17 2000

UNPACED FLYING START

200 m: 10.831, Olga Slyusareva (Russia), Moscow, Russia, April 25 1993

MEN'S WORLD RECORDS

UNPACED STANDING START

1 km: 1:00.148, Arnaud Tournant (France), Mexico City, Mexico, June 16 2000
4 km: 4:11.114, Chris Boardman (UK), Manchester, UK, Aug 29 1996

UNPACED FLYING START

200 m: 9.865, Curtis Harnett (Canada), Bogotá, Colombia, Sept 28 1995
500 m: 26.649, Aleksandr Kiritchenko (USSR), Moscow, Russia, Oct 29 1988

TEAM PURSUIT

4 km: 3:59.710, Germany (Robert Bartko, Guido Fulst, Jens Lehmann, Daniel Becke), Sydney, Australia, Sept 19 2000

SKIING

WOMEN'S RECORDS

MOST OLYMPIC TITLES

Alpine: 3, Vreni Schneider (Switzerland), giant slalom, slalom

1988; slalom 1994; Katja Seizinger (Germany), downhill 1994; combined, downhill 1998; and Deborah Campagnoni (Italy), super giant slalom 1992; giant slalom 1994; giant slalom 1998
Nordic: 6, Lyubov Yegorova (Russia), 10 km, 15 km, 4 x 5 km 1992; 5 km, 10 km, 4 x 5 km 1994

MOST WORLD CUP ALPINE TITLES

Overall: 6, Annemarie Moser-Pröll (Austria), 1971–75, 1979
Downhill: 7, Annemarie Moser-Pröll (Austria), 1971–75, 1978–79
Slalom: 6, Vreni Schneider (Switzerland), 1989–90, 1992–95
Giant slalom: 5, Vreni Schneider (Switzerland), 1986–87, 1989, 1991, 1995
Super giant slalom: 5, Katja Seizinger (Germany), 1993–96, 1998

MOST WORLD CUP NORDIC TITLES

Cross-country: 4, Yelena Välbe (USSR/Russia), 1989, 1991–92, 1995

MEN'S RECORDS

MOST OLYMPIC TITLES

Alpine: 3, Anton 'Toni' Sailer (Austria), downhill, slalom, giant slalom, 1956; Jean-Claude Killy (France), downhill, slalom, giant slalom, 1968; Alberto Tomba (Italy), slalom, giant slalom, 1988; giant slalom, 1992
Nordic: 8, Bjørn Dæhlie (Norway), 15 km, 50 km, 4 x 10 km, 1992; 10 km, 15 km, 1994; 10 km, 5 km, 4 x 10 km, 1998
Jumping: 4, Matti Nykänen (Finland), 70 m hill, 1988; 90 m hill, 1984, 1988; Team 1988

MOST WORLD CUP ALPINE TITLES

Overall: 5, Marc Girardelli (Luxembourg), 1985–86, 1989, 1991, 1993
Downhill: 5, Franz Klammer (Austria), 1975–78, 1983
Slalom: 8, Ingemar Stenmark (Sweden), 1975–81, 1983
Giant slalom: 7, Ingemar Stenmark (Sweden), 1975–76, 1978–81, 1984
Super giant slalom: 4, Pirmin Zurbriggen (Switzerland), 1987–90

MOST WORLD CUP NORDIC TITLES

Jumping: 4, Matti Nykänen (Finland), 1983, 1985–86, 1988
Cross-country: 5, Gunde Svan (Sweden), 1984–86, 1988–89; Bjørn Dæhlie (Norway), 1992–93, 1995–97

SPEED SKATING

WOMEN'S RECORDS

500 m: 37.29, Catriona LeMay Doan (Canada), Salt Lake City, USA, March 9 2001
1,000 m: 1:14.13, Monique Garbrecht-Enfeldt (Germany), Salt Lake City, Utah, USA, March 10 2001
1,500 m: 1:54.38, Anni Friesinger (Germany), Calgary, Canada, March 4 2001
3,000 m: 3:59.26, Claudia Pechstein (Germany), Calgary, Canada, March 2 2001
5,000 m: 6:52.44, Gunda Niemann-Stirnemann (Germany), Salt Lake City, USA, March 10 2001

LOWEST WORLD CHAMPIONSHIP SCORE
161.479 points, Gunda Niemann-Stirnemann (Germany), Hamar, Norway, Feb 6–7 1999

SHORT TRACK
500 m: 43.873, Evgenia Radanova (Bulgaria), Lake Placid, NY, USA, Feb 18 2000
1,000 m: 1:31.991, Yang Yang (China), Nagano, Japan, Feb 21 1998
1,500 m: 2:25.146, Evgenia Radanova (Bulgaria), Szekesfehervar, Hungary, Nov 6 1998
3,000 m: 5:01.976, Eun-kyung Choi (South Korea), Calgary, Canada, Oct 22 2000
3,000-m relay: 4:16.260, South Korea (An Sang-mi, Chun Lee-kyung, Kim Yun-mi, Won Hye-kyung), Nagano, Japan, Feb 17 1998

MEN'S RECORDS
500 m: 34.32, Hiroyasu Shimizu (Japan), Salt Lake City, USA, March 10 2001
1,000 m: 1:08.28, Jeremy Wotherspoon (Canada), Salt Lake City, USA, March 11 2001
1,500 m: 1:45.20, Kyu-Hyuk Lee (South Korea), Calgary, Canada, March 15 2001
3,000 m: 3:42.75, Gianni Romme (Netherlands), Calgary, Canada, Aug 11 2000
5,000 m: 6:18.72, Gianni Romme (Netherlands), Nagano, Japan, Jan 30 2000
10,000 m: 13:03.40, Gianni Romme (Netherlands), Heerenveen, Netherlands, Nov 26 2000

LOWEST WORLD CHAMPIONSHIP SCORE
152.651 points Rintje Ritsma (Netherlands), Hamar, Norway, Feb 6–7 1999

SHORT TRACK
500 m: 41.938, Nicola Franceschina (Italy), Bormio, Italy, March 29 1998
1,000 m: 1:28.23, Marc Gagnon (Canada), Seoul, South Korea, April 4 1997
1,500 m: 2:15.50, Kai Feng (China), Groningen, Netherlands, Nov 11 1997
3,000 m: 4:46.727, Kim Dong-sung (South Korea), Szekesfehervar, Hungary, Nov 8 1998
5,000-m relay: 6:49.618, South Korea Chang Chun, China, Dec 5 1999

FIGURE SKATING

GRAND SLAM RECORDS
The figure-skating grand slams make up the European, World, and Olympic titles.

MOST FIGURE-SKATING GRAND SLAMS
Women: 2, Sonja Henie (Norway), 1932, 1936; and Katarina Witt (West Germany), 1984, 1988
Men: 2, Karl Schäfer (Austria), 1932, 1936

WORLD CHAMPIONSHIP RECORDS

MOST TITLES
Individual titles, women: 10, Sonja Henie (Norway), 1927–36
Individual titles, men: 10, Ulrich Salchow (Sweden), 1901–05, 1907–11

World titles, pairs: 10, Irina Rodnina (4 with Aleksey Nikolayevich Ulanov, 1969–72; 6 with Aleksandr Gennadyevich Zaitsev, 1973–78)
Dance titles, pairs: 6, Lyudmila Alekseyevna Pakhomova and husband Aleksandr Georgiyevich Gorshkov (USSR), 1970–74, 1976

YOUNGEST WORLD CHAMPION
Individual title: 14 yr 286 days, Tara Lipinski (USA), March 22 1997

COMPETITION RECORDS

HIGHEST MARKS
Women: 7 perfect 6.0s, Midori Ito (Japan), World Figure Skating Championships, Paris, France, 1989
Men: 7 perfect 6.0s, Donald George Jackson (Canada), Prague, Czechoslovakia, 1962
Pairs (dancing): 29 perfect 6.0s, Jayne Torvill and Christopher Dean (both UK), Ottawa, Canada, March 22–24 1984

SWIMMING

WOMEN'S SHORT-COURSE RECORDS

BACKSTROKE
50 m: 27.25, Haley Cope (USA), Indianapolis, USA, March 7 2000
100 m: 58.45, Mia Nakamura (Japan), Sagamihara, Japan, March 23 2001

200 m: 2:06.09, He Cihong (China), Palma de Mallorca, Spain, Dec 5 1993

BREASTSTROKE
50 m: 30.60, Penny Heyns (South Africa), Durban, South Africa, Sept 26 1999
100 m: 1:05.40, Penny Heyns (South Africa), Durban, South Africa, Sept 26 1999
200 m: 2:19.25, Hiu Qi (China), Paris, France, Jan 28 2001

BUTTERFLY
50 m: 25.36, Anne-Karin Kammerling, (Sweden), Stockholm, Sweden, Jan 25 2001

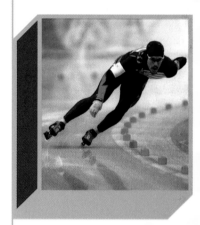

100 m: 56.56, Jenny Thompson (USA), Athens, Greece, March 18 2000
200 m: 2:04.16, Susan O'Neill (Australia), Sydney, Australia, Jan 18 2000

FREESTYLE
50 m: 23.59, Therese Alshammar (Sweden), Athens, Greece, March 18 2000
100 m: 52.17, Therese Alshammar (Sweden), Athens, Greece, March 17 2000
200 m: 1:54.17 Claudia Poll (Costa Rica), Gothenburg, Sweden, April 18 1997
400 m: 4:00.03, Claudia Poll (Costa Rica), Gothenburg, Sweden, April 19 1997
800 m: 8:15.34, Astrid Strauss (GDR), Bonn, Germany, Feb 6 1987
1,500 m: 15:43.31, Petra Schneider (GDR), Gainesville, FL, USA, Jan 10 1982
4 x 50 m relay: 1:38.21, Sweden (Annika Lofstedt, Therese Alshammar, Johanna Sjöberg, Anna-Karin Kammerling), Valencia, Spain, Dec 15 2000

4 x 100 m relay: 3:34.55,
China (Le Jingyi, Na Chao,
Shan Ying, Nian Yin),
Gothenburg, Sweden,
April 19 1997
4 x 200 m relay: 7:49.11,
Great Britain (Claire Huddart,
Nicola Jackson, Karen Legg,
Karen Pickering), Athens,
Greece, March 16 2000

MEDLEY
100 m: 59.30, Jenny
Thompson (USA), Hong
Kong, April 2 1999
200 m: 2:07.79, Allison
Wagner (USA), Palma de
Mallorca, Spain, Dec 5 1993
400 m: 4:29.00, Dai Gouhong
(China), Palma de Mallorca, Spain,
Dec 2 1993
4 x 50 m relay: 1:48.31, Sweden
(Therese Alshammar, Emma
Igelström, Anna-Karin Kammerling,
Johanna Sjöberg), Valencia, Spain,
Dec 16 2001
4 x 100 m relay: 3:57.46, University
of Georgia, USA (Courtney Shealy,
Kristy Kowal, Keegan Walkley,
Maritza Correia), Indianapolis, USA,
March 16 2000

MEN'S SHORT-COURSE RECORDS

BACKSTROKE
50 m: 23.42, Neil Walker (USA),
Athens, Greece, March 16 2000
100 m: 50.75, Neil Walker (USA),
Athens, Greece, March 19 2000
200 m: 1:51.62, Matt Welsh
(Australia), Melbourne, Australia,
Oct 13 2000; and Gordon Kozulj
(Croatia), Berlin, Germany,
Jan 21 2001

BREASTSTROKE
50 m: 26.70, Mark Warnecke
(Germany), Sheffield, UK,
Dec 11 1998
100 m: 57.66, Ed Moses (USA),
Minneapolis, USA, March 24 2000
200 m: 2:06.40, Ed Moses (USA),
Minneapolis, USA, March 25 2000

BUTTERFLY
50 m: 22.87, Mark Foster (UK),
Sheffield, UK, Jan 17 2001
100 m: 50.44, Lars Frolander
(Sweden), Athens, Greece,
March 17 2000
200 m: 1:51.58, Franck Esposito
(France), Antibes, France,
Jan 13 2001

FREESTYLE

50 m: 21.13, Mark Foster (UK), Paris, France, Jan 28 2001
100 m: 46.74, Aleksandr Popov (Russia), Gelsenkirchen, Germany, March 19 1994
200 m: 1:41.10, Ian Thorpe (Australia), Berlin, Germany, Feb 5 2000
400 m: 3:35.01, Grant Hackett (Australia), Hong Kong, April 2 1999
800 m: 7:34.90, Kieren Perkins (Australia), Sydney, Australia, July 25 1993
1,500 m: 14:19.55, Grant Hackett (Australia) Sydney, Australia, Sept 27 1998
4 x 50 m relay: 1:26.78, USA (Bryan Jones, Matt Ulricksson, Robert Bogart, Leffie Crawford), Minneapolis, USA, March 23 2000
4 x 100 m relay: 3:09.57, Sweden (Johan Nystrom, Lars Frolander, Mattias Ohlin, Stefan Nystrand), Athens, Greece, March 16 2000
4 x 200 m relay: 7:01.33, USA (Josh Davis, Neil Walker, Scott Tucker, Chad Carvin), Athens, Greece, March 17 2000

MEDLEY

100 m: 52.79, Neil Walker (USA), Athens, Greece, March 18 2000
200 m: 1:54.65, Jani Sievinen (Finland), Kuopio, Finland, Jan 21 1994; and Atilla Czene (Hungary), Minneapolis, USA, March 23 2000

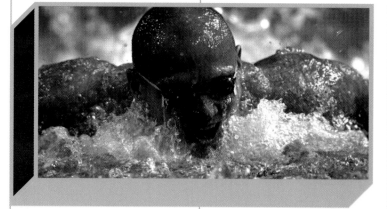

400 m: 4:04.24, Matthew Dunn (Australia), Perth, Australia, Sept 24 1998
4 x 50 m relay: 1:35.51, Germany (Thomas Rupprath, Mark Warnecke, Alexander Luderitz, Stephane Kunzelmann) and Sweden (Daniel Carlsson, Patrik Isaksson, Jonas Akesson, Lars Frolande), Sheffield, UK, Dec 13 1998
4 x 100 m relay: 3:29.88, Australia (Matt Welsh, Phil Rogers, Michael Klim, Chris Fydler), Hong Kong, April 4 1999

WOMEN'S LONG-COURSE RECORDS

BACKSTROKE

50 m: 28.25, Sandra Voelker (Germany), Berlin, Germany, June 17 2000
100 m: 1:00.16, He Cihong (China), Rome, Italy, Sept 10 1994
200 m: 2:06.62, Krisztina Egerszegi (Hungary), Athens, Greece, Aug 25 1991

BREASTSTROKE

50 m: 30.83, Penny Heyns (South Africa), Sydney, Australia, Aug 28 1999
100 m: 1:06.52, Penny Heyns (South Africa), Sydney, Australia, Aug 23 1999
200 m: 2:22.99, Hiu Qi (China), Hangzhou, China, April 3 2001

BUTTERFLY

50 m: 25.64, Inge de Bruijn (Netherlands), Sheffield, UK, May 26 2000

100 m: 56.61, Inge de Bruijn (Netherlands), Sydney, Australia, Sept 17 2000
200 m: 2:05.81, Susan O'Neill (Australia), Sydney, Australia, May 17 2000

FREESTYLE

50 m: 24.32, Inge de Bruijn (Netherlands), Sydney, Australia, Sept 23 2000
100 m: 53.77, Inge de Bruijn (Netherlands), Sydney, Australia, Sept 20 2000
200 m: 1:56.78, Franziska van Almsick (Germany), Rome, Italy, Sept 6 1994

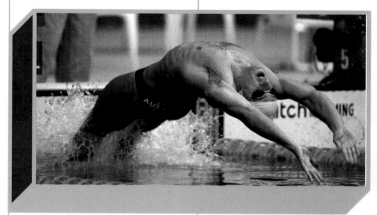

400 m: 4:03.85, Janet Evans (USA), Seoul, South Korea, Sept 22 1988
800 m: 8:16.22, Janet Evans (USA), Tokyo, Japan, Aug 20 1989
1,500 m: 15:52.10, Janet Evans (USA), Orlando, USA, March 26 1988
4 x 100 m relay: USA (Amy van Dyken, Dara Torres, Courtney Shealy, Jenny Thompson), Sydney, Australia, Sept 16 2000

4 x 200 m relay: 7:55.47, East Germany (Manuela Stellmach, Astrid Strauss, Anke Möhring, Heike Friedrich), Strasbourg, France, Aug 18 1987

MEDLEY

200 m: 2:09.72, Wu Yanyan (China), Shanghai, China, Oct 17 1997
400 m: 4:33.59, Yana Klochkova (Ukraine), Sydney, Australia, Sept 16 2000
4 x 100 m relay: 3:58.30, USA (Megan Quann, Jenny Thompson, BJ Bedford, Dara Torres), Sydney, Australia, Sept 23 2000

MEN'S LONG-COURSE RECORDS

BACKSTROKE

50 m: 24.99, Lenny Krayzelburg (USA), Sydney, Australia, Aug 28 1999
100 m: 53.60, Lenny Krayzelburg (USA), Sydney, Australia, Aug 24 1999
200 m: 1:55.87, Lenny Krayzelburg (USA), Sydney, Australia, Aug 27 1999

BREASTSTROKE

50 m: 27.39, Ed Moses (USA), Austin, USA, March 31 2001
100 m: 1:00.29, Ed Moses (USA), Austin, USA, March 28 2001

200 m: 2:10.16, Mike Barrowman (USA), Barcelona, Spain, July 29 1992

BUTTERFLY

50 m: 23.60, Geoff Huegill (Australia), Sydney, Australia, May 14 2000
100 m: 51.81, Michael Klim (Australia), Canberra, Australia, Dec 12 1999
200 m: 1:54.92, Michael Phelps (USA), Austin, USA, March 30 2001

FREESTYLE

50 m: 21.64, Alexander Popov (Russia), Moscow, Russia, June 16 2000
100 m: 47.84, Pieter van den Hoogenband (Netherlands), Sydney, Australia, Sept 19 2000
200 m: 1:44.69, Ian Thorpe (Australia), Hobart, Tasmania, Australia, March 27 2001
400 m: 3:40.59, Ian Thorpe (Australia), Sydney, Australia, Sept 16 2000
800 m: 7:41.59, Ian Thorpe (Australia), Hobart, Tasmania, Australia, March 26 2001
1,500 m: 14:41.66, Kieren Perkins (Australia), Victoria, Canada, Aug 24 1994
4 x 100 m relay: 3:13.67, Australia (Michael Klim, Chris Fydler, Ashley Callus, Ian Thorpe), Sydney, Australia, Sept 16 2000
4 x 200 m relay: 7:07.05, Australia (Ian Thorpe, Michael Klim, Todd Pearson, Bill Kirby), Sydney, Australia, Sept 19 2000

MEDLEY

200 m: 1:58.16, Jani Sievinen (Finland), Rome, Italy, Sept 11 1994
400 m: 4:11.76, Tom Dolan (USA), Sydney, Australia, Sept 17 2000
4 x 100 m relay: 3:33.73, USA (Lenny Krayzelburg, Ed Moses, Ian Crocker, Gary Hall Jr.), Sydney, Australia, Sept 23 2000

ROWING

ROWING EIGHT (NONTIDAL WATER)

FASTEST 2,000 M (2,187 YD)
Women: 5:58.50 (12.48 mph; 20.08 km/h), Romania, Duisburg, Germany, May 18 1996
Men: 5:20.92 (13.94 mph; 22.43 km/h), Poland, Plovdiv, Bulgaria, Aug 5 1999

ROWING SINGLE SCULLS

FASTEST 2,000 M
Women: 7:17.09 (10.23 mph; 16.47 km/h), Silken Laumann (Canada), Lucerne, Switzerland, July 17 1994
Men: 6:35.67 (11.30 mph; 18.19 km/h), Leonid Gulov (Estonia), Plovdiv, Bulgaria, Aug 5 1999

RIVER THAMES SCULL
Roundhouse, Lechlade to Gravesend Pier, UK (146 miles; 234 km): 60 hr 23 min, Peter Goodchild (UK), Dec 15–17 1996

CONCEPT II INDOOR ROWER

FASTEST 1,000,000 M
Men's team (of 12): 66 hr 44 min 54 sec, HMP Downview team, Sutton, Greater London, UK, Aug 3–6 1999

FASTEST 2,000 M
Women: 6:33.4, Kathrin Boron (Germany), 1998
Men: 5:38.3, Rob Waddell (New Zealand), 1998

CRICKET

INNINGS RECORDS

LONGEST INDIVIDUAL CRICKET INNINGS
16 hr 55 min, Rajiv Nayyar (India), scoring 271 for Himachal Pradesh, India, Nov 1–3 1999

LONGEST INNINGS WITHOUT SCORING
First class: 101 min, Geoff Allott, New Zealand *v.* South Africa, Auckland, New Zealand, March 2 1999. Allott faced a total of 77 deliveries

HIGHEST CRICKET INNINGS
Score: Brian Lara, 501 not out in 7 hr 5 min for Warwickshire *v.* Durham at Edgbaston, UK, June 3 and 6 1994. Innings included: most runs in a day (390 on June 6), most runs from strokes worth four or more (308, 62 fours and 10 sixes)
Test: Brian Lara, 375 in 12 hr 48 min for West Indies *v.* England, St. John's, Antigua, April 16–18 1994

WICKET-KEEPING RECORDS

MOST CAREER CATCHES
First class: 1,473, Bob Taylor, Derbyshire/England, 1960–88.
Test: 353, Ian Healy, Australia, 1988–99 (111 Tests)

MOST CAREER STUMPINGS
First class: 418, Leslie Ames, Kent/England, 1926–51.
Test: 52, William Oldfield, Australia, 1920–37 (54 tests)

MOST CAREER DISMISSALS
First class: 1,649, Bob Taylor, Derbyshire/England, 1960–88
Test: 381, Ian Healy, Australia, 1988–99 (111 Tests)

One Day International: 234 (195 ct, 39 st), Ian Andrew Healy, in 168 matches, 1988–97

BOWLING RECORDS

MOST WICKETS
Innings (test): 10–53, Jim Laker (UK), England *v.* Australia, July 31 1956; and 10–74, Anil Kumble, India *v.* Pakistan, New Delhi, India, Feb 7 1999
Match (first class): 19 for 90 (9–37 and 10–53), Jim Laker, England *v.* Australia, July 27–31 1956
Career (first class): 4,187, Wilfred Rhodes (av 16.71) Yorkshire/England, 1898–1930

FASTEST BOWLING
99.7 mph (160.45 km/h), Jeffrey Robert Thomson, Australia *v.* West Indies, Dec 1975

BATTING RECORDS

MOST CENTURIES
First class: 197, Jack Hobbs (in 1,315 innings), Surrey/England, 1905–34
Test: 34, Sunil Gavaskar (in 214 innings), India, 1971–87

FIELDING RECORDS

MOST CATCHES
Test: 157, Mark Taylor (in 104 tests), Australia, 1989–99

BLIND CRICKET RECORDS
The first Cricket World Cup for the blind was held in New Delhi, India in November 1998.

HIGHEST INDIVIDUAL SCORE
262 not out, Mansood Jan, Pakistan *v.* South Africa, Nov 19 1998

BEST BOWLING ANALYSIS
3–12, Bhalaji Damor, India *v.* Sri Lanka, Nov 18 1998

PLAYERS

YOUNGEST CAPTAIN
Test: 21 yr 77 days, the Nawab of Pataudi (later Mansur Ali Khan), India *v.* West Indies, Barbados, March 23 1962

YOUNGEST PLAYERS
First class: 11 yr 261 days, Esmail Ahmed Baporia (India), Gujarat *v.* Baroda, Ahmedabad, India, Jan 10 1951
Test: 15 yr 124 days, Mushtaq Mohammad, Pakistan *v.* West Indies, March 26 1959

OLDEST CAPPED CRICKETER
International Cricket Council member country: 65 yr 269 days, Wally Glynn, Malta *v.* Greece, Aug 21 1997

ARCHERY
Archery featured in the Olympic Games of 1900, 1904, 1908, and 1920, with participating countries using their own rules. Due to the confusion, archery was removed from the Olympics. In 1972 it returned to the Games, with the Fédération Internationale de Tir à l'Arc (FITA) as the international governing body for the sport, and with standardized international rules.

WOMEN'S RECORDS

HIGHEST SCORES IN SINGLE FITA ROUNDS
FITA: 1,384 of 1,440 points, Chung Chang-sook (South Korea), Wonju, South Korea, Nov 2000
Team: 4,094 of 4,320 points (3 x 144), South Korea (Cho Youn-jeong, Kim Soo-nyung, and Lee Eun-kyung), South Korea, 1992

30 m: 360 of 360 points, Ha Na-young (South Korea), Wonju, South Korea, Aug 1998
50 m: 345 of 360 points, Kim Moon-sun (South Korea), Ch'ungjo, South Korea, Nov 1996
60 m: 350 of 360 points, Kim Jo-soon (South Korea), Ye-chun, South Korea, Sept 1998
70 m: 345 of 360 points, Choi Nam-nak (South Korea), Wonju, South Korea, Aug 2000

MEN'S RECORDS

HIGHEST SCORES IN SINGLE FITA ROUNDS

FITA: 1,379 of 1,440 points, Oh Kyo-moon (South Korea), Wonju, South Korea, Nov 2000
Team: 4,053 of 4,320 points (3 x 144), South Korea (Oh Kyo-moon, Lee Kyung-chul, and Kim Jae-pak), Jakarta, Indonesia, Aug 1995
30 m: 360 of 360 points, Han Seuong-hoon (South Korea), Seoul, South Korea, June 1994; and

Oh Kyo-moon (South Korea), Wonju, South Korea, Nov 2000
50 m: 351 of 360 points, Kim Kyung-ho (South Korea), Wonju, South Korea, in Sept 1997
70 m: 345 of 360 points, Jackson Fear (Australia), Kyongju, South Korea, June 1997
90 m: 332 of 360 points, Oh Kyo-moon (South Korea), Wonju, South Korea, Nov 2000

HORSE SPORTS

OLYMPIC RECORDS

MOST OLYMPIC GOLDS
Dressage: 6, Reiner Klimke (Germany), team: 1964–88, individual: 1984
Show jumping: 5, Hans Günter Winkler (Germany), team: 1956, 1960, 1964, 1972, individual: 1956

MOST INDIVIDUAL GOLDS
Dressage: 2, Henri St. Cyr (Sweden), 1952, 1956; and Nicole Uphoff (Germany), 1988, 1992

MOST TEAM GOLDS
Dressage: 10, Germany (West Germany 1968–90), 1928, 1936, 1964, 1968, 1976, 1984, 1988, 1992, 1996, 2000

MOST TEAM MEDALS
Show jumping (Prix des Nations): 7, Germany, 1936, 1956, 1960, 1964, 1996 (as Germany), and 1972, 1988 (as West Germany)

LOWEST SCORE (NO FAULTS)

Show jumping: Frantisek Ventura (Czechoslovakia), 1928; Alwin Schockemöhle (West Germany), 1976; and Ludger Beerbaum (Germany), 1992

WORLD RECORDS

MOST WORLD SHOW JUMPING CHAMPIONSHIP TITLES

Women: 2, Janou Tissot (*née* Lefebvre, France), 1970, 1974
Men: 2, Hans Günter Winkler (Germany), 1954, 1955; and Raimondo d'Inzeo (Italy), 1956, 1960
Team: 2, France, 1982, 1990; and Germany, 1994, 1998

SHOOTING

WOMEN'S RECORDS

RIFLE

50 m (3 x 20 shots): 689.7 (592 + 97.7), Vessela Letcheva (Bulgaria), Munich, Germany, June 15 1995; and 689.7 (591 + 98.7), Wang Xian (China), Milan, Italy, May 29 1998

AIR RIFLE

10 m (40 shots): 503.5 (398 + 105.5), Gaby Buehlmann (Switzerland), Munich, Germany, May 24 1998

PISTOL

25 m (60 shots): 696.2 (594 + 102.2), Diana Jorgova (Bulgaria), Milan, Italy, May 31 1994

AIR PISTOL

10 m (40 shots): 493.5 (390 + 103.5), Jie Ren (China), Munich, Germany, May 22 1998

TRAP

100 targets: 95 (71 + 24), Satu Pusila (Finland) Nicosia, Cyprus, June 13 1998;.and Delphine Racinet (France), Sydney, Australia, March 26 2000

DOUBLE TRAP

120 targets: 150 (115 + 35), Yafei Zhang (China), Nicosia, Cyprus, Oct 20 2000

SKEET

100 targets: 99 (75 + 24), Svetlana Demina (Russia), Kumamoto City, Japan, June 1 1999

MEN'S RECORDS

RIFLE

50 m (3 x 40 shots): 1,287.9 (1,186 + 101.9), Rajmond Debevec (Slovenia), Munich, Germany, Aug 29 1992
50 m prone: 704.8 (600 + 104.8), Christian Klees, (Germany), Atlanta, USA, July 25 1996

AIR RIFLE

10 m: 700.7 (597 + 103.7), Artem Khadjibekov (Russia), Munich, Germany, Nov 18 2000

RAPID FIRE PISTOL

25 m: 699.7 (596 + 103.7), Ralf Schumann (Germany), Barcelona, Spain, June 8 1994

AIR PISTOL

10 m: 695.1 (593 + 102.1), Sergey Pyzhyanov (former USSR), Munich, Germany, Oct 13 1989
50 m: 676.2 (577 + 99.2), William Demarest (USA), Milan, Italy, June 4 2000

RUNNING TARGET

10 m: 687.9 (586 + 101.9), Ling Yang (China), Milan, Italy, June 6 1996

TRAP

125 targets: 150 (125 + 25), Marcello Tittarelli (Italy), Suhl, Germany, June 11 1996

DOUBLE TRAP

150 targets: 194 (prelim 146 + 48), Daniele di Spigno (Italy), Tampere, Finland, July 7 1999

SKEET

125 targets: 150 (125 + 25), Jan Henrik Heinrich (Germany), Lonato, Italy, June 5 1996; Andrea Benelli (Italy), Suhl, Germany, June 11 1996; Ennio Falco (Italy), Lonato, Italy, April 19 1997; Harald Jensen (Norway), Kumamoto City, Japan, June 1 1999; Franck Durbesson (France), Sydney, Australia, March 31 2000; and Mikola Milchev (Ukraine), Sydney, Australia, Sept 23 2000

BENCH REST (CLOSEST GROUP)

10 shots at 1,000 yd (914 m): 3.151 in (8.003 cm), John Voneida (USA), Williamsport, PA, USA, July 8 1995
5 shots at 500 m (546 yd): 1.048 in (26.6 mm), Dave Goodridge (Australia), Canberra, Australia, Aug 29 1998

SPORTING CLAY TARGETS

500 shot and broken: 30 min 31 sec, Scott Hutchinson (USA), NY, Lake Placid, NY, USA, Sept 18 1999
Broken in one minute: 27, Scott Hutchinson (USA), Lake Placid, NY, USA, Sept 18 1999

OLYMPIC RECORDS

MOST INDIVIDUAL GOLD MEDALS

3, Gudbrand Gudbrandsönn Skatteboe (Norway), 1906

MOST MEDALS

Women: 5 (2 gold, 1 silver, 2 bronze), Marina Logvinenko (*née* Dobrancheva, Russia), 1988–96
Men: 11 (5 gold, 4 silver, 2 bronze), Carl Townsend Osburn (USA), 1912, 1920, and 1924

WEIGHTLIFTING

Since Jan 1 1998, the International Weightlifting Federation (IWF) introduced modified bodyweight categories, thereby making the then world records redundant. This is the new listing with the world standards for the new bodyweight categories. Results achieved at IWF-approved competitions exceeding the world standards by 0.5 kg for snatch or clean & jerk, or by 2.5 kg for the total, are recognized as world records.

WOMEN'S IWF RECORDS

48 KG BODYWEIGHT

Clean & jerk: 113.5 kg, Donka Mincheva (Bulgaria), Athens, Greece, Nov 21 1999
Snatch: 87.5 kg, Liu Xiuhua (China), Montreal, Canada, June 6 2000
Total: 197.5 kg, Liu Xiuhua (China), Montreal, Canada, Sept 6 1999

53 KG BODYWEIGHT

Clean & jerk: 125 kg, Yang Xia (China), Sydney, Australia, Sept 18 2000
Snatch: 100 kg, Yang Xia (China), Sydney, Australia, Sept 18 2000
Total: 225 kg, Yang Xia (China), Sydney, Australia, Sept 18 2000

58 KG BODYWEIGHT

Clean & jerk: 131.5 kg, Ri Song Hui (North Korea), Osaka, Japan, May 3 2000
Snatch: 105 kg, Chen Yanqing (China), Athens, Greece, Nov 22 1999
Total: 235 kg, Chen Yanqing (China), Athens, Greece, Nov 22 1999

63 KG BODYWEIGHT

Clean & jerk: 132.5 kg, Xiong Meiyin (China), Athens, Greece, Nov 23 1999
Snatch: 112.5 kg, Chen Xiaomin (China), Sydney, Australia, Sept 19 2000

Total: 242.5 kg, Chen Xiaomin (China) Sydney, Australia, Sept 19 2000

69 KG BODYWEIGHT
Clean & jerk: 143 kg, Sun Tianni (China) , Athens, Greece, Nov 24 1999
Snatch: 112.5 kg, Erzsebet Markus (Hungary), Sydney, Australia, Sept 19 2000
Total: 252.5 kg, Lin Weining (China), Wuhan, China, Sept 3 1999

75 KG BODYWEIGHT
Clean & jerk: 142.5 kg, Sun Tianni (China), Osaka, Japan, May 6 2000
Snatch: 116 kg, Tang Weifang (China), Wuhan, China, Sept 4 1999
Total: 257.5 kg, Sun Tianni (China), Osaka, Japan, May 6 2000

+75 KG BODYWEIGHT
Clean & jerk: 160.5 kg, Ding Meiyuan (China), Osaka, Japan, May 6 2000
Snatch: 135 kg, Ding Meiyuan (China), Sydney, Australia, Sept 22 2000
Total: 285 kg, Ding Meiyuan (China), Athens, Greece, Nov 27 1999

MEN'S IWF RECORDS

56 KG BODYWEIGHT
Clean & jerk: 168 kg, Halil Mutlu (Turkey), Trenčín, Slovakia, April 24 2001
Snatch: 138.0 kg, Halil Mutlu (Turkey), Sydney, Australia, Sept 16 2000
Total: 305.0 kg, Halil Mutlu (Turkey), Sydney, Australia, Sept 16 2000

62 KG BODYWEIGHT
Clean & jerk: 180.5 kg, Le Maosheng (China), Athens, Greece, Nov 23 1999
Snatch: 152.5 kg, Shi Zhiyong (China), Osaka, Japan, May 3 2000
Total: 325 kg (world standard)

69 KG BODYWEIGHT
Clean & jerk: 196.5 kg, Galabin Boevski (Bulgaria), Sydney, Australia, Sept 20 2000
Snatch: 165 kg, Georgi Markov (Bulgaria), Sydney, Australia, Sept 20 2000
Total: 357.5 kg, Galabin Boevski (Bulgaria), Athens, Greece, Nov 24 1999

77 KG BODYWEIGHT
Clean & jerk: 210 kg, Oleg Perepetchenov (Russia), Trenčín, Slovakia, April 27 2001
Snatch: 170.5 kg, Khach Kyapanaktsyan (Armenia), Athens, Greece, Nov 25 1999
Total: 375 kg, Oleg Perepetchenov (Russia), Trenčín, Slovakia, April 27 2001

85 KG BODYWEIGHT
Clean & jerk: 218 kg, Zhang Yong (China), Tel Aviv, Israel, April 25 1998
Snatch: 181 kg, Georgi Asanidze (Georgia), Sofia, Bulgaria, April 29 2000
Total: 395 kg (world standard)

94 KG BODYWEIGHT
Clean & jerk: 232.5 kg, Szymon Kolecki (Poland), Sofia, Bulgaria, April 29 2000
Snatch: 188 kg, Akakios Kakiashvilis (Greece), Athens, Greece, Nov 27 1999
Total: 417.5 kg (world standard)

105 KG BODYWEIGHT
Clean & jerk: 242.5 kg (world standard)
Snatch: 197.5 kg (world standard)
Total: 440 kg (world standard)

+105 KG BODYWEIGHT
Clean & jerk: 262.5 kg (world standard)
Snatch: 212.5 kg, Hossein Rezazadeh (Iran), Sydney, Australia, Sept 26 2000.
Total: 472.5 kg, Hossein Rezazadeh (Iran), Sydney, Australia, Sept 26 2000

be a record breaker!

We are always on the look out for interesting new records and categories, so if you think you could break or make a record, get in touch, and we will tell you whether your idea is suitable and what you have to do. Make sure you contact us early so that we can consult our experts and draw up new guidelines if necessary.

Getting in touch has never been easier – contact us via the web, or by letter, fax, or phone, and we will consider your claim and send you all the relevant rules, guidelines, and a list of all the documentation you will need as valid proof for your record claim.

Remember that you must follow these, otherwise your record attempt will not be accepted by our rigorous judges!

Once you know what you have to do to make or break a world record, get in touch with us just before you make your attempt to ensure that no one else has broken the record in the meantime.

CONTACT US!

• Via our website at:
http://www.guinnessworldrecords.com

Our online service is a fast-track way of submitting your record application. Just fill in the form and we'll give you a personal I.D. number so that you can track your claim's progress on the website.

• Write to:
Records Research Services
Guinness World Records
338 Euston Road
London NW1 3BD

• Phone/fax:
To contact us from the US, ring +44 870 241 6632.

Calls will be charged at the international rate set by your telecommunications provider.

To fax us from the US, ring +44 20 7891 4501.

Please note that if you contact us by letter, fax, or phone, it will take us longer to acknowledge your claim.

The world's largest ice-cream cake (left)

GUINNESS WORLD RECORDS™

stop press!

Records are being broken all the time, and our meticulous verification process means that we cannot always include all the latest details in the main body of the book. Here are some of the records that had just been confirmed as we went to press.

CITY WITH THE MOST NO.1 HIT SINGLES PER CAPITA
According to Guinness World Records *British Hit Singles*, the city with the most No.1 hit singles on the UK chart per head of population is Liverpool (pop. 461,481), UK, with local groups achieving a record 53 hits – one for every 8,707 Liverpudlians. The most recent No.1 was Atomic Kitten's 'Whole Again.' The City of Liverpool was presented with a *British Hit Singles* No.1 Award on June 28 2001.

MOST NO.1 BILLBOARD CHART ACTS PERFORMING ON SAME STAGE IN ONE DAY
A total of 53 artists with *Billboard* chart No.1 hits performed on 'Beatstock 2000' on Staten Island, New York, on Aug 19 2000. Acts at the record-breaking event included Pink, the Outhere Brothers, C+C Music Factory, Thelma Houston, and Deborah Gibson (all USA).

FASTEST TIME TO MAKE ONE LITER OF ICE CREAM
On June 10 2001 Peter Barham (UK) made one liter (1.75 pint) of ice cream in a record 54.5 seconds, as part of the 'Ice Cream Sunday' event, organized by the Royal Institution and the Royal Society of Chemistry. The ingredients – light cream, heavy cream, confectioner's sugar, and vanilla extract – were mixed with liquid nitrogen at approximately –320°F (–196°C) until they reached the right temperature and consistency.

LARGEST CROQUEMBOUCHE
Chefs from the Dubai World Trade Center prepared a 16-ft (5-m) tall croquembouche (tower of profiteroles), containing 137,000 cream puffs, on March 23 2001. It weighed approximately 20,000 lb (9 tonnes) and was created during the Dubai Shopping Festival, UAE.

MOST DONUTS EATEN IN THREE MINUTES
Ben Munday-Chanin (UK) ate two sugar jam donuts in three minutes, without licking his lips, on the set of Channel 4's *The Big Breakfast*, London, UK, on March 7 2001.

LARGEST SERVING OF FISH AND CHIPS
Tadeusz Hupa (Poland), chef of the Wrockaw Hotel, prepared the world's largest serving of fish and chips at the Third Cookbook Fair held at the Wroclaw Hotel, Wroclaw, Poland, on Dec 1 2000. The fish, once battered and fried, weighed 12.13 lb (5.505 kg) and the chips weighed 11.98 lb (5.435 kg).

LARGEST SNOW CONE
Mammoth Mountain Ski Area created the world's largest snow cone weighing 4,640 lb (2,104.66 kg) with 71 gal (322.77 liters) of syrup (cherry, grape, and lemon flavors) at Mammoth Lakes, California, on Nov 11 2000. It took five hours to fill the 11 ft 2-in (3.43 m) cone with ice and syrup. The contents of the cone were served to 1,000 guest skiers.

MOST EXPENSIVE WATERMELON
In June 2001 approximately 400 square watermelons were put on sale for $85 (£60) each, by growers from a farmers' association in Zentsuji on the western Japanese island of Shikoku. The unusual shape, chosen to make storing the fruit easier, was achieved by placing a segment of vine bearing a bud inside a flexible square glass container. As the fruit grew it was forced into the square shape by the glass, which also acted as a hothouse and protected and encouraged the fruits to grow.

LARGEST KING CAKE
SAV-A-CENTER Food Market New Orleans Division, in partnership with Pillsbury Bakeries Food Service, made the world's largest king cake at the Lakeside Mall, Metairie, Louisiana, between March 3 and 4 2000. It was 186 ft 3 in (56.76 m) long, 9 in (22.86 cm) wide, and weighed 1,024.69 lb (464.79 kg). King cakes are special sponge cakes baked to celebrate Mardi Gras in New Orleans, Louisiana.

MOST CANDLES ON A CAKE
On March 23 2001 chefs at the Al Bustan Rotana Hotel, Dubai, UAE, made a cake with a record 2,100 candles to celebrate the same number of rooms at the hotel.

LARGEST SHOT SLAM
A total of 190 people took part in the world's largest shot slam at the Delta King Hotel, Sacramento, California, on April 9 2001. JB Scotch was used for the attempt.

LARGEST FORMAL DINNER
The world's largest formal dinner party took place on April 28 2001, when 11,483 people were guests at a dinner party hosted by Vodafone Group plc at Earls Court, London, UK. The event was organized by Skybridge Group plc and the caterers were Beeton Rumford Ltd.

TALLEST SUGAR-CUBE TOWER
Dean O'Loughlin (UK), a contestant on Channel 4's *Big Brother*, London, UK, built a sugar-cube tower (one cube at a time) to a height of 47.24 in (1.2 m) on June 27 2001, breaking the existing record by 7.12 in (18.1 cm).

MOST SWEETCORN EATEN IN THREE MINUTES
On July 5 2001 Paul Ferguson, alias 'Bubble' (UK), a contestant on the UK *Big Brother* television show ate a total of 185 sweetcorn kernels in three minutes using an ordinary wooden toothpick to individually stab each kernel. The record was broken

at the studios of E4's *Little Brother*, Bromley-on-Bow, London, UK. He broke his own UK record by 20 and the world record by 16.

LARGEST SHOPPING BAG
The world's largest shopping bag measures 6 ft (1.80 m) high, 4 ft (1.20 m) wide, and 7.8 in (20 cm) deep. It was made by the luxury goods store Paris Gallery and presented on March 23 2001, during the Dubai Shopping Festival, UAE.

LARGEST LABEL
On May 1 2001 Germark SA, a label company based in Cornellà de Llobregat, Barcelona, Spain, produced the world's largest label, measuring 328 ft x 11.4 in (100 m x 29 cm). Once it had been printed, it took approximately 100 people standing side-by-side to hold it up.

LARGEST KIMONO
The largest kimono in the world was created as part of the National Kimono Festival in Cho Kagoshima City, Japan, on March 23 2001. The giant kimono was 38 ft 3 in (11.72 m) wide, 41 ft 11 in (12.80 m) high, and weighed 220.4 lb (100 kg).

LARGEST INCENSE BURNER
A handcrafted ash wood and brass incense burner (*mabkhara*) measuring a record 10 ft (3 m) tall and weighing 2,200 lb (1,000 kg) was made by fragrance company AJMAL on March 23 2001, during the Dubai Shopping Festival, UAE.

TALLEST TOWER OF WALKERS
Staff and residents of The Royal Palm Retirement Center, Port Charlotte, Florida, built a tower 9.1 m (30 ft) high with 103 walkers on Oct 21 2000.

FASTEST TIME TO PUNCH TEN TV SETS
Mike Yikealo (Japan) punched ten 21-in (53-cm) television sets placed on tables in a time of 7.66 seconds on Feb 3 2001. He wore boxing gloves.

picture credits

4	Vincent Yu / AP	41	Torsten Blackwood/AFP
4	Kevork Djansezian / AP	42	Corbis
4	Fox Broadcasting	42	Rex
5	Rex	43	Mike Derer / AP
5	Brian Spurlock / Empics	44	Tom Ewart / AP
5	Fox Broadcasting (6)	44	Rex
5	Nordisk Film and TV	45	Corbis
10	Brett Coomer / AP	46	Christie's South Kensington
10	Lon Beale / Sandboard.com	46	Playmaxx
11	Playstation	47	Rex
11	Tom Hauck / Allsport	48	Popperfoto / Reuters
14	Ron Tom / Fox Broadcasting	48	Rex
14	Thaddius Harden	49	Vincent Yu / AP
15	Ross Parry	50	Rex
16	Mr Mahendra	50	Corbis
16	Corbis	51	Matt Campbell / AFP
17	Rex	54	Bob Martin/Allsport
18	Hasan Jamah/ AP	55	Tom Bennett
18	David Scott	55	Eric Jamison / AP
19	Antonio Todde	56	Barry Norman / WKVL
20	Mike Jones / Fox Broadcasting	56	James Janssen
20	Rex	57	Fiona Hanson / PA
21	Rex	58	Kim Stallknecht / AFP
22	Rex	58	Ted Stevens
22	Rex	59	Stone
23	James Webb / Robert Harding	60	Ramon de la Rocha / AP
24	Rex	60	Donald Stampflis / AP
24	Popperfoto / Reuters	61	Rex
25	Axel Koester	61	Franck Prevel / AP
26	Gregory Smith / AP	62	McKinlay & Murrie
26	Hank Morgan / SPL	62	Corbis
27	Rex	63	TF1/Sipa/Rex
28	Nancy Palmeri / AP	64	Steven Darvill
28	Corbis	64	Abakash
29	Bill Janscha / AP	65	Gary Wixom
32	Rex	65	John Stillwell / PA
32	Rex	66	Mike Jones / Fox Broadcasting
33	Lucy Nicholson / AFP	66	Dave Harris/Picture Link
33	Gregorio Borgia / AP	67	Mike Jones / Fox Broadcasting
34	Rex	68	Corbis
35	Brooke Bond	69	Sutton Motor Sports Images
35	Rex	69	Rex
36	Rex	70	Peter Poole
36	Rex	70	Rhett Bobzien
37	Corbis	71	TF1/Sipa/Rex
38	Rex	72	Stacey Studio
38	Garth Vaughan / AP	72	Taipei Twins Association
39	Mark J.Terrill / AP	73	Denis Doyle / AP
40	Rex	74	Stuart Claxton
40	Rex	75	Carlos Virgili Ribe
41	Rex	75	The Independent/ Syndication/ Tom Pilston
		78	NASA
		78	Anglo-Australian Observatory
		79	Science Photo Library
		80	NASA
		80	NASA
		81	NASA
		82	Paulo Santos / AP
		82	Carol Kane

83	Still Pictures	126	Neil Barnes
84	Oxford Scientific Films	126	Ramesh Chand Dhiman
84	Theresa Schuch / AP	127	Supercircuits, Texas
85	Matt York / AP	128	Suhail Mohd. Al Zarooni
85	Corbis	128	Jeri Pace
86	NASA	129	The Gnome Reserve
87	NASA	130	John Reznikoff
87	Corbis	130	Peter Lavinger
88	Rex	131	Graham Barker
88	Hulton Archive	134	The Ronald Grant Archive
89	Still Pictures	134	Rex
90	Patrick Valasseris / PA	135	Universal Pictures
90	Ch. Roshan	136	The Ronald Grant Archive
91	Getty / Image Bank	136	The Ronald Grant Archive
92	Corbis	137	PA Photos
92	Corbis	138	HO / Apple / AP
93	FLPA	139	Warner Bros. Television
94	Corbis	140	AP
94	Corbis	140	Popper/Reuters/Kieran Doherty
95	Corbis	141	NBC Photo
96	Corbis	142	Fox Broadcasting
97	Rex	142	Miramar Air Show
98	Corbis	143	The Ronald Grant Archive
98	Corbis	144	Corbis
99	PA Photos	145	Pictorial Press
100	Rex	145	Popperfoto / Reuters
100	Oxford Scientific Films	146	Popperfoto / Reuters
101	The Gorilla Foundation	146	Popperfoto
102	Jeff Morris	147	Pictorial Press
102	Dr Chai Khanchanakom	148	Corbis
103	Rex	148	Mark J Terrill / AP
106	Popperfoto / Reuters	149	Corbis
106	Honda	150	Rachel Johnson
107	Edson Silva-Gazeta de Povo / AP	150	Rex
108	Katsumi Kashara / AP	151	Stefan Hesse / AFP
108	Pat Wellenbach / AP	152	Shochiku Co. Ltd.
109	Still Pictures	153	Fox Broadcasting
110	Popperfoto / Reuters	153	Rex
110	Rex	154	Bankers Audition Ltd.
111	Corbis	154	Corbis
112	Hulton Archive	155	Cliff Wright/Harry Potter & the Prisoner of Azkaban
112	AeroVironment Inc.	156	Sigma-Tau Pharmaceuticals Inc.
113	Corbis	156	Rex
114	Newspix / News Limited	157	Still Pictures
115	Toshihiko Sato / AP	158	The Ronald Grant Archive
116	STR / AP	159	Carole Kane
116	Hulton Archive	159	Corbis
116	Hulton Archive	160	AS Rekato Ltd.
117	Koji Sasahara / AP	160	SAC Neil Armstrong/RAF Leeming
120	Kampgrounds of America	161	Lazaros Pilarinos/Audio Visual Ent.
120	Gremi Provincial de Patisseria, Confiteria I Bolleria School	162	Rex
121	Corbis	162	Rolf Kay Photography
122	Monika Gumm/White Star, Hamburg	163	Corbis
122	David Leeson	164	Corbis
123	Bethel Chamber of Commerce	164	AP Photo/TimFleck/ Sandusky Register
124	Science Museum, London	164	Tania Gardner
124	Sergio Rodriguez Villarreal	165	Nagashima Kanko Kaihatsu
125	Rocketbuster Boots, Texas		

FASTEST TIME TO CLEAR TWO POOL TABLES USA

The fastest time to clear two pool tables is 1 min 36 sec, achieved by Dave Pearson, Las Vegas, on March 12 2001. Dave is a full-time professional pool player and world champion.

LARGEST NUDE PHOTO SHOOT

On May 5 2001 over 2,500 people bared their all in the name of art, lying naked on the streets of Montreal, Quebec, Canada, for US photographer Spencer Tunick. The brave volunteers lay outside the city's Place des Arts, shivering in temperatures as low as 55°F (13°C). Tunick's project, shot from above, was intended to illustrate the vulnerability of humanity.

MOST PUSH-UPS USING BACK OF HANDS IN ONE HOUR

Mario Sirotiæ (Bosnia-Herzegovina) completed a record 671 push-ups, using the back of his hands, in one hour, at the Hotel Sol Park, Rovinj, Croatia, on March 8 2001.

LONGEST KEYBOARD PLAYING MARATHON

Between March 30 and April 1 2001, Ginés Borges Belza (Spain) played a Yamaha MC-600 electric organ for a record 49 hours 15 min (including six breaks of 15 min) at the Royal Nautical Club of Santa Cruz de Tenerife, Canary Islands, Spain. He played a total of 800 individual arrangements, each lasting approximately three minutes.

LARGEST OUTDOOR PHOTOGRAPHIC EXHIBITION

A total of 10,610 photographs based on the theme 'One Family' were displayed on the 'Kodak DSF Wall of Fame' on March 23 2001, during the Dubai Shopping Festival, UAE.

MOST SYSTEMATIC SCIENTIFIC STUDY INTO 'HAUNTED' LOCATIONS

Between April 4 and 17 2001 psychologist Richard Wiseman (UK) led an in-depth scientific experiment to test the reactions of more than 250 volunteers who were exposed to supposed 'haunted' locations in Edinburgh, Scotland, UK. Equipment used included a magnetometer, thermal imager, movement sensors, and a light meter as well as photographic and video cameras.

MOST ENDANGERED WILDCAT

In 2000 it was estimated that the number of Iberian lynx (*Lynx pardinus*) – once widespread in Spain – had dwindled to just 600. A major cause of the decline has been the introduction of the disease myxomatosis to reduce the rabbit population. As rabbits are the Iberian lynx's main food source, this had a devastating impact on the population. The lynx or wild cat is now legally protected and efforts are being made to increase numbers.

MOST ENDANGERED CANID

In 2000 there were less than 400 Ethiopian Wolves (*Canis simensis*) left in Ethiopia – their main habitat – making this the most endangered genus of the canid (dog) family. Their numbers have been greatly reduced because of agricultural activities and they exist only in a few mountain ranges. They are so scarce that they are in danger of extinction.

MOST HAIR WASHED AND BLOW-DRIED IN EIGHT HOURS BY 60 PEOPLE

On Jan 15 2000, 948 people had their hair washed and blow-dried by 60 hair stylists in eight hours during the Rejoice Shampoo-a-thon organized by Procter & Gamble in Singapore. The event attracted large crowds of people who lined up to have a free shampoo and blow-dry in one of the four salons taking part.

TALLEST FLOWER ARRANGEMENT

On June 3 2000 the Campaign for the Promotion of Flowers and Plants created a flower arrangement in Cadiz, Spain, measuring a record 42 ft 5 in (13 m) tall and weighing 374,000 lb (170,000 kg). The arrangement took 40 florists 3,000 hours in total to make and consisted of 31,500 blooms.

TALLEST TREE TRANSPLANTED

David Fountain and former pop star Kim Wilde (both UK) transplanted a 60-year-old London plane tree (*Platanus acerifolia*) measuring 57 ft 11 in (17.65 m) high from The Big Tree Company Ltd. in Houtvenne, Belgium to Warrington, Lancashire, UK, in Jan 2001.

MOST HEADS ON ONE SUNFLOWER

Rose Marie Roberts Waterford, Michigan, USA, grew an 8-ft (2.4-m) sunflower that bloomed a record 129 heads in Oct 2000.

MOST GLASSES BALANCED ON CHIN

Ashrita Furman (USA) balanced 75 one-pint (20-oz) beer glasses on his chin for 10.6 seconds in his backyard, in Jamaica, New York, on April 26 2001.

LARGEST ROCKING CHAIR

A giant, solid-wood rocking chair measuring a record 13 ft (3.9 m) tall, 8 ft (2.4 m) wide, and weighing 1,700 lb (771 kg) was constructed by The Solid Wood Bed and Table Company, Ontario, Canada, in Feb 2001.

LARGEST LEGO FLAG

On July 29 2000 a Saudi Arabian flag measuring a record 15 ft 1 in x 24 ft 10 in (4.62 x 7.57 m) was made by 12,000 children using 470,000 LEGO® bricks. The feat took place at the Jeddah Science and Technology Museum, Saudi Arabia.

LONGEST FLIGHT OVER WATER BY A POWERED PARAGLIDER

The longest flight over water in a powered paraglider (PPG) is 164 miles (264 km), achieved by Haim Raveh (Israel) on May 12 2001, between Haifa, Israel, and Larnaca, Cyprus. A powered paraglider is a standard paraglider with a light, three-wheeled frame slung below it. A small engine is attached to the frame and the aircraft has a maximum airspeed of around 31 mph (50 km/h). Haim's PPG was modified to carry emergency equipment and enough fuel for a 12-hour flight.

OLDEST COMPETING AEROBATIC PILOT

Ian Metcher (Australia) was 85 years old when he won the basic aerobatics section of the Western Australia Light Aircraft Championships at Jandakot Airport near Fremantle, W.A., Australia, on Feb 24 2001.

FURTHEST DISTANCE WALKED ON HANDS IN EIGHT HOURS

Roger Rank (USA) walked on his hands a record-breaking distance of 2,100 ft (640.08 m) between 9:30 a.m. and 5 p.m. at the Wal-Mart Super Center, Pittsburg, Kansas, on March 17 2001.

LARGEST FULLY-MOVEABLE MOTOR-DRIVEN STRUCTURE ON LAND

The Robert C. Byrd Green Bank Telescope is a radio telescope at the National Radio Astronomy Observatory in West Virginia. It is fully moveable and its highest point stands 480 ft (146 m) tall. The dish measures 328 x 360 ft (100 x 110 m) and can move to observe the whole sky from five degrees above the horizon.

YOUNGEST PERSON TO TRAVEL TO EACH CONTINENT

By Dec 2000, at age 12, Mario Casuga II (USA), had visited all seven continents in the world, becoming the youngest person ever to have done so. Traveling with his parents Mario and Rebecca, Mario Jr. had visited nearly 40 countries before completing his quest in Antarctica.

indeH

GUINNESS
WORLD RECORDS

acknowledgments

Guinness World Records would like to thank the following for their contributions to *Guinness World Records 2002*:

Airports Council International (ACI); Al Turner, World Waterparks Association; Andy Milroy; Ashrita Furman; Attilio Costaguta, ICAO; Barry Norman, WKVL Amusement; Research Library; Bill Palantonio, Eric Schotz, Marty Tenney for LMNO Productions; British Antarctic Survey; Christie's; Clive Everton; Craig Hilton Taylor, Coordinator of Red List Program, UK; Darrell Kirk Nordstrom and Charles Alpers, US Geological Survey; Dave McAleer; Dave Roberts; David Wallechinsky; Emma Dixon; Eric Schlosser; Estève Font Canadell; Ewan Vinnicombe; Forbes; Fortune; Fox Television; Giles Marion; Guinness - Die Show Der Rekorde, ARD; Guinness Rekord TV, TV3; Guinness World Records, Channel 4; Guinness World Records, ITV; Guinness World Records, NTV; Guinness World Records: Primetime, Fox Television; Hoover's; Ilumi; International Road Federation (World Road Statistics 2000); International Union for the Conservation of Nature; James Carlyle, Casella CEL Inc.; Jeff Sniegowski; Jill Paski, North Coast Redwood; Interpretive Association, USA; Jo Steel; Karl Shuker; Karola Gadja; Kate Stuart-Cox; Kevin Warwick; L'Émission des Records, TF1; L.M. Cunningham; Malcolm Smith; Mark Carwardine; Mark Hertsgaard; Maureen Kane; Mike Foster, Jane's Information Group; Mike Cowley; Munich Re; NASA; National Science Foundation; NetNames; Nigel Richards; Nik Bambrick; One Bad Monkey Limited; Peter Matthews; PPARC; Rebecca Adcock; RIAA; Roger Hawkins; Roger Launius; Salvador Pujol; Simon Gold; Sir Peter Johnson; Sotheby's; Stan Greenberg; Suzanne Collins; The Economist; Tim Footman; World Tourism Organisation; World Wildlife Fund; W.B.J. Rees; Yamaha

The TOTALLY 2002!! Guinness World Record Competition Instant Win Game

No purchase necessary to enter or win. Open only to legal residents of the 50 United States and the District of Columbia. Game starts at 12:00 PM Eastern Time (ET) on September 1, 2001 and ends at 4:59 PM Eastern Time (ET) on January 14, 2002 (the "entry period") or when the supply of games cards is exhausted, whichever is earlier. Minors must get their parent or legal guardian's permission before entering this Game or submitting any personally identifiable information in connection herewith.

1. TO PLAY

To play online, go to www.GuinnessWorldRecords.com http://www.GuinnessWorldRecords.com, click on the TOTALLY 2002 Guinness World Record Competition banner/button during the entry period and you will be taken to the Instant Win Game. Provide the requested information and follow the instructions to enter the "secret" number (found in your 2002 edition of Guinness World Records) and receive your online game play. Follow directions to play the game. If you are a potential winner (subject to verification), you will receive information on how to claim your prize. Winning game plays will appear at randomly selected times each day during the promotion. All prize claims are subject to verification and eligibility confirmation. In the event that there are no Game players during a winning time period, instant win prizes for that time period will be awarded as specified in rule #4. Or, to play without making a purchase or going online, hand print your full name, complete address, zip code, daytime phone number, email address (if any), and age on a 3" x 5" piece of paper and mail in an envelope to: The TOTALLY 2002!! Guinness World Record Competition Instant Win Game, P.O. Box 5490, Ellenton, FL 34222-5004. On the day an eligible mail-in request is received, a designated representative of the Sponsor will play one (1) Game play on behalf of the applicable eligible request, provided it is postmarked between August 27, 2001 and January 7, 2002 and received by January 14, 2002. Only those mail-in entrants that are winners will be notified by either email or regular mail. Each play request must be mailed in a separately stamped envelope. Any potential winners selected via the mail-in method will be notified by email or regular mail. All such potential winners must follow the instructions provided to claim their prize, or prize will be considered unclaimed and awarded as specified in rule #4. No photocopies, reproductions or facsimiles of Game materials allowed. Limit one (1) Game play per person/email address per day whether plays are online or by regular mail for the duration of the promotion. For the purpose of the promotion, an online day shall mean a 24-hour period beginning at 12:00 AM ET and ending at 11:59 PM ET, except that on September 1, 2001, the first day of the promotion, the period will begin at 12:00 PM ET and on January 14, 2002, the last day of the promotion, the period will end at 4:59 PM ET. Sponsor is not responsible for telecommunications, network, electronic, technical, or computer failures of any kind, or for entries that are stolen, misdirected, garbled, delayed by computer transmissions, lost, late, damaged, or postage due. Entries that are late, inaccurate, incomplete, illegible, lost, or corrupted are void and will not be accepted. All entries become the property of the Sponsor and will not be acknowledged or returned. Entrants using electronic entry must be registered subscriber of the email account from which Game is played. The "registered subscriber" shall be deemed the natural person who is assigned to an e-mail address by an Internet access provider, online service provider, or other organization (e.g., business, educational institution, etc.) that is responsible for assigning e-mail addresses for the domain associated with the submitted e-mail address. Sponsor may require proof to its satisfaction of entrant's registered subscriber status.

2. ELIGIBILITY AND NOTIFICATION

Game open to legal residents of the 50 United States and the District of Columbia. Void in Puerto Rico and where prohibited or restricted by applicable federal, state, or local laws or regulations. Employees of Guinness World Records, Promotions.com, their respective advertising and promotion agencies and members of their immediate families (parents, children, siblings and their respective spouses) and any of their household members are not eligible. Winners may be required to sign and return to Sponsor an affidavit of eligibility and liability and (where legal) publicity release within 14 days of issuance of these documents. If any such prize documentation is undeliverable, or if winner fails to timely return the properly signed affidavit and releases, or in the event of non-compliance with any other requirements, the prize will be forfeited and may be awarded in the Second Chance Drawing described below. Guests of Grand Prize winner must be 18 years of age or older unless an immediate family member of winner and will be required to submit and return a liability and travel release before the awarding of prize. If a prize is won by a minor, it will be awarded to the parent or legal guardian of the winner who must sign all required documentation on behalf of their child or ward. Minors must travel with parent or legal guardian.

3. PRIZES AND ODDS OF WINNING

Grand Prize (1): A trip for four (4) to Orlando, Florida. Prize consists of round trip coach air transportation for 4 from the closest major U.S. gateway airport to the winner's home to Orlando, Florida, based on 21-day advance purchase of non-refundable tickets; round trip land transfers between the airport and the hotel in Orlando; 4 days/ 3 nights hotel accommodations, based on quad occupancy; 4 day park hopper passes for 4 to a national theme park; one day admission for 4 to the Guinness World Records Museum and a total of $500 spending cash (Estimated Retail Value $5000) - Odds: 1 in 2,000,000. First Prize (6): Sony PlayStation 2 consoles (Estimated Retail Value $499 each) - Odds: 1 in 333,333. Second Prize (100): Hasbro "Monster XL Super Soakers" - the world's largest water pistol (Estimated Retail Value $49) - Odds: 1 in 20,000. Third Prize (395): Music packages provided by music artists who have received a Guinness World Records book. Package includes: autographed CD's, concert tickets, back stage passes (Estimated Retail Value $40 each) - Odds: 1 in 5,063. Fourth Prize (1,500): Posters by musical artists who have received a Guinness World Records book (Estimated Retail Value $15 each) - Odds: 1 in 1,333. Total estimated retail value of all prizes is $51,194. Odds of winning any prize are 1 in 999. All details of all prizes shall be in Sponsor's sole discretion (including, without limitation, all autographs provided, as well as all travel arrangements, which must be made through Sponsor and on a carrier of Sponsor's choice), and certain restrictions may apply. The prizes are only as detailed above, with no substitution, cash equivalent or transfer of prize permitted by winner. Sponsor reserves the right to substitute a similar prize of equal or greater value in its sole discretion. Grand Prize Travel must be completed by January 31, 2003, and winner and all of his/her guests must travel together and on the same itinerary, and participate in all Prize-related activities together. Reservations must be completed 60 days prior to travel. Certain blackout periods and additional travel restrictions may apply. Some of the prizes being awarded in this promotion were purchased by the Sponsor for use as prizes. The manufacturers of these prizes are not associated or affiliated with, nor have they endorsed, the Sponsor or this promotion. Any trademarks used in this promotion are the property of the respective trademark owners and are used herein for identification purposes only. Winners are solely responsible for paying all applicable federal, state, and local taxes, and all other expenses associated with any prize not explicitly stated herein. Limit one major prize per person/email address or household. Winners agree that all prizes are being provided "as is." Any and all warranties and/or guarantees on a prize (if any) are subject to the manufacturer's terms therefor, and all winners agree to look solely to such manufacturer for any such warranty or guarantee.

4. SECOND CHANCE DRAWING

Any Grand, First and Second Prizes not claimed will be awarded in a Second Chance random drawing conducted by Promotions.com on or about January 21, 2002. Any unclaimed Third and Fourth Prizes will not be awarded. Any eligible participant who plays but does not win instantly will automatically be entered into the second chance drawing for any unclaimed prizes available. Odds of winning a prize in the Second Chance Drawing (if such a drawing is held) are dependent on the number of unclaimed Grand, First, and Second prizes available and the number of eligible entries received. Winner will be notified by email or mail. All major prize winners (and the Grand Prize winner's guests (and their parent or legal guardians), as applicable) will be required to sign and return all required affidavits and releases as set forth above.

5. DISCLAIMER

By entering, entrants assume all liability for any injury or damages caused or claimed to be caused by his or her participation in this Game and/or the acceptance and/or use of any prize (or any prize-related travel or activities), and release and hold harmless Guinness World Records, Promotions.com, their respective parents, affiliates, divisions, subsidiaries, advertising and promotions agencies and each of their respective officers, directors, shareholders, agents, and employees (the "Released Parties") from and against all claims, actions, damages, and any such liability, in connection therewith. The Released Parties assume no responsibility for any injury or damage to participants or to any other persons' computer (whether hardware or software), relating to or resulting from entering or downloading materials or software in connection with this Game. The Released Parties are not responsible for technical, hardware, software, or telephone malfunctions or failures of any kind, lost or unavailable network connections, or failed, incorrect, incomplete, inaccurate, garbled or delayed electronic communications caused by the user or by any of the equipment or programming associated with or utilized in this Instant Win Game or by any human or other error which may occur in the serving of game pieces in this Game, or for entries or mail which are late, lost, stolen, damaged, illegible, or postage due. Entry constitutes permission (except where prohibited by law) to Guinness World Records and its designees' use of winner's name, city, state, likenesses, and/or voice for purposes of advertising, promotion, and publicity without additional approval, notification, or compensation, unless prohibited by law. In the event more winning game cards are issued and prize claims are received than the number of prizes set forth in these rules, due to computer, printing, seeding, human or other error or problem, Promotions.com reserves the right to conduct a random drawing from among all eligible, valid prize claims for the prize at issue to award the proper number of prizes as set forth in these rules. In no event will more prizes be awarded than set forth in these rules.

6. ADDITIONAL RULES

This Game is sponsored by Guinness World Records ("Sponsor"), 338 Euston Road, London, NW1 3BD, England. Sponsor reserves the right to withdraw the transmission of this Game at any time and award the prizes previously claimed. Entrants agree to abide by these Official Rules and by the decisions of the Sponsor and Promotions.com, which shall be final. Failure to comply with these rules may result in disqualification from this promotion. Sponsor reserves the right to permanently disqualify from this and any other any promotion it sponsors, any person it believes has intentionally violated these rules or otherwise tampered with any element of this Game, or acted in a manner which compromises the integrity, fairness, or proper play of this Game.

7. WINNERS LIST

For a list of Grand and First prize winners, available after February 21, 2002, send a self-addressed, stamped envelope to be received by April 21, 2002 to: The TOTALLY 2002!! Guinness World Record Competition IWG Winners, P.O. Box 5140, Ellenton, FL 34222-5004.